WOODROW WILSON CENTER SERIES

The Truman presidency

The Truman presidency

Edited by
MICHAEL J. LACEY

WOODROW WILSON INTERNATIONAL CENTER
FOR SCHOLARS

AND

CAMBRIDGE UNIVERSITY PRESS
Cambridge
New York   Port Chester   Melbourne   Sydney

Published by the Press Syndicate of the University of Cambridge
The Pitt Building, Trumpington Street, Cambridge CB2 1RP
40 West 20th Street, New York, NY 10011, USA
10 Stamford Road, Oakleigh, Melbourne 3166, Australia

© Woodrow Wilson International Center for Scholars 1989

First published 1989
Reprinted 1990
First paperback edition 1991

Printed in the United States of America

Library of Congress Cataloging-in-Publication Data
The Truman presidency / edited by Michael J. Lacey.
p.   cm. – (Woodrow Wilson Center series)
Papers presented at a symposium at the Wilson Center, Sept. 1984
organized by the Center's Program on American Society and Politics
and the staff of the National Museum of American History of the
Smithsonian Institution.
Includes index.
ISBN 0-521-37559-2 (Cambridge University Press)
1. United States – Politics and government – 1945–1953 – Congresses.
2. United States – Foreign relations – 1945–1953 – Congresses.
3. Truman, Harry S., 1884–1972 – Congresses.   I. Lacey, Michael
James.   II. Program on American Society and Politics (Woodrow Wilson
International Center for Scholars)   III. National Museum of American
History (U.S.)   IV. Series.
E813.T74   1989
973.918 – dc20   89–1045
CIP

British Library Cataloging in Publication Data
The Truman presidency. – (Woodrow Wilson Center
series)
1. United States. Political events 1945–1953
I. Lacey, Michael J.   II. Series
973.918

ISBN 0-521-37559-2 hardback
ISBN 0-521-40773-7 paperback

WOODROW WILSON INTERNATIONAL CENTER FOR SCHOLARS

The Center is the "living memorial" of the United States of America to the nation's twenty-eighth president, Woodrow Wilson.

The U.S. Congress established the Woodrow Wilson Center in 1968 as an international institute for advanced study, "symbolizing and strengthening the fruitful relationship between the world of learning and the world of public affairs." The Center opened in 1970 under its own presidentially appointed board of directors.

Each year the Woodrow Wilson Center holds open international competitions to select approximately fifty residential fellows to conduct advanced research, write books, and contribute to seminars, conferences, and discussions with other scholars, public officials, journalists, and business and labor leaders.

Research at the Woodrow Wilson Center ranges across the entire spectrum of the humanities and social sciences. Staff and fellows employ comparative, multidisciplinary approaches. The process of discovery that operates at the Woodrow Wilson Center frequently illuminates new understanding of the world in which we live, an expanded awareness of history, choices, and future consequences.

Results of the Center's research activity are disseminated internationally through the book-publishing programs of the Wilson Center Press, of Cambridge University Press's Woodrow Wilson Center Series, and of other co-publishers as appropriate; and through *The Wilson Quarterly,* a scholarly journal published four times a year. Additional dissemination in the United States includes *The Woodrow Wilson Center Calendar,* published monthly; *The Woodrow Wilson Center Report,* published periodically throughout the year; and Radio DIALOGUE, a weekly FM series of half-hour programs.

In all its activities the Woodrow Wilson Center is a nonprofit, nonpartisan organization, supported financially by annual appropriations from the U.S. Congress, and by the contributions of foundations, corporations, and individuals. The Center seeks diversity of scholarly enterprise and points of view. Conclusions or opinions expressed in Center publications and programs are those of the authors and speakers and do not necessarily reflect the views of the Center staff, fellows, trustees, advisory groups, or any individuals or organizations that provide financial support to the Center.

Dedicated
to
the memory of
Charles S. Murphy
(1909–1983)

Contents

Part II. Foreign policy and national defense

Acknowledgments

This volume is the result of a scholarly symposium organized by the Woodrow Wilson Center's Program on American Society and Politics and the staff of the National Museum of American History of the Smithsonian Institution. Thanks are due first to the authors whose work appears in the pages that follow, not merely for their scholarly acumen, but for their patience and good humor in suffering publication delays. The editor wishes to thank formally the members of the planning committee for the symposium, who helped to sort out themes, topics, and possibilities for participation and did so much to bring the conference to fruition: Michael Beschloss, Robert Donovan, John Gaddis, Robert Griffith, and particularly Robert Pollard.

The symposium project was undertaken at the urging of the Truman Centennial Committee, established in 1983 to coordinate the activities held in observance of the one-hundredth anniversary of Harry Truman's birth. We are especially grateful to the committee's chairman, Clark M. Clifford, and his colleagues, particularly the late Charles S. Murphy (to whose memory the volume is dedicated), George M. Elsey, Francis Heller, Philleo Nash, Elmer B. Staats, David Stowe, Benedict Zobrist, and the late Leon Keyserling, for their advice, encouragement, and support. The critics and commentators at the conference sessions also made important contributions to the arguments developed; this group included Richard J. Barnet, Robert Collins, Bruce Cummings, Steven Fraser, Louis Galambos, James Gilbert, Gary Hess, Michael Hogan, Vojtech Mastny, Aaron D. Miller, Howard Schonberger, Harvard Sitkoff, Ronald Steel, and Nancy Tucker. And a final word of thanks is in order for Sam Hughes, former under secretary of the Smithsonian Institution, for his guidance in getting everything arranged and under way.

Introduction and summary:
The Truman era in retrospect

MICHAEL J. LACEY

The essays in this volume were presented as papers in September 1984 at a scholarly symposium at the Woodrow Wilson Center, one of many events that occurred in that year to commemorate the centennial of Harry Truman's birth. As a scholarly gathering, its aim was not to celebrate those aspects of President Truman's outlook and temperament that had earned for him in the decades after he left office such a respected place in political folklore and popular consciousness, but instead to reflect critically on the major developments of the Truman era in light of recent scholarship.

Important historical questions are seldom finally settled, but rather are constantly reinterpreted. Their status changes not only with the discovery of new sources, but with the changing perspective of the historians themselves, as influenced by the currents of their own contemporary experience. In the academic community, to take the case in point, the meaning of the Truman era—its achievements and failures and its placement in the developing political tradition—is a more complex, controversial, and ambiguous problem than in the popular mind. For some, Truman represented high achievement, the protection and extension of New Deal impulses, the orchestration of the great success story in American diplomacy in the reconstruction of Europe and restructuring of a viable world economy, and the establishment of a system for the defense of the free world.

From others, in what came to be called the revisionist school of the 1960s and 1970s, a new set of themes appeared. Writing in the turbulent years of the Vietnam War and domestic protest, the civil rights and wom-

1

en's movements, the Watergate investigations, the revelations of CIA misdeeds, and the FBI's close monitoring of domestic dissent, the revisionists saw the Truman years as the unfortunate point of origin for the evils of the day. According to this interpretation, Truman and his colleagues were sometimes seen as the authors of the cold war, rather than as participants in the story, and Truman himself was suspected of presiding, however uneasily, over the elaboration of an undiscriminating political culture of anticommunism that failed to make important distinctions in social thinking and worked toward the suppression of dissent, the foreclosure of indigenous political possibilities, and the commitment of the country to dubious foreign struggles.

Although perhaps less militant than it was a decade ago, the revisionist attitude is still a factor in the writing of contemporary political and diplomatic history, and its presence has resulted in a more cautious approach to problems and their assessment on the part of all who participate in the conversation at its academic level. The essays in this volume were written by scholars who are familiar with both the liberal and revisionist currents of thought and hold diverse views about them. Whereas the papers do not represent an overall synthesis on the period and the emergence of a new consensus, they do offer an authoritative look at some of the major developments of the time, and they correct some of the excesses of both schools that grew up in the more strident controversies of early revisionist argument. More than that, these authors share a realization, based on a decade and more of rich scholarship on corporatism in America, that there were issues of central concern to the Truman administration that were not understood in earlier analysis to be so important, the most significant being the relationship in postwar America between the public and private sectors, the state and society. This concern to define the quality, character, and institutions of postwar liberalism did not stop at the water's edge. It provided the linkage between domestic and foreign policy in the early cold war years, and the underlying challenge in rebuilding the economies of Europe and Asia.

For all the differences of interest and emphasis the essays represent, they agree on an important starting point, that is, the overriding importance of the Truman years as the watershed for our understanding of the contemporary political system. It was Truman's misfortune to take up his duties in the shadow of Franklin D. Roosevelt and to be measured during his days in office against the memory of the most dominant American political personality of the twentieth century. Historians, too, have worked in this shadow, and there has long been a tendency to organize thought about modern statecraft around the controversies, achievements, and failures of the New Deal—to use it, however selectively, as a yardstick in estimating subsequent development. And there is no doubt about the importance of the New Deal in inaugurating key elements of the modern system of social policy.

It is becoming increasingly clear, however, that for all its motion and drama and color, the New Deal is less important as a source of underlying changes in the political order than were World War II and the Truman years that followed it. Although it is true that Truman's most important mentor was FDR and that Truman was deeply committed to many elements of the New Deal heritage, the differences between the two men are what now stand out.

The postwar world and new international order that Harry Truman helped to shape is very different from the world of FDR and places a different agenda, both domestic and foreign, at the center of political concern. Succeeding presidents have found themselves to have more in common with the experience and outlook of Truman, as he attempted to come to terms with the new agenda, than with his more dynamic and formidable predecessor.

Economic recovery was the central aim of the New Deal, and the failure to generate prosperity was its major shortcoming. From 1937 onward it was in a stalemate position, stymied by the Supreme Court, confronted by an increasingly suspicious Congress, and vilified by a discredited but hostile business community. Thereafter the problems of diplomacy and preparation for war came to the fore, and the urgencies of mobilization and wartime production gradually generated the recovery that had been out of reach. Truman entered the New Deal political establishment rather late on his arrival in the Senate in 1935; as a freshman senator he was predictably loyal to the party line but nonetheless rather aloof from the more dramatic front-line controversies of the hour. He became an expert on national transportation policy and took an interest in the developing problems of defense mobilization. After his reelection in 1940, he was thoroughly immersed in defense issues and came to national prominence as the chairman of the Senate's Special Committee to Investigate the National Defense Program. It was from this angle that his political education in governance at the national level took shape and he first encountered the intricate problems of state and economy.

The state he inherited with the death of Roosevelt in April 1945 had been swollen by the exigencies of war and was far more extensive, powerful, deeply enmeshed in the operations of society and the economy than had been known before in this country. Those who worked within it were preoccupied with new problems and possibilities, which seemed increasingly remote from the early recovery and reform strategies of the New Deal. After the surrender of Japan, the agenda was dominated by the politics of reconversion, and it is clear that for Truman the important lessons of government were tied to the performance of the state in wartime. As he put it in his first major message to Congress, which contained his "Twenty-one Point" program for the reconversion period, "When we have reconverted our economy to a peacetime basis, . . . we shall not be satisfied with merely our prewar economy. The American people have set high goals for their own future. They have set these goals high because they have seen how great can be the productive capacity of our country."

The economy of abundance that had been dreamed of by old progressives and New Dealers was now in view. Sustaining prosperity and generalizing it in the transition to peace were the central concerns of the new administration, and thus, as several of the essays here make clear, Truman and his advisers embarked upon the search for a new order that would enable the political leadership to cope with the problems and opportunities of the postwar world. One aspect of that search—an attempt to set the government's house in order—is reflected in the drive to consolidate the bureaucratic heritage of the New Deal and the wartime experience; to develop the institutional apparatus for the modern, managerial presidency; and to equip the office with new capacities to handle both domestic and foreign affairs, as symbolized by the emergence of the National Security Council, the Council of Economic Advisers, and the embryonic domestic policy staff that stemmed from the roles played by Clark Clifford and his associates. A second aspect of the search was the evolution of the containment doctrine and the cold-war pattern of foreign relations. A third aspect, which was not so much the fulfillment of a plan as the outcome of conflict, points to the balance in relations between the public and private sectors that arose in the wake of the generally unsuccessful effort to advance the Fair Deal program. Truman's losses in policy battles often provided starting points for his successors, however, indicating the existence of deep-seated, complex drives within the maturing system of interest-group politics. It is the interaction of these three aspects of the search for a new order that gives to the politics of the past four decades their distinctive texture and coherence, the feeling that the decades mark different phases in the same period.

New Deal models and memories proved to be of limited help to Truman and his aides in the construction of the postwar order. On matters of domestic economic and social policy, the aim was not to resuscitate the 1930s but to avoid the confrontational politics and stalemate that had plagued the later New Deal years. Truman's relations with the business community were stormy and often bitter, and the antibusiness rhetoric of his 1948 campaign even more strident than had been Roosevelt's tilting at "the money changers and economic royalists"; on the whole, however, the new emphasis was less confrontational, less dominated by the imagery of labor and capital locked in struggle over distribution, and less concerned with reform than with the ongoing mediation of conflicts.

Despite the excesses and anxieties of the period and the suspicious intolerance of dissent fostered by the government, there was more than anticommunism at work in the muting of radicalism in the early postwar years. Attention was shifting to new topics. The drive to stabilize prosperity focused attention not only on problems of production, which traditionally pitted labor against capital, but on removing impediments to high levels of consumption as well. This concern brought with it a new attentiveness to the needs and interests of a large and expanding middle class, and the desire to swell its ranks even further through adaptive, compensatory, and stimulative programs of government.

In the Truman era, many of what would come to be known as "quality of life" issues surfaced on the national agenda—the concern with urban blight, mass housing, medical care, and education among them. The democratic coalition forged by Roosevelt expanded, became more pluralistic, and placed new demands on the political system. Although his critics may wish that he had done more, Truman plainly deserves credit for placing civil rights and social justice for minorities in a more prominent place on the agenda than previous administrations had done.

Despite occasionally severe disagreements with both labor and industry, Truman and his Fair Dealers were generally reconciled to the existing structure of the economy. Feats of wartime production had restored the public image of business leadership, and a general willingness to concede economic leadership to the corporate sector reemerged.

Truman clearly belongs in the statist tradition that culminated in the New Deal, but he and his aides conceived the tasks of government as compensatory, designed to forestall problems and to remedy those that arose from the normal workings of the system. He, like all his successors in office, hoped for voluntary cooperation on the part of the principal participants in the economic system, and his hopes, like those of his successors, were often disappointed, but command models of political economy held no allure. From the "Twenty-one Points" message onward, Truman was chiefly concerned to discover what government might do to build up the infrastructure of the economy without competing with the private sector—through transportation; federal aid to housing and agriculture; regional development of public works (with stockpiled plans for public employment, if necessary, as a last resort); federal aid to education; and a powerful emphasis on government's responsibility to nurture research in science, technology, and medicine.

In foreign policy, the United States had, since Woodrow Wilson's tenure, participated as one of several Western powers in negotiating the terms of international trade, flows of capital, and investment. In the post-World War II years, a bipolar world arose out of the chaos and destruction in Europe and Asia, and the United States had the luxury—or perhaps the responsibility—of dictating and financing postwar economic arrangements.

The essays in this volume depict the experience of the Truman administration in the struggles at home and abroad that marked the emergence of the new system. They are divided into two groups, the first concentrating on domestic politics and issues, and the second on questions of foreign policy and national defense.

As the focus of most of the essays is on the Truman *administration,* it is well to recall that *administration* is a collective noun, often personified in misleading ways that conceal the pluralism and ambiguity of communication (and the failure to communicate) on the part of those who make up the collectivity.

Domestic politics and issues

To help establish a biographical context on the president himself, Alonzo Hamby offers a concise, synoptic account of Truman's experience. He calls attention to what seems to have been an unusually long period of maturation in Truman's case, many years of drift filled with dead-end jobs, failed business ventures, family tensions, and uncertainty about his vocation. Truman's first feelings of significant accomplishment and momentum came, as Hamby points out, when he was in his mid-thirties, during his service as an infantry officer in World War I. Not long after his return from the war he found he had the makings of a political career in Missouri's Democratic party machine dominated by Thomas Pendergast. Thereafter came many years of intensive political education and the search for professional competence—years, as Hamby puts it, of "Niebuhrian compromise" that blended loyalty to the machine with the wish for some distance from it and an enthusiasm for the progressive tradition and a host of "good government" causes. The education would continue after Truman entered the Senate in 1935, in the whirlpool of New Deal politics, where he showed himself to be reserved, eager to learn, and more respectful of policy expertise and specialization than of popular oratory and reformist talk. The reputation he earned in the following several years for competence and reliability in Senate circles would land him on the ticket in 1944 as FDR's running mate.

In trying to separate the realities presented by the increasingly copious collections of public and private documentary sources from the legend that grew up around Truman's memory in the years after he left office, Hamby offers a balanced account of the discrepancies involved. He concedes that Truman's vaunted decisiveness sometimes shaded off into impulsiveness and poor judgment that generated difficulties for him and his subordinates; that although outwardly affable and accessible, Truman sometimes harbored feelings of paranoia and was excessively sensitive to slights, real or imagined; and that his private opinions, even on matters of great moment, could be naive and ill-informed. Nonetheless, Hamby concludes, Truman's public record was one of considerable achievement, and, despite his shortcomings, there was something in Truman's temperament that appealed to the people, sustained support for him in office, and has deepened popular admiration for him since.

Robert Griffith turns his attention to the domestic scene during the years of the Truman presidency and provides a *tour d'horizon* of the Fair Deal battlefield, a many-sided conflict involving in confusing combinations the administration, the Congress, and the most powerful elements in the maturing interest-group system. It was here that Truman's hopes for mutual restraint and voluntary cooperation on the part of contending groups within the private sector were shown to be naive. The administration's attempts to find roles for government that would enable it to stabilize the economy through projects to shore up infrastructure at various points were often stymied, and Truman learned to his dismay that most attempts to alter the placement of the jumbled lines separating public affairs from private would be hotly contested.

Scholars are accustomed to seeing cold-war economic and military diplomacy in terms of the emergence of a new, postwar international order, and in comparison with these topics the basic dynamics of development on the home front have been understudied. Griffith makes the important point that the "emerging order" theme provides an equally valuable framework for organizing thought about the trend of domestic social and economic policy. The new order is marked by a fairly stable set of public-private relationships that arise out of the struggles of the Truman period and represent a kind of "balance of power" that settles on the scene in the early 1950s. Drawing on a wide range of both published and unpublished sources, Griffith sees the new order as principally shaped by the most powerful and best financed components of the interest-group system. He concentrates on the political mobilization of the business community, which he suggests represented the most massive and systematic deployment of corporate power in the history of the country. And he draws attention to a series of coordinated efforts to determine the contours of public policy via lobbying, campaign financing, litigation, public relations, and advertising.

With a focus on the actions of the National Association of Manufacturers, the U.S. Chamber of Commerce, the Committee for Economic Development, and the Advertising Council, Griffith traces the ways in which the struggle was joined not just over the election of public officials and the passage of legislation, but also over the leadership and direction of executive agencies, the composition and rulings of regulatory commissions, and even over the massive diffusion of probusiness ideas and images that pervaded the discussion of public affairs. The topics that provided the occasions for struggle included fiscal and monetary policy, labor relations, farm policy, antitrust policy, natural resources and public power proposals, medical care, and housing and urban development.

Truman, as Griffith points out, was only dimly aware, as were his officials, of the scope, scale, and organization of business opposition to administration initiatives. The president harbored powerful resentments of certain features of the new corporate order, but it was only with the increasing frustrations of 1948 and the election that he rallied his supporters and launched a sustained rhetorical attack on business. On issue after issue, however, especially after the outbreak of war in Korea and the rising tide of McCarthyism at home, his administration was burdened with an overriding need for support from many conflicting groups, and so proved to be no match for the more narrowly focused goals of the opposition.

Whereas Griffith's account brings the influence of business and industry groups to the forefront, Craufurd Goodwin focuses on how events appeared from within the world inhabited by government's economic policy-making officials. He discusses the choices with which administration officials wrestled in searching for a workable public-private relationship, because that relationship makes up the core of the "mixed" economy and is always imperiled by the need to constrain inflation without causing a recession. Mining the papers in the Truman Library and the National Archives, Goodwin isolates the economic policy conversation under way within the administration, a conversation that involved divergent and sometimes contradictory voices of Keynesians, marginalist laissez-faire advocates, and "institutionalist" reformers urging greater intervention in the doings of the private sector.

The Truman administration had invested a good deal of hope in the developing capacity of the government to influence activity at the macroeconomic level through fiscal and monetary policy. Goodwin makes it clear that the hope for a macroeconomic approach to social affairs came to a head in 1944, preparatory to support for what eventually became the Employment Act of 1946. That hope was heavily influenced by the "Americanized" Keynesian views of Alvin Hansen, who emphasized the need for government policy (1) to create the conditions under which the private economy could reach its maximum development and (2) to supplement the activities of the private sector in areas where only government could do the job.

At the center of his account are the newly created Council of Economic Advisers (CEA) and its attempts to find an effective role within the administration. Conceptions of the office ranged, as Goodwin demonstrates, from that of a mere fact-finding body, at one extreme, to an economic "general staff," at the other.

Officials would learn during the first Truman administration that macroeconomic tools by themselves were inadequate to curb inflation and shape the direction of development; the failures of the macroeconomic approach caused them to turn their attention to problems at the microeconomic level. There they found the corporations, the labor unions, the professions, and other organized groups locked in conflict. They came to appreciate the need for both fiscalist macroeconomic measures and more interventionist approaches to microeconomic behavior. Conceiving and justifying the latter approaches and making them politically specific turned out to be an impossible task. Goodwin identifies a brief period, 1949 to 1950, in which officials began speculating about new ways of

achieving cooperation between government and the principal participants in the private sector. It was symbolized by CEA Chairman Leon
Keyserling's concern for a new "cooperative partnership" between business and industry and Commerce Secretary Charles Sawyer's espousal of
an unfortunately undefined "new liberalism" to be based on public-
private cooperation. The coming of the Korean war and the incipient
militarization of the economy, however, ended the administration's search
for new peacetime relationships. Goodwin concludes that the Truman
administration must be judged to have left the question of the proper
relationship between the public and private sectors with little more of an
answer than when it first took the matter up, an appraisal that converges
with Griffith's view.

Nelson Lichtenstein's study of labor in the Truman era fits into the
same pattern of emphasis. Lichtenstein traces the decline of labor's power
from its peak in the early 1940s—when it was regarded by many as the
voice of the working class as a whole, and some elements of its leadership
spoke for a broad social agenda that represented the left wing of what
was politically possible in the United States—to more recent decades,
when labor has come to be regarded as just another interest group, one
among many. Labor's social agenda, Lichtenstein argues, was a good
deal broader than collective bargaining over wages and working conditions, which had been secured and underwritten by the state in the New
Deal's Wagner Act and in wartime production arrangements; it constituted a gradual assault on management's prerogatives and the attempt to
shift power relations in a more democratic direction.

For a time those who represented this impulse within the labor movement, like some people in the business sector and in government, entertained visions of corporatist governmental arrangements, but to no avail.
Lichtenstein argues that the Congress of Industrial Organizations profoundly underestimated the scope, resources, organization, and militancy
of the business mobilization and the conservative political support for it.
In the ensuing struggles, the enactment of the Taft-Hartley Act over the
president's veto became a symbol of the shifting relationship between
unions and the government. Despite his veto of the Taft-Hartley Act,
Truman was deeply ambivalent about the new unionism; Lichtenstein
sees him as both an architect and a victim of the labor-management stale-
mates of his early years in office.

When "social unionism" failed to find any traction in the emerging
polity, Lichtenstein argues, the unions turned their attention away from

Congress and the possibilities of government support for the welfare and security needs of workers. They concentrated instead on obtaining automatic cost-of-living adjustments—annual "improvement factors" tied to productivity, pension, medical, and other benefits for their members—through the collective bargaining process itself, thus contributing to the "privatization" of welfare in the United States at a time when welfare was increasingly being factored into the list of government's *public* responsibilities in Europe. The result of this shift of attention away from broad social concerns and toward the immediate needs of members of unions served to assure stable prosperity and relative security for union members.

But, as Lichtenstein points out, the shift had other important consequences as well, among them the decreasing mobility of workers within American industry, the growing split within the working class between the unionized and the nonunionized, the growing number of women and minorities who were left out of the system, and the decreasing pressure on the state for the development of comprehensive and equitable welfare arrangements. Many workers in the private sector found they could do without such arrangements and thus were tempted to view social policy in terms of "us against them," rather than in terms of a more inclusive public interest.

In his essay "Postwar American Society: Dissent and Social Reform," William Chafe takes up Lichtenstein's contrast between Americans who were participating in prosperity and those whose needs for various reasons were neglected, principally minorities and women. Women, particularly, suffered from the loss of the remunerative jobs of wartime and the return to the clerical or sales jobs that awaited them in a discriminatory peacetime labor market. With the problems of women and minorities in mind, Chafe sees the Truman era as one of paradox and ambiguity, rather than steady advance. The circumstances of the typical American family significantly improved, largely because of government policy; the GI Bill, which brought the federal government into the support of higher education on a massive scale for the first time, was especially important. So were low-cost Veterans Administration housing loans, which spurred both supply and demand in the housing sector. But regardless of whether the prosperity stemmed from skillful government policy making or was the natural result of free enterprise, most Americans were concentrating on private matters, on job, home, family, and participation in the new abundance. Chafe points out that the centerpiece of the new consumer culture was the TV. In 1947, at the beginning of diffusion of the new technology, 7,000 sets were sold in this country; by 1950, the figure had climbed to 7 million. The industry operated on the receipts from corporate advertising, and its programming generally depicted an "American way of life" that was benign, inclusive, and free of conflict and anxiety.

Questions of foreign policy and national defense

In a chapter serving as a bridge from the discussion of domestic policies and issues to foreign ones, "Some Sort of Peace," Paul Boyer points out that for all the controversy over the character of atomic diplomacy in the Truman years, little has been written about Truman's view of the bomb per se. In his study he draws on a variety of sources to fill this gap and relates Truman's public and private reactions to the bomb and atomic energy to the pattern of responses in American culture as a whole, as reflected in public opinion and media treatment of the issues at the time. Boyer concentrates on three topics: the decision to drop the atomic bomb on Japan, the question of the peaceful uses of atomic energy, and the possibility of using the bomb again in the early stages of the cold war.

On the decision to bomb Japan, an issue that received considerable attention in the revisionist literature on the Truman years, the picture of Truman's intentions that emerges from Boyer's account is strongly at variance with Truman's public presentations of the matter. From early on, Truman had given as his reasons for dropping the bomb the Japanese rejection of the Allies' surrender ultimatum at Potsdam and the need to save American lives that would have been lost in an invasion of the Japanese islands, and he never thereafter confessed to doubts on the matter. Boyer makes clear, however, that Truman's position involved some rationalization on his part and that his motives were a good deal more complex. He shows that Truman was aware of Japan's hopeless position and its intention to surrender; eager to demonstrate the power of the new weapon; vengeful toward the Japanese for their wartime behavior; and, most important, concerned to bring the war to a close with an American victory before the Soviets entered the war against Japan and earned a voice in postwar policy making for Asia. Whatever Truman's motivation, the arguments that he advanced at the time struck a responsive chord with the public.

In interpreting the larger meaning of atomic energy, too, the public and private responses of Truman paralleled and helped shape the views of the public. Although Truman strongly endorsed efforts to turn public attention from weapons to the promise of peaceful uses of atomic energy—one of the important areas which his administration was seeking cooperation with the private sector—his diary indicates that he was occasionally skeptical of the claims of science and industry and worried that "machines are ahead of morals."

On the question of the possible use of the bomb in Korea, Boyer makes it clear that Americans enjoyed a risky flirtation with the idea, as did their president. Truman could readily state compelling arguments against such use, but when levels of frustration rose, so did thoughts of his "ace in the hole." But Truman's last official comment on the atomic dilemma, in January 1953, nine weeks after the explosion of the first hydrogen bomb and a few weeks before he left office, was a far cry from his earlier statements about the beneficence of science. His vision of a fearful, inexorable nuclear future possibly beyond human control was a long way from his exultant mood of August 1945.

Robert Pollard considers Truman's philosophy of defense as it bore on the complex politics of federal budgeting and examines the key episodes behind the emergence of what came to be called the national security state. Arguing against the trend of revisionist historiography, Pollard finds that Truman's legacy was one of restraint—that in his concern with the domestic economy and control of the federal budget, and in his hopes for the economic aspects of containment doctrine, he erred on the side of inadequate military preparedness. In his first four years in office, Truman favored a strong mobilization capacity over keeping large forces in being, worked to keep manpower costs as low as possible, and favored measures such as universal military training and a reliance on air and atomic power rather than the alternative requirements of a large, standing military establishment. What finally shifted momentum toward large-scale rearmament, says Pollard, was a change in the official view of the Sino-Soviet threat in late 1949, after the Soviets' development of atomic weapons and Mao's victory in China. It was in the subsequent preparations for war in Asia, Pollard argues, that the structure of the national security state took shape; thus the Korean problem represents the watershed for its development.

In the first of two essays on the cold war in Europe, John Gaddis traces the evolution of U.S. perceptions of the Soviet threat and the resulting policy of containment. He looks at the movement away from the traditional "Continentalist" view of balance-of-power relations to the more global and far-flung "rimlands" philosophy that marks the postwar world order. Gaddis examines the wartime reluctance of Americans to view the Soviets as a threat, the growth of concern over the Soviets' postwar intentions, and the gradual emergence of a "totalitarian-ideological" model within administration circles as the context for public thought on dealing with the Soviet Union as a global adversary.

After discussing the development of containment strategy and considering the reinterpretations of the period that have been advanced in recent decades, Gaddis concludes that, on occasion, the United States undoubtedly overreacted to the perceived threat of communist expansion. But he also argues that this judgment should not obscure the fact that there were demonstrable grounds for concern in the unilateral behavior of the Soviet Union. He calls attention to the fact that the concern was shared by most of the nations of Europe, and cites recently declassified British Foreign Office documents indicating that the British assessment of the Soviet threat was even more sweeping and anxious in character than anything in the record of U.S. statements at the time.

In his chapter on "Alliance and Autonomy: European Identity and U.S. Foreign Policy Objectives in the Truman Years," Charles Maier examines the broader context for the workings of the Marshall Plan and the search for order and economic recovery in the war-torn states of Europe. In his reassessment of the "Pax Americana" thesis regarding the postwar world, a staple of revisionist historiography, Maier exposes the peculiarly collaborative character of the new American "empire," reviewing both the components and the limits of U.S. ascendancy. The twin pillars of American policy, Maier points out, were military containment and the emphasis on economic productivity in orchestrating the economic recovery.

Containment meant "writing off" Eastern Europe, a concession that increased the importance of sustaining a successful alternative to the Soviet-dominated system within the states of Western Europe. There the fear of economic collapse or stagnation, and the prospect that either would boost left-wing influence within the area, led to an emphasis on stabilization, economic integration, the isolation of radical movements, and the politics of productivity, which became the upbeat "ideological watchword of a coalition that would unite progressive management with collaborative labor."

In sorting out the complex bargaining of the period, balancing the different needs, resources, and vulnerabilities of the nations of Western

Europe and the many-sided objectives of American policies, Maier concentrates on the collaborative, compromising, pluralistic aspects of development. He concludes that the historical results of this episode in American diplomacy were indeed remarkable: "In an era when Europe seemed initially demoralized and devastated, the groundwork was laid not just for imperial subordination to Washington, but for a genuine revival of national traditions and of autonomous historical possibilities for Europeans."

In the first of two essays on U.S. policy toward the third world, Bruce Kuniholm tackles several interlocking issues that absorbed the attention of Truman administration officials in the Near East: the problem of maintaining the balance of power as British influence waned in the region, the Palestine problem and the origins of Israel, and the tensions between nationalist movements and the concern over the security of oil reserves. Kuniholm applauds Truman's commitment to maintain the balance of power in the region and argues that the inclusion of Greece and Turkey in NATO after the Korean War began helped to contain Soviet influence in the area. On the Palestine issue, however, he finds U.S. policy to have been muddled and ineffective, tending to postpone decisions and to mitigate problems, rather than solving them. Government officials were divided on the issue; the State Department's regional experts feared that American support for Zionist goals would alienate the Arabs and undermine containment policy, whereas other U.S. policy makers favored support for Israel. Truman himself, Kuniholm suggests, had an inadequate command of the problem, sometimes failed to understand the distinctions between one diplomatic formula and another, and clung to the "unwarrantedly optimistic" belief that he could simultaneously support the efforts of Holocaust victims to find a home in Palestine, protect his political future in the United States, and safeguard American interests in the Near East.

On the problem of response to the area's nationalist movements, complicated by worries over the security of oil reserves and the uncertain consequences of Britain's waning power to influence the course of affairs, Kuniholm finds the results of U.S. policy to be mixed. American officials were caught in conflicting pressures to collaborate with the British and thus maintain their support for containment policies, on the one hand, and the desire to improve relations with the emerging nationalist forces of the region, on the other. In Egypt, Kuniholm argues, the administration had few alternatives. But in Iran, events could have taken a different course if the administration had found a basis to support Iran before the crisis over the nationalization of the Anglo-Iranian Oil Company erupted. Because U.S. support for British policy limited Mossadeq's options, "precluding a viable liberal-democratic alternative to the Shah," Kuniholm argues, U.S. policy contributed to the impasse that existed in Iran when Truman left office, and he suggests that a more "assertive and fair-minded role" in mediating the conflict might have resulted in shaping subsequent U.S.-Iranian relations along different lines.

Robert McMahon deals with the Truman administration's record in South and Southeast Asia, areas in which the U.S. government had little experience and understanding and which would be transformed into critical cold-war battlegrounds. The central problems, as McMahon makes clear, were nationalism and decolonization, and again the United States found itself pulled in different directions; it needed support for its containment policies from Europe's reluctant colonial powers (British, French, and Dutch), on the one hand, and it recognized the wisdom of supporting "liberation" from colonialism, on the other. Within this context McMahon considers the twists and turns and checkered results of American policy toward Indonesia, India, Pakistan, the Philippines, and Indochina.

By 1949–50, with the increasing subordination of all other diplomatic goals to the requirements of cold-war solidarity, the administration's achievements in the region were partially negated. The efforts to align India and Indonesia with the West led to strained relations with both countries. The proposed military aid pact with Pakistan "promised to cement relations with the world's largest Muslim nation, but only at enormous cost." And the cause in Indochina to which the administration had committed itself in its increasing support for the French appeared doomed, with consequences that would long haunt American politics. In his conclusion McMahon points to the irony of the fact that in its efforts to "contain" Southern Asia without any deep and discriminating knowledge of the history and politics of the region, the administration occasionally undermined its own diplomatic goals.

In his chapter on occupied Japan and the cold war in the Far East, John Dower provides a richly detailed and tightly focused overview of American policy development in the 1945–52 period. His paper reflects his knowledge of Japanese sources as well as American ones and emphasizes the gradually changing perceptions in Washington of the importance of economic problems in Asia and the "containment" role that might be played by a successful Japanese economy as a counter to the increase of communist influences in the region. In considering the transformation of Japan from bitter enemy to cold war ally, Dower traces the complex, piecemeal evolution of U.S. policy from reform to rehabilitation and the establishment of mechanisms for regional military and economic integration. According to Dower, the most important point that emerges from recent research on the problem is the discovery of the extent to which, by the early 1950s, U.S. planners had come to see Japan and Southeast Asia as inseparable parts of the evolving U.S. containment strategy. The premises of that strategy held that Southeast Asia needed the "Japanese workshop" and that Japan, in turn, needed secure access to the markets and raw materials of the region, especially if it was to be denied close economic relations with China. Thus still another level of complexity in the tangled global and regional politics of the period is brought to the surface.

In the final essay in the volume, Barton Bernstein examines the Truman administration's handling of the Korean War, a set of developments that, as other papers have indicated, had watershed effects on domestic economic and social trends as well as on military and foreign affairs. Pointing out that Korea was *the* test case of containment doctrine, Bernstein reviews the discord and confusion within the military and diplomatic bureaucracies of the administration over the components of the doctrine and their implications for dealing with the Korean problem. In organizing his account of the Korean episode, Bernstein focuses on three critical decisions: the entry into the war in late June 1950; the commitment during the same summer and autumn to expand the war across the thirty-eighth parallel to the Yalu River; and the determination in 1952 to insist on voluntary repatriation of prisoners of war before accepting an armistice.

In his account of the decision to enter the war, Bernstein develops the view that Truman could have avoided committing the United States without disrupting the alliance system or producing domestic backlash by shaping "the dialogue within the anti-Communist culture at home," but that he and Dean Acheson had so expanded the terms of containment that they failed to consider the prospect. Acting contrary to the advice of their military advisers and responding to MacArthur's appeals, Truman and Acheson decided, Bernstein argues, that Korea was "the first of the dominoes." They determined to send troops to Korea in order to establish the credibility of the U.S. commitment and to block likely Soviet moves elsewhere.

Bernstein stresses that when the decision to cross the thirty-eighth parallel was made later in the war, the originally modest aim of restoring military balance was quickly transformed into a quest for the liberation of the North and the unification of Korea. According to Bernstein, the Truman administration believed that unification of Korea would weaken communist morale elsewhere and protect and expand markets for Japan. Bernstein notes that although MacArthur has often been blamed for the subsequent military debacle, Washington shared MacArthur's information, aims, and misguided estimates of the likelihood of Chinese intervention.

With respect to the third critical choice, Bernstein suggests that Truman and Acheson insisted on voluntary repatriation as a largely symbolic gesture with no roots or resonance in domestic politics, did not foresee that so few enemy prisoners of war (just over half) would agree to repatriation, and hence caused unnecessary prolongation of the war. He concludes with an excursion into "counterfactual history" and suggests that if Truman and his aides had not entered the war in 1950, domestic politics in the period would have been less rancorous and that rapprochement with China might have occurred under a Republican administration in the late 1950s rather than decades later.

1

The mind and character of Harry S. Truman

ALONZO L. HAMBY

Twenty-five years ago, nothing of academic consequence had been written on the Truman presidency. Today, one could fill a six-foot shelf with the books on Truman's White House years. They range from tightly defined monographs on peripheral issues to Robert Donovan's excellent two-volume history of the Truman presidency. Yet, although we know much about the Truman years, we know comparatively little of Harry S. Truman. Most Truman-era historians have little or nothing to say about the first sixty-one years of Truman's life. The monographic writers may work him into their story almost as a supporting actor for other figures deeply involved in this or that special issue. But whether their objectives are narrow or broad, the Truman historians generally begin with a well-defined set of assumptions. Some writers have picked up the idea that he was at heart a conservative know-nothing; others have the conviction that he was a constructive democratic leader with a sound grasp of elemental truths. Very few have done the sort of research necessary to establish a solid base for their assumptions.

Harry Truman remains a problem in biography for which historians have yet to produce an entirely satisfactory book. Here a point of explanation may be in order. By the term *biography* I refer to a work that centers on an individual's life. A biographer is interested above all in explaining his subject's growth and development, personality, character, and view of his times. The proper object of biography is to explore the subject's historical identity and to examine his sense of selfhood. (The two may be different.) The task of the biographer is twofold: first, to display and critically examine his subject's interaction with the larger world from the subject's angle of vision, and, second, to place his subject in the larger context of his times.

19

By these criteria, no entirely successful biography of Truman has yet appeared. We have a nicely written book by Jonathan Daniels that is very good for the prepresidential period, an adequate journalistic account of Truman's life into the 1960s by Alfred Steinberg, an admiring piece of family history by Margaret Truman, a solid academic work by Harold Gosnell, and a slim volume by Robert Ferrell.[1] All have their merits, but none has entirely fulfilled what I consider the biographer's mission. Other volumes frequently mentioned as Truman biographies, most notably those by Cabell Phillips and Robert J. Donovan, seem to me more properly classified as histories.[2]

A big part of the problem is that until recently we faced a paucity of the sources that biographers require. It was not until the opening of the President's Secretary's File at the Truman Library in the mid-1970s that the president's personal material was accessible. Even then, it was difficult to find out much about the first fifty-five years of Truman's life. The recent acquisition at the Truman Library of the long-undiscovered family, business, and personal papers has gone far toward filling that enormous gap. At last we have the sources and the perspective for a measured biography of one of the most important of American presidents.

Early life and experiences

During the first thirty-five years of his life, Harry Truman was above all a product of the experiences of the two generations of his family that had preceded him. His definitions of success and self-realization, his conceptions of masculinity, and his values were inherited from his parents and

[1] Jonathan Daniels, *The Man of Independence* (Philadelphia and New York: J. B. Lippincott, 1950); Alfred Steinberg, *The Man from Missouri* (New York: G. P. Putnam's Sons, 1962); Margaret Truman, *Harry S. Truman* (New York: William Morrow, 1972); Harold Gosnell, *Truman's Crises* (Westport, Conn.: Greenwood, 1980); Robert H. Ferrell, *Harry S. Truman and the Modern Presidency* (Boston: Little, Brown, 1983). The first substantial book on Truman's prepresidential years, Richard Lawrence Miller's *Truman: The Rise to Power* (New York: McGraw-Hill, 1986), which appeared after this essay was written and revised, rests on exhaustive research in local materials. It is not without its weaknesses in use of sources and seems to me overly inclined toward a simple debunking of its subject rather than a coherent attempt at an understanding of him. Still, it contains valuable information and succeeds at times in raising provocative questions.
[2] Cabell Phillips, *The Truman Presidency* (New York: Macmillan, 1966); Robert J. Donovan, *Conflict and Crisis: The Presidency of Harry S. Truman, 1945–1948*, and *Tumultuous Years: The Presidency of Harry S. Truman, 1949–1953* (New York: W. W. Norton, 1977, 1982). My own book on Truman, *Beyond the New Deal: Harry S. Truman and American Liberalism, 1945–1953* (New York: Columbia University Press, 1973), is frequently mentioned as a "biography." I take this occasion to reject the accusation.

grandparents. His education and boyhood life provided reinforcement. Other formative influences included a rather difficult childhood and the ambiguous social status of his family.[3]

As a boy, Harry Truman learned the experience of pioneer Missouri from his grandparents, who had come to Missouri in the 1840s from Kentucky, acquired land, speculated successfully, and done well for themselves. His maternal grandfather, Solomon Young, was the epitome of the self-made man of the nineteenth century. His example and the ambience of Harry Truman's youth imparted a simple nineteenth-century definition of how to get ahead in the world. It was an ideal that Woodrow Wilson glorified in the presidential campaign of 1912. Economic success was the product of a solitary entrepreneur, risking a small stake, working hard, and eventually prospering.

The Youngs and the Trumans were Baptists who attended church regularly, shunned liquor, paid their debts, and worked hard. They were practical Baptists of a type rather common in rural America. They distrusted extravagant emotionalism and disliked hypocrisy. Neither of Harry Truman's parents appears to have been a regular churchgoer when he was growing up in Independence. He consequently most fully absorbed the ethical aspects of old-time Protestant Christianity. Throughout his life, he felt a strong sense of identification with his Protestant heritage. He was prone to refer to the Ten Commandments and the Sermon on the Mount as the most perfect guides to moral behavior ever put forth. Occasionally, he would declare in times of difficulty that the United States or the world needed "a new Martin Luther."[4] He valued the Baptist faith, however much as an adult he ignored Baptist preachings against alcohol, gambling, and profanity. The Baptists allowed the common man direct access to God; their lines of church authority ran from the bottom

[3] The biographies listed in note 1 all contain some material on Truman's early life. For his own version, see Harry S. Truman, *Memoirs*, vol. 1, *Year of Decisions* (Garden City, N.Y.: Doubleday, 1955), chaps. 9–10, and *The Autobiography of Harry S. Truman*, ed. Robert H. Ferrell (Boulder: Colorado Associated University Press, 1980). *"Dear Bess": The Letters from Harry to Bess Truman, 1910–1959*, ed. Ferrell (New York: W. W. Norton, 1983), is an excellent source for the farm and World War I years.

[4] See, e.g., Truman's remarks at the Young Democrats dinner, 14 May 1948, *Public Papers of the Presidents of the United States: Harry S. Truman, 1948* (Washington: U.S. Government Printing Office, 1964), 259–61. Truman told Alfred Steinberg that Solomon Young was not himself a church member, although he contributed to several different denominations that used a nearby church house and presumably attended services with some regularity. Young's daughter, Martha, Harry Truman's mother, was a Baptist, but her attachment to the organized church was so provisional that she enrolled Harry in Presbyterian Sunday School because the Presbyterian minister had gone out of his way to welcome the Trumans to Independence. (Steinberg, *Man from Missouri*, 18, 23.)

up, and their worship services were simple and unadorned. Even as an old man, Truman was wary of a Catholic president.[5]

It is so well known that Harry Truman's family was fervently attached to the Democratic party that a biographer risks boring his readers by repeating the stories of his grandparents' affection for the Confederacy or of his father's rough-and-tumble partisanship. In Missouri, which had endured some of the nastiest guerrilla activities of the Civil War, the difference between Democrat and Republican was more than a difference of opinion. It was a deeply felt social rift that affected marriage decisions, friendships, and business associations.

The Democratic party to which the Trumans gave their loyalty was personified by Andrew Jackson, Jefferson Davis, William Jennings Bryan, and Jesse James.[6] (James and his brothers were heroes to many Missourians who had supported the Confederacy.) The Truman view of political parties transcended most questions of socioeconomic ideology. Harry's father, John Truman, apparently found it possible to back Cleveland and Bryan with equal enthusiasm. Harry Truman's Democratic legacy was even more deeply instilled than his Baptist heritage.

Truman's mother and father deeply affected him in other ways about which we can be reasonably confident. All Truman scholars are familiar with the stories that are told about his father—a feisty little man with a high-pitched voice and a quick temper ready to take on burly adversaries twice his size; a speculative businessman who gambled almost everything he possessed in the commodities markets and lost it all; a shrewd, persuasive livestock trader who rarely came out on the short end of any deal. John Truman, as Harry described him in many letters to Bess Wallace, must have been a difficult man to live with in the later, bitter years of his life. We have firm evidence that Harry was not his favorite son, and we know that Harry had reservations about the ethics of horsetrading as well.[7]

Yet it appears that John had considerable power over his elder son, who seems to have been more dutiful and solicitous toward him than

[5] For Truman's candid feelings about a Catholic president, see the transcripts of his taped interviews with William Hillman and David Noyes during the preparation of *Mr. Citizen* (New York: Bernard Geis Associates, 1960). The relevant passages are Tape 8, 11 September 1959, 5–7, and Tape 10, 21 October 1959, 29–31.

[6] Alonzo L. Hamby, "Harry S. Truman: The Liberal Democrat" (Carroll Lecture, Mary Baldwin College, 24 October 1979; published with a companion lecture in booklet form by Mary Baldwin College); "The Commoner: Harry S. Truman," chap. 2 of *Liberalism and its Challengers: FDR to Reagan* (New York: Oxford University Press, 1985).

[7] See the many references to John Truman in Ferrell, ed., *"Dear Bess,"* especially 178.

was younger brother Vivian. John Truman gave Harry a definition of masculinity as a simple, rough-and-ready willingness to speak bluntly and be ready to fight. He passed along a reputation for honesty that Harry took pride in. Even as a failure, he passed along to Harry the family way of trying to move up in the world—taking big risks with relatively small stakes, in the hope of big gains. Perhaps because Harry was not his favorite, John appears to have been a dominating presence whom Harry worked hard to accommodate. It seems likely that the father got in the way of his son's emotional maturation, especially in those years they spent together out on the farm in Grandview when the older man called the shots and the son did his bidding. It is hard to escape the feeling that the death of his father was a liberating experience that finally gave Harry Truman a chance to function as a full adult.

What did he receive from his mother? One has the impression that her influence was greater but is hard pressed to explain in what way. There is little doubt that Harry was her favorite son. She seems to have been responsible for such intellectual interests as he developed and, of course, for his piano lessons. It probably was from her and her side of the family that Harry acquired the intense distaste for New England and the Northeast that was the obverse side of the family's Southern sympathies. Above all, however, she gave Harry a set of values and characteristics that in general reinforced those that he got from his father, those of the honest, hard-working, plain-speaking rural culture of the Midwest. Especially as she grew older, she seems to have become a person of great symbolic value to him, a representative of older, more pristine "pioneer" times.[8]

One other aspect of Truman's family experience strikes me as critical to an understanding of his character and personality development. John Truman's family was a marginal family functioning in a pseudo-egalitarian environment—marginal not in the sense that it was poor but in the sense that it was striving for upward mobility and was new in the city of Independence. It was marginal in the sense that John Truman was striving to equal or surpass the success and stability achieved by his father and father-in-law. It was marginal in the sense that the Trumans could not be counted among the older, established, well-to-do families. In brief, the Trumans were trying to get ahead financially and achieve social recognition; hoping to be more than just another middling family, they were striving for admission to the local elite.

No one can measure the effect of this situation on Harry Truman's

[8] See, e.g., Truman's remarks about his mother, ibid., 502.

personality with anything approaching quantitative precision. One can make some plausible guesses. The boy must have grasped, however inarticulately, the sense of not having fully arrived, of his parents being not quite in the same league as the parents of some of his schoolmates. A young man whose life was disrupted by his father's financial failure must have felt the setback deeply. He seems to have resolved to reverse it and to accomplish what his father had been unable to do. We know that he became remarkably touchy about himself and his family as others saw them, ready to take the slightest criticism of his wife or daughter as a personal insult, almost always prone to feel that he was being overlooked or slighted by others.

To this insecurity-inducing set of circumstances, one must add the special physical and medical circumstances of Truman's childhood. He wrote of his boyhood so happily and nostalgically in his memoirs that it appears to a casual reader something like a chapter from Tom Sawyer. But of course it was not. There were those thick eyeglasses that restricted his activities and set him apart from most other children. There was the reading—and the piano lessons. As he admitted in more candid moments, he had to endure periodic taunts of "sissy" or "four-eyes" and on occasion had to run from fights. One suspects that such humiliations were not frequent, however, because young Harry seems to have worked hard at getting along with others. What may have been more important was the early realization that he was different and that he had to *work* at getting along.[9]

Next to his family and his physique, Truman's education probably was most important in molding his character. What we know of his schooling indicates that it was strictly traditional, with plenty of attention to the three R's and a rudimentary grounding in the classics, including the study of Latin. It appears to have been the basis for much of young Harry's serious reading and for a lifelong interest in ancient history. His reading of Plutarch and other ancients commended to bright young students in those days appears to have given him whatever ideals he did not pick up from his mother and father and to have reinforced

[9] Norman Podhoretz, "Truman and the Idea of the Common Man," *Commentary* XXI (May 1956): 469–74; Merle Miller, *Plain Speaking: An Oral Biography of Harry S. Truman* (paperback ed.; New York: Berkley, 1974), 19, 31–32. Truman's one boyhood illness was an attack of diphtheria that temporarily paralyzed him and seems to have nearly killed him. He was ten years old and for a time was utterly helpless; when he had to be moved, his family wheeled him around in a baby carriage. His recovery took months. Whether the trauma left any psychological marks is hard to say.

others. It was at this stage of his life that he chose Cincinnatus, the farmer-soldier who returned to his plow, as his hero over Alexander the Great, whom he was prone to cite in later years as an example of the sins of pride and gluttony. It was here also that he came to believe that the purpose of education was the instillation of moral values. (In his memoirs he wrote of his teachers, "They gave us our high ideals.") Finally, it was here that he came to envision history as a story of men, battles, and leadership, a uniquely personal process with little room for intangible forces.[10]

The life of Harry Truman in the thirteen years after his graduation from high school—the period in which most young men test their powers in the world, find a wife, take on the responsibilities of family, and settle on a career path—appears to have been one of remarkable drift and immaturity. It is easier to discern the pattern than the reasons for it. What we know of his life in those days is sketchy; it gives us a basis only for speculation about his innermost motives. What we can say is that he behaved in most respects as if he were still an adolescent.

After working at a couple of dead-end jobs, he seemed finally to hit on promising employment with a leading Kansas City bank. His supervisors liked him and he was pretty clearly on the way to steady advancement when he left to join his parents on the farm at Grandview.[11] He spent the next eight years of his life being bossed around by his father; he even agreed to assume half of his father's debts.[12]

According to all sources, moreover, he never had anything approaching a serious relationship with any woman other than Bess Wallace, which means he had no serious relationship with a young woman from 1901 to 1910. Throughout his life, in fact, he was unusually inhibited in dealing with women.[13] Whatever the reasons, Harry Truman from early on clearly wanted to be a man's man. Perhaps because of the difficult socialization he had experienced as a boy, he seems to have developed a talent for mixing with other men. To older men, he probably seemed a solid hard-working young fellow who was going to move up in the world, to men

---

[10] Truman, *Year of Decisions,* 118–19. Copies of the Independence high school yearbooks at the Harry S. Truman Library (hereafter, HSTL) present a good picture of the style of Truman's education.

[11] The personnel records of Harry and Vivian Truman from the Commerce Bank are in Files 308 and 309 of Miscellaneous Historical Documents, HSTL.

[12] For Truman's attitude toward farm life, see Ferrell, ed., *"Dear Bess,"* part 1.

[13] William Hillman, ed., *Mr. President* (New York: Farrar, Straus, and Young, 1952), 190; Eben Ayers, Diary, 14 September 1952, Ayers Papers, HSTL; Robert Alan Aurthur, "Harry Truman Chuckles Dryly," *Esquire,* September 1971, 136–39, 256–62.

his own age, an amiable guy who was good company at vaudeville shows, Kansas City steak houses, or poker games. He was an avid joiner; at the age of thirty, he was a member of the Masons, the Farm Bureau, the Woodmen of the World, the Grandview Commercial Club, and the Kansas City Athletic Club. He seems to have been popular in all of them as a willing worker and a congenial member.[14]

In later years, Truman and his supporters were prone, understandably enough, to romanticize his days as a farmer, but in fact young Harry Truman conceived of the family farm as a means to an end, not as an end in itself. From 1916 to 1922, he participated in three business ventures—an Oklahoma zinc mine, various oil-drilling activities, and the Truman-Jacobson haberdashery. They all were obvious indications of his ambition to get off the farm and to establish himself as a prosperous businessman. They also tell us other things about him.

Harry Truman in his mid-thirties was a nineteenth-century entrepreneur trying to get rich in a twentieth-century world. He was in many respects attempting to follow the example of his Grandfather Young. It is in his business activities that we find the strongest early indications of his irrepressible optimism. He poured what capital he had into these enterprises, managed to raise money from others, worked very hard, failed, and invariably went on to something else, apparently confident that the next try would work out. In fact every activity he undertook was so thinly funded that, if he thought his way through in advance, he must have assumed that nothing would go wrong. Of course, life is seldom so kind. The price of zinc stayed low, the oil company drilled too many dry holes, the haberdashery got caught in a sharp recession.[15]

In the first two cases, Truman attributed the failure to bad luck; in the last, he blamed Andrew Mellon. In this attitude, he was typical of most provincial small entrepreneurs, who tend to stake their hopes for success on lots of luck and easy credit. It is unclear whether he understood the dimensions of the risks he was taking with his own and other people's money, but in this respect he was similar to thousands of other men willing to take chances with small enterprises in areas of the economy dominated by Anaconda and Kennicott, by the Standard Oil companies, and by Sears Roebuck and Montgomery Ward. His forays into business

---

[14] Ferrell, ed., *"Dear Bess,"* contains many references to Truman's social activities. See, e.g., 144, 155–57.

[15] Ibid., chap. 5 for the mining and oil ventures. For the haberdashery, see relevant material in the Family Business, Personal File, Truman Papers; Eben Ayers Papers; and Eddie Jacobson Papers—all at HSTL.

exemplified yet one more way in which he so easily identified with the ordinary American.

His World War I experiences completed his long maturation process. Certainly no one can accuse him of a sophisticated understanding of the geopolitical issues behind the war. Like most Americans, he was caught up in Wilsonian idealism and was an easy mark for the simplistic propaganda of the Creel Committee. The war had to be fought to destroy the evil Hun. And once the war was over, in typical American fashion, he could think only of getting back home.[16]

However naive he may have been about the wider meaning of the Great War, there can be no doubt that he was an effective officer who made himself into a first-rate leader of men. Years older than most of his troops, strong and hard-muscled from a decade of farm work, courageous to the point of foolhardiness, a firm disciplinarian who promoted or demoted men freely, an older-brother figure who counseled his soldiers on personal matters and managed American Express savings accounts for them, he assuredly won the respect and affection of a large majority of his battery. The experience was the first major, unqualified success of his life and must have strengthened his self-confidence enormously.

He took home something else from World War I—a strong belief in the ideal of the citizen-soldier and an unquenchable contempt for most professional military brass. His letters reek with hostility toward the senior careerists obsessed with spit-and-polish inspections and so utterly lacking in common sense that one ordered that the horses be fed only boiled oats. France ended whatever thoughts he may still have possessed about a military life. But his own experience and that of his battery convinced him of the importance of the National Guard. For the next twenty years, he was a devoted reservist who enjoyed the camaraderie of summer camp while feeling that he was performing a useful and important duty as a citizen. The sense of self-improvement and opportunity for service as a citizen would be prime motivations behind his universal military training proposals as president.[17]

When Harry Truman married Bess Wallace on 28 June 1919, he was thirty-five years old; when his haberdashery closed its doors toward the

[16] Ferrell, ed., *"Dear Bess,"* chaps. 6–8 for the World War I experience.
[17] The newly accessioned Family, Business, Personal File, Truman Papers, HSTL, contains valuable material documenting Truman's World War I service. Of special interest are a small diary that he kept and a "little black book" in which he recorded his estimates of the men who served under him.

end of September 1922, he was thirty-eight. Like most men at his age, he possessed a fully developed sense of values that, in the main, had come to him in one way or another through his family. They encompassed the outlook of the nineteenth-century American as enterpreneur, as citizen, and as believer in Victorian, Protestant morality. He had taken an unusually long time to reach a stage of full emotional maturity, and the special circumstances of his childhood and his family setbacks left him with a residue of insecurity. Nonetheless, the war must have given him a considerable measure of self-confidence, and he had long found it easy to win the friendship and respect of other men. As he approached middle age, he found himself forced by business failure turning to politics—and reconciling a deeply internalized value system with a new and morally ambiguous profession.

Political education

Politics came naturally to Harry Truman; if not his first goal in life, it seemed a perfectly plausible second. His family had inclined him naturally toward political interests, and he had long possessed half-serious ambitions. In male company, he was a natural mixer with a near photographic memory for names and faces, and by 1922, he possessed friends and relatives throughout Jackson County.[18]

At first, he probably saw political office as a temporary expedient; somewhere along the line, however, his latent political ambitions became dominant. Hounded by creditors throughout the twenties, embarrassed by the insolvency of one of the banks with which he was associated, he faced abundant reminders that he had been a failure as a businessman. But he was a conspicuous success as a politician. By 1931, as he tried for a gubernatorial nomination or possibly a seat in the U.S. Congress, he clearly had changed his goals and had done so over what must have been the expressed doubts of his wife.[19]

Politics forced Truman to face a new set of moral problems. He re-

[18] Ferrell, ed., "Dear Bess," 142–43, 277; Rufus Burrus, interview, 17 February 1984. Colonel Burrus, a prominent Independence attorney, was a close friend and associate of Harry Truman's.

[19] Daniels, Man of Independence, chaps. 7–11; Steinberg, Man from Missouri, chaps. 7–15; and Gosnell, Truman's Crises, chaps. 5, 8–10, provide coverage of Truman's political and business career in the 1920s and early 1930s. A special section of Midcontinent American Studies Journal VII (Fall 1966): 3–39, features articles on Truman's abortive gubernatorial campaign, his relations with the Pendergast machine, and his 1934 senatorial race by Franklin Mitchell, Lyle Dorsett, Gene Schmidtlein, and Richard Kirkendall.

solved them with what one might call a series of Niebuhrian compromises. His own ideals of public service were rather typical of what George B. Tindall has called "business progressivism." He believed in honesty and efficiency, expanded public services, responsible funding, management that would give the public top value for the dollar, and comprehensive planning for the general welfare.[20] Throughout his career in county politics, he almost quixotically took up one "good government" cause after another, including regional planning, tax reform, state zoning codes— even a drastic consolidation of Missouri's 114 counties. But in order to be elected, he had to associate with and loyally support a political machine notorious for election fraud and graft derived from improper public contracts, speakeasies, gambling establishments, and bawdy houses.

He resolved the dilemma in two explicit ways: He made his loyalty to the Pendergast machine into an elemental virtue narrowly based on his own dealings with the Boss. Pendergast, whatever he had expected, never demanded dishonesty of Truman and always kept whatever promises Truman could extract from him. Truman, in turn, ignored the many varieties of antisocial behavior in which Pendergast engaged. It was a tenuous position. Throughout the 1930s, the world outside Jackson County, when it noticed Truman at all, tended to write him off as a complacent tool of what had become one of the most malevolent political forces in the United States. Yet his attitude may have been the only way he could justify to himself an association that was absolutely necessary to his own advancement.

He took care to keep his own hands clean. Perhaps now and again his position gave him a bit of leverage into business deals, but he never took payoffs and never handled political money. In his own position and in the public projects he controlled, he consistently followed through on his own ideals. He constructed a county road system, a hospital, and a courthouse and undertook numerous lesser endeavors with rigid honesty and efficiency. Pendergast was a bit astonished and not at all amused that a

[20] George B. Tindall, *The Emergence of the New South, 1913–1945* (Baton Rouge: Louisiana State University Press, 1967), 225–29. Tindall's coverage of Cameron Morison, Bibb Graves, and Austin Peay provides some obvious similarities in style and aspiration. For primary documentation of Truman's values as presiding judge, see Truman, "Property Assessment in Jackson County" (handwritten), Longhand Notes, President's Secretary's file (PSF), Truman Papers, HSTL; Truman, speeches to Club Presidents Round Table, 7 October 1929; Real Estate Board of Kansas City, 25 September 1931; Committee on Taxation and Governmental Reforms, 28 November 1931, all in Presiding Judge File, Truman Papers, HSTL; Truman, speeches to Women's Government Study Club, [10 March 1930]; Colburn Road Rotary Boys Club, 1 October 1930; Club Presidents Round Table [probably spring, 1931], all in Lou E. Holland Papers, HSTL.

debt-ridden underling would pass up a chance to enrich himself. (Truman always declared publicly that the Boss had amiably gone along with his honesty in building the Jackson County road system, but he wrote privately that he had faced down Pendergast's anger.)[21] Still, the machine went along with him—it had many other sources of graft to tap—because increasingly he could command support among independent voters.

An implicit judgment lay beneath his arrangement with the Pendergast machine. He had decided that the world was neither perfect nor perfectable. One lived in it as it was and did the things necessary to preserve one's own sense of honor. Understanding that human nature was mixed, he realized that the Boss had his virtues as well as his vices. These attitudes, which appear to have developed primarily from practical experience rather than from any conscious philosophical study, foreshadowed the "Vital Center" liberalism that would set the theme for the Truman presidency.

In many respects the most partisan of men, Truman as a county judge routinely dispensed jobs to Pendergast followers; as senator and president, he flailed away at the Republican opposition, giving no quarter. Yet at critical points in his career, he displayed a remarkable talent for bipartisanship. During his first term as presiding judge, he built support for his road and construction bonds by appointing two professional engineers—one Republican, one Democrat—as consultants to develop a comprehensive highway plan. He won over the *Kansas City Star* and the business community, got voter approval of his bond issues, and gave the county an excellent highway system. In other crucial episodes of his career—the World War II Truman Committee, the postwar economic rehabilitation of Europe—he displayed a talent for nonpartisan persuasiveness on issues that he thought lay beyond the bounds of ordinary partisan politics.

He learned something else as presiding judge. His entire family background and most of his own experience in politics had been of rural small-town democracy with its old stock provincial suspicions of urban America. As a young man, he was a typical rural bigot whose correspondence abounded with references to bohunks, kikes, and niggers. Of course,

---

[21] At some point, probably beginning in 1930, Truman wrote several undated, untitled memoranda to himself filled with caustic reflections on his political and business associates. All were done on Pickwick Hotel stationery and are hereafter referred to as the Pickwick memos. Typed copies may be found in Presiding Judge File and Post-Presidential File, Truman Papers, HSTL. One of these contains the somewhat franker account of the Truman-Pendergast relationship.

he wrote and spoke the language of his time and place; the eventual direction of his career provides compelling evidence that his early bigotry was not deeply felt. He moved away from it without noticeable difficulty as his political career encompassed all of Jackson County. He worked easily with the Irish and Italian Catholics who were Pendergast's lieutenants and learned to deal with the black vote on a relatively sophisticated basis. As Richard Kirkendall observed years ago, Truman's progression paralleled that of the Democratic party: He moved from the country to the city in the 1920s. But he made the transition without renouncing his old identity; he simply layered the new over the old. It is little wonder that so many Democrats would find him acceptable for the vice-presidency in 1944.[22]

His Senate career displayed some of the same characteristics as his county judgeship. Coming into a Senate top-heavy with Democrats, he did not find it necessary to cultivate the few surviving Republicans, but he did position himself somewhere to the left of the broad center of his party. Like most newly elected senators, he was eager to make his mark; what is interesting is the way in which he went about it. He consciously sought the respect of his peers rather than the attention of the public. He wanted to be a doer, not a talker. He detested Gerald Nye and Huey Long as irresponsible rabble-rousers and decided the conspicuous progressives were ineffective.[23] He respected the Senate establishment and worked to ingratiate himself with its leaders. Presenting himself as a freshman who had a lot to learn, he sought mentors. The most important among them was Burton K. Wheeler, who encouraged his investigation of the Missouri Pacific railroad financing scandal.

Truman's first term in the Senate was by any standard one of considerable accomplishment. Pushing himself to the verge of exhaustion, he

[22] Ferrell, ed., *"Dear Bess,"* contains numerous examples of Truman's routine use of ethnic slurs in his earlier days; it is interesting to observe the way they taper off as he becomes a state and national figure. His longtime associate Rufus Burrus believes that his bigoted language was little more than routine employment of the vernacular in which he had been brought up. Burrus interview. Richard S. Kirkendall, "Truman's Path to Power," *Social Science* XLIII (April 1968): 67–73, is an excellent brief survey of the larger political meaning of Truman's prepresidential career. Larry Groathaus, "Kansas City Blacks, Harry Truman and the Pendergast Machine," *Missouri Historical Review* LXIX (October 1974): 65–82, is a valuable piece that both sketches in the details of Truman's accommodation to the black vote and explains the context of black politics in Missouri.

[23] Truman's Senate career is surveyed in Daniels, *Man of Independence,* chaps. 12–15, and Steinberg, *Man from Missouri,* chaps. 16–24, and Gosnell, *Truman's Crises,* chaps. 12–16; but the most ambitious account to date is Gene Schmidtlein, "Truman the Senator" (Ph.D. diss., University of Missouri, 1962). For Truman's remarks about Nye, Long, and the progressives, see Ferrell, ed., *"Dear Bess,"* 374.

made himself the chamber's expert on transportation policy, conducted a major investigation, and contributed heavily to the Civil Aeronautics Act and the Transportation Act of 1940. Yet his achievements were all but unnoticed, and he barely prevailed in a tough contest for renomination. One cannot explain this situation solely as a reflection of the fact that transportation was not a glamour issue. Truman's "do—don't talk" style made him all but politically invisible, and the few times he surfaced publicly were, as often as not, counterproductive.

By senatorial standards, Harry Truman suffered from a serious case of anemia of the ego. He always had been uncomfortable speaking before large groups, in part because his myopic eyesight made it difficult for him to read a speech, but also because he still did not fully believe in himself. His modesty and determination to involve himself in the lasting work of the Senate were appealing and won him many friends among his colleagues, but they also were evidence that he felt an uncommonly strong need to prove himself.

When he probed financial mismanagement of the Missouri Pacific, he appears to have had no sense of how to turn a congressional investigation into an ongoing media event that would focus public attention on the issues, as well as give him valuable publicity. The other issue on which he gained attention in his first term became a political disaster. He attacked the prosecutors of the Pendergast machine and made an abortive attempt to block the reappointment of U.S. Attorney Maurice Milligan; he gained perhaps some personal satisfaction but only at the cost of lowering his public reputation.[24]

Truman was renominated in 1940 in an 8,000-vote victory over Governor Lloyd C. Stark and U.S. Attorney Milligan. In part, he was fortunate in his opponents—Stark displayed blatant opportunism and egomania as the state's chief executive and Milligan was too pigheaded to settle for the gubernatorial nomination. Nonetheless, the way in which Truman waged his campaign tells us much about his political style as it had developed by then. It also in many ways foreshadowed the strategy he would use in 1948.[25]

---

[24] *Congressional Record*, 75th Cong., 2d sess. (10 Dec. 1937), 1912–24; ibid., 75 Cong., 3d sess. (15 Feb. 1938), 1962–64.

[25] The following paragraphs on the 1940 primary and Missouri politics are based upon my research in the papers of Bennett Champ Clark, Russell Dearmont, and Lloyd Stark, all at the Western Historical Manuscripts Collection, jointly administered by the State Historical Society of Missouri and the University of Missouri. For Milligan's refusal to run for governor, see Ralph Coughlan to Joseph Pulitzer II, 24 April 1940, "Missouri Poli-

First, Truman consciously adopted an underdog role. I do not mean to imply that observers should have considered him the odds-on favorite. Stark was a formidable opponent—wealthy, ambitious, nationally known, the possessor of carefully cultivated friendships in the worlds of business, politics, and journalism across the country. He stood at the controls of a well-oiled machine manned by state workers. He and Milligan had smashed the Pendergast organization, gained control of the Jackson County election board, and made ballot-box stuffing impossible in Kansas City. Nonetheless, the edge with which he began the campaign was hardly so great as Truman made it appear.

Truman possessed considerable assets. Pendergast had allies throughout the state, seething with resentment against Stark and untouched by his antimachine politics. Stark had failed to root Pendergast men out of the Missouri federal relief bureaucracy, and in one county after another local WPA offices functioned as adjuncts to the Truman campaign. Stark had alienated Senator Bennett Champ Clark, who considered himself the leader of the Missouri Democrats and had come to see the governor as a dangerous rival to his presidential ambitions. Clark swung his considerable influence behind Truman with a series of speeches devoted mostly to denouncing Stark. Milligan deprived the governor of part of the anti-Pendergast vote. (Truman promised not to stand in the way of his reappointment as a U.S. attorney if he lost.) Truman had the support of labor, especially of the railway brotherhoods. Several of his Senate colleagues came into the state to speak in his behalf. Senator Clyde Herring of Iowa staged an investigation of Stark's campaign finances and charged that his effort was partly funded by a "lug" levied on state employees. At the urging of James F. Byrnes, Bernard Baruch contributed $4,000 to the Truman effort.

Shrewd observers realized early on that, although Truman was in a tough fight and would have to come from behind, he had a good shot at winning. Truman must have known this also. In many respects, I believe, he found the role of underdog appealing, both as a matter of style and a matter of political tactics. Without questioning his hardheaded shrewdness as a strategist, we may conclude that this tells us something about his self-image after one term in Washington.

His campaign was waged on at least three levels. The first of these involved barnstorming the state. He went after the rural vote all across

tics," Business File, Pulitzer Papers, Library of Congress. For the Baruch contribution, see James F. Byrnes, *All in One Lifetime* (New York: Harper & Brothers, 1958), 101.

Missouri the same way he had sought it in Jackson County and, indeed, the only way a candidate could seek it in the pretelevision era. He spoke at the county fairs and local picnics that constituted the primary summer recreations for most rural Missourians in the final days of the Great Depression. On a second level, he did all he could to appeal to the interest groups that made up the New Deal coalition, especially organized labor and blacks. On a third level, he dealt with machine leaders throughout the state, rallying not only those honest votes that the remnants of the Pendergast machine could command in Kansas City but all the outstate Pendergast allies. Most importantly, he reached an understanding with portions of the St. Louis machine, which had been willing to support Stark only so long as he appeared to be a winner with whom one had to do business. Bob Hannegan and other St. Louis leaders saw Truman as one of their own and swung to him what probably was the decisive bloc of votes in the election.

In this intense personal campaigning, most of it in a folksy, rural style, in this appeal to the New Deal interest groups, in this mobilization of organizational support, Truman established a campaign modus operandi that he would transfer to the national level in 1948. The stage would be bigger, the names different, his political situation more precarious; but then also he would face a smooth, well-organized opposition confident of victory, would adopt the role of the fighting underdog, and conduct a national campaign much as he had run his Missouri campaign in 1940.

Once he was reelected, he rapidly became a national figure through his chairmanship of the Special Committee to Investigate the National Defense Program. Interpreting its mandate broadly, the committee poked into almost every aspect of the domestic war effort, made its criticisms in a constructive, nonsensational way, and won nearly universal acclaim. To a biographer, the following points about its origins and conduct stand out:

1. The committee originated out of Truman's concern for the way in which the military procurement agencies were passing over small businesses, especially those based in Missouri. It was an outgrowth not simply of his real concern for honest, efficient administration but also of his hostility toward big business and Wall Street.

2. He managed the committee with extraordinary skill, avoiding investigative paths that might embarrass any of the committee members, keeping on good terms with all of them, and usually achieving a consensus on committee findings. "In the case of each senator," Gregory Silver-

master observed, "he would conduct an investigation in their states, applying a light coat of whitewash to some local or state problem, but in return he would receive from them their unanimous support on his national policy recommendations." Moreover, he was able to see to it that most of his committee members were like himself—relatively junior senators, activist-minded, ambitious, and a bit disdainful of the tired, older Senate establishment. They were men with whom he could work and who were willing to accept his leadership.[26]

3. He now had people around him who knew how to publicize his activities, and he himself was less reluctant to claim the power and prestige that his new position brought him. He extracted his share of patronage, perhaps a bit more, from a White House that had ignored him during the 1930s; he even successfully pressed the selection of Bob Hannegan as chairman of the Democratic National Committee. The committee staff put out a steady series of press releases detailing its activities in a way that usually featured Senator Truman. The senator himself spoke on a wide range of issues, including foreign policy. He engineered the notable B^2H^2 (Burton, Ball, Hatch, Hill) resolution in favor of postwar participation in an international body. By 1944, he was the leader of a bloc of two dozen or so younger senators, generally in agreement on foreign and domestic policy. His image was still fuzzy to the general public, but his name and achievements were widely known. Among Washington insiders, he had gained enormous respect and was well positioned for a national leadership role in the Senate, the cabinet, or the vice-presidency.[27]

The new Truman, now a mature, self-confident, highly regarded legislator, had changed little in his approach to politics since his initial run for county judge, eastern district. As always, he regarded virtually every significant interest group as possessing a measure of legitimacy. Once a

[26] The only published scholarly book on the Truman committee, Donald H. Riddle, *The Truman Committee: A Study in Congressional Responsibility* (New Brunswick, N.J.: Rutgers University Press, 1964), suffers from the tendency of many political scientists to focus on problems that are, to say the least, rather abstract—in this instance the problem of defining "committee responsibility." Harry Toumlin, *Diary of Democracy* (New York: Richard R. Smith, 1947), is an uncritical celebration by a former Truman Committee staffer. The Silvermaster analysis is N. Gregory Silvermaster, Memorandum to Henry Morgenthau, Jr., June 1945, Morgenthau Papers, Franklin D. Roosevelt Library; I am grateful to Alfred E. Eckes, Jr., for bringing this item to my attention and supplying me with a copy.

[27] The Truman Committee Papers, Legislative Records Center, National Archives, contain a large file of press releases that clearly indicate that the committee staff was skilled at publicizing its work and that of the senators who led it. Robert A. Divine, *Second Chance: The Triumph of Internationalism during World War II* (New York: Atheneum, 1967), 92, 128, 148, discusses Truman's new standing as a leader of the internationalists.

farmer and a businessman, he found it easy enough to accept the claims of labor unions, ethnic minorities, and blacks as worthy of consideration. Yet he possessed an absolute identification with no single interest and was willing to deliver sharp rebukes to both businessmen and labor leaders whom he considered greedy or irresponsible. When he thought in theoretical terms, he clearly accepted the idea that there existed a general welfare that transcended the claims of any single interest.

To the extent that he placed devils in his vision of American politics, they reflected the quasi-populist heritage of his youth. He intensely distrusted the northeastern financial and corporate establishment and with equal intensity cherished the virtues of the American heartland and its people. He saw the purpose of American politics as the creation of opportunity for the common man, whom he envisaged in various ways: a blue-collar worker who wanted a job without having to buy a union card or pay off a labor leader in advance, a small businessman threatened by monopolistic practices (whether by corporate bigness or by labor unions), a member of a white ethnic minority or a black struggling against discrimination. The business of representative government, he told a constituent in 1941, was "to see that everyone had a fair deal."[28]

It was consistent with this outlook that he considered politics to a large extent a matter of personal relations, whether he was campaigning before small groups or dealing with his colleagues in the Senate. Just as he was popular throughout the party, he felt that the party should be as nearly all-inclusive as possible. He had no sympathy with the efforts of ideologues to exclude this or that hated enemy. The few senators with whom he did not get on well tended to be dogmatists, such as Harry Byrd or Robert A. Taft. His friendships tended to be closest with moderates; it is apt to describe him, as has Samuel Lubell, as a "border-state senator" who generally supported the New Deal with some qualms about its more radical tendencies and little disposition to assume the leadership in fighting for its landmark proposals.[29]

In the closest analysis of his Senate voting record, James Hilty and Gary Fink have perceived a shift in Truman's position within the New

[28] Truman to E. J. Wallace, 16 July 1941, Senatorial File, Truman Papers, HSTL. The correspondence in this file is fascinating and refreshing in its bluntness. Truman did not hesitate to tell his correspondents what he thought during his second term in the Senate. (The papers for much of his first Senate term were lost when placed in storage during World War II.)

[29] Samuel Lubell, *The Future of American Politics*, 3d ed. rev. (New York: Harper & Row, 1965), 26–37.

Deal coalition. At the beginning, he was on its "right wing"; during his second term in the upper house, he was sharply visible on the left, "a change due not only to movement on Truman's part, but also to the gradual but perceptible drift of the Democratic party to the right, the declining strength of the liberal insurgency, and the Republican reascendancy."[30]

The question of what politics did to Truman's personality is more interesting. Indications are that the compromises he was forced to make did not always weigh easily with him. Reared and educated as a moral absolutist, he was forced to function in a shadowy world in which honest public service coexisted uneasily with graft, organized crime, electoral dishonesty, and police-protected vice. However much he kept his own hands clean, he could not escape the stigma of guilt by association. The result surely was to magnify the insecurity that stemmed from such earlier experiences as the nature of his childhood, his family's setbacks, and his own business failures. Politics intensified his drive for recognition and became also a quest for vindication against unfair critics.

One response was the unrelenting hard work that characterized his political career from Jackson County to the White House. Other byproducts were less desirable. A man of great stamina and excellent health, he nonetheless suffered from periodic bouts of exhaustion apparently brought on by extreme stress. The most pervasive character trait that his political career intensifed was a capacity for sheer rage that was unhealthy in a public leader. Outwardly, Harry Truman was the most affable of men, invariably greeting others with a big grin and a modest demeanor. Inwardly, he cultivated a belief that half the world was against him or at least letting him down, while the other half was conducting a smear campaign against him and his family. He simmered over slights, real or imagined, from others, and occasionally broke off relationships on flimsy grounds. At times, his capacity for resentment could seem boundless; there could be little doubt that he unnecessarily made a few enemies and lost a few friends.[31]

---

[30] Gary M. Fink and James W. Hilty, "Prologue: The Senate Voting Record of Harry S. Truman," *Journal of Interdisciplinary History* IV (Autumn 1973): 207–35. Steinberg, *Man from Missouri*, 144–45.

[31] See Pickwick memos, cited above, note 21, for examples of Truman's anger. Some notable episodes that illustrate Truman's tendency to become angry with friends are his relationships with Bernard Baruch, Victor Messall, and Hugh Fulton. For Baruch, see Ferrell, ed., *"Dear Bess,"* 483, 526, 560–61, and Ferrell, ed., *Off the Record: The Private Papers of Harry S. Truman* (New York: Harper & Row, 1980), 134; Hillman, ed., *Mr. President*, 134. For Messall, see Messall to Truman, 19 August 1938, Senatorial File,

Perhaps the single biggest private resentment that Truman contained within himself before becoming president was his hatred and distrust of the press. He long had disliked the *Kansas City Star,* and very quickly after taking the statewide political stage in Missouri he developed an even fiercer hatred of the *St. Louis Post-Dispatch.* (As Rufus Burrus recalls it, his bitterness toward the *Star* became all but cast in concrete when it ran prominent stories about the foreclosure of the mortgage on his mother's home.) Although he was on friendly terms with most working reporters, he seems privately to have distrusted just about all of them.[32]

The Harry Truman who was elected vice-president of the United States in 1944 had come a long way in the twenty-two years since his business had failed and he had won his first election to county office. He had reoriented his life from the simple work-hard, get-ahead ambitions of his younger years into the more ambiguous world of politics. By virtue of talent and effort, he had achieved a measure of success that must have been beyond his dreams. But his new career appears to have exacted a psychic toll also, exhibited in episodes of anger and depression that seem quite unlike anything we know of in his earlier life. For all his good qualities, he also had become an inordinately touchy man whose suspicions of others were easily aroused. Perhaps these characteristics demonstrated little more than the truism that politics is among the least security-inducing of professions. Nevertheless, they would haunt his presidency and repeatedly lead to behavior that would undermine his authority.

Personality, politics, and the presidency

"Well, I'm getting organized now," the new president told his wife some eight weeks after taking office. "It won't be long until I can sit back and study the whole picture and tell 'em what is to be done in each department. When things come to that stage there'll be no more to this job than there was to running Jackson County and not any more worry."[33] The remark was characteristic of Harry Truman's determined—one is tempted to say, desperate—optimism. But it equally reflected an initial lack of understanding about the nature of the presidency itself.

Truman Papers, HSTL; Ferrell, ed., *"Dear Bess,"* 443–44, 492; Daniels, *Man of Independence,* 225. For Fulton, see Margaret Truman, *Harry S. Truman,* 215.
[32] Burrus interview; Ferrell, ed., *"Dear Bess,"* 426.
[33] Ferrell, ed., *"Dear Bess,"* 514.

There can be no doubt that from the time he accepted the vice-presidential nomination Truman had repeated intimations that he very likely would soon be president of the United States.[34] He probably was emotionally prepared for the shock of Roosevelt's death, but there was little he could do to ready himself for the presidency, given Roosevelt's seeming indifference toward discussing other than immediate political problems with him. And, of course, no one had expected FDR's death to come so quickly. As a result, Truman fell back on his instincts during his early months in office.

The most obvious of these was to surround himself with friends he knew and trusted. Some were able, others beyond their depth, but neither the liberal nor the conservative press discriminated among them. Both reflexively asserted, with obvious historical parallels, that the president was surrounding himself with a "Missouri gang."[35] Truman's reaction was a normal one and the "Missouri gang" stereotype a blatant distortion of reality. He very much wanted to keep some Roosevelt people whom he liked and trusted (among them Harry Hopkins, Jonathan Daniels, and Sam Rosenman), and neither his cabinet nor his staff was ever as top-heavy with people from his home state as was commonly alleged. All the same, those highly visible Missourians created a negative impression, however unjustified, that haunted the Truman presidency for the next seven years.

Truman related most easily and fully to men like himself—products of the American heartland or the border South, educated in their home states and possessing appearances and mannerisms that evidenced their origins. He enjoyed their company, liked an occasional after-hours drink with them, and felt free to use rough, rural language around them. But he valued even more highly another quality. As in the Senate, he preferred doers to posturers, and he sought quiet achievers. He detested prima donnas (a favorite epithet) or people afflicted with "Potomac fever." As his administration progressed, he increasingly found such men from backgrounds quite different from his own.

By his second term, in fact, the White House staff would consist almost entirely of non-Missourians, many of them with Ivy League educations. They were, of course, men of liberal Democratic political sympa-

---

[34] See, e.g., Daniels, *Man of Independence*, 255; Harry Easley, Oral History Memoir, 41, HSTL.

[35] Daniels, *Man of Independence*, 266–67; Steinberg, *Man from Missouri*, 242–43; Hamby, *Beyond the New Deal*, 54–59; Eben Ayers, Diary, 17 April, 18–19 April, 12 June, Ayers Papers, HSTL.

thies, but they may fairly (and nondisparagingly) be described as pragmatists and technicians rather than ideologists. Truman may not have cottoned to their northeastern intellectual style, and he maintained a formal relationship with them, rarely using profanity in their presence or inviting any of them for an after-hours drink. But he took them seriously, used them effectively, and won their loyalty.

Another wholly understandable reaction in the first months was a determination to represent himself as a decisive leader, both because he needed to think of himself as such and because he understood that the public wanted reassurance. In the beginning, this undertaking was on the whole successful. Yet it soon wore thin. He was not the sort of person who was adept at dodging tough questions, keeping silent, or simply saying that something was under consideration. Soon, his dialogue with reporters in press conferences and on other occasions led to reversals that transmuted his public image from one of decisive leadership to one of impulsiveness. The examples are legion; one thinks immediately of the unhesitating endorsement of Henry Wallace's Madison Square Garden speech, the "red herring" characterization of the early accusations against Alger Hiss, the offhand remarks about the possibility of using the atomic bomb in the Korean War.[36]

Then there were his temperamental outbursts, the most memorable example of which was that letter to the *Washington Post* music critic. Many will also recall the angry characterization of the Marine Corps at about the same time. But these were only two of many incidents that made him appear less than presidential to much of the public. By 1952, an editorial cartoonist was able to win the Pulitzer Prize with an effort that depicted an angry president confronting a group of journalists and telling them: "Your editors ought to have more sense than to print what I say!"[37]

Yet on important matters Harry Truman was neither impulsive nor prone to act in spasms of anger. In one crisis after another, he moved with caution and deliberation, invariably seeking a wide range of informed advice and attempting to construct as broad a consensus as pos-

---

[36] *Public Papers of the Presidents of the United States: Harry S. Truman,* 1946 (Washington: U.S. Government Printing Office, 1962), 426–27; *Public Papers, 1948,* 432–33; *Public Papers, 1950* (Washington: U.S. Government Printing Office, 1965), 727.

[37] Donovan, *Tumultuous Years,* 311–12; Franklin D. Mitchell, "An Act of Presidential Indiscretion: Harry S. Truman, Congressman McDonough, and the Marine Corps Incident of 1950," *Presidential Studies Quarterly* 11 (Fall 1981): 565–75; *New York Times,* 6 May 1952, for Pulitzer cartoon.

sible. His administration took two years to arrive at a coherently formulated, publicly stated goal of containing the expansion of Soviet
Communism. Until finally forced to the wall in September 1946, he hoped
to keep both James Byrnes and Henry Wallace in his cabinet. He took
nearly a week to commit ground troops to Korea. The decision to relieve
General MacArthur was all but forced upon him by behavior that skirted
the limits of constitutional government. It was peculiar that his circum-
spection on the big things was obscured by his tendency to be impulsive
and temperamental on the little ones, and unfortunate for both himself
and the nation that this characteristic disproportionately damaged his
presidency.

Truman was above all a man of orderly habits and thought patterns.
Once the initial shock of becoming president had worn off, once he had
begun to develop a grasp of issues he had to master from scratch, once
he began to feel comfortable handling the levers of power, he set about
the task of restructuring both a disorderly White House and the entire
executive branch.

The patterns of jurisdiction that had characterized the Roosevelt administration disturbed him. Within the White House, Roosevelt had relied heavily on unofficial advisers (most notably Harry Hopkins) and had
established few clear lines of authority or issue-jurisdiction among his
official staff. Whether this messiness resulted from the application of a
conscious plan and whether it possessed the hidden virtues that Arthur
Schlesinger, Jr., and others have attributed to it, are questions beyond the
scope of this paper. (Much probably depended on the mutual tolerance
of the personalities who worked in the White House.) Truman established a much greater degree of orderliness, although unlike Eisenhower
he refused to name a single chief of staff with near-total control over the
information and people to be granted access to the president. The staff
organization that evolved might be described as one of structured decentralization.

John Steelman, the assistant to the president who had handled administrative routine, frequently found himself called on in his area of special
expertise, labor relations. The special counsel to the president (Clark
Clifford, 1946–50; Charles Murphy, 1950–53) functioned as general
legal adviser and chief speech writer; especially during Clifford's tenure,
he was informal chief of staff of the administrative assistants, each of
whom was given reasonably well defined areas of responsibility. The press
secretary (Charles Ross, 1945–50; Joseph Short, 1950–52; Roger Tubby,

1952–53) continued a job that had been well defined, and Ross especially could have an impact on policy decisions.

Other aides handled appointments to see the president (Matthew J. Connelly), formal correspondence (William D. Hassett), and patronage (Donald Dawson). Truman seems to have reserved most important congressional contacts for himself, with the special counsel or other aides involved according to the specific issue. The director of the budget and the chairman of the Council of Economic Advisers appear always to have had direct access to the president, although Leon Keyserling realized that his effectiveness could be enhanced by maintaining a close liaison with the special counsel. With the exception of Admiral Robert L. Dennison, who exercised great influence over maritime and shipping issues, the military aides do not seem to have played significant policy roles.[38]

Truman equally sought clear and precise relations with the cabinet. When he became president, many of the functions for which cabinet departments normally were responsible had been preempted by emergency war agencies. He wanted to phase them out as soon as possible and bring the cabinet back to what he considered its appropriate level of responsibility. His use of the cabinet, or at least his ideas on how it should be used, are interesting. He was a constitutional formalist who approached the workings of government from almost a civics-textbook viewpoint. At the beginning, he assumed that the executive branch was run by the president with his cabinet members acting as aides. He formed cabinet committees to lobby for pending legislative proposals, such as the full employment bill, and to carry out policy decisions.

After observing this system for several months, Truman's first director of the budget, Harold Smith, a holdover from the Roosevelt administration and a perceptive analyst of the governmental process, made bold to deliver a lecture to the president on the fallacies of his modus operandi: "I pointed out that the President should think of his Cabinet members as operating commanders in their particular fields; that the Cabinet should never be used as a Staff and that it was disastrous to attempt to do so." The president, he went on, should look to his cabinet for policy and political recommendations, but he needed to remember that their judgment would be colored by their particular viewpoints and personal ambitions.

---

[38] Richard E. Neustadt's contribution to Francis H. Heller, ed., *The Truman White House: The Administration of the Presidency, 1945–53* (Lawrence: Regents Press of Kansas, 1980), is an excellent summary of the staff situation at the end of the Truman presidency. Unfortunately, there is no study of the evolution of the staff system from 1945 to 1953.

It was absolutely necessary for the president "to have a separate staff operating in a detached, objective atmosphere to supply him with information and to check all the information that came to him."[39]

Something resembling a coherent White House staff operation did become discernible in the months after this conversation. Truman would learn in time that in the main the cabinet officers had to be left to run their own departments. (It was neither possible nor desirable for a small White House staff to monitor most day-to-day operations.) Realizing that the interests of the president were not always identical with those of any given cabinet member, he sought as large a degree of loyalty, as great a sense of teamwork, and as much efficiency as he could extract from them.[40]

From the beginning, however, he was firm on a point most clearly illustrated by his rocky relationship with Secretary of State James F. Byrnes: On matters that he considered of presidential importance, he expected close consultation, deference, and respect. He knew that on many issues he was not well enough informed to make a decision without expert advice. He does not appear even to have required his cabinet members to present him with alternatives. What he did require was the final power to say yes or no, even when this amounted to little more than the power to approve that which inevitably would be approved. And he wanted his office and himself to receive the respect he felt it deserved. A "border-state politician" like Byrnes could erase years of respect and admiration by behaving as if he were a business partner rather than a subordinate. A northeastern patrician like Dean Acheson could win the president's ineradicable loyalty and friendship by giving him, and the office, every measure of regard that Truman needed.[41]

When Truman became president, he felt that his ten years in Washington had taught him that the federal bureaucracy was wasteful, inefficient, and encumbered with too many overlapping lines of jurisdiction. "The

[39] Harold D. Smith, Diary, 8 February 1946, Smith Papers, HSTL. The Smith and Ayers diaries, taken together, give a valuable sense of Truman's mind and the workings of the White House during the first year of his presidency.

[40] As late as 1949, however, Truman expected to be able to name Jonathan Daniels secretary of the navy. When he found himself forced to accede to the refusal of Louis Johnson, secretary of defense, he offered Daniels the consolation prize of an authorized biography, a recognition of cabinet responsibility especially beneficial to historians.

[41] On the Truman-Byrnes relationship, see Truman, *Year of Decisions*, 546–53, and Byrnes, *All in One Lifetime*, especially 399–403. Robert L. Messer, *The End of an Alliance: James F. Byrnes, Roosevelt, Truman, and the Origins of the Cold War* (Chapel Hill: University of North Carolina Press, 1983), is a fine scholarly account. On the Truman-Acheson relationship, see Dean Acheson, *Present at the Creation: My Years in the State Department* (New York: W. W. Norton, 1969).

longer I am here the more I hate the Bureaucrats," he told an old friend in 1944. "They have neither common sense nor judgment." A man who had possessed a passion for administrative neatness since his years as a county judge, he took some matters into his own hands.

He made the unification of the armed forces and the consolidation of foreign intelligence activities primary White House objectives. He appointed the Hoover Commission to undertake a study of the entire executive branch with an eye to greater efficiency, secured an executive reorganization act, and did as much as he could to implement its recommendations. The results were limited but useful. William Pemberton has argued that Truman left the executive branch more manageable than he found it but ran up against interest-group politics in his attempt to create an administrative model. Pemberton also notes one by-product of the administrative reform drive: "Support for the [Hoover] commission proposals, which turned into a national fad, allowed the people to ratify the New Deal by trying to insure that its programs were effectively administered."[42]

The president, of course, is not simply a chief administrator; he is probably most in view as chief legislator. Truman had been acceptable to Roosevelt for the vice-presidency in large measure because of his popularity in Congress. FDR assumed that, unlike Henry Wallace, Truman would be an effective lobbyist for administration proposals and a purveyor of goodwill for the White House. As much as possible, he seems to have fulfilled this function during his brief vice-presidency.[43] Throughout his term as president, he seems to have maintained friendly relations with almost everyone on Capitol Hill, however bitter the political differences between himself and some of his former colleagues. Yet his domestic record is generally recalled for what it did not achieve, and he is most commonly remembered as flailing away at a hostile, unresponsive Congress. Here, as in other aspects of his life, appearances were deceiving.

Congress is not a neutral, inert mass waiting to be stirred by presidential leadership. Who could argue with such a truism? Yet the historians who speak in general terms about Truman's lack of leadership appear to

---

[42] Truman to Marvin Gates, 28 January 1942, Senatorial File, Truman Papers, HSTL; William E. Pemberton, *Bureaucratic Politics: Executive Reorganization during the Truman Administration* (Columbia: University of Missouri Press, 1979), 174.

[43] Truman's brief vice-presidency is covered in Daniels, *Man of Independence,* 255–57; Steinberg, *Man from Missouri,* 228–235; and Gosnell, *Truman's Crises,* 209–214. See also Arthur F. McClure and Donna Costigan, "The Truman Vice Presidency: Constructive Apprenticeship or Brief Interlude?" *Missouri Historical Review* LXV (April 1971): 318–41.

proceed from the opposite assumption, arguing that a talented and vigorous president, presumably one capable of making a good speech and somehow persuading or forcing Congress to follow him, could have marshaled the American people behind him and obtained passage of the entire Fair Deal agenda. It is ironic that their example, usually implicit, at times explicit, is Franklin D. Roosevelt, for it was precisely Roosevelt's steadily declining leverage with the Congress that had made Truman seem so attractive as a running mate.

Different Congresses have different structures, and Truman adopted a different stance toward each of the four Congresses he faced. But a few generalizations appear in order. In each Congress, the controlling elite ("the establishment") and the center of ideological gravity were located to the right of Truman's Fair Deal. With the possible exception of the Eightieth Congress, this situation roughly reflected the attitude of most Americans, who, opinion data demonstrated, were conservative in the simplest sense of that word—wanting to preserve the society in which they lived and undisposed toward major change in either ideological direction. Even if Congress had somehow been unrepresentative, its institutional mechanisms, particularly the filibuster and the power of the House Rules Committee, made it possible for a determined minority to block new departures.

From his first message to Congress to the end of his presidency, Truman advocated proposals for which no majority or potential majority can be discerned—national health insurance, civil rights, aid to education, repeal of Taft-Hartley, the Brannan plan. His Senate leaders (Alben Barkley, Scott Lucas, and Gerald McFarland) were amiable, ineffectual men; his House leader (Sam Rayburn) was too attached to the mores of the chamber to make himself the consistent instrument of a presidential attempt to dominate it.,

Finally Truman, like Roosevelt and every other president before him, faced the decentralized nature of the U.S. party system, a fact of life that made party discipline, as it is customarily exercised in parliamentary democracies, all but nonexistent. A system in which lines of authority run directly from voters to individual legislators, rather than from voters to party to legislator, deprives a party leadership of the most effective means of discipline (control of nominations) and may deprive the leadership itself of coherence or even any generally accepted identity.

In general, presidents before Truman had brought Congress down major new paths only when they could display apparent overwhelming approval or when they were acting to meet an overriding national emergency. Like most presidents, Truman possessed only slim resources in his efforts to work his will on Congress. In this perspective, what he achieved looms larger than most scholars believe.[44]

He was at the beginning overoptimistic about his chances with the Seventy-ninth, or "reconversion," Congress. Quickly he learned that his influence and popularity as a senator were not transferable to 1600 Pennsylvania Avenue on most matters of substance. Nevertheless, he did secure a major piece of legislation, the Employment Act of 1946. He did not get what most people in truth did not want, the extension of wartime economic controls.

The Eightieth Congress, the "Republican" Congress, gave him his most enduring image. Facing an opposition-controlled legislative body almost certain to reject any domestic program he proposed, he adopted the role of an oppositionist. Displaying amazing virtuosity, he persuaded most of the Republicans to support a "bipartisan foreign policy." Yet he never attempted serious negotiations with Republican leaders on any domestic issue, and he blamed them for every difficulty in American life. Concentrating on building a record that played to the interest groups that made up the Democratic presidential party, he took his case directly to the people and won in 1948.[45]

His success was accompanied by the election of the Eighty-first Congress, in many ways the most complex and interesting of all. Truman worked hard at legislative leadership with this Congress, even obtaining curbs on the power of the House Rules Committee. Yet it was here that his major Fair Deal issues, with the exception of a not entirely successful housing program, met defeat. What are frequently overlooked are his

[44] These generalizations are based on my research in a wide range of primary and secondary sources over the past twenty years. A few of the most important and accessible sources for them are George H. Gallup, *The Gallup Poll: Public Opinion, 1935–1971*, vols. 1 and 2 (New York: Random House, 1972); James MacGregor Burns, *The Deadlock of Democracy* (Englewood Cliffs, N.J.: Prentice-Hall, 1963); David R. Mayhew, *Party Loyalty Among Congressmen* (Cambridge: Harvard University Press, 1966); Samuel Lubell, *Future of American Politics, and Revolt of the Moderates* (New York: Harper & Brothers, 1956); and Richard E. Neustadt, *Presidential Power: The Politics of Leadership* (New York: John Wiley, 1960). Relevant chapters of the following two books strike me as particularly effective in displaying the character of the postwar (1945–c. 1963) Congresses: Rowland Evans and Robert Novak, *Lyndon B. Johnson: The Exercises of Power* (New York: New American Library, 1966), and Harry McPherson, *A Political Education* (Boston: Little, Brown, 1972).

[45] Susan M. Hartmann, *Truman and the 80th Congress* (Columbia: University of Missouri Press, 1971), does an excellent job of examining the way in which the White House dealt with this Congress.

successes. The Eighty-first Congress was most revelatory of the underlying social-political climate of the Truman administration, and Truman's final record was congruent with what we know of public opinion.

The White House predictably lost on the big issues for which there was no majority in the country at large, but it consistently won on issues for which there was widespread support. Aid to middle-class housing was the most obvious, but there were numerous other victories that might be described as major additions to or updatings of existing New Deal legislation. Arthur J. Altmeyer has described the Social Security Act of 1950, for example, as almost as significant as the original legislation itself. Truman's experience with the Eighty-first Congress displayed the legislative side of his role as president in domestic policy, as a consolidator who built constructively onto the edifice erected by his predecessor.[46]

The Eighty-second Congress reflected Democratic setbacks in the 1950 elections and ran through the domestic trauma of the unwinnable stalemate in Korea. Here Truman faced a situation almost as intractable as that posed by the Eightieth Congress. For the sake of achieving party unity behind his foreign policy, he abandoned any serious attempts at major domestic legislation. Instead, he contented himself with a series of pronouncements designed to keep his program before the electorate and to see that it remained part of the agenda of the Democratic party.[47]

Truman, Samuel Lubell has suggested, purposely zigzagged in an effort to appease all the diverse groups of the Democratic party and ultimately kept it on dead center, the only position in which it could remain unified. As a description of the Truman presidency, the Lubell thesis has something to be said for it. As a description of Truman's motivation, it is superficial. It has a grain of truth in this respect: As a nonideological man with a fierce attachment to his party, Truman was an inclusionist rather than an exclusionist. He wanted the Democratic party to embrace as many diverse groups as possible and hoped to reconcile even northern blacks and southern whites.[48]

[46] On the housing issue, see Richard O. Davies, *Housing Reform during the Truman Administration* (Columbia: University of Missouri Press, 1966). On Social Security, see Arthur J. Altmeyer, *The Formative Years of Social Security* (Madison: University of Wisconsin Press, 1968), 7. The Eighty-first Congress is among the most studied by political scientists, but both David B. Truman, *The Congressional Party* (New York: John Wiley, 1959), and Duncan MacRae, Jr., *Dimensions of Congressional Voting* (Berkeley: University of California Press, 1958), may strike historians as less than satisfactory.

[47] Hamby, *Beyond the New Deal*, chap. 20.

[48] Lubell, *Future of American Politics*, chap. 2.

Lubell also implies that Truman did not really believe in much of what he advocated. That judgment rests, I think, on a fundamental misreading of his personality. Harry Truman was the sort of person who *had* to believe in positions he advocated publicly. Sometimes belief did not come naturally or easily, but either because Truman wanted to believe for political reasons or because he underwent a change of heart, it came. The classic example is civil rights. Consider the arguments that came most naturally to him—the unacceptability of mob violence directed toward black war veterans and the need to give everyone, black or white, a fair chance in life. These arguments came from deep within his family background and experience. He may have used these arguments so often because he needed to convince himself as well as the broader electorate. Personal letters that he wrote after leaving the presidency and his public membership in the Democratic Advisory Council provide convincing evidence that after it made no political difference, he continued to believe in civil rights, national health insurance, and all the rest—that in fact he took pride in his identification with them.[49]

Discussions of Truman's congressional leadership have rarely said much about his foreign policy record. Yet here he was as shrewd and as effective as any American president. Throughout his years in office, Truman consistently had his way with Congress on the top priority of his administration, foreign policy. Throughout his first term and into the beginning of his second, he enlisted the support of a majority of the Republican party. As the Republicans succumbed to McCarthyism and began to take advantage of the political opportunities presented by the Korean War, he brought his own party behind him on such difficult issues as the MacArthur dismissal and the dispatch of additional ground forces to Europe. Truman's success in the Eightieth Congress was especially remarkable. The key to it, I think, was this: The Truman Doctrine and the Marshall Plan won the vociferous opposition of the far Right and the far Left, but Truman preempted the center. Here he found himself in the position in

---

[49] The best and most thorough study of Truman and civil rights is Donald R. McCoy and Richard T. Ruetten, *Quest and Response: Minority Rights and the Truman Administration* (Lawrence: Regents Press of Kansas, 1973); representative counterparts to their generally favorable evaluation of Truman may be found in William C. Berman, *The Politics of Civil Rights in the Truman Administration* (Columbus: Ohio State University Press, 1970), and Harvard Sitkoff, "Harry Truman and the Election of 1948: The Coming of Age of Civil Rights in American Politics," *Journal of Southern History* XXXVII (November 1971): 597–616. For Truman's private feelings after he left the presidency, see Ferrell, ed., *Off the Record*, 370.

which he was most comfortable and from which it was easiest to build majority support.

When Truman became president, he possessed some well-defined impulses about U.S. foreign policy. Foremost among these was a strong commitment to what people vaguely and rather naively called "internationalism"—the belief that the United States should exercise vigorous leadership in postwar world affairs and work for the betterment of mankind. He claimed to have carried with him for years lines of poetry from Tennyson describing mankind's last apocalyptic war and the establishment of universal law. He was capable of genuine eloquence when he spoke to visitors of envisaging TVAs for the Euphrates, the Yangtze, or the Danube. He also was predisposed toward suspicion of all totalitarian states, the Soviet Union as well as Nazi Germany.[50]

But his actual experience in diplomacy was nil. He wanted to establish himself as a leader and make key decisions, but he also realized that he needed expert advice. In private, he could make statements so naive and ill-informed that they bordered on the bizarre: Stalin reminded him of Tom Pendergast, Stalin was a prisoner of the Politburo, Soviet foreign policy followed the dictates of "the will of Peter the Great." He seems to have been about as tolerant of Third World neutralism as was John Foster Dulles and may have been more prone to confuse it with communism. Perhaps it was shallow, perhaps understandable, that his conceptualization of most problems depended more on specific examples than generalized understanding. For example, his contempt for the regime of Spanish *caudillo* Francisco Franco deepened into strong personal outrage when he learned that the fascist dictator persecuted Baptists and Masons.[51]

Still, it is hard to discern any significant diplomatic decision of his presidency based simply on personal whim. Although he might vent his prejudices and misinformation to friends, aides, and occasional journalists, he relied heavily on the experts for policy advice. Especially after General George C. Marshall became secretary of state, it was the State Department that did the basic thinking about U.S. foreign policy, gave

---

[50] John Hersey, "Profiles [Harry S. Truman]," *New Yorker,* 14 April 1961; David Lilienthal, *The Atomic Energy Years* (New York: Harper & Row, 1964), 475; Ferrell, ed., *"Dear Bess,"* 471, 474.

[51] Daniels, *Man of Independence,* 23; J. Garry Clifford, "Harry Truman and Peter the Great's Will," *Diplomatic History* IV (Fall 1980): 371–85; Truman, Memo to Dean Acheson, 2 August 1951, and attached letter, Thomas Harkins to Fred Land, 25 July 1951, Foreign—Spain, President's Secretary's File, Truman Papers, HSTL.

the president most of his information, and presented him with the alternatives. Truman's style of decision making provided ample play for the expression of his temperament as a constructive force in U.S. foreign policy, even as it assured that he would not undertake initiatives based on ignorance.

It was this temperament that also determined his response to McCarthyism and the civil liberties crisis of his second term. No one can claim that Truman's record was flawless. His loyalty program was poorly conceived and his Smith Act prosecutions ill-advised. He felt compelled by political considerations to praise J. Edgar Hoover and the FBI, although he privately detested both the man and the institution. But his personal experience, his reading of history, his partisanship, his sense of commitment to his friends, and his civil libertarian advisers all combined to produce a president instinctively opposed to anti-communist excesses.

He had suffered investigations into his own finances and personal life in the Pendergast years and resented the experience bitterly. An avid reader of American history, especially influenced by the partisan Democratic works of Claude Bowers, he identified with the Jeffersonian principles of the 1790s. As the Internal Security Act of 1950 came to the White House, he resisted pressure from his own party to go along with it and told his advisers he would not sign "a sedition bill." And surely it was not by accident that he chose primary advisers on civil liberties and national security—Clark Clifford, Charles Murphy, Stephen Spingarn, and Max Lowenthal—who consistently displayed more concern about civil liberties than about communist subversion. So did Truman. Despite revisionist claims that he initiated McCarthyism by exaggerating the dangers of communism at home, any thorough examination of his pronouncements on the subject demonstrates that he consistently argued that the communist threat was primarily external.

Perhaps his fundamental impulses, however, were his sense of obligation to his associates and his need to defend his administration against the partisan opposition. He denounced McCarthyism and Senator McCarthy himself more strongly and regularly than almost any other politician in Washington, albeit to little effect. Defending General Marshall against McCarthy's smears after Dwight Eisenhower had backed away from doing so, he revealed his most elemental feelings when he told a crowd in Boston, "I stand by my friends."[52]

---

[52] Hamby, *Beyond the New Deal*, 410–14, 502.

Here, as was usually the case during his presidency, his temperament served him well.

Reality and legend

Harry Truman was not the closet conservative so frequently depicted by revisionist historians, nor was he simply a nonideological pol who happened to have an aversion to cheap cigars. He possessed a complex political identity, composed of elements that were not entirely compatible. He was an intensely partisan Democrat who identified with the reformist wing of his party. He lived and assimilated within himself all the contradictory currents of the Age of Reform, from Bryan through FDR. He began his adulthood as a neopopulist entrepreneur, picked up the principles of "business progressivism" in public administration, and moved into the urban-labor liberalism of the New Deal. Along the way, he had to compromise his more idealistic values, made a virtue of doing so, and took pride in considering himself a practical politician.

For a man often remembered for his cockiness, he had a remarkable understanding of his limitations. His political campaigns were attuned to issues, not to his personality. Assuming that people would be inclined to vote less for his personality than for the causes with which he identified himself, he practiced the politics of the hard sell: "I am not asking you to vote for me alone," he declared in a 1948 whistle-stop speech at Fresno, California, "I want you to vote for yourselves. Vote for your own interests."[53]

He practiced interest-group politics with considerable skill but never identified fully with any one interest and felt it imperative to preserve his sense of independence from all of them. Inclined to accept the designation "liberal," he nonetheless had little patience with liberal intellectuals and their pet politicians. When asked to define the term, he never got much further than the proposition that liberalism meant a concern for the welfare of all the people. By instinct more than by theory, he was what came to be called a Vital Center liberal with a mixed view of human nature, a distrust of excessive centralization, and a skepticism about all absolutes.

In dealing with domestic problems, this attitude translated into a belief in equal opportunity, a suspicion of bigness, a rather broad view of just who was the "little man," a distaste for bureaucratic government that

[53] *Public Papers, 1948, 550.*

coexisted uneasily with advocacy of the welfare state, and a mixed bag of fiscal attitudes in which budget balancing and easy money bumped against each other. In foreign policy, an area in which he was untrained and not very knowledgeable, there were two elements at the core of his faith: a belief in an American mission throughout the world and a conviction that the totalitarianism of the Left was as menacing as that of the Right.

When Harry Truman went into retirement in 1953, he was unpopular and discredited. There can be little doubt that most Americans felt that he had not been big enough for his job. Slowly, his public reputation recovered. By the end of the 1950s, he had a good press and considerable public esteem. Through the 1960s and 1970s his standing grew steadily. By 1974, it was so high that a new and unsure Republican president would attempt to gain public favor by comparing himself to the man who once had been the scourge of the Grand Old Party.

Good substantive reasons existed for the Truman renaissance among those who undertook serious comparisons of his presidential performance with that of most of his successors. But these were less important than the increasing attractiveness of the Truman image. To a generation in which individuality was all but smothered by bigness, bureaucracy, and impersonality, he represented an era of small communities, sincere relationships, and elemental values. To a generation alienated by transparently synthetic and devious leadership, the man who said what he thought and sneered at the pollsters seemed to possess a quality of authenticity that had departed from American political life.

Truman liked to imagine himself as a composite of the American common man, and in many ways he was the ordinary American in his beliefs, his tastes, and his behavior. He represented as vividly as any American political leader the American democratic man. A Baptist, an intense cultural traditionalist, a man who could seem obsessed with the need for recognition, an inner-directed personality who managed to put his imprint on an other-directed world, Truman in many ways was a magnified image of the American democrat with his virtues, his limitations, his insecurities.

Democracies tend to oscillate between self-glorification and self-doubt. In their search for political leadership, especially in difficult times, they are most receptive to extraordinary individuals who display powers well beyond those of the common man. It was Truman's misfortune to follow such a man, and his presidency suffered by comparison. At times, as in

1948, his talent for striking a sense of identification with the ordinary American became a political asset; more often it was a liability. Nonetheless, Truman left behind a record of considerable achievement, and however much historians may continue to debate it, it seems likely that he will remain enshrined in the popular consciousness as an example of the potential of American democracy.

Part I

Domestic politics and issues

2

Forging America's postwar order:
domestic politics and political economy
in the age of Truman

ROBERT GRIFFITH

As often happens in the search after truth, if we have answered one question, we have raised many more; if we have followed one track home, we have had to pass by others that opened off it and led, or seemed to lead, to far other goals.

Sir James George Frazer, The Golden Bough

Almost every book written on the presidency of Harry S. Truman includes, if indeed it does not begin with, an account of that afternoon of 12 April 1945, when the vice-president, having just left the Senate chamber, where he had been presiding, headed for the Capitol Hill office of House Speaker Sam Rayburn to join a small group of Democratic leaders who met there regularly to open a bottle and "strike a blow for liberty." "Before I could even begin a conversation with the half a dozen fellows that were there," Truman later recalled, "Sam told me that [White House aide] Stephen Early had called and wanted me to call right back. I did, and Early said to come right over to the White House." Minutes later, at the other end of Pennsylvania Avenue, Truman was taken directly to Eleanor Roosevelt's study. "Harry," Mrs. Roosevelt said, "the president is dead." There was a long pause as Truman struggled to collect himself. Then he asked, "Is there anything I can do for you?" Mrs. Roosevelt gently replied, "Is there anything *we* can do for *you*? For you are the one in trouble now."[1]

[1] Harry S. Truman, *Memoirs,* vol. 1, *Year of Decisions* (Garden City, N.Y.: Doubleday, 1955), 5; Robert H. Ferrell, ed., *Off the Record: The Private Papers of Harry S. Truman* (New York: Harper & Row, 1980), 14–16; Robert J. Donovan, *Conflict and Crisis: The Presidency of Harry S. Truman, 1945–1948* (New York: W. W. Norton, 1977), 4–8.

Yet neither Eleanor Roosevelt nor the new president understood just how great those troubles would prove or how critical the years that followed would be in shaping the history of the modern United States. The world that Harry Truman and other Americans had inherited was strange and in some ways rawly new. In Europe, more than three decades of violent upheaval had not only taken an enormous toll in lives and material but had irreparably weakened the old, European-led world system that had ordered international affairs for more than a century. Germany, whose economic and military power had dominated the continent throughout much of the twentieth century, now faced virtual annihilation, as Allied armies closed from both the east and the west. France and Britain, once great imperial powers and now ostensibly victorious, were but little better off than the vanquished. By contrast, the Soviet Union had emerged from the war a major, if battered, new world power. In the Far East, the imminent defeat of Japan promised to change the balance of power radically in the Pacific, while throughout the colonial world of Asia and Africa the collapse of imperial Europe released powerful revolutionary stirrings among peoples seeking self-determination and economic development.

The United States, which alone of the great powers had escaped the destruction wrought by war, was now the most powerful nation in the world, both militarily and economically. In victory, however, Americans and their leaders would confront myriad difficult questions: What would be the character of the postwar relations between the United States and its allies, especially the Soviet Union? With its vanquished enemies, Germany and Japan? With the war-devastated nations of Europe? And with the peoples of Latin America, Africa, and Asia? What role would the United States play in the reconstruction of world affairs? And how would the costs and burdens of that role be distributed? What implications would all this, in turn, have for the ordering of politics and economics at home?

Harry Truman and other Americans faced an equally difficult set of problems in their domestic affairs. The Depression that had preceded World War II had produced enormous, if piecemeal and at times contradictory, changes in U.S. politics and political economy. The New Deal had sought to impose social discipline on U.S. capitalism, to protect individuals from arbitrary and impersonally inflicted deprivation, and to mobilize the common people in pursuit of a more democratic social and economic order. But the New Deal had also aroused powerful economic and political interests that were determined, if not to destroy reform, then at least to turn it to their own purposes. World War II had shown some of them how this might be accomplished through the accommodation of business and government, but many important issues remained unresolved at war's end.

The power and reach of the national government had grown enormously during the Depression and war, but the question of how and in whose interest that power would be used remained largely unanswered. Could the U.S. economy be harnessed to democratic and egalitarian goals, or would it serve as a powerful engine of inequality and special privilege? Would insurgents, aroused by the economic collapse of the 1930s, succeed in emptying private ownership of its meaning through progressive taxation, vigorous proconsumer regulation, and public ownership? Or would the powers of government be used instead to secure and defend patterns of privilege? Would the state be employed to redistribute power by encouraging the organization of the powerless, or would its authority now be used to restrain the new power of workers, farmers, and urban minorities?

Beyond these explicitly political issues lay yet a third set of questions, again at least partially open to resolution, involving the day-to-day lives of ordinary citizens. In 1945, Americans lived in the midst of a great, though as yet uncompleted, revolution, as the continued spread of industrial organization, mass communications, and secular values transformed the nation from a patchwork of local cultures into a single mass society. Both the Depression and World War II, moreover, had imposed their own powerful influences on the lives of ordinary Americans. "The great knife of the depression . . . cut down through the entire population cleaving open the lives of rich as well as poor," wrote Robert and Helen Lynd on their return to "Middletown" in the 1930s. "The experience has been more nearly universal than any prolonged recent emotional experience in the city's history; it has approached in its elemental shock the primary experiences of birth and death." The experience of war was scarcely less profound or far-reaching. More than 12 million men and women entered the armed forces, nearly a million of whom were killed or wounded. More than 15 million others left their homes to find work in the burgeoning defense industries. In 1945, as the war drew to a close and the nation began conversion to peacetime, these and other Americans anxiously faced a future over which they had only partial control. Would they find jobs, and if so on what terms? Would they find decent housing, and if so where and at what costs? What would be the character of relationships between men and women, parents and children, friends and neighbors? How would balances be struck between private and public consumption, between development and preservation, between competition and community?

The way in which all these questions (foreign and domestic, political and economic, social and cultural) were answered; the way in which the conflicts of nations and classes and interests were resolved or institutionalized; the myriad compromises, arrangements, accommodations, bargains, and truces (both armed and otherwise) that were struck; the balances of power (however dynamic or fragile) that resulted—all this would mark the emergence of a fundamentally new era in U.S. and world history and of a fundamentally new order created out of the instability of war and depression.

Profound changes, of course, seldom advertise themselves, and neither Harry Truman nor indeed most Americans were fully aware of the transformation that was taking place in their time. All Truman knew was that the weight of complex problems now bore down heavily on him. He felt, he told reporters the day after Roosevelt's death, as though "the moon, the stars and all the planets had fallen on me." Years later he confessed, "I was plenty scared, but, of course, I didn't let anybody see it."[2] Nervous and uncertain of his own capacity for leadership, the new president anxiously if unknowingly faced the beginning of a new era in U.S. history.

The postwar order

The idea of a postwar order is, of course, hardly new. During the war itself Americans as dissimilar as Henry Luce and Henry Wallace confidently predicted the advent of what they respectively called "the American Century" and "the Century of the Common Man." Indeed, even before America's entry into the war, sophisticated observers such as Dean Acheson had called on Americans to assume "some responsibility for making possible a world of order." Thirty years later he would modestly title the memoir of his State Department years *Present at the Creation*.[3] Several generations of diplomatic historians, orthodox and revisionist alike,

---

[2] Donovan, *Conflict and Crisis,* 15–18; Merle Miller, *Plain Speaking: An Oral Biography of Harry S. Truman* (New York: Putnam, 1973), 36.
[3] Dean Acheson, *Present at the Creation: My Years in the State Department* (New York: W. W. Norton, 1969).

have agreed. Whatever their differences over the relative responsibility of U.S. and Soviet leaders, the role of ideals and self-interest, the contingent effect of personality and chance, or the relative importance of economics, politics, and bureaucracy, they appear virtually unanimous on the determinative influence of the early postwar years and on the way in which the calculus of U.S. and Soviet power brought into being a new, if perilous, international system.

What has been somewhat less obvious, at least until recently, is that an analogous process was taking place at home as well—that here, too, a new postwar world was being created. To be sure, social scientists have not lacked for terms to describe this new order; a partial listing would include new or "modern" capitalism, the mixed economy, liberal or societal corporatism, the New Industrial State, the Welfare State, the Warfare State, and the Broker State. The recent efforts of political economists to define the postwar era have been especially provocative. In *Segmented Work, Divided Workers: The Historical Transformation of Labor in the United States* (1982), David Gordon, Richard Edwards, and Michael Reich argue that the postwar era constituted a new "social structure of accumulation," by which they mean the political and institutional environment within which economic processes occur. Similarly, Samuel Bowles, David Gordon, and Thomas Weisskopf, in *Beyond the Wasteland: A Democratic Alternative to Economic Decline* (1983), describe "a postwar corporate system" made up of a series of "accords" in international economics, in the relations between capital and labor, and in domestic politics.[4]

Yet even the best of these efforts have been but thinly historical. Few social scientists have paid more than passing attention to the system's origins or fully captured the complexity or political dynamism through which it was created. With a few important exceptions, historians have generally eschewed broad generalization or have been content to depict

[4]David Gordon, Richard Edwards, and Michael Reich, *Segmented Work, Divided Workers: The Historical Transformation of Labor in the United States* (Cambridge: Cambridge University Press, 1982). The authors tie the creation of such structures to the so-called long swings of world capitalism and to a new theory of labor market segmentation, neither of which is addressed in this paper. Their concept of a postwar "accord" or "social structure of accumulation," however, with its emphasis on politics and institutional environment, provides a lively point for interdisciplinary exchange with historians of recent U.S. politics. For a thoughtful discussion of the relevance of their work to labor history, see Ron Schatz, "Labor Historians, Labor Economics, and the Question of Synthesis," *Journal of American History* 71 (June 1984): 93–100. Samuel Bowles, David Gordon, and Thomas Weisskopf, *Beyond the Wasteland: A Democratic Alternative to Economic Decline* (Garden City, N.Y.: Doubleday, 1983).

postwar politics as either a relatively unimportant adjunct to the cold war or as a mildly reformist interlude between the New Deal and the New Frontier. One of the principal arguments of this paper is that the concept of a new postwar order (or "accord," or "social structure of accumulation") provides a useful framework for organizing our knowledge of postwar domestic politics and perhaps for better understanding the integral character of the era.

Having said this, let me quickly add three important qualifications:

First, I do not wish to claim too much for the years under consideration. Historical processes are neither discrete nor discontinuous. The construction of America's new order did not begin in 1945 or, for that matter, end in 1953. Indeed, it seems clear that many of the materials for that order had been assembled during the preceding decades of depression and war, if not during the near-century of industrial and urban growth that had gone before. Nevertheless, the argument of this essay is that the postwar years *were* important and not just as a holding action or era of political stalemate.

Second, although the processes by which America's postwar *domestic* order was created were intimately connected to the processes through which the postwar *international* order was created, I have (resisting great temptation) restrained myself from discussing either international affairs or the complex relationships between foreign and domestic politics. Nor, for that matter, have I addressed the politics of the workplace, the school, or the home, even though the themes I have attempted to develop are intimately related to developments in each of these other historical venues.

Finally, let me warn the reader that this may seem a somewhat odd essay for me to have contributed to a volume on Harry Truman, because Truman himself appears relatively infrequently in its pages. In part this is because Professor Hamby provides a biographical profile of Truman elsewhere in this volume, in part because so much has already been written from various angles about the president and his presidency, but mainly because of my own desire to explore what I believe are the deeper currents that shaped American politics in the early postwar era, and for this a biographical approach is inadequate.[5]

---

[5] The best general account of the Truman presidency is the two-volume study by journalist Robert J. Donovan, *Conflict and Crisis: The Presidency of Harry S. Truman, 1945–1948,* and *Tumultuous Years: The Presidency of Harry S. Truman, 1949–1953* (New York: W. W. Norton, 1982). See also Alonzo L. Hamby, *Beyond the New Deal: Harry S. Tru-*

The political mobilization of U.S. business

The second major theme of this essay is that America's new postwar domestic order was shaped not just by the inertial momentum of a declining New Deal or by the exigencies of World War II and the cold war but rather, to a degree far too little studied or understood, by the political mobilization of U.S. business. This mobilization began during the late 1930s, was at least partially adjourned during the war, but was greatly expanded in the years immediately following the war's end. U.S. business leaders had been badly shaken by the political and economic upheavals of the 1930s and were deeply troubled by the disorderly and sometimes threatening world in which they found themselves. Indeed, despite the waning of the New Deal and the wartime collaboration with the Roosevelt administration, they entered the postwar era fearing that the continued popularity of New Deal liberalism at home and the spread of socialism abroad foreshadowed drastic and undesirable changes in the U.S. economic system. The political mobilization of business was designed to arrest such alarming possibilities and to create instead a secure and orderly environment for the expansion of business enterprise.

The scope of this mobilization and the multiplicity of actions that it encompassed almost defy generalization. Its sources included the activities of individual firms; trade associations and other industrywide organizations; "peak" associations such as the National Association of Manufacturers (NAM) and the U.S. Chamber of Commerce; other national business groups such as the Committee for Economic Development (CED), the Business Advisory Council (BAC) and the Advertising Council; and a variety of associations, foundations, and other organizations dependent, in varying degrees, on business support and reflective, also in varying degrees, of business opinion. Its targets ranged from the work forces of individual firms and the local communities surrounding individual plants to the legislative, executive, and judicial branches of the national government. Its techniques included lobbying, campaign financing, and litigation as well as the whole new arsenal of professional public relations—

man and American Liberalism (New York: Columbia University Press, 1973), and, for a more critical appraisal, Bert Cochran, *Harry Truman and the Crisis Presidency* (New York: Funk & Wagnalls, 1973). For a comprehensive bibliography of the Truman years, see Richard Dean Burns, *Harry S. Truman: A Bibliography of His Times and Presidency* (Wilmington, Del.: Scholarly Resources, 1984). For a discussion of the scholarly literature on the Truman presidency, see Robert Griffith, "Truman and the Historians: The Reconstruction of Postwar American History," *Wisconsin Magazine of History* 59 (Autumn 1975): 20–50.

institutional advertising, philanthropy, sponsorship of research, and industrial and community relations. Collectively, these activities constituted the largest and most systematic deployment of corporate power in
the history of the United States.[6]

Much of this power was deployed by the owners and managers of
individual firms, who organized political contributions and corporate
philanthropy, dispatched lobbyists and other representatives to Washington, or expanded their companies' public relations budgets. Some of these
efforts were limited to specific goals, as when the Great Atlantic and
Pacific Tea Company (A&P) launched a public relations campaign to
help defeat an antitrust suit or when Weyerhaeuser, disturbed over the
possibility of constricting regulation, employed advertisements of idyllic
forest scenes to tout its timber management policies. Some were more
general, as when Standard Oil of New Jersey, embarrassed by the expo-
sure of its prewar ties with the German company, I. G. Farben, hired the

[6] On lobbying, see especially the *Hearings of the House Select Committee on Lobbying
Activities*, 81st Cong., 2d sess., 1950; and Karl Schriftgiesser, *The Lobbyists* (Boston:
Little, Brown, 1951). Although hardly a new phenomenon, lobbying was expanded and
professionalized to a degree unprecedented in earlier years as corporations established
their own government affairs departments or, as was more often the case, retained the
services of one of the many Washington law firms that proliferated and grew during the
early postwar era. By 1949 prominent political scientists would argue that lobbyists constituted a "third house" or chamber of government. Robert Lane, "Notes on the Theory
of the Lobby," *Western Political Quarterly* 2 (1949): 154–62; and James MacGregor
Burns, *Congress on Trial: The Legislative Process and the Administrative State* (New
York: Harper, 1949), 31. The preponderance of business interests among the lobbyist'
Lane concluded, was a "travesty of representation." See also *Congress and the Natio*.
which concluded (p. 1553) that "taken in the aggregate, business groups were probably
the single most powerful pressure force and tended toward a 'conservative' position on
most legislation." On campaign contributions, see especially Alexander Heard, *The Costs
of Democracy* (Chapel Hill: University of North Carolina Press, 1960), although most of
the data for this study are drawn from the 1952 and 1956 campaigns. On public relations,
see Richard S. Tedlow, *Keeping the Corporate Image: Public Relations and Business,
1900–1950* (Greenwich, Conn.: JAI Press, 1979); and Robert Griffith, "The Selling of
America: The Advertising Council and American Politics, 1942–1960," *The Business History Review* 57 (Autumn 1983): 388–412; as well as earlier works such as J. A. R. Pim-
lott, *Public Relations and American Democracy* (Princeton: Princeton University Press,
1951) and Edward L. Bernays, *Public Relations* (Norman, Okla.: University of Oklahoma
Press, 1952). On institutional advertising, see George A. Flanagan, *Modern Institutional
Advertising* (New York: McGraw-Hill, 1967). On philanthropy, see Morrell Heald,
The Social Responsibilities of Business (Cleveland: Press of Case Western Reserve University, 1970). On business sponsorship of research, see David W. Eakins, "The Development of Corporate Liberal Policy Research in the United States, 1885–1965" (Ph.D.
diss., University of Wisconsin, 1966). On industrial and community relations, see
Wayne Hodges, *Company and Community* (New York: Harper, 1958); and William H.
Form and Delbert C. Miller, *Industry, Labor and Community* (New York: Harper,
1960).

Earl Newsom Agency to create for it a new corporate image of social responsibility.[7]

Not all such efforts were so overtly political. In fact, many Washington representatives of large firms spent their time not on lobbying or public relations but on marketing their companies' goods and services to the government. Indeed, the resulting emergence of what H. L. Nieburg has called "the contract state" must in itself be understood as one of the critical ways in which business succeeded in containing and disciplining the political effects of the large budgets created by the New Deal and World War II.[8]

Trade associations or other industrywide organizations often organized the more overt politics of business. Thus the American Petroleum Institute and its public relations arm, the Oil Industry Information Committee, spearheaded the drive to preserve the industry's complex arrangement of noncompetitive production from threatening antitrust, tax, and regulatory policies. The National Association of Electric Companies, together with the Edison Electric Institute, the Electric Companies' Advertising Program, and a variety of "front" organizations such as the National Tax Equality Association led the campaign against public power. The Cement Institute and the American Iron and Steel Institute led the fight to preserve the "basing point" system of discriminatory freight rates, while the National Association of Real Estate Boards led a broad coalition of business groups opposed to public housing.[9]

The broadest of issues were tackled, finally, by the large "peak associations" and other national business groups. The oldest and most conservative of these, the National Association of Manufacturers (NAM), had organized major campaigns against the New Deal during the late 1930s and was perhaps the most active of the large associations in the immediate postwar period. With an annual budget of more than $5 million, it was instrumental in ending price controls and in securing passage of the Taft-Hartley Act. The U.S. Chamber of Commerce was also strongly conservative, although its views were moderated somewhat during the mid-1940s under the influence of Chamber President Eric Johnston. The chamber was especially influential in the passage of the Employment Act

[7] Flanagan, *Modern Institutional Advertising*, 23–28; Robert Engler, *The Politics of Oil: Private Power and Democratic Directions* (New York: Macmillan, 1961), 464–66.
[8] H. L. Nieburg, *In the Name of Science* (Chicago: Quadrangle Books, 1970), 184–99.
[9] See below.

of 1946. The Business Advisory Council, since 1933 an advisory committee of the Department of Commerce, included among its members the leaders of many of the nation's largest business enterprises and played an important, though often informal, role through its intimate contacts with government and through its sponsorship of groups such as the Committee on Postwar Taxation and the Committee for Economic Development.

The CED, spun off from the BAC during the war, was the most liberal of the large business associations. Its leaders welcomed at least limited cooperation between business and government and recognized that the state could serve as a powerful positive instrument for moderating economic conflict, regulating domestic markets, promoting international trade, and sustaining economic growth. Like more conservative business leaders, however, the CED also worried that the continued advance of New Deal liberalism might lead to a semisocialist state whose fiscal and regulatory policies would ultimately destroy private enterprise. As William Benton, one of the founders of the CED, wrote in 1944, U.S. leaders ought to "rid the economy of injurious or unnecessary regulation, as well as administration that is hostile or harmful," and pursue "constructive fiscal, monetary and other policies that provide a climate in which a private enterprise system can flourish." The great influence wielded by the CED derived not only from the skill and moderation of its leadership but also from the strategic place the organization occupied within both political parties and from the manner in which its corporatist ideology served to rationalize the emerging political economy of the postwar era.

The last of the large associations, the Advertising Council, was created during World War II by major advertisers and advertising agencies and was reorganized in 1945 when, as council leader Theodore S. Repplier put it, American business was "again being pictured as the 'villain' in the American drama" and when "everybody agree[d] that the American enterprise system need[ed] 'reselling.' " Espousing relatively moderate views ("You might say that whereas CED is concerned with the *manufacture* of information in the public interest, the Advertising Council is concerned with the *mass distribution* of such information," declared Repplier), the council became the principal source not only of so-called public service advertising but also of propaganda extolling the "economic miracle" of U.S. enterprise.[10]

---

[10] On the NAM, see especially Richard W. Gable, "NAM: Influential Lobby or Kiss of Death?" *Journal of Politics* 15 (1953): 254–73; as well as the more recent discussion of

Neither business nor its politics was, of course, monolithic. Small retail grocers and druggists battled the chains, independent oil producers challenged the majors, small steel manufacturers chafed at the domination of the big steel companies who were both their suppliers and, through manufacturing subsidiaries, their chief competitors. The railroads made war on the truckers and the big New York bankers sought to discipline or destroy upstarts such as the West Coast-based Bank of America. Even the large peak associations differed among themselves on such critical issues as international trade, labor relations, and the role of the state. Yet the differences among business interests could easily be exaggerated and their power to shape the postwar world easily underestimated.

Much of political conflict among individual firms was brokered, if not always resolved, by trade associations and other industrywide bodies. Powerful alliances were frequently forged across industry lines, moreover, as business leaders traded support for key objectives among themselves and with other powerful groups such as the American Farm Bureau Federation, the American Bar Association, and the American Medical Association. Broader conflicts were often mediated, if not always eliminated, by the peak associations. The differences among these powerful associations have probably been exaggerated, moreover, given their overlapping memberships, financial support, and shared assumptions. And even when real differences persisted, they often gave rise to a powerful dialectic in which, for example, the more conservative attacks of the NAM enhanced the influence of the more moderate CED. As Stephen Bailey observed of the struggle over the Employment Act of 1946, the Right "opened the hole through which more moderate conservative spokesmen ran."[11] Despite real differences in interest and ideology, most business leaders shared a body of broad common assumptions, and, although they disagreed among themselves over many important questions of strategy and tactics, they also shared a commitment to arresting the disorderly momentum of New Deal liberalism and to refashioning the New Deal state in their own interests.

NAM politics in Howell John Harris, *The Right to Manage: Industrial Relations Policies of American Business in the 1940s* (Madison: University of Wisconsin Press, 1982). On the Chamber of Commerce, see Robert Collins, *The Business Response to Keynes, 1929–1964* (New York: Columbia University Press, 1981). On the CED, see Collins, as well as Karl Shriftgiesser, *Business Comes of Age* (New York: Harper, 1960). On the BAC, see especially Kim McQuaid, *Big Business and Presidential Power: From FDR to Reagan* (New York: Morrow, 1982). On the Advertising Council, see Griffith, "The Selling of America."

[11] Stephen K. Bailey, *Congress Makes a Law* (New York: Vintage Edition, 1964), 238.

The politics of the new order

America's new postwar order was the product of struggle, of a historical process heavily freighted with political values—not a neutral quest for order and rationality. It was a struggle fought on many fronts—not just over the election of public officials and the passage of legislation but also over the leadership and direction of executive agencies, over the composition and rulings of regulatory commissions, and even over the ideas and images that constituted the nation's political culture. The power of the business mobilization was contested at almost every point, moreover, by the legatees of the New Deal—in Congress, the federal bureaucracy, and the White House and especially among the trade unions, rural cooperatives, and other groups that constituted the infrastructure of New Deal liberalism. The struggle was an unequal one, however, in which the New Dealers, divided by the older cultural cleavages of race, religion, and modernism as well as by the newer anti-communist politics of the cold war, were no match for the power of American business. Most resulting patterns of settlement, as we shall see, were thus conservative, as was the system they served to create.

Fiscal policy. Among the greatly enhanced powers of the new state created by the New Deal and World War II were its powers to tax and spend. The postwar struggle over the exercise of these powers was central to the character of the postwar order. Much of this struggle was shaped, of course, by seemingly discreet contests over the funding of individual programs. Much of it was also shaped by the debate over taxation, over who should pay and how much. The broad issue of federal fiscal policy was most directly addressed, however, during the long debate that culminated in passage of the Employment Act of 1946.[12] Originally titled the "Full Employment Act," the measure was rooted in the economic liberalism of the late New Deal, but was by no means synonymous with that liberalism. As Herbert Stein has noted, "The assurance of full employment was only one of the many ways in which the earlier New Dealers proposed to reform the old order, and fiscal policy was only one of the many ways by which they hoped to accomplish the reform."[13] Early

---

[12] See especially the fine studies by Bailey, *Congress Makes a Law;* Herbert Stein, *The Fiscal Revolution in America* (Chicago: University of Chicago Press, 1969); and Collins, *The Business Response to Keynes.*
[13] Stein, *The Fiscal Revolution,* 174.

drafts of the bill, nevertheless, sought to commit the federal government both to full employment and to a policy of compensatory spending for public works, health, education, conservation, rural electrification, and urban renewal.

Given such an agenda it was hardly surprising that the bill quickly attracted strong business opposition or that the NAM launched a major campaign to block its passage. More moderate business organizations such as the CED and the U.S. Chamber of Commerce, however, had begun to accept the necessity for at least some management of economic activity by the state. Indeed, they saw in fiscal policy a highly desirable alternative to more interventionist policies such as wage and price controls.

Rather than defeat the bill, therefore, the moderate organizations sought to modify it. The crucial issue, from their point of view, was not whether the state ought to discharge this obligation but rather *how* it ought to do so. Thus whereas the New Dealers sought to tie fiscal policy to public spending, business leaders extolled the virtues of cutting taxes. As business economist Beardsly Ruml patiently explained to a group of CED leaders in 1947, the initial debate over compensatory fiscal policy had been largely obscured because each side in the debate had sought to justify "less explicit desires and motivations." Those who had championed compensatory spending believed in Keynes but "were much more interested in getting rid of slums, or in doing something about public health, or in extending electrification in rural areas," whereas those who argued in support of balanced budgets were more interested in "getting government expenses down, in keeping the federal government from competing with private enterprise, in making sure the states maintained their sovereign rights. . . . Then something happened," concluded Ruml, and business leaders who believed in the need for a compensatory policy but opposed the public spending program of the New Deal "began to be interested in the possibilities of tax reduction as an alternative to public spending."[14]

Business leaders also sought to insulate fiscal policy from the potential activism of a New or Fair Deal administration by stressing the importance of the "automatic stabilizers" created by Social Security and tax legislation, and by emphasizing the importance of monetary policy as a

---

[14] Minutes, meeting of the Board of Trustees, Committee for Economic Development, 16 October 1947, Box 40, Paul G. Hoffman Papers, Harry S. Truman Library (hereafter HSTL).

brake on federal spending. Even the new Council of Economic Advisers, later hailed as one of the act's most important features, had its origins in a conservative attempt to vest economic policy in an independent "board of experts."[15]

The final bill, shorn of its commitment to "full" employment as well as to a specific policy of public spending, was largely the product of these business moderates. Indeed, the version of the bill that finally passed the House of Representatives and was subsequently enacted had been drafted in large part by the Government Affairs Department of the U.S. Chamber of Commerce.[16]

Despite, or perhaps because of, its lack of specifics, the new act symbolized the gradually emerging consensus on postwar economic policy. For business leaders, as we have seen, it marked the beginning of the acceptance of a carefully circumscribed role for the state in the management of economic activity. For liberals, it marked the beginning of a steady retreat from the redistributive and structural reforms of the New Deal and an acceptance of the conservative Keynesianism being hammered out by moderate business leaders. On both sides the intellectual and programmatic assumptions of the new era were falling into place.

Monetary policy. Monetary policy, too, played an important role in the emerging consensus over federal economic policy and occasioned a major struggle over the role of the Federal Reserve Board in governing the nation's economic life. Presidential authority over the Federal Reserve system had been increased by the New Deal and World War II. Indeed, during the war the Federal Reserve had been forced to support the price of government securities at predetermined levels, thus subordinating the board's powers to the debt management policies of the Treasury Department and effectively preventing the use of interest rates to guide economic activity (or to check federal spending). After the war, the

[15] Fred M. Vinson to Truman, 22 October 1945, Box 884, O.F. 264, Truman Papers, HSTL. As CED economist Theodore O. Yntema declared in 1947, "We have a strong preference for building a sound institutional structure which will work automatically with a minimum of *ad hoc* government interference." *CED Digest* (January 1947): 7.

[16] Collins, *The Business Response to Keynes*, 105–07. The House version was drawn up by conservative Mississippi Democrat Will Whittington working from a series of drafts prepared by the Chamber of Commerce. It diluted the bill by broadening it to include not just employment but also productivity and maintenance of purchasing power (meaning price stability), by limiting the spending provisions to loans and public works expenditures consistent with "sound fiscal policy," and by replacing the planning features of the National Production and Employment Budget with the much weaker and less specific President's Economic Report.

big New York banks, led by the powerful Federal Reserve Bank of New York, launched a campaign to "liberate" the board from its subordination to the Truman administration and to revive its ability to act more or less independently. These efforts were strongly supported by the CED and other moderate business leaders, who looked to a flexible monetary policy to help stabilize the economy and who preferred to insulate such policies from direct presidential authority. "There was undoubtedly some self-interest here," Herbert Stein has understatedly concluded, because the heads of banks and insurance companies had "a natural predisposition towards higher interest rates." But the nation's financial leaders were also influenced by "a strong aversion to inflation, a dislike of direct controls whether over prices or over lending, and a skepticism of the government's determination to follow anti-inflationary fiscal policies."[17]

Truman, backed by the Treasury Department and the Council of Economic Advisers, fought back, defending the administration's debt management policy and commitment to low interest rates, and the authority of the president. "For my part I can't understand why the bankers would want to upset the credit of the nation," he wrote Morgan partner Russell C. Leffingwell.[18] Led by Federal Reserve Board Chairman (and CED member) Thomas McCabe, however, the Federal Reserve finally overcame the opposition of the Truman administration in 1951. Following this victory the Federal Reserve would reemerge as a powerful arbiter of economic policy and a check on the management of fiscal policy by Truman and subsequent presidents. Here too, then, the emerging outlines of the new U.S. postwar order could be discerned.

Tax policy. Taxation was the final element in the construction of the new fiscal environment. The evolution of a new tax policy was vastly complicated by the great variety of conflicting interests and strategies— between those who seemed to want immediate tax reduction at any price and those who, like Truman, emphasized retirement of the federal debt; between those who saw progressive taxation as confiscatory and socialistic and those who saw it as a means of more equitably distributing the

---

[17] Stein, *Fiscal Revolution*, 241–80, contains the best discussion of the struggle over the postwar Federal Reserve System, despite the author's enthusiasm for what he calls "the liberation of monetary policy."

[18] Truman to Leffingwell, 10 February 1951, Box 124, President's Secretary's Files, Truman Papers, HSTL. See also Joseph G. Feeney, memorandum for the president, 26 January 1950; and Council of Economic Advisers to the president, 2 February 1950, both in Box 143, ibid.

costs of government; and between those who increasingly saw taxes as an important instrument of fiscal management and were willing to abandon the idea of an annually balanced budget and the many others who still clung doggedly to a federal fiscal policy modeled on household economics.

Even before the war was over, the question of taxation had become the subject of much research and propaganda. Virtually every business group in the country offered its recommendations, including the Committee for Economic Development, which became the first major business group to stress the role of taxation in modern fiscal management, and the Committee on Postwar Tax Policy, which sought to use tax cuts to control the federal budget and whose 1945 proposal, "A Tax Program for a Solvent America," became the basis for congressional tax policy. Yet despite real differences, the specific recommendations of the CED did not diverge greatly from those of the more conservative Committee on Postwar Taxation. Both stressed reductions in the higher brackets, repeal of many wartime taxes on business, and elimination of the so-called double taxation of corporate dividends. Indeed, a liberal journalist correctly described the CED proposal as "an intelligent Rich Man's Guide to Profits and Prosperity."[19]

Truman, in vetoing successive Republican-sponsored tax bills, stressed his own deeply held belief in orthodox economics and the importance of retiring the federal debt, the new international obligations he was calling on the United States to assume, and the inequitable character of Republican-sponsored proposals. His own alternative—a forty-dollar individual tax credit offset by increased corporate taxes—was denounced by the *New York Times* as a "political device [for] redistributing a country's wealth" and was ignored by Congress, as Truman had perhaps expected. Tax reduction finally passed over Truman's third veto in 1948, although a related attempt to revise the Internal Revenue Code was postponed until after the election and was not enacted until the early Eisenhower years.[20]

---

[19] For a general discussion of early postwar taxation, see Randolph E. Paul's encyclopedic *Taxation in the United States* (Boston: Little, Brown, 1954), 393–629. On the Committee for Economic Development, see especially Collins, *The Business Response to Keynes*, 122–35; and Shriftgiesser, *Business Comes of Age*, 77–85, 100–07. For an analysis of the recommendations of the Committee on Postwar Tax Policy, see H. L. Gutterson to Robert Taft, 11 January 1946, Box 746, Taft Papers, Manuscripts Division, Library of Congress (hereafter LC). Taft's papers contain much material on the role of the committee in shaping GOP tax policy, especially during the Seventy-ninth and Eightieth Congresses.

[20] Paul, *Taxation in America*, 416–17. For analyses of tax legislation, see John Snyder to

The role of taxation in the new order would not be fully realized until 1964, as Herbert Stein, Robert Collins, and others have correctly noted. The continuing orthodoxy of businessmen, congressional leaders, and, not least, Presidents Truman and Eisenhower, would delay the final integration of tax policy into what Collins has aptly called "commercial Keynesianism." Nevertheless, here, too, in the debates over federal tax law, the principal outlines of the postwar period were emerging.

Labor relations. No issue was more central to the reconstruction of America's postwar political economy than that of labor relations. The 1930s had been a watershed in U.S. labor history, in David Montgomery's words, "one of the greatest chapters in the historic struggle for human liberties in this country." The New Deal, the great organizing drives, and World War II all served to transform U.S. labor relations and to alter sharply the balance of power between workers and managers. By war's end, the dramatic growth and rising militancy of unionized workers had produced a powerful assault on management's control of wages and the workplace, and even threatened to spill over into the areas of corporate pricing, investment, and plant location.[21]

The leaders of U.S. business were deeply worried by such challenges to their authority and were fearful (perhaps unnecessarily) that such actions prefigured even bolder and more radical changes in the relationship of labor and management. Although they differed among themselves on strategy and tactics—from the accommodation preached (if not always practiced) by the corporatist leaders of the CED to the unreconciled antiunionism of many small-to-middling firms outside the great industrial centers—almost all of them agreed on the need to contain the challenge of union power and to compel a major revision in the relations of labor and management.

After the war many companies sought to recapture lost power and authority through aggressive collective bargaining, the introduction of new industrial relations and personnel administration techniques, and intensive public relations drives.[22] Exploiting public reactions to the

James E. Webb, 15 July 1947; "Some Suggested Themes for Veto Message on Tax Bill," (n.d. but c. June–July 1947); and Norse, Keyserling, and Clark to Truman, 5 June 1947; all in Box 2, Clark Clifford Files, HSTL.

[21] David Montgomery, *Workers' Control in America: Studies in the History of Work, Technology, and Labor Struggles* (Cambridge: Cambridge University Press, 1980), 163–65; David Brody, *Workers in Industrial America: Essays on the Twentieth Century Struggle* (New York: Oxford University Press, 1979), 173–214; and especially Harris, *The Right to Manage.*

[22] Harris, *The Right To Manage,* 105–204; and Ronald Schatz, *The Electrical Workers: A*

postwar strike wave and capitalizing on the growing clamor of cold war anticommunism, they also launched a major campaign to revise the National Labor Relations Act. Led by the NAM, business leaders played a decisive role in shaping the new Taft-Hartley Act of 1947. And although the new law was not all that many of them had hoped it would be, it nevertheless helped contain the power and scope of industrial unionism and signal the passing of an era in labor relations. "Coming out of the long period of confusion under the Wagner Act is something like coming out of a tunnel wherein one has grasped toward the light," declared one business executive. "There is suddenly much more clarity, much more assurance of sound footing, much fresher air to breathe. We sense a closing of the confusion."[23] The labor movement, thrown on the defensive by the business mobilization and deeply divided by the emerging cold war, turned increasingly toward compromise and accommodation. Although much of the new law's meaning remained to be hammered out through bargaining and litigation, the main contours of postwar labor relations had nevertheless been forged and a critical venue of the new postwar order secured.

Farm policy. American farmers, too, became part of the new postwar order. Since the early 1930s farm policy had been shaped by a loose alliance between the Democrats and the powerful American Farm Bureau Federation. During the late 1930s, however, federal farm policies threatened to escape the bureau's grasp. As a consequence, the bureau and its allies launched savage attacks on the Farm Security Administration and other New Deal programs. By the late 1940s, under the leadership of Allan Kline, the bureau was increasingly making common cause with conservative Republicans and Democrats in Congress. Indeed, in 1951 Charles F. Brannan, Truman's secretary of agriculture, would complain

History of Labor at General Electric and Westinghouse, 1923–1960 (Urbana: University of Illinois Press, 1983), 167–240.

[23] Harris, *The Right to Manage,* 127. On Taft-Hartley, also see R. Alton Lee, *Truman and Taft-Hartley: A Question of Mandate* (Lexington: University of Kentucky Press, 1966); and especially Harry A. Millis and Emily Clark Brown, *From the Wagner Act to Taft-Hartley: A Study of National Labor Policy and Labor Relations* (Chicago: University of Chicago Press, 1950). On the NAM, see Gable, "NAM: Influential Lobby or Kiss of Death?" 254–73. For an example of the important role played by public relations counselors in the bill's passage, see especially James P. Selvege to Robert A. Taft, Box 830, Taft Papers, Manuscripts Division, LC. The impact of the NAM campaign was clearly revealed in editorial and press response, which almost overwhelmingly favored revision of the labor law. See Editorial Reaction to Current Issues, Labor Legislation, Parts I and II (2, 31 January 1947), Box 126, President's Secretary's Files (PSF), Truman Papers, HSTL.

of Kline's "effort to make the Farm Bureau a political adjunct of the Republican Party and especially the Taft faction."[24] The smaller but more liberal National Farmers Union (NFU), on the other hand, remained closely tied to the Democrats.

When Truman proposed a major reorganization of agriculture policy in 1949—the so-called Brannan Plan—he immediately encountered strong opposition from the Farm Bureau and its many business and political allies. While some of this opposition may have simply reflected the bureau's determination to maintain its primacy in the drafting of farm legislation, there was far more at stake than just this. By supporting farm income rather than farm prices, the Brannan Plan sought to maintain high farm income while reducing food prices to consumers. It restricted benefits to large commercial growers, moreover, by limiting assistance to the first $27,500 of production. Drafted by NFU leader James G. Patton and strongly endorsed by the AFL and CIO, the new legislation was designed, in Allen Matusow's words, "to cement the tentative alliance of farmers and laborers that [had] elected Truman in 1948."[25] Opposition to the plan was led by the Farm Bureau, by food processors and other middlemen, and by business organizations such as the U.S. Chamber of Commerce and the National Association of Manufacturers. Republicans and conservative Southern Democrats, fearing the power of a liberal farmer-labor alliance, charged it was a socialistic attack on "bipartisanship" in agriculture.

The defeat of the Brannan Plan symbolized important changes both in farm politics and farm economics. The Brannan Plan marked the last hurrah of an older vision of the role of farmers and farming in American life, a vision based on the notion that farmers, as men and women who worked with their hands, had more in common with workers than with the leaders of business. Its defeat marked the triumph of the very different view that farming was primarily a business and that its future, both economic and political, rested with its growing integration into U.S. agribusiness. The specter of a farmer-labor alliance was thus dissipated and the organization of agriculture, like that of labor, conservatively secured.

The antitrust revival. The efforts by business leaders to fashion a secure new postwar environment for American enterprise were also threatened

[24] Brannan to Matthew J. Connelly, 30 October 1951, Box 155, PSF, Truman Papers, HSTL.
[25] Allan J. Matusow, *Farm Policies and Politics in the Truman Years* (Cambridge, Mass.: Harvard University Press, 1967; paperback edition, 1970), 200.

by the antimonopoly revival of the Truman years. Although the policies of the Truman administration, like those of the New Deal before it, were fraught with ambivalence and although Truman himself vacillated in his tactics between the Fabian and the Napoleonic, the activities of the Justice Department, the Federal Trade Commission, and congressional antimonopolists nevertheless threatened to disrupt a broad range of business practices.[26]

The industrial counteroffensive against the antitrust revival, fought simultaneously in Congress, the courts, and the press, as well as in the administration itself, constituted a major battle in the struggle to define the postwar order. When, for example, the Justice Department attempted to revive a court suit, abandoned during World War II, to outlaw the rate bureaus long used by railroads and other common carriers to establish rates through routes, schedules, and equipment standards, the industry responded by sponsoring legislation (the Bulwinkle Bill) to exempt such practices from the antitrust laws. Opponents charged that the bill would "legalize conspiracy" and lead to the "cartelization of the basic industry of our economy." Supporters, led by the Association of American Railroads, replied that the measure would simply recognize practices that the railroads had been engaging in for four decades and that such arrangements were absolutely necessary for the management of an efficient and integrated transportation system. The bill was eventually passed over Truman's veto.[27]

[26] During his first two years Truman sought rapprochement with business and other conservatives. During the 1948 campaign, however, he vetoed a bill to legalize railroad rate-setting bureaus and repeatedly attacked big business on the hustings. During the first eighteen months of his second administration he supported the antitrust activities of the Justice Department and the Federal Trade Commission, vetoed a bill to legalize the basing point system, and supported passage of the Cellar-Kefauver amendment to the Clayton Act. Following the 1949 recession and the onset of war in Korea, he once again drew back from vigorous support for antitrust. Moreover, as a student of the Truman antitrust program has concluded, "Never during the Truman administration did the traditional antimonopoly agencies receive enough money to fulfill adequately the terms of the antitrust laws" (Robert L. Branyon, "Anti-Monopoly Activities During the Truman Administration," Ph.D. diss., University of Oklahoma, 1961, 237). Nevertheless, antitrust investigations and indictments touched many of America's largest industrial enterprises, including General Electric and other electrical manufacturers, U.S. Steel, AT&T, the large motion picture producers (Paramount, RKO, Fox, Loew's and Warner), Standard Oil and the other large oil companies, RCA, ALCOA, the National Football League, A&P, the big three soap manufacturers (Procter and Gamble, Lever Brothers, and Colgate-Palmolive-Peet), International Business Machines, General Motors, DuPont, as well as railroads, banks, insurance companies, and newspaper publishers.

[27] For an analysis of the bill and its many business supporters, see "Memorandum Re: Bulwinkle Bill—Senate Bill 110," in Box 569, Taft Papers, LC. For an attack on the bill and on the railroad companies' "use, as dummies, [of] all sorts of chambers of commerce,

In 1948, to take another example, the Federal Trade Commission secured a ruling from the Supreme Court outlawing the long-standing "basing point" system employed by the steel and cement industries, a decision that threatened, in the words of the U.S. Chamber of Commerce, to "exert a disruptive influence on the pricing and distribution system of many important industries." The affected industries, led by U.S. Steel, immediately sought legislation that they claimed would merely "clarify" the decision but that critics charged would legalize the basing point system in steel and other concentrated industries as well as allow large distributors such as the oil companies and the drug and grocery chains to smash their small-business competitors. Truman vetoed the bill, however, and no effort was made to override.[28]

Not all the antitrust battles of the Truman era were fought as directly as those over rate bureaus and railroads. Business lobbyists were unable, for example, to prevent passage in 1950 of the popular Cellar-Kefauver amendment to the Clayton Act preventing restraint of trade through the acquisition of the assets of one corporation by another. The following year, however, they succeeded in cutting funds for enforcement, effectively crippling implementation of the law and contributing to what Congressman Emanuel Cellar charged was an attempt "to get as many mergers consummated as possible before the Commission is able to begin enforcement." In fact, the commission launched only one prosecution under the new law during the final two years of Truman's presidency.[29]

Some cases were tried in the press as well as in the courts, moreover,

tax payers' leagues, shippers associations, etc.," see Max Lowenthal, Special Memorandum for Judge Murphy, Box 21, Charles S. Murphy Files, HSTL. For Truman's veto, see especially Charles S. Murphy to Truman, 25 March 1948, in Box 14, Charles S. Murphy Papers, HSTL. For a compact discussion of the measure, see *Congress and the Nation,* 454–55. In 1945, in a somewhat similar fashion, insurance companies secured exemption from the antitrust laws following a 1944 Supreme Court ruling.

[28] *Congress and the Nation,* 453–54. The basing point system was designed to assure price uniformity throughout the country (or in some instances, a region) by basing prices on a geographical reference point. In the case of steel, for example, prices were calculated on the basis of the Pittsburgh steel mill price plus the cost of transportation from Pittsburgh, no matter where the steel was produced. For a proindustry analysis of the Court's decision, see Chamber of Commerce of the United States, "The Cement Decision of 1948," in Box 561, Taft Papers, LC. For the role played by some members of the Truman administration in drafting the bill, see especially John D. Clark to Truman, 6 June 1950, Box 127, PSF, Truman Papers, HSTL. For opposition to the bill, see Senator Paul Douglas to Stephen J. Spingarn, 6 June 1950, Box 51, and Spingarn to Truman, 7 June 1950, Box 50, Spingarn Papers, HSTL.

[29] Stephen J. Spingarn to Charles S. Murphy, 26 September 1951; and Emanuel Cellar to Truman, 28 September 1951; both in Box 906, O.F. 277, Truman Papers, HSTL. J. Howard McGrath to Truman, 12 December 1951, Box 2, Murphy Papers, HSTL.

as corporations increasingly resorted to the use of sophisticated public relations campaigns. When, for example, the Justice Department filed an antitrust suit against A&P, A&P responded with a campaign designed by Carl Byoir, one of the nation's foremost public relations counselors. Advertisements and flyers asked shoppers, "Do you want higher prices?" "Do you want your A&P put out of business?" Although during the early 1930s A&P had been seen as "a greedy, monopoly-hungry, chain store monster, devouring small businesses," the new campaign pictured the company as "a public benefactor, providing food for all at lower prices than would be possible otherwise." The campaign not only produced a deluge of mail but even increased the chain's sales at a time when business was off for other large food retailers. In 1954 the Justice Department abandoned its attempt to break up the chain and settled instead for the divestiture only of its produce subsidiary.[30]

One of the most spectacular assaults on antitrust enforcement, however, was launched during the closing months of the Truman administration by the oil industry. For nearly two decades, large U.S. oil companies had joined British and Dutch rivals in an international oil cartel to control the international development, production, and pricing of petroleum. In 1949, however, the Federal Trade Commission (FTC) initiated a study of the cartel that resulted in the filing of both civil and criminal proceedings by the Justice Department. The oil industry fought back through the courts; through oil-state leaders in Congress; through its many close contacts with top officials in the Department of State, Defense, and Interior; and through a massive public relations campaign spearheaded by the American Petroleum Institute's Oil Industry Information Committee. This campaign produced a flood of articles, press releases, canned editorials, and "pattern speeches" linking the industry with free enterprise and the national security. Truman, convinced by his advisers that only through the cartel's continued operation could the United States maintain its access to foreign oil, ordered the criminal proceedings dropped in early 1953, shortly before leaving the White House. Eisenhower showed even less enthusiasm for prosecution, and the case was finally closed out nearly fifteen years later with a series of virtually meaningless consent decrees. It was, as John Blair, one of the authors of the FTC report, later concluded, "a textbook example of how to bring about the evisceration of an anti-trust case." More important, it secured from

---

[30] Flanagan, *Modern Institutional Advertising*, 23–38. For background on Byoir's work for A&P, see also Richard S. Tedlow, *Keeping the Corporate Image*, 91–97.

public disruption the carefully worked-out arrangements of the international oil industry, thus setting yet another pillar of America's postwar order.[31]

Business leaders sought throughout the Truman years to replace what they called the "witch hunting" of antitrust prosecutions with an approach that featured cooperation and consultation, and at least some members of the Truman administration seemed to agree. Conservative FTC Commissioner Lowell Mason, for example, sought unsuccessfully to replace prosecution of individual firms by the FTC with industrywide conferences to draw up codes of fair competition. Secretary of Commerce Charles Sawyer, another administration conservative, launched a similar program. Even the Department of Justice initiated a small, premerger clearance program. The triumph of this approach, however, would await the Eisenhower administration, the antitrust policies of which would be characterized by the widespread use of prefiling conferences, consent decrees, and premerger clearances and by a consistent emphasis on cooperation and quiet negotiation.[32]

Natural resources. The new order also depended, in the view of many business groups, on secure access to the nation's natural resources. Thus ranching, mining, and timber interests, for example, battled conservationists over access to western lands in a struggle that anticipated by several decades the "Sagebrush Rebellion" of the late 1970s. The most controversial natural resource battles of the early postwar era, however, revolved around oil and electric power.

Although the oil industry had prospered during World War II, indus-

---

[31] On the oil cartel case, see especially John M. Blair, *The Control of Oil* (New York: Pantheon Books, 1976); and Burton I. Kaufman, *The Oil Cartel Case: A Documentary Study of Antitrust Activity in the Cold War* (Westport, Conn.: Greenwood, 1978). See also Stephen J. Spingarn, memorandum for the president, 12 January 1953, Box 144, PSF, Truman Papers, HSTL. For the industry's position, see especially "The Progressive Threat to the U.S. Position in Oil," 25 July 1952, in Box 102, Oscar L. Chapman Papers, HSTL.

[32] On Mason's efforts to reform the FTC, see especially Mason to Truman, 3 October 1946, Box 128; 8 October 1947, Box 144; 26 October 1948, Box 199, all in PSF, Truman Papers, HSTL. Truman supported Mason's efforts in 1946 and 1947 but later changed his tack, appointing strong antimonopolists such as John Carson and Stephen Spingarn to the commission. On Sawyer's efforts, see *The Journal of Commerce*, 5 December 1949; and Estes Kefauver to Truman, 5 December 1949, Box 906, O.F. 277, Truman Papers, HSTL. On the Justice Department's program, see H. G. Morison, annual report, 30 June 1952, in Box 155, PSF, Truman Papers, HSTL. For the views of large business leaders, see especially the Business Advisory Council, "Effective Competition," 14 December 1952, in Box 561, Taft Papers, LC. On Eisenhower, see Robert Griffith, "Dwight D. Eisenhower and the Corporate Commonwealth," *American Historical Review* 87 (February 1982): 104–05.

try leaders entered the postwar period fearful that antitrust prosecutions might threaten their elaborate system of regulated production, that federal control of offshore oil might deprive them of ready access to large deposits, that they might lose the generous depletion allowance, or that federal regulatory activities might impinge on their profits or autonomy. An extremely complex industry whose interests were by no means unitary, oil was nevertheless dominated both economically and politically by the large integrated companies.

Led by the American Petroleum Institute and its public relations arm, the Oil Industry Information Committee, the oil industry was perhaps the most politically active single industry in the postwar era. Enlisting skilled lobbyists and public relations firms and making especially good use of powerful oil-state representatives such as Lyndon Johnson and Robert Kerr, the industry succeeded in protecting the depletion allowance from Truman's attacks and in blocking the renomination of Leland Olds to the Federal Power Commission (FPC). Truman twice vetoed "tidelands" legislation, which would have turned over to the states title to all "submerged lands" between the low-water mark and the states' historic boundaries. Not until 1953, under the Eisenhower administration, would this industry-supported measure be signed into law. Truman also blocked attempts to exempt natural gas producers from FPC regulation. At the same time, as we have seen, he abandoned criminal proceedings against the international oil companies when his national security advisers convinced him that prosecution might imperil U.S. access to oil in the Middle East. Although not all industry objectives were achieved, oilmen nevertheless succeeded in protecting their many interests and securing an environment conducive to rapid and profitable postwar expansion.[33]

[33] *Congress and the Nation*, 1401–04, 980–84, and passim. The best book on the politics of the oil industry remains Robert Engler, *The Politics of Oil*. On tidelands, see especially Oscar Chapman to Truman, 22 May 1951, in Box 158, PSF, Truman Papers, HSTL; and Truman to Harold Ickes, July 1951, Box 40, Ickes Papers, LC. "I really don't think they have enough votes to pass the 'big steal' over my veto," wrote Truman. On the natural gas issue, see Robert Kerr to Truman, 11 August 1949, copy, Box 34, Clinton Anderson Papers, LC: Memorandum [of conference on the Kerr Bill], Box 12, Clark Clifford Papers, HSTL; and Charles S. Murphy to Truman, 13 April 1950, Box 25, Murphy Files, HSTL. On the defeat of Leland Olds, see especially Olds, memorandum for the president, 10 October 1949; and Truman to Senator Edwin C. Johnson, 6 October 1949; both in Box 132, PSF, Truman Papers, HSTL. The campaign against Olds was rooted in his opposition to efforts to exempt independent producers of natural gas from FPC regulation. In their campaign against Olds, Johnson and Kerr dredged up a series of radical articles Olds had written in the 1920s and accused him of following the Communist Party line. Olds' nomination was also opposed by the private electric utilities, who charged that

The public power programs of the New Deal (Tennessee Valley Authority, Rural Electrification Administration, and other regional projects) were among the decade's most popular innovations, and the construction of new hydroelectric and steam-generating plants expanded rapidly during the Truman years when nearly 5 million kilowatts were added to federal generating capacity. Yet the very success of these programs aroused powerful opposition from the private utilities. On the defensive during most of the 1930s, the industry launched a major counteroffensive after the war.[34]

The campaign was led by the National Association of Electric Companies, which opened a Washington office in 1945 and quickly became one of the largest lobbies in the capital. Its activities were supplemented by those of the Edison Electric Institute, the Electric Companies Advertising Program, and a host of other groups subsidized by the industry or otherwise recruited to its banner.[35] The industry no longer opposed the increase of federal generating power or even the construction of transmission lines in areas of uncontested federal supremacy such as the Tennessee Valley. Instead, industry spokesmen concentrated their attack on the construction of new steam-generating plants and transmission lines that would extend the scope of federal activity into new regions. The issue was particularly important because the long-distance transmission of power and the creation of regional power pools promised enormous economies (and thus profits) in the distribution of electric power. As Congressman Frank Buchanan observed, the industry sought to "fix public policy so that the distribution of power, which is the big profit end of the business, will be regarded as 'private' enterprise as compared with

his attitude toward their industry was "discriminatory and socialistic." "I am extremely sorry that the special interest group seems to have completely and thoroughly smeared a good public servant," Truman wrote. "I am also sorry that Senators seem to have been taken in by that approach."

[34] Ambitious political campaigns were hardly new to the industry, which had mounted a series of major drives against the development of public power during the 1920s and early 1930s. Indeed, investigations of these activities helped spur passage of the Public Utilities Holding Company Act of 1935. See Summary, "Nation-wide Propaganda Campaign of the Electric and Gas Utility Companies, 1919–1934," in Box 56, Stephen J. Spingarn Papers, HSTL.

[35] Congressman Frank Buchanan, "Operations of the Private Power Lobby," 25 August 1950, in Box 10, Charles S. Murphy Papers, HSTL. Among the more active groups spawned by the industry were the National Tax Equality Association, organized in 1943, and National Associated Businessmen, Inc., which began operation in 1946. The two organizations were closely linked and concentrated most of their attacks on rural electric cooperatives, which they claimed posed a menace to small businessmen. See U.S. Congress, House Select Committee on Small Business, "Small Business Organizations," 81st Cong., 2d sess., 21 February 1950, 9–15.

generation which even they concede may in some instances properly be done by public agencies." Industry success in blocking construction of new transmission lines compelled federal power projects to enter into so-called wheeling agreements under which private utilities would purchase all federally produced power at the dam and distribute it over their own lines. Frozen into law by the Keating Amendment, these agreements served to prevent the extension of public power into any new areas of the country.[36]

The industry also succeeded, in alliance with local reclamation interests and rival federal bureaucracies, in preventing the creation of new valley authorities such as those proposed for the Missouri and Columbia River valleys and thus compelling the abandonment of the New Deal goal of publicly directed regional planning and development. Perhaps most important, it succeeded, in the Atomic Energy Act of 1954, in excluding the federal government from the development of nuclear power and in ensuring that the new, nuclear-based technologies would be almost exclusively controlled by the large private utilities.[37] The complex integration of public and private governance of nuclear energy, although not concluded until the early years of the Eisenhower administration, was an excellent example of the kind of arrangements that were being so extensively forged during the postwar years and that would serve to contain and discipline the power of the state.

Housing and urban development. A somewhat analogous development occurred in federal housing and urban development, as the real estate, banking, and home construction lobbies sought to block some liberal initiatives and to contain and control others. These powerful interests failed to block the public housing provisions of the Housing Act of 1949, although they contributed to delaying its implementation in the years that followed. (By 1964 only 365,000 units had been constructed, out of the 800,000 units authorized fifteen years earlier.) But almost all the business lobbies supported the act's expansion of the Federal Hous-

[36] John R. Waltrip, "Public Power during the Truman Administration" (Ph.D. diss., University of Missouri, 1965), 1–3, 64–68, 122–24, 134. *Congress and the Nation*, 771–832. For a critical view of such arrangements, see Richard L. Boke to Harold Ickes, 20 February 1951, Box 46, Ickes Papers, LC. For a defense of them, see Sam Rayburn to Clyde T. Ellis, 22 January 1948, Box 134, PSF, Truman Papers, HSTL. Also see Gordon Clapp, "Electricity and the Public Interest," 7 March 1950, Box 3, Kenneth Hechler Files, HSTL.

[37] Waltrip, "Public Power," 30–36, 57–59, 124–219; *Congress and the Nation*, 832–966.

ing Authority's mortgage insurance program, which they rightly believed would provide a powerful stimulus to the real estate and home construction industries. Similarly, most realtors and downtown bankers supported the act's urban renewal title, especially because its stress on private construction and local control assured them a major role in the program's implementation. As housing authority Charles Abrams wrote in *The Nation*, the "building and lending fraternity" wanted "federal money to be the great lubricant for business. Government should become business's handmaid, subsidize business undertakings, remove the element of chance from 'venturing,' and socialize business losses." Or, as Herbert U. Nelson, chief lobbyist for the National Association of Real Estate Boards, bluntly put it, "In our country we prefer that government activity shall take the form of assisting and aiding private business rather than undertake great public projects of a governmental character." Once again then, and on another important front, the modestly redistributive and democratic momentum of the 1930s had been arrested and the New Deal state made safe for private enterprise.[38]

Social Security and health care. The battle over public housing, however, was but one of many struggles to contain and limit the social welfare initiatives of the New Deal. Truman was able to expand the Social Security system by including large numbers of people previously excluded, easing eligibility requirements, and increasing benefits. He was unable to expand coverage of the Fair Labor Standards Act, however, and in fact Congress in 1949 voted to exclude a million workers previously covered by the law.[39] The fiercest of all such battles, however, was over his call for a comprehensive national health insurance program. The American Medical Association (AMA) in particular saw in Truman's proposal a dangerous threat to its autonomy and control of the nation's health industry. When Truman's upset election in 1948 made passage of

[38] On housing and urban development, see especially Richard O. Davies, *Housing Reform During the Truman Administration* (Columbia: University of Missouri Press, 1966); and Mark I. Gelfand, *A Nation of Cities: The Federal Government and Urban America, 1933–1965* (New York: Oxford University Press, 1975), 105–56. Much information on the real estate lobby was collected by the Buchanan Committee in its 1950 investigation of lobbying. See House Select Committee on Lobbying Activities, *Hearings*, Part 2 (Washington, D.C., 1950). For an analysis based on these hearings, see CIO National Housing Committee, "The Republican Party and the Real Estate Lobby," n.d., Box 4, David D. Lloyd Files, HSTL. For a critical congressional perspective on the evolution of postwar housing policy, see Boxes 727–32, Robert A. Taft Papers, LC.

[39] *Congress and the Nation*, 1243–46, 639.

the legislation more likely, the AMA organized one of the most extensive lobbying and public relations campaigns in American history. Flooding the country with literature accusing the Democrats of supporting "socialized medicine," the AMA not only blocked the bill's enactment but contributed heavily to the defeat of a number of Democratic liberals in the 1950 elections. With the election of Eisenhower in 1952, the entire issue dropped from the national agenda for a decade. Although the federal government would support hospital construction and medical research, the delivery of health care itself would remain securely in private hands. As Paul Starr has concluded, "Government financing increased, but it was channeled into avenues that did not . . . threaten professional sovereignty."[40]

The politics of culture. The struggle to forge a new postwar America was accompanied, finally, by a campaign to capture not just votes but hearts and minds, to shape not only the political economy but also the economy of ideas and images. As a Standard Oil executive said at a meeting of the American Petroleum Institute in 1946, "Public sentiment is everything. . . . He who molds public sentiment goes deeper than he who enacts statutes or pronounces decisions. He makes statutes and decisions possible or impossible to be executed."[41]

In the years following the close of World War II, the leaders of American business employed their vast power over the channels of communication not merely to advance their own immediate interests but to shape a new and acquiescent political culture. Thus the NAM launched a massive campaign to "sell free enterprise," to which businesses contributed an estimated $37 million. The NAM was joined, moreover, by the U.S. Chamber of Commerce; by many individual firms and trade associations; and by conservative, business-financed groups such as the Committee for Constitutional Government, the National Economic Council, the Foun-

[40] On the struggle over health care, see especially Monte M. Poen, *Harry S. Truman versus the Medical Lobby: The Genesis of Medicare* (Columbia: University of Missouri Press, 1979); and Paul Starr, *The Social Transformation of American Medicine: The Rise of a Sovereign Profession and the Making of a Vast Industry* (New York: Basic Books, 1982), 280–89. On the AMA campaign, see also Stanley Kelley, *Professional Public Relations and Political Power* (Baltimore: Johns Hopkins Press, 1966), 87–99. For an outline of the AMA's 1949 campaign, prepared by the West Coast public relations firm of Whitaker and Baxter, see "A Simplified Blueprint of the Campaign Against Compulsory Health Insurance," Box 721, Taft Papers, LC.

[41] Engler, *The Politics of Oil*, 428.

dation for Economic Education, and the American Economic Foundation.[42]

More moderate business groups were also active. The Committee for Economic Education, for example, joined the Ford Foundation in sponsoring the Joint Council for Economic Education, which sought to influence the teaching of economics and business in the nation's schools. The Advertising Council launched the first of a series of multimillion-dollar campaigns to promote "the American enterprise system." Worried that Americans were "staggeringly ignorant" of their nation's economy, council leaders hoped that by showing people "what our private enterprise system has done for us," it would make them poor prospects for "swapping this system for government ownership and control."[43]

By the early 1950s, according to *Fortune* editor William Whyte, American businesses were spending more than $100 million annually for such campaigns, littering the cultural landscape with books, articles, and pamphlets; billboards and posters; radio and television spots; ads on buses, trains, and trolleys; even comic books and matchbook covers. The content of these offerings varied from the sophisticated research reports of CED to the hard-sell comics of NAM, but the underlying purpose was almost invariably the same: to halt the momentum of New Deal liberalism and to create a political climate conducive to the new corporate order.

To an extent that historians have not fully appreciated, the postwar intellectual and cultural consensus was manufactured by America's corporate leaders, packaged by the advertising and public relations industries, and marketed through the channels of mass communication. Although many ordinary Americans remained skeptical of and resistant to such a sell, they nevertheless found themselves surrounded by a pervasive and constantly reiterated vision of the United States as a dynamic, classless, and benignly consensual society. In culture, as in politics, the new order reigned.

---

[42] See especially William H. Whyte, Jr., *Is Anybody Listening?* (New York: Simon and Schuster, 1952); and C. W. McKee and H. G. Moulton, *A Survey of Economic Education* (Washington, D.C.: Brookings Institution, 1951).

[43] On the CED-JCEEC project, see Marion B. Folsom to Lou Holland, 11 September 1951, Box 79, Holland Papers, HSTL. On an earlier CED and Carnegie Foundation program of cooperative research between businessmen and educators, see Gardner Cowles to Helen Rogers Reid, 27 January 1948, Box D84, Reid Papers, LC. On the Advertising Council, see especially Griffith, "The Selling of America."

The last hurrah of New Deal liberalism

America's new postwar order was thus the product of a struggle fought on many fronts and by many combatants. The particular alignment of forces varied from one battlefield to another, as did the outcomes. Total victories were less common than compromises, and the result was thus a series of arrangements, accords, and accommodations. The resulting system was neither complete nor static. Just as the process of its creation had begun well before 1945, so did its articulation continue after 1953. Many issues remained to be negotiated; indeed the system seemed to depend on a constant process of negotiation and fine-tuning. Yet the underlying similarities among the many contests, the overall pattern of the outcomes, the dense interconnectedness of the process and its cultural rationalization marked the emergence of a new and conservative order, the contours of which would define and delimit American political life for the next quarter-century.

Harry Truman presided over this transformation uneasily at best. As I have suggested elsewhere, his was a life deeply riven by the great polar tensions of twentieth-century American culture.[44] His presidency was shaped not just by the clash of liberals and conservatives, Democrats and Republicans, southerners and northerners, but also by the deeper tensions between the provincial and the metropolitan, between the small-town America of shops and farms and the modern United States of cities and large corporations. Truman harbored powerful resentments toward the new corporate order, fueled in part no doubt by the loss of his own business during the 1921 recession. He later blamed his losses on the Republicans and on the deflationary policies of Secretary of the Treasury Andrew Mellon, a man who, as Truman put it, "would do everything in his power to make the rich richer and the poor poorer."[45] During the first two years of his presidency, Truman nevertheless sought to accommodate conservatives both in Congress and in the business community. In 1948, however, driven by the dynamics of electoral politics, he embarked on a sharply different course, rallying the still-potent armies of the New Deal coalition and attacking business with a ferocity since unmatched in U.S. politics. "Wall Street expects its money to elect a Repub-

[44] "Harry S. Truman and the Burden of Modernity," *Reviews in American History* 9 (September 1981): 295–306.
[45] Miller, *Plain Speaking*, 113.

lican Administration that will listen to the gluttons of privilege first, and not to the people at all," he declared, in a typical speech.[46]

Business leaders were stunned by his reelection. *Business Week* freely predicted the repeal of Taft-Hartley, while the dispirited director of the Business Advisory Council wrote a prominent corporate executive that the president would probably not wish to receive a delegation of business leaders before the announcement of his legislative program. "After all, he doesn't owe his present occupancy of the White House to any business support, he was elected on what amounts to an anti-business platform and he knows that business opposes most of his legislative program." *Fortune* magazine concluded that "business isn't out of the dog house yet. Sixteen turbulent years have rolled by since the New Deal began to rescue the People from the Capitalists, and no one can say that business has retrieved the authority and respect it ought to have if the drift to socialism is to be arrested. Every U.S. businessman, consciously or unconsciously, is on the defensive." At least one prominent executive took his case directly to the president. General Electric President Charles E. Wilson wrote Truman that the economic downturn that had begun in November stemmed from the fact that stockholders and customers were worried that "business [was] in for some rough going if not a beating." Only by abandoning his legislative program, which could lead only to "an incentive-destroying and competition-destroying collectivism," could Truman assuage the fears of the business community.[47]

Although Truman did offer business an olive branch of sorts, sending Leon Keyserling and Clark Clifford out to preach the gospel of cooperation and a painless "politics of growth," he not only declined to abandon the Fair Deal agenda but he revived the administration's flagging antitrust program, inspired a congressional investigation of business lobbying, and even "read the riot act" to a delegation from the U.S. Chamber of Commerce.[48]

---

[46] *Public Papers of the Presidents, Harry S. Truman, 1948* (Washington: U.S. Government Printing Office, 1964), 504 and passim. See also Irwin Ross, *The Loneliest Campaign: The Truman Victory of 1948* (New York: New American Library, 1968), 171–98.

[47] *Business Week* (18 December 1948), 124; Walter White to John L. Collyer, 22 December 1948 (copy), Box 135, PSF, Truman Papers, HSTL. *Fortune* (May 1949), 67. Wilson to Truman, 1 December 1948; Truman to Wilson, 18 December 1948, both in Box 135, PSF, Truman Papers, HSTL.

[48] See especially Cabell Phillips, "Truman's New Romance: The Businessman," *Colliers* (3 June 1950); and Hamby, *Beyond the New Deal*, 297–303. See also address by Clark Clifford, 15 November 1949, Box 5, Charles S. Murphy Papers, HSTL; and address by

Truman's intentions, however, were no match for the powerful forces arrayed against his administration; and as we have seen, he lost on issue after issue, especially following the outbreak of war in Korea and the rise of McCarthyism. Meanwhile, a steady stream of powerful business and political leaders were pouring through the offices of Columbia University President Dwight D. Eisenhower. "Many hundreds of people were urging me to go into politics," Eisenhower later recalled in a letter to his brother Edgar. "Scores of different reasons were advanced as to why I should do so, but in general they all boiled down to something as follows: 'The country is going socialistic so rapidly that, unless Republicans can get in immediately and defeat this trend, our country is gone. Four more years of New Dealism and there will be no turning back. This is our last chance!' " No one put their issue more bluntly than New York Governor Thomas E. Dewey, who told Eisenhower that only he could "save the country from going to Hades in the handbasket of paternalism-socialism-dictatorship. We must look around for someone of great popularity . . . who has not frittered away his political assets by taking positive stands against national planning, etc." Dewey concluded, "Elect such a man to the Presidency, *after which* he must lead us back to safe channels and paths."[49]

With the election of Dwight D. Eisenhower in 1952, the final triumph of the new order would be sealed.

Leon H. Keyserling, 18 September 1949, Box 143, PSF, Truman Papers, HSTL. For Truman's encouragement of the lobby investigation, see Charles Murphy to Truman, 14 May 1949, 12 September 1949, both in Box 3, Murphy Papers; and Truman to James W. Gerard, 13 September 1949, in OF 277, Truman Papers, HSTL. For his meeting with the Chamber of Commerce leaders, see *Washington Star,* 13 August 1949.

[49] Griffith, "Dwight D. Eisenhower and the Corporate Commonwealth," 99.

3

Attitudes toward industry in the Truman
administration: the macroeconomic origins of
microeconomic policy[1]

CRAUFURD D. GOODWIN

During the 1980s a seemingly endless series of troubles plagued the economy of the United States, some new in Americans' experience and others
supposedly banished long ago. The problems, often interrelated, included
intractable unemployment combined with inflation, slow growth in national output and in output per worker-hour, loss of international competitiveness in major industrial sectors, and uncontrollable increases in
the cost of social services such as medical care. During the same decade
the United States saw other countries, notably Japan but also West Germany, South Korea, and a few others, deal successfully with some or all
of these problems. And Americans have wondered why. Various hy-
potheses have been put forth, including suggestions that the size of the
U.S. defense effort reduced the nation's capacity to cope with other difficulties, that victory in war paradoxically led to sclerosis of the economic
system, that the distinctive "spirit" of American society constrains it from
dealing effectively with late twentieth-century challenges, and finally that
somewhere along the way the American people consciously chose to accept a relationship between the private and public sectors that damaged
the two and made them unable to formulate effective, cooperative responses to new challenges. This American social dilemma is contrasted

[1] Laborers in the Truman vineyard are fortunate to have the services of several exceptionally
skilled and cooperative archivists. I am especially grateful for assistance in this project to
Benedict Zobrist and his colleagues at the Harry S. Truman Library (HSTL), including
Dennis Bilger, Warren Ohrvall, and Elizabeth Safly, and to Gerry Hess of the National
Archives in Washington (NA). Research for this chapter was supported by a grant from
the Harry S. Truman Library Institute.

with "Japan Inc." and West Germany and the close relationships there among government, business, and labor.

In this essay the choice of a public-private relationship during the administration of President Truman is explored, for those eight turbulent years following World War II. The discussion on the subject is placed among events of the times.

Emerging from war

The two large economic questions facing President Truman when he assumed office were, first, how best to convert from a wartime to a peacetime economy—to wrench the system for the second time in four years into a different mode with the least possible dislocation—and, second, how to make certain that the postwar world would be better than the prewar one. The second question to some people (especially the Keynesian, or "fiscalist," economists, as they were then called) meant simply maintenance of full employment; but to others (notably the Institutionalist heirs of the New Deal) it implied creation of a more efficient and just system through structural change or public intervention if need be.

World War II, unlike its predecessor, was fought under a system of tight price and quantity controls administered by a network of temporary organizations with an alphabet of acronyms. Prices rose remarkably little and virtual miracles of production were accomplished. During the war, discussion of the sanctity of the free market seemed academic at best, and only a few people took the time to worry whether the war effort was permanently damaging the underlying structure of the economy. One exception concerned the possibility that mobilization would increase the pace of industrial concentration and force out the "little guy."

The Smaller War Plants Corporation (SWPC) was created to address this concern, and it became a thin but insistent voice bemoaning monopoly and warning that competition was much easier to arrest than to create. The SWPC carried on to a limited degree the crusade against economic bigness conducted in the 1930s by the Temporary National Economic Committee. The SWPC, led by its feisty chairman Maury Maverick, reported on mergers and acquisitions and appealed for programs of credit and special services to small business. Perhaps sensing that in the mood of the postwar period successful policy required a link to the achievement of full employment, SWPC staff member John M. Blair pointed out that small firms were typically more labor-intensive than large ones. Hence "the key to full employment—and the guiding light for the management of industrial reconversion—must be found in the expansion of small business."[2]

The Special Senate Committee to Investigate the National Defense Program in 1944, chaired by Senator Harry Truman, also probed wartime threats to small enterprise and to competition. But the mood of the hour was to encourage and cajole business to produce as swiftly and efficiently as possible, not to speculate about its darker sins.

In May 1943 an Office of War Mobilization was created; this was replaced in October 1944 by an Office of War Mobilization and Reconversion (OWMR) with responsibility for policy planning concerning the unification of industrial and civilian mobilization and reconversion activities. The office was abolished in June 1947.[3] Over a three-year period, the OWMR was the center of discussion of how reconversion should be carried out. Although mobilization had blocked much discussion of long-term public policy toward private industry, the prospect of reconversion returned it prominently to view. In a letter to James F. Byrnes, head of OWMR, Chester Bowles, head of the Office of Price Administration, argued in 1944 that fear about whether peace would bring depression was demoralizing to both workers and businesses and was affecting the war effort. Like many others, Bowles called for a "bold and vigorous" national economic program to combat "unemployment, insecurity and disunity."[4]

Keynesians and traditional free-market advocates tended to come together on the recommendation that controls should be removed sooner rather than later. The best hope for a smooth conversion to peacetime, they believed, was simply to restore market freedom with all the flexible

[2] E.g., Harrison F. Houghton, "Concentration of Industry during the War Years," 27 December 1944, Folder: U.S. Government-Smaller War Plants Corporation, Records of the Office of the Deputy Director for War Programs, Entry 34-PI-25, Records of the Office of War Mobilization and Reconversion, Record Group 250 (hereafter RG 250), NA: Maury Maverick to J. A. Krug, 12 June 1945, Smaller War Plants Corporation File, OF 92-B, HSTL; John Blair to Maury Maverick, "Small Business and Full Employment," 26 April 1945, Folder: Small Business, General Files of Robert R. Nathan, Entry 38-PI-25, RG 250, NA.

[3] See Herman Miles Somers, *Presidential Agency, The Office of War Mobilization and Reconversion* (Cambridge, Mass.: Harvard University Press, 1950), and Homer L. Calkin, *Records of the Office of War Mobilization and Reconversion* (Washington, D.C.: NA, 1951).

[4] Bowles to Byrnes, 8 December 1944, Folder: U.S. Government-Office of Price Administration, Records of the Office of the Deputy Director for War Programs, Entry 34-PI-25, RG 250, NA. Bowles's experience in OPA is described in his autobiography *Promises to Keep* (New York: Harper & Row, 1971).

response to rapid change that is implied. The best way to contain the danger of inflation was to "let her rip" with the production of goods and services. Inequities and inconsistencies that had grown up under controls would in this way be reduced as painlessly as possible through the free play of market forces. Only the clever entrepreneur could react precisely to the wants of consumers and grasp the opportunities presented by demobilization. For Keynesians, who most feared unemployment and stagnation, there seemed little reason to continue leashing businesses who wanted to generate production of consumer goods and employment.

The case for more cautious reconversion seems to have been made by people with "Institutionalist" perspectives, who believed that at critical times the state was simply more efficient and fair than a market system. They had come to believe almost viscerally that relatively tight planning and controls would be best for a little while longer. The case for retention of controls rested on the sense that in the hurly-burly of precipitate decontrol, the rich and powerful would come out on top at the expense of the weak and disorganized. Fred Vinson, director of the Office of Economic Stabilization, made the case in 1944 that because conditions during reconversion would be excessively disorderly, with government "fighting against deflationary pressures in some sectors of the economy and against inflationary pressures in other sectors," controls must be retained.[5] Frances Perkins, secretary of labor, making the countercase for the free market as the best structure for reconversion, responded to Vinson that controls should be lifted swiftly on wages at least, if not on all prices: "Human as distinct from economic needs and standards are involved in wages," she said, "and those can always be best achieved by the free human relationship in bargains made directly by the workers and employers involved." Moreover, "the time when an increase in wages will promote, instead of choking off, employment will differ from industry to industry and from plant to plant. Governmental control, depending as it does on a universal rule or precedent and effective, as it is, only after considerable delay, cannot meet the needs of this sort of situation."[6] Because there was little empirical evidence at hand about how best to move economically from war to peace, the arguments about how long to retain controls tended to have this broad theoretical character.

[5] Vinson to William H. Davis, chairman, National War Labor Board, 10 August 1944, Folder: Post War Planning Committee, Records of the Office of Economic Stabilization, Entry 141-PI-25, RG 250, NA.

[6] Perkins to Vinson, 13 September 1944, Folder: Reconversion-Wages and Salaries, Records of the Office of Economic Stabilization, RG 250, NA.

In general, government officials recognized that reconversion tactics involved judgments about events that were impossible to predict with any confidence. For example, OWMR Director James Byrnes wrote in February 1945 to Cap Krug, chairman of the War Production Board rather hesitantly, as follows: "The effective method of checking inflation is to produce quantities of goods rapidly, but an uncontrolled scramble for materials and components may impose a heavy strain on the price structure." Byrnes urged Krug to relax controls "to the full extent deemed possible without a real threat of interference with essential programs." But he did not explain how to determine when this "threat" existed or which "programs" were essential.[7]

The War Production Board (WPB) consulted widely among business and industrial leaders about how best to accomplish a smooth reconversion. The board also solicited the views of professional economists, who were found to be "more voluble on these subjects than most of the more specialized business men"; moreover, they "specialize in perspective and sometimes see things that are overlooked internally in the pressure of details."[8] The obvious need for coordination among the major agencies during the move into peace led one OWMR staff member to recommend creation of an economic "general staff."[9] But naturally this notion appealed only to those who favored retention of controls at all. Krug was widely perceived as the most vehement advocate of speedy termination of controls and a return to peacetime conditions. Robert Nathan in OWMR described as "reckless" a statement by Krug that "regulations . . . automatically put ceilings on initiative, imagination and resourcefulness."[10] In August 1945 a public letter from President Truman, presumably instigated by OWMR, asked Krug and the WPB to continue some of their functions at least for a while so as "to help industry to obtain unprecedented civilian production."[11]

The end of a victorious war, just as the war itself, was not the occasion for profound reflection on the proper role for government in the econ-

---

[7] Byrnes to Krug, 1 February 1945, Folder: Victory Planning-Post V-E Day, Records of the Deputy Director for War Programs, Entry 34-PI-25, RG 250, NA.
[8] Edwin B. George to J. D. Small, 21 April 1945, Folder: Eddie George, General Files of Robert R. Nathan, Entry 38-PI-25, RG 250, NA.
[9] William H. Davis to O. Max Gardner, 23 July 1945, Folder: Advisory Board-Correspondence, Records of the Director's Office, Entry 145-PI-25, RG 250, NA.
[10] Draft (unsent) by Nathan for memorandum, Fred M. Vinson to J. A. Krug, attached to Nathan to Vinson, 6 June 1945, Folder: Controls, Office of the Deputy Director for Reconversion, Entry 38-PI-25, RG 250, NA.
[11] Truman to Krug, in press release, 9 August 1945, OF 172, HSTL.

omy. Nevertheless, the makings of controversy were present, and the fact that the preference for rapid decontrol seemed to prevail over preferences for retention of some controls into peacetime was a hint of things to come.

The Keynesian conversion

The effect of Keynesian economic ideas on American economists, although not immediate, was ultimately akin to a religious experience.[12] In part the appeal was strictly intellectual: An elegant new body of theory explained hitherto puzzling facts. But the appeal was emotional as well: Here, the believers became convinced, was the answer to the enormous human suffering of the 1930s that had almost brought the nation to its knees. Moreover, the Keynesians believed, this end to economic woes would permit the survival and strengthening of liberal democracies and arrest the growth of new dictators.[13] The personal allegiance of many economists, especially young ones, to Keynes is clear, but it is striking that in government documents about macroeconomic policy during and just after the war, Keynes's name is almost never mentioned.

Several reasons can be suggested why. First, the American masses seldom take kindly to newfangled foreign ideas, and this was sensed by the Keynesians, who presented the ideas without attribution. But in addition there was a distinctly and uniquely American flavor to the macroeconomic discussions during this period. Instead of a focus exclusively on the tools of fiscal policy characteristic of the British discussion, there was a much wider emphasis on the context in which fiscal policy would operate. This feature of the American discussion may have been influenced by the "mature economy" thesis of Professor Alvin Hansen of Harvard University, who foresaw problems of "secular stagnation" associated with the closing of the frontier and other phenomena lying behind the inadequacy of effective demand in the United States. Finally, there was an appreciation of the political difficulties associated with selling a theory

[12] A great deal has been written on this topic. Many of the early appraisals are collected in Seymour E. Harris, *The New Economics* (New York: Alfred A. Knopf, 1952). An examination of Keynes's reception in the private sector is Robert M. Collins, *The Business Response to Keynes, 1929–1964* (New York: Columbia University Press, 1981).

[13] An eloquent statement of this position was prepared by Walter Salant, entitled "Full Employment and Political Democracy," 2 February 1945, Memoranda File, 1945, Salant Papers, HSTL.

as radical as that of Keynes and a policy instrument as heretical as deficit finance. So better bury the radical ideas in a more conventional larger program!

Discussion of macroeconomic policy came to a head in the summer of 1944 when Chairman Marriner Eccles of the Federal Reserve Board and Director Harold Smith of the Budget Bureau convened an informal group of economists in, and on the edge of, government to explore the preparation of an American white (or "pink") paper on a postwar employment program. The group consisted of Gerhard Colm, Arthur Smithies, Emile Despres, Richard Gilbert, Walter Salant, Kenneth Williams, Richard Musgrave, and Alvin Hansen.[14]

Various members of the group prepared draft statements. To get a sense of their thinking, it is worth examining one statement by Hansen dated 18 September 1944 in some detail. It began by deploring the Depression and marveling at economic accomplishments during the war. "It [the war production achievement] presents both hopes and fears for the future—hopes of a new high level of prosperity and living standards; fears of vast unemployment." The role of the federal government after the war, Hansen wrote, should be to "establish the framework within which families, private business, and state and local governments can plan and execute effectively their part." This task consisted first of all of the "responsibility to so manage its fiscal operations that the total flow of expenditures, public and private, will be adequate and stable." So far, so good, and very Keynesian. But the Hansen memo went on, "The role of the government is to create conditions under which free enterprise can reach its maximum possible development, and to supplement its activities in areas where only the government can do the job." The government "job" in this regard was defined to include promotion of

investment outlets for private enterprise . . . by a comprehensive program of regional resource development, by urban redevelopment, and by a thoroughgoing modernization of our highway and airport system. . . . To encourage new products, new processes, and new industries the government should undertake a large program of scientific research . . . to promote the most efficient use of labor and

[14]The "pink" paper is reprinted in *History of Employment and Manpower Policy in the United States; Twenty Years of Experience under the Employment Act of 1946,* Subcommittee on Employment and Manpower of the Senate Committee on Labor and Public Welfare, 89th Cong., 2d sess. (1966), vol. 7, pt. I, 1–27. Many of the documents leading up to the paper are in Employment Act Symposium File, Colm Papers, HSTL.

resources. . . . It should promote comprehensive planning with respect to land use, both urban and rural.

Government must undertake an expanded program of Social Security, including unemployment and old-age insurance, and make provision for temporary and permanent disability. "It must greatly improve and extend the facilities for public health and education, especially in the backward areas in our country. It must carry through a comprehensive veterans program. It must enforce minimum wages and improving labor standards."

This agenda was certainly far beyond the pure milk of John Maynard Keynes. It owed as much to the old American Institutionalists and the New Deal as to the "New Economics" from across the water. The influence of free-market advocates could also be discerned in the advocacy of "automatic stabilizers" such as unemployment insurance to limit dependence on discretionary fiscal measures.[15]

There was a distinctly optimistic tone to the Hansen memo. Inflation could be avoided by "an orderly upward adjustment of wages and money incomes generally in proportion to the over-all increase in per capita productivity. Industries which enjoy a more rapid increase in productivity than the general average should reduce prices." Happily, Hansen noted, "there is a close community of interest between all the groups of our economy." Even in this maturing economy, he could discern few uncertainties or clouds on the horizon.

The final "pink" paper was much more elaborate than the original Hansen draft but there were strong similarities. The authors declared firmly that their concern was with "long-range" problems, and they had purposely "side-stepped" the "demobilization" issues. For this they were criticized for tendering "lack of guidance."[16] Elsewhere in government, however, others were thinking through the administrative implications of macroeconomic reasoning. One staff member of OWMR urged the construction of a large national macroeconomic model (with assumptions "to accord with political or social realism") and the appointment of a "planning staff . . . to outline policies for each major segment of the economy so as to accommodate the interests and pressures of each segment into an overall program."[17]

[15] Alvin Hansen, "Postwar Employment Program," 18 September 1944, Postwar Employment Program File, Colm Papers, HSTL.
[16] J. Weldon Jones to the director, "Progress Report on Full Employment Report," 25 August 1944, Employment Act Symposium File, Colm Papers, HSTL.
[17] "Proposed Research Project: Policy Yardstick for OWMR," undated and unsigned, prob-

During 1944–45 there was everywhere a yearning for "cooperation" rather than conflict among the institutions and sectors of American society. The "hostilities" of the 1930s and the wartime conflict itself had left deep scars; many people seemed exhausted by the struggles and yearned for a new sense of domestic and international community. Moreover, they believed that this change in mood could be brought about relatively easily. Paul Hoffman wrote to the president in August 1945 that "there is a deep anxiety among all segments of our population over the availability of jobs after the war. That anxiety is matched by a desire on the part of an overwhelming majority of our people for the preservation and strengthening of our system of free competitive enterprise." He advocated creation of a "Presidential Full Employment Commission" to make recommendations about public policies and programs.[18]

As the war came to a close, then, debates over "industrial policy" occurred at two levels. Economists argued over when to remove wartime controls. At the same time a vision of new macroeconomic policy was formed with a component of constructive intervention in the private sector that, like the case for retention of controls, owed as much to the old tradition of New Deal planning and to home-grown Institutionalism as to the new macroeconomic messiah.

Adjusting to peace

Disillusionment toward the economy might be the best way to describe the mood of the Truman administration during the first term. The good news was that the dreaded depression did not return. This in itself was cause for rejoicing. But the bad news was that, in place of unemployment, fear of inflation became a constant complication for government policy and its direction. Moreover, the hoped-for cooperation among business, labor, and government, which had been dreamed of so often during the war, failed to materialize. Indeed, the parties all seemed bound on courses that, taken together, were malignant and self-destructive.

During this period it was necessary not only to diagnose the problems

ably 1944, marked "Livingston or Hagen," Folder Programming, General Files of Robert R. Nathan, Entry 38-PI-25, RG 250, NA.

[18] Hoffman to Truman, 4 August 1945, Folder: Committee for Economic Development, Office of the Deputy Director for Reconversion, Entry 38-PI-25, RG 250, NA. A typical letter from a businessman pleading for a "spirit of cooperation" to replace the "hostile attitudes" of the 1930s is B. C. Black, president, Mayflower Doughnut Corporation, to the president, 3 May 1945, OF 172 (1945), with attachment.

but to sort out the instruments and mechanisms to be used against them. As war ended, the air was full of suggestions for ways in which the parts of the economy could cooperate for their mutual benefit. Discussion was stimulated by the yeasty contents of the Murray Full Employment Bill then before Congress. There were proposals for such new bodies as a National Board of Economic Development, rather like an Estates General, with representatives from agriculture, business, consumers, government, and labor. The National Planning Association (NPA), which had issued during the war a "Declaration of Interdependence" of agriculture, business, and labor, kept up a stream of conferences and publications after war's end calling for "a course of conduct in terms of reason, unity, and justice." President Truman wrote to the NPA in October 1945 to endorse this initiative: "I want every businessman, farmer, and worker to know that joint action in developing solutions to the challenging problems that lie ahead has my most sincere and determined support."[19]

But it was precisely joint economic action for the common good that Truman was to see little of for several years to come. The first policy debacle and manifestation that unbridled self-interest would be the order of the day concerned the issue of when and how to effect decontrol after V-J Day. There was as high a level of disagreement within the government as without. Cap Krug from the WPB continued to argue that the best approach was to go to the free market cold turkey. "Once unleashed from governmental control," he said,

American industrial experience and ingenuity will find the speediest way to clear the tangles, break the bottlenecks and get civilian production rolling again. . . . The trouble with continued centralized Government control over industrial production and distribution is, first, that the American consumer is deprived of freedom of choice in what he can buy, and second, that American management and local public agencies are deprived of their demonstrated ability to exercise initiative and judgement in determining the shape and timing of economic activities.[20]

Chester Bowles and others, especially the staffs of OPA and OWMR, repeated the contrary view about the necessity for government planning and coordination over an extended transitional period.

But more important than this difference of view in determining the

---

[19] Alva Meyers, Jr., and Oscar Meier, "Proposal for the Establishment of a National Board of Economic Development under the Terms of the Full Employment Act of 1945," 15 October 1945, attached to Bill Devlin to Robert R. Nathan, 6 November 1945, Folder: E. E. Hagen, General files of Robert R. Nathan, Entry 38-PI-25, RG 250, NA; and Truman to the National Planning Association, 15 October 1945, PPF 2099, HSTL.

[20] J. A. Krug, "Should Uncle Sam Program Civilian Production?" Article prepared for *New York Times* Sunday Magazine, 22 July 1945, Folder: Press Releases, General Files of Robert R. Nathan, Entry 38-PI-25, RG 250, NA.

final outcome was the way in which events unfolded. Truman appealed for public-spirited behavior but believed that he received the reverse. At the urging of Chester Bowles he convened a Labor-Management Conference in November 1945 to plot common strategy, but this broke up in disarray. From then on through 1946 it must have seemed to the embattled president that he was like the little Dutch boy with his finger in the dike resisting firms, industries, unions, farm groups, and others who were striking, locking out, lobbying Congress, and in all respects making it impossible for him to stem the tide of inflation. At the same time members of his staff were giving conflicting advice that would have been difficult for the most sophisticated professional, let alone a new chief executive inexperienced in economic affairs, to sort out.

A moment of crisis occurred in July 1946 when the president was faced with a weak and attenuated price control bill whose advocates in Congress made what would be called today "supply side" arguments. The bill might seem to be inflationary, they said, but in fact the stimulus it would give to industry would merely generate a compensatory deflationary flow of goods. A "demand side" staff member in OWMR responded, "This assertion is not supported by quantitative evidence concerning supply and demand—as you will realize if you try to remember reading or hearing such evidence—but instead it is sold like soap by repetition." This critic said that, to the contrary, "an inflationary boom and collapse would occur under the bill."[21] A second, tougher price control bill was finally passed, but after this incident the end of restraints was near. A strike by meat producers placed intolerable pressure on that one crucial market, and in November 1946 President Truman announced to the American people the end of all controls.

The Employment Act and its effect

While the reconversion to peace was being accomplished in 1945 and 1946, the new advisory institutions that Congress finally agreed were needed to meet the mounting economic challenges were formed and put

---

[21] E.g., James R. Newman to Robert Nathan, "Memorandum: The Bureau of the Budget Statement on Reconversion Policies," 8 May 1945, Folder: Bureau of the Budget, Office of the Deputy Director for Reconversion, Entry 38-PI-25, RG 250, NA. Events of the times were described in a report by Philip E. Coombs, "Factors Contributing to Collapse of Stabilization Program," 10 April 1947, Folder: OES-History Notes, Records of the Office of Economic Stabilization, Entry 127-PI-25, RG 250, NA.

Everett E. Hagen to John R. Steelman, "The Price Control Extension Bill, HR 6042," 27 June 1946, Folder: General-Price Control, Reports and other Records on Economic Problems of Reconversion, Entry 31-PI-25, RG 250, NA.

into effect. As is often the case, what was put in place was substantially a reaction to what had gone before. Despite hopes harbored by some in the early days of discussions about the Murray Bill that a large new planning and directive agency would be created (perhaps a successor to OWMR), or at least an "Economic General Staff," unhappy recollections of the New Deal, together with departmental jealousies, joined with other factors, among them an activist group of alarmed business lobbies, to make certain that the Employment Act, when passed, contained nothing more threatening than a three-person Council of Economic Advisers (CEA) to the president, a Joint Economic Committee of Congress, and an annual economic report by the president. With memories of the recently deceased National Resources Planning Board still strong—and of its penchant for large studies that seldom entered the policy process—the new CEA was placed squarely within the Executive Office of the President, and the members had status approaching that of cabinet members.[22]

The Employment Act (S. 380) in its final form set out to declare national policy on three subjects: employment, production, and purchasing power. It did not contain the words "full employment" and avoided direct reference to the use of public expenditures to supplement private expenditures. The requirement that the president submit an annual economic report to Congress replaced an earlier proposal for a "National Production and Employment Budget." Nevertheless the CEA remained substantially an outgrowth of Keynesian, or fiscalist, thinking, and this character was to become both its strength and its weakness. It was a source of strength, because by 1946 many business leaders had come to recognize that full employment achieved through a flexible fiscal policy could be the best of all worlds—they would have buoyant markets and minimal governmental intervention. As one business consulting group told its clients as S. 380 came up for passage, "So far as the bill may achieve its goal of sustaining employment through greater purchasing power, it will mean more prosperous business—though total profits may not increase proportionately. To the extent that the goal is achieved by stimulating business investment it will in fact be a 'business bill.' "[23]

[22] The standard account of passage of the Employment Act is Stephen K. Bailey, *Congress Makes a Law* (New York: Columbia University Press, 1950). Plans for a new and expanded executive office of the president, which would contain "a sort of economic general staff," were set forth by Thomas I. Emerson, general counsel of OWMR, to Director John W. Snyder in a memorandum "Administration of Full Employment Legislation," 30 November 1945, Folder: Full Employment Bill, General Files of Robert R. Nathan, Entry 38-PI-25, RG 250, NA.

[23] Policy memorandum prepared by The Research Institute of America staff for executive

The weakness growing out of the Keynesian origins was the precise emphasis on output, employment and price levels. The CEA, in effect, would be asked to do both too much and too little. The Budget Bureau recognized this problem immediately and pointed it out to the president, while at the same time advising him to sign the Employment Act. Harold Smith, the director, explained:

The establishment of the Council is based on the theory that policies designed to create and maintain maximum employment, production, and purchasing power can be separated from other aspects of the Federal Program, and that responsibility for advising the President on employment policies can be separated from responsibility for counseling him on other aspects of his economic and fiscal program. This again is a very serious defect of the bill.[24]

In fact none of the first three CEA members was a strict Keynesian, although all knew and were sympathetic to Keynes's ideas. Edwin Nourse, the chairman, was an agricultural economist from The Brookings Institution who had specialized in studying the behavior of individual markets. He had long had a research interest in cooperatives, a market form not easily subsumed by traditional price theory. Although not properly categorized as an Institutionalist, he had distinct Institutionalist roots and affiliations, and he described the neoclassical and Keynesian traditions as, respectively, the laissez-faire and fiscal policy schools. Leon Keyserling was a product of Columbia University Institutionalism and a veteran of many New Deal battles. John D. Clark had been a businessman and business school dean.

In his letter of acceptance to President Truman, Chairman Nourse redefined the CEA's functions as he saw them. First, he said, it was necessary to collect facts. Then it was necessary

to interpret all available literal facts into the soundest possible diagnosis as to the state of the nation's economic health and the causes which explain any evidence of current ill health or which threaten to produce unhealthy conditions in the future. Since even the best of doctors are often in disagreement as to what the picture actually shows is going on in a bodily organism, we must draw many economic specialists into consultation on the special phases of our diagnosis.[25]

No orthodox Keynesian here! In fact this response from Nourse sounded like a classic statement of American Institutionalist methodology. The

members, 30 August 1945: "The Meaning of the Full Employment Bill," General Files of Robert R. Nathan, Entry 38-PI-25, RG 250, NA.

[24] Harold D. Smith, memorandum for the president: "The Employment Bill of 1946," 15 February 1946, Program on Full Employment File, Colm Papers, HSTL.

[25] Nourse to the president, 29 July 1946, Daily Diary, Nourse Papers, HSTL. See also oral history interview with Dr. Edwin G. Nourse, 7 March 1972, 5, 16–17, HSTL.

following account of strategy by senior CEA staff member Gerhard Colm only strengthens this sense of pervasive Institutionalist thinking:

Somehow we begin to look at free enterprise as an institutional arrangement that permits us to accomplish broad economic objectives with a greater degree of individual freedom than any other economic organization. In order to be able to judge whether the decisions of free enterprise do or do not accomplish these objectives we need to know them. Under this philosophy it will be necessary for a free enterprise country to establish economic goals of a character not so different from those that are needed to develop a five-year plan for a socialist economy. Yet the use made of these goals is fundamentally different in both cases.[26]

The CEA began life with its gaze fixed, as charged, on issues of employment. But events drew it inexorably toward the issue of the time, inflation. In fact, it soon seemed to CEA members that uncontrollable price increases were the Achilles' heel of a free-market system. Normal macroeconomic policies to maintain employment could not be pursued so long as there was great danger of inflation, and if prices were allowed to get out of hand, crisis and collapse would soon follow. Like most of the economics profession at the time, the CEA members did not consider seriously a monetary basis for inflation. Instead they turned to macroeconomic variables for an explanation and for a solution. In this way microeconomic issues were forced on President Truman's economic advisers and much of the "industrial policy" of his first term came into being by default.

The two market sectors that drew the attention of the economists as a source of inflation were those for productive factors and for finished goods and services. Views about the labor market changed perceptibly over the course of the first term. Right after the war, younger economists in particular pictured labor as victimized by the Depression and by arrangements during wartime, which they claimed had been "tilted" toward employers; it was time now for workers to get their own back. A declining relative share of wages in total national income was bound to reduce aggregate purchasing power, they pointed out, and to bring on a recession. In a series of memos on "the wage situation" discussed widely in OWMR during 1945, Richard Gilbert spoke of labor as "seething with unrest," and he called for "immediate and substantial wage increases . . . if we are to avoid a crippling decline in national income and purchasing power and in employment." He recommended a restoration of free col-

[26] Excerpts from letter of G. Colm to P. T. Homan, 31 July 1947, Daily Diary, Nourse Papers, HSTL.

lective bargaining within a system of controls on product prices. In part he looked for a shift in factor shares away from profits to wages, but he also depended on another optimistic and unsubstantiated supply-side argument, that higher wages in some sectors would not be inflationary because "dissatisfied workers will slow down on the job; satisfied workers will pull their own weight. Wage increases have always paid for themselves in productivity. They will do so now."[27] Another economist, Walter Salant, made a supplementary supply-side case when he claimed that productivity gains had accumulated during the war and a pay-out now would be "compatible with the maintenance of existing costs and prices."[28]

In reporting the results of this overall discussion to OWMR Director and presidential confidant John Snyder, Robert Nathan gave greatest weight to the macroeconomic, or demand-side, arguments for wage increases. "The only solution to mass production and full employment in America," he said, "lies in mass consumption which requires a much higher standard of living and a much higher income for those who will use their income for consumption purposes." Accordingly, "a high wage policy is a prerequisite to overcoming this basic weakness of our system. We must give meaning and substance to the concept of large production and low prices and high wages." Nathan seemed to imply that accomplishment of this goal of income redistribution and a new national wage policy should not be difficult to achieve. He explained confidently, "We should arrive at a wage policy which will help us to avoid disputes, moderate the impact of reduced take-home pay upon the workers, and avoid a run-away inflation."[29] As it turned out, the government was unable to achieve any of these goals over the next few years.

What stood in the way of these dreams of applied reason in industrial relations was the disorderly and imperfect character of the labor market, where bilateral monopoly made the outcome of wage disputes indeterminate. As long as a single seller of labor (a union) dealt with a single buyer (a large corporation), there was no way to predict the outcome precisely or to prescribe a "just" wage. Political forces within the unions and corporations led to actions that could not be anticipated on any

[27] Richard V. Gilbert, two memoranda on "The Wage Situation," 3 and 16 October 1945, Folder: Wage Policy, General Files of Robert R. Nathan, Entry 38-PI-25, RG 250, NA.

[28] Walter S. Salant to Thomas I. Emerson, "Background for Determination of Wage Policy," 28 September 1945, Folder: Wage Policy, General Files of Robert R. Nathan, Entry 38-PI-25, RG 250, NA.

[29] Nathan to Snyder, 27 September 1945, with attached memorandum "The Labor and Wage Problem," Folder: Wage Study, General Files of Robert R. Nathan, Entry 38-PI-25, RG 250, NA.

simple economic ground. Economists spoke of ranges of indeterminacy. But this was cold comfort to a beleaguered and inexperienced president trying to steer the economy away from rocks that appeared everywhere he looked. Struggles involving coal miners, steelworkers, and other labor organizations led to some of the most frustrating moments President Truman experienced during his years in office, and he grew increasingly bitter about them. He felt that he was himself a "little guy" and a president for all the working people, yet time and time again relatively small groups of union members would either impede crucial production that would benefit all or block efforts to fight inflation.

Some attention to the long run

The administration was too busy putting out economic fires of all kinds during the first term to think hard about fundamental changes that might have to be made in the system as a consequence of undesirable individual actions. Some people, however, did wonder whether even current trends in wage and price determination were compatible with the continuation of economic freedom. Occasionally, interesting suggestions for reform came along; for example, John Dunlop wrote to Chester Bowles from the Federal Reserve in 1946 that it might be necessary for government to issue "guideposts to the parties of collective bargaining" based on improvements in technology. This proposal for a formal link between wage increases and productivity growth was an idea that lay dormant for almost twenty years before reappearing in the Johnson administration.[30]

President Truman himself was naturally receptive to thinking that grew out of disillusionment with powerful economic actors. His experience as chairman of the Senate Special Committee to Investigate the National Defense Program had left him dubious about both the competitive instincts and the patriotism of big business and labor leaders. He reminisced years later: "I saw cliques in labor and in capital, each greedy for gain, while small production plants by the hundreds were being pushed aside and kept inactive by big business. The big fellows, in the name of the government, were putting thousands of small concerns out of business that should have been producing for the total war effort."

The Truman Committee had discovered that selfish and monopolistic actions in product and labor markets fed off each other.

---

[30] Dunlop to Bowles, "Tomorrow without Fear," 12 March 1946, Folder: John Dunlop, General Files of Chester Bowles, Entry 142-PI-25, RG 250, NA.

The Committee found that leadership in both labor and industry had been too much concerned with its own interests and too little concerned with the national welfare. The defense program was very seriously handicapped by strikes and threatened strikes. I felt that many demands for wage increases were inspired by the reports of tremendous profits being made by companies with defense contracts.[31]

President Truman speculated that those same monopolists who had impeded the war effort might also be behind the problems of conversion to peace.

The one serious inquiry into a possible reformulation of conditions in the labor market during Truman's first term focused specifically on proposals for a guaranteed annual wage in industry. The study originated in a request for a guaranteed annual wage by the United Steelworkers of America in a case before the War Labor Board in 1944. The board responded by recommending that the president examine the whole subject in detail, and this task was assigned to the OWMR. The idea for a guaranteed annual wage drew support from at least three quarters. The labor movement, and especially the Congress of Industrial Organizations, saw it as a device to increase job security and perhaps even take-home pay when averaged over the business cycle. Macroeconomists thought it a promising automatic stabilizer to sustain effective demand and thereby to supplement discretionary public policy in recessions. Those worried over the increasingly acrimonious state of labor relations generally, including some business leaders, thought that strikes and unreasonable wage demands might be reduced and productivity increased with a more secure and self-confident labor force. By late 1946 an OWMR research team led by Murray Latimer had undertaken a series of case studies and general explorations that seemed to imply that all three objectives might indeed be gained by a guaranteed annual wage.[32]

One of the most interesting components of the study was a chapter by Alvin Hansen and Paul Samuelson on the macroeconomic implications of the scheme. They found it likely to be a stabilizing force but certainly not a panacea.[33] Continued inquiry into the device from all angles, how-

---

[31] Harry S. Truman, *Memoirs*, vol. 1, *Year of Decisions* (Garden City, N.Y.: Doubleday, 1955), 165, 176.

[32] The origins of the Guaranteed Annual Wage Study are discussed in a document prepared for congressional hearings, dated 14 March 1946. Folder: Appropriations (1946), General Correspondence and other Records, Entry 104-PI-25, RG 250, NA. A "Statement of CIO Executive Board on Guaranteed Wage Study" is in Folder: Labor Unions— Correspondence, ibid. The findings of the study were set forth in a summary document by Latimer, "Principal Conclusions of the Interim Report of the Guaranteed Wage Study," Folder: Advisory Board on Annual Wage Study, ibid.

[33] The views of Hansen and Samuelson are reflected well in the detailed minutes of a meet-

ever, began to suggest that it would present innumerable problems and side effects, and the advocates fell away as they thought about other possible structural reforms. The supply-side arguments for the scheme claimed it would be costless and noninflationary, but remained unsupported by evidence. A number of distinguished economists—including Jacob Viner, J. M. Clark, E. S. Mason, Sumner Slichter, Everett Hagen, Richard Musgrave, Walter Salant, and Lloyd Metzler—criticized the scheme with varying degrees of vigor.

The coup de grace to the study may have come from the brilliant young labor lawyer Benjamin Ginsburg, who wrote a devastating critique expressing concern that a focus on a labor market gimmick might reduce the national commitment to macroeconomic planning, the only course that he believed would really bring about economic justice, full employment, and growth: "It is the unconscious reversal of our thinking that does the harm."[34] During 1947 the study was wound up, prematurely in the eyes of its director, with responsibility for examining the matter further transferred to the CEA, and at the practical level to the Departments of Labor and Commerce.[35]

Even though, as Chairman Nourse wrote to Presidential Assistant John Steelman in 1948, it was generally understood that a labor dispute was not "a situation in which you or the President conceive that my duties need concern me or that the services of the Council are called for," it was becoming increasingly plain that the notion of a macro-micro policy split was impractical. Nourse argued that, for example, a generous settlement of the current railway strike "would have serious inflationary repercussions" and therefore was of vital significance to accomplishment of the macroeconomic goals of the CEA. He pointed out that the broad purpose of the Employment Act was to "substitute methods of reason and social engineering for resort to force." It was appropriate, therefore, to follow this principle to its natural conclusion by inquiring into the affairs of all units possessing "monopoly power." Fiscal policy as a macroeconomic tool could not be expected to work smoothly in the absence of a truly competitive economic system, and this condition, he concluded, was absent in America. "The situation confronting our democratic government today is quite similar to that which France was faced by—and failed to

ing of economists in which they took part dated 17 May 1946. Folder: Economic Analysis of Guaranteed Wages, ibid.

[34] Ginsburg to Latimer, "Basic Policy on Guaranteed Wage Study," 14 October 1946, Folder: Analysis of Guarantee Plans, ibid.

[35] Harry Truman to Edwin G. Nourse, 7 March 1947, Daily Diary, Nourse Papers, HSTL.

meet effectively—between the World Wars and since. It is the danger that follows the growth of strong factions and the revelation of weak government."[36]

The CEA position on the Taft-Hartley Act, which eventually became law despite President Truman's veto, was that it did not deal effectively with the problem of labor market monopoly, not that the problem was unimportant. "It provides no genuine solution for those industrial conflicts which threaten to paralyze the economy because of their size or the vital points at which they strike." The CEA believed that the way had yet to be found to ensure "labor peace and high productivity and the adjustment of wages and working conditions through the process of smoothly running collective bargaining."[37]

The CEA shared at least as much unease about the prevalence of market imperfections among business firms in product markets as among workers. But, as in the case of labor markets, they were not sure what to do about the situation. Addressing the War Contracts Subcommittee of the Senate Military Affairs Committee in May 1944, long before the CEA existed, Nourse had argued that "changes in business philosophy or current policy and practice" would be necessary if peace were to bring "high efficiency, smooth operation, and well-sustained prosperity." Nourse worried that

free enterprise has in fact often been interpreted as a demand by those of greater strength, better location, more favorable situation, or greater ruthlessness that they be allowed to exercise their full power toward advancing their individual or group interests even when the effect is to restrain the enterprise of others. . . . No one who will honestly look at the past and present record of America can doubt that the majority of businessmen are in fact afraid of competition, just as they are afraid of really free enterprise.

Nourse discovered two major dangers in this condition. First, timid businessmen, when combining to exert monopoly power, tended to associate stable prices with stable profits and therefore created an inflationary bias in the economy. Prices were encouraged to go up, but never down. Administered prices became inflationary prices. Second, the fears of businessmen in situations of imperfect competition could combine with the fears of workers to encourage a policy of restriction of output rather than of growth. Misunderstanding of how a competitive economy could

[36] Nourse to Steelman, 7 May 1948, Daily Diary, Nourse Papers, HSTL.
[37] Nourse, Keyserling, and Clark to President Truman, 16 June 1947, Letters and Memos 1946–47 File, Clark Papers, HSTL.

work led to pressures to "share" limited markets and jobs. Unemployment and stagnation then became self-fulfilling prophesies. The danger was manifested by

the reassertion of the doctrine by various interest groups that their welfare is to be promoted by lines of action which retard rather than enhance production.

This danger stems from the prevailing fears of workers that there are not enough jobs, of capitalists that there are not enough investment opportunities, and of producers and distributors generally that there is not enough market demand to go around.

Paradoxically, Nourse said, if all parts of the economy behaved optimistically and competitively, prosperity would be assured: "If the policies of the government and of owners and managers of business vigorously and skillfully follow lines that make for maximum production, this will assure the largest possible number of jobs, the steadiest possible work, and the lowest possible prices for consumer goods."[38]

Over the course of President Truman's first term, while the administration was finding its feet, sorting out responsibilities for new institutions such as the CEA, and responding to the innumerable crises of the moment, various parts of government kept one eye, at least, cocked toward "long-run problems" and long-term solutions. Typically they had in view undesirable microeconomic characteristics of the economic system. For example, Lowell Mason, President Truman's first appointee to the Federal Trade Commission (FTC), offered a controversial proposal for the convening of a series of "industry-wide trade practice conferences to be held under the aegis of the Federal Trade Commission," wherein business leaders would work out the means to achieve "a reign of law" in their particular industries and, as it were, acquire "a self-imposed vaccination against bad business habits."[39] Mason was affirming, in effect, that some degree of monopoly, as of sin, was natural to the human condition and that it was far more reasonable and promising to seek to limit and channel impure motives than to strive unsuccessfully for their total elimination. Mason's accommodationism was greeted with stern disapproval by his colleagues on the FTC and others who thought that the only proper approach to market concentration was hot pursuit.[40]

[38] Testimony of E. G. Nourse before the War Contracts Subcommittee of the Senate Military Affairs Committee, 2 May 1944, CEA Staff File, Nourse Papers, HSTL.
[39] Mason to Matthew J. Connelly, 24 November 1947, OF 100, HSTL.
[40] Critical discussions of Mason's approach are John D. Clark to John R. Steelman, 22 October 1947, OF 100, HSTL.; and unsigned memo titled "Federal Trade Commission," 2 January 1948, OF 100, HSTL.

Senior staff member Gerhard Colm, in presenting material on long-range economic policies to the new CEA members in 1946, explored how it might be possible "to strengthen the basic structure of the economy so that it will become less vulnerable to fluctuations and will require a lesser amount of compensating Government measures than otherwise may become necessary." Even though he was an immigrant from Germany in the 1930s, Colm used familiar Institutionalist language in calling for "a well-balanced economy." He saw a large potential agenda for government action to "strengthen the structure of the American economy," broken into the following four categories:

(1) To promote adaptation of the labor force to the opportunities and requirements of the modern economy;
(2) To promote maximum production by broadening the production base of the American economy;
(3) To promote maximum purchasing power by lifting the bottom of the pyramid;
(4) To promote maximum production and maximum purchasing power by cooperating in the development of world economics and world trade.[41]

This constituted a distinctly demand-side shopping list, in which long-term as well as short-term problems were perceived as growing out of the need to sustain aggregate purchases of goods and services. Only the second of these four categories was aimed directly at improving the productivity of the private sector of the economy. And even there the principal supply-side issue raised was the old stagnationist concern for new investment outlets to maintain employment. Colm noted the benefits of regional development programs like the Tennessee Valley Authority, the need to accomplish "adjustments" in agriculture to large-scale production, and only last of all "the development of new industries," such as atomic energy, and encouragement to free competition and small enterprise. In any event the CEA was not able to take up these questions for some time to come.

The most clear-cut "industrial policy" expressed by a government agency during Truman's first term came from the FTC, which insisted that "unfair practices of competition in commerce" were a danger to the society and must be exposed and either discouraged or prohibited. Small businesses in particular must be protected from the predatory practices of their larger brethren and should receive special encouragement from gov-

[41] "Long-Range Economic Policies," 3 December 1946, G. Colm Draft, Daily Diary, Nourse Papers, HSTL.

ernment. Lowell Mason was in a minority on the FTC in suggesting that government, in effect accept the inevitability of some concentration and try to work out ways of making firms with monopoly power act "responsibly." The other FTC members wished to pull up monopoly wherever it could be found, root and branch. President Truman himself seems not to have become especially interested in the details of this dispute over the best approach to market concentration except to keep calling for protection of the little guy. Several presidential addresses, including the 1947 State of the Union, condemned bigness more as a cause of inflation than as a source of inequities and inefficiencies. President Truman wrote to the chairman of the FTC on one occasion as follows: "The Commission can perform an extremely important service to the American people by directing the spotlight at this time on those members of the business community who are jeopardizing the jobs and welfare of all Americans by maintaining unreasonably high prices in relation to costs."[42]

By the end of Truman's first term, as the CEA continued to wrestle unsuccessfully with inflation, all the members had concluded that structural issues must lie at the root of the problem and that serious inquiry into microeconomic behavior was an essential prerequisite for the formation of effective macroeconomic policy. So long as just the right amount of aggregate effective demand was present, they believed, vigorous and growing production would take place—that is, unless struggles among monopolistic groups in the economy for a larger share of the pie caused inflation. In June of 1948 a CEA staff economist, Donald H. Wallace, began an ambitious study of "wage-price policy" so as to develop recommendations for tactical supplements to fiscal policy. Wallace began from the position that although pressure might reduce the degree of concentration and potential for monopolistic behavior throughout the economic system, substantial market imperfections were bound to remain. If alternating inflationary surges and recessions were not to be the consequence of this condition, government intervention was essential. A first step, he thought, should be research and analysis to show how, in theory at least, the economy could be assured of stability and growth. He set out to prepare "a statement of general balance for the economy which would be a kind of general code or charter" and "a statement of guiding rules for particular firms or segments of the economy."[43]

The Wallace Report generated vigorous discussion within the CEA.

[42] Truman to Chairman Ferguson, n.d., OF 100 (1947–48), HSTL.
[43] Donald H. Wallace to Edwin G. Nourse, "A Tentative Work Outline," 29 June 1948, Daily Diary, Nourse Papers, HSTL.

Vice-Chairman Keyserling prepared a detailed critique in which he called for greater empirical study to be made of just how prices really were set before the jump was made to policy. He also pointed out a schizophrenia that was beginning to attack many economists who were calling for, at the same time, greater competition in markets and public intervention in price making. "I would like to see a greater effort to fish or cut bait," he said. "Either we must say that private adjustments *can* be effectual or we must say that more intervention is needed." Finally, Keyserling warned against making the macroeconomic norms of price stability and full employment the sole criteria for judging microeconomic performance. "A stable price level and high employment are undoubtedly all to the good, but it is certainly true that economic analysis can find a lot wrong with the economy even under such conditions and that economic policy cannot be held in abeyance during such time."[44]

John D. Clark, the third CEA member, took stock of the advisers' capacity to throw light on sources of the nation's macroeconomic problems and concluded they had a long way to go. For Clark the relationship between income distribution and economic performance remained largely a mystery:

The [Wallace] study to determine what relations of wages, prices, and profits contribute to prosperity and economic progress has produced no conclusion, even tentative in character. The Council continues to use the same broad phrases in its admonitions to business and labor, but it leaves their meaning as obscure as ever, unlighted by suggestions of any standard by which either proper wages or proper prices can be recognized.

The same obscurity held for Clark with respect to the effects of concentration of industry:

During the inflation of 1947 and 1948, expansion of production was of vital importance, and it did not occur despite the high profits which in a competitive economy would usually bring it about. Did the concentration of much of our manufacturing in a few large business firms account for the failure of production to increase? . . . We can only speculate about the managerial decisions about volume of output which would have been made if normal competition had prevailed.

The issue of antitrust policy, Clark reported, had "been studied by the Council for two years with no satisfactory result."[45]

[44] Leon H. Keyserling to Edwin G. Nourse, 14 August 1948, Daily Diary, Nourse Papers, HSTL.

[45] John D. Clark, "The President's Economic Council" (unpublished manuscript), chapter X, 15, chapter XI, 9, Clark Papers, HSTL.

Events during President Truman's first term drew the attention of policy makers and analysts to public policy toward industry in a way that was not anticipated at the start. The stimulus lay in seemingly insoluble macroeconomic problems whose solution, if to be found at all, must lie at their microeconomic roots. But the result of the preliminary attention to this point was little more than the formulation of questions. The answers lay ahead.

A time for brave thoughts

President Truman's second term brought important changes for economic policy makers in Washington. The election of 1948 coincided roughly with an appreciation that after three years the postwar inflationary surge had run its course and the long-awaited return of recession might be at hand at last. At the same time, there appeared a pervasive new mood of self-confidence and of excitement about fresh opportunities and vistas ahead. President Truman had at last won a decisive mandate, and the challenge was to design programs worthy of the opportunity.

Elements both of continuity and of change in the policy toward industry emerged during this second term. First, the commitment to antitrust remained, and a message was presented to Congress to this effect. The earlier wartime encouragement to small business was also sustained through a special charge to the Commerce Department. The administration's concern was addressed particularly to the difficulty small firms faced "in obtaining access either to longer-term credit or to equity capital." The question remained of how to remedy this situation, whether through tax concessions, a loan insurance program, a special loan agency such as the Reconstruction Finance Corporation, or some other device.

In preparation for a presidential message to Congress on small business, delivered 5 May 1950, the White House staff paid attention also to the relationship between technical change and the maintenance of competition. A report from the Commerce Department concluded, "The continued progress of science and technology, fundamental as it is to improvement in living standards, seems to work in the direction of stimulating further business concentration." Alternative forms of "public action to offset this trend" were discussed, including "concentration of research and development in the hands of the Federal and State Governments and . . . to make the results available to all business" on the model of agriculture. But the report came down, instead, in favor of an expansion of various Commerce Department projects such as a clearinghouse for scientific and technical data for business use, expansion of such government laboratories as the National Bureau of Standards, and authorization of new programs for a business extension service, a grant-in-aid program for engineering schools to carry on small-business technical research, and a series of "business clinics" to address current problems.[46]

When the small-business program was opened for wide discussion during the summer of 1950, the thinness of its support was evident. White House staff member Richard Neustadt reported after an interdepartmental session on 6 June that "there is likely to be considerable opposition from bankers' and businessmen's organizations" while within the government, "atmospherically, there was very little enthusiasm." The financial community, in particular, was skeptical: "You can't find much fire for the program in the eyes of Mr. McCloy and his aides. The Treasury technicians present merely scowled. . . . I made a stump speech but nobody changed expression." Neustadt noted that the presentations to date had contained little effective "economic rationale for the program."[47] His observation undoubtedly reflected the general view held by market economists as far back as Adam Smith that, in order to remedy inequities in the economy, it was better to deny special favors to all than to give them to some. Schemes of special assistance, no matter how exalted their goals, were likely to become merely devices to generate economic rents for their beneficiaries.

In addition to the elements of continuity in policy represented by the continuing endorsement of antitrust and assistance to small business, the Truman second term witnessed change reflected both in the expanded role that the CEA sought for itself and a fundamentally different conception of the proper place for government in the economy that began to emerge in the thinking of CEA members and other leaders in government.

The new mood of exhilaration and expectation evident in the CEA in 1949 was complicated by the departure of Chairman Nourse. Nevertheless, the strong sense of the remaining members, especially Leon Keyser-

---

[46] Charles S. Murphy, memorandum for the president: "Formulation of legislative program and presidential message on aid to small business," 7 February 1950. Finance and Industry, Small Business Program File, Spingarn Papers, HSTL; Stephen J. Spingarn, Memorandum for the Director of the Budget, 27 February 1950, ibid.; Office of Program Planning, Department of Commerce, "Technical and Expert Assistance to Small Business," 28 February 1950, ibid.

[47] R.E.N., memorandum for Mr. Spingarn: "Interdepartmental Session on Small Business Testimony-Tuesday," 6 June 1950, Small Business Program File, Spingarn Papers, HSTL.

ling, who became the new chairman, was that they had an opportunity and responsibility to exert leadership in economic policy among the various parts of government. The first term had demonstrated both the intractability of macroeconomic problems, notably inflation, and the need to develop coordinated strategies. The task now was to develop an appropriate response. In a draft communication shortly after the election Keyserling reminded the president that nowhere "available to the President [was there] a detached agency which could review these programs and proposals for the President from the general viewpoint of the good of the whole economy and the whole nation." He recommended that the CEA be encouraged now to perform this central staff role with vigor.[48]

The emerging activist economic philosophy, which motivated the desire of the CEA to redefine its role, implied that the nation absolutely required a centrally administered macroeconomic policy with both demand and supply sides. The demand side dictated attention to aggregate governmental expenditures and revenues based on the kinds of forecasts that the CEA had learned to prepare during its first three years. The supply side was far more uncertain and challenging but, as an increasing number of senior advisers counseled, it too required a positive program of intervention to make certain that the flow of goods and services continued at maximum physical limits and stable prices.

The turn to the supply side grew out of several concerns. First, a mounting sense of the large and increasing calls on American productive capacity made any kind of waste through less-than-full utilization of resources seem intolerable. The U.S. economy had accepted responsibility to fill the consumption needs of its people, still starved after wartime abstinence, and in addition to help rebuild Europe under the Marshall Plan, assist development in the poorer nations, and undertake rearmament under the North Atlantic Treaty. The old worries of whether aggregate effective demand would be present in a "mature" economy were replaced by a troubled sense that this mature system could never respond adequately to these demands put upon it.

The second reason for greater attention to the supply side was a strengthened appreciation, which had grown during the first term, that this was in fact where solutions lay to the most intractable macroeconomic problems of recent decades. In particular there was a mounting

[48] The Council of Economic Advisers to the President, "Recommendations for Improved Utility and Service to the President (draft)," 4 November 1949, Quarterly and Monthly Reports 1947–49 File, Clark Papers, HSTL.

sense that a misguided restrictionism throughout the economy, growing out of the terrors of the Great Depression, could explain the intense inflationary pressures of the postwar years and the continuing vulnerability of the system to cyclical fluctuations. Virtually all parts of the economy—businesses, unions, and farmers—had become conditioned, often by government policy, to react to pressures by restricting output. This response tended only to worsen the problem overall. Somehow these units had to be persuaded to produce without restraint, with consequent benefit to everyone. But changes in attitudes required reform of practices, institutions, and policies, and the federal government must take the lead. To an important degree, these years saw the beginnings of the movement for deregulation that required another three decades to reach maturity.

John D. Clark argued that the CEA was the obvious locus for leadership in supply-side reform, because this would require presidential intervention in virtually all parts of government:

There has been no staff organization plan for the constant survey of policies and programs from the point of view of integration within the master plan of the President for economic stabilization. The void is especially flagrant in the case of the so-called independent boards and commissions, whose activities cannot be permitted, under the claim of autonomy, to escape the knowledge or avoid the leadership of the President.

Clark pointed out that demand-and-supply policies were inextricably linked. Effective guarantees of adequate demand would sustain the optimism of decision makers and keep them from taking actions and pressing for restrictive public policies that would be socially destructive overall:

The most difficult programs of our domestic economy can be met only if the economy expands continuously. In our free economy, steady expansion is possible only if the great army of individuals who, by their personal decisions, create the economic situation in every period have confidence at all times that the minor variations which can never be eliminated are not forerunners of serious trouble. Then the individual need not feel that he should protect himself by withholding action or plans which he would carry out if assured that business would continue at the prosperity level.[49]

To an important extent, President Truman's own life experience had equipped him to provide leadership in this search for new economic structures. His disillusionment with the current system had begun in the depression after World War I, when his own business failed. Then from

---

[49] John D. Clark, "The Role of the Council of Economic Advisers," 7 November 1949, Quarterly and Monthly Reports 1947–49 File, Clark Papers, HSTL.

the vantage point of the wartime Truman Committee he witnessed powerful firms and unions using the emergency to improve their lot at the expense of the public welfare. He had begun his own presidency by appealing for "the machinery for a continuous full-employment policy based on the co-operation of industry, agriculture, and labor, and between Congress and Chief Executive, and between the people and their government." Instead it seemed to him that he had encountered only obstruction and selfishness at every turn. For example, those who stood to gain helped to prevent a smooth phasing out of wartime controls. He reported angrily in March 1947 as follows: "If certain interests were not so greedy for gold, there would be less pressure and lobbying to induce the Congress to allow the Price Control Act to expire, or to keep down minimum wages, or to permit further concentration of economic power."

Moreover, he found that selfishness and shortsightedness were not confined to the business world. In explaining the failure of the "Brannan Plan" for reform of agricultural policy to pass Congress he wrote:

The American Farm Bureau Federation, which represented the special-interest farmers . . . attacked the price-support programs on the same grounds that the private utilities companies fought every attempt of the government to make public power available to the people, and as the American Medical Association fought the health program which would benefit all the people.[50]

President Truman believed instinctively that individual American citizens as economic actors would do the public-spirited and patriotic thing. It was only when gathered together within interest groups that greed overcame them. In markets these monopolies restricted output to raise prices, and they held back stocks from sale, thereby bringing about the price increases they sought. In the political process they brought pressure to bear on legislators and public servants to make and implement policy in their own rather than the public interest. The policy of the second term was in essence to call again for cooperation among the individual units of the economy and to seek relationships in which their self-interested behavior would contribute collectively not to the creation of public problems but to the common good.

As the second term began, the strategy chosen to identify promising new supply-oriented policies was to engage industry in a "cooperative partnership." The CEA took on a new role as coordinator of an interdepartmental effort involving participants from Commerce, Treasury, In-

[50] Harry S. Truman, *Year of Decisions*, 485, 489; vol. 2, *Years of Trial and Hope*, 267.

terior, Agriculture, Labor, and other agencies that touched on the private economy. White House aide David Bell reported as follows after the first organizational meeting to discuss this "rather new departure" in the work of the CEA: "The Council's intention to establish these talk groups and to take a more positive role in developing economic policy met with general approval from those present."[51]

An indication of the CEA's intent to try working with the private sector rather than scolding it was the advice from John D. Clark to Clark Clifford to remove threats to increase the scope of public enterprise from the 1949 State of the Union Message. He noted, "If the free economy cannot be readjusted to bring about adequate production in basic industries, we are indeed in a bad way."[52]

In discussing draft legislation "to effectuate stabilization policies" during 1949, the CEA advised that too much attention need not be paid to "certain apprehensions expressed by the Department of Justice" over proposed "voluntary agreements" within industries to allocate scarce commodities. On the contrary, these agreements were consistent with the declared policy "to rely to the greatest extent possible on the voluntary action of private business agencies and to develop cooperation between private business and government." Moreover, "we believe that the voluntary allocations program is an outstanding example of success in developing such cooperation and, if continued, might furnish valuable experience for other types of voluntary cooperation between business and government."[53]

The CEA's fourth annual report, titled *Business and Government*, set forth the new philosophy in detail. Cabell Phillips reviewed this document in an article in *Collier's* magazine titled "Truman's New Romance: The Businessman." He marveled, "Methods are actually being devised to help businessmen live with the antitrust laws and federal trade practices; to cut new paths through the jungle of bureaucratic red tape; to open up the cornucopia of government purchases to thousands of new suppliers."[54] There was controversy in the press over whether this new ap-

[51] David E. Bell, memorandum for Messrs. Elsey, Spingarn, and Lloyd, 10 November 1949, Finance and Industry (Domestic) File, Spingarn Papers, HSTL.
[52] Clark to Clifford, 3 January 1949, Letters and Memos to President File, Colm Papers, HSTL.
[53] The Council of Economic Advisers to the President, "Memorandum: Legislation to Effectuate Stabilization Policies," 14 January 1949, Letters and Memos to President File, Colm Papers, HSTL.
[54] Cabell Phillips, "Truman's New Romance: The Businessman," *Collier's*, 5 June 1950, 11.

proach was a retreat from the New Deal commitment to "planning." Keyserling denied that it was.[55] There were also suspicions that this new friendliness was the prelude to new controls. The president himself complained in a letter to Rexford Tugwell that although his objective was to preserve a free economy, those who stood to benefit the most were reluctant to recognize the fact: "Our business community is so touchy and so afraid that the Government will really function for the welfare of the people that they take every means possible to misrepresent what we are trying to do."[56]

Understandably, the Commerce Department was given point duty in developing a new public-private relationship. Secretary of Commerce Charles Sawyer began the campaign with a series of speeches after the election in 1948. On 3 December, he told the National Association of Manufacturers about "Teamwork for Prosperity." He called for patriotism as the motivating principle in economic affairs:

During the war we organized a national team that confounded our enemies and amazed the whole world—including ourselves—with its efficiency and power. Industry, labor, agriculture, and government worked together to support our armed forces and to keep our economy sound and strong. Our objective was clear, and the motivation for team play was powerful. We must find a substitute for that motivation in time of peace. Back in my college days I was deeply impressed by an essay written by a great American philosopher, William James. It was entitled, "The Moral Equivalent of War." James said that we must find ways to make peace as thrilling as war. We should transfer the excitement and the all-out sacrifice and cooperation of war to the pursuits of peace.

The translation of these lofty sentiments into the needs of the contemporary economy, Sawyer explained, required selective "restraint" in price and wage setting and in consumption of goods in short supply.[57]

At President Truman's request, Secretary Sawyer set out on an odyssey across the country from which he reported periodically about the basic soundness of the private sector and of its wish to move ahead rapidly with a minimum of government entanglements.[58] As a strategy for dealing with the ever-present danger of monopoly, Sawyer called for "a positive program for preventing violations by actively fostering and promoting competition in industry." He urged "educational and promotional

[55] Barr King, "Leon Keyserling's New Look," *The Nation,* 14 January 1950; Leon Keyserling, "No Retreat from Planning," ibid., 21 January 1950.

[56] Truman to Tugwell, 7 February 1949, President's Personal Files (PPF), 768, HSTL.

[57] OF 3, HSTL, and also Bernard L. Gladieux to the secretary, "Accomplishments in 1949," 9 January 1950, BLG 1950 File, Gladieux Papers, HSTL.

[58] Sawyer to John R. Steelman, 17 October 1949, OF 172, HSTL.

activity" and less adversarial action through the Federal Trade Commission and Department of Justice. All federal agencies should be required to work "as a team."[59] Sawyer reminded the president repeatedly that the welfare of the nation as well as that of the Democratic party depended on the health of the private sector.[60] A report prepared for the secretary in 1949 urged that in the future concentration in industry be judged not by form but by results. "Effective competition" should be the objective, meaning a market form that contributed to the growth of the system.

One *positive* test of whether competition is to be deemed "effective competition" is whether the business performance in such competition tends to serve the public interest increasing values in goods and services for more people. . . . It is inconsistent with the policy of this country in favor of a progressive dynamic economy to prescribe in detail a rigid pattern for business to follow. . . . The public policy of this country is taken to be one in favor of dynamic economic growth and development, creative innovations, improvements in values, and fluidity and change, as such. Where such conditions exist there should be a presumption of effective competition so long as other evidence is consistent therewith.[61]

Sawyer called the philosophy represented in this doctrine "new liberalism." "Above all," he said, "the new liberal is open-minded. He is willing to consider new approaches to our problems. At all times he guards his mind against the danger of thinking in formulas." Sawyer saw political as well as economic salvation in his new liberalism. "The best safeguard against the growth of communism is the growth of our own economy and the participation of all our people in the benefits of our increasing power to produce." Ironically, in light of what was soon to transpire, Sawyer suggested that the success of the Kuomintang in China over their communist rivals was likely because of their adoption of a progrowth policy (picked up by Sun Yat-sen, he said, from a book written by a New York dentist!).[62]

Thomas C. Blaisdell, Jr., assistant secretary of commerce, appears to have been the principal departmental interpreter of the new macroeconomic philosophy with its microeconomic dimension. An address he delivered to the Chamber of Commerce of Chester, Pennsylvania, in June

[59] Sawyer to the president, 17 October 1949, OF 172, HSTL.
[60] Sawyer to the president, 31 October 1949, OF 3, HSTL.
[61] "Antitrust Law Project: Explanatory Report to Business Advisory Council," draft, 9 May 1950, 6, 9, and 10, Anti-Trust Law Project (draft) File, Blaisdell Papers, HSTL.
[62] Charles Sawyer, "A New Liberalism for the Next Half Century: Address before the Second Annual Dinner of the Public Relations Society of America," 5 December 1949, 10, 11, 12, and 13, OF 3, HSTL.

1950 is illustrative. In parts it is remarkably anticipatory of later ideas both in economic theory and economic policy. He began by observing that after four years it was clear that government could not achieve full employment through fiscal policy alone; the public sector was simply too small a part of the total economy. Government was like a small boy floating down a fast-moving river, able to change the direction of his boat but unable to affect its forward progress very much. But business and government working together in "an essential partnership" should be able to change both direction and velocity and thereby accomplish the goals set forth in the Employment Act. The big question still was how this partnership could be achieved:

We in our system of private capitalism have learned something about how to handle this great society. For one thing, we know that business and government cannot operate separately in two distinct worlds. We know also that we have not yet worked out a perfect means of understanding between business and government. Just as our knowledge concerning the relations of government and business has been limited, so has our knowledge of the kind of society in which we live been limited.

Blaisdell outlined generally what he took to be appropriate public responsibilities. First, government should attend to the "technological base of our whole system—a base which is laid down by our schools and colleges." He drew attention to opportunities ahead in mechanical power, transportation, and communication. Second, a government must examine the structure of the economy to minimize its inflationary potential. Blaisdell recognized the trade-off between unemployment and inflation that would be expressed years later in the "Phillips Curve," and he suggested that the partnership of government and business could shift this relationship inward. He explained:

There is a close relationship between the size of unemployment and inflation. It is a fact of which we must be aware at all times. No one is going to advocate the inhumane policy of allowing unemployment to rise in order to prevent inflation. This, however, does not mean that we should blind ourselves to the inflationary dangers of an economy in which employment stays continually at unusually high levels. . . . We can have flexibility with high levels of employment but, when employment stays high we must be unusually vigilant to make sure we are taking all possible steps to avoid the danger of inflation.

Finally, in terms reminiscent of today's controversies among macroeconomic theorists, Blaisdell worried that business expectations were a crucial variable to which government must attend with great care:

On its part, government must hold steady and make as few changes as possible so that business can know what to expect. If changes are to be made, they must be made with expedition and finality. Knowledge that something will be done is usually fully as important as what is done. Thus confidence is created which is so indispensable to maintaining business activity at high levels.

It is significant that, as authority for the position he set forth, Blaisdell cited not Keynes, or Veblen, or any microeconomic theorist, but rather the classical political economist John Stuart Mill. "He knew what we know now even better—that government and business are inseparable. They must work together toward the same end—the building of a great society."[63]

Reversion to war

It is not unreasonable to speculate that if the policy path set down in 1949 and 1950 had been followed throughout the second term, the Truman administration might have solved, or at least laid the base for solution of, macroeconomic problems that bedeviled later administrations and in some cases remain unanswered still. The sense of exploration and creativity was present not only in the White House, the CEA, and the Commerce Department but in other parts of government as well, such as the Interior and Agriculture Departments and some committees of Congress. Among the principal issues that were clearly identified for serious attention in these early years were, first, how to specify the appropriate public-private division of labor in providing for technical change and international competitiveness, and, second, how to develop a partnership between business and government that would not embody conflict of interest and would not reduce the competitiveness of markets. To this end, several parts of government, notably the CEA, Commerce, and Interior, experimented during these years with different kinds of private sector advisory committees.[64] Finally, the search was on for institutional change within the economy that would shift inward what we now call

[63] Thomas C. Blaisdell, Jr., "Business and Government—an Essential Partnership," before the Chamber of Commerce, Chester, Pennsylvania, 15 June 1950, Speeches and Articles 1950 File, Blaisdell Papers, HSTL.

[64] See, for example, Bertram M. Gross, "The Operations of the Council of Economic Advisors," 15 May 1950, CEA Operations of the Council File. Blough Files, HSTL; Gerhard Colm, "The Task of Economic Stabilization in Perspective," 5 July 1950, CEA Benjamin Kaplan File, Blough Papers, HSTL; and on the efforts of the Interior Department, Craufurd D. Goodwin, ed., *Energy Policy in Perspective* (Washington, D.C.: The Brookings Institution, 1981), 98–101.

the Phillips Curve, through alteration in the pricing behavior of firms, trade unions, farmers, and government agencies, so that expansive fiscal policy could be allowed to raise the level of economic activity close to full employment without triggering inflation.

The tragedy was, of course, that the path sketched out in 1949–50 came to an abrupt end with the return to a war footing by the end of the latter year. There were two consequences: First, the mounting tensions of the cold war, which turned hot in Korea, simply soaked up most of the energy and initiative of the senior figures in government whose attention was required for any serious reform of the economic system. In addition, the crisis of mobilization, as it did in World War II, placed the federal government much in the debt, or even the thrall, of private sector leaders. Not only did senior industrialists like Charles Wilson of General Electric come to Washington with their impressive executive skills, but entire industrial sectors such as the petroleum industry agreed to deliver goods required in the conflict and in effect to operate those parts of government (e.g., the Petroleum Administration for Defense) that would accomplish the task. Just as World War II virtually terminated the reflective thinking and experimentation that had characterized the New Deal, so the Korean War brought to an end the brief but highly promising period of creative opportunity during the Truman years.

As the United States geared up for war once again, using many of the practices and institutions that had worked so well in World War II, the role of the CEA necessarily receded. No longer could the advisers think of themselves as architects of structural reform at the ear of the president. Now they must take a back seat, preparing studies on issues of importance to the mobilization but essentially out of the center of the action. Moreover, with the arrival of what one CEA staff member called a "decade of defense," it was necessary to prepare a different work plan. Buoyant defense spending and the imposition of various controls soon removed the challenges of how to maintain full employment and price stability in a free economy that had motivated the 1949–50 period. Attention turned instead to topics such as "Resources Development in a Defense Decade" and the productive potential of various regions of the country.[65]

The Commerce Department seemed much less disposed in the atmo-

[65] John C. Davis to Leon H. Keyserling, "Work Program," 26 February 1950, CEA Midyear 1951 Economic Report File, Blough Papers, HSTL.

sphere of war than it had been two years before to ponder a brave new and creative public-private partnership. Secretary Sawyer now pressed much harder, and seemingly with a different purpose, his demand for "a new, modern definition of competition." The former appeals for a "new liberalism" were replaced with an insistence that very practical questions be addressed and that, when in doubt, government should leave well enough alone. Before government considered any interference with a private firm, it should ask: "In what way is our business body not functioning properly? Is it failing to maintain or raise our standard of living? Is it selling its products at fair prices? Is it giving employment at good wages? Is it considering the welfare of its employees? Is it earning money for its shareholders? Is it contributing its share of taxes for the support of the government? Is it doing its part in time of war?" Symbolically, whereas Thomas Blaisdell had turned in 1950 to the epitome of classical economists, John Stuart Mill, for guidance on business policy, Sawyer complained in 1952: "Some people think and talk as if nothing had changed since the classical economists first talked about competition in its theoretical 'pure' form. The old Adam Smith type of simple competition no longer exists, if it ever did."[66]

By 1952 Charles E. Wilson, president of General Motors, could reveal in an address to the Commerce Department's Business Advisory Council that alternative explanations were now available for the macroeconomic enigmas of two years before. He agreed that wage determination under trade unions was a potentially inflationary force, but he also asserted (using charts) that both inflation and business fluctuations were mainly monetary phenomena. For their elimination the public need look no further than reform of monetary policy: "It is clear to me that government must now exercise some controls over what we now speak of as the total money supply."[67] Even at this early date, incipient monetarism was used to deny the need for other forms of economic change.

The abandonment of any serious discussion of reform of the public-private relationship together with the introduction of wartime economic conditions raised again the familiar tensions of World War II. Small businesses complained bitterly, and evidently with justification, that govern-

[66] Charles Sawyer to the Business Advisory Council for the Department of Commerce, 18 December 1952, Business Advisory Council File, Snyder Papers, HSTL.

[67] C. E. Wilson, "Some Aspects of Economic Stability," a talk to the Business Advisory Council, Washington, D.C., 9 January 1952, Business Advisory Council File, Snyder Papers, HSTL.

ment procurement practices under mobilization increased industrial concentration and threatened their very survival. A complex set of administrative arrangements was put in place to meet the problem.[68]

Within the two parts of government with special responsibility to protect the free competitive economy, the Antitrust Division of the Department of Justice and the FTC, the war brought a sense of betrayal and of beleaguerment. H. Graham Morrison, assistant attorney general for antitrust, wrote to the president in June of 1952 that the antitrust laws were "being subjected to attacks by groups whose objective is to shake the faith of the American people in our laws against illegal monopolies and restraints of trade." He feared that if these groups succeeded, "we shall lose the real source of our expanding enterprise system—the economic freedom of the individual." He called for nothing less than a successor to the Temporary National Economic Committee appointed in 1938. Morrison was concerned both that government procurement tended to favor "big" firms and that "industry advisory committees" employed in some parts of government had become simply a cloak for price fixing.[69] Evidently in a mood of desperation by 1952, Morrison poured out his anguish to the newspaper columnist Drew Pearson:

I need help, but I think I am merely an instrument of calling for help for the American people. We may be sitting upon the end of the free competitive economic system that has been the mainspring of America's might and preeminence in the world. The competitive system was never under more serious threat than it is during these days of defense buildup in which the short-term thinkers abandon fundamental principles under the pressure of expediency. I am sure that no thinking American would tolerate the abandonment of our basic rules of political freedom during a time of defense activity and yet there seems to be a callousness about economic freedom. In brief, I must somehow find a way to arouse the American people to their plight.[70]

After first viewing mobilization as an opportunity for service and as an occasion in which the effectiveness of an equitable public-private cooperation could be demonstrated, the FTC grew increasingly uneasy about what it took to be a steady movement toward monopoly and concentra-

[68] See Robert M. Macy to Richard E. Neustadt, "Review of Small Business Activities," 13 April 1951; and J. E. Reeve and William K. Condrell, "Possible Steps to Strengthen Small Business Program," 16 April 1951, both in OF 172, HSTL.
[69] H. G. Morrison to the president, 25 June 1952, Department of Justice, Anti-Trust Division 1951–52 File, Morrison Papers, HSTL.
[70] Morrison to Pearson, 8 January 1952, Department of Justice, Anti-Trust Division 1951–52 File, Morrison Papers, HSTL.

tion. By September 1951, Commissioner John Carson was casting around for new devices wherewith to "dramatize the issues very soon." He found the "liberal forces" on the run and "the reactionary groups . . . winning the fight." In the spirit of World War II, Carson proposed a major national conference on the topic "The Welfare of Bona Fide Free Enterprise." He suggested also that five prominent academic economists be impaneled as a "Court of Public Opinion," to report on the destruction of the free-market economy then in progress and to suggest what might be done.[71]

By 1952 the mood of one FTC commissioner at least can only be described as approaching hysteria. In 1950 the FTC had begun an investigation of cartel behavior by the integrated petroleum companies overseas. The study raised fundamental issues about pricing policies, market sharing, the conduct of foreign policy, and the capacity of big business to influence domestic policy making. The study was completed in 1951 and released to the public by a Senate committee in 1952. The issues raised by the report were complex, involving national security, long-run energy policy, and Middle East strategy, in addition to industrial policy.

FTC Commissioner Stephen J. Spingarn who, while a White House aide in 1950 had been closely involved in discussions of a new relationship between government and industry, was horrified by the tactics the oil companies used in pressing their case. He charged them with misrepresentation, underhanded actions of various kinds, and even efforts to subvert the normal processes of democratic government. For Spingarn the issue became far more than one of monopolistic behavior. It was a fundamental question of fairness and of "ethics in government." The final capitulation of the administration to unbridled monopolistic forces came for Spingarn when President Truman in January 1953, just before handing over the reins of office, ordered that criminal prosecutions be dropped against the companies. In a memorandum to the president, which he released to the press, Spingarn suggested that the communists might be right after all in their portrayal of the "subservience of democratic governments to financial and industrial interests."[72] He saw the public-private relationship at a new low ebb.

---

[71] Charles S. Murphy to John Steelman, 29 January 1951, with excerpt from letter of 19 January 1951 from John Carson; and Charles S. Murphy to Joe Short, 24 July 1951, with copy attached of undated letter from Carson to Short, OF 100, HSTL.

[72] Spingarn to the president, 12 January 1953, Subject File: FTC, President's Secretary's File, HSTL. This incident is treated in greater detail in Goodwin, *Energy Policy*, 119–27.

Conclusion

The Truman administration left the question of what should be the proper relationship between government and the private sector with little more of an answer than when it first took the matter up. President Truman entered office at a time when suspicions ran high that business had profited unfairly from war and was prepared to profit even more in peace. His first term seemed only to strengthen suspicions. As the president attempted to build a stable peacetime economy and to restrain the unexpected forces of inflation, it seemed that all the decision makers in the private sector worked against him. Businesses, unions, farmers, others, all scrambled for a larger piece of the economic pie, with the result that the pie itself was imperiled. What use were macroeconomic tools, the government policy makers wondered, if microeconomic obstacles stood in the way of their success?

In a sense domestic and international concerns came together at this time over the question of policy toward the private sector, with the international clearly predominant. The unexpected depth of America's involvement in all aspects of world affairs explains the almost complete disappearance of Alvin Hansen's mature economy thesis during Truman's first term. Here was a mature economy with needs to build up the war-ravaged nations of Europe, to assist development in the new countries of a postcolonial era, to take the leadership in rearmament of the free world, and to be prepared to fight a cold (if not a hot) overseas war. In this case, where the size of "G" (government spending) in the famed Keynesian equation Y (national income) = C (consumption) + I (private investment) + G, seemed likely to become, if anything, insupportable, it was no longer sensible to worry about aggregate demand as a whole, and therefore the adequacy of private effective demand (C and I).

To the contrary, the issue now became one of how to make certain that the U.S. economy would indeed run full tilt and meet its many obligations. One of the principal obstacles to achievement of this performance was perceived to be a restrictionist mentality carried over inappropriately from the Great Depression in firms, unions, and the government itself in the form of market-sharing schemes such as those in agriculture. The second major obstacle to full employment and growth, discovered quickly by the Truman macroeconomists, was the distressing tendency of the economy to generate inflation when operating near full employment. With monetary policy constrained by limitations placed on the

Federal Reserve, the economists looked for some other alternative to the disinflationary fiscal policy that they knew would destroy the full employment and rapid growth that were their paramount goals in the first place. During 1949 and 1950 the economists turned tentatively to structural reform of the economic system for a solution, to a guaranteed annual wage, to limits on collective bargaining, and to greater competition in markets for goods and services. There was also murmuring about the need for a more interventionist wage-price policy if full employment, growth, and price stability were ever to be achieved together in a free society.

The two years 1949 and 1950 were a brief, golden, halcyon period when the problems of the previous four years could be examined calmly and creatively. The time ended only too soon. Under the pressure of war once again the public-private nexus returned to its early postwar character of bitter confrontation in some places and unhealthy intimacy in others. Large and important questions about how the mixed economy could best adapt to technical change or constrain inflation by means other than recession were placed once more on the back burner. And there they remained to bubble and overflow repeatedly in the years to come—even unto this day.

4

Labor in the Truman era:
origins of the "private welfare state"

NELSON LICHTENSTEIN

Stranded somewhere between the activism of the New Deal and the bureaucratic routine of the Eisenhower years, the labor politics of the Truman era has seemed a chaotic interregnum. In the minefield of postwar
reconversion politics, the new president floundered, unable to prevent
either a massive strike wave or a surge of inflation. And when Truman
did act decisively, as in his veto of the Taft-Hartley Act in 1947 and his
seizure of the steel mills during a 1952 strike, he was repudiated either
by the Congress or the Supreme Court. These failures were compounded
by the defeat of most of his Fair Deal social program and of his effort to
repeal Taft-Hartley. Finally, Truman's personal relations with the powerful trade union leaders of the era were erratic: bitter in 1946, cordial
during the presidential campaign, chilly again during the Korean War.[1]

But such a seemingly dismal record belies the historical import of the
Truman years, for it was under his administration that the experimentation of the New Deal era ended and a remarkably stable settlement that
would govern the relationship among capital, labor, and the state became
part of the unwritten constitution of the postwar United States. The turning point came between 1946 and 1948 when a still-powerful trade union
movement found its efforts to bargain over the shape of the postwar

---

[1] Standard works on the labor policy of the Truman administration include Arthur F. McClure,
The Truman Administration and the Problem of Postwar Labor (Cranberry, N.J.: Fairlie
Dickenson University Press, 1967); R. Alton Lee, *Truman and Taft-Hartley: A Question
of Mandate* (Lexington: University of Kentucky Press, 1966); Maeva Marcus, *Truman
and the Steel Seizure Case: The Limits of Presidential Power* (New York: Columbia University Press, 1977), 195–227; and several of the essays of Barton Bernstein, especially,
"The Truman Administration and Its Reconversion Wage Policy," *Labor History* 6 (Fall
1965), 214–31.

political economy decisively blocked by a powerful remobilization of business and conservative forces whose collective strength weighed heavily on the man who occupied the Oval Office. Labor's ambitions were thereafter sharply curbed, and its economic program was reduced to a sort of militant interest-group politics. This forced retreat laid the basis for a crisis-free quarter-century of union-management relations, but it also narrowed the appeal of labor liberalism as a coherent social force and contributed to the atrophy of the once-hopeful effort to expand the welfare state and refashion industrial America along more genuinely democratic lines.[2]

Union power

The dramatic growth of the organized working class put the U.S. system of industrial relations at a crossroads in 1945. In the years since 1933 the number of unionized workers had increased more than fivefold to more than 14 million. About 30 percent of all American workers were organized: This density was greater than at any time before or since in this country and for the first time equal to the density in northern Europe. Unions seemed on the verge of recruiting millions of new workers in the service trades, in white-collar occupations, across great stretches of the South and Southwest, and even among the lower ranks of management. Thus few disagreed when the noted Harvard economist Sumner Slichter declared U.S. trade unions "the most powerful economic organizations which the country has ever seen."[3]

It was not size alone that contributed to this assessment. The élan so noticeable in many sections of the labor movement rested on a degree of union consciousness, in some cases amounting to working-class loyalty, that would today seem quite extraordinary. The mid-1940s were no period of social quiescence, for the war itself had had a complex and dichotomous impact on working Americans. It had provided them with a taste of postwar affluence and had attuned them to the daily influence of large, bureaucratic institutions like the military and the government mobiliza-

---

[2] Michael Piore, "Can the American Labor Movement Survive Re-Gomperization?" *Proceedings, Industrial Relations Research Association 35th Annual Meeting* (1982), 30–39; Samuel Bowles, David M. Gordon, and Thomas E. Weisskopf, *Beyond the Waste Land: A Democratic Alternative to Economic Decline* (Garden City, N.Y.: Anchor Press/Doubleday, 1983), 70–75; and David Brody's influential synthesis, *Workers in Industrial America: Essays on the 20th Century Struggle* (New York: Oxford University Press, 1980), 173–257.

[3] Sumner Slichter, *The Challenge of Industrial Relations* (Ithaca, N.Y.: Cornell University Press, 1947), 4.

tion agencies. But full employment itself had also created the conditions for a remarkable burst of rank-and-file activity. Led by shop stewards and local union officers, hundreds of thousands of workers had taken part in a wildcat strike movement that had focused on a militant defense of union power in the work place itself. The massive, largely peaceful, wage strikes called by the big unions in 1945 and 1946 have obscured this more local sense of militancy and solidarity, but the now-forgotten series of postwar general strikes called by central labor councils in Oakland, California; Lancaster, Pennsylvania; Stamford, Connecticut; and Akron, Ohio, are indicative of the extent to which working-class activity retained an occasionally explosive character even in the later half of the 1940s.[4]

Because the contemporary trade unions have often been equated with "special interest politics," it is important to recognize that the trade union movement of the immediate postwar era in the United States, and especially its industrial union wing, held a social agenda that was broad, ambitious, and not without prospects for success. The unions sought a greatly expanded welfare state, a political realignment of the major parties, and a powerful voice in both the management of their industry and the planning of the overall political economy. Even the traditional demand for higher wages held a larger social content, for it now meshed easily with the Keynesian view that demand must be sustained to avoid a new slump. To an extent greater than at any other time in U.S. politics, the union movement defined the left wing of what was possible in the political affairs of the day. Hence, this broad vision was shared by a species of political animal hardly extant today, the "labor liberal," whose mid-1940s ranks included such well-known figures as Henry Wallace, Wayne Morse, Eleanor Roosevelt, and Ronald Reagan. "Labor's role in our national progress is unique and paramount," affirmed Supreme Court Justice William O. Douglas as late as 1948. "It is labor, organized and independent labor, that can supply much of the leadership, energy and motive power which we need today."[5]

The economic power wielded by U.S. trade unions was by its nature political power, for the New Deal had thoroughly politicized all relations

---

[4] For a discussion of the war years, see Nelson Lichtenstein, *Labor's War at Home: The CIO in World War II* (Cambridge: Cambridge University Press, 1982); and George Lipsitz, *Class and Culture in Cold War America: "A Rainbow at Midnight"* (South Hadley, Mass.: J. F. Bergin, 1982), 37–86.

[5] *Proceedings of the Tenth Constitutional Convention of the CIO*, Portland, 22–26 November 1948, 270.

among the union movement, the business community, and the state. The New Deal differed from previous eras of state activism in this area not only because it created a relatively favorable political and legislative environment for organized labor, but—perhaps even more important—because the New Deal provided a set of semipermanent political structures in which key issues of concern to the trade union movement might be accommodated. Thus the National Recovery Administration of 1933 and 1934 had done much to legitimize the idea of mass production unionism; the National Labor Relations Board had established the legal basis of union power and provided the arena in which jurisdictional disputes between the unions might be resolved; and the National War Labor Board had provided a tripartite institution that both set national wage policy and contributed to the rapid wartime growth of the new trade unions. The policies of all of these institutions changed over time, and none was uniformly favorable to the interests of a mass union movement. But the successive appearance of these agencies seemed to signal the fact that in the future, as in the past, the fortunes of organized labor would be determined as much by a process of politicized bargaining in Washington as by the give-and-take of contract collective bargaining in Pittsburgh, Detroit, and other industrial centers.[6]

Labor's vision

As a result of the wartime mobilization, the United States seemed to advance toward the kind of labor-backed corporatism that would later characterize social policy in northern Europe and Scandinavia. In these societies, full employment policies combined with a relatively high social wage to provide a supportive environment in which "peak" associations of industry and labor could reach broad accords that established industry or regional wage levels, eased union organization, and facilitated the informal resolution of shop level disputes over wages and working conditions.[7] In the United States the War Labor Board (WLB) and its wartime

---

[6] For contrasting discussions of the way in which state functions accommodated and influenced the new labor movement, see Theda Skocpol, "Political Response to Capitalist Crisis: Neo-Marxist Theories of the State and the Case of the New Deal," *Politics and Society* 10 (1980): 155–201; and Christopher Tomlins, *The State and the Unions: Labor Relations, Law, and the Organized Labor Movement in America, 1880–1960* (Cambridge: Cambridge University Press, 1985).

[7] Robert Kuttner, *The Economic Illusion: False Choices Between Prosperity and Social Justice* (Boston: Houghton Mifflin, 1984), 136–86; Margaret Weir and Theda Skocpol, "State Structures and the Possibilities for 'Keynesian' Response to the Great Depression in Swe-

companion, the Office of Price Administration (OPA), had substituted
for the market a highly politicized administrative regime that socialized
much of the trade union movement's prewar agenda, making night-shift
supplements, sick leave, and paid mealtimes standard "entitlements"
mandated for an increasingly large section of the working class. Although union officials often denounced both agencies for their accommodation to politically resourceful business and producer groups, the
maintenance of such institutions was nevertheless seen by most liberal
and labor spokesmen as the kernel of a postwar "incomes" policy that
would set profit and price guidelines and continue the progressive rationalization of the labor market begun during the war. Thus the WLB's
equal pay for equal work guidelines attacked race and sex wage discrimination; and its "Little Steel" wage formula, although bitterly resisted by
the more highly paid and well-organized sections of the working class,
helped dramatically increase the relative wages of workers in agriculture,
cotton textiles, and retail trade.[8]

In the early postwar years most unionists, and especially those in the
key Congress of Industrial Organizations (CIO) industrial unions, continued to believe that the social welfare of their members would be advanced not only by government-led wage bargaining but by significant
structural changes in the distribution of political and economic power.
As Neil Chamberlain put it in his widely read *Union Challenge to Management Control,* "Union leaders no longer regard themselves as a force
merely reacting to managerial decisions in certain areas of business operation, but as a force which itself can influence the whole range of industrial economic activity."[9] This perspective was most graphically manifest in the recurrent demand for tripartite industry governance, embodied
in the industry council plan put forward by President Philip Murray at
each meeting of the CIO. The industry council idea represented an ad-
mixture of Catholic social reformism and New Deal-era faith in business-
labor-government cooperation. With public representatives appointed by
a friendly president, the drafters of the industry council plan contem-

den, Britain and the United States," in Peter B. Evans, Margaret Weir, and Theda Skocpol,
  eds., *Bringing the State Back In* (New York: W. W. Norton, 1984), 132–49.
[8] Paul Sultan, *Labor Economics* (New York: Henry Holt and Company, 1957), 71; U.S.
  Department of Labor, *Termination Report of the National War Labor Board* (Washington, D. C.: U.S. Government Printing Office, 1947), 150–55, 211–91, 338–402; Timothy
  Willard, "Labor and the National War Labor Board, 1942–1945: An Experiment in Corporatist Wage Stabilization" (Ph.D. diss., University of Toledo, 1984), 51–117.
[9] Neil Chamberlain, *The Union Challenge to Management Control* (New York: Harper
  Brothers, 1948), 306.

plated a high-level fusion of economic and political bargaining. The plan was an American version of the sort of social democratic industrial planning many northern European nations adopted in this era. In its postwar elaboration of this scheme the CIO sought a national production board to plan peacetime production and establish wage-price guidelines. Sounding not at all unlike Britain's Labour government or the social democrats of Sweden, Philip Murray declared the CIO plan "a program for democratic economic planning and for participation by the people in the key decisions of the big corporations." Thus such key issues on the union movement's wartime agenda as the guaranteed annual wage, rationalization of the wage structure, and industry-wide bargaining would be won only if the unions secured a direct role in industry governance.[10]

If the CIO plan had something of an abstract air about it, the proposals put forward by the young auto worker leader, Walter Reuther, had a good deal more political bite. Although still only a vice president of the United Automobile Workers (UAW), Reuther rose to national prominence in 1940 and 1941 by linking a bold UAW assault on the traditional prerogatives of the auto corporations with President Franklin Roosevelt's ambitious call for the production of 50,000 military aircraft a year. Reuther's famous "500 planes a day" plan would have solved the production bottleneck through a state-sponsored coordination of the entire auto-aircraft industry. Reuther proposed a tripartite aircraft production board that would have the power to reorganize production facilities without regard for corporate boundaries, markets, or personnel. It would have conscripted labor and work space where and when needed and secured for the UAW at least a veto over a wide range of managerial functions. Winning wide support among old New Dealers and social planning liberals, the Reuther plan was ultimately delayed and then defeated by an automobile industry both hostile to social experimentation and increasingly well represented within the government's wartime production agencies.[11]

The Reuther plan nevertheless cast a long shadow, for it contained hallmarks of the strategic approach so characteristic of labor-liberalism in the 1940s: an assault on management's traditional power made in the

---

[10] Philip Murray, "Industry Councils: the CIO Prosperity Program," 22 October 1946 in Box A4, Murray Papers, Catholic University of America. See also Merton W. Ertell, "The CIO Industry Council Plan: Its Background and Implications" (Ph.D. diss., University of Chicago, 1955).

[11] David Brody, "The New Deal in World War II," in John Braeman et al., *The New Deal: The National Level* (Columbus: Ohio State University Press, 1975), 281–86.

name of social and economic efficiency, an appeal for public support in the larger liberal interest, and an effort to shift power relations within the structure of industry and politics, usually by means of a tripartite government entity empowered to plan for whole sections of the economy. Thus did auto executive George Romney declare, "Walter Reuther is the most dangerous man in Detroit because no one is more skillful in bringing about the revolution without seeming to disturb the existing forms of society."[12]

Labor and the search for a reconversion wage program

The CIO hoped to take this tripartite, corporatist model and use it to bridge the uncertain political currents of the immediate postwar era. Reuther wanted a peace production board that would preside over the reconversion of defense plants to civilian production, while the CIO forecast the continuation of a strong labor board that would impose a government-backed accommodation with industry, along with a somewhat more liberal wage-price formula. As CIO President Philip Murray told a 1944 labor meeting, "Only chaos and destruction of our industrial life will result if employers look to the war's end as an opportunity for a union-breaking, wage-cutting, open-shop drive and if labor unions have to resort to widespread strikes to defend their very existence and the living standards of their members."[13]

To forestall such a prospect, the CIO in March 1945 sponsored a "labor-management charter" with William Green of the American Federation of Labor (AFL) and Eric Johnston, the corporate liberal president of the U.S. Chamber of Commerce. Consisting of a list of often irreconcilable platitudes hailing the virtues of unfettered free enterprise and the rights of labor, the charter nevertheless symbolized the CIO's hope for cooperation with the liberal wing of U.S. capitalism in stabilizing postwar industrial relations along roughly the lines established during the war. "It's Industrial Peace for the Postwar Period," headlined the CIO NEWS. In return for management support for the unamended Wagner Act and a high-wage, high-employment postwar strategy, the unions pledged to defend "a system of private competitive capitalism" including

[12] George R. Clark, "Strange Story of the Reuther Plan," *Harper's* 184 (May 1942), 649.
[13] Victor Reuther, *The Brothers Reuther and the Story of the UAW* (Boston: Houghton Mifflin, 1976), 247–48; Walter Reuther, "The Challenge of Peace," Box 1, UAW Ford Department Collection, Archives of Labor History and Urban Affairs (ALHUA), Wayne State University, Detroit; CIO, *Proceedings of the Seventh Constitutional Convention*, Chicago, 20–24 November 1944, 39.

"the inherent right and responsibility of management to direct the operations of an enterprise."[14]

The charter represented the general CIO belief that the trade unions could secure an accord with progressive industrialists that might institutionalize some of the cooperative arrangements worked out on government boards and agencies during the war. The businessmen with whom the CIO hoped to work were collective bargaining progressives and moderate Keynesians who favored a countercyclical fiscal policy and a degree of structural reform as the minimum program necessary to stabilize postwar capitalism. Often influenced by the Committee for Economic Development and the Twentieth Century Fund, they also supported the 1946 Full Employment Act in something like its original, liberal form. Among these progressive industrialists with whom the CIO sought an alliance were not only the Chamber of Commerce's Eric Johnston, who called for a "people's capitalism" in the postwar era, but also Paul Hoffman of the Studebaker Corporation, who took pride in his company's harmonious relationship with organized labor. The most famous of these progressives was undoubtedly Henry J. Kaiser, the maverick West Coast industrialist who had built his empire on New Deal construction projects and wartime contracts. Hardly an opponent of government planning or public works spending, Kaiser's good relations with the unions and pioneering health-care facilities at his shipyards and mills added to his reputation as a social liberal. In 1945 he won strong UAW cooperation in his well-publicized effort to convert the giant Willow Run bomber plant to civilian car production.[15]

Implementation of a new wage-price policy was one of the key elements in such an accord with the liberal wing of the business community, so state action was essential. The CIO wanted an immediate 20 or 30 percent wage increase at the end of the war to make up for the elimination of overtime pay, and many old New Dealers like Commerce Secretary Henry Wallace and Robert Nathan of the Office of War Mobilization and Reconversion considered such an increase essential to maintain living standards and avoid the long-feared postwar downturn.[16]

Such forecasts were music to CIO ears, but the political and social

---

[14] *The New York Times*, 29 March 1945; *CIO News*, 1 April 1945.
[15] Howell Harris, *The Right to Manage: Industrial Relations Policies of American Business in the 1940s* (Madison: University of Wisconsin Press, 1982), 110; on Henry Kaiser, see Eliott Janeway, *The Struggle for Survival* (New Haven: Yale University Press, 1950), 249–53; and "Adventures of Henry and Joe in Autoland," *Fortune* 38 (1946), 96–103.
[16] Barton Bernstein, "The Truman Administration and Its Reconversion Wage Policy," *Labor History* 4 (1965): 216–25.

base for such a liberal postwar prospect had already been eroded. President Franklin Roosevelt's death on the eve of reconversion did not fundamentally alter the framework of domestic politics, but it did undermine the self-confidence of those who identified with the labor movement and the New Deal. Although Truman's moderation on labor issues had made him an acceptable vice-presidential candidate in 1944, the new president was not a New Dealer, but instead a border-state Democrat who represented that increasingly powerful wing of the Party that was willing to live with the political stalemate that now structured domestic politics. Truman certainly recognized that for him to govern, the unions had to be a core constituency of his administration, yet the President had none of the patrician equanimity with which FDR faced the leaders of this movement.[17] Although Truman prided himself on his humble origins, he found emotionally jarring and somehow illegitimate the power and resources now commanded by trade union leaders. Thus Clark Clifford remembered a bitter 1946 showdown with the United Mine Workers' (UMW) John L. Lewis as "the moment when Truman finally and irrevocably stepped out from the shadow of FDR to become President in his own right."[18]

Truman's inadequacies aside, the CIO profoundly misjudged the tenor of the postwar business community. The progressive industrialists with whom the industrial union federation hoped to achieve an accord were in fact a relatively uninfluential minority. Key business spokesmen were the practical conservatives who presided over the core manufacturing firms in the unionized steel, electrical, auto, rubber, and transport industries. Led by men such as John A. Stephens of U.S. Steel, Ira Mosher of the National Association of Manufacturers, and Charles E. Wilson of General Motors (GM), these industrialists had emerged from the war with enormous sophistication and self-confidence. Unlike many of their counterparts in continental Europe or even in the British Isles who had been tarred with the brush of collaboration or appeasement, U.S. business leaders had found lasting commercial success and political advancement in their wartime experience. They felt little need for the kind of state-sponsored labor-management collaboration that helped legitimize a mixed capitalist economy in Germany, France, and Italy in the immediate postwar era.

[17] Robert Garson, *The Democratic Party and the Politics of Sectionalism, 1941–1948* (Baton Rouge: Louisiana State University Press, 1974), 94–130; Richard Polenberg, *War and Society: The United States, 1941–1945* (New York: J. B. Lippincott, 1972), 44–87.
[18] Bert Cochran, *Harry S. Truman and the Crisis Presidency* (New York: Funk and Wagnalls, 1973), 208.

These industrialists recognized the potential usefulness of the new industrial unions as stabilizers of the labor force and moderators of industrial conflict, but they also sought the restoration of managerial prerogatives that wartime conditions had eroded in the areas of product pricing, market allocation, and shop-floor work environment. Looking forward to a postwar boom, these industriali ts wanted to be free of government or union interference in determining the wage-price relationship in each industry.[19] Thus the long-awaited Labor-Management Conference that President Truman convened in November 1945 was doomed to failure. Although management and labor could agree that collective bargaining would continue as a bedrock institution of U.S. democracy, no accord proved possible on either the prerogatives of management or the scope of legitimate union demands. On the crucial issue of a general wage policy, the CIO got nowhere. Philip Murray offered industry a de facto policy of labor peace in return for a pattern wage increase that Truman had endorsed in a speech on 30 October, but the opposition was so great that the issue never secured a place on the formal conference agenda.[20]

The CIO faced resistance not only from industry but from within the labor movement itself. American Federation of Labor unions had never been so committed as the CIO to the tripartite bargaining arrangements of the war era, and these unions demanded a return to free and unrestricted collective bargaining. In part this attitude stemmed from the AFL's tradition of Gompersarian voluntarism, but it also reflected the contrasting organizational base of the two labor federations. The CIO unions were overwhelmingly concentrated in the manufacturing sector of the economy, where they faced oligopolistically organized employers who were themselves capable of imposing a new wage pattern. Such was not the case with the AFL unions, for only about 35 percent of their members in 1945 were in manufacturing. The organizational and political weight of the AFL lay in construction, transportation, and service trades—decentralized and now booming sectors of the economy less subject to the pattern-setting guidelines established by core firms like General Motors

[19] Harris, *The Right to Manage*, 111–18, 129–58; Robert M. C. Littler, "Managers Must Manage," *Harvard Business Review* 24 (1946): 366–76; see also David Brody, "The Uses of Power I: Industrial Battleground," in his *Workers in Industrial America*, 173–214; and Ron Schatz, *The Electrical Workers: A History of Labor at General Electric and Westinghouse, 1923–60* (Urbana: University of Illinois Press, 1983), 167–71.

[20] U.S. Department of Labor, *The President's National Labor-Management Conference*, Bulletin 77 (Washington, D.C.: U.S. Government Printing Office, 1945), 12–24; *The New York Times*, 9 November 1945; *CIO News*, 26 November 1945; for a larger analysis of the postwar corporate offensive, see Robert Griffith, "Forging America's Postwar Order: Domestic Politics and Political Economy in the Age of Truman" in this volume.

and U.S. Steel. The AFL, with almost 7 million members in 1945, also was some 30 percent larger than the CIO. And it was growing more rapidly because the contours of the postwar economy, with its booming service and transport sectors, fit the flexible AFL model of mixed craft and industrial unionism more closely than the CIO brand of mass organization. This meant that although CIO unions like the United Steelworkers (USW) and the UAW remained innovative and powerful institutions, their political and organizational weight was often less impressive than it seemed.[21]

Although he was an industrial unionist, John L. Lewis spoke forthrightly for the AFL viewpoint. The founder of the CIO, Lewis had, in the early 1930s, successfully advocated a greater role for the state in the labor-management arena. But the repeated clashes between the UMW and the Roosevelt administration during the war had soured the mine leader on the kind of tripartite planning arrangements the CIO still advocated, and Lewis was now determined to exercise his union's power unfettered by a new set of federal regulations. "What Murray and the CIO are asking for," declared Lewis at the Labor-Management Conference, "is a corporate state, wherein the activities of the people are regulated and constrained by a dictatorial government. We are opposed to the corporate state."[22]

The General Motors strike and American liberalism

This stalemate led directly to the General Motors strike, actually begun while the conference remained in session, and then to the general strike wave that spread throughout basic industry in the winter of 1946. Like Walter Reuther's other wartime "plans," the GM strike program made a strong appeal to the "national" interest, this time not so much in terms of rationalized production and democratic control, but as part of the emerging Keynesian consensus that a substantial boost in mass purchasing power would be necessary to avoid a postwar depression. The UAW's demand that industry pacesetter GM raise wages by some 30 percent without increasing the price of its product seemed adventuresome in a collective bargaining negotiation; even more so did Reuther's demand that

---

[21] U.S. Department of Labor, *Labor-Management Conference*, 18–19; Christopher L. Tomlins, "AFL Unions in the 1930s: Their Performance in Historical Perspective," *Journal of American History* 65 (March 1979): 1021–42.

[22] As quoted in Melvyn Dubofsky and Warren Van Tine, *John L. Lewis: A Biography* (New York: Quadrangle, 1978), 456–57.

GM "open the books" to demonstrate its ability to pay. GM quickly denounced these UAW demands as European-style socialism, but they were in fact little more than standard OPA price-setting procedures now translated into the language of collective bargaining.[23]

Although this program was formally directed against the giant automaker, it was in practice a union demand against the state as well, for its ultimate success depended on the willingness of an increasingly embattled Office of Price Administration to resist industry pressure and enforce price guidelines well into the postwar era. These demands won Reuther a wave of support, both within the UAW, where it prepared the way for his election as union president, and among influential liberals who identified with the union effort. A group of economists and clergymen that the UAW organized into a "National Citizens Committee on the GM-UAW Dispute" lauded the union's determination to lift "collective bargaining to a new high level by insisting that the advancement of labor's interest shall not be made at the expense of the public."[24]

Reuther's UAW and most other big unions won an 18½-cent wage increase during the postwar round of strikes and negotiations that ended in the late winter of 1946. But the effort to turn this struggle into a downward redistribution of real income was decisively repulsed, first by the adamant opposition of industrial management, second by Truman administration vacillation, and finally by division and timidity within trade union ranks, especially after Philip Murray made it clear that the USW would not turn its mid-winter strike into a political conflict with the government over the maintenance of price controls.

The GM strike represented the apogee of the UAW's effort to make a radical transformation in its bargaining relationships with the large automakers. Its defeat signaled the destruction of an effective price control program, and with it the end of CIO hopes that organized labor could play a direct role in shaping class relations for society as a whole. Thereafter, Reutherite social unionism gradually linked its fate more closely to that of the industry and moved away from a strategy that sought to use

[23] Walter Reuther, "Our Fear of Abundance," in Henry Christman, ed., *Walter Reuther: Selected Papers* (New York: Macmillan, 1961), 13–21; Barton Bernstein, "Walter Reuther and the General Motors Strike of 1945–46," *Michigan History* 49 (September 1965): 260–77; Irving Howe and B. J. Widick, *The UAW and Walter Reuther* (New York: Random House, 1949), 97–101; Donald Montgomery, "The Product Standard in OPA Price Ceilings," 16 January 1945; and Montgomery to Philip Murray, 6 March 1945, both in Box 10, UAW-Montgomery Collection, ALHUA.

[24] "Report of the National Citizens Committee, December 1945," in file UAW-CIO, Box 29, Paul Sifton Papers, Library of Congress.

union power to demand structural changes in the political economy. Instead, the UAW worked toward negotiation of an increasingly privatized welfare program that succeeded in providing economic security for employed auto workers but that left unchallenged essential power relationships in the industry. Just as postwar liberalism gradually reduced its commitment to national planning and eschewed issues of social and economic control, so too did the UAW abandon the quest for labor participation in running the automobile industry. And just as liberalism increasingly came to define itself as largely concerned with the maintenance of economic growth and an expansion of the welfare state, so too did the UAW and the rest of the CIO come to define their mission in these terms as well.[25]

Taft-Hartley and American politics

Although the immediate postwar strike wave had proved to be the largest since 1919, the pattern wage increases won by the UAW and other major unions soon evaporated under the galloping inflation that occurred when government price controls were loosened during the summer. In the fall, therefore, all the major unions had to return to the bargaining table to demand another round of wage increases. Unions that sought to improve on such postwar wage patterns, such as the Railway Brotherhoods and the UMW, now found that "free" collective bargaining of the sort advocated by John L. Lewis brought them into bitter confrontation with the government. The frequent strikes and annual pay boosts of this era, which industry used to raise prices, were at least partially responsible for creating the conservative, antilabor political climate that culminated in the passage of the Taft-Hartley Act in 1947.[26]

President Truman was both an architect and a victim of this rightward shift in public sentiment. Unable to muster the political resources necessary to deploy an effective wage-price policy, the administration turned to accommodate the conservative voices calling for administrative or legislative limitations on union power. At the same time, however, Truman recognized the necessity for maintaining at least a semblance of a politi-

---

[25] Barton Bernstein, "The Truman Administration and Its Reconversion Wage Policy," *Labor History* 6 (Fall 1965): 214–31. For a good discussion of the changing character of the liberal economic agenda, see Alan Wolfe, *America's Impasse: The Rise and Fall of the Politics of Growth* (Boston: South End Press, 1981), 13–79.

[26] Joel Seidman, *American Labor From Defense to Reconversion* (Chicago: University of Chicago Press, 1953), 233–44.

cal alliance with organized labor—thus his inconsistency and vacillation. For example, during the same month when Truman threatened to draft railroad strikers—May 1946—he also vetoed the Case bill, which embodied much of the spirit, if not the precise content, of the administration's own proposal. Truman claimed that he had favored only temporary, emergency antistrike legislation, whereas the Case bill would have enacted a permanent statute, but the distinction seemed of dubious political weight.[27]

Truman's inability to project a constructive labor policy contributed to the alienation of much of the trade union leadership, to the demobilization of liberal-labor forces, and to the conservative antilabor breakthrough represented by the congressional elections of 1946. The subsequent enactment of the Taft-Hartley Act—over the president's veto— would prove a milestone, not only for the actual legal restrictions the new law imposed on the trade unions but as a climax to and symbol of the shifting relationship between the unions and the state during the late 1940s.

From the point of view of the trade unions, the Taft-Hartley Act had a dual character. In the first instance it was a law that sought to curb the practice of interunion solidarity, eliminate the remaining radical cadre that still held influence within trade union ranks, and contain the labor movement to roughly its existing geographical and demographic terrain. The anti-communist affidavits, the prohibition against secondary boycotts, the enactment of a section (14b) allowing states to prohibit the union shop, the ban on foreman unionism—all these sections of the law had been on the agenda of the National Association of Manufacturers and other conservative groups since 1938. Of course, Taft-Hartley was not the fascistlike "slave labor law" denounced by AFL and CIO alike. In later years unions like the Teamsters prospered quite well even in right-to-work states, while the bargaining relationship between their employers and big industrial unions like the UAW and the USW was relatively unaffected by the new law. But if Taft-Hartley did not destroy the union movement, it did impose upon it a legal-administrative straitjacket that encouraged organizational parochialism and penalized any serious attempt to project a class-wide political-economic strategy.[28]

---

[27] Lee, *Truman and Taft-Hartley*, 22–48.
[28] James A. Gross, *The Reshaping of the National Labor Relations Board: National Labor Policy in Transition, 1937–1947* (Albany: State University of New York, 1981); see also Harris, *Right to Manage*, 121–25; Lee, *Truman and Taft-Hartley*, 236.

This explains the union movement's enormous hostility to Taft-Hartley. As Lee Pressman put it in 1947, "When you think of it merely as a combination of individual provisions, you are losing entirely the full impact of the program, the sinister conspiracy that has been hatched." Union leaders correctly recognized that Taft-Hartley represented the definitive end of the brief era when the state served as an arena in which the trade unions could bargain for the kind of tripartite accommodation with industry that had been so characteristic of the New Deal years. At the highest levels a trust had been broken, which is why Philip Murray declared the law "conceived in sin."[29] Lurking in the background, of course, was the fear endorsed even by *Business Week* that "Given a few million unemployed in America, given an administration in Washington which was not pro-union—and the Taft-Hartley Act conceivably could wreck the labor movement." But even without a new depression or an outright assault on the unions, Taft-Hartley had altered the whole texture of the political-social environment, and the failure of the congressional Democrats to repeal the law in 1949 proved the final blow for many unionists. As Arthur Goldberg, the CIO counsel who replaced Lee Pressman, sadly put it in late 1949, the law had "in its most fundamental aspect created great changes in our industrial *mores* with incalculable effects."[30]

The search for political realignment

If the tide of public sentiment, congressional votes, and administration policy all seemed to be shifting against the unions, these organizations were not without the resources to mount a counterattack. There were two elements in this strategy: (1) Operation Dixie, the CIO campaign to organize the South, which was carefully planned and well funded, and (2) labor's search for a political alternative to Truman, and quite possibly to the Democratic party, which represented more of an unfocused mood than a program of action. Both of these efforts might have had some real effect on the body politic, but in both cases failure became almost inevitable when the communist issue and the cold war became the focus of domestic politics in postwar America.

In the spring of 1946 the CIO sought to break the political power of

[29] CIO, *Proceedings of the Ninth Constitutional Convention*, Boston, 13–17 October 1947, 22, 186, 189.
[30] *Business Week*, 18 December 1949; CIO, *Proceedings of the Eleventh Constitutional Convention*, Cleveland, 31 October–4 November 1949, 124.

the Bourbon South, both at home and in Congress, by striking at its heart, the bastions of racial segregation and low-wage labor in the Deep South. During the war, both labor federations had made substantial inroads in the South, organizing more than 800,000 new workers. Black workers proved particularly union-conscious, for they recognized that union seniority rights and grievance procedures promised them a kind of civic equality and political participation in a shop-floor society governed by the rules inherent in most union contracts. Hence unionization of such key industries as textiles, tobacco, and furniture therefore seemed possible.[31]

The South always represented more than just another source of union recruits. It was the chief political obstacle to the creation of a realigned Democratic party and the stumbling block to progressive legislation in general. In 1944, the CIO's new Political Action Committee had mobilized newly unionized war workers in Alabama and Texas shipyards to defeat such well-known labor baiters as Martin Dies and Joe Starnes. In Winston-Salem, wartime organization of the heavily black R. J. Reynolds Tobacco Company overnight transformed that city's NAACP chapter into one of the largest and most vital in the Seaboard South, which in turn opened local politics to black participation for the first time since the Populist era. Beginning in 1946, Operation Dixie sought to replay these local breakthroughs on an even larger scale, in the process mobilizing an interracial electorate that could realign the shape of Southern politics.[32] "When Georgia is organized," predicted Van Bitter, CIO southern organizing director, "you will find our old friend Gene Talmadge trying to break into the doors of the CIO conventions and tell our people that he has always been misunderstood."[33]

But Operation Dixie was a thorough failure. The CIO put up a million dollars, recruited some 200 organizers, and opened scores of offices throughout the South. Not to be outflanked, the AFL almost immediately opened its own rival campaign to bring authentic "American" unionism

[31] Barbara Griffith, *The Crisis of American Labor: Operation Dixie and the Defeat of the CIO* (Philadelphia: Temple University Press, 1988), 22–45, 62–87; F. Ray Marshall, *Labor in the South* (Cambridge, Mass.: Harvard University Press, 1967), 225–27.

[32] James Foster, *The Union Politic: The CIO Political Action Committee* (Columbia: University of Missouri Press, 1975), 28–29; Robert Korstad, "Daybreak of Freedom: Tobacco Workers and the CIO in Winston-Salem, North Carolina, 1943–1950" (Ph.D. diss., University of North Carolina, 1987), 112–233; "CIO Will Seek End of Poll Tax," *New York Times*, 11 April 1946, 30; "Unionized South Will Oust Reaction, Murray Declares," *Wage Earner*, 12 April 1946, 3; "Murray Says Labor Should Be in Politics," *New York Times*, 21 April 1946, 46.

[33] CIO, *Proceedings of 1946 Convention*, 19 November 1946, 194.

to the region. Although some inroads were made in 1946 and 1947, the resistance from the political and industrial leadership of the white South proved overwhelming, and the CIO ended up with fewer southern members in 1952 than it had in 1944. In all, the proportion of union, nonfarm labor in the South declined from just above 20 percent in 1945 to somewhat under 18 percent ten years later. Nor did the unions build a political base in the Deep South. White supremists made the CIO-PAC a whipping boy of the 1946 election season, and with the rise of the Dixiecrats and the defeat of such prounion racial moderates as Claude Pepper and Frank Graham, the southern congressional delegation was even more monolithically reactionary in 1950 than it had been five years before.[34]

Operation Dixie's failure was cause and consequence of the stalemate in domestic politics that characterized the early postwar years. To have organized the South in the late 1940s would have required a massive, socially disruptive interracial campaign reminiscent of the CIO at its most militant in the late 1930s, indeed a campaign not dissimilar from that which the modern civil rights movement would wage in the 1960s. Moreover, it would have required the kind of federal backing, both legal and ideological, offered by the Wagner Act in the 1930s and the Supreme Court's *Brown* v. *Board of Education* decision thirty years later.

Although some of the political ingredients for a social revolution of this sort were available just after the war, such a campaign proved beyond labor's strength in 1946 and 1947. The white South was economically and politically stronger than it had been ten or twelve years before. Traditional elites in both agriculture and industry had been financially strengthened, first by the New Deal's massive intervention in the farm economy of that region, then by the military industrialization of the early 1940s. Moreover, direct federal pressure on the white South would remain quite timid in the postwar years, not withstanding the celebrated bolt of the Dixiecrats at the 1948 Democratic convention. Reluctant to fragment the fragile Democratic coalition, Truman tried long and hard to accommodate both civil rights liberals and Southern white supremists. "The strategy," presidential aide Philleo Nash later explained, "was to start with a bold measure and then temporize to pick up the right-wing forces."[35]

---

[34] Marshall, *Labor in the South*, 229–66, 276; Griffith, *Crisis of American Labor*, 161–66; Michael Honey, "Labor and Civil Rights in the Postwar South: The CIO's Operation Dixie," paper delivered at the Southern Labor Studies Conference, Atlanta, September 1982.

[35] Weir and Skocpol, "State Structures," 143–45; quote taken from Joseph Huthmacher, ed., *The Truman Years* (Hinsdale, Ill.: Franklin Watts, 1972), 111.

The government's timidity was matched by that of organized labor and its liberal allies. Red-baiting had long been a staple of southern anti-unionism, but instead of confronting these attacks when they launched the campaign, CIO leaders sought to deflect and accommodate southern xenophobia by excluding communists and other radicals from participation in Operation Dixie. The resources of the communist-led trade unions and of Popular Front institutions like the Southern Conference for Human Welfare and the Highlander Folk School were shunted aside, and under the pressure of segregation's counteroffensive, union leaders often ignored the continuation of Jim Crow practices within their organizations.[36]

CIO anticommunism was not alone responsible for the defeat of Operation Dixie: the decisive battles in the key textile mill towns were over by the end of 1946, before this issue became all-consuming. But the labor movement's internal conflict may well have turned a tactical defeat into a disorganized rout. For example, two of the most dynamic unions in the postwar South, the Mine, Mill, and Smelter Workers and the Food and Tobacco Workers, were heavily black organizations hospitable to the communists. By 1947, locals of these unions were being systematically raided by anticommunist CIO unions. The crisis came to a head in Alabama when Murray's own Steelworkers broke the Mine Mill local that represented militant black iron miners around Birmingham. Recruiting their cadre from elements close to the Ku Klux Klan, USW locals in northern Alabama blended anticommunism with overt racism to raid the Mine Mill union and destroy one of the black community's most progressive institutions. The legacy of this fratricidal conflict extended well into the 1960s when Birmingham became synonymous with brutal white resistance to the civil rights movement.[37]

The cold war's chilling effect on domestic politics also sealed the fate of liberal-labor efforts to find an effective vehicle to stem the rightward drift in national politics. Although the formation of the CIO's Political Action Committee in 1943 had put the most politicized wing of the union movement into a close working relationship with the Democratic party, the failure of the CIO's reconversion strategy and the decline of Demo-

[36] Griffith, *Crisis of American Labor,* 139–60; Anne Braden, "Red, White and Black in Southern Labor," in Ann Fagan Ginger and David Christiano, eds., *The Cold War Against Labor* (Berkeley: Meiklejohn Civil Liberties Institute, 1987), 648–60.
[37] Korstad, "Daybreak of Freedom," 276–408; Marshall, *Labor in the South,* 258–60; Neil Irvin Painter, *The Narrative of Hosea Hudson* (Cambridge, Mass.: Harvard University Press, 1979), 329–34. Hudson was a black Communist, purged by the CIO, whose graphic account of Southern labor illustrates both the potential and the tragedy of its history in the 1930s and 1940s.

cratic party liberalism reopened the issue of labor's attitude toward party politics. In the fluid period after the death of Roosevelt and before the 1948 elections, unionists searched for some alternative strategy that might give them a more articulate and forceful political voice.

Until the spring of 1948 labor liberals almost uniformly repudiated Truman as their presidential candidate and proposed as a replacement men as different as Dwight D. Eisenhower and William O. Douglas. The structure of the Democratic party also came under scrutiny. The CIO, the new Americans for Democratic Action, and the AFL favored its "re-alignment" either by liberalization of the South or, if that failed, the expulsion of the Dixiecrats. Moreover, there was still enough interest in the formation of a third party to create at least a serious debate within some of the major unions—notably the UAW—and within sections of the liberal community. Mainstream union leaders had always held a dichotomous view of this subject. In the short run (that is, before the next election) unionists rejected the third-party idea on the ground that it would "divide progressive forces." But when unionists looked further down the line the labor party idea seemed more attractive. In 1946 sociologist C. Wright Mills found that 65 percent of the CIO's national officers favored such a new political initiative in ten years' time.[38]

Yet as the Democratic party declined in both its liberalism and its electability, the union determination to preserve the unity of "progressive" forces seemed increasingly tenuous. Thus in the spring of 1946, John Dewey, Norman Thomas, and Walter Reuther, all identified with the anti-communist wing of American liberalism, issued a call for a National Educational Committee for a New Party. A year later, the UAW's secretary-treasurer, the socialist Emil Mazey, told local union presidents to take "concrete action in building an independent labor party of workers and farmers." So unsure was Reuther of Truman's election that he scheduled a unionwide political education meeting for January 21, 1949, the day after Thomas Dewey's presidential inauguration.[39]

Ironically, it was the actual formation of a third party—the Progressive party, which ran Henry Wallace for president—that decisively ended such political experimentation and wedded trade unionism even more closely to the Democratic party. For nearly a decade Wallace had enjoyed

[38] Brody, "The Uses of Power II: Political Action," in *Workers in Industrial America*, 215–221.

[39] Ibid., 222–25; *United Automobile Worker*, 1 October 1948; see also Mike Davis, *Prisoners of the American Dream* (London: Verso, 1986), 52–101.

remarkable support in liberal-labor circles; as late as 1947, both his domestic program and his foreign policy views coincided closely with those of the bulk of the labor movement. But his candidacy brought into sharp relief two issues that would prove crucial to the political reformation of postwar labor-liberalism. The first was the Marshall Plan, and more generally the effort to integrate into a U.S.-dominated world order the shattered economies of the industrial west. Although initially greeted with some skepticism even by anticommunist union leaders like Walter Reuther, the Marshall Plan won strong endorsement from most liberals as their hopes for the construction of a purely domestic full-employment welfare state declined and as the Truman administration promoted the European Recovery Program as a key to international trade and North Atlantic prosperity. In addition, the government's recruitment of scores of American unionists to help staff the new program appeared to assure significant labor participation in the reshaping of U.S. foreign policy in this crucial area.[40]

The second issue raised by the Wallace candidacy was the legitimacy of the communists in U.S. political life, and more broadly the possibility that Popular Front politics might have a continuing relevance in postwar America. Wallace, who now spoke for these forces, refused to accept the postwar settlement that was emerging abroad and at home. He wanted détente with the Soviet Union (accepting its control of East Europe) and saw the Marshall Plan as little more than an effort to drive Western Europe into the straitjacket constructed by a newly hegemonic American capitalism. At home he denounced Taft-Hartley, defended those unions that defied its sanctions, and tried to ally himself with the most advanced forms of civil rights militancy.[41]

By early 1948 the Wallace candidacy was therefore anathema, for it broke with what was becoming fundamental in the postwar United States: alignment with the government in the battalions of the new cold war and exclusion of the communists from the political arena. This was made explicit in a January 1948 CIO executive council resolution rejecting the Progressive party and endorsing the Marshall Plan. A powerful Wallace

---

[40] Alonzo Hamby, *Beyond the New Deal: Harry S. Truman and American Liberalism* (New York: Columbia University Press, 1973); Michael Hogan, "American Marshall Planners and the Search for a European Neocapitalism," *American Historical Review* 86 (April 1981): 44–72; Federico Romero, "Postwar Reconstruction Strategies of American and Western European Labor," Working Paper No. 85/193, European University Institute, Department of History and Civilization, San Somenico di Fiesole, Italy.

[41] Norman Markowitz, *The Rise and Fall of the People's Century: Henry A. Wallace and American Liberalism, 1941–1948* (New York: Free Press, 1973), 242–60.

movement threatened to taint the CIO with the badge of disloyalty. "The real issue," asserted the ever-cautious Philip Murray, "is the jeopardy in which you place your Unions." Although the trade unions might still differ on bargaining strategy and their approach to Taft-Hartley, any divergence from the CIO election strategy was tantamount to organizational treason.[42]

A remarkably enthusiastic labor campaign on behalf of the president proved feasible in 1948 because of Truman's veto of Taft-Hartley in June 1947 and his carefully calibrated shift to the left in the year before the November elections. Inaugurating his campaign with a massive AFL-CIO rally in Detroit's Cadillac Square, Truman shored up liberal support and won potential Wallace voters back to the Democratic fold with a populist "Give 'em Hell, Harry" appeal that solidified union ties with the Democratic party. The president's unexpected success in November sealed the fate of the communist-influenced unions within the CIO. With the Wallace supporters routed and the Republicans at least temporarily subdued, the industrial union federation could clean house with the least possible institutional damage. CIO expulsion of unions considered communist, which dominated the next year, proved decisive, not so much because these dissident unionists represented a progressive alternative leadership but because the purge drastically narrowed the scope of political debate within the labor movement and those sections of the community who looked to labor for leadership.[43]

Privatization of the welfare state

COLA. After 1947 the defensive political posture adopted by even the most liberal of the CIO unions enhanced the apparent appeal of a narrowly focused brand of private-sector collective bargaining. For example, the conservative victory in the 1946 congressional elections forced Walter Reuther to temper his call for government economic planning. In a radio debate of May 1946, well before the elections, Reuther told his audience that rhetoric about a "government controlled economy" was a big-business scare tactic. The real question, he said, is "How much govern-

---

[42] CIO Executive Board Minutes, 22–23 January 1948, 220, ALHUA; see also Mary Sperling McAuliffe, *Crisis on the Left: Cold War Politics and American Liberalism, 1947–1954* (Amherst: University of Massachusetts Press, 1978), 3–47.

[43] McAuliffe, *Crisis on the Left*, 41–47; Harvey A. Levenstein, *Communism, Anticommunism and the CIO* (Westport: Greenwood Press, 1981), 280–97, 330–40; Brody, "The Uses of Power," 226–28.

ment control and for whose benefit." But in the wake of the massive Republican victory of November 1946 Reuther made a rhetorical about-face, now urging "free labor" and "free management" to join in solving their problems or a "superstate will arise to do it for us."[44] Or as Reuther put it in another context, "I'd rather bargain with General Motors than with the government. . . . General Motors has no army."[45]

This retreat to a more privatized conception of what labor could accomplish meant that the UAW and other progressive unions were forced to make agreements with employers on less favorable economic terrain. By the spring of 1948, in the wake of Taft-Hartley, in the midst of a difficult third round of postwar wage negotiations, and in a bleak pre-election political season, Reuther and other top UAW leaders found themselves confronted with a contract settlement from General Motors that seemed remarkably attractive. GM had long sought the containment of UAW power, and to achieve this end it was willing to make substantial economic accommodation to the union and its newly unified leadership. At the same time the Chez coup in February, congressional debate over a peacetime draft, and the administration's request for a supplemental $3.3 billion military procurement package convinced men like GM President Charles Wilson that inflationary pressures generated by cold-war military expenditures would be a permanent feature of the postwar scene. Since General Motors faced little effective competition, either foreign or domestic, it could easily "administer" the higher prices in an orderly fashion.[46]

But inflationary pressures were destabilizing in the labor relations realm. The corporation had staved off the UAW's effort to link company pricing policy to a negotiated wage package in 1946, but GM realized that disruptive strikes and contentious annual wage negotiations, especially if couched as part of a broader offensive against corporate power, merely served to embitter shop-floor labor relations and hamper the company's long-range planning. In 1948 GM therefore offered the UAW a contract that included two pillars of the postwar social order: (1) an automatic cost-of-living adjustment (COLA) keyed to the general price index, and

[44] "Are We Moving Toward a Government Controlled Economy" 30 May 1946; and UAW Press Release, 7 December 1946, in Box 542, Walter Reuther Collection, ALHUA.
[45] Lester Velie, *Labor, U.S.A.* (New York: Random House, 1958), 64.
[46] Stephen Amberg, "Liberal Democracy and Industrial Order: Autoworkers under the New Deal" (Ph.D. diss., Massachusetts Institute of Technology, 1987), 118; Kathyanne El-Messidi, "Sure Principles Midst Uncertainties: the Story of the 1948 GM-UAW Contact" (Ph. D. diss., University of Oklahoma, 1976), 48–79; Daniel Bell, "The Subversion of Collective Bargaining: Labor in the 1950s," *Commentary* (March 1960), 697–713.

(2) a 2 percent "annual improvement factor" (AIF) wage increase designed to reflect, if only partially, the still larger annual rise in GM productivity.[47]

The agreement was a dramatic, even a radical, departure from past union practice. Reuther himself had rejected wage escalation until early 1948, and a Twentieth Century Fund survey of union leaders taken later that same year revealed that more than 90 percent opposed COLA clauses in their contracts. With the general wage declines of 1921, 1930–32, and 1938 still a living memory, most union leaders instinctively rejected the premise on which the GM-UAW contract was based: the emergence of a new era of inflationary prosperity and relative social peace. Labor leaders thought such schemes foreclosed the possibility of a large increase in the real standard of living, and they continued to fear that such a wage formula would become a downward escalator when the inevitable postwar depression finally arrived. As one industrial union leader put it, "If living costs move, our people must earn more. But it can't go on. One reason we want to strengthen our position is that in case living costs drop we must be in a position to make a determined demand to retain our wages and working conditions."[48]

When the 1949 recession turned out to be less than the depression many had expected, the gateway was open to the further elaboration of such an accommodation between the big unions and the major corporations. Again, the UAW pioneered the way with a new agreement, a five-year "Treaty of Detroit" that provided an improved COLA and AIF and a $125-a-year pension. *Fortune* magazine hailed the 1950 UAW-GM contract as "the first that unmistakably accepts the existing distribution of income between wages and profits as 'normal' if not as 'fair'. . . . It is the first major union contract that explicitly accepts objective economic facts—cost of living and productivity—as determining wages, thus throwing overboard all theories of wages as determined by political power and of profits as 'surplus value.' " By the end of the 1950s the COLA principle had been incorporated in more than half of all major union contracts, and in the inflationary 1960s and 1970s it spread even wider—to Social Security, some welfare programs, and to wage determination in the government and nonunion sector.[49]

[47] El-Messidi, "Sure Principles," 80–107.
[48] W. S. Woytinsky, *Labor and Management Look at Collective Bargaining: A Canvas of Leaders' Views* (New York: Twentieth Century Fund, 1949), 105–9; El-Messidi, "Sure Principles," 60.
[49] Russell Davenport, *U. S. A.: The Permanent Revolution* (New York: Fortune Magazine,

Health insurance and pensions. Just as the negotiation of COLA agreements came in the wake of the union movement's forced retreat from the effort to reshape the Truman administration's early economic policy, so too did the new interest in pension and health and welfare plans represent a parallel privatization of the labor movement's commitment to an expanded welfare state. Once it became clear that the unions would be unable to advance their social agenda within the halls of Congress, trade unionists who had been in the forefront of the fight for national health insurance and a more liberal Social Security program now turned to collective bargaining to build the social safety net their members required.

Although company-sponsored or union-negotiated benefit plans had not been entirely absent in U.S. industry, the dramatic growth of these welfare schemes began only after World War II. The issue had become a pressing one for two reasons: First, both the coverage and the benefit level of the Social Security system were extraordinarily meager. "Nothing more clearly distinguishes the post-war political climate of the USA from that of Great Britain than the almost unqualified refusal of its legislature to respond to proposals for social reform," wrote the British political scientist Vivian Vale.[50] The United States devoted about 4.4 percent of gross national product to Social Security in 1949, less than half the proportion of even the austere economies of war-torn Western Europe. In 1948 nearly half of the country's working population remained excluded from any federal retirement income, while the inflationary surge of that era had reduced purchasing power of old age beneficiaries to well below the payment levels of 1940.[51]

Second, the relative aging, and the greater social visibility of older workers in the ranks of the blue-collar work force, exacerbated the Social Security crisis. Union seniority procedures instituted over the previous decade had given workers something of a legal ownership to their jobs, thus lengthening the tenure most workers spent in the employ of a particular company and reducing the characteristic mobility of workers in such heavily unionized industries as automobiles, packinghouses, and coal

---

1951), 94; George Ruben, "Major Collective Bargaining Developments: A Quarter Century Review," reprinted from Bureau of Labor Statistics, *Current Wage Developments* (Washington, D.C.: U.S. Government Printing Office, 1974), 46–47.
[50] Vivian Vale, *Labour in American Politics* (London: Barnes and Noble, 1971), 97.
[51] Harold Wilensky, *The Welfare State and Equality* (Berkeley: University of California Press, 1975), 24–26; Oscar R. Ewing, Federal Security Administrator to Harry S. Truman, 13 April 1948, Box 535, HST Official File, Harry S. Truman Library.

mining. Retirement pay for these workers would be an obvious issue. Moreover, during World War II many older workers stayed on the job past the ages of sixty-five or seventy; the average age of workers at the Ford Motor Company stood at almost forty-seven in 1945, nearly a full decade above prewar estimates. In the coal mines, the average age had risen from thirty-two to forty-nine during the war, and more than 11,000 men age 65 or over were still working in 1944.[52]

Trade unionists overwhelmingly favored a public, federal system for financing social benefits like pensions. Both the CIO and the AFL worked for the passage of the Wagner-Murray-Dingell bill, a proposal that would have liberalized and federalized the U.S. social welfare system in a fashion not dissimilar to that envisaged by the British government's path-breaking Beveridge Report of 1942. Central elements of the bill included a national health insurance system and an expansion of Social Security coverage.[53] In the Twentieth Century Fund's 1948 survey, labor officials representing more than 8 million workers opposed collectively bargained pension and welfare schemes; instead, they argued for an adequate federal system of health insurance and old-age security. Workers mistrusted the complicated funding arrangements necessary for private plans, and they feared that in a major slump no pension guarantee could be immune from erosion. In one of the few rank-and-file "referenda" on the issue, a majority of the 107,000 workers at the Ford Motor Company rejected a union-negotiated pension plan in 1947 in favor of a contract with a larger straight wage increase.[54]

Pensions and other fringe benefits, like health insurance and vacation rights, had been put on the union bargaining agenda during World War II, when these schemes were given important tax advantages in 1942 and again in 1944 when the War Labor Board exempted the cost of fringe benefits from the government's wage ceiling in a politically adroit maneuver designed to take the steam out of the more explosive union effort to break the government's wage freeze.[55] The UMW made the first impor-

---

[52] Minutes, National Ford Council Meeting, 28 July 1947, 2–37, and "Pensions—Elimination of Company Security Clause," both in Box 5, Bert Matthews Collection, ALHUA; Dubofsky and Van Tine, *John L. Lewis*, 459.

[53] Monte M. Poen, *Harry S. Truman versus the Medical Lobby* (Columbia: University of Missouri Press, 1979), 29–43; author's telephone interview with Nelson Crunkshank, former AFL Director of Social Insurance Activities, 18 July 1984.

[54] Woytinsky, *Labor and Management Look at Collective Bargaining*, 128–40; "Ford Workers Couldn't Afford Pension," *Wage Earner*, 26 September 1947.

[55] Sumner Slichter, James J. Healy, and E. Robert Livernash, *The Impact of Collective Bargaining on Management* (Washington, D.C.: The Brookings Institution, 1960), 372–76; Donna Allan, *Fringe Benefits: Wages or Social Obligation?* (Ithaca: Cornell University Press, 1964), 99–152.

tant postwar commitment in this area when John L. Lewis demanded an employer-funded health and welfare system in the spring of 1946. Several wartime years of conflict with the government had soured Lewis on the whole idea of the liberal administrative state. He mistrusted not only government efforts to regulate industrial relations but the federal bureaucracy's efficacy in the maintenance of labor and social welfare standards as well. He found, for example, that when federal administrators seized actual control of the coal mines in 1943 and 1946, little changed in terms of the safety or health of UMW workers. Lewis would feel confident only if the UMW itself played the decisive role in providing safety, health, and retirement benefits in the mines. His struggle over this issue entailed a series of strikes and legal confrontations with the administration, but the UMW's ultimate success proved crucial in reducing labor's support of a federal effort in this area. Thus in 1948, after Lewis had finally established the UMW health and welfare program, he told the embattled advocates of Truman's national health insurance scheme that the UMW would no longer support this initiative.[56]

This retreat to a more parochial outlook also took place, if more subtly, among the mainstream unions like the UAW and the Steelworkers. Immediately after the disastrous midterm elections of 1946, CIO leaders announced that they were not going to wait "for perhaps another ten years until the Social Security laws are amended adequately." Instead, they would press for pensions and health benefits in their next collective bargaining round. Some unionists of a more explicitly social democratic outlook, like Walter Reuther and William Pollock of the Textile Workers, theorized that if employers were saddled with large pension and health insurance costs, they would join "shoulder to shoulder" with labor-liberal forces to demand higher federal payments to relieve them of this burden.[57] But such assumptions proved naive. After the steel and auto unions established the heavy industry pension and health benefit pattern in 1949, most of the large unions carved out a similar private welfare state for their own members. Not surprisingly, these organizations no longer saw an increase in federal welfare expenditures as an urgent task. Moreover, managers recognized that company-specific benefits built employee loyalty, and at some level they understood that a social wage

---

[56] Dubofsky and Van Tine, *John L. Lewis*, 454–72; Edward Berkowitz and Kim McQuaid, *Creating the Welfare State: A Political Economy of Twentieth-Century Reform* (New York: New York University Press, 1980), 137.

[57] CIO, *Proceedings of the Eighth Constitutional Convention*, Atlantic City, 18–22 November 1946, 186–87.

of minimal proportions was advantageous to their class interest, even if their own firm had to bear additional costs as a consequence.[58]

The postwar legacy

The consequences of this U.S. version of the welfare state have been far-reaching. Within two decades private pension plans covered more than 30 million workers and approached $900 billion in value.[59] Corrupt or negligent mismanagement of these plans has been a well-publicized fruit of this system, but of far greater consequence has been its social effects on the character of work, employment, and class. First, health and pension benefits, along with the new seniority systems, have dramatically reduced employment mobility in the core firms of the economy. Because neither seniority nor pension benefits were adequately vested, they have tended to re-create a kind of feudal relationship between the worker and his firm. Second, the weakness of the postwar welfare state and the creation of a privatized substitute for workers in organized industry did much to redivide the American working class into a unionized segment, which until recently enjoyed an almost West European level of social welfare protection, and a growing group—predominantly young, minority, and female—who were left out in the cold. The absence of COLA protection for nonunion or weakly organized workers meant that during the inflationary surge of the years 1967–83, wage differentials expanded steadily between industrial, service, and white-collar workers. Moreover, the classic resentment felt by many blue-collar workers toward people on state-supported welfare has at least one of its roots in the system of double taxation the organized working class has borne in the postwar era. Unionized workers pay to support two welfare systems: their own, funded by a "tax" on their total pay periodically renegotiated in the union con-

---

[58] Peter Drucker, *The Unseen Revolution: How Pension Fund Socialism Came to America* (New York: W. W. Norton, 1976), 5–10; Ruth Glazer, "Welfare Discussion Down-to-Earth," *Labor and the Nation* (Spring, 1950), 30–36. Author's interview with Nelson Crunkshank; Martha Derthick, *Policymaking for Social Security* (Washington, D.C.: The Brookings Institution, 1979), 110–31. According to Crunkshank and Derthick, the AFL proved a stronger advocate of higher welfare spending than did the CIO in the years after 1950, because its influential craft unions found pension and health insurance systems difficult to establish in multi-employer industries.

[59] U.S. Department of Commerce, *Statistical Abstract of the U. S.* (Washington, D.C.: U.S. Government Printing Office, 1975), 286.

tract, and that of the state and federal government, paid for by a tax system that grew increasingly regressive with the passing of time.[60]

Among its other consequences, this division has progressively weakened political support for the structures of the welfare state erected in the New Deal era. American unions remain supporters of Social Security, national health insurance, and minority-targeted welfare programs, but their ability to mobilize either their own members or a broader constituency on these issues declined during most of the postwar era. A militant civil rights movement, not the unions, put these issues back on the national agenda for a time in the 1960s. Moreover, labor's postwar abdication from any sustained struggle over either the structure of industry or the evolution of the work process has had its own debilitating consequences. As older industries decline, it has both sapped the loyalty of the union movement's original blue-collar constituency and deprived the unions of any effective voice in the contemporary debate over the deployment and organization of the new technology or the reindustrialization of the economy.

[60] For additional consideration of these issues see Paul Blumberg, *Inequality in an Age of Decline* (New York: Oxford University Press, 1980), 65–107; Robert Gordon, Richard Edwards, and Michael Reich, *Segmented Work, Divided Workers* (Cambridge: Cambridge University Press, 1982), 165–227; Hugh Mosley, "Corporate Benefits and the Underdevelopment of the American Welfare State," *Contemporary Crisis* 5 (Fall 1981): 139–54.

5

Postwar American society:
dissent and social reform

WILLIAM H. CHAFE

When Harry Truman became president, one of the first questions asked about him was whether he would carry on, with enthusiasm, the liberal agenda of social reform associated with Franklin Roosevelt's New Deal. Although the process of idealizing the Roosevelt record already may have been reflected in the question, there were many Americans on the left side of the political spectrum who pointed to the Tennessee Valley Authority, the Works Progress Administration, the Farm Security Administration, and the National Youth Administration (among others) as evidence of a commitment by FDR to greater social and economic equality in America. The war had also raised hopes for such equality, especially among black Americans, women workers, and organized labor. Although FDR said he was replacing Dr. New Deal with Dr. Win-the-War during the actual fighting, he had campaigned for reelection in 1944 on a platform calling for a new economic bill of rights at home, a message that sounded to many like a rallying cry to carry forward the New Deal. What would happen to these hopes now that Roosevelt was dead and the Man from Missouri had assumed the reins of power?

Truman, of course, understood the political problem of holding the allegiance of Roosevelt's liberal followers. Within a few months of taking office he announced a legislative program fully consistent with Roose-veltian activism—national health insurance, full employment, higher minimum wages, and more. The new president also faced the difficult task of reviving a coalition in Congress that would be capable of enacting such a program—all this in the context of massive fears of a new depression, domestic instability due to demobilization, and a series of foreign policy crises that would eventually result in the cold war. For the most part, historians have given Truman high grades for his performance during these difficult months. Not only did he vigorously defend his Fair Deal and oversee a peaceful transition to an era of prosperity, but he also fought heroically against the forces of reaction and in 1948 preserved and maintained the New Deal tradition.[1]

This essay, however, argues for a more paradoxical, complex assessment of the Truman years. Without question, the Truman period was a time of unprecedented social change, much of it traceable directly or indirectly to Truman administration policies. Whether the issue be economic growth, alterations in the work force, shifts in gender roles, the transformation of popular culture, education, or the mass migration to suburbia, the years from 1945 to 1953 witnessed extraordinary developments. Moreover, the positive nature of the changes that occurred in these areas—particularly the fact that millions of Americans for the first time had a chance to own their own home and their own car and to seek a college degree—made this an era of significant improvement in the lives of the average family.

Yet it is also important to remember that during these same years many of the hopes for substantial progress toward social and economic equality were disappointed. The Truman rhetoric on such issues as civil rights, labor, and full employment was often not matched by performance. Many women who expected to retain decent jobs after the war saw their hopes dashed. Black veterans who came home seeking democracy in America to match that for which they had fought in the Pacific and in Europe found less support than they wished. And as others in this volume have shown, labor's agenda of social reform was not achieved.

Thus the Truman period presents a set of mixed results. Important social change and progress occurred for millions. But for two of the groups who in the past had been most victimized by discrimination, women and blacks, there was no comparable progress. Ironically, the two results may have been connected; the absorption of millions of Americans in new

[1] The most comprehensive overview of politics in the postwar years can be found in Alonzo L. Hamby, *Beyond the New Deal* (New York: Columbia University Press, 1973). See also Cabell Phillips, *The Truman Presidency* (New York: Macmillan, 1966); Bert Cochran, *Harry Truman and the Crisis Presidency* (New York: Funk and Wagnalls, 1973); Robert Donovan, *Conflict and Crisis* (New York: Norton, 1977); and Robert Ferrell, *Harry Truman and the Modern American Presidency* (Boston: Little, Brown, 1983). Samuel Lubell presents a provocative interpretation of the political climate of the postwar years in *The Future of American Politics* (New York: Harper, 1952). On the cold war, see John Gaddis, *The United States and the Origins of the Cold War, 1941–1947* (New York: Columbia University Press, 1972).

material opportunities made the continued inequality of some seem less significant and less deserving of political attention, particularly in an era that all too often associated social protest with pro-communist sympathies.

Postwar affluence

With the end of World War II, millions of Americans eagerly anticipated a return to peacetime patterns, traditional family relationships, and the pursuit of long-deferred advances in living standards. To a striking degree, their hopes were realized. Between 1945 and 1960, the gross national product (GNP) jumped 250 percent, consumption of personal services increased three times, and new construction multiplied almost tenfold. By the mid-1950s nearly 60 percent of American families had achieved a "middle class" standard of living (defined as an income of $3,000 to $10,000 in constant dollars), in contrast to only 31 percent in 1929, the last year of prosperity before the Great Depression. Between 1946 and 1957, short-term credit soared almost 600 percent and by the end of the 1950s, 75 percent of Americans owned a car and washing machine, while 87 percent had a television set. The country, economist Walt Rostow said, had entered the "high mass consumption" stage of economic development.[2]

To a large extent, the war itself served as a primary catalyst for such growth. For the first and only time in the twentieth century, there was a redistribution of income during the war years, with the share of the total national income held by the top 5 percent of the nation's wage earners declining from 22 percent to 17 percent and the share of the bottom 40 percent substantially increasing. Savings accounts increased by 300 percent in the same years; $140 billion was available at the end of the war for consumer spending, compared with just $50 billion at the end of 1941.[3]

Wartime spending also helped to generate the technological and managerial breakthroughs that increased productivity in the nation's facto-

---

[2] For a general discussion of postwar economic conditions, see William E. Leuchtenburg, *A Troubled Feast* (Boston: Little, Brown, 1973); John Kenneth Galbraith, *The Affluent Society* (Boston: Houghton Mifflin, 1958); and Walt Rostow, *The Stages of Economic Growth* (Cambridge: Cambridge University Press, 1960).

[3] On the impact of the war on income distribution, see John Blum, *V Was for Victory* (New York: Harcourt Brace Jovanovich, 1976); and Robert Lampman, *The Share of Top Wealth Holders in National Wealth, 1922–1956* (Princeton: Princeton University Press, 1962).

ries and facilitated the development of new products. Innovations in electronics, aerospace, and chemicals created new jobs and products. Electronics spurted from forty-ninth to fifth place among the nation's industries; the airplane industry boomed; and automakers took advantage of new plants and pent-up consumer demand to start the second stage of the automobile revolution. In the decade after the war, the number of cars on the road increased by 100 percent.[4]

Continued government involvement in the economy, as well as specific federal programs, helped to sustain postwar growth. The GI Bill, in particular, provided crucial ingredients for long-term prosperity. Veterans returning from the war had available to them a variety of benefits. Those who wished to continue their schooling received tuition as well as subsistence pay. The Veterans Administration (VA) offered loans of up to $2,000 for those who wanted to start businesses. And perhaps most important, the government helped veterans buy homes. A GI returning home was guaranteed access to $2,000, with the Federal Housing Administration (FHA) willing to underwrite mortgages of up to 80 or 90 percent of a home's value. With the average home costing less than $20,000, millions of veterans had the opportunity to buy a house without even having to make the down payment from their own savings. Nothing proved more important to the booming housing market of the late 1940s and 1950s. Indeed, the construction industry, together with the automobile industry, served as a critical foundation for the entire postwar economy. Directly and indirectly, federal funds were fueling an unprecedented era of economic growth—providing financing for mortgages, stipends for education, and investment in scientific research destined to produce massive economic dividends. In 1929 federal expenditures had amounted to 1 percent of the GNP. By 1955 that figure had increased to 17 percent. The results were remarkable.[5]

Significantly, the new economy was one in which the distribution of jobs shifted rapidly from blue-collar to white-collar. Through productivity breakthroughs, the assembly line actually required fewer workers to produce larger numbers of goods. The number of factory operatives fell 4 percent between 1947 and 1957. The number of clerical workers, meanwhile, increased 23 percent. Most new jobs were in areas that served

[4] See Leuchtenburg, *A Troubled Feast;* and John Rae, *The American Automobile* (Chicago: University of Chicago Press, 1965).
[5] For the GI Bill, see Hamby, *Beyond the New Deal;* and Jack Goodman, ed., *While You Were Gone* (New York: Simon and Schuster, 1946). See also Leuchtenburg, *A Troubled Feast.*

consumers—salespeople in automobile showrooms, advertising executives, telephone operators, government bureaucrats—thus reflecting the emergence of an economy geared to the production of human services rather than basic necessities.

Simultaneously, a new managerial class emerged. Between 1947 and 1957 the number of salaried middle-class workers increased by 61 percent. These may not have been executives in the sense of deciding the fate of a company. But they were specialized and salaried workers who increasingly became a feature of the huge corporate structures that developed in postwar years, with personnel trained to take charge of a particular niche within the large corporate structure. A marketing analyst made decisions on the sales potential of a new product, a specialist in "management science" coordinated personnel, and a research engineer oversaw the development of new inventions and design ("R&D," or research and development). In huge companies such as General Motors there were more than 100,000 salaried workers by the mid-1950s, and some corporations took on the power and the character of nation states. What sociologists called the "organization man" (there were few, if any, organization women) had become an economic reality as well as a cultural stereotype.[6]

Many of the members of this new "salariat," as Daniel Bell called it, led the way in the greatest migration to occur in American history since the massive influx of European immigrants in the early twentieth century—the move to suburbia. During the late 1940s and 1950s more than a million people per year moved to the "Levittowns" that sprouted up in ever-widening circles around every metropolitan area. As a result of the postwar housing crunch, 2 million couples were living with relatives in 1948. It was here that the housing programs spawned by the VA and FHA made a critical difference. Families wanted new homes; building contractors wanted cheap land; county governments wanted an expanding tax base and new developers. Overnight a new community would come into existence—not perhaps the spacious manor houses surrounded by trees that inspired advertisers but nevertheless comfortable homes with new appliances and yards, places that represented, in the eyes of millions of people, a giant stride forward.

The growth of suburbia, of course, was also associated with children

---

[6] Daniel Bell, *The Coming of Post-Industrial Society* (New York: Basic Books, 1973); John Rasmussen, ed., *The New American Revolution* (New York: Wiley, 1972); William Whyte, *The Organization Man* (New York: Simon and Schuster, 1956); and Eleanor B. Sheldon and Wilbert E. Moore, *Indicators of Social Change* (New York: Russell Sage, 1968).

and family life. By 1950 nearly 60 percent of all women eighteen to twenty-four years old were married, compared with only 42 percent in 1940. Most of these new families participated in the baby boom, perhaps the single largest growth industry of postwar America. During the 1940s, America's population grew by 19 million, more than twice the growth of the 1930s. But in the 1950s that figure faded into insignificance as the nation grew by almost 30 million people and approached a level of population growth identical to that of India. Prior to World War II the fertility rate was 80 and the birthrate only 19 per 100,000 people. By 1957 the fertility rate peaked at 123 and the birthrate was 25 per 100,000. The birthrate for third children doubled between 1940 and 1960, while that for fourth children tripled. Advertisers now portrayed the five- or six-person family as ideal, not the three- or four-person family. Moreover, this new family was supposedly the realization of America's dream, with contented mothers delighting in chauffeuring their children from ballet classes to Scouts all day and hard-working, fulfilled fathers returning home at night to romp with the kids and settle down to a happy dinner with the family. As we shall see, the stereotype obscured conflicts, tensions, and contradictions that would later explode into public visibility, but for the time, at least, it seemed that the world of the postwar suburbs had brought a measure of satisfaction and joy never before available to such a large number of people.[7]

One of the principal vehicles for reinforcing this impression was the centerpiece of postwar consumer culture, the television. In 1947, 7,000 TV sets were sold to American customers; three years later, the figure was 7 million. By the mid-1950s, two-thirds of all families had their own set. TV, columnist Max Lerner said, had become "the poor man's luxury because it is his psychological necessity." Junior high school students watched TV twenty-seven hours per week by 1950, advertisers used the new medium to multiply exponentially the sales of their products (Hazel Bishop went from $50,000 per year of revenue to $4.5 million in sales through TV advertising), and nightclub owners and movie houses mourned the loss of customers who stayed home Saturday night to watch Sid Caesar and Imogene Coca's "Show of Shows" rather than leave the house for their entertainment.[8]

For the most part, TV celebrated the values of the dominant culture.

[7] On suburbia, see A. C. Spectorsky, *The Exurbanites* (Philadelphia: Lippincott, 1955); Whyte, *The Organization Man;* Herbert Gans, *The Levittowners* (New York: Pantheon, 1967); and Scott Donaldson, *The Suburban Myth* (New York: Columbia University Press, 1969).

[8] Erik Barnouw, *Tube of Plenty* (New York: Oxford University Press, 1974).

"I Remember Mama" portrayed a story of immigrant assimilation, upward mobility, and ethnic nostalgia far removed from the eighty-four-hour work weeks of the Pittsburgh steel mills or the Lower East Side garment factory. "Father Knows Best," in turn, told viewers that middle-class respectability was a noble goal and that traditional sex roles were the major route to happiness. When Margaret, the wife, worried on one show that she had "failed" because she had not pursued a career as a doctor as her high school girlfriend had, the woman doctor assured her that "no," it was the doctor who had failed because she had given up the chance for marriage by seeking a career. Margaret, it turned out, had achieved the only success that really mattered to a woman.

There were, of course, many critics of the values and institutions of suburbia, corporate America, and consumerism. To writers such as William Whyte and Lionel Trilling, postwar culture represented a devastating blow to individuality, diversity, and freedom. Even religion, Trilling said, had become "what the ideal modern house is called, a machine for living." Others indicted the social life of the suburban development, where everyone knew everyone else's business, people wore the same clothes, bought the same cars, ate the same food, and read the same books (if they read at all). It was all a "split-level trap," one group of authors claimed.[9]

But in fact, many Americans had found a way of life that *did* seem better than what they had experienced before. Although the critics were correct in denouncing conformism for its own sake, many suburbanites exhibited imagination and courage in their effort to create communities where none had existed before. Through voluntary associations, parent groups, church activities, and shared social life, people who moved to the new communities surrounding the nation's cities had attempted to give substance to their quest for a better way of life. Moreover, for many Americans who had not known prosperity or optimism for more than a decade, the new emphasis on acquiring consumer goods and moving up the economic ladder had an excitement all its own. Perhaps the life of suburbia was as stifling and tyrannical as James Dean portrayed it in *Rebel Without a Cause,* but for many, suburban existence (and the postwar world out of which it grew) had attractions and excitement enough to enlist their energies and allegiance.

[9] For critics of suburbia, see, for example, Whyte, *The Organization Man;* Richard E. Gordon et al., *The Split-Level Trap* (New York: Dell, 1962); Gibson Winter, *The Suburban Captivity of the Churches* (Chicago: University of Chicago Press, 1961).

The other side of the picture

Still, it would be a mistake to overlook the other visions and dreams that thrived in America at the end of World War II. During the war, women, blacks, and organized labor had experienced substantial gains. As the war drew to a close, many who had benefited from the fact that war jolts older social patterns hoped that they could continue to build on these advances. But it was not to be. From the perspective of many of these people, the Truman years were more ones of stalemate or regression than of progress, especially in light of the onset of anti-communist hysteria in 1947.

Women workers in particular had experienced dramatic change during the war. All through the 1930s, government officials, business leaders, and magazine editorial writers had insisted that women stay in the home and not threaten the position of male breadwinners by seeking jobs. School systems fired women teachers who married, and the federal government prohibited more than one member of a family from having a civil service job (a prohibition that functioned almost exclusively to hurt women). More than 80 percent of the respondents in a Gallup Poll declared that wives should not be employed if their husbands had jobs. As *McCall's* magazine argued, only as a wife and mother could the American woman "arrive at her true eminence."[10]

With the onset of the war, all that changed. As more than 10 million men joined the armed services, the call went out for women, especially married women, to leave the home and take the jobs of soldiers going to war. Over 6 million women responded. Wages leaped upward, unionization among women grew 400 percent, and the number of married women holding jobs doubled. Under the new propaganda, women were patriots only if they took jobs. As one government filmstrip said, "Men are needed at the battlefront. Women are needed at the homefront. Men are needed with minds clear and hands steady. Women are needed with attention to their work undivided." Rosie the Riveter became a new national heroine, and as the female labor force increased by 57 percent, millions of women had the opportunity for the first time to make a decent living and at the same time receive approval of their employment by the culture around them.

---

[10] On women in the 1930s, see William Chafe, *The American Woman* (New York: Oxford University Press, 1972); Lois Scharf, *To Work and to Wed* (Westport, Conn.: Greenwood, 1981); and Susan Ware, *Holding Their Own* (Boston: Twayne, 1982).

Perhaps the greatest change was in the age and marital status of those going to the factory. Nearly three out of four women workers were married, and more than 60 percent were over age thirty-five. From the very beginning of industrialization, the average woman worker was young, single, and poor. Now working women were more frequently married, middle class, and middle aged. These were often women who had been discouraged from seeking employment in the past. Now they sought jobs, leading some observers to conclude that a social revolution was in the making. "In the long years ahead," wrote one *Christian Science Monitor* editor, "we will remember these short years of ordeal as a period when women rose to full stature." Expressing a similar view, the labor leader Jennie Matyas said, "We are building up an entirely different social climate. . . . What we didn't consider the nice thing to do after the last war will become the regular thing to do after this one." And most women war workers agreed. Although, when the war began, most told pollsters that they would happily return to the home after the war was over, more than 80 percent told the Women's Bureau in 1945 that they wanted to hold onto their jobs and continue to play an active, socially approved role outside the home. Rosie the Riveter and thousands of her sisters hoped that the end of the war would not bring an end to progress but would become the occasion for expanding and solidifying the new opportunities that they had experienced from 1941 to 1945.[11]

Many black Americans as well experienced great change. Black employment increased dramatically in response to the same manpower pressures that resulted in women's soaring labor-force participation. Overall, the number of blacks employed in manufacturing grew from 500,000 to 1.2 million; blacks who were skilled craftsmen and foremen doubled in number, and black membership in labor unions grew 100 percent. Black Americans also joined the armed forces in percentages far higher than their proportion in the population. Although they encountered the same racism that existed prior to the war, including total segregation of blood supplies and fighting units, the military experience produced sufficient contact with more liberal racial situations, including the more tolerant environment of Europe, that hopes were raised for a better life after the war. Migration out of the South also brought a new sense of liberation.

[11] For various points of view on women's experience in World War II, see Leila Rupp, *Mobilizing Women for War* (Princeton: Princeton University Press, 1978); D'Ann Campbell, *Women at War with America* (Cambridge, Mass.: Harvard University Press, 1984); Susan Hartman, *The Home Front and Beyond* (Boston: Twayne, 1982); Karen Anderson, *Wartime Women* (Westport, Conn.: Greenwood, 1981); and Chafe, *The American Woman*.

Even if northern ghettos offered little in the way of decent housing or treatment, there was at least the chance to vote, to express dissenting opinion, and to have a sense of greater possibilities in the future.[12]

Black protest increased significantly during the war. The new militancy found early expression in A. Philip Randolph's March on Washington Movement in 1941 that led directly to FDR's executive order creating a Fair Employment Practices Committee (FEPC) to fight discrimination in defense industry hiring. The militancy continued as word spread during the war of both new opportunities and continued discrimination. National Association for the Advancement of Colored People (NAACP) membership soared 900 percent, to more than 500,000 people; black newspapers sounded the cry for a "Double V" campaign—victory at home as well as abroad. With renewed vigor, civil rights groups challenged segregation. "We die together," read signs at one demonstration in Washington, "let's eat together." Southern blacks meeting in Durham, North Carolina, even demanded an end to segregation, a statement that would have been unheard of ten years earlier.

Not all wartime developments were positive, of course. The FEPC had a budget of only $80,000 and for the most part used exhortation rather than force to secure fair treatment of blacks in hiring. Brutality in the armed forces also was frequent, with blacks often terrorized in boot camp. But the juxtaposition of some progress with continued discrimination helped to fuel the demands of black Americans for greater progress. "World War II has immeasurably magnified the Negro's awareness of the disparity between the American profession and practice of democracy," the NAACP's Walter White declared, and black Americans seemed intent on acting on that gap, closing it, and moving to create at home the democracy they had fought for abroad.[13]

In the case of both blacks and women, however, the immediate postwar years brought frustration and disappointment. When black veterans returned home, they often headed for the county courthouse to register to vote. Medgar Evers went to cast his ballot in Mississippi even though

---

[12] Harvard Sitkoff, "Race Relations: Progress and Prospects," in James T. Patterson, ed., *Paths to the Present* (Minneapolis: Burgess Publishing Co., 1975); Richard Dalfiume, "The Forgotten Years of the Negro Revolution," *Journal of American History* 55 (June 1968): 90–106; and William Chafe, "The Civil Rights Revolution," in Robert Bremner and Gary Reichard, eds., *Reshaping America* (Columbus: Ohio State University Press, 1982).

[13] Dalfiume, "The Forgotten Years"; Chafe, "The Civil Rights Revolution"; Jervis Anderson, *A. Philip Randolph* (New York: Harcourt Brace Jovanovich, 1973); Herbert Garfinkel, *When Negroes March* (Glencoe, Ill.: Free Press, 1959).

he was warned that he would be shot if he did so. In Terrell County, Georgia, black soldiers did the same, and places like Winston-Salem, North Carolina, and Atlanta even saw attempts to build substantial black political machines that could defend the rights of black people without having to succumb to manipulation of the polls by whites. But despite some success, white intransigence was the most common response to these efforts. Armed whites drove Medgar Evers and others from the polls in Mississippi. In Georgia, the only black to seek to vote in one district was murdered in his front yard. A race riot greeted blacks in Columbia, Tennessee, who challenged traditional racial patterns, and, after seventy blacks were arrested, a mob broke into the jail and murdered two of the prisoners.

Where violence was not employed, other equally effective means of social control could be exercised. More than 90 percent of blacks depended on whites for their employment, the head of the White Citizens Council of Mississippi pointed out. Hence all a white person needed to do to keep blacks in line was to send them "for a vacation." Credit lines were canceled, sharecroppers were evicted from the land, and food and seed were withheld. Surrounding all this was the pervasive attitude of white racism. As the former president of the Alabama Bar Association declared, "No Negro is good enough and no Negro will ever be good enough to participate in making the law under which white people in Alabama have to live."[14]

Clearly, the hopes of black Americans for change in such attitudes depended in large part on receiving encouragement and protection from government officials higher up than their state representatives—in short, from the federal government. Harry Truman had a decent record in civil rights. He had supported the FEPC, voted to abolish the poll tax, endorsed antilynching legislation, and paid attention to his black constituents in Missouri. Now, as president, he intervened boldly with Congress on behalf of legislation to create a permanent FEPC, writing a key congressional leader that abandonment of the FEPC was "unthinkable."

But Truman was also adept at backtracking. Despite his avowed support as a senator for antilynching legislation, he allegedly told one south-

[14] Steven Lawson, *Black Ballots: Voting Rights in the South, 1944–1969* (New York: Columbia University Press, 1976); William Berman, *The Politics of Civil Rights in the Truman Administration* (Columbus: Ohio State University Press, 1970); Yollette Jones, "The Columbia Race Riot of 1946" (M.A. thesis, Duke University, 1978); and C. Vann Woodward, *The Strange Career of Jim Crow*, 3d ed. rev. (New York: Oxford University Press, 1974).

ern colleague, "My sympathies are with you." After urging enactment of a permanent FEPC, Truman, as president, did little else, even refusing to permit the FEPC to order Washington's transit system to hire black operators. In protest, black lawyer Charles Houston resigned from the FEPC, denouncing the government's failure "to enforce democratic practices and protect minorities in its own capital."

The same ambivalence appeared in Truman's response to the brutal repression of black efforts to register to vote after the war. During the spring and summer of 1946, black protest groups and their white allies demanded a response from Truman. More than fifteen thousand people marched to the Lincoln Memorial, and a national emergency committee pleaded with the president to intervene. In reply, Truman created a Committee on Civil Rights to investigate the entire situation facing blacks in America. The committee's report, *To Secure These Rights,* boldly called for a series of actions to end discrimination and racism, including enactment of antilynching legislation, creation of a permanent FEPC, integration of the armed forces, and passage of laws to protect the rights of qualified voters. Truman endorsed the report and told an NAACP rally, "Every man should have the right to a decent home, . . . the right to a worthwhile job, the right to an equal share in making public decisions through the ballot."

Yet rhetoric did not quickly translate into action. Truman retreated from his strong embrace of civil rights, hoping to retain the support of white southern Democrats for his foreign policies, and failed to introduce any legislation to implement the recommendations of his civil rights committee. Nor did he issue executive orders to end segregation in the military or in federal employment until he had to do so in the midst of the 1948 presidential campaign in order to appeal to black voters in the North. In the South, meanwhile, the Justice Department did little to investigate or prosecute violations of civil rights. In the end, the Truman administration may have encouraged civil rights protests on a national level by giving renewed attention to the issues raised by civil rights groups; but in substance the situation facing those who challenged white supremacy in the South had not changed. A Truman aide perhaps summarized the record best when he said, "The strategy was to start with a bold measure and then temporize to pick up the right-wing forces. Simply stated, backtrack after the bang."[15]

[15] Lawson, *Black Ballots;* Berman, *The Politics of Civil Rights;* Lewis Ruchames, *Race, Jobs and Politics* (New York: Columbia University Press, 1953); Harvard Sitkoff, "Harry

In the case of women, the situation was more complicated. There was far less political organization among women workers, there were fewer vehicles for protest, and there was an absence of a sense of gender solidarity for collective advancement of women as women. Nevertheless, four out of five women war workers did express a desire to continue on the job, and there was some support, even in official quarters, for the desire to continue and build on wartime gains. The War Department, for example, issued a pamphlet calling on returning veterans to share household responsibilities and to support such innovations of the domestic war experience as child care centers and community laundries. The Women's Advisory Committee to the War Manpower Commission, in the meantime, urged similar measures. "No society can boast of democratic ideals," the committee said, "if it utilizes woman power in a crisis and neglects it in peace."

On balance, however, the dominant theme of postwar discussion was the necessity for women to return to the home. Ironically, even the propaganda that during wartime had exhorted women to enter the job market contained a subtheme that, once the war was over, women should leave their jobs and go back to the home. "When will mother return home?" one ad said. "Just as soon as Daddy comes back safe and sound from fighting the war," was the reply. In such a situation, a return to domesticity seemed the only logical—and natural—way for women to fulfill their biological roles. Those who wished to pursue careers and compete with men in peacetime, one prominent psychiatrist said, were "stimulated by neurotic competition."[16]

Demobilization created a set of circumstances where such propaganda could take hold. As war plants converted to peacetime production, women who were the last ones hired were also the first ones laid off. Almost a million workers were sent home from aircraft industry jobs after V-J Day, most of them women. In the automobile industry, women's proportion of the labor force fell from 25 percent in autumn 1944 to under 8 percent by the spring of 1946. Some companies also reinstated provisions that restricted the hiring of married or older women. Federal support for

Truman and the Election of 1948," *Journal of Southern History* 37 (November 1971): 597–616; Barton J. Bernstein, "The Ambiguous Legacy: The Truman Administration and Civil Rights," in Barton Bernstein, ed., *Politics and Policies of the Truman Administration* (Chicago: Quadrangle Books, 1970); and Donald McCoy and Richard Ruetten, *Quest and Response: Minority Rights and the Truman Administration* (Lawrence: University Press of Kansas, 1973).

[16] See Chafe, *The American Woman;* Hartman, *The Home Front and Beyond;* and Rupp, *Mobilizing Women for War.*

child care facilities was withdrawn, and in the absence of strong unions committed to women's rights, there was little organized resistance to the changeover.

Significantly, no active feminist movement existed to offer a counter-point to official and unofficial supporters of women's return to traditional roles. The National Women's Party, the primary organization advocating the Equal Rights Amendment, was viewed by the Women's Bureau of the Department of Labor as "a small, . . . militant group of leisure class women venting their resentment at not having been born men." If an alternative ideology with broad-based support was needed to mount a challenge to traditional definitions of women's proper roles, the popular view of feminists as a "lunatic fringe" was clearly not help-ful. Nor did the pace and atmosphere of demobilization provide any as-sistance. There were few who did not genuinely welcome men back to their old jobs, and there was little opportunity for women who wished to share these jobs to meet together and find a common agenda of ac-tion.[17]

In the meantime, what Betty Friedan would later dub the "feminine mystique" was sweeping the nation. According to a popular best-seller, *Modern Woman: The Lost Sex,* the independent woman was a "contra-diction in terms." Mass-circulation magazines repeated the message that women would secure fulfillment only by devoting themselves to home-making, reclaiming the lost arts of canning, preserving, and interior dec-orating, and making household work into a creative adventure. The psy-chiatrist Helen Deutsch noted that only "masculinized" women sought careers. The path of "normal femininity" was for a woman to accept her distinctive sexuality, repress her masculine strivings, and relate to the outside world through her husband and children.

Yet there was something profoundly suspicious about such rhetoric. The celebration of traditional norms seemed almost frantic, as though under the surface something very threatening to traditional values was occurring. Indeed, all during the late 1940s and early 1950s the same magazines that exhorted women to rediscover happiness in the home were also asking, "What's the trouble with women?" In an article bear-ing that title, Margaret Mead declared, "Choose any set of criteria you

---

[17] Chafe, *The American Woman;* Sheila Tobias and Lisa Anderson, "What Really Hap-pened to Rosie the Riveter," MSS Modular Publications, Module 9 (1974); and Leila Rupp, "The Survival of American Feminism," in Bremner and Reichard, eds., *Reshap-ing America.*

like, and the answer is the same: women—and men—are confused, uncertain, and discontented with the present definition of women's place in America." When a 1946 *Fortune* poll asked American women whether they would prefer to be born again as women or men, a startling 25 percent of women declared that they would rather be born men (only 3.3 percent of men, by contrast, said they would prefer to be born women).[18]

In retrospect, then, the "feminine mystique" appears to represent just one side of a tug-of-war occurring between traditional and modern roles. *Life* magazine, commenting on the tension, observed that in the past women had had to make only one major decision—choosing a husband. Now, the magazine observed, they had to decide how they would participate in the world beyond the home as well. Yet there were few guideposts to assist them in this process, especially in a world in which autonomy for women was viewed as deviant and books urged women to study the "theory and preparation of a Basque paella" rather than post-Kantian philosophy.

Further compounding the confusion was the fact that women's labor force participation continued to grow, flying in the face of the stereotypes of the "feminine mystique." By 1960 twice as many women were employed as in 1940, and nearly 40 percent of all women over age sixteen held a job. Female employment increased at a rate four times faster than the rate for men throughout the 1950s. Perhaps most important, the women taking jobs were married and increasingly middle class. By the end of the 1950s, 39 percent of mothers with children ages six to seventeen held jobs. In 1960, 30 percent of married women were employed, in contrast to only 15 percent in 1940. Although concentrated in low-paying, sex-segregated jobs, many of these women could no longer adequately be described as from low-income families. In households where the husband earned from $7,000 to $10,000 per year (comparable to $25,000 to $30,000 today), the rate of women's participation in the job market rose from 7 percent in 1950 to 25 percent in 1960. By the early 1950s more than half of all women with college degrees were employed, while only 36 percent of those with just a high school diploma held a job. Thus not only was the increase in women's employment continuing; it was also being led by many of the same middle-class wives who allegedly had found new contentment in domesticity.[19]

---

[18] See Chafe, *The American Woman;* and Ferdinand Lundberg and Marynia Farnham, *Modern Woman: The Lost Sex* (New York: Grosset and Dunlap, 1947).

[19] See Juanita Kreps, ed., *Women and the American Economy* (Englewood Cliffs, N.J.: Prentice-Hall, 1976).

Two points stand out from this seemingly paradoxical process. First, the women who were taking jobs in no way participated in any improvement of women's economic status. Most were holding "jobs," not pursuing "careers." Their opportunities were limited to segregated positions such as sales or clerical jobs defined as "women's work." In 1950, for example, women made up 64 percent of the workers in the insurance industry, but fewer than 20 percent of those held decent paying positions. Moreover, they said they were working for reasons of "economic necessity." Because their work was defined as "helping the family"—not "competing with men"—it became more acceptable.

Second, and just as important, the jobs these women took provided an indispensable ingredient to the drive of millions of families to acquire middle-class status. Although it was rarely noted at the time, the concentration of new women workers in families where the husband already earned an income close to the national median provided the crucial margin that made it possible for families to move to a new house, take a vacation out of state, or send a child to the college of their choice. In effect these women were charting the only path available to them for resolving the contradiction between traditional and "modern" definitions of women's proper roles. The result was major social change—a big boost toward the consumerism that attracted so many in the postwar years—but that change could not be defined as substantive progress toward sex equality.

Conclusion

Any overall assessment of social change in the Truman period therefore must acknowledge the ambiguity and paradox of these years. Certainly for millions of Americans, perhaps a large majority, this was a time of enlarged opportunities and new discoveries. Anyone who was a child at the time can recall vividly the excitement of seeing one's first television show, laughing at Milton Berle getting hit by a powderpuff or a cream pie, going to a drive-in movie in the family's new car—the first one it had ever owned. They were years of exhilaration for many: The chance to go to college and the acquisition of a home on a plot of ground with trees and a garden were benefits that the government, directly or indirectly, helped to make possible.

But for a person who was black and disenfranchised or for women who had discovered a new sense of pride and identity as welders during the war, these were years of disappointment. To be sure, there were changes. It was important to have a president endorse civil rights and speak to the NAACP. It was also important that millions of women who had not worked before were now taking jobs, even if the jobs were a far cry from those they had been exhorted to take during the war. But the president's civil rights rhetoric meant little to Isaac Nixon of Georgia who was murdered in the fall of 1948 because he insisted on the right to vote. And the fact that women were employed in record numbers by the 1950s had to be balanced against the fact that the jobs they now held paid far less than their wartime positions and offered far fewer psychological and material rewards. As one former welder said, "Is it so much to ask that I should have had the chance to make an ornamental iron gate?"

Part of the reason that these aspirations were not realized had to do with the absorption of most people in all the good things that were occurring. When exciting new developments were happening everywhere, it was difficult to focus on the frustrations of those who were left out, especially when, as in the case of women, there were no major protest organizations to call attention to their grievances. (Ironically, the movement of many families into the middle class was contingent upon women's working in jobs that reflected the persistence of inequality.)

A second reason was the growth of political hysteria about communism that resulted in many social activists being dismissed or persecuted as "fellow travelers" or communist sympathizers. As the Soviet Union and the United States entered a stridently adversarial relationship in 1947, the rhetoric of policy makers became moralistic, with communism (and any ideas associated with it) pilloried as subversive, atheistic, and evil. Concern grew that communists were infiltrating American society and that there must be a connection between people who criticized America from within and those who attacked the country from abroad.

As the phenomenon later called "McCarthyism" increased in fervor, red-baiting became a vehicle for casting suspicion on activists who insisted that the United States was falling short of its ideals of equality and freedom. Supporters of feminism were sometimes identified as communists; when women in New York fought for retention of day-care centers, a major New York newspaper charged that the entire program of child care was conceived by communists operating out of social work cells. In Georgia, Governor Eugene Talmadge attributed civil rights protests to "communist doctrines from outside the state," and in Washington, FBI agents questioned bootblacks at the Pentagon who had donated money to the defense of the Scottsboro Boys (blacks who had been erroneously accused of rape and who were defended by communist attorneys). As one intelligence officer said, "A liberal is only a hop, skip, and a jump from a communist. A communist starts as a liberal." Such sentiments had a devastating impact on the reception given social activists.

Whether or not a majority of the population, especially those who benefited so much from the positive social changes that occurred in the 1940s and 1950s, would have favored significant social reform under any circumstances we will never know. The fact remains that in light of a cold war siege that discredited movements for social reform, it was difficult to secure cultural sanction for discussion of collective reforms involving racial and sexual equality. Positive social changes and a negative political environment combined to defer attention to these issues until another decade when a civil rights movement, rooted in the black church, which could not easily be tarred with the brush of communism, provided a new opportunity to raise the issue of equality in American society.

6

"Some sort of peace": President Truman,
the American people, and the atomic bomb

PAUL BOYER

For millions of Americans born before World War II, memories of President Truman are inextricably interwoven with memories of the atomic bomb. To be sure, Franklin D. Roosevelt had launched the Manhattan Project, but that was all in secret. It was Truman who announced the staggering news to the world on 6 August 1945, who was central to the controversies of 1946–47 over both domestic and international control of atomic energy, who announced the first Russian atomic-bomb test in September 1949, and who in January 1950 authorized development of the hydrogen bomb.

For anyone interested in Harry Truman and his presidency, the question of the atomic bomb is clearly central. For the historian concerned with the bomb's effect on American thought and culture, Truman inevitably looms as a key figure. Curiously, however, neither Truman scholars nor historians studying the evolution of popular attitudes toward nuclear weapons have given Truman's comments about the atomic bomb the close attention that one might expect. We have excellent studies of Truman's role in the diplomacy, strategy, and domestic politics of the early postwar period as they related to the atomic bomb, but relatively little attention has been given to a systematic analysis of his views on the atomic bomb per se.

One reason for this is probably the elusive nature of the evidence. Truman had a good deal to say about the atomic bomb, as about most subjects, but much of it was ad hoc and fragmentary. Rarely if ever did he offer a comprehensive account of the development of his view of the bomb and its meaning. Adding to the challenge is the fact that Truman commented on the bomb at three quite distinct levels of discourse, and two of these levels have only gradually become accessible to historians. The first level (public pronouncements, formal addresses, messages to Congress, and so on) has, of course, been known for decades. Indeed much of it is so familiar as to be difficult to read with a fresh eye. The second level (oral and written communication that passed between Truman and his advisers) has unfolded only gradually and in piecemeal fashion with the publication of memoirs by participants and the opening of various manuscript and archival collections. Finally, there is the intensely interesting level of Truman's relatively uncensored private reflections expressed in diary jottings or in personal letters to his wife, Bess, or his daughter, Margaret. Much of this material, often in striking variance to his public pronouncements, has become available only in the past few years. Thus it is perhaps not surprising that we have yet to see a comprehensive and systematic analysis of Truman's views of, and feelings about, the atomic bomb.

This brief essay will not attempt that exhaustive treatment, but it will draw together some of what we know about Truman's thinking on this subject and relate it to the larger pattern of American attitudes toward the atomic bomb in the early postwar years. Such an effort is revealing in several ways. First, it brings into sharp focus aspects of Truman's character and his mode of dealing with issues. Second, it illustrates how profoundly the advent of this awesome new force could disrupt and disorient even so down-to-earth a man as Truman, producing some quite striking contradictions and inconsistencies. Third, Truman's response to the bomb, in all its ambiguity, mirrors to an uncanny degree the larger response of the American people. The uncertainties and ambivalences within Truman's own mind on this subject were simultaneously being played out on the larger stage of public discourse and cultural expression in this early post-Hiroshima period. Finally, of course, the views expressed by Truman and top members of his administration on the atomic bomb are important to the cultural historian not only because they mirror the broader national response, but also because they directly helped shape that response.

Let us turn, then, to Truman's expressed views on the atomic bomb and the way those views both reflected and molded the larger responses of the American people. The focus here is on three general areas: the justifications offered for the decision to drop the bomb on Japan, the larger meaning of atomic energy for mankind, and the possible use of atomic weapons in the early cold war period.

Justifications for dropping the bomb

President Truman was lunching with the crew of the USS *Augusta* on 6 August 1945, steaming westward across the Atlantic en route home from the Potsdam conference, when a radio message from Secretary of War Henry L. Stimson informed him that the atomic bombing of Hiroshima had been a "complete success." "This is the greatest thing in history," he spontaneously exclaimed. After breaking the news to the cheering sailors, he rushed to the wardroom to tell the officers, amid more cheers and excitement.[1]

Meanwhile, in Washington, D.C., a prearranged news release had been issued that morning by the White House under Truman's name, informing the world that an atomic bomb had been "loosed against those who brought war in the Far East." In this critically important announcement, which shaped Americans' initial perceptions of the bomb, Truman offered only two brief justifications for its use against Japan: First, he cited Tokyo's surprise attack on the United States in 1941: "The Japanese began the war from the air at Pearl Harbor. They have been repaid manyfold." Second, he noted that the Japanese had rejected the Allied surrender ultimatum issued at Potsdam on 26 July 1945—an ultimatum that had warned them of "complete and utter destruction" if they did not surrender unconditionally.[2]

In less formal comments at this time, Truman further justified the atomic bombing on two additional grounds: Japan's wartime atrocities and the racist assertion that the Japanese were subhuman creatures to whom the moral restraint that nations at least professedly observed in wartime need not apply. These interwoven themes emerged most clearly in Truman's response to a post-Hiroshima telegram from an official of the Federal Council of Churches, an association of liberal Protestant denominations, urging that no further atomic bombs be dropped. Truman's answer (written on 9 August with the knowledge that a second atomic bomb would in fact be dropped momentarily) declared, "Nobody is more disturbed over the use of the atomic bomb than I am, but I was greatly disturbed over the unwarranted attack by the Japanese on Pearl Harbor and their mur-

[1] Harry S. Truman, *Memoirs*, vol. 1, *Year of Decisions* (Garden City: Doubleday, 1955), 421.

[2] "White House Press Release on Hiroshima, 6 August 1945," in Robert C. Williams and Philip L. Cantelon, eds., *The American Atom: A Documentary History of Nuclear Policies from the Discovery of Fission to the Present 1939–1984* (Philadelphia: University of Pennsylvania Press, 1984), 68–70.

der of our prisoners of war. The only language they seem to understand is the one we have been using to bombard them. When you have to deal with a beast you have to treat him as a beast. It is most regrettable but nevertheless true."[3]

As the inflamed wartime passions subsided after Japan's surrender, a further justification emerged: The atomic bomb was the only alternative to an invasion of Japan that would have cost many American lives. The gist of this argument was contained in Truman's message to Congress of 3 October 1945, on the subject of atomic-energy legislation. "We know," the president declared unequivocally, "that [the atomic bomb] saved the lives of untold thousands of American soldiers who would otherwise have been killed in battle." Truman became more specific in his address at the annual Gridiron Dinner in Washington on 15 December 1945. Purporting to describe his thought process at the time he made the atomic-bomb decision, Truman declared, "It occurred to me, that a quarter of a million of the flower of our young manhood were worth a couple of Japanese cities, and I still think they were and are."[4]

This argument was most fully elaborated in an extremely influential February 1947 *Harper's* magazine article by former secretary of war Stimson. Had the atomic bomb not been employed as it was, Stimson contended, a full-scale invasion of Japan, first of Kyushu and then of the main island of Honshu, would have been necessary. This would have extended the war through 1946, he insisted, and entailed horrendous losses: "I was informed that such operations might be expected to cost over a million casualties to American forces alone. Additional large losses might be expected among our allies, and of course, if our campaign was successful and if we could judge by previous experience, enemy casualties would be much larger than our own."[5] Repeating this argument in his 1953 memoirs, Winston Churchill inflated Stimson's projection of a million American *casualties* (i.e., killed, wounded, and missing) into a million American *deaths*, plus a half-million British deaths.[6]

With the passing years, Truman insisted ever more rigidly that the atomic-bomb decision was totally justified, that he had never had a

[3] Robert J. Donovan, *Crisis and Conflict: The Presidency of Harry S. Truman 1945–1948* (New York: W. W. Norton, 1977), 96–97.
[4] Ibid., 133; Truman, *Year of Decisions*, 530.
[5] Henry L. Stimson, "The Decision to Use the Atomic Bomb," *Harper's*, February 1947, 102.
[6] Winston S. Churchill, *The Second World War*, vol. 6, *Triumph and Tragedy* (Boston: Houghton Mifflin, 1953), 638–39.

moment's second thoughts, and that he would unhesitatingly make the same decision again. "I regarded the bomb as a military weapon," he wrote in his memoirs in 1955, "and never had any doubt that it should be used."[7] A fundamental element of Truman's public persona was his cocky self-confidence, with never a hint of self-doubt or even of second thoughts about his major decisions. As he wrote in 1957, "I hardly ever look back for the purpose of contemplating 'what might have been.'"[8] Nothing illustrates this trait more clearly than the tone of absolute assurance he adopted in all public comment on the atomic-bomb decision. From 6 August 1945 until his death in 1972, Truman invariably rejected with great vehemence any suggestion that the atomic destruction of two cities may have been unnecessary militarily, tragic in its long-range implications, or problematic on ethical grounds. When J. Robert Oppenheimer, in a White House meeting with Truman shortly after the war, expressed remorse over the dropping of the atomic bomb and alluded to scientists' feelings that they had blood on their hands, Truman wrote to Dean Acheson contemptuously ridiculing this "crybaby" reaction. (According to one version of the encounter, Truman pulled a handkerchief from his pocket and derisively offered it to Oppenheimer to wipe the blood off his hands.)[9]

So intent was Truman on maintaining his posture of absolute certitude regarding this question that he eventually erected a kind of invisible shield around the subject, to ward off any probing by himself or anyone else. In one of his now-famous unmailed letters, he in 1962 unleashed a memorable blast at diplomatic historian Herbert Feis, who was raising troublesome questions as he sought to re-create the strategic considerations that had underlain the bomb decision. Wrote Truman to Feis:

It ended the Jap War. That was the objective. Now if you can think of any other . . . egghead contemplations, bring them out.

You get the same answer—to end the Jap War and save ¼ of a million of our youngsters and that many Japs from death and twice that many on each side from being maimed for life.

[7] Truman, *Year of Decisions*, 419.
[8] Truman to Dean Acheson, 15 March 1957, in Monte M. Poen, ed., *Strictly Personal and Confidential: The Letters Harry Truman Never Mailed* (Boston: Little, Brown, 1982), 33.
[9] Nuel Pharr Davis, *Lawrence and Oppeheimer* (New York: Simon and Schuster, 1968), 260.

It is a great thing that you or any other contemplator "after the fact" didn't have to make the decision. Our boys would all be dead.[10]

The following year, in another unsent letter, this one to *Chicago Sun Times* columnist Irv Kupcinet, Truman wrote, "I knew what I was doing when I stopped the war that would have killed a half million youngsters on both sides if those bombs had not been dropped. I have no regrets and, under the same circumstances, I would do it again—and this letter is not confidential." Toward the end of his life, when the producers of a TV special on his career suggested a trip to Hiroshima in connection with the atomic-bomb episode, Truman proclaimed, "I'll go to Japan, if that's what you want, but I won't kiss their ass."[11]

Why did Truman react so violently to even the whisper of doubt about his atomic-bomb decision? Why the insults, ridicule, contempt, and abuse toward those who tried to penetrate his shell of self-righteous certitude? In part, of course, this was simply another manifestation of the cocky self-confidence so central to Truman's public image. Was more involved? Did the strident certainty that eventually reached a level of self-parody perhaps mask a bad conscience? Despite the evidence of Alamogordo, did Truman still not wholly grasp prior to 6 August the bomb's full destructive magnitude? In his memoirs, he makes clear that he carefully went over the atomic-bomb target list of Japanese cities with his military leaders, and in retrospect he insists that he was fully aware that the bomb "would inflict damage and casualties beyond imagination" and was "potentially capable of wiping out entire cities." Yet on 5 July as the final order for the bomb's use was being drawn up, he wrote in his diary, "I have told the Sec. of War, Mr. Stimson, to use it so that military objectives and soldiers and sailors are the target and not women and children. . . . He and I are in accord. The target will be a purely military one." In the same vein, the prearranged news release of 6 August described Hiroshima (a city of 350,000) simply as "an important Japanese Army base."[12]

In the days immediately after 6 August, before the brittle shell of certitude enveloped Truman's pronouncements about the bomb decision, there

---

[10] Truman to Herbert Feis [late April 1962], Poen, ed., *Strictly Personal and Confidential*, 34.

[11] Merle Miller, *Plain Speaking* (New York: Berkley, 1974), 248; Truman to Irv Kupcinet, 5 August 1963, in Poen, ed., *Strictly Personal and Confidential*, 35.

[12] "White House Press Release on Hiroshima," Williams and Cantelon, eds., *The American Atom*, 68; Truman, *Year of Decisions*, 87, 420, 419; Robert H. Ferrell, ed., *Off the Record: The Private Papers of Harry S. Truman* (New York: Penguin Books, 1982), 55.

are hints that he was shaken and dismayed as the full horror of the civilian toll sank in. On 7 August (in significant contrast to his assertion two
days later that "When you deal with a beast you have to treat him as a
beast"), Truman rejected Senator Richard B. Russell's demand that the
Japanese must be brought "groveling to their knees," commenting: "I
can't bring myself to believe that because they are beasts we should ourselves act in the same manner." And, according to Henry Wallace's diary,
at the cabinet meeting of 10 August, the day after the Nagasaki bombing,
"Truman said he had given orders to stop atomic bombing. He said the
thought of wiping out another 100,000 people was too horrible. He didn't
like the idea of killing, as he said, 'all those kids.' "[13]

Obviously, such sketchy evidence as this does not prove conclusively
that Truman felt more uneasy about his decision than he revealed publicly. Yet if the full evidence of the bomb's power to obliterate entire
cities did shock and somewhat unnerve him, making a mockery of his
earlier insistence on "purely military" targets, the very stridency of his
later efforts to place his decision beyond the reach of criticism or even
discussion may have been his way of dealing with fugitive doubts that he
never openly expressed and perhaps never fully acknowledged even to
himself.

How successful were Truman's efforts to explain and justify his atomic-
bomb decision? From the first, the president's contention that the atomic
bomb was the only alternative to an invasion of Japan aroused skepticism in some quarters. As early as 1946, on the basis of a detailed study
of the state of the Japanese war effort by the summer of 1945 and
exhaustive interviews with high Japanese officials, the United States Strategic Bombing Survey concluded that Japan would have surrendered
"certainly prior to 31 December 1945, and in all probability prior to 1
November 1945 . . . even if the atomic bombs had not been dropped,
even if Russia had not entered the war, and even if no invasion had been
planned or contemplated."[14]

Beginning with Gar Alperovitz's *Atomic Diplomacy: Hiroshima and
Potsdam* (1965) and continuing with such works as Martin J. Sherwin's

---

[13] John M. Blum, ed., *The Price of Vision: The Diary of Henry A. Wallace 1942–1946*
(Boston: Houghton Mifflin, 1973), 474 (entry for 10 August 1945); Truman to Senator
Richard B. Russell, 9 August 1945, with attached telegram, Russell to Truman, 7 August
1945, Folder 197, misc., Official File, Harry S. Truman Library, quoted in Robert L.
Messer, "New Evidence on Truman's Decision," *Bulletin of the Atomic Scientist*, August
1985, 56.

[14] United States Strategic Bombing Survey, *Japan's Struggle to End the War* (Washington,
D.C.: U. S. Government Printing Office, 1946), 13.

A World Destroyed: The Atomic Bomb and the Grand Alliance (1977), a considerable body of historical scholarship has emerged that reinforces the conclusion of the Strategic Bombing Survey and convincingly shows that calculations involving the Soviet Union were more fundamental to the decision-making process than Truman's or Stimson's version of that process acknowledged. These works have made clear that Japan was almost desperately seeking to end the war by July 1945 and that, thanks to the breaking of the Japanese communications code, these efforts were known to President Truman. Indeed, Truman's own memoirs acknowledge that as early as the end of May, after the Okinawa campaign, Acting Secretary of State Joseph Grew (the only high administration official with extended experience in Japan) informed Truman of his belief that the Japanese would surrender if they were assured the emperor could remain on his throne.[15]

The Truman diaries and family letters that have become available to scholars in the past few years further support the revisionist critique of the Truman-Stimson version of the atomic-bomb decision. For example, when Stalin reaffirmed at Potsdam his Yalta pledge to declare war on Japan three months after Germany's surrender, Truman was exultant. "He'll be in Jap War on August 15," Truman wrote in his diary on 17 July; "Fini Japs when that comes about." To Bess he wrote: "I've gotten what I came for—Stalin goes to war on August 15. . . . I'll say that we'll end the war a year sooner, now, and think of the kids who won't be killed. That is the important thing."[16] By mid-July, in short, Truman knew that Japan was on the verge of surrender, and he was convinced that the Soviet Union's forthcoming declaration of war would provide the final push. As historian Robert Messer has recently argued, the issue occupying Truman's mind in these critical days was not the nightmare of a costly land invasion of Japan, but the precise means by which Japan's imminent collapse would be achieved.

As the stunning success of the Alamogordo test became apparent, Truman realized that the United States, and not the Soviets, could provide the final blow. "Believe Japs will fold up before Russia comes in," Truman wrote in his diary on 18 July; "I am sure they will when Manhattan [the atomic bomb] appears over their homeland." When Stimson flew to

[15] Truman, *Year of Decisions*, 416–17.
[16] Harry Truman to Bess Truman, 16 July 1945, in Robert H. Ferrell, ed., *"Dear Bess": The Letters from Harry to Bess Truman, 1910–1959* (New York: W. W. Norton, 1983), 519; Truman diary entry, 17 July 1945, in Ferrell, ed., *Off the Record*, 153.

Potsdam and gave Truman a full briefing on Alamogordo, the president
was (according to Stimson's diary) "tremendously pepped up" and displayed "an entirely new feeling of confidence." Repeatedly Truman thanked
Stimson for the report and for "being present to help him in this way."
In a 1948 letter to Margaret, Truman regretted that he had worked so
hard at Potsdam to get Stalin to reaffirm his pledge to enter the Pacific
war: "All of us wanted Russia in the Japanese War. Had we known what
the Atomic Bomb would do we'd have never wanted the Bear in the
picture."[17]

Even the precise casualty estimates that Truman cited so authorita-
tively whenever he discussed the hypothetical invasion that the atomic
bomb allegedly prevented have come in for critical scrutiny. After an
exhaustive study of this aspect of the debate over the atomic-bomb decision, Rufus E. Miles, Jr., a former senior fellow of Princeton's Woodrow
Wilson Center, concluded in 1985 that the figure of a quarter-million
casualties was "an 'off-the-top-of-the-head' estimate made in the early
spring of 1945, before the War and Navy departments realized how rapid
was the deterioration of Japan's capacity to resist, and then uncritically
repeated on various occasions after the situation had radically changed."[18]

Truman's immediate purpose, however, was to persuade not historians but the American electorate that the atomic bombing of Japan had
been necessary and praiseworthy, and in this he succeeded brilliantly.
Public opinion polls in the autumn of 1945 revealed approval ratings of
80 to 85 percent, with what *Fortune* magazine called "a considerable
minority of disappointed savagery" wishing that even more cities had
been wiped out. In newspaper editorials, approval was practically unanimous.[19]

All the arguments advanced by Truman in justifying his action struck
a responsive popular chord. The moral symmetry of the president's link-

---

[17] Harry Truman to Margaret Truman, 3 March 1948, in Margaret Truman, *Letters from
Father: The Truman Family's Personal Correspondences* (New York: Arbor House, 1981),
107; Messer, "New Evidence on Truman's Decision," 55–56; Truman diary entry, 18
July 1945, in Ferrell, ed., *Off the Record*, 54; Stimson diary entry, 21 July 1945, Yale
University Library, quoted in Gar Alperovitz, *Atomic Diplomacy: Hiroshima and Pots-
dam* (New York: Random House, 1965), 150.

[18] Rufus E. Miles, Jr., "Hiroshima: The Strange Myth of Half a Million American Lives
Saved," *International Security* 10 (Fall 1985): 136–37.

[19] "The Fortune Survey," *Fortune*, December 1945, 305; Sydnor H. Walker, ed., *The First
One Hundred Days of the Atomic Age* (New York: Woodrow Wilson Foundation, 1945),
35 (Gallup Poll); Michael J. Yavenditti, "The American People and the Use of Atomic
Bombs in Japan: The 1940s," *The Historian* 36 (February 1974): 225 (newspaper
editorials).

ing of Pearl Harbor and Hiroshima appealed strongly to a nation that recalled vividly the treachery of 7 December 1941 and for whom "Remember Pearl Harbor" had been the most powerful of wartime slogans. A *Chicago Tribune* cartoonist, on 8 August 1945, pictured a long fuse running from Pearl Harbor to Hiroshima, with a severed head flying over Hiroshima murmuring "So Sorry." William L. Laurence of the *New York Times*, the Manhattan Project's official chronicler, struck the same note in his 1946 history *Dawn over Zero*. Describing his emotions aboard the plane carrying the atomic bomb to Nagasaki, Laurence wrote, "Does one feel any pity or compassion for the poor devils about to die? Not when one thinks of Pearl Harbor and of the Death March on Bataan."[20]

Similarly, countless post-Hiroshima editorials, cartoons, and letters to the editor enthusiastically endorsed Truman's assertion that the atomic bomb was fair retribution for Japanese atrocities in the Philippines and the brutal island campaigns of the Pacific. Some of this commentary reflected the same racism that underlay Truman's description of the Japanese as "beasts." As John Dower has shown, American anti-Japanese propaganda during the war was deeply racist, and it is hardly surprising that racist arguments and images should have been employed in the rush to justify the atomic bomb. "Hirohito is the representative of the devil," a North Dakota listener wrote radio news commentator H. V. Kaltenborn after Hiroshima; "He and his palace should be blowed off the map with an atomic bomb." A *Philadelphia Inquirer* cartoon on 7 August portrayed a brutish, apelike creature staring up in dumb wonder as an atomic bomb burst overhead. Many newspaper letters expressed regret that atomic bombs had not been used to destroy all human life in Japan. A Milwaukee woman expressed her genocidal impulses this way: "When one sets out to destroy vermin, does one try to leave a few alive in the nest? Certainly not!"[21]

Truman's insistent claim that the only alternative to the atomic bomb would have been a protracted land invasion of Japan was also widely accepted. An editorial cartoon in the *Louisville Courier-Journal*, captioned "Bloodless Invasion," pictured a GI striding ashore in Japan as a phantom corpse representing "Avoided Costs" sprawls on the sand

[20] William L. Laurence, *Dawn over Zero: The Story of the Atomic Bomb* (New York: Alfred A. Knopf, 1946), 234.
[21] Leonie M. Cole to editor, *Milwaukee Journal*, 16 August 1945; W. J. Rademacher, New Leipzig, N. D., to H. V. Kaltenborn, 12 August 1945, Kaltenborn Papers, State Historical Society of Wisconsin, Box 107; John Dower, *War Without Mercy: Race and Power in the Pacific War* (New York: Pantheon Books, 1986).

beside him. Some commentators went further, arguing that the atomic bomb was actually a blessing for the Japanese, sparing them the enormous losses the hypothetical land invasion would have entailed. A *Chicago Tribune* editorial praising Truman and his advisers for deciding to drop the bomb expressed this point succinctly: "Being merciless, they were merciful."[22]

Why did most Americans accept so eagerly and uncritically Truman's claim that if the atomic bomb had not been used the war would have dragged on for perhaps another eighteen months at a hideous cost in blood and suffering? Why, in the face of the mounting body of historical evidence to the contrary, do many, perhaps most, Americans still remain firmly convinced that the bomb "saved hundreds of thousands of American lives"? The answer, presumably, is that myths of this tenacity serve necessary psychological functions. As Rufus E. Miles, Jr., has observed:

The use of these figures [estimating invasion casualties] by Truman and others can be explained by a subconscious compulsion to persuade themselves and the American public that, horrible as the atomic bombs were, their use was actually humane inasmuch as it saved a huge number of lives. The larger the estimate of deaths averted, the more self-evidently justified the action seemed. Exaggerating these figures avoided, in large part, the awkward alternative of having to rethink and explain a complex set of circumstances and considerations that influenced the decision to drop the bomb.[23]

Not everyone accepted the government's attempts to rationalize the nuclear annihilation of well over a hundred thousand men, women, and children of a defeated nation teetering on the brink of surrender. Even in the perfervid emotional climate of the war and its immediate aftermath, a small minority of Americans expressed grave reservations about the official deeds performed in their name. Others who did not condemn Truman's decision categorically were nevertheless unprepared to accept his strident insistence that the action was so obviously justified as not even to merit reflection or debate.[24] These responses, too, constituted a part of the post-Hiroshima cultural and moral landscape, and as such they deserve attention and study. But the fact remains that the overwhelming majority of Americans, as well as the nation's principal media outlets, found little to question in the atomic bombing of Hiroshima and

[22] "For This We Fight," *Chicago Daily Tribune*, 11 August 1945; "But for the Grace of God" (cartoon), *Louisville Courier-Journal*, 30 August 1945.
[23] Miles, "Hiroshima," 138.
[24] Paul Boyer, *By the Bomb's Early Light: American Thought and Culture of the Dawn of the Atomic Age* (New York: Pantheon Books, 1985), 196–210.

Nagasaki. In short, the pattern of Truman's own response to the bomb—vociferous public justification with an undercurrent of barely acknowledged uneasiness and doubt—quite accurately reflected and encapsulated the reaction of the larger American public.

The larger meaning of atomic energy

What of the atomic future? What were the implications of the unleashing of the atom? And what larger meanings could one extract from this momentous event? Here, too, the responses of President Truman, both public and private, paralleled and helped shape those of the larger public. Again, Truman's initial announcement of 6 August 1945 must be the starting point. This 1,100-word message provided no information, even of the sketchiest sort, about the probable human or physical toll at Hiroshima. The Alamogordo test, and the scale of destructiveness it had demonstrated, was passed over in silence. Radiation was unmentioned.

Rather, the theme of the message was upbeat and positive. The drama and vast scope of the Manhattan Project were vividly evoked, underscoring the supremacy of U.S. industrial might and technological know-how:

We now have two great plants and many lesser works devoted to the production of atomic power. Employment during peak construction numbered 125,000 and over 65,000 individuals are even now engaged in operating the plants. Many have worked there for two and a half years. Few know what they have been producing. They see great quantities of material going in and they see nothing coming out of these plants, for the physical size of the explosive charge is exceedingly small. We have spent two billion dollars on the greatest scientific gamble in history—and won.[25]

Even more than on the technological wonder of the Manhattan Project, Truman's announcement dwelled on the scientific achievement. For the United States in 1945, news of the atomic bomb came embedded in a glowing hymn of praise to science:

The greatest marvel is not the size of the enterprise, its secrecy, nor its cost, but the achievement of scientific brains in putting together infinitely complex pieces of knowledge held by many men in different fields of science into a workable plan. . . . The brain child of many minds came forth in physical shape and performed as it was supposed to do. . . . What has been done is the greatest achievement of organized science in history.[26]

[25] "White House Press Release on Hiroshima, 6 August 1945," Williams and Cantelon, eds., *American Atom*, 69.
[26] Ibid; *New York Times*, 7 August 1945, 4.

This dramatic scientific breakthrough, Truman continued, held vast promise for enlarging human knowledge; indeed, it had ushered in "a new era in man's understanding of nature's forces." Truman reiterated the point in his atomic-energy message to Congress of 3 October 1945. Although the atom posed "potential danger," it was "at the same time . . . full of promise for the future of man and for the peace of the world."[27]

As for the immediate practical benefits to be expected from this triumph of science, Truman's 6 August announcement struck a cautious note, warning that only after "a long period of intensive research" would atomic energy be available for nonmilitary purposes. But soon the cautionary note faded in a glow of hyperbole. Atomic energy, proclaimed Truman in his 3 October congressional message, "may someday prove to be more revolutionary in the development of human society than the invention of the wheel, the use of metals, or steam or internal combustion engines." Speaking extemporaneously at a county fair in Missouri at about the same time, Truman predicted that knowledge of the atom would lead to "the happiest world that the sun has ever shone upon."[28]

The positive note was emphasized, too, in several of Truman's state-of-the-union messages. Significantly, the advent of the atomic bomb, surely a major event of 1945, was not even mentioned in Truman's first such message, in January 1946. When the subject of atomic energy *was* first raised, in the January 1947 message, it was in the context of the atom's great promise: "In the vigorous and effective development of peaceful uses of atomic energy," the president declared, "rests our hope that this new force may ultimately be turned into a blessing for all nations." With variations, similar bright hopes are expressed in the remainder of Truman's state-of-the-union messages through the end of his term of office.[29]

If Henry Stimson was Truman's principal collaborator in the campaign to justify the decision to drop the atomic bomb, his most effective lieutenant in promulgating the message of the peaceful atom was David E. Lilienthal. As head of the Tennessee Valley Authority in the 1930s, Lilienthal had emerged as a tireless public advocate for the vision of large-scale federal development projects. As chairman of the Atomic Energy

[27] Truman, *Year of Decisions*, 530.
[28] Ibid; Donovan, *Crisis and Conflict*, 132.
[29] State of the Union Message, 6 January 1947, in Fred L. Israel, ed., *The State of the Union Messages of the Presidents, 1790–1966* (New York: Chelsea House, 1966), III, 2948.

Commission from its creation in 1946 until 1950, Lilienthal brought the same zeal and eloquence to spreading the vision of a world transformed by atomic energy. Often featured in the press as "Mr. Atom," Lilienthal labored mightily to flesh out Truman's upbeat message and give a benevolent aura to the new atomic reality. While debunking the more ludicrously exaggerated claims of some popularizers, Lilienthal extolled the atom's peacetime promise in countless speeches and magazine articles. In a nationally broadcast 1948 high school graduation address delivered at Gettysburg, Pennsylvania, Lilienthal spoke with almost strident optimism of the vast future benefits of atomic energy. Ignore the prophets of doom and their "predictions of dire and utter calamity," Lilienthal advised. With "knowledge, love, [and] faith," the atomic age could be "one of the blessed periods of all human history."

Lilienthal frequently described atomic energy as simply a form of solar energy—and potentially as beneficial. As he put it in another high school commencement speech, this one in Crawfordsville, Indiana: "I suppose there is nothing of a physical nature that is more friendly to man, or more necessary to his well-being than the sun. From the sun you and I get . . . the energy that gives life and sustains life, the energy that builds skyscrapers and churches, that writes poems and symphonies." Yet this same benevolent, life-giving sun, Lilienthal concluded triumphantly, was nothing but "a huge atomic-energy factory."[30]

Such pronouncements reflected Lilienthal's almost mystical belief in the power of positive thinking—his conviction that merely to turn people's thoughts from the atomic bomb to speculation about possible peacetime applications, whatever the actual reality, was a significant social achievement. The psychological value of atomic energy as a "stimulus to the imagination, an awakening force," observed Lilienthal in a 1947 diary entry, was much more important than any specific practical use. After an address to 4,500 delegates at the annual convention of the American Farm Bureau in Chicago later that year, Lilienthal reflected, "It was wonderful to see how profoundly moved these people are when one talks about eliminating this as a weapon, putting it to beneficial uses. . . . I added a conclusion, reverting to the note of 'service to humanity

---

[30] David E. Lilienthal, "Youth in the Atomic Age," *NEA Journal* (September 1948): 370–71 (Gettysburg Speech); Lilienthal, "Atomic Energy is *Your* Business," *Bulletin of the Atomic Scientists* (November 1947): 335–36 (Crawfordsville speech); Boyer, *By the Bomb's Early Light*, 125, 294–95, 302.

and the Kingdom of God,' and that audience seemed to merge into a single picture, . . . a unified presence, you might say; it was like uttering a benediction."[31]

President Truman strongly backed Lilienthal's efforts to turn the public mind from atomic weapons to the promise of atomic energy. Dramatizing this theme, Truman at the initiative of the Atomic Energy Commission (AEC) sent a telegram to an international conference of cancer specialists meeting at St. Louis in 1947, announcing that scientists all over the world would be given access to radioactive isotopes (by-products of the government's nuclear-weapons program) to aid in the fight against cancer. During a February 1950 meeting with Truman, two weeks after the president's hydrogen-bomb decision, Lilienthal noted in his diary Truman's full agreement "that my theme of Atoms for Peace is just what the country needs."[32]

Reflecting Lilienthal's upbeat emphasis, the AEC in the late 1940s initiated the preparation of booklets, films, exhibitions, and curricular materials publicizing the atom's beneficent promise. Prominent in this effort was the Brookhaven National Laboratory, a Long Island facility jointly funded and administered by the AEC and nine large eastern universities. Much of the AEC's limited nonmilitary research was centered at Brookhaven, and members of its staff frequently spoke to public gatherings and the press, "trying to prove, against heavy odds [as a skeptical New Yorker reporter put it] that atomic energy has its attractive side." Brookhaven's public-relations office assembled two traveling exhibits featuring movies, audiovisual displays, and live demonstrations. Exhibitions were mounted in a number of cities and at the American Museum of Natural History in New York. Reporting on a Brookhaven road-show presentation in Stamford, Connecticut, under the title "Main Street Meets the Atom," Science Illustrated described the fascination of adults and the delighted reaction of children to such exhibits as a Van de Graff generator and an "atomic pinball machine"—an atomic-pile simulation complete with gong and blinking lights.[33]

The high point of this exercise in government-inspired positive think-

[31] David E. Lilienthal, The Atomic Energy Years (New York: Harper & Row, 1964), 160, 269 (15 March and 16 December 1947 diary entries).

[32] Ibid., 635 (14 February 1950 diary entry); Harry M. Davis, Energy Unlimited: The Electron and the Atom in Everyday Life (New York: Murray Hill Books, 1947), 3.

[33] "Main Street Meets the Atom," Science Illustrated, April 1948, 19–23, 68–69; Daniel Lang, "The Long Island Atoms," New Yorker, 20 December 1947, 33; Michael Amrine, "Exhibits as a Technique in Atomic Education," Journal of Educational Sociology 22 (January 1949): 343–47.

ing came in the summer of 1948 with "Man and the Atom," a month-long exhibition in New York's Central Park. This show was jointly sponsored by the AEC and its major corporate contractors for nuclear-power development (General Electric and Westinghouse) and the New York Committee on Atomic Information—an umbrella group of various service organizations. The exhibit's centerpiece was Westinghouse's Theater of Atoms, featuring such eye-catching exhibits as a "real radiation detector"; a simulated chain reaction (with sixty interconnected mouse traps); and a model of an atomic nucleus that, according to a Westinghouse public-relations spokesman, resembled a "futuristic Christmas tree" and exploded harmlessly with a "blinding flash [and] an ear-splitting crash!"[34]

Visitors to the General Electric (GE) exhibit at the "Man and the Atom" show received free copies of "Splitting the Atom—Starring Dagwood and Blondie," a comic book produced by King Features Syndicate in consultation with the AEC, in which Mandrake the Magician reduced Dagwood and Blondie to molecular size to explain the wonders of the atom to them. The emphasis of this exhibition was almost entirely on stimulating positive public attitudes toward the peacetime promise of atomic energy. In the GE comic book, for example, when Mandrake demonstrates a chain reaction (as silly Dagwood rushes off in a panic shouting "Blondie!"), the "BANG!" in the center of the picture is balanced by drawings of a power plant, a factory, a grain field, a medical lab, and a ship—depicting the many uses of the peaceful atom. Even if most of the nonmilitary applications featured in the exhibit either lay far in the future or had already proven infeasible, Westinghouse's public-relations spokesman disingenuously insisted, surely this was "a better note to strike . . . than emphasizing the destruction of bombs."[35]

Following the lead of Truman, Lilienthal, and the AEC, the American media in these years heavily promoted the vision of an atomic utopia ahead. Although the "Atoms for Peace" program as a formal U.S. policy initiative dates from President Dwight Eisenhower's United Nations speech of December 1953, the theme was in fact omnipresent in the Truman years as well. In one of its more dramatic expressions, CBS radio in June 1947 broadcast an hour-long documentary, "The Sunny Side of the Atom," designed to publicize the vast promise of radioactive isotopes and,

---

[34] Richard C. Hitchcock, "Westinghouse Theater of Atoms," *Journal of Educational Sociology* 22 (January 1949): 353–56.

[35] Ibid., 354, 355; Richard C. Robin, "Power from the Atom," ibid., 350–53; Louis M. Heil and Joe Musial, "'Splitting the Atom' Starring Dagwood and Blondie: How It Developed," ibid., 331–36.

according to a publicist, counteract "the 'scare' approach to atomic education." With Agnes Moorehead as narrator, the program featured visits to a physician's office, where isotopes help in the diagnosis of a patient; a great medical facility, where researchers seek "a cure for cancer with the aid of isotopes"; a southwestern oil field, where isotopes seek out residual oil in abandoned wells; and an "atom farm," where vast agricultural research projects use isotopes. After a fleeting reference to the horror of nuclear war, Moorehead's narrative ended on a note of soaring triumph: "Everything I have seen, everything I have heard, everything I have felt has given me this faith: We are bigger than the atom, and if we face the future boldly, we will enter a world made bright by the sunny side of the atom."[36]

Numerous magazine feature articles struck the same note, portraying the enormous promise of the atomic age. The applications of atomic energy to the treatment of cancer and other ills, reported *Collier's* in May 1947, offered "cures for hitherto incurable diseases" and opened the door to a "golden age of atomic medicine." Once "atomic medicine" became universally available, this article concluded, "much of the pain and premature death which now face so many of us may prove to be avoidable." This feature was illustrated with a composite photograph of a former cripple, healed by atomic energy, emerging smiling from a mushroom-shaped cloud, his empty wheelchair in the background. Writing in the *American* magazine at about the same time, Chancellor Robert M. Hutchins of the University of Chicago gave his imagination full rein: "The atomic city will have a central diagnostic laboratory, but only a small hospital, if any at all, for most human ailments will be cured as rapidly as they are diagnosed."[37]

Thanks to atomic energy, declared *Operation Atomic Vision*, a 1948 high school study unit prepared by the National Education Association, "It is unlikely that you or any of your classmates will die prematurely of cancer or heart disease, or from any contagious diseases, or from any other human ills that afflict us now. Many of our generation will reach the century mark. . . . No one will need to work long hours. There will be much leisure, and a network of large recreational areas will cover the country, if not the world." In "Atom: Key to Better Farming," *U.S. News*

[36] "The Sunny Side of the Atom," CBS radio broadcast, 30 June 1947, script in Papers of the Atomic Scientists of Chicago, Regenstein Library, University of Chicago, Box 19, Folder 14.

[37] Robert M. Hutchins, "The Bomb Secret Is Out!" *American Magazine*, December 1947, 137; Albert Q. Maisel, "Medical Dividend," *Collier's*, 3 May 1947, 14, 44.

and World Report in June 1948 enthusiastically described the amazing agricultural breakthroughs that isotopes would make possible, including vastly increased crop yields through radioactive fertilizer; the synthesizing of gasoline, coal, and food; and further wonders "bigger and more important than the scientists themselves can imagine right now."[38]

A capstone of sorts to this genre was "A World Worth Waiting For," a 1948 article in *Coronet* magazine offering a breathless and uncritically positive "glimpse into the future of the Atomic Age." Isotope tracers, *Coronet* predicted, would one day decode the basic metabolic processes of animals, leading to "the fantastic possibility . . . of directing that growth into channels most useful to man. And then may come the control of growth in man himself!" Like many other visionary atomic-energy articles in these years, this one concluded on a note of high inspiration and promise: "Atomic energy is to us what the Atlantic Ocean was to Columbus when he sailed from Spain. He set out to find India but discovered the Western Hemisphere instead. Who can tell where our voyage into this unknown realm will lead?"[39] Who indeed?

This government and media blitz had its effect. In a 1948 Gallup Poll, 61 percent of college-educated Americans answered affirmatively the question: "Do you think that, in the long run, atomic energy will do more good than harm?" Other surveys produced similarly positive results.[40] This emphasis on a thrilling if somewhat amorphous atomic utopia ahead, tentatively advanced in President Truman's initial atomic-bomb announcement and then massively reinforced by official and media sources in the succeeding months and years, had a profound influence in shaping the initial responses of the American people to the nuclear reality.

On a more general plane, the positive view of science that pervades Truman's 6 August announcement also mirrored and helped shape the broader public response. In the early post-Hiroshima period, newspapers, magazines, and radio were full of glowing accounts of the Manhattan Project as a crowning triumph of the Age of Science. Photographs of J. Robert Oppenheimer and other leading physicists stared from every

[38] "Atom: Key to Better Farming," *U.S. News and World Report,* 4 June 1948, 26–27; Hubert M. Evans, Ryland W. Crary, and C. Glen Hass, *Operation Atomic Vision* (Washington, D.C.: Committee on Curriculum Planning and Development, National Association of Secondary School Principals, 1948), 6–7.

[39] Harold Wolff, "A World Worth Waiting For," *Coronet,* November 1948, 31–38. For a more extended discussion of the campaign to encourage positive public perception of atomic energy, see Boyer, *By the Bomb's Early Light,* 291–302.

[40] George N. Gallup, ed., *The Gallup Poll: Public Opinion, 1935–1971* (New York: Random House, 1972), vol. I, 767.

page, and the pronouncements of scientists ranging from Albert Einstein down to the lowliest physics graduate students caught up in the Manhattan Project were given almost reverent attention. "Hats off to the men of research," declared the *Milwaukee Journal* on 8 August 1945. Never again, proclaimed the *St. Louis Post-Dispatch,* should the nation's "science-explorers . . . be denied anything needful for their adventures." The scientists themselves did little to discourage this adulation. "However deplorable the human deficiencies that made it necessary for American and British scientists to develop the atomic bomb," observed the American Association for the Advancement of Science in September 1945, "we must admire their glorious achievement. . . . Modern Prometheans have raided Mount Olympus again and have brought back for man the very thunderbolts of Zeus."[41]

In post-Hiroshima editorial cartoons, scientists typically appear as awesome, larger-than-life figures. In one, a scientist, represented as a person so gigantic only his lower legs are visible, passes the knowledge of atomic energy to a dwarf-like figure labeled "The Statesmen." Another cartoon portraying a somber scientist offering the atomic secret to the human race represented as a crawling, diaper-clad infant was captioned, "Baby Play With Nice Ball?"[42]

But as the mixed messages of such cartoons suggest, there was a darker side to the post-Hiroshima view of science, and this, too, was anticipated by President Truman. Characteristically, however, Truman did not reveal his bleaker reflections publicly. On 16 July, the day he first learned of the successful test at Alamogordo, he wrote in his diary: "I hope for some sort of peace—but I fear that machines are ahead of morals by some centuries and when morals catch up perhaps there'll be no reason for any of it. I hope not. But we are only termites on a planet and maybe when we bore too deeply into the planet there'll [be] a reckoning—who knows?" On 25 July, after Stimson had flown to Potsdam with a detailed account of the Alamogordo blast by eyewitnesses, Truman characterized the report as "startling—to put it mildly." Brooding on this "most terrible bomb in the history of the world . . . the most terrible thing ever discovered," he expressed his fear of apocalypse in biblical imagery: "It

---

[41] F. L. Campbell, "Science on the March," *Scientific Monthly,* September 1945, 234; "A Decision for Mankind," *St. Louis Post-Dispatch,* 7 August 1945.

[42] *Time,* 20 August 1945, 19; *New Republic,* 11 February 1946, 179. See also Boyer, *By the Bomb's Early Light,* 266–68.

may be the fire destruction prophesied in the Euphrates Valley Era, after Noah and his fabulous Ark."[43]

In these sober reflections on Alamogordo, Truman anticipated in an uncanny way a spontaneous popular response to the Hiroshima news that would come a few days later—a response of profound apprehension and even terror, often expressed in nightmarish images of universal destruction. The Reverend John Haynes Holmes of New York City, vacationing at his summer cottage in Kennebunk, Maine, on 6 August, shortly afterward described his response to the news: "Everything else seemed suddenly to become insignificant. I seemed to grow cold, as though I had been transported to the waste space of the moon. The summer beauty seemed to vanish, and the waves of the sea to be pounding upon the shores of an empty world. . . . For I knew that the final crisis in human history had come. What that atomic bomb had done to Japan, it could do to us."[44]

Millions of Americans had the same instantaneous, intuitive prevision of holocaust—a realization that could coexist, strangely enough, with grim satisfaction over the atomic bombing of Japan and even with fantasies of an atomic utopia ahead. Radio newscasters compared Hiroshima with U.S. cities of similar size like New Haven and Denver. Newspapers printed maps of their own communities overlaid by concentric circles showing the pattern of devastation at Hiroshima. Photographs of Hiroshima and Nagasaki were transmuted into images of American cities in smoldering ruin. "As we listen to the newscast, as we read our newspapers tomorrow," intoned H. V. Kaltenborn on 17 August 1945, "let us think of the mass murder which will come with World War III." Physically untouched by the war, the United States at the moment of victory perceived itself as naked and vulnerable. The life expectancy of the human species, said the *Washington Post* on 26 August, had "dwindled immeasurably in the course of two brief weeks."[45]

This fear pervaded all levels of society, from Nobel laureates and government leaders to persons who scarcely grasped what had happened but sensed that it was deeply menacing. The "strange disquiet" and "very great apprehension" the atomic bomb had aroused, wrote theologian

[43] Truman diary entries, 16 and 25 July, 1945, in Ferrell, ed., *Off the Record*, 52–53, 55, 56.
[44] John Haynes Holmes, "Editorial Comment," *Unity*, September 1945, 99.
[45] *Washington Post*, 26 August 1945; Kaltenborn broadcast script, 17 August 1945, Kaltenborn Papers; Boyer, *By the Bomb's Early Light*, 6–8, 13–26.

Reinhold Niebuhr, was particularly intense among "the more sober and thoughtful sections of our nation." Eugene Rabinowitch, a chemist with the Manhattan Project, later recalled walking the streets of Chicago the summer of 1945 haunted by visions of "the sky suddenly lit by a giant fireball, the steel skeletons of skyscrapers bending into grotesque shapes and their masonry raining down into the streets below, until a great cloud of dust rose and settled over the crumbling city." "The 36-Hour War," a November 1945 *Life* magazine article describing the nuclear annihilation of America's cities, was illustrated with chillingly realistic drawings of a mushroom cloud rising over Washington, D.C., and of the marble lions of the New York City Public Library gazing sightlessly over the rubble of a demolished city.[46]

As they did for Harry Truman, these visions of atomic destruction often summoned up apocalyptic images remembered from the Bible. A 1945 country-music hit entitled "Atomic Power" spoke of divine judgment and brimstone fire raining down from heaven. Biblical prophecies of universal destruction in the last days ("The heavens shall pass away with a great noise, and the elements shall melt with fervent heat, the earth also and the works that are therein shall be burned up") were much quoted in 1945, their familiar cadences taking on a new and ominous meaning.[47]

Truman's diary jottings of July 1945 also revealed a far more ambivalent view of science than he conveyed in his public proclamations—a view not of brilliant researchers unlocking the atom's secrets for the ultimate benefit of mankind but of voracious termites burrowing into the planet with unpredictable but probably catastrophic consequences. Here again, Truman's response anticipated an important thread in the larger cultural reaction to the atomic bomb. Accompanying the post-Hiroshima praise for the scientific miracle workers who had accomplished this marvel was a strain of nagging apprehension about where science and its handmaiden technology were leading humankind. If, as Truman was boasting, the atomic bomb was "the greatest achievement of organized science in history," wrote Dwight Macdonald in his one-man journal of opinion *politics* a few days after Hiroshima, then "so much the worse for organized science." It was grotesque, he suggested, to present this city-

[46] "The 36-Hour War," *Life,* 19 November 1945; Reinhold Niebuhr, "Our Relations with Japan," *Christianity and Crisis,* 17 September 1945, 5; Eugene Rabinowitch, "Five Years After," *Bulletin of the Atomic Scientists* (January 1951): 3.

[47] Charles Wolfe, "Nuclear Country: The Atomic Bomb in Country Music," *Journal of Country Music* 7 (January 1978): 7–13. The biblical passage quoted is II Peter 3:10.

destroying machine as a giant leap forward in the march of science. Macdonald's view of the Manhattan Project was closer to Truman's private apprehensions than to the president's expansive public pronouncements. For Macdonald, the horror of the atomic bomb was immeasurably deepened by the fact that it represented the end product of an elaborately bureaucratized project involving the uncoerced labor of 125,000 people, only a handful of whom had the slightest idea what they were doing.[48]

Dwight Macdonald expressed with particular vehemence one extreme of a complex and ambivalent set of public attitudes toward science in the early postwar period. In powerful counterpoint to the enthusiasm for scientists as technological wonder-workers that Truman insisted (in public) was the true meaning of Hiroshima, one also finds strong currents of fear, mistrust, and disillusionment. "Grave doubts are in many minds, and science is being regarded both with greater respect and with greater apprehension than ever before," observed *Scientific Monthly* in September 1945. The atomic bomb had "entirely transformed lay thinking regarding science," wrote the Manhattan Project physicist Louis Ridenour early in 1946; "[People] are beginning to hate and fear [it]."[49]

Much evidence supports these assessments of the public mood. Newspaper editorials and letters to the editor, for example, reflected praise and fear of science in about equal proportions. "Science a Menace" and "Science Moving Too Fast" were the captions of typical letters. A letter published in the *Portland Oregonian* called the bomb "the idiot child of science and the machine age." A *St. Louis Post-Dispatch* editorial could simultaneously praise this scientific "triumph" and brood that it may have "signed the mammalian world's death warrant." The very search for truth that was science's "noblest attribute," observed Raymond B. Fosdick, the president of the Rockefeller Foundation, in a November 1945 radio address, "has brought our civilization to the brink of destruction. ... What do we do," Fosdick asked, "curb our science or cling to the pursuit of truth and run the risk of having our society torn to pieces?"[50] It is a dilemma that remains with us still, and one that Harry Truman, in

---

[48] Dwight Macdonald, editorial, *Politics*, August 1945 (quoted passage); "The Bomb," ibid., September 1945.

[49] Louis N. Ridenour, "Science and Secrecy," *American Scholar* (Spring 1946): 151; Campbell, "Science on the March," 234.

[50] Raymond B. Fosdick, "A Layman Looks at Science," radio address, 4 November 1945, extracts in Walker, ed., *First One Hundred Days of the Atomic Age*, 62; *Portland Oregonian*, 12 August 1945; "A Decision for Mankind," *St. Louis Post-Dispatch*, 7 August 1945. See also Boyer, *By the Bomb's Early Light*, 268–72.

the privacy of his diary, was already struggling with before the rest of the world had even heard of the atomic bomb.

The contemplated uses of atomic weapons

One final question merits attention in this brief exploration of the inter-woven responses of the American people and their president to the atomic bomb. What postwar diplomatic and military uses, if any, were envis-aged for what Bernard Baruch in 1946 called America's "winning weapon"? On this critical question, too, Truman vacillated in ways that reflected the larger uncertainty of the American people. In his post-Hiroshima public pronouncements, Truman always insisted that a fun-damental objective of U.S. policy was to devise a system of international control that would end the U.S. atomic supremacy, forestall a dangerous nuclear arms race, and ensure that the bomb would never again be used. The Acheson-Lilienthal plan of March 1946, to which historians have given much attention, was presented to the world as an expression of this high-minded objective.

At the same time, Truman was clearly prepared to gain whatever stra-tegic advantage he could from the U.S. atomic monopoly that continued until September 1949 and the overwhelming U.S. atomic superiority that lasted considerably longer. As he wrote jauntily to Bess from Potsdam on 31 July 1945, using a metaphor drawn from his favorite game: "I rather think Mr. Stalin is stallin' because he is not so happy over the English elections. [Clement Attlee had replaced Winston Churchill as prime min-ister.] He doesn't know it but I have an ace in the hole and another one showing—so unless he has threes or two pair (and I know he has not) we are sitting all right."[51] As numerous studies have now demonstrated, all Truman's thinking and decision making regarding nuclear weapons from July 1945 through the end of his term invariably reflected his preoccu-pation with the U.S.-Soviet power nexus.

As the cold war worsened, did Truman ever envisage the atomic bomb not only as a diplomatic asset in his maneuverings with the Soviets but as something that actually might be used again? In various public pro-nouncements, as well as in occasional private communications within the government, Truman firmly rejected such an option. Thus when Army Secretary Kenneth Royall urged a preemptive nuclear strike against the Soviets during the 1948 Berlin blockade crisis, Truman made plain that

[51] Harry Truman to Bess Truman, 31 July 1945, in Ferrell, ed., *"Dear Bess,"* 522.

he considered such an action not only unthinkable morally but appalling in its strategic and diplomatic short-sightedness: "You have got to understand that this isn't a military weapon. It is used to wipe out women and children and unarmed people, and not for military uses. You have got to understand that I have got to think about the effect of such a thing on international relations. This is no time to be juggling an atom bomb around."[52]

When the cold war turned hot in Korea, however, Truman himself toyed with the nuclear option. At a news conference on 30 November 1950, after the Chinese invasion across the Yalu River, Truman was asked about the possible use of the atomic bomb. He replied: "There has always been active consideration of its use. I don't want to see it used. It is a terrible weapon and it should not be used on innocent men, women, and children who have nothing whatever to do with this military aggression." When the respected Merriman Smith of the United Press asked the president explicitly to confirm whether dropping the atomic bomb was, indeed, under "active consideration," he answered tersely: "Always has been. It is one of our weapons." When asked whether the targets being considered were civilian or military, he responded that this was a "matter that the military people have to decide. I'm not a military authority that passes on those things. . . . The military commander in the field will have charge of the use of weapons, as he always has."[53]

The newspapers reported the story in banner headlines. A United Press bulletin proclaimed: "PRESIDENT TRUMAN SAID TODAY THE UNITED STATES HAS UNDER ACTIVE CONSIDERATION USE OF THE ATOMIC BOMB IN CONNECTION WITH THE WAR IN KOREA." An alarmed Prime Minister Attlee flew to Washington to dissuade the president from precipitate action.[54]

In her biography of her father, Margaret Truman describes this episode as "all ridiculous, and very disheartening." It was, she writes, a classic example of journalistic distortion and sensationalism. Indeed, she implicitly blames the press's handling of this story for the fatal heart attack suffered a few days later by Truman's old friend and press secre-

[52] Quoted in Gregg Herken, *The Winning Weapon: The Atomic Bomb in the Cold War, 1945–1950* (New York: Alfred A. Knopf, 1980), 260. Compare this statement with the one from Truman's memoirs, quoted earlier, justifying the decision to drop the bomb on Hiroshima and Nagasaki: "I regarded the bomb as a military weapon, and never had any doubt that it should be used."

[53] Truman news conference, 30 November 1950, quoted in Margaret Truman, *Harry S. Truman* (New York: William Morrow, 1973), 495–96.

[54] Ibid., 497.

tary Charlie Ross.[55] Yet when one reads Truman's clear answers to a series of clear questions, it is difficult to see how the reporters distorted or misrepresented his views. Truman's comments seemed clearly to indicate that use of the atomic bomb in the Korean War, while deeply deplorable, was indeed under active consideration and that targeting decisions would be left to "the military commander in the field"—General Douglas MacArthur, well known for his advocacy of turning the Korean conflict into a war of destruction against communist China.

In 1952, with his popularity sagging at home and the armistice talks bogged down at Panmunjom, Truman again considered the nuclear option, this time in the form of two memorandums evidently written to clarify his own thinking and spelling out in specific detail a nuclear ultimatum to the Soviets. The first, dated 27 January 1952, says:

It seems to me that the proper approach now would be an ultimatum with a 10-day expiration limit, informing Moscow that we intend to blockade the China coast from the Korean border to Indochina, and that we intend to destroy every military base in Manchuria by means now in our control—and if there is further interference we shall eliminate any ports or cities necessary to accomplish our purposes.

This means all-out war. It means that Moscow, St. Petersburg, Mukden, Vladivostok, Peking, Shanghai, Port Arthur, Darien, Odessa, Stalingrad, and every manufacturing plant in China and the Soviet Union will be eliminated.[56]

In the second of these two remarkable memos, this one written in May 1952, Truman actually drafted his ultimatum to "the Commies": "Now do you want an end to hostilities in Korea or do you want China and Siberia destroyed? You may have one or the other; whichever you want, these lies of yours at this conference have gone far enough. You either accept our fair and just proposal or you will be completely destroyed."[57]

It is important to place these documents in context. Apart from the 1950 news conference mentioned above, Truman in his public pronouncements dismissed all talk of employing atomic weapons in the Korean War. Indeed, he had recalled General MacArthur in April 1951 in part over MacArthur's insistent calls for a wider war. And the Truman administration had firmly rejected NSC 100, the 1951 proposal by Stuart Symington, chairman of the National Security Resources Board, to the National Security Council calling for a nuclear attack on China and pos-

[55] Ibid., 498–99.
[56] Quoted in "Truman Considered All-out War in 1952," *New York Times*, 3 August 1980, 20.
[57] Ibid.

sibly the Soviet Union. In this context, Gregg Herken is probably correct in suggesting that Truman's Rambo-like private musings are best seen as "more an expression of pique than of policy."[58] Yet in a nuclear age, even such "pique" by a U.S. president cannot be dismissed lightly.

Clearly, Truman's view of the military and diplomatic utility of the atomic bomb was ambivalent. He could readily state the compelling arguments against using the bomb (except when looking back on Hiroshima and Nagasaki) and he recognized the terrible dangers of nuclear threats and bluster. Yet when his frustration level rose high enough— whether against Stalin at Potsdam or the communists in Korea—his thinking invariably circled back to the alluring option of resolving his frustrations once and for all with his ace in the hole.

In this respect, too, Truman's ambivalence mirrored to a striking degree the ambivalence of the American public: fearful of the bomb, aware of the horror of nuclear war, yet longing to translate the nation's atomic supremacy into a decisive stroke against the new postwar enemy. Here it is important to note that, at least for some Americans, Truman's ringing defense of the use of the atomic bomb against Japan had larger implications. If the bomb was justified against one enemy, they plausibly asked, why not against another? As one reader wrote the *New Yorker* after the publication of John Hersey's *Hiroshima* in August 1946, "I read Hersey's report. It was marvelous. Now let us drop a handful on Moscow." A letter published in the *New York Daily News* at about the same time drew the same linkage: "Russia shows by its spy activities in Canada that it badly wants the atom bomb, so I say give the bomb to Russia the same way we gave it to the Japs."[59]

During the Korean War, a strong current of opinion emerged in favor of using the atomic bomb. In August 1950, a few weeks after the war began, 28 percent of Americans favored this option. When the Chinese entered the war in November, *U.S. News and World Report* noted a "wave of demand" for an atomic response. By November 1951, with the war in a costly, frustrating stalemate, 51 percent of Americans supported dropping atomic bombs on "military targets."[60]

[58] Herken, *Winning Weapon*, 334.
[59] John Gunther, *Inside USA* (New York: Harper and Brothers, 1947), 544 (*New York Daily News* quoted); Joseph Lutt and W. M. Wheeler, "Reaction to John Hersey's 'Hiroshima,' " *Journal of Social Psychology* 28 (August 1948): 138.
[60] *Gallup Poll*, II, 938, 1027 (in the November poll, 41 percent of those questioned favored the atomic bombing of military targets without qualification; 10 percent qualified their answer in various ways); "A-Bomb Will Not Beat China: Crowded Military Targets Scarce in Far East," *U.S. News and World Report*, 8 December 1950, 23.

Although some periodicals like the *Saturday Evening Post* warned that use of the atomic bomb in Korea would surely trigger World War III, others discussed the matter quite coolly, as a viable option to be carefully weighed. *Science News Letter* concluded that North Korea's urban-industrial centers were so few as probably not to "warrant" using the atomic bomb on them. After an assessment of the tactical pros and cons that ignored any larger strategic (not to mention ethical) considerations, *U.S. News and World Report* concluded in December 1950 that U.S. use of the bomb in Korea would probably be "sparing."[61]

On a different cultural front, composer Fred Kirby's 1950 country tune "When the Hell Bomb Falls" mingled images of nuclear destruction with the wish that God would "lend a helping hand" in Korea. In Roy Acuff's "Advice to Joe" (1951) the wish becomes explicit, as Acuff warns the Russians that when Moscow lies in ashes they will regret their aggressions. "When the atomic bombs start falling," the song rhetorically asks Stalin, "do you have a place to hide?"[62]

The American people and their president displayed strikingly parallel patterns of response in their risky flirtation with the atomic bomb during the Korean War. This was only the latest manifestation of a congruence of outlook that had been evident for years. From the time he learned of the Alamogordo test in July 1945, Truman's attitude toward the atomic bomb was a bundle of contradictions. He could express awe, fear, caution, bluster, or bravado, depending on his mood, his audience, and the circumstances of the moment. The very diversity and unpredictability of these reactions accurately mirrored the mood of the nation as a whole. Reacting to their political leaders, to the media, and to their own instincts, the American people displayed a wide and sometimes quite contradictory range of responses as they struggled to come to terms with the endless, ramifying implications of the news they first heard from President Truman on 6 August 1945.

Epilogue: January 1953

Truman's final and most complete comment on the atomic dilemma as president came in his state-of-the-union message of 7 January 1953, nine

---

[61] Ibid. "No Worthwhile Target for A-Bomb in North Korea," *Science Newsletter*, 22 July 1950, 50.

[62] Wolfe, "Nuclear Country," 19.

weeks after the United States exploded the world's first hydrogen bomb at Eniwetok Atoll in the South Pacific. It was an exceptionally depressing appraisal:

Now we have entered the atomic age, and war has undergone a technological change which makes it a very different thing from what it used to be. War today between the Soviet Empire and the free nations might dig the grave not only of our Stalinist opponents but of our own society, our world as well as theirs.

War's new meaning may not yet be grasped by all the peoples who would be its victims; nor, perhaps by all the rulers of the Kremlin. . . . The war of the future would be one in which man could extinguish millions of lives at one blow, demolish the great cities of the world, wipe out the cultural achievements of the past—and destroy the very structure of a civilization that has been slowly and painfully built up through hundreds of generations.

Such a war is not a possible policy for rational man. We know this, but we dare not assume that others would not yield to the temptation science is now placing in their hands.[63]

Truman went on to insist that the United States had done everything in its power to avoid a nuclear arms race; the fault lay entirely with the Soviet Union. But beneath the cold-war rhetoric lay another theme: the inevitability of an upward spiral of nuclear menace rooted in the nature of science itself. "Science and technology have worked so fast," Truman suggested, that mere presidents and premiers were helpless in the face of its inexorable advance:

The progress of scientific experiment has outrun our expectations. Atomic science is in the full tide of development; the unfolding of the innermost secrets of matter is uninterrupted and irresistible. Since Alamogordo we have developed atomic weapons with many times the explosive force of the early models, and we have produced them in substantial quantities. And recently in the thermonuclear tests at Eniwetok, we have entered another stage in the world-shaking development of atomic energy. From now on man moves in a new era of destructive power, capable of creating explosions of an order of magnitude dwarfing the mushroom clouds of Hiroshima and Nagasaki.

We have no reason to think that the stage we have now reached in the release of atomic energy will be the last. Indeed, the speed of our scientific and technical progress over the last 7 years shows no sign of abating. We are being hurried forward in our mastery of the atom, from one discovery to another, toward yet unforeseeable peaks of destructive energy. . . . It is no wonder that some people wish that we had never succeeded in splitting the atom.[64]

[63] State of the Union Message, 7 January 1953, in Israel, ed., *State of the Union Messages of the Presidents*, 3006–07.
[64] Ibid.

Truman attempted to summon up once again the soothing vision of the peaceful atom as "an instrumentality for human betterment," but the words rang hollow in this strikingly bleak panorama of nuclear menace.

Absent from these passages is the aura of confidence and mastery so characteristic of the public Truman; muted is the reassuring image of a beneficent science. Other than stoic fortitude, Truman offered no advice or hints in this farewell message as to how the nation might avoid the fate toward which an inexorable "science" was propelling it. The message was not only bleak but deeply passive and acquiescent in tone, as it described a fearful nuclear future that seemed destined to play itself out beyond human control. Harry Truman—and the American people—had come a long way since that exciting August afternoon aboard the USS *Augusta* a little more than seven years before.

Part II

Foreign policy and national defense

7

The national security state reconsidered:
Truman and economic containment, 1945–1950

ROBERT A. POLLARD

On 13 May 1948, a dramatic conference took place at the White House. Ever since the communists had seized power in Czechoslovakia in March 1948, a war scare had gripped Washington. President Harry S. Truman had already agreed to add more than $3 billion to the Pentagon's fiscal 1949 budget, raising it to $13 billion, but the Joint Chiefs of Staff (JCS) and the military services were demanding much higher sums for the following years. Now the president had had enough. Supported by Budget Director James E. Webb, Truman flatly told Secretary of Defense James V. Forrestal that he was putting a $14.4 billion ceiling (excluding stockpiling) on the fiscal 1950 defense budget.

As Truman explained to Forrestal, "Military strength is dependent on a strong economic system and a strong industrial and productive capacity." Before considering higher defense budgets, "the effect on our national economy must be weighed." Increased military expenditures could bring runaway inflation, taxes, and deficit spending. In fact, unless "world conditions deteriorate and tensions increase," the president intended to *cut* the Pentagon budget.[1]

Truman's showdown with Forrestal over the defense budget poses interesting questions about the origins of the cold war. Some of the most decisive battles of the postwar era were fought not along the iron curtain but along the Potomac. The combatants consisted of contending factions within the U.S. government, each with differing ideas about how best to

[1] According to Truman, the administration's priorities were "efficiency, economy and getting a dollar's worth of value for each dollar expended." See Truman to Forrestal, 13 May 1948, Papers of Clark M. Clifford (hereafter cited as Clifford Papers), File: National Military Establishment-Miscellaneous, Harry S. Truman Library (HSTL).

achieve the national security and world peace. Although the debate centered on the choice between a big standing military and nonmilitary instruments of foreign policy, such as economic pressure and traditional diplomacy, the fight over the budget also addressed larger issues, notably a decision about long-term U.S. strategy for dealing with Soviet expansionism. To prevail, policy advocates had to win the support of the president, for although Truman was not the only player, he was the most important player, the one who could tip the scales in favor of one group or another.

Truman's defense philosophy was based on lessons learned before the war. Like Gen. George C. Marshall, he favored a strong mobilization capacity over large forces in being, because he believed that the American public, as in the 1920s and 1930s, would not tolerate a big standing military establishment. The president also worried that high Pentagon expenditures might bankrupt the country, and he favored measures such as universal military training and heavy reliance upon air and atomic power to reduce manpower costs as much as possible. Finally, Truman believed that this country's unrivaled economic resources and political prestige made it possible to achieve its most important postwar security aims after the war without a large military.

The Truman years clearly witnessed epochal changes in U.S. foreign policy—the outbreak of the cold war, the buildup of U.S. strategic air power, and the assumption by the United States of unprecedented commitments overseas. Yet there is a common misconception about this period, namely that the "national security state" (or "military-industrial complex") first emerged during the Truman presidency.[2] It is true that many key U.S. military officials, both uniformed and civilian, called for a massive expansion of the nation's war machine after 1945. Undoubtedly, too, the United States acquired dozens of new naval and air bases around the world, particularly on the periphery of the Soviet Union.[3] There is even evidence that some (minor) White House officials sought,

[2] Some revisionist scholars contend that the Truman administration had created by late 1947 a "national security state" organized "for perpetual confrontation and for war" with the Soviet Union. NSC 68, the top-secret blueprint for U.S. rearmament developed by Dean Acheson and Paul Nitze during the first half of 1950, was supposedly the culmination of that crisis mentality. Hence massive rearmament by the United States was inevitable, with or without the Korean invasion. Quotation from Daniel Yergin, *Shattered Peace: The Origins of the Cold War and the National Security State* (Boston: Houghton Mifflin, 1978), 5. Also, see Michael S. Sherry, *Preparing for the Next War: American Plans for Postwar Defense, 1941–45* (New Haven, Conn.: Yale University Press, 1977).

[3] See Melvyn P. Leffler, "The American Conception of National Security and the Beginnings of the Cold War, 1945–1948," *American Historical Review* 89 (April 1984): 346–81.

in classic "military Keynesian" fashion, to increase the defense budget in order to fight domestic recession.[4]

None of this adds up to the national security state that critics have associated with the Vietnam War era, however. A comparison of what the administration said with what it actually did demonstrates that Truman's legacy in defense policy was, on balance, one of restraint. Although some elements of the military-industrial complex were already in place by the late 1940s, economic power remained the mainstay of U.S. security until the eve of the Korean War. And the president remained determined to balance the budget, if necessary by cutting defense spending, right up to the day that North Korean tanks crossed the thirty-eighth parallel. The United States most likely would not have rearmed on the scale that it did during the early 1950s without the Korean invasion. In view of four critical episodes early in the cold war—the enunciation of the containment doctrine in 1946, the abortive rearmament of 1948–49, the creation of NATO in 1949, and the formulation and implementation of NSC 68 in early 1950—it is perhaps more plausible to argue that if the president and his advisers erred, they erred on the side of not doing enough for military preparedness.

Demobilization

First, one should recall the problems and constraints that the new president inherited upon the death of Franklin D. Roosevelt. The unexpectedly rapid collapse of Germany in May and Japan in August 1945 had caught the administration unprepared for a series of pressing foreign and domestic decisions. In particular, the lingering isolationism in Congress and among the public, manifested in sentiment for rapid demobilization and against large-scale foreign aid and defense programs, limited the administration's ability to meet worldwide U.S. responsibilities. Secretary of the Navy Forrestal and Secretary of War Robert P. Patterson

---

[4]Some historians view the shift, beginning in 1948, from economic to military containment and the corresponding growth of defense spending as the product of U.S. economic imperatives. According to some historians, the United States rearmed in 1950 to fight domestic recession. Still others regard the U.S. military aid program to the NATO allies as a roundabout way of closing Europe's severe dollar gap in the early 1950s. See, e.g., Fred L. Block, *The Origin of International Economic Disorder: A Study of United States International Monetary Policy from World War II to the Present* (Berkeley: University of California Press, 1977), 103–07; Joyce and Gabriel Kolko, *The Limits of Power: The World and United States Foreign Policy, 1945–1954* (New York: Harper & Row, 1972), chapter 18 passim. All these variants of the national security thesis share the notion that the militarization of U.S. foreign policy was driven by its own internal dynamic.

warned Truman in October 1945 that the pell-mell disengagement of U.S. servicemen from overseas bases jeopardized the U.S. strategic position in the world. In January 1946, Under Secretary of State Dean Acheson added that demobilization "was a matter of great embarrassment and concern" to his own department in the conduct of foreign affairs.[5]

Yet the Truman White House was unable to contain the overpowering public and bipartisan congressional outcry (accompanied by riots at overseas military bases in January 1946) for the early return home of American soldiers. Only a serious foreign crisis could have reversed this trend, and, for the time being, the administration did not publicize its misgivings about Soviet behavior. As a result, the U.S. armed forces shrank from about 12 million in June 1945 to 1.5 million in June 1947. Across-the-board cuts of specialists and combat veterans eroded the effectiveness of units even more than these figures would suggest.[6]

Meanwhile, legislation for universal military training (UMT)—the White House-sponsored program that would have required virtually all young men to undergo paramilitary instruction—went nowhere on Capitol Hill. The War Department, reflecting army interests, recommended UMT over forces in being on the grounds of fiscal prudence and military efficacy. Yet some members of Congress strongly suspected that UMT, with its wholesale calling up of the country's youth for military training, was somehow "un-American." In April 1946, Congress extended the draft through March 1947 but forced the services to resort to voluntary recruitment between April 1947 and August 1948. The United States continued to maintain the largest navy and air force in the world and to retain a monopoly on the atomic bomb. But after one takes into account the U.S. commitments in occupied territories, this country lacked the ground forces required to intervene in anything greater than a minor conflict, such as the territorial dispute between Italy and Yugoslavia over Venezia Giulia.[7]

[5] Acheson quotation cited in Walter Millis, ed., *The Forrestal Diaries* (New York: Viking Press, 1951), 129; also, see Robert J. Donovan, *Conflict and Crisis: The Presidency of Harry S. Truman, 1945–1948* (New York: W. W. Norton, 1977), 128; James F. Schnabel, *The Joint Chiefs of Staff and National Policy, 1945–1947* (hereafter *JCS*), vol. 1 of *The History of the Joint Chiefs of Staff* (Washington, D.C.: JCS Joint Secretariat, Historical Division, 1979), 195–226.

[6] Donovan, *Conflict and Crisis*, 129, 165, and 285; H. Bradford Westerfield, *Foreign Policy and Party Politics: Pearl Harbor to Korea* (New Haven, Conn.: Yale University Press, 1955), 197–99. On across-the-board demobilization, Schnabel notes, "Less than two months after Japan's capitulation, millions of Americans remained in uniform but the combat effectiveness of most units had declined from 50 to 75 percent although their authorized strength had declined by only a small percentage." Schnabel, JCS, 212.

[7] Donovan, *Conflict and Crisis*, 200; John Lewis Gaddis, *The United States and the Origins*

Although the pace and scale of demobilization dismayed the president and his advisers, almost everyone agreed that major cuts in defense spending were in order. Administration officials perceived no immediate threat to U.S. security and feared that the continuation of wartime expenditures and deficits, or anything approaching them, would mortgage the country's future. Although the war had demonstrated the power of expansionary fiscal policies to spur enormous growth and high employment, Keynesian economics (in the sense of major compensatory spending to stimulate the economy) had made little headway with the general public or Truman's cabinet, which assigned priority to balancing the budget. Hence, the annual rate of military spending plunged from $90.9 billion in January 1945 to $10.3 billion during the second quarter of 1947.[8] The cessation of hostilities would have prompted sharp defense cutbacks in any case, but the fiscally conservative mood of the country caused what, in retrospect, appears to have been a precipitous dismantling of the U.S. military machine.

No pervasive, national security "ideology" characterized U.S. military thinking in the early post-World War II period.[9] The disorganization, misconceptions, and infighting that had disrupted the military services before and during the war continued well into the postwar period. This does not mean that Pentagon officials did not engage in contingency planning for wars of the future, against the Soviet Union among other hypothetical enemies. Military planning, however, was not the same thing as actual defense programs, for the Truman administration did not believe that the Soviet Union posed a direct *military* threat to the United

of the Cold War, 1941–1947 (New York: Columbia University Press, 1972), 262. On the administration's commitment to UMT, see War Department [unsigned], "Notes on Universal Military Training," n.d. [September 1945], Papers of Harry S. Truman, President's Secretary's File, Subject File, File: Agencies: Military Training, HSTL (hereafter cited as Papers of HST-PSF-Subject File); Stimson Statement before Cabinet meeting, 7 September 1945, ibid. On the link between failure of UMT and expansion of the atomic program, see Lynn Eden, "Capitalist Conflict and the State: The Making of United States Military Policy," in Charles Bright and Susan Harding, eds., *Statemaking and Social Movements: Essays in History and Theory* (Ann Arbor: University of Michigan Press, 1984).
[8] Alan Sweezy, "The Keynesians and Government Policy, 1933–1939," *American Economic Review: Papers and Proceedings* 62 (May 1972): 116–24; Byrd L. Jones, "The Role of Keynesians in Wartime Policy and Postwar Planning, 1940–1946," ibid., 129–32; Herbert Stein, *The Fiscal Revolution in America* (Chicago: University of Chicago Press, 1969), 169–75; Robert M. Collins, *The Business Response to Keynes, 1929–1964* (New York: Columbia University Press, 1981), 77–141; Donovan, *Conflict and Crisis,* 285. Ayers also notes Treasury Secretary John W. Snyder's skepticism toward navy and army air force plans for defending "all the world," at an annual price tag of $10 to $12 billion. See Ayers Diary, 24 August 1945, Papers of Eben A. Ayers, File: January 1, 1945 to December 31, 1945, HSTL (hereafter cited as Ayers Papers).
[9] Cf. Sherry, *Next War,* passim; Yergin, *Shattered Peace,* passim; and Leffler, "American Conception of National Security," passim.

States at the end of the war. Instead, the containment doctrine that evolved from early confrontation with the Soviet Union prescribed primary reliance upon the greatest U.S. asset of all, its economic power.

Kennan and containment

By early 1946, Soviet depredations in Eastern Europe, notably in Poland, had persuaded most U.S. policy makers that a lasting settlement with the Soviet Union was nearly impossible. Yet U.S. misgivings about Soviet conduct lacked coherent expression until February 1946, when George F. Kennan formulated the containment thesis from the vantage point of the U.S. embassy in Moscow.[10] In his famous "long telegram," Kennan argued that the Soviet foreign outlook postulated an unremitting hostility toward the West. In combination with Marxist-Leninist ideology, the current phase of Soviet expansionism was "more dangerous and insidious than ever before." The Kremlin used Marxism, "the fig leaf of their moral and intellectual respectability," and the capitalist encirclement thesis to justify the increased military and police power of the Soviet state. According to Kennan, the Soviets favored peaceful coexistence only to give them a breathing spell to recover from the war and a low-cost means to subvert the West: "We have here a political force committed fanatically to the belief that with US there can be no permanent *modus vivendi,* that it is desirable and necessary that the internal harmony of our society be destroyed, the international authority of our state be broken, if Soviet power is to be secure."[11]

Given the impressive resources at the command of the Kremlin and the inflexibility of its outlook, what could the West do? Kennan first reassured Washington that the Soviets would respond to the logic of force, if not the logic of reason. The West was collectively stronger than the So-

[10] Even so, U.S. policies toward Eastern Europe continued to vacillate until late 1946 because American officials never systematically defined U.S. goals and interests there. See Lynn Davis, *The Cold War Begins: Soviet-American Conflict Over Eastern Europe* (Princeton, N.J.: Princeton University Press, 1974), 22–23, 70–75, 160; Geir Lundestad, *The American Non-Policy Towards Eastern Europe, 1943–1947: Universalism in an Area Not of Essential Interest to the United States* (New York: Humanities Press, 1975), 429. In addition, bureaucratic momentum, or what Hugh De Santis terms "the image of ideological cooperation," discouraged American diplomats from responding aggressively against the Soviets in the early postwar period. De Santis's argument challenges Yergin's thesis concerning the "Riga axioms." Compare Hugh de Santis's "Conflicting Images of the USSR: American Career Diplomats and the Balkans, 1944–1946," *Political Science Quarterly* 94 (Fall 1979): 475–94 passim, with Yergin, *Shattered Peace,* 17–41.

[11] Quotations from Kennan to SecState, 22 February 1946, *Foreign Relations of the United States, 1946,* VI, 700–01, 706 (hereafter cited as *FRUS*).

viet Union, and the Kremlin had yet to consolidate its rule. Above all, the administration needed to educate the public about the realities of Soviet power and intransigence, to secure its allies against communist subversion, and to project a more positive image of American society to the world.[12]

Interestingly, Kennan's telegram, generally considered the harbinger of the containment doctrine, offered no concrete recommendations for U.S. policy, other than a plea for the reeducation of the American public. Nowhere in the telegram, for instance, did Kennan prescribe greater economic or military aid to countries threatened by communist takeover. Nor did Kennan's famous "X" article in the July 1947 issue of *Foreign Affairs* clarify the distinction between economic and military containment.[13]

To Kennan's surprise, the telegram created a sensation in official Washington. Unfortunately, the ambiguity of Kennan's thesis allowed for varying interpretations. The author had not intended to imply that negotiations with the Soviets were futile or that Moscow's foreign policy was unalterably dedicated to war according to some set timetable. Yet some policy makers, notably Navy Secretary Forrestal, seized on its more militant passages to argue for much tougher policies against the Soviet Union and a general escalation in U.S. defense programs. Others were more restrained. Although Kennan's "predictions and warnings could not have been better," Dean Acheson comments in his memoirs, "we responded to them slowly."[14]

Containment deferred

Indeed, the Truman White House did not implement Kennan's containment doctrine for more than a year. And when it did, the administration

---

[12] Ibid., 706–09.

[13] In addition, Kennan's argument was ambiguous in that it identified, with varying degrees of emphasis, three major sources of Soviet conduct: traditional Russian imperialism; Marxist-Leninist (or Stalinist) ideology; and the insecurity of the Kremlin rulers stemming from the fragility of their internal power base. See X [George F. Kennan], "The Sources of Soviet Conduct," *Foreign Affairs* 25 (July 1947): 566–82; C. Ben Wright, "Mr. 'X' and Containment," *Slavic Review* 35 (March 1976): 7–9, 15–16, 28–31; Daniel F. Harrington, "Kennan, Bohlen, and the Riga Axioms," *Diplomatic History* 2 (Fall 1978): 425–27.

[14] Acheson quotation from Dean Acheson, *Present at the Creation: My Years in the State Department* (New York: New American Library, Signet Books, 1970), 209. On Forrestal, see Yergin, *Shattered Peace*, 170–71; Millis, ed., *Forrestal Diaries*, 136, 140; Wright, "Mr. 'X.' " 12–16. For examples of "militarist" interpretations of Kennan's telegram, see Matthews to SWNCC, 1 April 1946, *FRUS*, 1946, I, 1167–71; JCS Memo, 27 March 1946, ibid., 1160–65; McFarlane for JCS to SecState, 29 March 1946, ibid., 1165–66.

did little to build up U.S. military capabilities, in effect opting for a policy of economic containment—the use of foreign aid, economic sanctions, and liberalization of trade and currency to block further Soviet expansion and to help America's allies. Military containment—the rapid buildup of U.S. military power and the spread of the U.S. military presence around the globe to deter Soviet aggression—would not be adopted for several more years.

The story of the Clifford-Elsey report illustrates the gap between official thinking and action in this period. In the summer of 1946, President Truman ordered Clark M. Clifford, his special counsel, to prepare a study on U.S.-Soviet relations. The senior officials whom Clifford and his aide, George M. Elsey, consulted generally painted an even gloomier picture of Soviet intentions and capabilities than had Kennan. Secretary of War Patterson, for example, warned, "We must envisage the possibility of the U.S.S.R. adopting open use of armed forces on a global scale." He called for the development of "long range air power, supplemented by atomic and long range weapons, and adequate ground forces to hold and seize key areas." Similarly, the State Department recommended the integration of all foreign economic, political, and defense programs for the purpose of deterring Soviet expansion. The final report denigrated negotiations with Moscow and fell just short of predicting war before long between the superpowers.[15]

When Clifford submitted the report to the president in September 1946, however, Truman said it was too "hot" to be circulated and locked away all the copies in his office safe. The president did not necessarily disagree with the report, but he realized that the public and the Congress were still unprepared for either an open confrontation with the Soviet Union or a military buildup so soon after the war. And Truman himself remained ambivalent about what action to take. As he wrote former vice-president John Nance Garner in September 1946, "There is too much loose talk about the Russian situation. We are not going to have any shooting trouble with them but they are tough bargainers and always ask for the whole earth, expecting maybe to get an acre."[16]

---

[15] Quotation from Robert P. Patterson to the president, 27 July 1946, Papers of George M. Elsey, File: Russia, HSTL. Also, see Yergin, *Shattered Peace*, 243.

[16] "Hot" quotation cited in Richard M. Freeland, *The Truman Doctrine and the Origins of McCarthyism: Foreign Policy, Domestic Politics, and Internal Security, 1946–1948* (New York: Schocken Books, 1974), 67. Also, see Yergin, *Shattered Peace*, 245; Donovan, *Conflict and Crisis*, 222. Truman had also backed down from publicizing the rift with the Soviet Union when Churchill delivered his "iron curtain" speech in March 1946. See ibid., 190–92. "Loose talk" quotation from Truman to Garner, 21 September 1946, Papers of HST-PSF-Subject File: Foreign Affairs, File: Russia 1945–48, HSTL.

For all the rhetoric about the Soviet threat, the administration sat on its hands. Although the president's chief military aide, Admiral William D. Leahy, and others had warned Truman that the armed forces were gravely undermanned, demobilization and defense cuts continued apace. Nor did the atomic program accelerate. Truman claimed in October 1946 that the United States had stationed no bombs in overseas bases, meaning that the then short-range U.S. "atomic" bombers could not reach the Soviet Union in a general war. The U.S. atomic arsenal in the summer of 1946 consisted of no more than seven Mark III (Nagasaki-type, "Fat Man") weapons. As late as April 1947, the newly operative Atomic Energy Commission told Truman that the armed forces still had very few bombs, none of them ready to be used, and that military bomb assembly teams were unprepared for a crisis.[17]

In the months preceding the enunciation of the Truman Doctrine, Forrestal repeatedly complained that U.S. overseas commitments greatly exceeded U.S. military capabilities. Yet for both political and bureaucratic reasons, Pentagon policies and programs continued to lag behind the containment doctrine. The struggle over the unification of the armed forces had exhausted much of the Pentagon's credibility on the Hill, as well as in the White House. Budgetary pressures also encouraged the administration to pin its hopes on a national defense built around atomic weapons, however few, and around UMT, however chimerical. Furthermore, the Clifford-Elsey report itself recognized that economic power was America's strong suit in the battle against communism.[18]

The main instruments of economic containment, of course, were the Truman Doctrine and the Marshall Plan. Discussion of these landmark programs lies largely outside the scope of this essay, but it is worth men-

[17] For Leahy's warning, see Leahy to Truman, 12 March 1946, Papers of HST-PSF-Subject File: Agencies, File: Military-Army-Navy unification, HSTL. Truman was commenting on a report by Drew Pearson about U.S. stationing of atomic bombs in Germany or England, a story the president branded a "lie." See Ayers Diary, 14 October 1946, Ayers Papers, File: Diary (Ayers) 1946, HSTL. Also, see Schnabel, JCS, 294. On the size and readiness of the U.S. atomic arsenal, see also David Alan Rosenberg, "U.S. Nuclear Stockpile, 1945 to 1950," *Bulletin of Atomic Scientists* 38 (May 1982): 261.

[18] On Forrestal, see Millis, ed., *Forrestal Diaries,* 198, 236, 239–40. On constraints on military programs, see Donovan, *Conflict and Crisis,* 138–140, 172, 200–02, 222, 265. CEA Chairman Nourse told Truman that a $3 to $5 billion "budget surplus is urgently called for" in this period. See Nourse to Truman, "Budget Estimate of Expenditures," 13 December 1946, Papers of Edwin G. Nourse, File: Daily Diary 1946–47, Memorandum of contacts with President and the White House Staff, December 3–28, HSTL (hereafter cited as "Nourse Papers"). Truman endorsed the JCS's view in January 1947 that UMT was necessary until scientists perfected "the so-called 'push button' type of warfare." Truman to Karl T. Compton, 17 January 1947, Papers of HST-PSF-Subject File: Agencies, File: Military Training, HSTL.

tioning here a few points about their relationship to U.S. security aims. First, whereas the Greek-Turkish aid bill focused on measures to counter the alleged communist aggression against those countries, the Truman Doctrine itself was designed primarily to overcome public and congressional opposition to direct U.S. involvement in Europe, notably a comprehensive reconstruction program. To Acheson, the significance of the Truman Doctrine lay as much in its impact on the morale and security of Western Europe as in its impact on Greece and Turkey.

Despite the president's universalistic rhetoric, moreover, the administration had neither the inclination nor the means to police the world against communism. Given continued budgetary constraints, U.S. containment policy before the Korean War consisted largely of nonmilitary measures to bolster Western Europe, rather than armed might. Thus, the Truman Doctrine did not herald either the militarization of American society or the commitment of the United States to contain communism everywhere.[19]

Similarly, the chief purpose of the Marshall Plan was to immunize Western Europe against the seeming contagion of communism without massive U.S. rearmament. Before the Senate Foreign Relations Committee in January 1948, Secretary of State Marshall testified that the European Recovery Program would fulfill U.S. aims in World War II by restoring the balance of power in Europe. As he put it, "The way of life we have known is literally in the balance." Without the aid program, the United States risked a world war that would require "tremendous appropriations for national security."[20]

The abortive rearmament of 1948 and defense budgets before the Korean War

The second episode that is commonly cited as a flashpoint in the cold war is the March 1948 war scare. Some scholars have detected a major shift in U.S. defense planning during this period. One historian, for instance,

---

[19] John Lewis Gaddis, "Was the Truman Doctrine a Real Turning Point?" *Foreign Affairs* 52 (January 1974): 386–92. Cf. Thomas G. Paterson, *Soviet-American Confrontation: Postwar Reconstruction and the Origins of the Cold War* (Baltimore: Johns Hopkins University Press, 1973), 206; Freeland, *Truman Doctrine*, 99–102; Kolko, *Limits*, 336–45.

[20] Marshall quotations of 8 January 1948 from U.S., Congress, Senate Committee on Foreign Relations, *European Recovery Program, Hearings on S. 2202*, pt. 1, 80th Cong., 2d sess., 1948, 10, 36.

states that the "events in Czechoslovakia provided impetus to move to a new level of military preparedness."[21] In fact, the crises of 1948 only exposed the limitations of U.S. conventional military forces and the over-reliance of U.S. military planners on atomic power.

It is true that the March crisis gave rise to a momentary enthusiasm in Washington for increased defense spending. Addressing a joint session of Congress on 17 March 1948, President Truman denounced the "pattern" of Soviet aggression and communist subversion in Czechoslovakia, Finland, Greece, and Italy and expressed support for the Brussels Pact. The president again sought authorization of a universal military training program because, he said, "we have learned the importance of maintaining military strength as a means of preventing war." Truman also asked Congress to restore the draft for five years in order to expand the regular armed forces. These conventional forces, the administration believed, would offer a more flexible deterrent against Soviet aggression than would atomic weapons.[22]

The military services sought to capitalize on the spring crisis by demanding a sharp boost in defense spending. "The President commented that every department of the government now has gone warlike," an aide noted in late March. Truman favored only a $1.5 billion supplement to the fiscal 1949 budget, with an emphasis on UMT and a limited increment of ground troops, because the Bureau of the Budget had convinced him that a sharp rise in military expenditures would create deficits and fuel inflation. Yet after intense lobbying by the services, Truman agreed to meet the Pentagon partway. On 1 April 1948, Truman requested $3 billion (subsequently raised to $3.2 billion) in supplemental defense appropriations from Congress, including $775 million more for aircraft procurement.[23]

The debate within the administration over the defense budget had just begun, however. Forrestal had persuaded the Joint Chiefs of Staff (JCS)

---

[21] Quotation from Yergin, *Shattered Peace,* 350.

[22] Truman quotations from Harry S. Truman, "Toward Securing Peace and Preventing War," Speech before Congress, 17 March 1948, DSB 18 (28 March 1948): 419, 420.

[23] For Truman quotation, see Ayers Diary, 23 March 1948, Ayers Papers, File: Diary 1948-Ayers, HSTL. On interservice rivalry and the supplemental appropriations of spring 1948, see Millis, ed., *Forrestal Diaries,* 435–39; Yergin, *Shattered Peace,* 357–60; Steven L. Rearden, "History of the Office of the Secretary of Defense, Volume 1: The Formative Years, 1947–1950" (Washington, D.C.: JCS Joint Secretariat, Historical Division, 1984; hereafter cited as Rearden, *OSD*), chapter 8; Warner R. Schilling, "The Politics of National Defense: Fiscal 1950," in Warner R. Schilling, Paul Y. Hammond, and Glenn H. Snyder, *Strategy, Politics and Defense Budgets* (New York: Columbia University Press, 1962), 1–266.

to drop their original, $9 billion supplemental request by promising that he could increase the supplement before Congress from $3 billion to $3.5 billion. Proponents of air power in Congress and the administration, notably Air Force Secretary W. Stuart Symington, also demanded increased funding for air procurement and a seventy-group force. Truman instead favored a gradual and balanced military buildup stressing defense mobilization capabilities over standing forces. When Forrestal later failed to persuade the services to accept the president's guidelines, Truman told his staff that he was "getting damn sore" at the secretary of defense. According to the president, the "three muttonheads" in the Department of Defense—Forrestal, Symington, and Army Secretary Kenneth C. Royall—were responsible for undermining UMT by stirring up congressional support for their own pet projects.[24]

The armed services gained $3.2 billion in supplemental appropriations in May 1948, but they had won a Pyrrhic victory. On 13 May 1948, President Truman summoned Forrestal, the service secretaries, the Joint Chiefs of Staff, and top budget officials to the White House. The commander in chief announced his intention to withhold procurement funds that the House had designated for a seventy-group air force and to put a ceiling of $14.4 billion (excluding $600 million in stockpiling) on the fiscal 1950 budget. Truman contemplated no more than "the development of a military posture which would give evidence of continuing firmness in world affairs"—a signal to Moscow that the United States was prepared to rearm if necessary. The White House program called for total manpower levels of 1,539,000 by September 1948 if Congress enacted selective service, only 165,000 more than the postwar low reached in February and well below what Forrestal and the JCS had recommended.[25]

The Berlin crisis, beginning just a month later, in June 1948, further exposed the weakness of U.S. forces, as well as, some would argue, the

---

[24] As Truman explained in an off-the-record talk in April 1948, he wished to avoid a repeat of the boom-and-bust cycle after World War I. In light of the rapid obsolescence of aircraft, he added, a sudden expansion of airpower would lead to waste. "The proper way to approach this thing," the president stated, "is to take the construction program on a basis that will keep us linked up all the time, so that we can put these factories to work immediately, if that is necessary." See Ayers transcript of Truman speech before American Society of Newspaper Editors, 17 April 1948, Ayers Papers, File: Foreign Policy: Russian Relations, HSTL. For Truman on Forrestal, see Ayers Diary, 21 April 1948, Ayers Papers, File: Diary 1948-Ayers, HSTL. For Truman on "muttonheads," see Ayers Diary, 26 April 1948, ibid.

[25] On the 13 May 1948 White House meeting, see Millis, ed., *Forrestal Diaries*, 435–38. Truman quotation from ibid., 436.

absence of a strategic concept in U.S. military planning. Although the United States deployed several dozen B-29s to forward bases in England during July and August 1948, none of the so-called atomic bombers had been modified to carry atomic weapons. Washington never seriously considered the use of armed convoys to break the Berlin blockade, moreover, in part because the army could not spare a sizable contingent of combat troops.[26]

By capping the fiscal 1950 defense budget at $14.4 billion, the president had seemingly ordered the military services to adapt their programs to prescribed budgetary limits, rather than to what the world situation seemed to require. Forrestal, responding to strong JCS pressure for more funds, sought to outflank Truman's economic advisers by soliciting the support of the State Department in November 1948. Secretary of State Marshall, however, told Forrestal, "We must expect for the current fiscal year a [world] situation which is neither better nor worse than that which we have found in 1948 insofar as it affects the ceiling of our military establishment." State Department Counselor Charles E. Bohlen added that the main deterrents to Soviet aggression remained strategic air power and the "productive potential of the United States." Following Forrestal's departure in early 1949, Truman actually sought to clip another $1 billion off the Pentagon's $14.4 billion budget.[27]

For its part, the Republican-controlled Eightieth Congress in effect opted for a strategy based on atomic weapons by soundly defeating UMT, cutting back the president's proposed selective service measure from five to two years, and voting start-up funding for a larger air force than Truman had requested. Although U.S. atomic capabilities had greatly improved by the fall of 1948, the bomb was still regarded as a weapon of last resort. Moreover, David Rosenberg has pointed out, "Through 1950, the nuclear stockpile was . . . too small and the weapons too large and unwieldy to be used against true tactical targets, such as troops and transportation bottlenecks." The United States, in short, lacked a credi-

---

[26] Yergin, *Shattered Peace*, 378–80.
[27] In October 1948, Forrestal argued for a defense budget of $17.5 billion, compared with Truman's $14.4 billion, for fiscal 1950. See Forrestal to Marshall, 31 October 1948, Clifford Papers, File: National Military Establishment-Miscellaneous, HSTL. In December, Forrestal requested, but failed to achieve, a $16.9 billion budget (compared with the JCS's request for $23 billion). "Productive potential" quotation from Bohlen to Carter, 7 November 1948, *FRUS*, 1948, I, pt. 2, 654. Marshall quotation from Marshall to Lovett (Forrestal), 8 November 1948, ibid., 655. Also, see Forrestal to Marshall, 31 October 1948, ibid., 644–47; Lovett to Marshall, 1 November 1948, ibid., 647–48; Lovett to Marshall, 2 November 1948, ibid., 648–54; Millis, ed., *Forrestal Diaries*, 492–95, 498–99, 501–05, 508–11, 535–36, 538; Rearden, *OSD*, chapter IX.

ble deterrent in Europe.[28] The quarrels within the U.S. government over military strategy, however, should not obscure the similarity in approach by the various parties to the budgetary question: Everyone was looking for a cheap alternative to forces in being.

Even in the face of greatly expanded U.S. commitments in Western Europe, the administration sought to keep defense budgets below $15 billion. In fact, at precisely the same moment that the administration was pressing for final passage of the North Atlantic Treaty (and was about to introduce military aid legislation), the president directed the National Security Council (NSC) to explore new ways to reduce spending in fiscal 1951 (NSC 52). With the onset of a recession, Truman argued in July 1949, the combination of declining revenues and rising expenditures had brought about "such a serious fiscal and economic problem that a complete reevaluation of current and proposed programs is required." Domestic expenditures, in Truman's estimation, had already been cut to the bone, so he instructed the NSC to look for fat in military and international programs. (He expected European recovery to reduce the need for extensive foreign aid programs.)[29]

The Bureau of the Budget sought to meet Truman's objectives by cutting the defense budget from $14.4 billion in fiscal 1950 to $13 billion in fiscal 1951. It also sliced Marshall Plan funds, military aid, and other international programs roughly in half. By the Budget Bureau's calculations in July 1949, military and international programs should have cost about $5 billion less in fiscal 1951 ($17.8 billion) than they did in fiscal 1950 ($23 billion).[30]

In late September 1949—as the communists were sweeping to victory in mainland China and the Truman administration was discovering that the Soviets had exploded an atomic device—the NSC determined that the Defense Department "can, under the $13 billion ceiling allocated to it in NSC 52/1, maintain substantially the same degree of military strength, readiness and posture during [fiscal] 1951 which it will maintain in [fiscal] 1950." The Council of Economic Advisers (CEA) did not foresee a

---

[28] Quotation from David Alan Rosenberg, "The Origins of Overkill: Nuclear Weapons and American Strategy, 1945–1960," *International Security* 7 (Spring 1983): 16. Also, see idem, "American Atomic Strategy and the Hydrogen Bomb Decision," *Journal of American History* 66 (June 1979): 62–87; Eden, "Capitalist Conflict," in Bright and Harding, eds., *Statemaking*.

[29] Souers to NSC, NSC 52, 5 July 1949, with attached Truman to Souers, 1 July 1949, *FRUS*, 1949, I, 350, 351.

[30] Lay to NSC, 8 July 1949, NSC 52/1, with attached Pace "Summary Tabulation," 8 July 1949, ibid., 352–57.

continuation of the current recession into 1950, and CEA Chairman Edwin Nourse made a strong pitch for austerity. "The strains on our economy of increasing the deficit with its attendant problems," notably higher inflation, would pose "no less a risk than our military and diplomatic risks," Nourse argued, and "any jeopardy to our domestic industry had also to be considered as jeopardy to our national security." The Treasury Department, too, pleaded for spending cuts to combat the widening federal deficits. With the CEA, Budget Bureau, Treasury, and even Defense Secretary Johnson squarely lined up against them, the JCS and other proponents of rearmament were fighting a losing battle.[31]

In the fall of 1949, the president, despairing of the chances for an agreement on the international control of atomic energy, reluctantly approved the substantial increase in nuclear weapons production that the JCS had requested. But Truman was determined to hold down other defense programs. In his annual budget message on 9 January 1950, the chief executive asked for $13.5 billion for the fiscal 1951 defense budget, a 10 percent cut from the previous year. (In May 1950, the House of Representatives went even further, voting only $12.9 billion for the Pentagon.) The result was a partial demobilization of the armed forces from 1,617,000 in July 1949 to 1,460,000 on the eve of the Korean War.[32]

The rationale behind the Truman administration's position on defense spending was the widely shared conviction that the Soviets would probably not launch a general war in the near future and that burdensome military expenditures were not a cost-effective way to meet the Soviet threat. Economic and military assistance was still regarded as the most efficient means of supporting the Atlantic alliance, although as Europe recovered, U.S. foreign aid programs could be scaled down. Surprisingly, this viewpoint prevailed even as key officials, notably Secretary of State Dean Acheson, became increasingly alarmed by the Soviet threat. In April

[31] The NSC approved the Bureau of the Budget's cut of the ECA budget (from $4.2 to $3 billion) but hoped to maintain MAP at about $1 to $1.5 billion. Altogether, the NSC adopted a package of foreign and military programs costing $19 to $20 billion. Nourse quotation from Memo to President on 46th Meeting of NSC, 30 September 1949, Papers of HST-PSF-Subject File: NSC Meetings, File: Memos for President—Meeting Discussions (1949), HSTL. On CEA, see also Clarence Yin-Hsieh Lo, "The Truman Administration's Military Budgets during the Korean War" (Ph.D. diss., University of California at Berkeley, 1978), 150; Nourse Memo, 30 September 1949, *FRUS*, 1949, I, 394–96. Quotation by NSC from NSC to Truman, NSC 52/3, 29 September 1949, 387; also, see ibid., 388–93. On Treasury Department, see Memo by Acting Secretary of Treasury, 29 September 1949, ibid., 393–94.

[32] On nuclear weapons production, see Rosenberg, "Overkill," 21–22. Also, see Robert J. Donovan, *Tumultuous Years: The Presidency of Harry S. Truman, 1949–1953*, 132.

1950, for instance, with deficits of $4 billion to $8 billion looming for each of the next three fiscal years, Budget Director Frederick J. Lawton contemplated cuts in fiscal 1953 of $500 million from defense expenditures (to $13 billion) and cuts of $3 billion from foreign aid programs. This evidence, incidentally, directly contradicts the view that Truman sought to fight the 1949–50 recession with rearmament.[33]

Defense Secretary Johnson has suffered more criticism for the inadequacy of U.S. defense programs on the eve of the Korean War than have Truman and his economic advisers—Nourse, Treasury Secretary John W. Snyder, and the successive budget directors, James E. Webb (1946–49), Frank Pace, Jr. (1949–50), and Lawton (1950–53). Whatever his record on other issues, Johnson probably has been unfairly maligned for his position on the defense budget, for he was simply following his chief's orders. If anyone deserved credit or blame for the U.S. military posture before June 1950, it was Harry S. Truman.[34]

Origins of the North Atlantic Treaty Organization

The one concrete accomplishment of the Truman administration in the defense field during the 1948–50 period was the North Atlantic Treaty Organization (NATO), but in its inception the "entangling alliance" was little more than a political adjunct to the Marshall Plan. The main impetus for the Western defense organization came from the European allies themselves rather than the United States. The Brussels Pact countries, particularly France and Britain, insisted that defense planning and coordination could not go forward without a firm U.S. commitment to European security. Membership in NATO was also part of the price that Washington had to pay before France would permit West German reconstruction and statehood—and eventual German rearmament. (The other U.S. inducement to Paris was the Marshall Plan.)[35] The British and the

[33] Lawton to Truman, "Current Issues Regarding the 1952 and 1953 Budgets," 19 April 1950, Papers of HST-PSF-Subject File, File: BOB: Budget Data—FY 1952–1953, HSTL.

[34] CEA members Nourse and Keyserling, who agreed on very little else, both contended that Truman, rather than Forrestal and Johnson, was primarily responsible for the low defense budgets before the Korean War. See Oral History Interviews with Edwin G. Nourse, 1972, HSTL, 45–49, and Leon H. Keyserling, 1975, HSTL, 116–18. Cf. Leon H. Keyserling, "The View from the Council of Economic Advisers," in Francis H. Heller, ed., *Economics and the Truman Administration* (Lawrence: Regents Press of Kansas, 1981), 89–90.

[35] For the Franco-German thesis on NATO's origins, see Timothy P. Ireland, *Creating the Entangling Alliance: The Origins of the North Atlantic Treaty Organization* (Westport, Conn.: Greenwood Press, 1981). On European initiative, see ibid., 48–79.

French had no illusions about Moscow's intentions and feared communist encroachment on a united, but neutralized, Germany. In January 1948, British Foreign Minister Ernest Bevin proposed the formation of a "West European Union" of states in association with the United States. "The plain truth," the British ambassador informed Under Secretary of State Robert A. Lovett, "is that Western Europe cannot yet stand on its own feet without assurance of support."[36]

U.S. policy makers at first gave only lukewarm encouragement to the Europeans. "Some form of political, military and economic union in Western Europe will be necessary," the Policy Planning Staff (PPS) concluded in a major review of U.S. foreign policy in February 1948, "if the free nations of Europe are to hold their own against the people of the east united under Moscow rule." But George F. Kennan believed that the Marshall Plan countries should consolidate their economic and political gains before proceeding to a military pact and argued that the United States should avoid a close association with any European security organization. Others, such as the director of the Office of European Affairs, John D. Hickerson, looked more favorably on an Atlantic pact but demanded European initiative and self-help (as in the Marshall Plan) before the United States participated.[37]

The Czech coup and the ensuing war scare of March 1948 catalyzed official opinion behind the Western alliance. On March 12, Secretary of State Marshall told the British that the United States was "prepared to proceed at once in the joint discussions on the establishment of an Atlantic security system." A week later, the NSC called for "a worldwide counteroffensive" against the Soviet bloc, including U.S. military aid to the West European Union. Secret consultations with British and Canadian officials began at the Pentagon shortly thereafter.[38]

The Americans were still not enthusiastic about an open-ended secu-

[36] On Bevin, see Inverchapel to Marshall, 13 January 1948, *FRUS*, 1948, III, 3–6. "Plain truth" quotation from Inverchapel to Lovett, 27 January 1948, ibid., 14. Also, see Inverchapel to Lovett, 6 February 1948, ibid., 19–20.

[37] Quotation from Kennan to Lovett, 24 February 1948, with attached PPS/23, *FRUS*, 1948, I, pt. 2, 510. Also, see Kennan to Marshall, 20 January 1948, *FRUS*, 1948, II, 7–8; Hickerson Memcon, 21 January 1948, ibid., 9–12.

[38] Marshall quotation from Marshall to Inverchapel, 12 March 1948, *FRUS*, 1948, III, 48; also, see Hickerson to Marshall, 8 March 1948, ibid., 40–42. NSC quotation from Souers to NSC, NSC 7, 20 March 1948, *FRUS*, 1948, I, pt. 2, 548, 550. The "Pentagon talks" resulted in recommendations for the expansion of the West European Union to include the Scandinavian countries; the eventual inclusion of Germany, Austria, and Spain; Anglo-American guarantees to Greece, Turkey, and Iran; and continuing political and military consultations between the U.S. and the West European Union. See Minutes of 6th Meeting of Pentagon Talks, 1 April 1948, *FRUS*, 1948, III, 71–75.

rity commitment to Western Europe, however. The JCS were wary of assuming commitments beyond U.S. military capabilities and concerned about the virtual exhaustion of World War II stocks of equipment. (As a result of JCS pressure, the later military aid legislation would specifically prohibit the depletion of matériel needed by U.S. forces.) Congress also disapproved of extensive military aid, let alone a hard-and-fast alliance with Western Europe, while Marshall Plan legislation was still pending. "The general feeling of Congress," Lovett reported to the NSC in May 1948, "is that we should not formalize our participation in Western Union military talks but that we should merely send observers."[39]

Senator Arthur H. Vandenberg (R-Mich.), a barometer of bipartisan opinion, finally drafted a Senate resolution (approved in June 1948) that opened the way to U.S. membership in NATO. The Vandenberg Resolution stated that U.S. participation in any collective security agreement did not automatically commit the United States to go to war in case of aggression against another member country. Congressional approval, in other words, was still necessary. Moreover, the European countries, as in the European Recovery Program (ERP), would have to provide reciprocal aid. In July 1948, the NSC approved military assistance to Western Europe on this basis.[40]

During the same month, amid the Berlin crisis, exploratory talks on Western defense began in Washington. Although the Europeans demanded concrete assurances of U.S. military support, U.S. officials at this point favored shipping matériel in lieu of more troops to Europe. Part of

[39] Opposition to a NATO-like organization came from several quarters, most notably Kennan, who did not participate in many of the decisions in this period because of a trip to Japan and a subsequent illness in March–April 1948. Kennan's ability to counter the strong tide in Washington favoring U.S. association with the West European Union was also tempered by the fact that in his absence, the PPS in PPS/27 had endorsed U.S. military consultations leading to a pact with the West European countries. See PPS/27, 23 March 1948, *FRUS, 1948*, III, 61–64; Kennan to Lovett, 29 April 1948, ibid., 109–10. The NSC substantially adopted the viewpoint of PPS/27 on the West European Union. See NSC 9, 13 April 1948, ibid., 85–88. For Kennan's misgivings about NATO, see also Kennan, *Memoirs*, 396–414. For JCS comments on NSC 7, see Forrestal to NSC, 17 April 1948, *FRUS, 1948*, I, pt. 2, 561–64; also, see Rearden, *OSD*, chapter XIII. For Lovett quotation, see Memo to the President on 11th Meeting of NSC, 21 May 1948, Papers of HST-PSF-Subject File: NSC Meetings, File: Memo for President—Meeting Discussions (1948), HSTL.

[40] For Vandenberg Resolution, see Senate Resolution 239, 11 June 1948, *FRUS, 1948*, III, 135–36. On NSC approval of an Atlantic pact along the lines of the Vandenberg Resolution, see NSC 9/3, 28 June 1948, ibid., 140–41. On military aid, see NSC 14/1, 1 July 1948, *FRUS, 1948*, I, pt. 2, 585–88; Lawrence S. Kaplan, *A Community of Interests: NATO and the Military Assistance Program, 1948–1951* (Washington, D.C.: U.S. Government Printing Office, 1980), 14–15, 19–23. Also, see Yergin, *Shattered Peace*, 354, 363–64.

their reticence was due to the lingering isolationism among the American public, but aside from domestic constraints, senior policy makers did not believe that a major U.S. military presence was necessary. Charles Bohlen, for example, doubted the Soviets would attack Western Europe and valued the new alliance primarily for its "psychological" impact, especially upon French morale. Thus, when the Washington talks concluded in September 1948, the U.S. role in the proposed Atlantic security pact was conceived largely in terms of political and material support. As Marshall told Defense Secretary Forrestal in November, "We should not, at this stage, proceed to build up U.S. ground forces for the express purpose of employing them in Western Europe." The administration still hesitated to make public its plans for military assistance. In testimony before the Senate Foreign Relations Committee in July 1949, Dean Acheson, the new secretary of state, affirmed that the treaty required the United States neither to provide military aid nor to send additional troops to Europe. On 21 July 1949, the Senate approved the North Atlantic Treaty by a margin of eighty-two to thirteen.[41]

Yet as the French never tired of pointing out, NATO remained no more than a paper treaty until Congress approved a military aid program (MAP) to help rearm Western Europe. European anxiety was understandable: about ten U.S. and West European divisions, for the most part ill-equipped and poorly trained, faced more than thirty Soviet divisions in Eastern and Central Europe alone. Interestingly, however, economic considerations played a prominent role even in Washington's planning for MAP. Policy makers above all wished to ensure that European rearmament did not undercut the Marshall Plan. As the Foreign Assistance Correlation Committee, an interdepartmental committee on military aid, stated in February 1949, "Economic recovery must not be sacrificed to rearmament and must continue to be given a clear priority. . . . Of basic importance is recognition of the limits of U.S. financial and economic aid available."[42]

---

[41] "Psychological" quotation from Memo of 3rd Meeting of Working Group, Washington Exploratory Talks, 15 July 1948, *FRUS*, 1948, III, p. 186. Also, see Bohlen Memcon, 6 August 1948, ibid., 206; Marshall to Truman, 23 August 1948, ibid., 221–22; Memo, "Washington Exploratory Conversations on Security," 9 September 1948, ibid., 237–48; Memo by Brussels Pact Ambassadors to Department of State, 29 October 1948, ibid., 270; Kennan to Marshall and Lovett, with attached PPS Report, 24 November 1948, ibid., 284–85; Lovett to Harriman, 3 December 1948, ibid., 305; Kaplan, NATO, 35. On Acheson's relations with Congress regarding the North Atlantic Treaty, see Acheson, *Present at the Creation*, 364–76. On SFRC testimony, see ibid., 375–76. On congressional debate on the NAT, see Ireland, *Alliance*, 119–48.

[42] Quotation from FACC Policy Paper, 7 February 1949, *FRUS*, 1949, I, 254–55. On MAP

Congress significantly revised the MAP legislation for fiscal 1950, tightly restricting executive discretion to disburse funds. The military aid initially intended for NATO countries was cut to $100 million, and as of April 1950, a mere $42 million of the total $1 billion in MAP funds authorized for NATO had been obligated, with only token shipments reaching European shores. Nonetheless, the administration had provided a major boost to European morale and unity at a time of military weakness and insecurity.[43]

The State Department, rather than the Defense Department, administered MAP because the program's main purpose was, like the ERP, to buttress the political and economic stability of Western Europe rather than to build a war machine capable of fighting the Red Army. Unfortunately, this concept of NATO as a politico-military adjunct to the Marshall Plan reinforced the European propensity to defer both rearmament and the formulation of an integrated defense plan. Wary of endorsing a strategy that could entail a prolonged and destructive "liberation" of the Continent from Soviet occupation, many Europeans persuaded themselves that the mere existence of a political alliance with the United States was a sufficient deterrent against Soviet aggression. Yet until the assignment of U.S. ground troops to NATO in 1951, Timothy Ireland observes, "none of the American policies for Europe . . . implied permanent American involvement in continental affairs." Indeed, the Marshall Plan and the military aid program had been specifically designed to restore the balance of power in Europe so that direct U.S. military intervention would be unnecessary.[44]

Business and rearmament

One might suppose that military leaders would have been able to recruit powerful backing for rearmament in the corporate boardrooms of Amer-

and security organization, see Ireland, *Alliance*, 153–63. Averell Harriman also linked U.S. support of West European Union to the success of the Marshall Plan. See Harriman to Lovett, 12 November 1948, 840.50 Recovery Series (Marshall Plan), Confidential Decimal File 1945–49, File: 840.50 Recovery/11-148, NA (hereafter cited as Recovery series). For fears that military aid could stall European recovery, see, e.g., Minutes of Third Meeting of Washington Exploratory Talks, 17 July 1948, *FRUS*, 1948, III, 157–58.

[43] Although the Congress authorized $1.3 billion in military aid for fiscal 1950 (with about $1 billion earmarked for NATO countries), it required the NATO countries to reach an integrated defense plan (achieved in January 1950) before the executive could release the bulk of authorized MAP funds. Other amendments limited the funds available to accelerate arms production in Europe. By delaying final passage of the Mutual Defense Assistance Act to October 1949, the Congress further slowed Western rearmament. See Kaplan, *NATO*, 41–49, 68, 77.

[44] Quotation from Ireland, *Alliance*, 183. Also, see Kaplan, *NATO*, 72–77.

ica. After all, it was commonly acknowledged that the fat government contracts during the war had ended the Great Depression and generated record profits for U.S. business. Yet business opinion was overwhelmingly opposed to both Keynesian fiscal policies and a large peacetime military establishment. "Business leaders recognized that the economic recovery brought about by World War II had provided them with a final chance to build a prosperous peacetime economy under private direction," one scholar found in his study of businessmen and national defense. Corporate leaders generally supported an end to government controls and the reduction of federal spending and taxes. Truman's decision to slash military expenditures at the end of the war met with applause on Wall Street, and most businessmen heartily approved the president's move in May 1948 to cap the defense budget at $14.4 billion. Even during the 1949 recession, organizations such as the Chamber of Commerce of the United States and the Committee for Economic Development (CED) continued to demand cuts in federal outlays, including military expenditures, in order to balance the budget.[45]

Some private groups, such as the National Planning Association, however, favored government intervention to ensure high levels of postwar employment and production. Yet by 1945, most business leaders no longer feared demobilization, because the massive accumulated savings of consumers during the war promised strong postwar demand. Although many government analysts were predicting a postwar depression, manufacturers were generally confident that they could quickly reconvert to civilian output and find markets. Indeed, just a year later, inflation clearly posed a greater danger to the U.S. economy than unemployment. The Chamber of Commerce and the National Association of Manufacturers (NAM) probably spoke for most businessmen in calling for an end to high taxes, wage-price controls, and deficit spending, which they associated with excess demand and inflation.[46]

Demobilization affected different industries in different ways. In August 1946, just one year after the war had ended, munitions procurement fell to less than 10 percent of wartime levels. Aircraft manufacturers were especially hard hit and clamored for federal relief. Production of military airplanes fell from 96,000 in 1944 to 1,800 in 1947, and civilian demand came nowhere close to filling the gap. The aviation industry finally re-

---

[45] Quotation from William S. Hill, Jr., "The Business Community and National Defense: Corporate Leaders and the Military" (Ph.D. diss., Stanford University, 1980), 16. Also, see ibid., 18, 20–21, 491; Collins, *Business Response,* 127–41; Paterson, "Economic Cold War," 41.

[46] Hill, "Business Community," 32, 51–59, 68; Collins, *Business Response,* 139–41.

vived after the March 1948 war scare, as the Congress more than doubled the budget for the air force and naval air in fiscal 1949, compared with the previous year.[47]

The aircraft industry was an exception to the rule, however. Steel and automobile manufacturers, for instance, easily reconverted to civilian production and had little or no desire for military business (which suffered from the boom-and-bust syndrome) when they were struggling to meet consumer demand. Steel shipments to the government for military purposes in 1946–50 amounted to less than 2 percent of total industry output. And the postwar boom in housing more than compensated for the drop in military base construction.[48]

Business sentiment on fiscal policy, let alone the defense budget, did not shift markedly even with the onset of the first postwar recession beginning in late 1948. When the economy took a turn for the worse, the CED, NAM, and Chamber of Commerce called for further decreases in defense spending in order to offset declining revenues. Secretary of Commerce Charles Sawyer reported that "business leaders everywhere expressed enthusiastic approval of reductions in the military budget." Even the aircraft industry was fairly acquiescent; by 1949, it was operating at high capacity and had a backlog of orders exceeding $2 billion.[49]

On most issues, the business community was divided into innumerable factions: large and small producers, internationally and domestically oriented sectors, New Dealers, and laissez-faire enthusiasts. But it is probably safe to say that private groups on the whole acted to restrain U.S. rearmament before the Korean War. The corporate leaders sternly shunned what was later called "military Keynesianism," the notion that defense spending was necessary to sustain production and employment. Even during and immediately after the Korean War, "they clung stubbornly to the idea that businessmen, not government, should be responsible for economic growth."[50]

---

[47] On munitions procurement, see Hill, "Business Community," 165. On aviation and shipbuilding, see ibid., 19, 69, 76, 88–89, 97–99, 110, 206–13, 230, 234, 247, 284; Yergin, *Shattered Peace*, 268–69, 341–43, 359–63.

[48] On steel, see Hill, "Business Community," 166, 179, 326, 409.

[49] Ibid., 333, 336, 342–43, 348–50, 399, 415. Sawyer quotation cited in ibid., 348. On aircraft industry, see Lo, "Military Budgets," 144.

[50] Quotation from Hill, "Business Community," 437. Also, see ibid., 429, 434–35.

NSC 68 and the debate over containment

What finally shifted the momentum toward rearmament was a subtle change in official thinking about the Sino-Soviet threat in late 1949. The president tried to put on a brave face in announcing the detection of a Soviet atomic explosion in September 1949, but Truman and his key aides were privately apprehensive about U.S. vulnerability to a devastating atomic attack. The Soviet bomb also weakened the deterrent effect of U.S. strategic air power against a Red Army attack on Western Europe. And Mao's triumph in China, once regarded as a sideshow in the cold war, suddenly appeared to be part of a renewed communist offensive masterminded by the Kremlin. Given Moscow's growing capacity for aggression, many of Truman's top advisers became persuaded that economic containment alone could no longer guarantee vital U.S. interests abroad and that an expansion of defense programs was necessary.[51]

The year preceding the Korean invasion thus witnessed the erosion of the consensus built around economic containment and the rise of a new one centered on military containment. The declining influence of George Kennan during late 1949 reflected the evolution of official thinking. Kennan thought that a number of the administration's policies from 1948 to 1950—the creation of NATO and the West German state, the decision to retain U.S. troops in postoccupation Japan, and the development of the hydrogen bomb—all were certain to freeze the division of Europe and Asia into existing spheres of influence. Without conciliatory, positive efforts to bring the Russians to the negotiating table, the United States would confirm Soviet hard-liners' worst fears about U.S. intentions and provoke an uncontrollable arms race. In an October 1949 meeting of the PPS with Acheson in attendance, Kennan criticized the "acceptance throughout the Government of the infallibility of the Joint Chiefs of Staff," who he believed tended to draw their conclusions from improbable, worst-case scenarios. Given Moscow's new atomic capability, the PPS chief argued, it was no longer feasible for the United States to respond to a Red Army attack on Western Europe with strategic air strikes against the Soviet Union. Yet Kennan continued to oppose a major rearmament of NATO's conventional forces.[52]

[51] Gregg Herken, *The Winning Weapon: The Atomic Bomb in the Cold War, 1945–1950* (New York: Vintage Books, 1981), 303–05; John Lewis Gaddis, *Strategies of Containment: A Critical Appraisal of Postwar American National Security Policy* (New York: Oxford University Press, 1982), 84–85.

[52] For Kennan quotation, see Minutes of 148th Meeting of PPS, 11 October 1949, *FRUS*,

Acheson countered that an agreement with the Soviets on atomic energy was unattainable "and made the point that to agree with the Russians not to use atomic bombs in warfare was to deprive yourself of the effect on the enemy of the fear of retaliation by atomic bombing against orthodox aggression."[53] The secretary of state also questioned Kennan's view that West European recovery was all that was needed to contain Soviet power and influence. As Acheson later wrote, "The threat to Western Europe seemed to me singularly like that which Islam had posed centuries before, with its combination of ideological zeal and fighting power." Acheson regarded MAP and the atomic bomb as essential deterrents to Soviet aggression and believed the Pentagon "was not so unresponsive to the idea that our war preparations are designed to keep us out of war." His real fear, however, was probably not a Soviet invasion but the "drift of Western Europe toward neutralism, prompted by the lack of credibility" of the U.S. deterrent.[54]

Like Acheson, Paul H. Nitze, who succeeded Kennan as PPS director on New Year's Day, 1950, believed that a meaningful settlement with Moscow was possible only if the United States approached negotiations from a position of military superiority. On 31 January 1950, a special NSC advisory committee chaired by Nitze recommended accelerated development of atomic weapons, including the hydrogen bomb, and a thorough review of U.S. national security policies. Truman approved both proposals, and work immediately began on the strategic review that would culminate in NSC 68.

On the same day, the Defense Department and CIA forwarded new, higher estimates of Soviet atomic capabilities (predicted to reach a stockpile of about 100 fission bombs by 1953). Nitze shortly thereafter warned that the "danger of war . . . seemed considerably greater than last fall." Citing Moscow's recognition of Ho Chi Minh and lesser evidence of a shift in the Kremlin's tactics, Nitze postulated that

recent Soviet moves reflect not only a mounting militancy but suggest a boldness that is essentially new—and borders on recklessness. . . . Nothing about the moves

1949, I, 401–02. Also, see Minutes of 171st Meeting of PPS, 16 December 1949, ibid., 414–15; Gaddis, *Strategies,* 71.

[53] Quotation from Minutes of 148th Meeting of PPS, 11 October 1949, *FRUS,* 1949, I, 402. Acheson also noted that the administration would need to decide by January 1950 whether to expand the U.S. atomic weapons program, depending upon negotiations with the Soviets on international control. See ibid., 403.

[54] "Islam" quotation from Acheson, *Present at the Creation,* 490. Quotation on Pentagon from 171st Meeting of PPS, 16 December 1949, *FRUS,* 1949, I, 415; also, see ibid., 416. "Drift" quotation from Lo, "Military Budgets," 168.

indicate that Moscow is preparing to launch in the near future an all-out military attack on the West. They do, however, suggest a greater willingness than in the past to undertake a course of action, including a possible use of force in local areas, which might lead to an accidental outbreak of general military conflict. Thus the chance of war through miscalculation is increased.[55]

This new line of reasoning reflected the emerging consensus that achieved official status in NSC 68. The State-Defense Policy Review Group that drafted NSC 68 contended that the differences between "free" and "slave" societies were irreconcilable and that the only way to achieve peaceful relations between the two spheres would be a fundamental change in the Soviet system. In contrast to Kennan and many Sovietologists of the day, the authors of NSC 68 portrayed the Kremlin leaders as unequivocally hostile and uncompromising, bent on "the domination of the Eurasian land mass," and dedicated to the destruction of the United States. Negotiations with the Soviets were out of the question because the United States, despite superior military potential, suffered from "a sharp disparity between our actual military strength and our commitments." Unlike Kennan, who wished to focus U.S. efforts on certain strongpoints in Europe and Asia, Nitze and the other architects of NSC 68 believed that "a defeat of free institutions anywhere is a defeat everywhere" and that the United States should be prepared to defend against communist aggression wherever it occurred. According to NSC 68, the only effective response to the communist challenge was a sharp U.S. buildup in both the atomic and conventional areas, creating what Acheson called situations of strength. "Without superior aggregate military strength, in being and readily mobilizable," the memo stated, "a policy of 'containment'—which is in effect a policy of calculated and gradual coercion—is no more than a policy of bluff."[56]

One of the most important legacies of NSC 68 was a new set of assumptions about the economic foundations of security. Despite its vastly larger industrial capacity, the authors of NSC 68 claimed, the United States spent only one-half what the Soviets did on defense and military-

[55] "Danger" quotation from Record of 8th Meeting of PPS, 2 February 1950, *FRUS, 1950*, I, 142–43. "Soviet moves" quotation from Nitze memo, 8 February 1950, ibid., 145–46. For Nitze's evidence of a new communist offensive, see "Recent Soviet and Soviet-Satellite Moves," addendum to Nitze memo above, Papers of HST-PSF-Foreign Affairs File, File: Russia 1949–52, HSTL. Also, see Samuel F. Wells, Jr., "Sounding the Tocsin: NSC 68 and the Soviet Threat," *International Security* 4 (Fall 1979): 119, 126–27.

[56] Quotations from NSC 68, 7 April 1950, *FRUS, 1950*, I, 238, 240, 253, 261; also, see ibid., 242, 245–46, 249–52, 282–85. For a summary of NSC 68, see Wells, "Tocsin," 131–35.

related programs as a proportion of gross national product. U.S. buildup need not entail a reduction in the standard of living, for the U.S. economy contained enough slack in the aftermath of the 1949 recession to permit substantial expansion of both civilian and military production. The report did not clarify whether stimulatory steps were necessary to expand the economy, for Keynesianism was still frowned upon. In a message clearly directed at the White House, however, the review group stated that "budgetary considerations will need to be subordinated to the stark fact that our very independence as a nation may be at stake." Citing the U.S. experience in World War II, the memo argued that the United States could afford both guns and butter.[57]

The authors of NSC 68 in fact may have deliberately exaggerated the Soviet threat—they estimated 1954 to be the year of greatest danger of an all-out Soviet attack upon the United States—in order to sway the president and his economic advisers. (The State-Defense group also may have focused on the Soviet military danger because West European neutralism, the more immediate object of their fears, was too amorphous a threat to catalyze the government.) Truman, after all, had repeatedly stated that only a national emergency could justify a major escalation of U.S. defense spending. As Acheson explains in his memoirs, "The purpose of NSC-68 was to so bludgeon the mass mind of 'top government' that not only could the President make a decision but that the decision could be carried out."[58]

Yet Truman did not fall for this gambit. His response to an early draft of NSC 68 in April 1950 was to call for "a clearer indication of the programs which are envisaged in the Report, including estimates of the probable cost of such programs." He instructed the Bureau of the Budget, the Treasury Department, the Economic Cooperation Administration, and the Council of Economic Advisers to participate in an ad hoc committee to review NSC 68. Under its new chairman, Leon Keyserling, the CEA was confident that the U.S. economy, with the proper fiscal and tax measures, could easily accommodate the rearmament programs outlined in NSC 68 "without serious threat to our standards of living," excessive inflation, or large deficits.[59]

---

[57] Quotation from NSC 68, 7 April 1950, *FRUS*, 285. Also, see ibid., 256–58, 286; Gaddis, *Strategies*, 93–94.

[58] Quotation from Acheson, *Present at the Creation*, 488; also, see ibid., 489–90; Wells, "Tocsin," 124; Lo, "Military Budgets," 137–38.

[59] "Cost" quotation from Truman to Lay, 12 April 1950, *FRUS*, 1950, I, 235. Also, see Memo to President on 55th Meeting of NSC, 21 April 1950, Papers of HST-PSF-Subject

The counterattack against NSC 68 was led by the Budget Bureau, joined to a lesser extent by Defense Secretary Louis Johnson and individuals at the State Department (such as Under Secretary James Webb, the former budget director). In addition to questioning the memo's dire portrayal of Soviet military power, the Budget Bureau in May 1950 pointed out that this country's extraordinary productivity during World War II was irrelevant to a drawn-out cold war. Massive rearmament in peacetime could disrupt the civilian economy. Even with the 3.5 million unemployed in 1949, the agency argued, inflation remained a danger. In its view, full-scale rearmament would divert resources from the civilian sector (and thus negate any growth in the defense sector), limit the funds available for foreign aid, and require higher taxes and deeper deficits. The president appeared to agree. "The defense budget next year will be smaller than it is this year," he stated at a press conference in early May 1950, "and we are continually cutting it by economies." As late as 5 June, Louis Johnson told Acheson that "he doubted that the over-all US defense budget would be increased."[60]

Even though the administration accepted the general premises and conclusions of NSC 68, many senior officials balked at full implementation of its recommendations. There is no way of knowing for certain what the president would have done if the Korean War had not intervened. Truman did not approve NSC 68 as U.S. policy until late September 1950, months after the Korean War had radically altered Western perceptions of the Soviet danger. Initial cost estimates of all the programs recommended in the report were around $50 billion annually, but without Korea, spending on defense and international programs probably would have risen by only a few billion dollars annually, if at all. As it was, defense outlays for fiscal 1950 totaled only $13.5 billion; deducting occupation costs, army civil expenditures, and Greek-Turkish military aid,

File: NSC Meetings, File: Memo for Pres.—Meeting Discussions (1950), HSTL. On CEA, see Dearborn to Lay, 8 May 1950, *FRUS, 1950*, I, 311. The NSRB also strongly supported NSC 68; see NSRB Memo, 29 May 1950, *FRUS, 1950*, I, 316–21.

[60] The Budget Bureau claimed that the total war effort achieved in 1944 had caused the deterioration of capital assets and inflationary pressures that the government could suppress only over the short term. See Schaub to Lay, 8 May 1950, *FRUS, 1950*, I, 304–05. On Webb, see McWilliams Memcon, 6 June 1950, ibid., 324. Truman quotation from Press Conference, 4 May 1950, in U.S., Office of the President, *Public Papers of the Presidents of the United States, Harry S. Truman, 1950* (Washington, D.C.: National Archives and Records Service, 1964), 286. For Johnson quotation, see Battle Memo of Telephone Conversation, 5 June 1950, Papers of Dean Acheson, File: Memos of Conversation May–June 1950, HSTL. Also, see Wells, "Tocsin," 137–38; Rearden, *OSD*, chapter XVII, 1–2, 15–19.

the Pentagon spent only $11.9 billion. "The real significance of NSC 68," Samuel F. Wells, Jr., observes, "was its timing—the tocsin sounded just before the fire."[61]

The Korean War was the true watershed in Truman's defense policy. The invasion of South Korea appeared to refute the central concept of economic containment, namely that communist political penetration of war-disrupted societies posed a greater danger to Western security than did communist military aggression. In the face of the enhanced Sino-Soviet military capabilities and the aggression in Korea, economic aid seemed a frail deterrent indeed. After the Korean invasion, U.S. policy makers no longer regarded economic power and multilateral institutions as the first line of defense in the cold war.

The new mood in the administration was reflected in an NSC meeting of late November 1950 that was called to discuss NSC 68 and the defense budgets of fiscal 1951 and 1952. Dean Acheson emerged as the main spokesman for accelerated rearmament. The secretary of state argued that the United States must be prepared simultaneously for a long war in Korea and additional military responsibilities in Western Europe, as well as a possible Soviet atomic attack as early as 1952, the year, in his estimation, of "the greatest danger."

The national emergency also made it easier to accept big deficits. In the November 1950 NSC meeting, CEA Chairman Keyserling made "no judgment regarding defense needs," but argued that "the economy could stand the job required by NSC 68 and . . . no reduction of effort was necessary." In an annex to NSC 68/3 dated 8 December 1950, Keyserling further argued that the country could easily meet the report's mobilization aims. "These programs . . . ," he wrote, "fall about half way be-

---

[61] NSC 68 did not substantially differ in its recommendations from NSC 20/4 in November 1948, the earlier assessment of U.S.-Soviet relations, of which NSC 68 was a review. The tone of NSC 68, however, was new in that the threat of Soviet attack was magnified; in this sense, the Soviet bomb was probably an important factor. The main objective of NSC 68, then, was a call to action, rather than a policy analysis. In retrospect, it is clear that NSC 68 grossly exaggerated the Soviet threat and distorted the nature of Soviet communism. Soviet ground forces, atomic weapons and deliverability were greatly exaggerated while U.S. retaliatory capacity and mobilization potential were understated. In contrast with the malevolent master plan that NSC attributed to the Soviet leaders, they may have been reacting to Western initiatives, such as the Berlin blockade, the creation of NATO and MAP, McCarthyism, and the superbomb. Indeed, the Soviets commenced a major military buildup only after the post-Korea U.S. rearmament had begun in earnest. Quotation from Wells, "Tocsin," 139; see also ibid., 138–39, 152–57; Acheson, *Present at the Creation*, 488. Statistics on fiscal 1950 budget from W. J. NcNeil to Louis Johnson, 5 July 1950, Papers of HST-PSF-Subject File, File: Bureau of the Budget: Budget-Military—1945–53, HSTL.

tween 'business as usual' and a really large-scale dedication of our enormous economic resources . . . , even when defining this large-scale dedication as something far short of an all-out . . . mobilization for war purposes." Following the massive Chinese intervention in Korea during late November and early December, Truman and the NSC moved up the target date for the completion of the military buildup from 1954 to 30 June 1952. The president and his top advisers probably had not become sudden converts to Keynesianism; rather, the Korean crisis had led them to discount the economic costs of rearmament. As Acheson put it in a December 1950 NSC meeting, "It would not be too much if we had all the troops that the military want [and] all of the things that our European allies want. . . . The danger couldn't be greater than it is."[62]

The Truman administration's declining faith in the ability of economic instruments to contain communism is reflected in statistics on U.S. foreign assistance. Whereas U.S. military aid had amounted to only $69 million in 1946 and $97 million in 1947, it reached $523 million in 1950. By 1952, 80 percent of U.S. assistance to Western Europe consisted of military matériel, and for the first time in the postwar era, U.S. military aid worldwide ($2.7 billion) exceeded economic aid ($2 billion), setting a pattern for the rest of the decade.[63] Economic assistance had become an adjunct to military programs, a reward for good behavior rather than a vital instrument in the renovation of an integrated and stable Western economy.

Still, one of the most remarkable features of U.S. foreign policy before the Korean War was the durability of economic containment. Officials in the Truman administration remained confident that American economic

[62] Acheson "greatest danger" and Keyserling "no judgment" quotations from Memo to President on 72nd Meeting of NSC, 24 November 1950, Papers of HST-PSF-Subject File: NSC Meetings, File: Memos for Pres.—Meeting Discussions (1950), HSTL. Acheson "troops" quotation from Memo to President on 75th Meeting of NSC, 15 December 1950, ibid. "Business as usual" quotation from Keyserling Memo, 8 December 1950, *FRUS*, 1950, I, 430. Also, see ibid., 427–31; Butler Memo, 13 December 1950, ibid., 466–67; NSC Report to President, 14 December 1950, ibid., 468–70; Memo to President on 105th Meeting of NSC, 18 October 1951, Papers of HST-PSF-Subject File: NSC Meetings, File: Memos for Pres.—Meeting Discussions (1951), HSTL; Lo, "Military Budgets," 152.

[63] Congress, which had authorized $1.23 billion for MAP before the Korean invasion, increased the total to $5 billion after war broke out. ECA, meanwhile, was cut by $208 million in June 1950. See Kaplan, NATO, 104–05; U.S. Department of Commerce, Bureau of the Census, *Historical Statistics of the United States: Colonial Times to 1970*, part 2 (Washington, D.C.: U.S. Government Printing Office, 1975), 87; Paterson, *Confrontation*, 232. U.S. military aid, incidentally, was not designed, as some revisionist scholars claim, to close the dollar gap in Western Europe. See Lo, "Military Budgets," 136, 154, 162.

power, backed by the deterrent power of atomic weapons, could almost single-handedly stabilize vital regions and countries against communist encroachment. Changing perceptions of the Soviet threat did not substantially affect U.S. defense policy before June 1950. The national security state, such as it was, emerged only with the outbreak of the Korean War.

Conclusion

President Truman perhaps can be faulted for his preoccupation with balanced budgets. To many contemporaries, the Korean invasion and the subsequent Chinese entry into the war exposed the lack of U.S. military preparedness and the folly of Truman's ceiling on defense expenditures. There is no doubt that the proliferation of U.S. global commitments after the war stretched U.S. armed forces to the limit and that the neglect of conventional forces encouraged overreliance on atomic weapons in military strategy.

In retrospect, however, the Truman administration's dependence on economic power (and the bomb) before Korea is understandable. The demise in Congress of the president's limited proposal for universal military training indicates the depth of popular resistance to the notion of a large military. The increments in the Pentagon budget that many congressional defense advocates desired were heavily oriented toward air and atomic power and would not have significantly relieved the shortage of ground forces that military leaders faced in June 1950. In the final analysis, moreover, economic containment worked: The Marshall Plan did restore European production and facilitate Franco-German cooperation, and Western economic growth did make possible an enduring and powerful alliance among the United States, Japan, and most of Europe. The United States achieved all this with a defense budget that never exceeded 5.7 percent of GNP during the fiscal years 1947 to 1950, compared with 9 to 10 percent during the late 1950s.[64] President Truman, in short, did not succumb to the temptations of what his successor would label the "military-industrial complex."

[64] Gaddis, *Strategies*, 359. The defense figures exclude veterans' benefits.

8

The insecurities of victory: the United States and the perception of the Soviet threat after World War II

JOHN LEWIS GADDIS

The cold war, whatever else one might say about it, has been a remarkably durable phenomenon. It has already exceeded in length the Peloponnesian War, the First and Second Punic Wars, the Thirty Years' War, the Wars of the French Revolution and Napoleon, and what Winston Churchill called the second Thirty Years' War that began with an assassin's gunshot at Sarajevo and ended with mushroom clouds over Hiroshima and Nagasaki.[1] Almost half of the twentieth century has now been taken up by one aspect or another of that conflict, a rivalry made all the more striking by the fact that at no point in its long history have its major antagonists actually come to blows.

"*De quoi s'agit-il?*" Marshal Foch used to ask his subordinates in World War I. "What is it all about?" The passage of time has made this no easy question to answer. The great antagonism between the United States and the Soviet Union has become encrusted, over the years, with successive layers of routine, custom, tradition, myth, and legend. Few of the men who shaped the affairs of nations at its outset are still alive; fewer still are able to recall with any precision what impelled them to act as they did at that time. Documents on the origins of the cold war abound in Western archives—though almost none are available in the Soviet Union—but these sources provide no guarantee that those who use them will be able to reconstruct the past "as it actually happened." Historians, like

I am indebted, for helpful comments, to Alonzo Hamby, Michael Hogan, Michael Lacey, and Vojtech Mastny.
[1] Winston S. Churchill, *The Gathering Storm*, Bantam Books (Boston: 1948), vii.

most other people, are prone to see what they seek; they do not always take care to insulate their accounts of what transpired from their concerns with what is transpiring.

To recapture what was in the minds of Western leaders as the cold war began requires, in addition to traditional methods of historical research, something of an imaginative leap. One must get a sense of how things looked at the time. One must free one's vision from the accumulated impressions of the most recent past, from the tyranny of knowing what came next. One must avoid at all costs imposing a contemporary frame of reference upon those who were in no position to anticipate the contemporary world. There are standards of judgment in history, but they should be standards derived from a range of historical experience that goes beyond what happened last month, or last year, or even in the last decade.

What follows is an attempt, in the spirit of this approach, to answer a single simple question: What was there in the behavior of the Soviet Union immediately after World War II to convince American statesmen that the security of the United States was once again in danger, as it had been in 1917 and again in 1940–41? Of the fact that they were so convinced, there can be no doubt: alarm, when projected so widely and when sustained for so long, would be difficult to feign. The reasons for that alarm, though, are not at all clear at this distance. It is necessary to reconstruct them if we are to understand.

I

Early in November 1945, subscribers to *Life* picked up their copies of the magazine to find depicted there, in lurid détail, a mushroom cloud rising over Washington, a view from space of rockets raining down on other American cities, an antiballistic missile system responding to the attack while retaliatory rockets were launched toward enemy targets from underground silos, an invasion of the United States by gas-masked airborne troops equipped with infrared goggles, and, finally, after the successful American counterattack, a depiction of weary technicians checking for radioactivity in front of the New York Public Library's marble lions, the only recognizable feature of the city left intact amid the rubble. The occasion for this apocalyptic vision was General Henry H. Arnold's final wartime report of Army Air Force activities, a document that pointedly looked as much to future dangers as to past victories.[2] The success-

[2] "The 36-Hour War," *Life,* 19 November 1945, 27–35. For Arnold's complete report,

ful conclusion of the war had brought with it no guarantee of lasting security, both Arnold and the editors of *Life* seemed to be saying. It was as if the United States had finally assumed a decisive role in world affairs, only to find that the price of preeminence is vulnerability.

This sense of vulnerability is basic to an understanding of how Americans perceived their interests—and potential threats to them—in the postwar world. Prior to World War II, the dominant view had been that the security of the United States required little more than insulating the Western hemisphere from outside influences. This "continentalist" vision arose from several sources: traditional American isolationism, reinforced in the 1920s by disillusionment with the results of World War I; an assumption of economic self-sufficiency, intensified in the early 1930s by a self-centered preoccupation with economic recovery; and, by the mid-1930s, the fear of new conflicts in Europe and Asia in which Americans appeared to have no visible stake.[3] It is an indication of the strength of this attitude that Franklin D. Roosevelt, who never wholly shared it, felt obliged nonetheless consistently to defer to it during his first two terms in office.[4]

The fall of France and the Japanese attack on Pearl Harbor provided a painfully abrupt education on the inadequacies of "continentalism." Isolationist arguments that events overseas would never imperil the security interests of the United States could hardly have been more thoroughly discredited. In their place, there arose a new "globalist" consensus among opinion shapers both within and outside government: that the primary American postwar interest now lay, not just in securing the Western Hemisphere, but in keeping its Eastern counterpart as well free from control by a single potentially hostile power.

The idea, of course, was hardly a new one. Such a strategy of denial

dated 12 November 1945, see *The War Reports of General of the Army George C. Marshall, General of the Army H. H. Arnold, Fleet Admiral Ernest J. King* (Philadelphia: 1947), 419–70, especially 452–70.

[3] The most succinct definition of "continentalism" is in Mark A. Stoler, "From Continentalism to Globalism: General Stanley D. Embick, the Joint Strategic Survey Committee, and the Military View of American National Policy during the Second World War," *Diplomatic History* VI (Summer 1982): 304. But see also Manfred Jonas, *Isolationism in America, 1935–1941* (Ithaca: 1966), 100–01; and Wayne S. Cole, *Roosevelt and the Isolationists, 1932–45* (Lincoln: 1983), 6–7. For the impact of this thinking on military planning, see Fred Greene, "The Military View of National Policy, 1904–1940," *American Historical Review* LXVI (January 1961): 354–77; and Michael S. Sherry, *Preparing for the Next War: American Plans for Postwar Defense, 1941–45* (New Haven: 1977), 27–31.

[4] Ibid., 8–12, 113, 243; Robert Dallek, *Franklin D. Roosevelt and American Foreign Policy, 1932–1945* (New York: 1979), 12, 68, 106, 152, 227.

had formed the basis of England's policy toward Europe since at least the days of the Spanish Armada, and as early as 1904 the British geopolitician Sir Halford Mackinder had extended the concept to imply that the world balance of power depended upon preserving Eurasian "rimlands" free from domination by the Eurasian "heartland."[5] What was new in the 1940s was the conversion of influential Americans to this viewpoint, with all that it implied for a more active postwar role by the United States in world affairs.

"The most important single fact in the American security situation is the question of who controls the rimlands of Europe and Asia," Frederick Sherwood Dunn, director of the Yale Institute of International Studies, wrote late in 1943. "Should these get into the hands of a single power or combination of powers hostile to the United States, the resulting encirclement would put us in a position of grave peril, regardless of the size of our army and navy."[6] Dunn's colleague at Yale, Nicholas John Spykman, had provided the earliest and most thorough statement of this argument in his 1942 book, *America's Strategy in World Politics,* and in a second shorter volume, *The Geography of the Peace,* published in 1944 shortly after his death. Drawing on Mackinder's insights, Spykman pointed out that North and South America were in effect islands, possessing slightly over a third of the Old World's land area but only a tenth of its population. Throughout its history the United States had depended for its security upon the maintenance of a balance of power in Europe and Asia. Previous challenges to that balance had elicited Anglo-American cooperation to restore it—tacitly at the time of the Monroe Doctrine in 1823, overtly in 1917. World War II had again called the balance into question: its outcome would determine "whether the United States is to remain a great power with a voice in the affairs of the Old World, or become merely a buffer state between the mighty empires of Germany and Japan."[7]

Spykman's professorial arguments refuted continentalism effectively

[5] Sir Halford Mackinder, "The Geographical Pivot of History," *Geographical Journal* XXIII (April 1904): 421–44. See also Mackinder, *Democratic Ideals and Reality: A Study in the Politics of Reconstruction* (New York: 1919).
[6] Frederick Sherwood Dunn, "An Introductory Statement," in Nicholas John Spykman, *The Geography of the Peace,* edited by Helen R. Nicholl (New York: 1944), x.
[7] Nicholas John Spykman, *America's Strategy in World Politics* (New York: 1942), 195. See also Spykman, *The Geography of the Peace,* 33. Other volumes representative of this line of argument include William T. R. Fox, *The Super-Powers: The United States, Britain, and the Soviet Union—Their Responsibility for Peace* (New York: 1944), and Robert Strausz-Hupé, *The Balance of Tomorrow: Power and Foreign Policy in the United States* (New York: 1945).

enough, but not at a level likely to reach a mass audience. That task was left to Walter Lippmann, whose brilliant 1943 popularization of the Mackinder-Spykman thesis, *U.S. Foreign Policy: Shield of the Republic,* became one of the most influential books published during the war. With characteristic disdain for his own previous Wilsonianism, Lippmann now found support in the writings of the Founding Fathers for a strategy based on an explicit recognition of power realities. "Like the idle rich who regard work as something for menials," Americans had too easily come to believe, "that a concern with the foundations of national security, with arms, with strategy, and with diplomacy, was beneath our dignity as idealists." In fact, "the first concern of the makers of foreign policy in a sovereign national state must be to achieve the greatest possible security." This required the projection of power beyond national borders: "The strategic defenses of the United States are not at the three-mile limit in American waters, but extend across both oceans and to all the trans-oceanic lands from which an attack by sea or by air can be launched." It also required allies, because "to be isolated is for any state the worst of all predicaments."[8]

This new determination to base policy upon the facts of power implied no necessary rejection of the campaign to commit the United States to membership in a new collective security organization after the war;[9] indeed "internationalists" and "realists" emphatically shared the goal of undercutting isolationism, whatever their differences as to the nature of the postwar world. But the new geopolitics did insist upon the continuing importance of power in international affairs, however effective the new world body might turn out to be.[10] And, indeed, architects of the United Nations themselves seemed to acknowledge the point by building into the structure of that organization explicit provision for permanent big-power membership on the Security Council, with the right of veto guaranteed.[11]

President Roosevelt himself had always been at least as sensitive to considerations of power as his more forthright colleagues in the Grand

---

[8] Walter Lippmann, *U.S. Foreign Policy: Shield of the Republic* (Boston: 1943), especially 49, 94, 105. For the origins and reception of this book, see Ronald Steel, *Walter Lippmann and the American Century* (Boston: 1980), 404–08.

[9] The best account of this development is Robert A. Divine, *Second Chance: The Triumph of Internationalism in America During World War II* (New York: 1967).

[10] See, for example, Spykman, *The Geography of the Peace,* 60; Lippmann, *U.S. Foreign Policy,* 165–68.

[11] See, on this point, Strausz-Hupé, *The Balance of Tomorrow,* 275–76; also Divine, *Second Chance,* 297–98.

Alliance, Churchill and Stalin. Despite his deference to isolationist opinion in the 1930s, FDR had never accepted the argument that events in the Old World had no bearing upon the security of the New. As early as January 1939, he had privately described the "first line of defense" for the United States as requiring the continued independence of those European states not then under German control and denial to Japan of islands from which that nation might seek to dominate the Pacific.[12] By 1941, Roosevelt was discussing a postwar settlement based upon joint action by the "Four Policemen"—the United States, Great Britain, the Soviet Union, and China—to keep the peace.[13] Although the president would later incorporate his "Four Policemen" concept into a collective security framework acceptable to Wilsonian idealists, he never lost his own insistence upon the importance of power relationships. "We cannot deny that power is a factor in world politics," he noted in his last State of the Union address in 1945, "any more than we can deny its existence as a factor in national politics."[14]

Military planners, too, moved during the war toward a recognition of global responsibilities. The Navy, under the influence of Alfred Thayer Mahan, had never questioned the importance of overseas bases, especially in the Pacific, an attitude now strongly reinforced by Pearl Harbor and the loss of the Philippines.[15] Of greater significance was the conversion of Army strategists, who in the interwar period had been prepared to deny the existence of vital American interests in both Europe and Asia, to an active concern with the balance of power in these areas. "General Eisenhower . . . does not believe that it would be in our interest to have the continent of Europe dominated by any single power," the American embassy in Paris reported late in 1944, "for then we would have a super-powerful Europe, a somewhat shaken British Empire and ourselves." The Joint Strategic Survey Committee had reached similar conclusions about Asia a year earlier.[16] Intelligence analysts agreed with these assessments,

---

[12] Roosevelt meeting with the Senate Military Affairs Committee, 31 January 1939, as cited in Cole, *Roosevelt and the Isolationists*, 304. See also ibid., 243; and Dallek, *Franklin D. Roosevelt and American Foreign Policy*, 321.

[13] See, on this point, John Lewis Gaddis, *The United States and the Origins of the Cold War, 1941–1947* (New York: 1972), 24–25.

[14] Roosevelt State of the Union Address, 6 January 1945, Samuel I. Rosenman, ed., *The Public Papers and Addresses of Franklin D. Roosevelt* (New York: 1941–50), XIII, 498. See also Roosevelt's fireside chat, 24 December 1943, ibid., XII, 558.

[15] Waldo H. Heinrichs, Jr., "The Role of the United States Navy," in Dorothy Borg and Sumpei Okamoto, eds., *Pearl Harbor as History: Japanese-American Relations, 1931–1941* (New York: 1973), 201–04.

[16] Jefferson Caffery to Cordell Hull, 20 October 1944, *Foreign Relations of the United*

As an Office of Strategic Services study put it in the summer of 1944, "Our interests require the maintenance of a policy designed to prevent the development of a serious threat to the security of the British Isles [and of the United States], through the consolidation of a large part of Europe's resources under any one power."[17]

But the most persuasive arguments in favor of a global rather than a continental perception of postwar interests came from the Army Air Force, which to the irritation of its ground- and sea-based counterparts was not hesitant to stress the strategic implications of the new technology of warfare. "Bombers can now range the world," General Arnold pointedly noted in his final report that so impressed the editors of *Life;* moreover, improved versions of the German V-2 rocket capable of reaching the United States from Europe or Asia were not at all impractical. The V-2 "is ideally suited to deliver atomic explosives because effective defense against it would prove extremely difficult." It was entirely possible, Arnold concluded, "that the progressive development of the air arm, especially with the concurrent development of the atomic explosive, guided missiles, and other modern devices, will reduce the requirement for our employment of mass armies and navies." But it would also create permanent vulnerability, because even with existing equipment an enemy air force could, "without warning, pass over all formerly visualized barriers or 'lines of defense' and . . . deliver devastating blows at our population centers and our industrial, economic or governmental heart."[18]

The demonstrated feasibility of atomic weapons, together with the long-range bombers and—in the not too distant future—the rockets necessary to carry them, created a security problem for postwar planners that went beyond concern for the Eurasian balance of power. It involved nothing less than the physical safety of the United States itself. No longer, it appeared, would Americans enjoy the luxury of mobilizing their strength after threats had materialized; military force now would have to be maintained on a permanent basis, and in a manner that would make possible

---

States (hereafter *FRUS*), 1944, III, 743. See also Stoler, "From Continentalism to Globalism," 311, 314.

[17] OSS Research and Analysis report #2284, "American Security Interests in the European Settlement," 29 June 1944, Office of Strategic Service Records, Modern Military Records Division, National Archives.

[18] *War Reports,* 452–53, 457, 263–64. See also Sherry, *Preparing for the Next War,* 39–42. Curiously, Arnold coupled his vision of future warfare with an enthusiastic account of Army Air Force experiments in the field of hydroponics. These had produced, without soil, gratifying quantities of "tomatoes, radishes, lettuce and cucumbers." (*War Reports,* 465–66.)

its quick use. As Arnold put it in his report, "Real security against atomic weapons in the visible future will rest on our ability to take immediate offensive action with overwhelming force. It must be apparent to a potential aggressor that an attack on the United States would be immediately followed by an immensely devastating air-atomic attack on him."[19]

All of this seemed to confirm, then, the wisdom of a postwar strategy based on denying control of the Eurasian continent to any potentially hostile power. As the experiences of 1917 and 1941 had shown, it was a strategy with deep—if not always clearly perceived—historical roots. Nor was it inconsistent with the objectives for which Americans liked to think of themselves as fighting: after all, maintaining a balance of power could only enhance the opportunities for self-determination, liberal trading policies, and collective security called for in the Atlantic Charter and in innumerable other wartime justifications for the wielding of military force. Americans, it appeared, could respond to their new-found preeminence in world affairs by following the designs of both Wilson and Mackinder at the same time.[20]

II

"The most important political development during the last ten years of localized and finally global warfare," columnist C. L. Sulzberger noted in the *New York Times* a week after Japan's surrender, "has been the emergence of the Union of Soviet Socialist Republics as the greatest dynamic and diplomatic force on the vast Eurasian land mass which stretches from the Atlantic to the Pacific oceans."[21] No one could quarrel with the conclusion, which had been foreseen for some time. Nor could there be any doubt that this situation carried with it profound implications for the future of American foreign policy, given the widespread consensus that the security of the New World now depended upon what happened

---

[19]Ibid., 464. For a sampling of civilian assessments of the implications of the new technology, see Bernard Brodie, ed., *The Absolute Weapon* (New York: 1946); Dexter Masters and Katharine Way, eds., *One World or None* (New York: 1946); William Liscum Borden, *There Will Be No Time: The Revolution in Strategy* (New York: 1946); and B. H. Liddell Hart, *The Revolution in Warfare* (New Haven: 1947).

[20]For a persuasive account of Wilson's ability to think in balance-of-power terms, see N. Gordon Levin, *Woodrow Wilson and World Politics* (New York: 1968), especially 8, 36–41. Daniel Yergin provides a succinct characterization of the new "gospel of national security" in *Shattered Peace: The Origins of the Cold War and the National Security State* (Boston: 1977), 193–204.

[21]*New York Times*, 9 September 1945.

in the Old. Interestingly, though, this concern with the postwar balance of power did not automatically translate into a conviction that the Soviet Union posed the most likely threat to it.

The danger in World War II, after all, had come from the Germans and the Japanese, not the Russians; it is significant that in 1943 Mackinder himself had modified his thesis, pointing out the hazards of "rimland" domination of the "heartland" and not the other way around.[22] American geopoliticians, noting Moscow's vigorous participation in the war against Germany and potential assistance against Japan as well, followed his lead. As Spykman himself put it: "The heartland [has become] less important than the rimland and it is the cooperation of British, Russian, and United States land and sea power that will control the European littoral and, thereby, the essential power relations of the world."[23] Lippmann agreed, pointing out that the primary American interest was to allow no *European* power to become capable of committing aggression *outside* of Europe. "Therefore our two natural and permanent allies have been and are Britain and Russia."[24]

Certainly this was the viewpoint of the Roosevelt administration. "I personally don't think there's anything in it," FDR commented early in 1944, when asked about rumors that the Russians were out to dominate all of Europe. "They have got a large enough 'hunk of bread' right in Russia to keep them busy for a great many years to come without taking on any more headaches."[25] Roosevelt had built his whole strategy upon the expectation that the wartime alliance would survive the end of the war. He had sought to ensure this through public deference to Soviet security interests, mixed with subtle behind-the-scenes pressures to encourage Moscow's cooperation. Although concerned during the last months of his life about the increasing frequency of misunderstandings with the Russians, he at no point sought to contest the substantial expansion of Soviet influence in Europe and Asia that the end of the war would bring. Rather, he hoped to maintain a balance of power by convincing the Rus-

[22]H. J. Mackinder, "The Round World and the Winning of the Peace," *Foreign Affairs* XXI (July 1943): 595–605.

[23]Spykman, *The Geography of the Peace*, 41–44. Although Spykman in 1942 had raised the possibility that the United States and Britain might seek to preserve some form of German power to balance Soviet influence in Europe, because "a Russian state from the Urals to the North Sea can be no great improvement over a German state from the North Sea to the Urals." (Spykman, *America's Strategy in World Politics*, 460.)

[24]Lippmann, *U.S. Foreign Policy*, 164. See also Fox, *The Super-Powers*, 103–06.

[25]Roosevelt's informal remarks to the Advertising War Council Conference, 8 March 1944, Rosenman, ed., *Roosevelt Public Papers*, XIII, 99.

sians that security could best be attained through cooperative rather than unilateral efforts to counter potential threats.[26]

Despite obvious differences in personality and style, Harry S. Truman continued Roosevelt's policy upon coming into office. A more dedicated Wilsonian than his predecessor, the new chief executive held high hopes that the United Nations would provide workable mechanisms for resolving world tensions. During his first months in office he firmly rejected proposals from Winston Churchill and from some of his own advisers that would have denied the Russians previously agreed-upon occupation zones in Central Europe and Northeast Asia.[27] "I was having as much difficulty with Prime Minister Churchill as I was having with Stalin," the new president noted in May of 1945. As late as the fall of that year, both Truman and his new secretary of state, James F. Byrnes, were still relying upon the establishment of a personal relationship with Stalin as the best way to overcome the difficulties that had already begun to emerge in the Soviet-American relationship.[28]

The State Department followed his lead, though from a somewhat different perspective. Still very much under the influence of the recently retired Cordell Hull, it saw potential threats to world order as arising, not specifically from Soviet ambitions, but from spheres of influence in general. Any such perpetuation of power politics could set off new international rivalries, weaken the United Nations, and, worst of all, provoke a disillusioned American public into a reversion to isolationism like the one that had followed the First World War. These dangers could arise as easily from British as from Russian activities, the department warned in July 1945: Any attempt by London to lure Washington into supporting a spheres-of-influence settlement in Europe would "represent power politics pure and simple, with all the concomitant disadvantages. . . . Our primary objective should be to remove the *causes* which make nations feel that such spheres are necessary to build their security, rather than to assist one country to build up strength against another."[29]

[26]See, on these points, Dallek, *Franklin D. Roosevelt and American Foreign Policy*, 533–34; and John Lewis Gaddis, *Strategies of Containment: A Critical Appraisal of Postwar American National Security Policy* (New York: 1982), 9–13.

[27]Gaddis, *The United States and the Origins of the Cold War*, 206–11. For Truman's faith in the United Nations, see Robert J. Donovan, *Conflict and Crisis: The Presidency of Harry S. Truman, 1945–1948* (New York: 1977), 49–50.

[28]Robert L. Messer, *The End of an Alliance: James F. Byrnes, Roosevelt, Truman, and the Origins of the Cold War* (Chapel Hill: 1982), 133–34. Truman's complaint about Churchill is from his appointment sheet, 19 May 1945, as published in Robert H. Ferrell, ed., *Off the Record: The Private Papers of Harry S. Truman* (New York: 1980), 31–32.

[29]Potsdam Briefing Book Paper, "British Plans for a Western European Bloc," 4 July 1945,

Military planners, too, saw the United States more as a mediator between Britain and Russia than as a permanent ally of either one of them.[30]
The Joint Chiefs of Staff had noted in the spring of 1944 that Soviet
influence in postwar Europe would far exceed that of the British. Indeed,
the shift in power was more comparable "with that occasioned by the
fall of Rome than with any other change during the succeeding fifteen
hundred years."[31] But the Chiefs did not draw from this the conclusion
that the United States itself should step in to redress the balance. Intelligence estimates tended to downplay the likelihood of Soviet hostility even
as they acknowledged the probability of Soviet hegemony. However re-
pugnant it might be for those on the receiving end, the expansion of
Russian influence would be taking place more for defensive than offensive reasons. Moreover, overt attempts to build countervailing power in
Europe might have the effect of a self-fulfilling prophecy, reinforcing the
Kremlin's suspicions and perpetuating its inclination toward unilateralism.[32] Since public opinion seemed likely to insist in any event upon the

FRUS: The Conference of Berlin (The Potsdam Conference), 1945 (Washington: 1960),
I, 262–63. For the general State Department viewpoint, see Hugh De Santis, *The Diplomacy of Silence: The American Foreign Service, the Soviet Union, and the Cold War,
1933–1947* (Chicago: 1980), 81–105. For evidence that the Republican party's chief
foreign policy expert shared this viewpoint at the time, see Ronald W. Pruessen, *John
Foster Dulles: The Road to Power* (New York: 1982), 272–76. The American aversion
to spheres of influence as a basis for the postwar settlement is discussed in chapter three
of John Lewis Gaddis, *The Long Peace: Inquiries into the History of the Cold War* (New
York: 1987).

[30]President Truman himself was publicly describing the United States as an "umpire" between Great Britain and the Soviet Union as late as April 1946. (Press conference, 18
April 1946, *Public Papers of the Presidents: Harry S. Truman*, 1946 [Washington: 1962],
211–12.)

[31]JCS 973/1, "Fundamental Military Factors in Relation to Discussions Concerning Terri-
torial Trusteeships and Settlements," 3 August 1944, *FRUS, 1944*, I, 699–703. See also
William D. Leahy to Cordell Hull, 16 May 1944, *FRUS: The Conferences at Malta and
Yalta, 1945* (Washington: 1955), 106–08. For evaluations of the significance of these
documents, see Stoler, "From Continentalism to Globalism," 312–13; Walter S. Poole,
"From Conciliation to Containment: The Joint Chiefs of Staff and the Coming of the
Cold War, 1945–1946," *Military Affairs* XLII (February, 1978): 12; and James F. Schna-
bel, *The Joint Chiefs of Staff and National Policy, 1945–47* (Wilmington, Del.: 1979),
13–16.

[32]JIC 250, "Estimate of Soviet Post-War Capabilities and Intentions," 18 January 1945,
Army Staff Records, ABC 336 Russia Section 1-A, Record Group 319, National Archives. See also the following Office of Strategic Services Research and Analysis reports
on Russian intentions: #1337S, "Russian Intentions in the Mediterranean and Danube
Basins," 20 October 1943; #2284, "American Security Interests in the European Settlement," 29 June 1944; #2669, "Capabilities and Intentions of the USSR in the Postwar
Period," 5 January 1945, all in O.S.S. Records; as well as O.S.S. Director William Donovan's optimistic report of Soviet intentions following the October 1943 Moscow Conference of Foreign Ministers, Donovan to Buxton, 22 November 1943, ibid., USSR Division—1945, Entry 1; also Stephen E. Ambrose, *Eisenhower: Soldier, General of the*

withdrawal of American forces from Europe after the war, there seemed to be few means by which the United States could expect to challenge the Russians on the ground there, even if it should become desirable to do so.[33]

Nor did Moscow appear to possess the potential to threaten the United States directly. Concern about the new technology of warfare had the paradoxical effect of reassuring American military planners about the Russians because they had so little of it. Their navy was little more than a coastal defense force; their air force had no capability for long-range bombing; and there seemed to be no imminent prospect of their building an atomic bomb.[34] "Our Allies of today may be leagued against us tomorrow," an Army Air Force study had cautiously concluded in 1944, but it might well take from 20 to 100 years for "an Eurasian nation to grow into an aggressive-minded power."[35] As late as July 1945, General Arnold himself, the most visible alarmist on the subject of technological vulnerability, could rule out the Russians as a serious threat because of the primitive nature of their military power.[36] The next war, Pentagon planners assumed, would be much like the last, with the danger more likely to come from a resurgent Germany or Japan than from a defensive and technologically backward Soviet Union.[37]

It is true that military planners attached a high priority to the acquisition and indefinite retention of overseas bases. But there is reason to think that these postwar base requirements were determined more by a generalized sense of vulnerability (and perhaps as well by the need to justify a large peacetime defense establishment) than by any specific per-

---

Army, President-Elect, 1890–1952 (New York: 1983), 399–404. For evidence that American military planners did not begin thinking seriously about trying to secure permanent bases on the European continent until the summer of 1945, see Elliott Vanvelnter Converse III, "United States Plans for a Postwar Overseas Military Base System, 1942–1948" (Ph.D. diss., Princeton University, 1984), 90–98, 137–38, 151–54. As late as December 1945, General Eisenhower informed the War Cabinet that "a General Zhukov [had] told him that Russia was determined to make friends with the United States, to raise its standard of living, and to live up to every agreement made." (War Council minutes, 3 December 1945, Robert P. Patterson Papers, Box 23, Library of Congress.)

[33]Sherry, Preparing for the Next War, 102–03. See also Forrest C. Pogue, George C. Marshall: Organizer of Victory (New York: 1973), 574–75.

[34]General Leslie R. Groves, never one to be complacent about the Russians, thought it would take them up to twenty years to develop an atomic bomb. (Gregg Herken, The Winning Weapon: The Atomic Bomb in the Cold War, 1945–1950 [New York: 1980], 98–99.)

[35]Quoted in Perry McCoy Smith, The Air Force Plans for Peace, 1943–1945 (Baltimore: 1970), 80–81.

[36]Ibid., 81.

[37]Sherry, Preparing for the Next War, 53, 84–87, 168.

ception of the Soviet Union as an immediate threat.[38] The locations chosen for these bases suggested a concern with defending the East and West Coasts of the United States and maintaining a sphere of influence in the Pacific, but little apparent interest in the fact that the shortest air route to and from the USSR lay to the north, or in the potential advantages of having bases in Europe and the Near East. Not until the summer of 1945 did consideration of the Russians as likely adversaries begin to influence the actual selection of bases, and even then interservice disagreements, the anticipation of tight postwar budgets, and delays in the negotiation of base rights severely retarded the process of acquisition.[39]

But the main reason both diplomatic and military planners failed to foresee the full implications of the shift in the balance of power that World War II was bringing about was precisely the fact that the war was still on, that the Soviet Union was still an ally, and that its cooperation was still needed to assure victory over Germany and Japan. Common enemies constituted the glue that held the Grand Alliance together, and until they had been laid low, the presumption in relations between Washington, London, and Moscow had to be in favor of cooperation rather than competition. Too candid a consideration of possible postwar antagonisms could impair prospects for victory in the war that was going on at the time; no one was yet prepared to let long-term geopolitical realities overwhelm the immediate necessity of victory.

III

Wartime lack of concern over the powerful position the Soviet Union would occupy in the postwar world had been predicated upon the assumption that the Russians would continue to act in concert with their American and British allies. So long as the Grand Alliance remained intact, Western statesmen could assure each other, Moscow's emergence as the dominant Eurasian power would pose no threat. But during the final

[38]Similar considerations led Air Force planners to give enthusiastic support to the concept of a postwar international police force, administered by the United Nations, that would depend heavily on air power to keep the peace. (Smith, *The Air Force Plans for Peace*, 43–51.)

[39]Smith, *The Air Force Plans for Peace*, 75–83, 111; Sherry, *Preparing for the Next War*, 45–46; Converse, "United States Plans for a Postwar Overseas Military Base System," 143–45, 151–54, 191–234. Converse argues that the Air Force was fully aware of the strategic importance of the polar regions, but did not push for bases there because of the technical difficulties of operating at such latitudes. ("United States Plans for a Postwar Overseas Military Base System," 71–74, 204–11.)

months of the war, there began to appear unsettling indications of a determination on Stalin's part to secure postwar interests without reference to the corresponding interests of his wartime associates. It was these manifestations of unilateralism that first set off alarm bells in the West about Russian intentions; the resulting uneasiness in turn stimulated more profound anxieties.

"I am becoming increasingly concerned," Secretary of State Hull warned Ambassador W. Averell Harriman in early 1944, "over the . . . successive moves of the Soviet Government in the field of foreign relations." Hull went on to observe in this message, drafted by Soviet specialist Charles E. Bohlen, that whatever the legitimacy of Moscow's security interests in Eastern Europe—"and as you know we have carefully avoided and shall continue to avoid any disputation with the Soviet Government on the merits of such questions"—unilateral actions to secure those interests "cannot fail to do irreparable harm to the whole cause of international collaboration." The American people would not be disposed to participate in any postwar scheme of world organization which would be seen "as a cover for another great power to pursue a course of unilateral action in the international sphere based on superior force." It was "of the utmost importance that the principle of consultation and cooperation with the Soviet Union be kept alive at all costs, but some measures of cooperation in relation to world public opinion must be forthcoming from the Soviet Government."[40]

This document reflects as well as any other the point from which American statesmen began to develop concerns about the postwar intentions of the Soviet Union. The United States had not challenged Moscow's determination to retain the boundaries it had secured as a result of Stalin's unsavory pact with Hitler in 1939, nor had it questioned the Russians' right to a postwar sphere of influence in what remained of Eastern Europe. It was prepared to grant similar concessions in East Asia in return for eventual USSR participation in the war against Japan. But because the Roosevelt administration had justified American entry into the war as a defense of self-determination, and because it had committed the nation to participation in a postwar world collective security organization as a means of implementing that principle, it required from the Soviet Union a measure of discretion and restraint in consolidating these areas of control. Unilateral action seemed likely to endanger the balance

---

[40]Hull to Harriman, 9 February 1944, *FRUS*, 1944, IV, 824–26. For Bohlen's role in drafting this document, see De Santis, *The Diplomacy of Silence*, 111.

of power, not by allowing the Russians to dominate areas beyond their borders—that domination was assumed—but rather by weakening the American capacity for countervailing action in the postwar world by provoking, first, public disillusionment and then, as a consequence, a revival of the isolationism the president and his advisers had fought so long and so hard to overcome.[41]

The Russians, to put it mildly, were less than sensitive to these concerns. As their armies moved into Eastern Europe in 1944 they immediately set out to undermine potential sources of opposition, not just in the former enemy countries of Rumania, Bulgaria, and Hungary, but most conspicuously of all in Poland, which had been, after all, an ally. The callousness with which the Red Army allowed the Germans to decimate the anti-communist resistance in Warsaw late that summer shocked Western statesmen; meanwhile British and American representatives on Allied Control Commissions in the Balkans found themselves denied any significant influence in shaping occupation policies there as well.[42] Moscow had interpreted Western restraint as a sign of weakness, Harriman reported in September: "Unless we take issue with the present policy there is every indication that the Soviet Union will become a world bully wherever their interests are involved. . . . No written agreements can be of any value unless they are carried out in a spirit of give and take and recognition of the interests of other people."[43]

Franklin Roosevelt made valiant efforts at Yalta to make Stalin aware of the need to observe the proprieties in Eastern Europe, but these proved unsuccessful almost at once when the Soviet leader interpreted agreements made to hold free elections there as in fact license to impose still tighter control on Poland and Rumania. "Averell is right," Roosevelt complained three weeks before his death. "We can't do business with Stalin. He has broken every one of the promises he made at Yalta."[44]

[41]For the American attitude on these points, see Gaddis, *The United States and the Origins of the Cold War*, 133–73; also Lynn Etheridge Davis, *The Cold War Begins: Soviet-American Conflict over Eastern Europe* (New York: 1974), especially 369–77.

[42]Although, on this point, the Russians could with some justice claim only to be following the precedent set by the Americans and British in refusing to grant the Russians any substantial role in the occupation of Italy after the surrender of that country in 1943.

[43]Harriman to Harry Hopkins, 10 September 1944, *FRUS, 1944*, IV, 989. See also the recollections of American observers to these events in Thomas T. Hammond, ed., *Witnesses to the Origins of the Cold War* (Seattle: 1982).

[44]Quoted in W. Averell Harriman and Elie Abel, *Special Envoy to Churchill and Stalin: 1941–1946* (New York: 1975), 444. For other evidence of Roosevelt's disillusionment with the Russians during the final months of his life, see Dallek, *Franklin D. Roosevelt and American Foreign Policy*, 523–27.

FDR had not been prepared, on the basis of these difficulties, to write off all possibilities of postwar cooperation with the Russians. But Soviet unilateralism does appear to have convinced him, by the time of his death, that efforts to win Stalin's trust had not worked; and that future policy toward the Soviet Union would have to be based on a strict quid pro quo basis.[45]

Harry S. Truman emphatically agreed. Although the new chief executive had had no direct experience in the conduct of foreign affairs, he could hardly have believed more firmly in the importance of keeping one's word. "When I say I'm going to do something, I do it," he once wrote, "or [I] bust my insides trying to do it." It was characteristic of him that he did not believe in divorce because "when you make a contract you should keep it."[46] Convinced that the Yalta agreements on free elections in Eastern Europe were in fact contracts, determined to demonstrate decisiveness in an awesome and unexpected position of responsibility, Truman resolved—probably more categorically than Roosevelt would have done—to hold the Russians to what they had agreed to. It was this determination that occasioned the new president's sharp rejoinder to Soviet Foreign Minister V. M. Molotov after less than two weeks in office: "Carry out your agreements and you won't get talked to like that." A month later he complained again that the Russians were not honoring their agreements: They were, he told Henry Wallace, "like people from across the tracks whose manners were very bad."[47]

The experience of meeting Stalin personally at Potsdam seems to have modified the president's attitude somewhat. The Soviet autocrat evoked memories of the Kansas City political boss Tom Pendergast, a man with whom deals could be made because he had always kept his word.[48] "I

---

[45]Gaddis, *Strategies of Containment,* 13–15.

[46]See William Hillman, ed., *Mr. President* (New York: 1952), 153; also Deborah Welch Larson, *Origins of Containment: A Psychological Explanation* (Princeton: 1985), 132–36.

[47]Wallace Diary, 18 May 1945, quoted in John Morton Blum, ed., *The Price of Vision: The Diary of Henry A. Wallace, 1942–1946* (Boston: 1973), 451. For Truman's 23 April 1945 confrontation with Molotov, see his own account in Harry S. Truman, *Memoirs,* vol. 1, *Year of Decisions* (Garden City, N.Y.: 1955), 79–82, which should be supplemented with Bohlen's minutes of the meeting, published in *FRUS,* 1945, V, 256–58.

[48]"People have stored within memory a wide collection of 'personae,' or cognitive structures representing the personality characteristics of stereotypical characters—the hooker with a heart of gold, the truck-stop waitress, the 'urban cowboy,' Archie Bunker. Often people assimilate casual acquaintances or public figures to these stereotypical characteristics, on the basis of a superficial resemblance. Influenced by the Pendergast persona, Truman expected Stalin—a revolutionary who had never visited the West—to understand American public opinion." (Larson, *A Psychological Explanation,* 178.)

can deal with Stalin," Truman noted in his diary at Potsdam. "He is honest—but smart as hell." Disturbed by rumors of the dictator's ill health, the president worried about what would happen "if Joe suddenly passed out," because his potential successors lacked sincerity.[49] For several years afterward, there persisted in Truman's mind the notion that difficulties with the Russians reflected Stalin's internal political problems—interference from a recalcitrant Politburo was the most frequent explanation—rather than any personal desire on the Soviet leader's part to violate his word.[50]

But deals had to be honored if they were to work, and with the return of peace, instances of Soviet unilateralism began to proliferate. Reasonably free elections took place in Hungary and Czechoslovakia, but only in those countries: Moscow's grip on Poland, Rumania, and Bulgaria remained as tight as ever.[51] The Russians joined the French in resisting central economic administration of occupied Germany; they also arbitrarily transferred a substantial portion of that country's eastern territory to Poland.[52] Attempts to reunify another divided nation, Korea, came to naught as the Russians refused to tolerate anything other than a satellite government there.[53] The Soviet Union rejected participation in the World Bank and the International Monetary Fund, institutions American planners regarded as critical for postwar economic recovery.[54] And Stalin was showing strong signs, as 1945 ended, of exploiting the presence of Soviet troops in northern Iran to carve out yet another sphere of influence there.[55]

[49]Truman Diary, 17 and 30 July 1945, Ferrell, ed., *Off the Record*, 53, 58. See also the Wallace Diary, 15 October 1945, Blum, ed., *The Price of Vision*, 490; and the Stettinius Diary, 22 October 1945, Thomas M. Campbell and George C. Herring, *The Diaries of Edward R. Stettinius, Jr., 1943–1946* (New York: 1975), 439–40. For the Pendergast analogy, see Donovan, *Conflict and Crisis*, 75; Jonathan Daniels, *Man of Independence* (Philadelphia: 1950), 285.

[50]See, for example, Truman's campaign remarks in Eugene, Oregon, 11 June 1948, *Public Papers of the Presidents: Harry S. Truman, 1948* (Washington: 1963), 329.

[51]For events in Eastern Europe, see Davis, *The Cold War Begins*, 288–334, 358–68; Geir Lundestad, *The American Non-Policy Towards Eastern Europe* (Oslo: 1978), 127–35, 159–64, 205–13, 235–47, 271–78; Richard C. Lukas, *Bitter Legacy: Polish-American Relations in the Wake of World War II* (Lexington, Ky.: 1982); Michael M. Boll, *Cold War in the Balkans: American Foreign Policy and the Emergence of Communist Bulgaria, 1943–1947* (Lexington, Ky.: 1984).

[52]Gaddis, *The United States and the Origins of the Cold War*, 325–31.

[53]Russell D. Buhite, *Soviet-American Relations in Asia, 1945–1954* (Norman, Okla.: 1981), 139–50; Charles M. Dobbs, *The Unwanted Symbol: American Foreign Policy, the Cold War, and Korea, 1945–1950* (Kent, Ohio: 1981); James Irving Matray, *The Reluctant Crusade: American Foreign Policy in Korea, 1941–1950* (Honolulu: 1985), 28–98.

[54]Alfred E. Eckes, Jr., *A Search for Solvency: Bretton Woods and the International Monetary System, 1941–1971* (Austin, Tex.: 1975), 205–28.

[55]Bruce R. Kuniholm, *The Origins of the Cold War in the Near East: Great Power Conflict*

He was "trying to find a basis for an understanding which would give him confidence that an agreement reached with the Russians would be lived up to," Truman told his advisers in December 1945. He had such confidence in dealing with the British, the Dutch, and the Chinese (though not the French), "but there is no evidence yet that the Russians intend to change their habits so far as honoring contracts is concerned."[56]

The chief executive's initial inclination had been to regard these difficulties simply as failures of communication;[57] with that explanation in mind, he had authorized Secretary of State Byrnes to make one more effort to settle them at a hastily called meeting of foreign ministers in Moscow in December. By that time, though, public and congressional impatience with Soviet unilateralism had considerably intensified. Sensitive to these pressures, irritated by Byrnes's eagerness to reach agreements without consulting him, Truman early in 1946 proclaimed to himself—if not directly to Byrnes, as he later claimed—his intention to stop "babying" the Soviets: "Unless Russia is faced with an iron first and strong language another war is in the making. Only one language do they understand—'how many divisions have you?' I do not think we should play at compromise any longer."[58]

There was, in fact, no compromise when the Russians failed to meet their agreed-upon deadline for removing their troops from Iran: Instead, the administration confronted Moscow publicly in the United Nations Security Council and forced a humiliating withdrawal.[59] Truman drew the appropriate conclusions: "Told him to tell Stalin I held him to be a man to keep his word," he noted in his appointment book after a meeting with the newly designated ambassador to the Soviet Union, Walter Bedell

and Diplomacy in Iran, Turkey, and Greece (Princeton: 1980), 270–98. For the two contemporary summaries of Russian unilateral actions as of late 1945, see "Summary of Russian Dispatches for the Secretary's Diary," 26 November 1945, James V. Forrestal Papers, Box 100, "Book II, Item 30," Seeley Mudd Library, Princeton University; and a Department of State memorandum, "Foreign Policy of the United States," 1 December 1945, *FRUS, 1946*, I, 1134–39.

[56]Forrestal Diary, 4 December 1945, Walter Millis, ed., *The Forrestal Diaries* (New York: 1951), 124. For a recent—and considerably less critical—reassessment of the Soviet record on keeping agreements during this period, see Melvyn P. Leffler, "Adherence to Agreements: Yalta and the Experiences of the Early Cold War," *International Security* XI (Summer 1986): 88–123.

[57]See Truman's press conference comments on 8 October 1945, *Truman Public Papers: 1946*, 384, 387; and the Stettinius Diary, 22 October 1945, Campbell and Herring, eds., *Stettinius Diaries*, 437.

[58]The best recent account of these developments is Messer, *The End of an Alliance*, 137–66. Truman's controversial memorandum of 5 January 1946 is printed in *Year of Decisions*, 551–52.

[59]Kuniholm, *The Origins of the Cold War in the Near East*, 304–42.

Smith, on 23 March. "Troops in Iran after March 2 upset that theory."[60] By June, he was writing to the author Pearl Buck that "the United States has performed no unfriendly act nor made a single unfriendly gesture toward the great Russian nation. . . . How has Russia met our friendly overtures?"[61] The following month, after *New York Times* correspondent Brooks Atkinson had published a series of articles highly critical of the Russians, Truman pointedly invited him to the White House.[62] That same day he told his advisers that he was "tired of our being pushed around," that "here a little, there a little, they are chiseling from us," and that "now is [the] time to take [a] stand on Russia."[63]

It was in this spirit that the president authorized the first comprehensive study of Soviet-American relations to be carried out within the government. Compiled under the direction of his special counsel, Clark M. Clifford, and written after consultations with the Departments of State, War, Navy, the Joint Chiefs of Staff, and the director of central intelligence, the report acknowledged that agreements between nations were at times susceptible to differing interpretations. Nonetheless, it argued, there existed a persistent pattern on Moscow's part of either unilaterally implementing such agreements in such a way as to serve Soviet interests, or encouraging satellites to do so. "There is no question," the report emphasized, "where the primary responsibility lies."

The implications could only be that the Soviet Union had no intention of cooperating with the West to maintain the existing balance of power; that it sought to expand its own influence as widely as possible without regard for the security requirements of its former allies; and that, when circumstances were right, it would be prepared to risk war to attain that objective. American policy could no longer be based upon the assump-

[60]Quoted in Hillman, ed., *Mr. President*, 107. Career Foreign Service officer Elbridge Durbrow noted the implications of the new tough line: "It is the general feeling here that it has been finally realized all across the board that the only way to have really good relations with the Soviet Union is to stand by our guns when we feel we are right. If we can hold this fort all along the line from Korea to Timbuktoo, we may start to get somewhere. . . . General Smith has got the proper attitude and will, in all probability, impress the boys profoundly that we are not just talking through our hats to hear our own voices." (Durbrow to Charles W. Thayer, 11 April 1946, Charles E. Bohlen Papers, Box 1 "Personal [CEB] 1946," Diplomatic Branch, National Archives.)

[61]Truman to Buck, 15 June 1946, Harry S. Truman Papers, OF 220 Miscellaneous, Harry S. Truman Library (hereafter HSTL).

[62]Atkinson's articles appeared in the *New York Times* on 7, 8, and 9 July 1946. For his White House visit, see ibid., 13 July 1946.

[63]George M. Elsey notes on a Truman conversation with Clark Clifford and Charles G. Ross, 12 July 1946, George M. Elsey Papers, Box 63 "Foreign Relations—Russia 1946—Report—Folder 1," HSTL.

tion of shared interests, therefore; priorities henceforth would have to be directed toward the accumulation of sufficient military strength to deter war if possible and to win it if necessary, while at the same time keeping open possibilities for dealing with the Russians should a change of heart in the Kremlin eventually occur. "It is our hope," the report concluded, "that they will eventually change their minds and work out with us a fair and equitable settlement when they realize that we are too strong to be beaten and too determined to be frightened."[64]

President Truman received the Clifford report on 24 September, four days after he had fired Henry Wallace from the cabinet for publicly advocating a more conciliatory policy toward the Soviet Union. There is no question that he agreed with its general conclusions: On the day before he dismissed Wallace he had complained in his diary about "Reds, phonies and . . . parlor pinks [who] can see no wrong in Russia's four and one half million armed forces, in Russia's loot of Poland, Austria, Hungary, Rumania, Manchuria. . . . But when we help our friends in China who fought on our side it is terrible. When Russia loots the industrial plant of those same friends it is all right. When Russia occupies Persia for oil that is heavenly."[65] But Truman chose not to use the Clifford report, as he might have, to justify increased military appropriations; instead he ordered all copies to be locked in the White House safe, where they remained for the duration of the administration.[66] "There is too much loose talk about the Russian situation," he had written former vice-president John Nance Garner on the day after Wallace's dismissal. "We are not going to have any shooting trouble with them but they are tough bargainers and always ask for the whole earth, expecting maybe to get an acre."[67]

The president's cautious reaction to the manifestations of Soviet unilateralism catalogued in the Clifford report reflected a desire to avoid hasty and ill-considered action, but certainly no continuing assumption of common interests. Repeated demonstrations of Moscow's callousness to the priorities and sensibilities of its former allies had by this time vir-

[64]The full text of the Clifford report can be found in Arthur Krock, *Memoirs: Sixty Years on the Firing Line* (New York: 1986), 419–82.
[65]Truman memorandum, 19 September 1946, quoted in Margaret Truman, *Harry S. Truman* (New York: 1973), 317–18.
[66]Ibid., 347.
[67]Truman to Garner, 21 September 1946, Truman Papers, PSF Box 187, "Russia: 1945–1948," HSTL.

tually drained the reservoir of goodwill toward the Russians that had built up during the war. American leaders had been inclined, for many months, to give the Kremlin the benefit of the doubt: to assume, despite accumulating evidence to the contrary, that difficulties with Moscow had arisen out of misunderstanding rather than fundamental conflicts of interest. But such charitableness could not continue indefinitely, as Winston Churchill pointed out in the summer of 1946: "The American eagle sits on his perch, a large strong bird with formidable beak and claws. . . . Mr. Gromyko is sent every day to prod him with a sharp sickle, now on his beak, now under his wing, now in his tail feathers. All the time the eagle keeps quite still, but it would be a great mistake to suppose that nothing is going on inside the breast of the eagle."[68]

IV

In fact, a good deal was going on inside the breast of the eagle, all of it related in one way or another to attempting to explain the motivation for Moscow's puzzling behavior. Throughout the period of wartime cooperation there had lingered in the minds of most Americans latent but persistent suspicions about Russia, suspicions that extended back to, and even beyond, the Bolshevik Revolution. These grew out of the fact that the Soviet Union combined—as no other country in the world at that time did—two characteristics that Americans found particularly objectionable: arbitrary rule and ideological militancy. As long as the direct Axis threat remained, Americans had been willing to overlook these shortcomings, even to hope that in time they would disappear.[69] But after 1945, with no common foe to compel unity, with ample evidence that the Russians intended to proceed on their own rather than in concert

[68]Quoted in *Time*, 17 June 1946, 26. Former Ambassador Joseph E. Davies, one of the Soviet Union's most sympathetic interpreters, commented early in 1946: "I know of no institution that needs a high pressure 'public relations' organization as much as the U.S.S.R. They do not seem able to get their case across, even when, as it happens sometimes, they have a good case." (Davies to Clarence Dykstra, 8 January 1946, Joseph E. Davies Papers, Box 22, Library of Congress.) For other indications of the extent to which Soviet behavior alienated even those inclined to give the Russians the benefit of the doubt, see Jonathan Evers Boe, "American Business: The Response to the Soviet Union, 1933–1947" (Ph.D. diss., Stanford University, 1979), 235–37; and, on Eleanor Roosevelt, Joseph P. Lash, *Eleanor: The Years Alone* (New York: 1972), 73–99.

[69]Gaddis, *The United States and the Origins of the Cold War*, 32–62. The best overall account of wartime attitudes toward the Soviet Union is Ralph B. Levering, *American Opinion and the Russian Alliance, 1939–1945* (Chapel Hill: 1976).

with their former allies to consolidate postwar interests, the predisposition to assume the worst about Moscow's intentions came out into the open once again.

Americans had not always found cooperation with authoritarian regimes to be impossible: The Russian-American relationship itself had been friendly throughout most of its early history, despite the vast cultural and political differences that separated the two countries. But toward the end of the nineteenth century a combination of circumstances—increasing repression within Russia, a keener American sensitivity to conditions inside other countries, growing rivalries between Washington and St. Petersburg over spheres of influence in East Asia—had produced in the United States the suspicion that a connection existed between autocratic rule at home and aggressiveness in foreign affairs.[70] Parallel concerns had accompanied the deterioration of relations with imperial Germany prior to World War I; certainly participation in that conflict, which Woodrow Wilson justified by stressing the linkage between autocracy and aggression, served powerfully to reinforce this idea.[71] Determination to remain aloof from European involvements caused Americans to worry less about such matters during the 1920s and early 1930s—indeed, the economic distress of the latter decade even produced in some circles a grudging respect for dictatorships[72]—but the experience of fighting Germany and Japan during World War II brought back repugnancy for arbitrary rule with a vengeance. It would not take very many signs of aggressiveness on the part of totalitarian regimes in the postwar world—even totalitarian former allies—to convince Americans that the connection between domestic despotism and international expansionism still prevailed.[73]

"If we fought Germany because of our belief that a police state and a democratic state could not exist in the same world," Rear Admiral Ellery

[70]See John Lewis Gaddis, *Russia, the Soviet Union, and the United States: An Interpretive History* (New York: 1978), 27–56; also chapter one of Gaddis, *The Long Peace.*

[71]The best discussion is in Levin, *Woodrow Wilson and World Politics,* 37–45. But see also Patrick Devlin, *Too Proud to Fight: Woodrow Wilson's Neutrality* (New York: 1975), 136–39.

[72]See, for example, John P. Diggins, *Mussolini and Fascism: The View from America* (Princeton: 1972).

[73]Michael Sherry points out the tendency of Pentagon planners during the war to assume that the next war would be fought against a totalitarian power, without any clear idea of which nation that might be. (Sherry, *Preparing for the Next War,* 52–53.) See also, for a contemporary expression of this idea, William Liscum Borden, *There Will Be No Time: The Revolution in Strategy* (New York: 1946), 181, 198. For further insights into the American tendency to connect totalitarianism with aggression, see Eduard Maximilian Mark, "The Interpretation of Soviet Foreign Policy in the United States, 1928–1947" (Ph.D. diss., University of Connecticut, 1978), 95–96, 326–29.

W. Stone told Secretary of the Navy James Forrestal in July 1946, then "it must necessarily follow that we could not afford to lie down before Russia."[74] The simple fact that the Soviet Union was a totalitarian state raised suspicions that its foreign policy would proceed from priorities incompatible with those of the democracies—priorities now elaborately enshrined in the procedures the United Nations had established for settling international disputes. Totalitarian states, Americans assumed, relied upon force or the threat of force to secure their interests; such nations could hardly be expected to share Washington's aspiration to see the rule of law ultimately govern relations between nations. "It is not Communism but Totalitarianism which is the potential threat," publisher Arthur Hays Sulzberger pointed out. "Only people who have a Bill of Rights are not the potential enemies of other people."[75]

The point, for Truman, was fundamental. "Really there is no difference between the government which Mr. Molotov represents and the one the Czar represented—or the one Hitler spoke for," he privately wrote in November 1946.[76] And, again, informally, in May 1947: "There isn't any difference in totalitarian states. . . . Nazi, Communist or Fascist, or Franco, or anything else—they are all alike. . . . The police state is a police state; I don't care what you call it."[77] The president's public speeches

[74]Quoted in Millis, ed., *The Forrestal Diaries*, 181. "It was not inconceivable," Forrestal himself noted in June, 1945, "that the real reactionaries in world politics would be those who now call themselves revolutionaries, because the dynamics of their philosophy all tended toward the concentration of power in the state, with the inevitable result of exploitation of the common man by the masses, or rather, by those who in such a system apply power over the masses—such as Hitler, Mussolini, Stalin and Hirohito." (Forrestal Diary, 30 June 1945, Millis, ed., *The Forrestal Diaries*, 72–73.)

[75]Sulzberger to Douglas MacArthur, 6 June 1946, Douglas MacArthur Papers, Record Group 10, Box 9, "Sulzberger Folder," MacArthur Memorial Library, Norfolk, Virginia. "It is becoming more and more evident to me," Secretary of War Henry L. Stimson noted in his diary while at the Potsdam Conference, "that a nation whose system rests upon free speech and all the elements of freedom, as does ours, cannot be sure of getting on permanently with a nation where speech is strictly controlled and where the Government uses the iron hand of the secret police." (Stimson Diary, 19 July 1945, Henry L. Stimson Papers, Yale University Library.)

[76]Truman letter of 11 November 1946, quoted in Margaret Truman, *Harry S. Truman*, 323. See also Truman to Margaret Truman, 13 March 1947, ibid., 343. The implication here is that a surviving tsarist Russia would have posed as much of a threat, in the eyes of Truman and his advisers, as a communist one. The amount of attention given in the White House to a spurious "will" of Peter the Great bears this out. "Pete must have been a great guy," Admiral William D. Leahy commented. (Leahy to Clifford, 21 September 1946, Clark M. Clifford Papers, Box 14, "Russia: Folder 3," HSTL.) For an analysis of this document and its impact upon administration thinking, see J. Garry Clifford, "President Truman and Peter the Great's Will," *Diplomatic History* IV (Fall 1980): 371–85.

[77]Truman's informal remarks to the Association of Radio News Analysts, 13 May 1947, *Truman Public Papers: 1947*, 238–39.

during 1947 provided virtually a running commentary on the dangers of totalitarianism: "Freedom has flourished where power has been dispersed. It has languished where power has been too highly centralized." More than that, excessive concentrations of power produced temptations to use them. "The stronger the voice of a people in the formulation of national policies, the less the danger of aggression. When all governments derive their just powers from the consent of the governed, there will be enduring peace." There was no conflict between the requirements of justice and order: "The attainment of worldwide respect for essential human rights is synonymous with the attainment of world peace."[78]

It was no accident, then, that when the president in the most famous speech of his career characterized the world as divided between two ways of life, one reflecting "the will of the majority," the other based "upon the will of a minority forcibly imposed upon the majority,"[79] it was the distinction between democracy and totalitarianism to which he referred. By so doing, he implicitly linked his own justification of American action to restore the balance of power in Europe to those advanced by Franklin Roosevelt in the Atlantic Charter and by Woodrow Wilson in the Fourteen Points; in each case the assumption was the ultimate incompatibility of autocratic and democratic institutions. The fact that this particular autocracy also embraced the ideology of communism was, for Truman, relatively insignificant.

That certainly was not the case for most Americans, though. Nothing—not even totalitarianism—did more to arouse suspicion about the Soviet Union's behavior than that country's long-standing and self-proclaimed intention to seek the overthrow of capitalist governments throughout the world. American hostility toward communism went back to the earliest days of the Bolshevik Revolution: to Russia's abandonment of the Allied cause in World War I; to the terror, expropriations, and executions that soon followed; to the postwar Red Scare, with its suggestion that even the United States might not be immune from the bacillus of revolution. The Soviet Union's commitment to communism had been the primary justification for Washington's refusal to recognize that country until 1933; and even after that date Moscow's claim to be

[78]Truman speeches at Baylor University, 6 March 1947; Monticello, 4 July 1947; and Rio de Janeiro, 2 September 1947; ibid., 170, 324, 429.
[79]Truman speech to Congress on aid to Greece and Turkey, 12 March 1947, ibid., 178. For a further discussion of this point, see Gaddis, *Strategies of Containment*, 65–66.

the vanguard of world revolution had continued to plague relations with Washington.[80] Stalin implicitly acknowledged the corrosive effects of ideology upon his dealings with the West in 1943 when, eager for an Anglo-American commitment to establish a second front, he abolished the Comintern, Lenin's designated instrument for bringing about the world proletarian revolution.[81] But there could be no guarantee that such restraint would continue once Moscow's enemies had been defeated. As a Department of State memorandum put it in 1944, it was necessary to keep in mind the Soviet conviction that "there is an irreconcilable chasm between 'socialism' and 'capitalism' and that any temporary association in a common interest [is] an association of expediency for a specific purpose but with no underlying affinity of fundamental interest, civilization, or tradition."[82]

"I expressed it as my view that it would not be difficult to work with Russia provided we were dealing with her only as a national entity," James Forrestal noted in his diary during the summer of 1945. "The real problem was whether or not Russian policy called for a continuation of the Third International's objectives, namely, world revolution and the application of the political principles of the dialectical materialists for the entire world."[83] Evidence that the Kremlin still harbored such ambitions arose from two sets of circumstances: the Russians' use of communist parties in Eastern Europe as instruments with which to create their sphere of influence there; and the increasing success of communist parties in Western Europe, the Eastern Mediterranean, and China. In retrospect, it is not at all clear that these phenomena were related: The popularity of communist parties outside the Soviet sphere grew primarily out of their effectiveness as resistance fighters against the Axis; in Eastern Europe the communists owed their prominence chiefly to Moscow's reliance on them

[80]Gaddis, *Russia, the Soviet Union, and the United States,* 65–145; see also chapter 1 of Gaddis, *The Long Peace.*

[81]At least Stalin's action was so regarded in the United States. (See Gaddis, *The United States and the Origins of the Cold War,* 47–49.) But Vojtech Mastny doubts that Stalin's primary motive was to improve cooperation with the West. (*Russia's Road to the Cold War: Diplomacy, Warfare, and the Politics of Communism, 1941–1945* [New York: 1979], 94–97.)

[82]Division of European Affairs memorandum, "Current Problems in Relations with the Soviet Union," 24 March 1944, *FRUS, 1944,* IV, 840. See also O.S.S. Research and Analysis Report #1552, "The Current Role of the Communist Party in the USSR," 12 June 1944, Office of Intelligence and Research Files, Department of State Records, National Archives.

[83]Forrestal Diary, 30 June 1945, Millis, ed., *The Forrestal Diaries,* 72.

to consolidate its control.[84] Nor was it obvious that the Soviet Union's use of foreign communist parties to promote its interests necessarily proved an ideological motivation for its policies.[85]

But these fine points were difficult to keep in mind as the end of the war brought increases in the militancy—and the anti-American rhetoric—of all communist parties, not least that of the Soviet Union itself.[86] When combined with the indisputable evidence of Moscow's unilateral expansionism, when considered against the record of how Nazi Germany had used "fifth columns" before the war, it is not surprising that concern about the ideological dimension of the Soviet challenge should have surfaced as well. "The tendency is increasingly marked," the British embassy in Washington reported in August 1946, "to detect the Soviet mind or hand behind every move which seems to threaten or embarrass the United States or its friends, and to link events in one part of the world with those in another."[87] The editors of *Newsweek* put it more bluntly: "U.S. officials in the best position to judge fear they have confirmation that the Soviet Government has made up its mind that capitalism must be destroyed if Communism is to live."[88]

Both the "totalitarian" and the "ideological" explanations of Soviet behavior had in common the assumption that one was dealing with a compulsive internally driven process, unresponsive to gestures of restraint or goodwill from the outside. There had been yet a third interpre-

[84]See, on this point, Mastny, *Russia's Road to the Cold War*, 194, 231; also William Taubman, *Stalin's American Policy: From Entente to Detente to Cold War* (New York: 1982), 75–82.

[85]A State Department report, drafted late in 1945 by Charles E. Bohlen and Geroid T. Robinson, noted with unhelpful even-handedness that: "It is by no means to be expected that in the future the foreign policy of the Soviet leaders will be determined entirely by Marxian theory. This has never been the case since the establishment of the Soviet government. . . . Yet it would be very unsafe to assume, on the other hand, that the future attitude of the Soviet leaders toward non-Soviet states and toward the domestic forces and movements within those states will not be influenced in any degree by Marxian ideology." ("The Capabilities and Intentions of the Soviet Union as Affected by American Policy," 10 December 1945, as published in *Diplomatic History* I [Fall 1977]: 395.)

[86]Particularly important in this regard was the Stalin "election" speech of 9 February 1946, which clearly gave the impression, whether intended or not, of a renewed ideological emphasis in Soviet policy. The impact of this speech is discussed in De Santis, *The Diplomacy of Silence*, 172–73; but see also, for earlier indications of concern about ideology, Gaddis, *The United States and the Origins of the Cold War*, 296–99.

[87]Inverchapel to Foreign Office, 31 August 1946, Foreign Office Records, FO 371/51609/ AN2657, Public Record Office, London.

[88]*Newsweek*, 9 September 1946, 27. For an illuminating discussion of how John Foster Dulles had come, by the summer of 1946, to an almost entirely ideological explanation of Soviet behavior, see Ronald W. Pruessen, *John Foster Dulles: The Road to Power* (New York: 1982), 276–87.

tation of Moscow's unilateralism, popular during the war, that had seen it as growing out of a quite understandable preoccupation with security capable of being alleviated by patient Western efforts to win the Russians' trust. President Roosevelt himself had made this "insecurity" theory the basis of his policy toward the Soviet Union, and it had remained very much alive—though under increasing challenge—during the first months of the Truman administration.[89] But theories require validation if they are to be sustained: however persuasive the "insecurity" model of Soviet behavior may be in retrospect, what struck most observers at the time was the utter imperviousness of Stalin's regime to the gestures of restraint and goodwill that emanated from the West during and immediately after the war.[90] Moscow's perceived failure to reciprocate these initiatives made it more and more difficult to sustain an interpretation of Soviet actions based on "insecurity," as Henry Wallace found out when he attempted, during the spring and summer of 1946, to revive it within the inner councils of the government.[91] The "totalitarian" and "ideological" models were the obvious alternatives.

It is ironic that the individual most influential in discrediting "insecurity" as an explanation of Soviet unilateralism shared many of its basic assumptions. George F. Kennan had never been inclined to interpret Soviet behavior in either strictly totalitarian or ideological terms. As a keen student of Russian history and culture, he was fully aware of the lack of self-confidence that plagued the Stalinist government, and of the extent to which its unilateralism was defensively motivated.[92] But he emphati-

[89]See sections II and III of this essay, above.

[90]See, on this point, Eduard Mark, "American Policy toward Eastern Europe and the Origins of the Cold War: An Alternative Interpretation," *Journal of American History* LXVIII (September 1981): 313–36.

[91]For the Wallace affair, see Blum, ed., *The Price of Vision*, 589–601, 612–32; also J. Samuel Walker, *Henry A. Wallace and American Foreign Policy* (Westport, Conn.: 1976), 146–65. Dulles's comment on Wallace is worth noting: "It is a good initial approach to say that if you pat the dog he will not bite you. If, however, after several times patting the dog he still nips you, then it is necessary to think of another approach. Wallace has been sitting behind the scenes and has not had to go through the experience of having his hand nipped." (Dulles to Irving Fisher, 23 September 1946, John Foster Dulles Papers, Seeley Mudd Library, Princeton University.)

[92]"Security is probably their basic motive," Kennan noted in the summer of 1946, "but they are so anxious and suspicious about it that the objective results are much the same as if the motive were aggression, indefinite expansion. They evidently seek to weaken all centers of power they cannot dominate, in order to reduce the danger from any possible rival." (Kennan paper, "Draft of Information Policy on Relations with Russia," 22 July 1946, Dean Acheson Papers, Box 27, "State Department Under Secretary Correspondence, 1945–7," HSTL.) Daniel Yergin's characterization of Kennan as an advocate of what he calls the "Riga axioms," an ideologically based explanation of Soviet behavior, strikes me as a considerable oversimplification. See his *Shattered Peace*, 27–28, 170.

cally did not share the view of Wallace and others that these attitudes could be modified from the outside. It was in an effort to bring official Washington to see that point that Kennan crafted the February 1946 "long telegram," to this day the single most influential explanation of postwar Soviet behavior, and one which powerfully reinforced the growing tendency within the United States to interpret Moscow's actions in a sinister light.

The "long telegram" had the great influence that it did because it provided a way to fuse concerns about totalitarianism and communism in dealing with the Soviet Union. It portrayed that state as one in which an autocratic tradition had become incorporated within an ideological compulsion to treat the outside world as hostile. The conclusion was clear: No actions the United States or its Western allies could take would alleviate Stalin's suspicion; the best one could do was to look to one's own defenses—and to the strength and self-confidence of one's own society—and wait for the internal forces of change within the Soviet system to have their effect.[93]

There is a definite psychological satisfaction, when confronted with a phenomenon one does not understand, in finding a simple but persuasive explanation.[94] Whatever the actual intentions of its author,[95] the "long telegram" performed that function within the government in 1946; a similar analysis would find a wider audience the following year in the form of the famous "X" article in *Foreign Affairs*.[96] The "totalitarianism-ideological" model of Soviet behavior provided a clear, plausible, and in many ways gratifying explanation of the Russians' failure to cooperate with their former allies in building a lasting peace: It absolved the United States of responsibility for the breakdown of wartime cooperation; it made any future relaxation of tensions dependent upon changes of heart in Moscow, not Washington. Americans did not welcome the onset of the cold war. But the rationale they worked out to account for its appearance at least had the advantage of allowing them to approach the coming contest with a reasonably clear conscience.

---

[93]The "long telegram" is published in *FRUS, 1946*, VI, 696–709.
[94]See Larson, *Origins of Containment*, 52–57.
[95]Kennan's own explanation of his intentions with respect to the "long telegram" and the "X" article are in his *Memoirs: 1925–1950* (Boston: 1967), 292, 354–67.
[96]"X" [George F. Kennan], "The Sources of Soviet Conduct," *Foreign Affairs* XXV (July 1947): 566–82.

V

The Soviet Union's emergence as a potential adversary closed an obvious gap in Washington's thinking about the postwar world. A generalized sense of vulnerability, related both to historical experience and to technological change, had caused United States officials to regard preservation of a global balance of power as a vital interest even before specific challenges to that balance had manifested themselves. This situation of perceived vulnerability in the absence of apparent threat accounts for the failure of the United States to deploy forces and establish bases in the way one might have expected had the Russians been seen as the enemy from the beginning.[97] But Soviet unilateralism, together with the conclusions about the roots of Soviet behavior that unilateralism provoked, had by 1947 created a credible source of danger, with the result that American strategy now took on a clearer and more purposeful aspect.

Central to it was the defense of Western Europe, a priority so basic that it was more often assumed than articulated. "[It] is not a question of what men think now," the Joint Chiefs of Staff noted in the spring of 1947; "[It] is something that has been demonstrated by what we have had to do, though tardily, and therefore at greater risk and cost, in actual warfare in the past. . . . The entire area of Western Europe is in first place as an area of strategic importance to the United States."[98] And yet, American planners had given remarkably little thought to the means by which that part of the world might be secured against Soviet expansionism. Their assumption—again mostly unstated—had been that Great Britain would provide the necessary counterpresence, and that the United States could concern itself with other matters.[99] It had done just that throughout 1946, concentrating on resisting Soviet pressures aimed at Iran and Turkey, consolidating its position in Japan and southern Korea, mediating the Chinese civil war, and attempting to resolve the diplomatic stalemate over Germany.

The British decision to withdraw military assistance from Greece and Turkey in February 1947 forced a reconsideration of these priorities, not

[97]My argument here follows that of Sherry, *Preparing for the Next War*, 215.
[98]JCS 1769/1, "United States Assistance to Other Countries from the Standpoint of National Security," 29 April 1947, *FRUS, 1947*, I, 740.
[99]One of the best discussions of this point is still that of William Hardy McNeill, *America, Britain & Russia: Their Co-operation and Conflict, 1941–1946* (London: 1953), 753–57, although the work of Sherry, Smith, and Converse, cited in the notes, makes it clear that McNeill somewhat exaggerated the eagerness of the American military to supplant British power.

because those two countries were of critical importance in and of themselves, but because of the way in which London's action dramatized the failure of Western Europe as a whole to recover from the war. A major consequence of that conflict has been, in Mackinder's terminology, a severe weakening of the "rimland" states surrounding the Soviet "heartland," leaving only the "world island"—effectively the United States—as a countervailing balance. But it was not until 1947 that Washington officials realized the full implications of that fact and set about taking corrective action.

At no point—despite references to the possibility of war in the 1946 Clifford report—did these officials seriously anticipate a Soviet military attack in Europe. Estimates of Moscow's intentions, whether from the Pentagon, the State Department, or the intelligence community, consistently discounted the possibility that the Russians might risk a direct military confrontation within the foreseeable future.[100] Several considerations contributed to that judgment, not least of which was the damage the Soviet Union itself had suffered during the war and the still relatively primitive character of its air and naval forces. But these estimates also suggested that the Russians would not need to use force to gain their objectives, because of the ease with which war-weakened neighbors could be psychologically intimidated. "If the countries of the world lose confidence in us," General George A. Lincoln of the War Department General Staff told the Senate Foreign Relations Committee early in April 1947, "they may in effect pass under the Iron Curtain without any pressure other than the subversive pressure being put on them."[101]

---

[100]For a sampling of official assessments on this subject, see JIC 250/7, "Capabilities and Intentions of the USSR in the Post-War Period," 7 February 1946, Army Staff Records, ABC 336 Russia, 22 Aug. 43, Section 1-B, Modern Military Records Branch, National Archives; Robert Murphy to H. Freeman Matthews, 3 April 1946, Department of State Records, 861.00/4-346, Box 6462, Diplomatic Branch, National Archives; War Department intelligence review, "Soviet Foreign Policy: A Summation," 2 May 1946, Elsey Papers, Box 63, "Foreign Relations—Russia 1946—Report—Folder 3"; Joint Chiefs of Staff to Truman, 26 July 1946, Clark M. Clifford Papers, Box 14, "Russia [folder 3]," Harry S. Truman Library; George F. Kennan lecture to Foreign Service and State Department personnel, 17 September 1946, George F. Kennan Papers, Box 16, Seeley Mudd Library, Princeton University; Joint Chiefs of Staff to Secretaries of Army and Navy, 13 March 1947, *FRUS, 1947*, V, 111–12.

[101]Lincoln executive session testimony, 2 April 1947, U.S. Congress, Senate, Committee on Foreign Relations, *Legislative Origins of the Truman Doctrine* (Washington: 1973), 160. "The Soviets still do not want war," State Department adviser Harley A. Notter noted in July, "but believe that despite us they can gain their strategic objectives of control not only of the heartland of Europe and Asia but actually of the shores of those

American planners assumed a direct correlation between economic health, psychological self-confidence, and the capacity for defense. As a State-War-Navy Coordinating Committee report noted that same month: "Economic weaknesses may give rise to instability and subsequently to political shifts which adversely affect the security of the U.S." This could happen through "boring from within" tactics or the threat of over-whelming external force, but in either event the outcome from the stand-point of American interests would be grim.[102] "Without further prompt and substantial aid from the United States," Under Secretary of State William Clayton argued, "economic, social and political disintegration will overwhelm Europe."[103]

A Soviet-dominated Europe would pose obvious military dangers, even if military means were not used to secure it. In a clear echo of the wartime Mackinder-Spykman analysis, the Joint Chiefs of Staff pointed out that the Western Hemisphere contained 40 percent of the earth's land surface but only 25 percent of its population. "The potential military strength of the Old World in terms of manpower ... and war-making capacity is enormously greater than that of our area of defense commitments, in which the United States is the only arsenal nation." It was obvious, there-fore, that in case of war "we must have the support of some of the coun-tries of the Old World unless our military strength is to be overshadowed by that of our enemies." Western Europe was particularly important, not just because that region contained "almost all potentially strong nations who can reasonably be expected to ally themselves with the United States," but also because without access to the eastern shore of the Atlantic, "the shortest and most direct avenue of attack against our enemies will almost certainly be denied us."[104]

The economic consequences of a European collapse were less clear. The Truman administration found it convenient to argue publicly that the effect on the American domestic economy, in terms of lost exports,

---

continents at every point of major vulnerability from sea and air." (Notter to Dean Rusk, 14 July 1947, U.S. Department of State, *Foreign Relations of the United States: 1947*, IV, 578.)

[102]State-War-Navy Coordinating Committee "Ad Hoc" Committee report, "Policies, Pro-cedures and Costs of Assistance by the United States to Foreign Countries," 21 April 1947, *FRUS, 1947*, III, 217.

[103]Clayton memorandum, "The European Crisis," 27 May 1947, ibid., 231.

[104]JCS 1769/1, 29 April 1947, ibid., I, 739. Although for the purpose of launching a stra-tegic bombing offensive, it is now clear that Pentagon planners regarded Middle Eastern bases as of primary importance. (Converse, "United States Plans for a Postwar Overseas Military Base System," 211–19.)

would be little short of disastrous.[105] What strikes one in retrospect, though, is how self-sufficient that economy actually was. Exports as a percentage of gross national product did not rise above 6.5 percent between 1945 and 1950, a figure lower than had normally been the case before the Great Depression, when the government had adamantly resisted any kind of official aid for European reconstruction. American investment in Western Europe in the early postwar years was actually less than European investment in the United States. It seems likely that administration officials stressed the economic implications of the crisis not because these stood out above the others, but because Washington had chosen economic assistance as the quickest and most effective way to respond to it.[106] It was easier to sell an unprecedented foreign-aid package as a program to ensure American prosperity than as a strategy for redressing the balance of power.

But it was the psychological implications of an extension of Soviet influence over Europe that probably most concerned American leaders. Although the term *domino theory* would not come into currency for another decade, administration officials worried deeply about the "bandwagon" effect that might ensue if the perception became widespread that the momentum in world affairs was on the Russians' side.[107] And despite the United States' own history of isolationism, despite its relative self-sufficiency, there was a very real fear of what might happen if the nation were left without friends in the world. In one sense, this fear grew out of the tradition of American exceptionalism. The United States had always viewed itself as both apart from and a model for the rest of the world; it could hardly have regarded with equanimity evidence that its example

[105]See, for example, Dean Acheson's speech to the Delta Council, Cleveland, Mississippi, 8 May 1947, Department of State Bulletin XVI(18 May 1947): 991–94. These arguments were not wholly a matter of public rhetoric, though. See Clayton's 27 May 1947 memorandum, *FRUS*, 1947, III, 231; also Joseph M. Jones to William Benton, 26 February 1947, Joseph M. Jones Papers, HSTL; and the State-War-Navy Coordinating Committee "Ad Hoc" report, 21 April 1947, *FRUS*, 1947, III, 209–10.

[106]See, on these points, Robert A. Pollard, *Economic Security and the Origins of the Cold War, 1945–1950* (New York: 1985), 60–61, 246–52; also Geir Lundestad, *America, Scandinavia, and the Cold War, 1945–1949* (New York: 1980), 32.

[107]See, for example, Acheson to Marshall, 21 February 1947, *FRUS*, 1947, V, 30; "Report of the Committee Appointed to Study Immediate Aid to Greece and Turkey," 26 February 1947, ibid., 51–52; Clayton memorandum, 5 March 1947, Frederick J. Dobney, ed., *Selected Papers of Will Clayton* (Baltimore: 1971), 198–200; Acheson statement before the Senate Foreign Relations Committee, 24 March 1947, U.S. Congress, Senate, Committee on Foreign Relations, *Assistance to Greece and Turkey* (Washington: 1947), 23–24.

was no longer relevant.[108] But, in another sense, it was precisely the unexceptional character of Americans in relation to the rest of the world that was at issue here: Who was to say that, buoyed by success in Europe, the totalitarian instinct might not take hold in the United States as well? "There is a little bit of the totalitarian buried somewhere, way down deep, in each and every one of us," George Kennan reminded students at the National War College in the spring of 1947. "It is only the cheerful light of confidence and security which keeps this evil genius down. . . . If confidence and security were to disappear, don't think that he would not be waiting to take their place."[109]

The strategy of containment brought together the new American interest in maintaining a global balance of power with the perceived Muscovite challenge to that equilibrium in a part of the world that could hardly have been more pivotal—Western Europe. It sought to deal with that danger primarily by economic rather than military means; its goal was not so much the creation of an American hegemony as it was a re-creation of independent centers of power capable of balancing each other as well as the Russians.[110] This is hardly the place to evaluate the success of that strategy or to trace its subsequent mutations and incarnations; these subjects have received excessively lengthy treatment elsewhere.[111] Suffice it to say that the strategy could not have evolved without the

[108]The British embassy in Washington noted in March 1947 that "The missionary strain in the character of Americans . . . leads many of them to feel that they have now received a call to extend to other countries the blessings with which the Almighty has endowed their own." But the following August it was reporting that "in spite of all the exuberant confidence and bombast with which much of the public has embraced the new role of world leadership, Americans are genuinely afraid of standing alone." (Inverchapel to Foreign Office, 13 March and 23 August 1947, Foreign Office Records, FO 371/67035/R3482 and 61056/AN2982, Public Record Office, London.)

[109]Kennan, 28 March 1947, lecture, quoted in Kennan, *Memoirs: 1925–1950*, 319.

[110]"Basically the stability of international relations must rest on a natural balance of national and regional forces. . . . I would not hesitate to say that the first and primary element of 'containment' . . . would be the encouragement and development of other forces resistant to communism. The peculiar difficulty of the immediate post-hostilities period has rested in the fact that . . . Russia was surrounded only by power vacuums. At the outset, these could be filled . . . only by direct action on the part of this Government. This is admittedly an undesirable situation; and it should be a cardinal point of our policy to see to it that other elements of independent power are developed on the Eurasian land mass as rapidly as possible, in order to take off our shoulders some of the burden of 'bi-polarity.' To my mind, the chief beauty of the Marshall plan was that it had outstandingly this effect." (George F. Kennan to Cecil B. Lyon, 13 October 1947, Department of State Policy Planning Staff Records, Box 33 "Chronological—1947," Diplomatic Branch, National Archives.)

[111]Most excessively, in Gaddis, *Strategies of Containment*, passim.

perception of vulnerability brought about by the war, and the all-too-successful—if inadvertent—efforts of the Russians to give that abstraction an alarming reality.

VI

Soviet historians have argued with unsurprising consistency through the years that the United States overreacted to the "threat" posed by the USSR in the wake of World War II.[112] During the late 1960s and early 1970s, a number of American students of the early cold war expressed agreement with that conclusion, though not with the methods that had been used to arrive at it.[113] In an inversion of Kennan's theory regarding Russian behavior, these accounts portray official Washington as having in one way or another fabricated the myth of a hostile Soviet Union in order to justify its own internally motivated drive for international hegemony. The difficulty with this argument is the impossibility of verifying it, for without access to Soviet sources there could be no definite conclusions regarding its accuracy. One cannot credibly assess responsibility when one can confirm the motives of only one side. The intervening years have brought us no nearer to a resolution of that problem, but they have witnessed the emergence of several new lines of historical interpretation that appear to call into question the thesis of American "overreaction."

One of these involves a reconsideration of Stalin's policy by a new generation of scholars equally conversant, not only with the very limited number of Soviet and East European sources that are available, but with the overwhelming array of recently declassified American and British documents as well. The effect of this work is to confirm neither the "totalitarian" nor the "ideological" explanations of Stalin's actions that were popular during the early cold-war years, but rather to see that dictator as having followed an "imperial" model of expansion: a pattern of be-

---

[112]The clearest recent example in English is Nikolai V. Sivachev and Nikolai N. Yakovlev, *Russia and the United States*, translated by Olga Adler Titlebaum (Chicago: 1979), especially chapter six.

[113]See, for examples of this "revisionism" in its purest form, Gabriel Kolko, *The Politics of War: The World and United States Foreign Policy, 1943–1945* (New York: 1968); and Joyce and Gabriel Kolko, *The Limits of Power: The World and United States Foreign Policy, 1945–1954* (New York: 1972). Other works that stress the "overreaction" theme in varying degrees include: William A. Williams, *The Tragedy of American Diplomacy*, rev. ed. (New York: 1962); Lloyd C. Gardner, *Architects of Illusion: Men and Ideas in American Foreign Policy, 1941–1949* (Chicago: 1970); Thomas G. Paterson, *Soviet-American Confrontation: Postwar Reconstruction and the Origins of the Cold War* (Baltimore: 1973); and, most recently, Yergin, *Shattered Peace*.

havior motivated by insecurity and characterized by caution, to be sure, but one that was also incapable of defining the limits of security requirements and that sought, as a result, to fill power vacuums where this could be done without encountering resistance. The effect of this policy was twofold: to incorporate within the Soviet sphere what Vojtech Mastny has called "a cluster of sullen dependencies" that probably contributed to more than they subtracted from Moscow's nervousness; and to alarm, and ultimately alienate, the United States and its Western European allies, who saw Stalin's inability to define the full extent of his security requirements as likely to undermine their own.[114]

It may well be, as William Taubman has argued, that the West gave up on the possibility of cooperation with Stalin before Stalin gave up on the possibility of cooperation with the West. But Taubman points out that any such cooperation would have been on the Kremlin leader's terms and for his purposes: It would have been designed

to foster Soviet control of Eastern Europe whether directly (in the case of Poland, Rumania, and Bulgaria) or indirectly (in Hungary and Czechoslovakia); to expand Soviet influence in Western Europe, the Near East and Asia; to position the USSR for even greater gains when the next Western economic crisis struck; and to achieve all this while subsidized to the tune of at least six billion dollars in American credits.[115]

Western statesmen may perhaps be pardoned for not having shared this particular vision of the postwar world.

Nor are they condemned, in the new historiography, for having resorted to a strategy of containment; indeed, Mastny goes so far as to suggest that the West's responsibility for the coming of the cold war lies more in the passive and dilatory character of its response than in its aggressiveness: "any Western policy likely to restrain [Stalin] would have had to follow a harder rather than a softer line; it would also have had a better chance to succeed if applied sooner rather than later."[116] Containment no doubt reinforced Stalin's suspicion of the West, but it can hardly be said to have created it; without containment, according to this new line of interpretation, the fears Western statesmen held at the time regarding Soviet expansionism might well have become reality.

Historians are also beginning to study the involvement of third parties

---

[114]Mastny, *Russia's Road to the Cold War*, especially 306–13. Mastny's book is the most prominent example of this new interest in the early cold-war policies of the Soviet Union, but see also Taubman, *Stalin's American Policy*, passim.

[115]Ibid., 74, 129.

[116]Mastny, *Russia's Road to the Cold War*, 306, 310–11.

in the early cold war. This work sheds new light on the question of who saw whom as a threat. What emerges from it so far is the extent to which states along the periphery of the USSR tended to share Washington's concern about Soviet intentions, and indeed to welcome American intervention in their affairs as a counterweight. The Norwegian historian Geir Lundestad has pointed out that Washington's influence actually expanded more rapidly than did that of the Russians in the postwar world, but he argues that this happened because the United States was *encouraged* to assert its power in order to balance that of the Russians.[117] Bruce Kuniholm has documented a similar pattern in the Near East: In 1946 the Iranian government was demanding not less but greater American interference in its internal affairs on the grounds, as the U.S. ambassador put it, that "the only way they can think of to counteract one influence is to invite another."[118] But the clearest case of all is the policy of Great Britain, which as Terry Anderson and Robert Hathaway have demonstrated, amounted almost to a conspiracy to involve the United States more actively in world affairs.[119]

"If we cannot have a world community with the Russians as a constructive member," a British Foreign Office official minuted early in 1946, "it seems clear that the next best hope for peace and stability is that the rest of the world, including the vital North American arsenal, should be united in defense of whatever degree of stability we can attain."[120] This is as good a summary of London's early cold-war policy, under both the Churchill and Attlee governments, as one is apt to find. The British had come earlier than their American allies to the conclusion that cooperation with the Russians was not going to be possible; certainly they welcomed—and, at times, sought to reinforce—the increasing indications from Washington throughout 1946 and early 1947 that the Truman administration had come to share that view.[121] Their analysis of the reasons

[117]Lundestad, *America, Scandinavia, and the Cold War*, 32, 335. See also Geir Lundestad, "Empire by Invitation?: The United States and Western Europe, 1945–1952," *Journal of Peace Research* XXIII (1986): 263–77.

[118]George Allen to Loy Henderson, 6 July 1946, quoted in Kuniholm, *The Origins of the Cold War in the Near East*, 345. Kuniholm's book sees a similar pattern in Turkey and Greece.

[119]Terry H. Anderson, *The United States, Great Britain, and the Cold War, 1944–1947* (Columbia, Mo.: 1981); Robert M. Hathaway, *Ambiguous Partnership: Britain and America, 1944–1947* (New York: 1981). The point is also made in Alan Bullock, *Ernest Bevin: Foreign Secretary* (New York: 1983), especially 347–48, 394.

[120]J. C. Donnelly minute, 5 March 1946, Foreign Office Records, FO 371/51606/AN587, London.

[121]See on this point, in addition to the Anderson, Bullock, and Hathaway volumes cited

for Soviet unilateralism roughly paralleled that of the Americans;[122] nor were they inclined to find fault—apart from some wincing at the rhetorical excesses involved—with the strategies Washington proposed to deal with that problem. Indeed, if anything, London's attitude was that the Americans were not doing enough: It was this conviction that led Foreign Secretary Ernest Bevin late in 1947 to propose to the United States a formal and permanent peacetime military alliance with Western Europe.[123]

It is, of course, easy to see self-serving motivations at work in the invitations the British government and its counterparts in Western Europe and the Near East extended to the United States to expand its influence in their parts of the world. It could be argued that had that desire for an American presence not existed, these "third party" assessments of Russian intentions might have been considerably less alarmist than they were. But that is missing the point, for it is also the case that had a credible Soviet threat not presented itself, these countries would not have been seeking the expansion of American power in the first place. "It has really become a matter of the defence of western civilisation," the British Foreign Office concluded early in 1948:

Not only is the Soviet government not prepared at the present state to co-operate in any real sense with any non-Communist ... Government, but it is actively preparing to extend its hold over the remaining portion of continental Europe and, subsequently, over the Middle East and no doubt the bulk of the Far East as well. ... [P]hysical control of the Eurasian land mass and eventual control of the whole World Island is what the Politburo is aiming at—no less a thing than that. The immensity of the aim should not betray us into believing in its impracticality. Indeed, unless positive and vigorous steps are shortly taken by those other states who are in a position to take them ... the Soviet Union will gain political and strategical advantages which will set the great communist machine in action, leading either to the establishment of a World Dictatorship or (more probably) to the collapse of organised society over great stretches of the globe.[124]

above, Peter G. Boyle, "The British Foreign Office View of Soviet-American Relations, 1945–46," *Diplomatic History* III (Summer 1979): 307–20.

[122]See the exceptionally perceptive discussion in Bullock, *Ernest Bevin: Foreign Secretary*, 6–12, 105–08, 115–18. It is worth noting in this connection the similarity in the viewpoints of Kennan and Frank Roberts, the British charge d'affaires in Moscow in early 1946. (See, on this point, Boyle, "The British Foreign Office View of Soviet-American Relations," 310; also Hathaway, *Ambiguous Partnership*, 369–70.)

[123]Bullock, *Ernest Bevin*, 529–30; also Timothy Ireland, *Creating the Entangling Alliance: The Origins of the North Atlantic Treaty Organization* (Westport, Conn.: 1981), 48–79; and Lawrence S. Kaplan, *The United States and NATO: The Formative Years* (Lexington, Ky.: 1984), 49–64.

[124]Bevin to Cabinet, C. P. (48) 72, "The Threat to Western Civilisation," 3 March 1948, Cabinet Records, CAB 129/25, Public Record Office, London.

It is significant that this top-secret Foreign Office document, circulated only with the highest levels of the British government and declassified only after the passage of more than three decades, should have revealed an assessment of the Soviet threat more sweeping in character and apocalyptic in tone than anything in the record of private or public statements by major American officials at the time. The progression from Mackinder to Spengler, it appears, was easier than one might think.

VII

History, inescapably, involves viewing distant pasts through the prism of more recent ones. The incontestable fact that the United States overreacted more than once during the subsequent history of the cold war to the perceived threat of Soviet and/or "communist" expansionism has, to an extent, blinded us to the equally demonstrable fact that in the immediate postwar years the behavior of the Russians alarmed not just Americans but a good portion of the rest of the world as well. How wellfounded that alarm was—how accurately it reflected the realities that shaped Soviet policy—are issues upon which there are legitimate grounds for disagreement. But to deny that the alarm itself was sincere, or that Americans were not alone in perceiving it, is to distort the view through the prism more than is necessary. Fear, after all, can be genuine without being rational. And, as Sigmund Freud once pointed out, even paranoids can have real enemies.[125]

[125] *The Basic Writings of Sigmund Freud,* trans. and ed. by A. A. Brill (New York: 1938), 163.

9

Alliance and autonomy: European identity and U.S. foreign policy objectives in the Truman years

CHARLES S. MAIER

"Pax Americana" is a resonant term that conceals a crucial question: How much power and control did the United States exert in postwar Europe? U.S. policy involved organizing a coalition of nations, encouraging European leaders who shared the political objectives of the United States, and seeking to isolate those who did not. It meant using economic assistance as well as the appeal of a liberal ideology to reinforce centrist political preferences among European voting publics and working-class movements. At the same time Washington policy makers were supposedly committed to encouraging European autonomy. How did alliance and autonomy mesh? In some instances one goal might have to yield, at least temporarily. Consider, for example, the dilemma presented as late as 1951 by government fecklessness in Greece (admittedly the feeblest of the regimes in the U.S. orbit). William Foster at Economic Cooperation Administration (ECA) headquarters in Paris might wire officials in Athens that "any further assumption of responsibility for managing Greek affairs, despite recurring evidence that a weak government prefers to pass responsibility for potentially unpopular decisions, . . . could ultimately evolve into colonial relationship between Greece and U.S. which, of course, is wholly contrary to American objectives." But the mission in Athens responded, "It appears to us that, US aid being decisive factor in maintaining Greek stability, 'intervention' is a concomitant of our position. Insistence on sound performance is obligation we cannot escape."[1]

[1] National Archives (NA): Federal Record Center, Suitland, Md.: RG 469, Office of the Special Representative, Confidential Incoming Cables.

273

An "obligation we cannot escape": the concept is a warning that to summarize the components and the limits of U.S. ascendancy in the post-war years is not easy. Pax Americana summons up the image of empire, with Washington assuming an exhausted London's mission. A historian who uses the phrase implies that the United States took up an imperial role, perhaps "accidentally," to borrow Ronald Steel's phrase, perhaps "reluctantly," to concur with John Gaddis's judgment, but the role is recognizably imperial nonetheless.[2] But does the imperial analogue help us to understand the U.S. role and Europe's own organization? Only if it is analyzed more carefully than is usually the case.

To begin with, European antiquity alone (leaving aside East Asia and the world of Islam) offers two models of classical empire, Athenian and Roman. Only the former is heuristically compelling. Rome forcibly incorporated other peoples in a common legal framework ruled from the center. Athens's empire, in contrast, arose out of a military coalition that split into two blocs once the Persian threat was repulsed. Although Athens could enforce its hegemony with cynical brutality ("The strong do what they will, the weak do what they must"), the city did not seek directly to rule other communities but to encourage friendly elites within them and preserve their alignment. For postwar U.S. policy, the analogue of empire becomes useful precisely to reveal the structure of coordination (a more precise word than control) across national boundaries.

What characterized such a structure of coordination, assuming that it did not rest on repression alone? One characteristic was the popular acceptance of shared values and a common commitment (tested by elections and by the absence of disabling public protest) to transnational ideals that motivate political behavior. Another was the formation of a new elite who had a personal and political stake in defending the values. When national sovereignty or local rule persists, an imperial framework rests less on crude domination from the center than on consensus concerning the policy objectives that motivate the influential groups within

---

[2] I agree with the idea of an imperial paradigm put forward by John Lewis Gaddis, "The Emerging Post-Revisionist Synthesis on the Origins of the Cold War," *Diplomatic History* 7, no. 3 (Summer 1983): 171–90, especially 182–83. In the discussion at the symposium, Ronald Steel used the term "accidental" empire. But from the viewpoint of Britain and Rome, empire also came "accidentally," as each power usually expanded more to safeguard the last foothold acquired than to follow any grand plan. (Of course, every empire defines its role as defensive; its apologists rarely improve on Virgil: "Remember, Roman, to rule the people under law, to establish the way of peace, to subdue the haughty, to spare the meek.")

each country. Certainly, the Atlantic Community provided the institutions to nurture such an elite, obviously the long-standing institutions of religion, representative government, and law but also the newer ones of the Organization for Economic Cooperation and Development (OECD), the Common Market, the North Atlantic Treaty Organization (NATO), and the continuing stream of semiofficial exchanges, such as productivity missions, student exchanges, the Council on Foreign Relations, foundations, city-twinning, and the like.

Does it make sense, however, to think of such a system of common purpose as "imperial"? Did not shared concerns about economic collapse and communist expansion merely provoke a democratic reflex that united the Atlantic Community? That is how the orthodox historiography tends to describe the developments in the late 1940s and 1950s. To answer the question requires more careful reflection about the relationship between the United States and Europe, between the center of power and wealth and those countries that (if inaccurately thought of as periphery or province) were at least relatively poor and weak. The premise of this essay is that, given the basic inequality of resources after World War II, it would have been very difficult for any system of economic linkages or military alliance not to have generated an international structure analogous to empire. Hegemony was in the cards, which is not to say that Americans did not enjoy exercising it (once they resolved to pay for it). To state this, however, is to explain little. The more intriguing issue remains the degree to which the U.S. ascendancy allowed scope for European autonomy. The relationship worked out between Washington and the European centers during the formative Truman years provided cohesive political purpose but simultaneously allowed significant national independence. To explain that dual result is the purpose of this essay.

From Washington's viewpoint as of 1950, U.S. policy might have been described as a process of growing coherence and resolution. From a confused postwar period in which most Americans thought primarily of winding down their wartime commitments, the Truman administration recognized the threat of Soviet communist expansionism, provided economic and military reassurances that we would not simply abandon those who wished to resist Soviet encroachment, launched a major coordinated plan for economic recovery, and then served as architect for a military alliance and tentative political cooperation. Under the aegis of containment and the leadership of Truman, Americans committed themselves to a continuing role in West European affairs. Whether one admires the process of leadership or deplores it as provocative, certainly the policy of the Truman years—carried through by a remarkable phalanx of internationalists such as Robert Lovett, Averell Harriman, George Marshall, and Dean Acheson, all trained to influence and command and convinced that Washington must in fact exert influence and command—is one of remarkable purposefulness.

To be sure, this policy could not have enjoyed success had there been no West European interlocutors, a team of partners who quickly became convinced that their own countries' interests, and perhaps their own personal political fortunes, were best served by alignment in the new field of U.S. strength. As noted, such a transnational elite forms the backbone of any imperial system. Nevertheless, Europeans had their own problems and their own priorities. These did not always coincide with American preoccupations, even when common interests prescribed the same overall policies. Moreover, Europeans from the different countries understood how to pursue their own independent agendas under the U.S. umbrella. This freedom of action did not weaken Washington's policies. On the contrary, it allowed U.S. actions to seem less dominating and less constraining and thus probably helped make for a more broadly accepted policy. Precisely this possibility for national divergence made American policies more supple and more attractive than they might otherwise have been. John Gaddis has used the term "empire by consent," and I have referred to "consensual hegemony." But how was that consent achieved? And how could there be national differentiation within an overarching U.S.-sponsored Atlantic structure?

The major slogan invented to describe U.S. policies was "containment." In some ways containment remained an American concept. It defined policy as seen from the great-power center. Europeans accepted the notion, but it did not motivate them in the same integrating and substantive way. They remained concerned about economic recovery, economic integration, and national autonomy as much within blocs as between them. Here we will attempt to see the interlocking of the U.S. agenda and the Washington conceptualization of foreign policy with some of the European agendas and their respective notions of foreign policy objectives. There was much shared purpose to be sure, perhaps more than in any earlier or subsequent period. But even with the extraordinary consensus of the late 1940s to the mid-1960s, different national objectives did not cease to exist.

Containment and productivity

U.S. policy obviously had a political and an economic aspect. I have described the economic aspect in an earlier paper as "the politics of productivity."[3] Unlike "containment," this was not a term applied by policy makers at the time. Nonetheless, the watchword of productivity became important in 1947 as the Marshall Plan (substantial aid to an integrated West European region) emerged out of the ad hoc aid characteristic of immediate postwar efforts. Before 1947 U.S. assistance had been funneled through the United Nations Relief and Rehabilitation Administration (UNRRA) and Government Aid and Relief in Occupied Areas. These grants represented large amounts even by later Marshall Plan standards, but they responded to the priorities of basic recovery that the war seemed to dictate. UNRRA aid remained relatively apolitical, although the failure to win political mileage made UNRRA financing increasingly unpalatable during 1946, as cold-war bipolarity became a major theme of U.S. foreign relations. Congress resented communist exploitation of U.S. funds in Eastern Europe. State Department officials disliked the Keynesian social activism of American UNRRA officials in Italy. Administration officials turned to anti-communist arguments to justify major loans to France; and overall more influential Americans agreed with David Rockefeller's argument in the Council on Foreign Relations that "we should decide which groups we favored . . . and we should let them know our attitude even to the extent of offering selective economic support."[4] Still, as late as the deliberations on the Foreign Relief Aid Bill in spring of 1947, Democratic senators found it an acceptable proposition that "a needy Communist ought to get relief."[5]

[3]Charles S. Maier, "The Politics of Productivity: Foundations of American International Economic Policy After World War II," in Peter Katzenstein, ed., *Between Power and Plenty: The Foreign Economic Policies of Advanced Industrial States* (Madison: University of Wisconsin Press, 1978), 23–49.

[4]Rockefeller's views summarized in Council on Foreign Relations Archives, Records of Groups/XII G, Discussion Group on Reconstruction in Western Europe, 18 December 1946. For the problems of UNRRA in Italy, see John L. Harper, "Reconstruction through Economics: The American Experience in Italy, 1945–1948" (revised Ph.D. diss., Johns Hopkins School of Advanced International Studies, 1984). For the debates on the Blum loan, see National Advisory Council on International Monetary and Financial Policies, 6 May 1946, in NA, Washington: Office of the Secretary of the Treasury, RG 56.

[5]C. Tyler Wood's testimony in Senate Committee on Foreign Relations, Historical Series: *Executive Hearings . . . on H.J. Res. 153 and Sen. 1774, Foreign Relief Aid: 1947* (Washington, D.C.: U.S. Government Printing Office, 1973), 19. The unsuccessful McClellan amendment did seek to exclude communist-controlled countries.

Aid through early 1947, moreover, was keyed to relief. But by the spring of that year, Washington planners, cold-war politics aside, believed that approach would remain insufficient. In effect, foreign assistance would have to recapitulate the earlier progress of the New Deal, going from the Federal Emergency Relief Administration to the Public Works Administration and Work Projects Administration—that is, from relief to job creation and to investment in infrastructure. To be sure, the proximate impulse in the spring of 1947 for Marshall's initiative arose from a balance-of-payments crisis. Europe simply lacked the dollars to import agricultural goods, coal, and other basic necessities. The severe winter of 1947 had choked off the initial recovery of 1946. European workers were losing patience with counsels of restraint; strikes broke out and political conflict flared. Fuel was catastrophically scarce because coal barges could not move on the frozen northern rivers and German miners were weakened by hunger. Factories had to be cut back to partial work weeks. With massive discontent among labor, all efforts appeared blighted. The need was to rebuild the European economy so it would not be in a state of perpetual dollar hemorrhage. Integration with East European agricultural areas appeared a dead letter given the breakdown of Soviet-American agreement on Germany. The moment had come for a concept of far more integrated West European assistance, if only to persuade Congress that relief would not be poured perpetually down a rathole.[6]

As the European Recovery Program (ERP) was established over the course of the following year, with its country missions and Washington ECA headquarters, the rationale of enhancing "productivity" was increasingly developed. Productivity was the allegedly apolitical criterion that motivated recovery assistance. Just as the idea of "totalitarianism" offered an explanatory construct that could account for Soviet behavior, as John Gaddis points out, so "productivity" could serve to sum up American economic aspirations. Productivity was an index of efficiency: It implied clearing away bottlenecks to production and getting the highest output from labor and capital, just as the United States had so obviously accomplished. Productivity supposedly dictated no political interference; for what groups could object to such a neutral measure of economic achievement?

Productivity, I have suggested elsewhere, derived from an American

[6] See Michael J. Hogan, "The Search for a 'Creative Peace': The United States, European Unity, and the Origins of the Marshall Plan," *Diplomatic History* 6, no. 3 (Summer 1982): 267–85.

ideological legacy from the Progressive Era. The American celebration of private enterprise was periodically punctuated by reform crusades, usually couched as attacks on the forces of monopoly on behalf of exploited farmers or virtuous small businessmen oppressed by corporations. Reform efforts, however, had to yield after a decade of conflict to political exhaustion and conservative revival. Precisely as the celebration of expansion, growth, efficiency, and then, in the late 1940s, of productivity legitimated the dismantling of ideological fervor and the renewed celebration of American capitalism, now outfitted with a set of reforms that had not earlier been present, so the prewar Progressive Era had spawned the efficiency movement and the crusade against "waste in industry" that the wartime production performance of 1917–18 seemed to vindicate.[7]

Similarly, the acrimonious reform period of the New Deal, especially the antibusiness rhetoric of 1936 to 1938, yielded to Roosevelt's "Dr. Win the War," the return of business executives as dollar-a-year men, and the suspension of antitrust concerns.[8] The wartime output of tanks, planes, and Liberty ships vindicated the promise of productivity. It brought into national service many of the businessmen who would set their stamp on the Truman administration. Productivity suggested that class conflict was not inevitable and that management and labor did not have to quarrel over the shares of wages and profits. If they only cooperated, the dividend of economic growth might reward them both. Thus, economic growth in a sense promised the adjournment of political and social conflict; it would transform basic struggles into cooperative searches for optimal economic solutions, "the one best way."

Of course, there was an implicit politics in productivity. It effectively declared out of bounds any Marxist or left-wing notion that capitalism itself might be inequitable. Only self-serving parties interested in their own selfish power could object to economic growth. Acceptance of productivity as a goal effectively froze the division of income and managerial power in a society, promising proportional increments of growth to

---

[7] On this, see Robert Cuff, *The War-Industries Board: Business-Government Relations during World War I* (Baltimore, Md.: Johns Hopkins University Press, 1973); and Ellis W. Hawley, *The Great War and the Search for a Modern Order* (New York: Saint Martin's, 1979), 24–27, and passim on associational efforts during the war and the next decade.

[8] On the suspension of antitrust, see Ellis W. Hawley, *The New Deal and the Problem of Monopoly* (Princeton, N.J.: Princeton University Press, 1966), 440–42; on businessmen, John Morton Blum, *V Was for Victory: Politics and American Culture during World War II* (New York: Harcourt Brace Jovanovich, 1976), 106–46; and, most revealing for labor, Nelson Lichtenstein, *Labor's War at Home: The CIO in World War II* (Cambridge: Cambridge University Press, 1982).

everyone but keeping the basic distributions of authority and wealth the same. Americans were willing to accept this bargain, as agreement on productivity-keyed wages indicated. The United States was a society whose immigrant base in effect wagered on growth alone for prosperity.

But applied to Europe, such a policy meant by 1947–48 that communist spokesmen must be viewed as obstructionist, especially after the Soviet Union decided that it could not participate in the Marshall Plan and in the fall of 1947 urged communist party leaders in the West to enter a new phase of long-term obstruction.[9] Instead, productivity served to rally social-democratic labor groups. French and Italian social democrats were dissatisfied with galloping inflation in their countries and wanted the restoration of wage differentials, which communists opposed. Leaders of the Force Ouvrière in France, the non-communist trade unionists in Italy, and the anti-communist Trades Union Congress in Britain looked to U.S. government assistance or sympathetic American Federation of Labor emissaries with well-upholstered checkbooks to help them resist communist politicization and subversion of their own unions.[10] Productivity thus came to Europe as the ideological watchword of a coalition that would unite progressive management and collaborative labor.

The slogan motivated exchanges of labor groups across the Atlantic,

[9] Communist policy has been interpreted differently. See Alfred Rieber, *Stalin and the French Communist Party, 1941–1947* (Cambridge, Mass.: Harvard University Press, 1962); Wilfried Loth, 'Frankreichs Kommunisten und der Beginn des kalten Krieges: Die Entlassung der Kommunistischen Minister im Mai 1947," *Vierteljahrshefte für Zeitgeschichte* 26 (1978): 9–65; J. P. Hirsch, " 'La seule voie possible': Remarques sur les comunistes du Nord et du Pas-de-Calais de la Libération aux grèves de novembre 1947," Actes du Colloque de l'Université de Lille III, 2–3 novembre 1974, in *Revue du Nord* 57 (1975): 563–78. Up to winter 1947 communists themselves followed a politics of productionism, seeking to establish their coalition bona fides in Western Europe by getting their unions to work hard and pursue wage restraint. That policy threatened to fragment their own ranks during the hard winter of 1947, and they were compelled to a more militant stance: precisely the demands that let the French and Belgian socialists argue for their exclusion from "Tripartite" coalitions in early 1947. Only in the fall of 1947 did the "orders" from Moscow seem to arrive, that henceforth they must remain noncooperative. Even then, however, the objective of the mass communist strikes of 1947–48 seems less to have been to seize power (they knew this was impossible) than to show the centrist parties, including the Socialists, that their countries could not be governed without their cooperation. Here, too, they miscalculated. In effect, U.S. capital replaced communist labor.

[10] For the European labor movement, from viewpoints critical of U.S. policy, see Peter Weiler, "The United States, International Labor, and the Cold War: The Breakup of the World Federation of Trade Unions," *Diplomatic History* 5, no. 1 (Winter 1981): 1–22; Ronald Radosh, *American Labor and U.S. Foreign Policy* (New York: Random House, 1969); and the essays by Borsdorf, Niethammer, and Lademacher, cited in note 12, below. For more sympathetic accounts, André Barjonet, *La C.G.T.* (Paris, 1968); Daniel L. Horowitz, *The Italian Labor Movement* (Cambridge, Mass.: Harvard University Press, 1963); also Irving Brown's detailed if partisan reports in the AFL papers, Florence Thorne collection, State Historical Society of Wisconsin, Madison.

joint productivity councils, and even productivity villages in Italy.[11] The politics of productivity thus marked the critical years of 1948 to 1950 as purposeful Western policy emerged from earlier contradictory or ambiguous initiatives. In the spring of 1947 communists were thrust out of the governing coalitions in France, Belgium, and Italy. Hungary and then, in February 1948, Czechoslovakia fell under communist control. The division of Germany was effectively confirmed with the introduction of the Western currency reform, which was answered by the Berlin blockade. The World Federation of Trade Unions went into schism, as did the union confederations in the continental countries.[12]

In the United States the idea of productivity was complemented by the theme of sustained economic growth; the first reference to this—outside academic journals—that I am aware of was in the speeches of the New Dealish chairman of the Council of Economic Advisers, Leon Keyserling.[13] Growth and productivity were to remain underlying guidelines for foreign policy. Even as they were being crowded out after Korea by more purely military and security-oriented concepts, Atlantic leaders invoked their efficacy. "The improvement of productivity, in its widest sense, remains the fundamental problem of Western Europe," OECD spokesmen wrote in 1952. And Thomas Cabot, the director of international security affairs in the State Department, insisted as he turned over the Mutual Security Program to its incoming director, Averell Harriman, "In my view we have been remiss in not giving productivity greater emphasis. . . . If we can sell Europe on the fundamental advantages of a *competitive* and reasonably free system of enterprise, I have no doubt the standard of living there will advance soon to a level where there is no danger whatever of its being subverted."[14]

The politics of productivity, however, formed only one key concept underlying U.S. policy in the years after 1947. The other was the more

[11] Cf. Charles S. Maier, "The Politics of Productivity"; David W. Ellwood, "Il Piano Marshall e il processo di modernizzazione in Italia," in Elena Aga Rossi, ed., *Il Piano Marshall e l'Europa* (Rome: Trecani, 1983), 149–61.

[12] See the papers by Ulrich Borsdorf and Horst Lademacher in Othmar Nikola Haberl and Lutz Niethammer, eds., *Der Marshall Plan und die europäischen Linke* (Frankfurt am Main: Europäische Verlagsanstalt, 1986), 194–211, 501–34; also Niethammer, Stukturreform und Wachstumspakt, in H. O. Vetter, ed., *Vom Sozialistengesetz zur Mitbestimmung* (Cologne: Bund Verlag, 1975), 303–58.

[13] Keyserling, "Prospects for American Economic Growth," address in San Francisco, 18 September 1949, in Harry S. Truman Library (HSTL), PSF, 143: "Agencies: Council of Economic Advisers."

[14] Organization for European Economic Cooperation (OEEC), *Europe: The Way Ahead*, 4th Annual Report (Paris, 1952), 195; Cabot to Harriman, 25 October 1951, in *Foreign Relations of the United States*, 1951, I, 440 (hereafter cited as *FRUS*).

geopolitical notion of containment and national security, which is the focus for John Gaddis's contribution to this volume and need not be emphasized here. Containment and security, however, drew on a more recent intellectual legacy. Productivity was as American as apple pie. Efficiency and cooperation, the fundamentals of the U.S. economy, had been repeatedly invoked. The tradition of containment developed instead what had previously been a minority current. True, Sir Halford Mackinder's geopolitics with its geographical determinism had found earlier apostles, and Brooks Adams's imperialism introduced more European tonalities. From the turn of the century different geopolitical concepts had clashed, notably the maritime idea of Admiral Alfred Mahan that justified navalism and the Mackinder emphasis on the continental heartland. During World War II, the War and Peace Study Groups of the Council of Foreign Relations included proponents of geopolitics eager to acquire foreign bases and maintain a strong postwar military force.[15]

Melvyn Leffler has recently demonstrated how the U.S. military and defense officials combined became imbued with a fusion of geopolitical and economic concerns in the late 1940s, to the extent that they discerned a unified Soviet goal to control the resources of Eurasia.[16] Kennan himself, the intellectual adumbrator of political containment, was trained in Sovietology by right-wing Germans in the 1920s and liked to indulge his penchant for analysis in terms of Spenglerian evocations of national psychology and climate and overpowering landscape: Russian expansion resulted from the "age-old sense of insecurity of a sedentary people reared on an exposed plain in the neighborhood of fierce nomadic peoples" and Moscow's security might be sought "only in patient but deadly struggle for total destruction [with the] rival power."[17]

Productivity and containment were the twin themes of postwar U.S. foreign policy: the one upbeat, can-do, confident that with the removal of bottlenecks, abundance could reconcile all political differences; the other somber, minor-key, predicting twilight struggles and the need for untiring resistance until rivulets of reform might eventually thaw the fro-

[15] Council on Foreign Relations Archives, Records of Groups. Cf. the study in progress by Carlo Santoro of the geopolitical component of American security thinking; and for a contrast between Mackinder and Mahan, Paul Kennedy, *Strategy and Diplomacy 1870–1945* (London: George Allen & Unwin, 1983), 41–85.

[16] Melvyn P. Leffler, "The American Conception of National Security and the Beginnings of the Cold War, 1945–48," *American Historical Review*, 89 (1984):346–81, comments and reply, 382–400. On the containment theme in general John Lewis Gaddis, *Strategies of Containment*, and his reply to Leffler, above, 382–85.

[17] Cf. George F. Kennan, "Russia's International Position at the Close of the War with Germany (May 1945)," and "Excerpts from Telegraphic Message from Moscow of February 22, 1946," in *Memoirs: 1925–1950* (Boston: Little, Brown, 1967), 533, 550.

zen Soviet political system. The simultaneous pursuit of both ideas allowed the bipartisan foreign-policy coalition enough unity at home to overcome isolationism, rallying former New Dealers confident of the blessings of Keynesianism abroad and interventionist strategic thinkers convinced that the future lay with NSC 68 (the plan for U.S. rearmament developed in early 1950). Moreover, the themes could cross-fertilize each other, so that adherents of one mode, the social engineers of the New Deal, could appeal to the imperatives of the other, the Catos of preparedness.

Keyserling argued that the communist threat mandated a larger tax bite in the economy and expressed confidence that the government could orchestrate this intervention.[18] Mobilization meant government activism, obviously in terms of greater government spending, but also in planning and organization, because "needs seem to me to call for further improvement and further centralization of the overall programming of requirements and supply." Conversely, among the celebrators of military security, National Securities Resources Board Chairman Stuart Symington could wax vague and rhapsodic about the urgency of long-range diplomatic, economic, and military planning to counter the decades-long Soviet move toward world domination.[19]

Finally, both themes spotlighted Western Europe. The military resisted initiatives that divided Europe longer than civilian planners in Washington. Eisenhower and other generals recalled wartime collaboration with the Soviets; in addition the army was responsible for a theoretical four-power administrative task force in Germany. Containment had to mean containment at the Elbe, had to imply the frank write-off of Eastern Europe and the acceptance of spheres of influence that had earlier been resisted. Similarly, productivity had to draw on the skilled labor and resources of Western Europe; it had little relevance for what would later be called the Third World.

The diversity of European vulnerabilities and resources

The objectives of containment and productivity characterized policy in general, but they also suggested different needs for different European societies. Washington policy makers worked to encourage an integrated

[18] Chairman of the CEA to the president, 2 November 1951, *FRUS*, 1951, I, 245–54.
[19] Undated Symington memo to the president. Truman showed astuteness in minuting, "My dear Stu, this is [as] big a lot of Top Secret malarky as I've ever read. Your time is wasted on such bunk as this. HST" FRUS, 1951, I, 33 n. 22.

Western Europe, but they also understood that each country had particular vulnerability and potential resources. A common urgency underlay the crisis of 1947—the conviction that Western Europe was an entity that in effect had to be created to be preserved. But there was no undifferentiated bloc; there were specific problems, opportunities, and missions.

The European countries seemed to pose three sorts of challenge for U.S. policy during the Truman period. The most urgent and brutal was that of direct communist takeover. The image of countries slipping behind the Iron Curtain, of being "lost" to communism, prompted the articulation of containment. Communist takeover could result from armed subversion, as the Truman administration beheld it in Turkey and Greece. Renewed civil war prompted the earliest declaration of anti-communist intent, the Truman Doctrine of March 1947. Given the fragility of the Greek regime, U.S. intervention soon led to the greatest degree of political penetration outside occupied Germany.[20] But communist takeover need not be military. The Italian government in 1947 and early 1948 seemed almost as precarious. Italy's Communist party appeared to have the power to paralyze economic reform—to be sure, reform carried out along classical deflationary lines that restored management's power to lay off workers, which had been effectively suspended at liberation. Even sober American observers believed that the April 1948 elections might return the communists to a dominant government role. A pessimistic Kennan suggested that it would be better to provoke a communist uprising that might seize the industrial north but would at least allow military intervention to save the south.[21]

Direct communist takeover was not the only danger, however. It might arise as the upshot of civil war or violence. (The Czech coup of February 1948 revealed that direct-action factory committees should spearhead a virtual coup d'état. Nonetheless, Prague's freedom from communist control had been understood as limited once Czechoslovakia withdrew from the Paris discussions designed to work out European cooperation with the Marshall Plan.) But after April 1948, the danger of takeover seemed less pressing. More threatening was the danger of political and economic paralysis. Institutional crises would continue to affect Italy even after the peril of outright takeover seemed to pass, and they threatened French

---

[20] See Mark M. Amen, "La pénétration des structures militaires et politiques de la Grèce par les Etats-Unis. juin 1947–octobre 1949," *Relations Internationales*, no. 11 (Autumn 1977): 173–99; Lawrence S. Wittner, *American Intervention in Greece* (New York: Columbia University Press, 1982); Bruce Kuniholm, *The Origins of the Cold War in the Near East* (Princeton: Princeton University Press, 1980).

[21] See Kennan to secretary of state, 15 March 1948, *FRUS*, 1948, III, 848–49.

governments as well. Although Americans worried briefly in 1947 that Gaullist electoral gains might prompt communist counteraction, they became more concerned that the government's inability to master inflation might force the centrist parties to readmit the Communist party to the ruling coalition of Catholics, Socialists, and center parties. The outcome that was dreaded was less direct takeover than an inability to generate productivity and recovery—a vicious circle of inflationary wage settlements and continuing state deficits, growing alienation of labor, and eventually a debilitating neutralism. Similar concerns held for Italy in 1947 and 1948. Although Luigi Einaudi, supported by Alcide De Gasperi, imposed a deflationary monetary reform in late 1947, unless communist-dominated unions were subdued, wage pressure would choke off investment.

These dangers overcome, a third order of difficulty still threatened Washington's overall design. By 1949, "integration" had become a major theme of economic and political aspirations.[22] Although some degree of integration had stamped the Marshall Plan from its inception, Paul Hoffman and ECA administrators pressed the idea vigorously as the ERP went into its postcrisis phase. Integration had traditionally implied working toward a common market, but in 1948–49, it referred specifically to achieving monetary convertibility. Without multilateral clearances, U.S. subsidies could not generate their most efficient stimulus. Under Washington's prodding, the issue of payments was finally resolved with the creation of the European Payments Union. If the "weak" countries were the problems of 1947 and 1949, it was Britain that would prove the most resistant to economic integration. Military integration, the challenge of the final three years of the Truman presidency, remained another matter. Potential German neutralism and French fears of a revived Germany would then become preoccupying, although never to a fundamental degree.

Communist takeover, economic paralysis, and resistance to integration thus emerged as successive perils to U.S. policy for Europe. The countries most worrisome in 1947 were the least-so later. The societies least vulnerable at first were to become more problematic when integration was at stake. But U.S. policy makers also understood that the European countries brought different assets as well as difficulties. The European nations would make diverse contributions to the common effort.

West Germany clearly had an economic vocation. Even as food short-

---

[22] On Washington's hopes for European integration in 1947–48, see Hogan, "Search for a Creative Peace"; also Armin Rappaport, "The United States and European Integration: The First Phase," *Diplomatic History* 5, no. 2 (Spring 1981): 121–49.

ages provoked demonstrations and coal output fell in the spring of 1947, Americans sought to draw on German mining and industrial potential. American businessmen, trade unionists, and political leaders alike believed that German resources could serve Western Europe as a whole. As Democratic Senator Tom Connally said, "We cannot afford to destroy Germany. She is the economic heart of Europe. . . . There is too much ability in Germany and too many people that know how to do things just to slam down on her and permit the destruction of her plants and the removal of machinery and things to Russia and to other countries."[23] Not everyone agreed with former President Hoover that denazification should be suspended and all restrictions on industry lifted (for Germany was still producing below the ceilings imposed). Nonetheless, there was a broad consensus on the need for production. "The best reparations our Western Allies can obtain is the prompt recovery of Germany," Secretary of Commerce Harriman reported to Truman after his investigations of the summer of 1947. "We cannot revive a self-supporting Western European economy without a healthy Germany playing its part as a producing and consuming unit."[24]

Assigning West Germany a role as an eventual economic "locomotive" was possible because politically the country remained under effective control. In light of developments in East Germany, communism exercised no mass appeal in the West. Although concern persisted through 1948 about the political loyalty of the West Berlin trade unions, there was little anxiety about communism within the western zones. Socialism was also an excluded alternative. Once the United States took a leading role within the British and American zones, British sympathizers had to defer their plans for the socialization of coal and steel industries in North Rhine–Westphalia, and the Social Democratic party (SPD) itself retreated into an opposition stance within the embryonic administrative agencies of West Germany. As the émigré political scientist and former SPD activist Franz Neumann astutely noted two years later, the possibilities of socialism had

---

[23] Senate Committee on Foreign Relations, Historical Series, *Foreign Relief Aid: 1947*, 18 April 1947, 41.

[24] W. Averell Harriman to Truman, 12 August 1947, in Harriman papers: Commerce File; Folder: "Germany." For hesitations about rushing too quickly toward German recovery, see Edwin Pauley's note to Truman, 15 April 1947. John R. Steelman digested Hoover's and Pauley's contrasting opinions for the president, conceded the need for a policy change, but hoped to avoid "the revival of a German colossus along the lines suggested by Mr. Hoover." See FRUS, 1947. The American Left, as represented by the Committee to Prevent World War III, *The Nation*, and so on, remained adamantly opposed to German revival, but along with Wallace adherents in general they remained in retreat. For the spectrum of opinion, see Alonzo L. Hamby, *Beyond the New Deal: Harry S. Truman and American Liberalism* (New York: Columbia University Press, 1973).

been minimal. SPD enthusiasm had been overrated, and the British had never really pressed for it; there was little Labour party involvement in occupation affairs.[25]

West Germany had an economic mission; France, Britain, and the small countries of Western Europe had political roles to play in the new Western Europe. Administration policy makers believed that these countries were needed to generate stability and Western cooperation. The initial response of both Foreign Secretary Ernest Bevin and French Foreign Minister Georges Bidault to Marshall's speech promised that both countries would take the lead in the new Europe. But France's cooperation was proffered precisely to head off too quick a rehabilitation of Germany. French leaders had to be persuaded to come to terms with the economic role that West Germany must logically play, just as two years later they would have to be pressed into accepting a German military role. As Robert Lovett, acting secretary of state, wrote Harriman in early December 1948, "Our objective should continue to be the progressively closer integration, both economic and political, of presently free Europe and eventually of as much of Europe as becomes free." France thus had to be persuaded to accept German recovery. "The goal of the European Recovery Program is fundamentally political, and France is the keystone of continental Western Europe."[26]

If France was to be the political keystone, stability had to be ensured inside the country. This meant creating the conditions for a noncommunist coalition to prosper. As early as October 1947, in a striking application of the politics of productivity, Under Secretary Lovett urged working-class schism: "Politically speaking the break must come to the left of or at the very least in the middle of the French Socialist Party. Translated into labor terms, the healthy elements of organized labor must be kept in the non-Communist camp. Otherwise the tiny production margin of the fragile French economy would vanish and the ensuing civil disturbances would take on the aspects of civil war."[27]

Once the schism did materialize, the task was to brake inflation and restrain wages. Emphasizing that Americans "did not want to take sides in internal French politics," Lovett said that it would be hard to continue aid unless "a strong, unified and cooperative non-Communist govern-

[25] Neumann statements in Council on Foreign Relations Archives, Records of Groups, vol. XIX 1949/50: Study Group on the Problem of Germany, meetings of 13 October and 9 November 1949.

[26] Lovett to Harriman, 3 December 1948, *FRUS,* 1948, III, 301–03.

[27] NA, Washington: RG 59, 851.00/10-2447.

ment . . . put the French house in order."[28] Such a "nonpolitical" agenda included balancing the budget and ending inflation. Ambassador Jefferson Caffery repeatedly warned that political stability and keeping the communists at bay required "social and political stabilization" (wages and prices, budgetary equilibrium, sound fiscal policy).[29]

Although inflationary pressures eased temporarily in early 1948, by the fall the ECA mission in Paris felt reluctantly compelled to endorse the demand by the French to dip into counterpart funds to meet their budget deficit rather than resort to the printing press. Nevertheless, the colorless Queuille government held on, Jules Moch smashed a new wave of severe strikes, and by the new year food prices had stabilized and industrial production rose. American Treasury officials were pleased with the anti-inflationary policies of René Mayer and Maurice Petsche. Acheson could turn to Paris again to work for European integration: "France and France alone can take the decisive leadership in integrating Western Germany into Western Europe."[30] Washington would be gratified with the bold proposal of Jean Monnet and Robert Schuman in May 1950 for a supranational Coal-Steel Authority. And although the proposal by René Pleven for a supranational army was more a way of making the German military role that Washington pressed for more palatable, U.S. officials such as David Bruce, John J. McCloy, and W. M. "Tommy" Tomlinson worked closely with Jean Monnet, Robert Schuman, and Hervé Alphand in incubating the concept.[31]

Britain also had a political vocation in American eyes. The United States looked to the British to continue the lead they had early shown when Bevin responded so enthusiastically to Marshall's initiative. Over the long term, European recovery required meshing resources and production, thus freeing trade and payments from early postwar restrictions. Britain had the least scarred economy and the closest cultural links to the Americans, hence it appeared as a natural leader. But the British devoted their cooperative efforts largely to military matters. With great fanfare Bevin called for a "consolidation of Western Europe" in January 1948, but he proposed building on the Treaty of Dunkirk directed against Germany and helped produce the West European Union, a rather empty institutional vessel designed to encourage Washington to enter a defense

[28] FRUS, 1948, III, 307.
[29] Caffery to secretary of state, 14 January 1948 in FRUS, 1948, III, 595.
[30] Acheson to U.S. embassy, Paris, 19 October 1949, FRUS, 1949, IV, 469–72.
[31] See Pierre Mélandri, "Les Etats-Unis et le plan Pléven. octobre 1950–juillet 1951," *Relations Internationales*, no. 11 (1977): 201–29.

commitment.[32] Emphasizing a military role would give Britain more parity with the United States, whereas economic integration would undermine the Commonwealth resources. By 1949 Americans were chafing at London's unwillingness to upgrade the political status of the Organization for European Economic Cooperation (OEEC) and at British resistance to monetary convertibility. "We have been too tender with Britain since the war," Bruce claimed. "She has been the constant stumbling block in the economic organization of Europe." In Bevin's cold reception to the Schuman plan, he found "a vacuum of comprehension and an ineptness of diplomatic intercourse."[33] British assistance in Korea and the post-1950 emphasis on military cooperation compensated for foot-dragging on economic integration. Nonetheless, London's reluctance to strengthen European institutions remained a disappointment.

The exercise of individual strategies

Washington policy makers thus dealt with a complex European agenda. They sought to overcome the dangers of communist paralysis in Italy and France, to mobilize the economic potential of West Germany, to press France as continental "keystone" to allow German integration, and to move Britain toward more far-ranging economic cooperation. They also relied on the small countries to provide a basis for Europe's new supranational agencies, the staffs of NATO, the Coal-Steel Authority, and the OEEC. This very differentiation of tasks, however, provided special political leverage for the European countries. Precisely because U.S. policy makers envisaged a differentiated set of national problems and contributions, scope was provided for each country's political strategies. It is these very strategies that make European history during the cold war more than just a mere shadow of U.S. power and motivation. European statesmen understood what Washington needed from them and could extract concessions in return. De Gasperi in Italy, the leaders of the French "third force" (from Bidault to Mayer to Monnet and Schuman), Konrad Adenauer in West Germany, and finally the British leadership (a combi-

[32] See Rappaport, "The United States and European Integration," 129–31. Bevin followed up his cabinet paper and speech in Parliament with queries to Washington on U.S. readiness to help in the defense of Western Europe. See Alan Bullock, *Ernest Bevin, Foreign Secretary 1945–1951* (New York: W. W. Norton, 1983), 518–22.

[33] Meeting of ambassadors at Paris, 21–22 October 1949, *FRUS*, 1949, IV, 492; and Bruce to State Department, 4 June 1950, *FRUS*, 1950, III, 716. For the OEEC controversy, see the exchanges in *FRUS*, 1949, IV, 440–43, 462–67, also *FRUS*, 1950, III, 613–22.

nation of Labour ministers and persuasive Treasury and Foreign Office officials) used the new Atlantic Community for national as well as cold-war ends.

For Italy, weakness was itself a strategy. By the spring of 1947, De Gasperi sought to reconstruct his government without the communists. Throughout 1946 the Christian Democrats had built up their machine in Italy but economic difficulties mounted. When the economic officer of the American embassy, Henry Tasca, returned to Washington in May 1947, he reported a "lack of confidence on the part of the strategic economic groups in the ability of the government to direct and control the country." The communists were benefiting from the very fear that they might come to power.[34] At the same time Italian Ambassador Alberto Tarchiani sought guarantees from Secretary of State Marshall: If De Gasperi reconstructed his government without the communists, would he be assured of the economic aid needed to counter the obstruction that was feared? No specific promises could be brought back from Washington, although the crisis lingered even as Marshall made his celebrated Harvard commencement address.

This implicit dependence continued through the 1948 elections. Italy sought aid from the United States by constantly stressing the precariousness of non-communist democracy. De Gasperi received fewer promises of special assistance than he desired, but he could work within the overall context of the emerging Marshall Plan. When Washington sought to press large amounts of military aid on Italy in early 1948, however, he was shrewd enough to understand that the Americans' fear of a military coup was exaggerated and that such an arsenal could only discredit him if it became public knowledge.

The Italian premier understood how to exploit the politics of dependence. More than elsewhere the fate of the Christian Democrats depended on American intervention; hence it was in De Gasperi's interest to insist on his country's political and economic fragility. He stressed his difficulties in seeking a favorable decision on Trieste and, less successfully, on the Italian colonies. By 1948–49, the Italian authorities' emphasis on deflationary stabilization, even at the cost of rising unemployment, dismayed ECA supervisors, while the State Department similarly resented subordinating Italian defense expenditures to the stability of the lira. But it was hard to exert too much pressure. Even when the Christian

---

[34]Tasca statement in part in *FRUS*, 1947, III, 898–901, and in part in NA, Washington: RG 59, 865.51/5–747, both cited in Harper, "Reconstruction through Economics," 247.

Democrats enjoyed a majority after April 1948, the internal party balance was precarious.

Washington sought to encourage the more cooperative and less right-wing and deflation-minded currents. It was also essential in Washington's eyes to keep the Saragat wing of the Social Democrats within the coalition so as to prevent the Italian working class from falling completely under communist domination.[35] Thus Italy's plea to be included in NATO had to be honored despite the extended defense commitment this entailed and the negligible military assistance the nation might provide. To keep Rome out would have signaled a continuing stigma and undermined the Italian government. Domestic stability was more at stake than military defense. In short, Italy was included in NATO not because of its strength but because of its weakness.[36]

Throughout 1947, French governments were constrained to pursue a tactic similar to that of De Gasperi. Until the winter of 1947–48, Bidault still entertained aspirations that France might retain control of the German Rhineland, the French zone of occupation, and a share in administering the Ruhr. The French minister repeatedly importuned the Americans and the British that unless they heeded French wishes toward Germany the fragile centrist government that had expelled the communists might collapse. Ambassador Caffery faithfully conveyed a sense of the Ramadier government's standing at the political brink: aid or Armageddon.[37]

Such pleading might win U.S. willingness to provide more coal and financial aid, but it could not do more than slow down Anglo-American insistence that Germany must be made a more paying concern. After long internal debate, in early 1948 the French openly came round, accepted that their older ideas of a hold on the Rhineland were unrealistic and that they had to endorse West German institutions. French political strategy became less supplicating, more autonomous. By 1948 it was hard to play

[35] For the poormouthing of 1947, see Ambassador Dunn to secretary of state, 3, 6, and 28 May, also memorandum of conversation, 16 May, and memoranda of conversation by the director of the Office of European Affairs, 20 May and 4 June 1947; also Marshall to U.S. embassy, Rome, 20 May 1947, in *FRUS*, 1947, III, 889–919. For later criticism of Italian policies but unwillingness to press too hard, see the ECA Country Report on Italy (1950) and Acheson to U.S. embassy in London on Italian politics, 18 January 1950, *FRUS*, 1950, III, 1984–85, and Acheson to U.S. embassy in Rome, 2 December 1950, ibid., 1501–02.

[36] See E. Timothy Smith, "The Fear of Subversion: The United States and the Inclusion of Italy in the North Atlantic Treaty," *Diplomatic History* 7, no. 2 (Spring 1983): 139–55.

[37] Caffery cables to State Department, 19 February 1947, and 12 May 1947, in *FRUS*, 1947, III, 690–92; also memorandum of conversation, Moscow, 20 April 1947, and Bidault to secretary of state, 17 July 1947, and Caffery to State Department, 18 July 1947, all in *FRUS*, 1947, II, 367–71, 991–92, 996.

the menace of the communists so convincingly. If Caffery could always signal alarms, Tomlinson and other U.S. economic officials wanted action to raise taxes and curb expenditures. Efforts to curb inflation won recognition from Washington.

But firming up policy at home was only part of the French response. The other was to carve out some limited scope for foreign policy autonomy. While British statesmen aspired to be the experienced, senior counselors in an Anglo-American military-political framework, the French in effect sought a secondary, subhegemony within NATO. Abandoning their early effort to retain control over a segment of West Germany, the French sought to satisfy U.S. demands that they take the lead in "integrating" West Germany back into the West. The political genius of the Schuman Plan lay in the fact that it could please Washington, even as it capitalized on the fact that Bonn was momentarily weak but would soon be industrially and perhaps politically resurgent. In effect, Monnet and Schuman offered to serve as Bonn's patrons at a point when Adenauer could not really carry out an independent foreign policy.

Paris also insisted on Italian membership in NATO over British and even American skepticism.[38] The theoretical reason was that France must otherwise defend its long Italian frontier; but the French also wished to become Rome's patron as well as Bonn's. To Rome, France offered military colleagueship; to Bonn, economic partnership. Thus France became the architect of an alignment within Western Europe that seemed advantageous to the United States while it also enhanced France's own role. The French were not able to achieve the tripartite OEEC or NATO directorates they periodically proposed; nevertheless, France, perhaps more than Britain, created a real European role that could serve national interests.

France retained political assets throughout the period; State Department spokesmen always recognized how crucial France was. But what about West Germany: a divided country, burdened by its recent history, distrusted by its neighbors, and, until 1955, limited in its sovereignty? Even when her cities were in ruins, Germany always retained industrial

---

[38] For the internal French reassessment of their German policy, see Ministère des Affaires Etrangères, Paris: Série Y: 55, dossier 1: Massigli (ambassador in London) to Bidault, 22 November 1947; and Série Y: 45, dossier 9: Ministre des Aff. Etr. à M. le Commissaire Général du Plan, 9 août 1948 (provisional classifications). For a jaundiced French view of the origins of the Schuman Plan by an adherent of an English orientation, see René Massigli, *Une Comédie des Erreurs 1943–1956* (Paris, 1978), chapter V; and on the question of Italian membership in NATO, see minutes of the tenth meeting of the Washington Exploratory Talks, 22 December 1948, in *FRUS*, 1948, III, 324–32.

potential. Typecast as the animator of West European recovery, Germany could continually emphasize her economic vocation. German industrialists and labor leaders joined forces in petitioning for an end to dismantling and to corporate deconcentration. They found sympathetic responses from Lucius Clay's assistant, General William Draper, and later High Commissioner McCloy. German firms pressed their plans for reconstruction and expansion by citing their fervent desire to serve as good Europeans: Thyssen would get its new rolling mills by proposing steel for the Marshall Plan.[39] When France held out the Schuman Plan, Adenauer set aside any opposition on details from his own industrialists. The crucial aspect, he understood, was not whether Germany might or might not extract a few more concessions; it was the political opportunity to achieve partnership with France.

After the outbreak of the Korean War the potential of the German economy became even more prized. Emphasizing economic potential also accorded with the political tasks within West Germany. The constant appeal was for working-class loyalty; labor had to be harnessed for production. In return for codetermination, the union federation effectively accepted wage restraint until the 1960s. Pay claims were subordinated for the evident need to reconstruct the country. Workers remained suspicious of ideology after the experience of the Third Reich and in light of the unwelcome totalitarian development of East Germany. Economics was a surrogate for politics for two decades after 1947, but it was also a way of conducting politics. Reconstruction provided a sense of national purpose at home, and under Adenauer's canny supervision, coal, steel, and skilled labor were bargaining chips for recovering international autonomy. The resources of the Ruhr, reconciliation with France, reparation for Israel, and rearmament for the West became the pillars of German policy.

Within the framework of the new Western Europe, the smaller countries and Britain chose opposite courses. The Dutch and the Belgians provided the leadership and enthusiasm for the supranational agencies Americans sought to strengthen. In part their ministers may have found this new scope of activity personally rewarding. Dirk Stikker and Paul Henri Spaak were the preeminent Europeanists, although Americans had to balance Spaak's utility to the OEEC with his importance in holding together Belgium's unraveling political coalitions. In addition, Spaak (like

---

[39] See the Thyssen plea for expansion in Duisburg-Hamborn, in Bundesarchiv, Koblenz: Z 41/23 Verwaltungsamt für Eisen und Stahl.

Gunnar Myrdal, chairman of the Economic Commission for Europe in 1947–48) was distrusted by London.[40] But beyond Spaak's personal contribution, Belgium was pivotal in U.S. calculations because of its international financial strength. U.S. Treasury advocates of multilateralism approved of Belgium's early postwar policies, and they found Camille Gutt, who went on to chair the International Monetary Fund after presiding over Brussels's successful currency reform in 1944–45, a congenial defender of hard-currency convertibility.

In contrast to Belgium, Britain resisted multilateralism and convertibility. Within the American "hegemony" British leaders chose what a classical historian might call the Polybian strategy—that is, attempting to become the Greeks in America's Roman Empire, wagering on the "special relationship" to prolong their influence and status. They brought to this role a certain historical mystique, the experience of managing an empire, the willingness to shoulder heavy defense commitments (which the Pentagon especially appreciated), memories of the wartime alliance, and the considerable resources of a common language and a prestigious culture. State Department officials recognized that the United States was often partial to London and that British leaders "are not on occasion averse to letting their continental colleagues know they are favored above others by us."[41]

Throughout the late 1940s and early 1950s U.S. policy makers struggled against their own partiality as they criticized Britain for its retention of expensive military forces (at least before Korea), its reluctance to accept the Coal-Steel Community, and its resistance to a European Payments Union. But the web of informal associations, probably accentuated by the Anglo-Saxon descent of U.S. foreign service officers, tempered a more ruthless approach. The British sometimes overestimated the deference that their wisdom should command and assumed that they retained the brains even if Washington commanded the money. Nonetheless, Bevin, Sir Stafford Cripps, and civil servants such as Sir Edwin Plowden understood how to create a sympathetic mood in high-level negotiations. (Congress proved more resistant to U.S. concessions than executive-branch

---

[40] See Kirk to State Department, 11 October 1948, and Lovett to Kirk, 13 October 1948, in *FRUS*, 1948, III, 489–92; memorandum by Perkins for secretary of state, 9 September 1949, *FRUS*, 1949, IV, 421–22, and related material following.

[41] Ambassador Bruce to secretary of state, 25 April 1950, in *FRUS*, III, 63–65; also the meeting of ambassadors, 21–22 October 1949, *FRUS*, 1949, IV, 490–94; and the minutes of the seventh meeting of the Policy Planning Staff, 24 January 1950, *FRUS*, 1950, III, 617–22.

officials did.) And although Britain continued to insist on the special needs of the Commonwealth, Bevin's early anticommunism and Cripps's continuing "austerity" dissipated American charges of self-indulgence.

Britain relied on more than cultural resources and the memory of wartime collaboration, however. It drew on the benefits of the Sterling bloc, which Americans regarded as a barrier to their own goods and an imperial relic that Washington was being asked to finance. During the period of Lend-Lease and the British loan, Washington had continually sought to tie assistance to British dismantling of Commonwealth preferences. In practice, however, Washington usually accepted vague promises rather than concrete results. The disastrous experiment with sterling convertibility in the summer of 1947 demonstrated that London just could not move precipitately toward a more open system.

Nonetheless, the Marshall Plan presented occasions for disagreement. For Washington, the greater the degree to which Europeans could diminish their balance-of-payments constraints by multilateral clearance of payments among themselves, the greater could be the effect of scarce dollars for Europe as a whole and the less Europe's overall dollar dependency would cost the American taxpayer. But Britain resisted moves toward free convertibility. To enter a multilateral clearing scheme threatened to require deflationary measures at home that would preclude Labour party commitments to full employment and generous social welfare. What is more, Britain wanted to pass along Marshall Plan dollars in 1948 to its former Asian dependencies so that they would not liquidate their sterling reserves kept in London. (Much of these reserves, in effect, represented wartime loans from the colonies for the British costs incurred in their defense. They provided London with the same credit facilities that dollar convertibility gave the United States until 1973.)

U.S. ECA and Treasury officials felt that the British were stinting on their own domestic investment for the sake of imperial grandeur, and they argued that Washington could not afford to subsidize the dollar shortages of the Third World. As with other similar issues, compromise solutions were negotiated, which is why the European Recovery Program remained workable, even if it moved less decisively toward the integration that Washington desired.[42]

---

[42] See "Extract of Current Economic Developments," 24 May 1948; Ambassador Lewis Douglas to State Department, 11 June 1948; Richard M. Bissell, Jr., "Memorandum," 22 September 1948, all in *FRUS*, 1948, III, 442–43, 450–52, 486–89; and Phillip S. Brown to Bissell, 23 September 1948, in RG 59: 840.50 Recovery/10–148. Background

Similar controversies underlay the conflicts between 1948 and 1950 on clearing schemes. In 1948 Belgian and British members of the OEEC working party proposed an intra-European payments plan that called on additional American dollars beyond the ERP allocation to help Europeans balance up to half of their own reciprocal balance-of-payments deficits. London wanted to protect its precarious reserves. The Belgians, who pursued deflationary policies and possessed a hard currency, feared that without extra dollars to Europe, they would have to run a miniature ERP inside Europe and finance its partners' deficits in Brussels. Marshall Plan economists urged instead that Belgium run a more expansive economy with greater investment at home and higher imports, whereas Britain should tighten up. Washington compromised again, in part because U.S. policy was far from monolithic. A similar process of compromise marked the arduous negotiations that finally produced the European Payments Union in 1950–51.

By and large throughout such negotiations U.S. Treasury spokesmen looked to restoration of currency convertibility, which meant establishing the dollar as a universal medium of exchange. ECA planners in Washington and Paris stressed the recovery of production and consumption. Their activist economists contemplated increasing intervention into European investment plans, and they asked that Marshall Plan aid be evaluated not in monetary aggregates or financial terms but in the "real" categories of national income.[43]

It was not surprising that expansionist concepts of domestic investment and international trade took root in the ECA, for the new agency recruited the young economists being trained in the "Keynesian revolution." But the division between ECA Keynesians and the more orthodox Treasury-IMF spokesmen testified to the ambiguities of the Truman administration, poised between New Deal legacies and a revival of more

---

of the earlier issues in Richard Gardner, *Sterling-Dollar Diplomacy*, rev. ed. (New York: McGraw-Hill, 1969).

[43] On Treasury views, see Acheson's summary of the views of Frank A. Southard, Jr. (U.S. executive director of the IMF), 12 April 1949, in *FRUS*, 1949, IV, 382; also Southard to Secretary of the Treasury John Snyder, 29 September 1949 and 16 January 1950, in HSTL, John W. Snyder Papers, Box 34, F. "U.K. Loan, 1946–48, Alphabetical File," and Box 11, F. "ECA and International Trade Organization, 1950." On the activism of the ECA, see Hoffman to Harriman, 6 October 1949, *FRUS*, 1949, IV, 426–29; and on enduse accounting see Richard M. Bissell, Jr., "Statement on the Long-Term Programme," to the Long-Term Working Group of the OEEC, 26 October 1948, in HSTL, Charles P. Kindleberger papers, Box 2, F. "General Correspondence." Admittedly, ECA administrators in the respective countries were often businessmen who held views less Keynesian than those of the young academic economists at headquarters.

traditional economic concerns. The two major ECA officials had unconventional business backgrounds: Harriman had joined the New Deal after administering railroads, shipping, and banking. Paul Hoffman had been an organizer of the activist Committee on Economic Development, a business coalition that welcomed demand management and macroeconomic intervention. In contrast, John Snyder was a midwestern banker.

The ambiguities in America's foreign economic policy reflected the spectrum of approaches within the Truman administration more generally. These conflicting tendencies meant that different European countries might appeal to different sources of American authority. The deflationary leaders of Italy or of Belgium implicitly aligned with the U.S. Treasury to resist ECA prodding; the British relied first on Marshall Plan leaders to compromise, and then on U.S. military and political concerns to buffer Washington's would-be financial disciplinarians.

The result of these and many other bargains in the administration's European policy was to allow significant flexibility for national objectives. Washington policy makers could not smash Britain's residual imperial position, which London relied on in part to finance its welfare state. Nor could Washington push De Gasperi's Italy toward the thoroughgoing political and social modernization the Americans would doubtless have preferred. Rather, the Italian Christian Democrats knew how to use American assistance as part of their own resources for domestic patronage and political networks. The need for industrial revival in Europe provided the West Germans with their opportunity to recover political independence as well, as did the felt need for rearmament after 1950. The overarching Soviet-American bipolarity concealed how much scope there was for customized national policies and strategies to flourish. As Bevin had done in early 1948, Europeans talked boldly of integration and unity. But the policies they pursued looked toward cherished national and particularist objectives as well. U.S. policy offered many footholds precisely because with all its stress on Western Europe as a region, it had to confront individual national needs, weaknesses, and potential resources. The Europeans responded reciprocally. On the one level, integration and unity flagged; the opportunity that the European federalists sought was not fully seized, although this slowing of impetus was more apparent in later years than during the Truman period. But the historical result of the period was truly remarkable. The scope for national political alternatives distinguished Western from Eastern Europe; it followed not from blueprints but from the compromises that policy pluralism required. In an era when Europe seemed initially demoralized as well as devastated, the groundwork was laid not just for an imperial subordination to Washington but for a genuine revival of national traditions and of autonomous historical possibilities for Europeans.

10

U.S. policy in the Near East: the triumphs and
tribulations of the Truman administration

BRUCE R. KUNIHOLM

U.S. policy in the Near East during the Truman administration was concerned primarily with the region's "Northern Tier" (Iran, Turkey, and
Greece) and Palestine. Events in these two areas provided the context for
several major policy decisions—the Truman Doctrine and U.S. support
for the creation and establishment of Israel—that were among the best
known and most controversial of the Truman years. In this essay I take
a close look at these decisions, examine major questions that have been
raised about the Truman administration's policies, and, in light of recent
scholarship, attempt to assess them. Before such an assessment can be
made, however, it is necessary to examine the geopolitical context within
which the Truman administration was forced to operate.

When President Truman took office, World War II was not yet over
but it already had radically altered the world power balance and shifted
the loci of world power to Washington and Moscow. Within a year Stalin was exploring his options along the Soviet Union's southern borders
and, it appeared, would continue to do so unless resisted. The British
Empire, meanwhile, was disintegrating. By 1948, the British would be
forced to withdraw their forces from Greece, Turkey, India, and Palestine. The combination of the rise of Soviet power and the demise of British influence presented the United States with new responsibilities and
difficult choices.

In the nineteenth century the expanding Russian and British empires
had played for high stakes. A consequence of their rivalry across an area
stretching from the Balkans to India was the creation of a zone of buffer
states between the two empires. The rulers of these buffer states tradi-

tionally opposed the ambitions of both empires and sought to survive by playing one off against the other. At the end of World War II this game became more difficult, and the survival of Turkey and Iran was threatened by the relative disparity between Soviet and British power. Of the thirteen non-communist states that bordered Russia before the war, only five were independent when it was over. Finland was neutralized, and Afghanistan retained its traditional role of a buffer state. Of the remaining three—Norway, Turkey, and Iran—the latter two were in serious jeopardy of being drawn into the Soviet fold, and the United States was the only power capable of assisting them. Although almost all the states in the Middle East welcomed the decline of British influence, those on the periphery of the Soviet Union recognized the need for a countervailing force to balance Soviet influence. Invariably, they asked the United States for help.

The choices that confronted President Truman shortly after he took office in April 1945 were worrisome. Should he commit the United States to maintaining the balance of power in the region? If he did, how would the Soviets respond? If he did not, what would be the result of inaction? The president's response was articulated publicly in March 1947 in a policy statement that received wide support at the time but that subsequently became the subject of considerable scholarly debate.

The Palestine problem, meanwhile, not only complicated geopolitical categories but, it was feared, threatened to undermine U.S. attempts to maintain the balance of power in the Near East. Some observers viewed President Truman's support for the new state of Israel as entirely appropriate and in no way conflicting with other U.S. interests. Others thought that the president's actions raised profound questions about the fundamental values and priorities of public officials. What were the most appropriate guidelines for determining the national interest? Who should determine what that interest was, and should one interest be balanced against another?

Additional problems for long-term American interests were posed by the necessity of Anglo-American cooperation in effecting the policy of containment. Were British and American interests in Iran and Egypt compatible? To what extent would cooperation with the British undermine rather than facilitate the containment of Soviet influence in the region? These and other questions were constantly raised in the management of three interlocking regional issues that absorbed administration attention during the Truman years: (1) the balance of power in the Near

East, (2) the Palestine problem, and (3) the emerging nationalist movements in Iran and Egypt.

The balance of power in the Near East

In the immediate postwar years, U.S. policy toward the Near East was shaped by developments in Iran and Turkey.[1] In Iran, the Soviets violated Allied understandings and exploited the opportunities that occupation afforded them in an effort to control the government in Teheran. Oil concessions, which the Soviets demanded, and Kurdish and Azerbaijani separatist movements, which the Soviets supported in occupied northwest Iran, were means to the same end. In Turkey the Soviets sought through a war of nerves and constant diplomatic pressure to annex Kars and Ardahan in eastern Turkey and gain control of the Turkish Straits (the Bosporus and the Dardanelles). Press and radio attacks against "hostile" governments, attempts to effect the ouster of various government leaders, and irredentist Armenian and Georgian claims, coupled with troop mobilization, all smacked of Hitler's tactics before the war.[2]

In addition to attempting to carve out spheres of influence in Iran and Turkey, the Soviets in fact obtained one in the Balkans where they supported Bulgarian irredentism in Macedonia and Thrace. Faced in Eastern Europe with models of how *not* to deal with the Soviets, the Truman administration turned its attention to the Near East, where analogies between Stalin's and Hitler's tactics were too strong to ignore. If these analogies gave the administration pause, so did increasing evidence of Soviet designs on Iran and Turkey, particularly when supplemented by revelations concerning negotiations between Nazi Germany and the Soviet Union

---

[1] For more detailed documentation of the discussion that follows, see Bruce R. Kuniholm, *The Origins of the Cold War in the Near East: Great Power Conflict and Diplomacy in Iran, Turkey, and Greece* (Princeton: Princeton University Press, 1980); and *The Near East Connection: Greece and Turkey in the Reconstruction and Security of Europe, 1946–1952* (Brookline: Hellenic Press, 1984).

[2] Melvyn Leffler, "The American Conception of National Security and the Beginnings of the Cold War, 1945–48," *American Historical Review* 89, no. 2 (April 1984): 346–81, asserts that the American conception of national security was a consequence not so much of Soviet actions as of America's perceived vulnerabilities and of its resulting strategic and economic imperatives; that implementation of this conception was unnecessarily provocative, and hence primarily responsible for many of the cold war's enduring characteristics. Leffler's concept, however, has serious flaws. For criticisms of Leffler's arguments, see the comments by Bruce Kuniholm and John Gaddis, as well as Leffler's reply and the references cited therein (which need to be examined with greater care and in a broader context than Leffler allows) in the same issue, 382–400.

over the Near East in 1940. Captured German records and interviews with Hitler's interpreter, made available to the secretary of state in January 1946, underscored the continuity of Russian ambitions and suggested the desirability of a more forceful policy in opposing them.[3]

Stalin, while acknowledging his designs on Turkey, in December 1945 had assured both Secretary of State James F. Byrnes and British Foreign Secretary Ernest Bevin that the Soviet Union had no designs, territorial or otherwise, on Iran and no intention of infringing on the sovereignty of Iran.[4] In March 1946, however, after the date set by the Big Three for evacuation of Iran and following extremely tough discussions with the Iranian prime minister in Moscow, Stalin had moved a Soviet armed force of at least 200 tanks into northern Iran in an attempt to intimidate the government in Teheran into bending to his will. Stalin's maneuvers were thwarted only by masterful Iranian diplomacy, firm U.S. policies, and the possibility that Stalin saw further confrontation in Iran as detrimental to his designs on Turkey.[5]

Stalin, like Hitler, the pope observed in 1946, frequently gave assurances of his peace-loving intentions. To U.S. officials, the negligible value of those assurances was illustrated by the drawn-out crisis in Iran, which also underscored the value of anticipating rather than reacting to Soviet moves. This view was reinforced by Stalin's former Foreign Minister Maxim Litvinov, who observed in June 1946 that the Soviet Union had returned to a concept of geographical security. Goodwill, Litvinov told CBS correspondent Richard Hottelet, would be ineffective in meeting the Soviets' security needs, because Soviet demands, if satisfied, would only be followed by others.[6]

Stalin's thinking, of course, is largely unknown, although Khrushchev's memoirs may give us a clue about Turkey. According to Khrushchev, Lavrenti Beria, head of Stalin's huge police network and, like Stalin, a Georgian, teased and goaded Stalin—who had negotiated the frontier between Turkey and the Soviet Union in 1921—into demanding the return of territories that had once (from 1878 to 1921) been part of

---

[3] Interview with Harry Howard. 3 January 1946 memo (mistakenly dated 3 January 1945) from Henderson to Byrnes, James F. Byrnes Papers, Clemson University, Clemson, S.C. Harry N. Howard Papers, Harry S. Truman Library (HSTL), Box 1, Folder: "Basic Aims of Soviet Policy in Eastern Europe, 1939–1941"; "Department of State Special Interrogation Mission in Germany," 15 August–15 November 1945; and transcript, Harry N. Howard Oral History Interview, 5 June 1973, HSTL.
[4] *Foreign Relations of the United States* (hereafter *FRUS*), 1945, II, 684–90; VIII, 510–11.
[5] Kuniholm, *Origins of the Cold War in the Near East*, 282–350; 378–99.
[6] *FRUS*, 1946, VI, 763–65, 795.

Georgia. Beria's thinking was that Turkey's international status had been weakened by World War II and that the Turkish government would be unable to resist such demands.[7] Whatever Stalin's motives, officials in the Truman administration grew increasingly skeptical of them. Faced with what they saw as a fait accompli in Eastern Europe, they eventually came to the conclusion that a similar fate should not await the countries of the Middle East's Northern Tier.

The process by which the Truman administration reached this conclusion was gradual. Declarations of idealistic principles and expressions of concern over Soviet intentions, made by U.S. representatives in the course of protracted, fruitless negotiations, had proved ineffective in moderating Soviet relations with Iran and Turkey. Direct negotiations between Iran and the Soviet Union, moreover, had failed to solve the Iranian problem in 1946 and had subjected the Iranians to heavy-handed intimidation. The exhaustive crisis in Iran, more than any other development, crystallized the Truman administration's growing understanding of Soviet tactics along the Northern Tier and conditioned its reaction to Soviet diplomatic maneuvering over Turkey in the late summer of 1946.

The Soviet Union's postwar policies toward Iran and Turkey had forced the continued mobilization of Turkey's 500,000-man army, necessitating military expenditures that consumed 38 percent of the country's budget and caused widespread discontent. In August 1946, the latest in a series of diplomatic maneuvers by the Soviets to put pressure on the Turks, in this case to agree to a joint Turco-Soviet system of defense for the Straits, precipitated what President Truman considered to be his most important decision since the bombing of Hiroshima.[8] Soviet control over Turkey, the president concluded, would make it virtually impossible to prevent extension of that control to the Near and Middle East. Resources and communications, administration officials judged, made it imperative that the Soviet Union not gain control over Turkey, whether through force or the threat of force. Believing, ultimately, that nothing would deter Soviet aggression except the conviction that the United States was prepared to

[7] For Stalin's "assurances" regarding Turkey, see, for example, *FRUS*, 1946, VII, 836; VI, 736. For Khrushchev's views, see *Khrushchev Remembers: The Last Testament* (Boston: Little, Brown, 1974), 295–96; and the interpretation in Kuniholm, *Origins of the Cold War in the Near East*, 358–59. Melvyn Leffler, "Strategy, Diplomacy, and the Cold War: The United States, Turkey, and NATO, 1945–1952," *Journal of American History* 71, no. 4 (March 1985): 807–25, interprets events in Turkey in the context of his interpretation of the American conception of national security, cited in note 2, with many of the same problems.
[8] *FRUS*, 1949, VI, 1649.

confront it, the president decided to resist any Soviet aggression against Turkey with all means at his disposal, including the force of U.S. arms. Americans might as well find out whether the Soviets were bent on world conquest now as in five or ten years, he told his advisers; he was prepared to pursue the policy "to the end."[9]

President Truman's decision, while implemented in a restrained and nonprovocative manner, reflected a fundamental change in attitude toward the Near East. President Roosevelt had followed a traditional policy of noninvolvement in the region, which he consigned to Britain's jurisdiction as he focused on the war against Germany and Japan. Events in the Near East after Roosevelt's death, however, had schooled the Truman administration in the region's traditional balance of power politics and educated it in the fundamentals of containment, even before the containment thesis was consciously propounded. Acting on the basis of this understanding, the White House approved the formal establishment of a Mediterranean force,[10] while Department of State guidelines underscored the importance of the independence and territorial integrity of Greece, Turkey, and Iran. These countries were seen as a bulwark against Soviet expansion and a means of protecting strategic U.S. interests in the Near and Middle East as a whole. The focal point of those interests was the Middle East's 15 billion barrels of proven oil reserves, 24 percent of which were controlled by the United States.[11]

These developments explain the immediate U.S. reaction to Britain's

[9] For the 15 August 1946 meeting, and the circumstances surrounding it, see *FRUS, 1946*, VII, 840–42; Dean Acheson, *Present at the Creation: My Years in the State Department* (New York: W. W. Norton, 1969), 195–96; Walter Millis, ed., *The Forrestal Diaries* (New York: Viking, 1951), 192; and Kuniholm, *Origins of the Cold War in the Near East*, 282–382. For a different view of the Truman administration's policies in the Near East in general and toward Turkey in particular, see Leffler, "Strategy, Diplomacy, and the Cold War."

[10] This policy statement, written at Secretary Forrestal's direction, was cleared by the State Department and the White House. Millis, ed., *The Forrestal Diaries*, 211. It is interesting to note that earlier in the year the JCS had agreed to avoid a military commitment in the Middle East because of problems posed by lines of communications. United States Army, Operations Division, Modern Military Records Branch, National Archives, Washington, D.C. CCS 092 United States 12–21–45, 10 February 1946 Report by Joint Strategic Survey Committee. See also Robert Albion and Robert Connery, *Forrestal and the Navy* (New York: Columbia University Press, 1962), 187; *New York Times*, 1 October 1946; Stephen Xydis, *Greece and the Great Powers, 1944–1947: Prelude to the Truman Doctrine* (Thessaloniki: Institute for Balkan Studies, 1963), 357–59, 644, 715–16; Arnold Rogow, *James Forrestal: A Study of Personality, Politics, and Policy* (New York: Macmillan, 1963), 179–80; Jonathan Knight, "American Statecraft and the 1946 Black Sea Straits Controversy," *Political Science Quarterly* 90 (Fall 1975): 453–55.

[11] At the time, 15 billion barrels was estimated to be approximately one-third of the world's supply. *FRUS*, Potsdam I, 217–18; Millis, *The Forrestal Diaries*, 81.

February 1947 decision to withdraw support from Greece and Turkey. In the previous month, a full-scale review of U.S. policy toward Greece concluded, on the basis of considerable circumstantial evidence, that the Greek National Liberation Front (EAM) was an instrument of Soviet policy. The broad objective of the Soviets appeared to be to undermine British influence in the eastern Mediterranean and to establish their own domination of the littoral countries of that region. If, in retrospect, evidence does not bear out the conclusion that EAM was an instrument of Soviet policy, there was and still is little question that the Soviets were indirectly supporting Albania, Yugoslavia, and Bulgaria—who *were* supporting EAM. There also can be no doubt that the Soviets would have taken advantage of any situation in the Balkans that proved favorable to their interests. For this reason, Loy Henderson, director of the Office of Near Eastern and African Affairs (NEA), and Under Secretary of State Dean Acheson both believed that the United States was confronted with its most important decision since the war; they also believed that the choice was clear and there could be only one decision.[12] It was voiced in the Truman Doctrine, which called for a $400 million appropriation to aid Greece and Turkey.

President Truman's 12 March 1947 address to a joint session of Congress expressed the necessity of choosing between alternative ways of life. One alternative, he said, was based on the will of the majority and was distinguished by free institutions. The other alternative was based on the will of a minority forcibly imposed on the majority and relied on terror and oppression. The president's declared aim was to make possible the messianic hope of everlasting freedom—through support of peoples resisting subjugation by armed minorities or by outside pressure. In retrospect, the president's high-minded definition of the national purpose was probably necessary to acquire support for the policies he was advocating.

---

[12] *FRUS,* 1947, V, 53; interview with Loy Henderson; Dean Acheson, *Present at the Creation,* 218. Lawrence S. Wittner, *American Intervention in Greece, 1943–1949* (New York: Columbia University Press, 1982), correctly notes that the grim specter of Soviet expansionism that haunted U.S. policy in the Near East was contradicted by the reality of Soviet policy in Greece. But it was not contradicted by Soviet policy toward Turkey, where the United States hardly had to press the Turks, as Wittner asserts, to reject Soviet demands, nor was it in Iran and Bulgaria. Events in Greece could not be separated from the complex international problems of which they were a part and made a negotiated settlement (which Wittner would have preferred) far more risky and difficult than he is willing to acknowledge. In fact, according to Vojtech, Mastny, Stalin as late as the end of 1947 had tentatively approved a confederation of communist states in the Balkans and possibly elsewhere in Eastern Europe with Yugoslavia as its chosen instrument. *International Security* 9, no. 3 (Winter 1984–85): 109–29, especially 113.

Although historians may long debate the necessity of presidential rhetoric, none doubt that the metaphoric representations President Truman used were effective in producing the consensus necessary to respond to Soviet threats along the Northern Tier.[13]

The only way that nations can function internationally is to use the kind of metaphoric representations that the president articulated, with their attending conceptions of morality and power. It is also true, however, that the moral and power components of such imagery can only be evaluated relative to the particularities of circumstance in which they are applied. This means that they must constantly be evaluated critically, so that the imagery a nation employs can be appropriate to new circumstances. Unfortunately for the United States, this process of evaluation and reconception was overlooked in subsequent years and the view of the world presented by the Truman Doctrine, accompanied by a failure to match rhetoric with concrete policies and a defensive inclination to pursue consistently hard-line policies, hardened into myth. The consequence was a somewhat simplistic and increasingly inflexible perception of international events that imposed itself on a world for which it was increasingly irrelevant.

At the time, however, the Truman administration's response to Soviet maneuvering along the Northern Tier was based on the realistic assumption that U.S. interests were best served by maintaining the balance of power in the Near East. A corollary of this assumption, based on Brit-

[13] The president's approval of the program of assistance to Greece and Turkey was by no means a decision to send American armed forces to the region. U.S. armed forces had been reduced from 12 million in June 1945 to 3 million in June 1946, and by June 1947 would be at 1.6 million. Defense expenditures, at $81.6 billion in fiscal year 1945, had been reduced to $44.7 billion in fiscal 1946, and $13.1 billion in fiscal 1947. Neither of these trends suggested that the United States had much with which to undertake global responsibilities. Nonetheless, the administration's decision constituted a qualified acceptance of the general responsibility for maintaining the balance of power in the Near East. *FRUS, 1947*, V, 47–58, 94; *Legislative Origins of the Truman Doctrine: Hearings Held in Executive Session Before the Committee on Foreign Relations, United States Senate, 80th Cong., 1st Sess., on S. 938* (Washington, D.C.: U.S. Government Printing Office, 1973). For elaboration of the process by which the Truman Doctrine was written and for an assessment of its implications, see Kuniholm, *Origins of the Cold War in the Near East*, 410–25. For the statistics cited, see John Gaddis, *Strategies of Containment: A Critical Assessment of Postwar American National Security Policy* (New York: Oxford University Press, 1982), 23. For Acheson's belief that the Truman Doctrine was a turning point, see *FRUS, 1949*, III, 174–75. The Truman Doctrine's thematic significance for the Marshall Plan is evidenced not in its ideological trappings (which Kennan, for example, sought to diminish) but in its emphasis on assisting free peoples in order that they may work out their own destinies in their own way and in the notion that misery, want, poverty, and strife destroy the hope of a people for a better life.

ain's continuing role in the region even as the British withdrew from selected areas, was the necessity of a close association between U.S. and British policies in the Near East. Exactly how this association would play itself out, however, was far from clear. In the two years that followed the enunciation of the Truman Doctrine, although considerable assistance flowed to the region, Near East issues were superseded by others. The administration's attention focused instead on Europe, and then on the Far East. The objective of U.S. policy during this time was to restore the balance of power in Europe and Asia[14]—initially through an emphasis on economic recovery (the Marshall Plan) and subsequently through a complementary emphasis on military security (the North Atlantic Treaty Organization, NATO).[15]

Reconstruction and rearmament in Europe forced the United States and Britain to reassess the value of assistance to the Near East and to give careful thought to the region's role in their overall strategic interests. The British regarded the Middle East, because of its lines of communication, oil, and strategic bases, as a strategic theater second in importance only to Europe. While acknowledging the importance of Greece, Turkey, and Iran as a line of defense, the British saw U.S. actions as relieving them of their burden in Greece and Turkey.[16] They clearly intended to maintain their special position in Iran if possible but were most interested in the Suez, where two-thirds of the canal's west bank was occupied by

[14] Gaddis, *Strategies of Containment*, 57; Millis, *The Forrestal Diaries*, 341, 349–51, 366–67. *FRUS*, 1947, I, 579–80, 770–71.

[15] Events in the Near East, meanwhile, crystallized many of the administration's attitudes toward the Soviet Union, and these attitudes, in turn, provided a framework for managing and interpreting subsequent events. The decision on Turkey, Acheson told the British and French foreign ministers shortly after the signing of the Atlantic Pact in April 1949, had been a turning point. It was the signal to go ahead. *FRUS*, 1949, III, 174–75. The decision also set a precedent for Europe, where the Greek-Turkish Aid Program served as a model for the European Recovery Program and as a litmus test for American determination. Failure to implement the Truman Doctrine, American officials believed, would jeopardize the success of the Marshall Plan—a perception which helped to cement the bond in official minds between Europe and the two Balkan/Near Eastern states to which Marshall Plan aid was soon extended.

The "Pentagon Talks" between Great Britain and the United States in October–November 1947, which bordered on collective security arrangements in fact if not in name, also proved a useful precedent. After the traumatic coup in Czechoslovakia in February 1948, the British sought conversations on Western security that were similar to those on the Middle East. *FRUS*, 1948, III, 12–16, 32-–33.

[16] *FRUS*, 1947, V, 321–23, 330–32, 488–96, 511–13, 532–33, 566–80, 592–93, 607–08. The Afghans, it should be noted, were interested in abandoning their traditional neutrality in return for military aid. *FRUS*, 1948, V (Part 1), 491–94; *FRUS*, 1949, VI, 46.

a 38,000-man British garrison (whose thirty-four military stations and ten airfields had supported the equivalent of forty-one divisions and sixty-five squadrons in World War II).[17]

U.S. officials, in contrast, wanted the British to maintain their strategic, political, and economic position throughout the Near East and to follow policies that were parallel to those of the United States.[18] The unsatisfactory bureaucratic result of these different perceptions was a vague Anglo-American commitment to cooperate, to exchange views, and to pursue parallel policies.[19] When prodded by Greek, Iranian, and particularly Turkish representatives about security problems,[20] U.S. representatives were concerned not to spread U.S. responsibilities too broadly.[21] The essence of the U.S. response to repeated Turkish requests for security commitments in 1948 and 1949 was that the Turks should be patient; their security problems would not be overlooked.[22]

[17] William Roger Louis, *The British Empire in the Middle East, 1945–1951: Arab Nationalism, the United States, and Postwar Imperialism* (Oxford: Clarendon Press, 1984), 714 and 721; Howard Sachar, *Europe Leaves the Middle East, 1936–1954* (New York: Knopf, 1972), 411, 427. Louis notes that one of the keys to understanding the era is the way in which the British attempted to sustain their regional hegemony by gaining American assistance and cutting their losses. He also observes that if the loss of India made Egypt more important to the British, the loss of Palestine underscored the lack of viable strategic alternatives to the base at Suez, while the advent of war in Korea seemed to confirm the necessity of continued access to the base (which the British desired for air offensives against the Soviet Union in the event of war). Louis, *The British Empire in the Middle East,* 122, 374, 588–89, 666, 740–41.

[18] *FRUS, 1947,* V, 561, 575–76. The cornerstone of Secretary of State George Marshall's thinking at this time continued to be the maintenance of Britain's position in the Middle East to the greatest extent possible. *FRUS, 1947,* V, 268, 274–78, 290, 301–02, 308, 313, 322, 327–29, 330–32; and *FRUS, 1949,* III, 174–75.

[19] *FRUS, 1947,* V, 580–85, 623–25, 1289.

[20] As discussions between Britain and the United States, and, later, negotiations among the eventual signatories of the North Atlantic Treaty proceeded throughout 1948 and early 1949, the question of how to ensure the security of Greece and Turkey was ever present. The possibilities examined included an extension of the proposed pact to cover Greece and Turkey; a pact that would initially exclude but eventually provide for their association with the original signatories; a North Atlantic-Mediterranean regional defense arrangement; a separate Mediterranean security system with which the United States would be associated; a treaty of reciprocal military assistance; unilateral declarations of assurances; and a protocol attached to the treaty to cover the two Near East countries and Iran. See *FRUS, 1948,* III, 41, 47, 59, 63–67, 85–88, 92, 97, 225, 331–32, 342; *FRUS, 1949,* IV, 13–14; *FRUS, 1949,* VI, 31–45.

[21] Limits, many believed, had to be drawn somewhere: If Italy were admitted to NATO, for example, Greece would want to be included; if Greece were admitted, Turkey would want in; and if Turkey were admitted, Iran too would seek admission. At the end of 1948 Turkey was requested not to press further; in the meantime, military aid and diplomatic support would provide ample evidence of Turkey's special place in U.S. policy.

[22] *FRUS, 1948,* III, 58, 103, 108, 129–31, 179, 202, 321–23, 326; *FRUS, 1948,* IV, 82–83, 213–15; *FRUS, 1949,* IV, 29, 43. Turkey's concerns, it should be noted, were well understood. As long as the United States had not made a commitment to any country,

In early 1949, following a full-scale review of U.S. strategic interests in Greece and Turkey, priority for military aid was given to Europe and the Near East above all other regions. The Mutual Defense Assistance Act, signed by the president in October 1949, suggests the importance of Greece and Turkey relative to Western Europe. The North Atlantic Treaty states were allocated $1 billion in military assistance; Greece and Turkey were allocated $211 million.[23] Despite increasing commitments in U.S. military assistance to Turkey and Greece, the Pentagon's short-range emergency plans for the defense of Western Europe in 1949 envisaged, as a minimum goal in the eastern Mediterranean, holding only the Cairo-Suez-Khartoum area as a base for air offensives against the Soviet Union; subsequently, the area might serve as a base for further operations to regain Middle East oil resources.

A National Security Council (NSC) report in July 1949 illustrated the importance of these resources: It estimated that in its last years the European Recovery Program (ERP) would depend on the Middle East for 80 percent of its oil; loss of Middle East oil, it asserted, would seriously jeopardize the ERP. In view of the need for oil, the U.S. government was considering the establishment of bases in other countries, including Turkey, although such plans were complicated by a lack of forces to ensure retention of them after the initial stages of a war. From a strategic point of view, the United States still saw the Northern Tier states as a buffer area in which to conduct holding actions against Soviet expansion in a retreat to more tenable positions along Britain's line of communications.[24]

there was no apparent difference between intentions to assure the security of one country or another. Once the United States had concluded a close defensive arrangement with Western Europe, however, as it did in 1949, what was one to do about countries such as Greece and Turkey—equally threatened, less able to defend themselves, but not similarly protected? The possibility existed that the foundations of resistance would be eroded and the Soviet Union tempted once again to increase its pressures on them. *FRUS, 1948*, IV, 172–76.

[23] In December 1948, the JCS approved $100 million in military assistance to Turkey and $200 million to Greece. *FRUS, 1949*, VI, 42, 269–79; *FRUS, 1949*, I, 259–67, 277, 317–18, 398.

[24] *FRUS, 1949*, VI, 32, 42, 549, 1644–45, 1654–55, 1681–82; *FRUS, 1948*, V (Part 1), 2–3, 244–46; *FRUS, 1948*, III, 933–34. The importance of Middle East oil to the implementation of the Marshall Plan was recognized almost immediately. *FRUS, 1947*, V, 665–66. Concern in 1948 that available forces could not retain major portions of the oil-producing areas from the outset of a war was mitigated somewhat by knowledge that Allied forces could deny use of oil-producing facilities in the Middle East to the Russians. *FRUS, 1948*, V (part 1), 2–3. In the event of Soviet occupation of Turkey, the British apparently contemplated denial operations through aerial bombing. *FRUS, 1949*, VI, 1681–82. In the event of Soviet occupation of Iran, the shah anticipated withdrawing to

Between the signing of the North Atlantic Treaty in early April 1949 and the beginning of the Korean War in June 1950, the urgency of U.S. support for Greece and Turkey was increasingly challenged by competing priorities.[25] Previous statements and policy objectives, attached as boilerplate to policy papers, continued to be reaffirmed throughout the first half of 1950, but U.S. policies were far from clear. The process of formulating national security problems required more coherence and would lead to discussion that eventually would result in NSC 68.[26] In the interim, the question that continued to confront the United States in the Near East was the extent to which it should accept its new responsibilities. One answer, provided in January 1950 by the U.S. deputy chiefs of staff, was that U.S. military strategic interests there were almost negligible. It was not that the importance of the area had changed; rather, higher

the mountain areas in the west and southwest of Iran in order to attempt a defense of the oil fields. *FRUS*, 1949, VI, 471–72. In November 1949, during a visit to the United States, the shah discussed this plan with the Joint Chiefs and was told by General Bradley that it was probably the best that could be devised under the circumstances. *FRUS*, 1949, VI, 581–82. See also *FRUS*, 1950, V, 508.

[25] Attempts to restore the balance of power in Europe continued to call into question the relative importance of the Near East. In the fall of 1949, Soviet testing of an atomic weapon and the collapse of Chiang Kai-shek's regime together focused the attention of government officials on even broader issues: the development of a thermonuclear bomb, the use of atomic weapons, national objectives, and strategic programs. *FRUS*, 1949, I, 399–403, 413–16. News of the Soviet explosion also ensured administrative requests on the Mutual Defense Assistance Act. Donovan, 103.

[26] *FRUS*, 1950, I, 234–92. For discussion of NSC 68, see Samuel Wells, Jr., "Sounding the Tocsin: NSC 68 and the Soviet Threat," *International Security*, Fall 1979, 116–58; John Gaddis, "NSC 68 and the Problem of Ends and Means"; and Paul Nitze, "The Development of NSC 68," *International Security*, Spring 1980, 164–70 and 170–76; and Gaddis, *Strategies of Containment*, 89–126. See also the chapter by Charles S. Maier in this volume, "Alliance and Autonomy: European Identity and U.S. Foreign Policy Objectives in the Truman Years."

During this period, subtle changes became apparent in U.S. regional policy toward Turkey, but the question of America's commitment remained unclear. Because Turkey could not be included in the Atlantic Pact, the United States earlier in 1949 had decided that it would be unwise to construct forward air bases or stockpile aviation gas in Turkey. It also had chosen not to expose Turkey to increased pressures from the Soviet Union. In October this policy was reversed. The United States and Turkey reached agreement in principle on the reconstruction of military airfields in Turkey. *FRUS*, 1950, V, 1234, 1241–47, 1250, 1256, 1270–71, and 1350. See also *FRUS*, 1946, VII, 561; George Kennan, *Memoirs: 1925–1950*, 411; and Leffler, cited in note 7.

Turkey's use of American aid, meanwhile, had been impressive. So was its willingness to cooperate. Further indication of Turkey's attitude was evident in April 1950 when the Turks, ever thoughtful about underscoring their value as allies, asked for an opinion about the legality of controlled mining of the Straits. In its new frame of mind, the United States saw no legal obstacle to such action. The United States was careful, however, to resist any cooperative initiatives that might make it vulnerable to pressures for participation in a pact with Turkey. *FRUS*, 1949, VI, 1639; *FRUS*, 1950, V, 1245–46, 1260–62, 1266–67, 1270, 1341–43, 1354.

priorities in other areas made it impossible to devote any substantial portion of limited U.S. resources to the Near East.[27]

The North Korean invasion of South Korea in late June 1950 again raised the question of how far the United States should go in accepting its responsibilities in the Near East. President Truman worried that the Soviets might next move into Iran. Discussing the breaking crisis with his assistant George Elsey on the day after the Korean War began, Truman bent over a globe and put a finger on Iran. "Korea is the Greece of the Far East," he told Elsey. "If we are tough enough now, if we stand up to them like we did in Greece three years ago, they won't take any next steps. But if we just stand by, they'll move into Iran and they'll take over the whole Middle East."[28]

[27] *FRUS*, 1949, VI, 55, 58, 63; *FRUS*, 1950, III, 975–76; *FRUS*, 1950, V, 122–23, 153–54, 157. Turkey's armed forces were now under 300,000. *FRUS*, 1950, V, 1236.

[28] The "loss of China"—followed as it was by the Sino-Soviet Treaty of 14 February 1950—precipitated a concern about U.S. commitments outside the North Atlantic area, including the Near East. Some officials, such as Army Chief of Staff General Lawton Collins, worried that Iran—which the British, too, acknowledged to be a "soft spot"—would develop into a "second China." *FRUS*, 1950, I, 314–15; *FRUS*, 1950, V, 523. See also the memo by John Foster Dulles, *FRUS*, 1950, I, 314–16. Truman's thinking clearly reflected his experience during the Iranian crisis of 1946 and the crisis in Greece in 1947. See the George Elsey Papers, Box 71, Folder: "Korea," 26 June 1950, memo on President Truman's conversations with George Elsey, HSTL. NSC assessments during this time ruled out the likelihood of overt Soviet aggression against Iran, Turkey, or Greece, but saw Soviet intimidation and testing of firmness as a real probability. *FRUS*, 1950, I, 331–41, 375–89; *FRUS*, 1950, V, 382–86, 572–74, 1289–92. In late July, General Bradley, chairman of the Joint Chiefs of Staff, and General Tedder, marshal of the Royal Air Force and Britisʰ Permanent Representative at the NATO Standing Group, agreed that in the Middle East the British would take the initiative in regard to any steps that needed to be carried out. *FRUS*, 1950, V, 188–89. The difficulty of relying on intelligence assessments during this period, it should be noted, is apparent throughout the documentation. During discussion between the British and American chiefs of staff, for example, General Vandenberg reported that there were such wide differences among experts in the oil companies on the importance of Middle East oil that he doubted any firm conclusions could be reached. *FRUS*, 1950, V, 237. When it came to Soviet intentions, the difficulty was even greater. In early August, shortly after the Korean War began, George Kennan, in a memo to the secretary of state, attempted to assess Soviet intentions in a qualitative manner. Available evidence, he said, suggested that the Soviets would carry on vigorously their war of nerves with Iran, possibly even demanding assent to the reentry of Soviet troops on the basis of their 1921 treaty with Iran. He did not judge this move likely, however, if the Iranians stood firm. He did not attempt to suggest what it would take to make the Iranians stand firm. In the Balkans, Kennan observed, evidence as to the Soviet intentions was inconclusive. He believed it probable that the Soviets themselves had not made up their minds about what to do in the area. He believed they would not come lightly to a decision to attack Turkey or Greece because of the formidable risks involved. By contrast, Kennan's replacement as director of the Policy Planning Staff, Paul Nitze, expressed his judgments quantitatively. In discussing the Near East in January 1951, he told the JCS that "no one knows just how to assess the risk of action this spring. Some of our people think there is a 30 percent chance, some a 50 percent chance, some a 60 percent chance that the Soviets will move somewhere in this area this spring." *FRUS*, 1951, V, 42. The

Although there was little that Iran could do to protect its interests, a new urgency seized the Turkish government, which now committed a 4,500-man combat force to serve in Korea, stressed joint defense projects, and pressed hard for Turkey's inclusion in the Atlantic Pact.[29] The Turks recognized the limitations of European aid and asserted that they would bring to the common pool more than they would draw from it.[30] Once the tide was turned in Korea, a short-term solution in October 1950 circumvented fundamental decisions in the Near East until NATO's strength would allow for additional commitments. With U.S. encouragement, NATO offered the Turks and, once Turkey accepted, the Greeks the opportunity to associate themselves with NATO's military planning on the defense of the Mediterranean.[31]

The increasing importance of the Middle East to the West at this time was underscored by the fact that Middle East oil was supplying 75 percent of all European requirements. The region's proven reserves—estimated in 1950 to be approximately 40 billion barrels—were now equal to those of the rest of the world and were almost double those of the United States. If "probable" or "possible" reserves were taken into account, estimates approached 150 billion barrels. Although these reserves were obviously important, their vulnerability to attack appeared to preclude an effective defense: Both U.S. and British officials believed that, regardless of who possessed them, the Gulf's refineries would be destroyed by bombing early in the war.[32]

difficulty, without hindsight, of acting on either of these judgments should be apparent. See, for example, the Department of State's analysis of Greece, *FRUS, 1950*, V, 382–87.

[29] *FRUS, 1950*, V, 1262, 1276, 1285–89, 1296, 1302–05, 1318, 1320.

[30] *FRUS, 1950*, V, 1296–1302, 1311; *FRUS, 1950*, III, 175, 248–49. British fears, initially, were that if the Turks were admitted as full members they would see how bare the cupboard actually was. *FRUS, 1950*, V, 1316. For Turkey's difficulties in joining the Council of Europe, see George Harris, *The Troubled Alliance: Turkish-American Problems in Historical Perspective, 1945–1971* (Washington, D.C.: American Enterprise Institute for Public Policy Research, 1972), 38.

[31] *FRUS, 1950*, III, 257–61; *FRUS, 1950*, V, 1306–09. Acting on the advice of the JCS, Acheson told the Turks that it was difficult to conceive of a Soviet attack on Turkey under conditions that would not bring on a general war. To ensure surprise, an attack, if it came, would be against the United States, Western Europe, and Turkey all together. *FRUS, 1950*, V, 1321. That Acheson believed this is evident not only from earlier NSC judgments, but by his remarks in conversation with the British and French foreign ministers. *FRUS, 1950*, III, 1218. See also *FRUS, 1950*, III, 279–84, 333–35, 357, 1217–20; *FRUS, 1950*, V, 426, 1313–15, 1320–22. For concern about assurances that would have to be given to Iran, see *FRUS, 1950*, V, 600–01.

[32] In 1950, the Middle East produced 1.8 million barrels of oil per day (bpd), with U.S. companies producing 45 percent, British (and Dutch) companies 50 percent, and French and other companies 5 percent of the total. The breakdown by country was as follows: Iran, 700,000 bpd; Saudi Arabia, 555,000 bpd; Kuwait, 350,000 bpd; Iraq, 125,000

During this period, the British focused on the defense of what they called the region's inner core, or "inner ring," around Suez. Available forces made defense of the "outer ring," consisting primarily of south-eastern Turkey and southwestern Iran, extremely difficult and led the British to express the hope that the United States would help.[33] The U.S. Joint Chiefs of Staff (JCS), however, pursued a low profile in order to encourage the Commonwealth to do more for the Middle East. Because of this tactical consideration and Army Chief of Staff General Lawton Collins's orientation toward Western Europe, the JCS planned no mili-tary sacrifices in the region and opposed any measures that, in the event of global war, would even tend to commit U.S. forces to the Middle East. As one American official explained to the British chiefs in October 1950, the word *vital* was applied freely to the Middle East in planning but in practice the United States seemed to question whether a large part of the Middle East could be held.[34] In the event of war, General Collins told the British chiefs, the Middle East was a British responsibility. While agree-ing that the Middle East, in war, was of importance second only to West-ern Europe, the JCS would not commit forces to the area during the first two years of war.[35]

The British understood the limitations of U.S. support but nonetheless attempted to persuade the United States to give the Middle East a higher priority. The Americans were unreceptive, although they agreed to un-dertake a joint review of their capabilities for the defense of the "outer ring." Defense of the region anchored on Turkey in the West and running southeastward along the Zagros Mountains of Iran, the British and American chiefs of staff believed, would provide some protection for the oil fields in southern Iran and the Arabian Peninsula. Although the Brit-

bpd; Qatar, 40,000 bpd; Bahrain, 30,000 bpd. *FRUS, 1950*, V, 72–73, 76–77. For a detailed discussion of the significance of Middle East Oil, see *FRUS, 1950*, V, 76–96, 233. For an examination of the importance of oil to Western Europe under peacetime conditions, see NIE-14, *FRUS, 1951*, V, 268–76, which asserts that Western Europe would not be able to compensate for the loss of Middle East oil.

[33] In August 1950 a supplemental appropriation request of $193 million for Greece, Tur-key, and Iran, and an NSC decision to deploy available forces to Greece and Turkey in the event of a Soviet attack could be seen as a recognition of British weakness and an attempt to shore up an area where the United States and Britain were each looking to the other for help. *FRUS, 1950*, I, 188–91, 352–53; *FRUS, 1950*, III, 1664–65; *FRUS, 1950*, V, 195, 218.

[34] *FRUS, 1950*, V, 217–39, 610–11; *FRUS, 1950*, III, 1686–89; *FRUS, 1951*, V, 9–11. The British, of course, frequently tried to get the United States to do more—an effort which, given past performances, generated some terse comments. See, for example, *FRUS, 1948*, IV, 147.

[35] *FRUS, 1950*, V, 232, 236, 611.

ish, in the event of a war, did not believe they could defend even the "inner ring" centered on Suez, growing evidence pointed to the need for obtaining at least some Middle East oil throughout the war. In their judgment, such a requirement would make defense of the outer ring essential.[36]

Defense of the outer ring, however problematic, necessitated closer coordination with Turkey. One of the objectives sought by the United States in joint defense planning with Turkey was the capacity to deny the Soviet Union exit from the Black Sea through the Turkish Straits. Meanwhile, objectives and programs embodied in NSC 68, whose adoption was made virtually certain by the Korean War, were approved by the president on 30 December 1950. The national security document endorsed the idea of perimeter defense and seemed to show, at least for a while, that distinctions between peripheral and vital interests were unnecessary.[37]

As the implications of NSC 68 were being absorbed in the foreign policy bureaucracy, discussions over Turkey and Greece were intensified by the People's Republic of China's intervention in Korea in late November. Complications in the Far East had led the United States increasingly to seek support for its policies in Korea and created the opportunity for the Turks to urge early implementation of defense planning in the Mediterranean as a quid pro quo. What the Turks wanted from the United States was clear: a security guarantee that would give them a credible deterrent against the Soviet Union. What they could offer in return was far more important than continued deployment of the Turkish brigade in Korea, whose role, although significant, was essentially symbolic of their support for the principle of collective security.[38] What the Turks had to offer the West was a strategic role in the defense of Europe that was only gradually coming to be appreciated.

[36] FRUS, 1950, III, 1691–95; FRUS, 1950, V, 233, 611; FRUS, 1951, V, 7.

[37] FRUS, 1950, I, 400; Wells, "Sounding the Tocsin," 157. See also John Gaddis, *Strategies of Containment*, 89–126; and Gaddis, "The Problem of Ends and Means," 167.

[38] The Turkish brigade, characterized by General Douglas MacArthur as "bravest of the brave," received unanimously high praise for its performance during the Korean War. See, for example, General Collins's briefing of President Truman and Prime Minister Attlee at the White House on 8 December 1950. *FRUS*, 1950, VII, 1469. Over 5,000 troops arrived in Korea on 18 October 1950, and the brigade's subsequent strength was raised to 7,000. Geoffrey Lewis, *Turkey*, 3d ed. (London: Praeger, 1965), 161. In the course of the war, a total of 29,882 Turks would serve in the brigade, suffering 717 killed and 2,246 wounded in action; 16 were missing in action, and 219 (none of whom yielded to psychological or physical torture) were taken prisoner. Altemur Kilic, *Turkey and the World* (Washington, D.C.: Public Affairs Press, 1959), 150–51. See also *FRUS*, 1950, II, 1486–87; *FRUS*, 1950, V, 1337–38, 1340–41, 1351–52; *FRUS*, 1950, III, 1706 ff.

In January 1951, General Dwight Eisenhower, who in the previous month had been appointed Supreme Allied Commander of Europe (SACEUR) and who was responsible for determining the strategic relations between the Middle East and Europe, gave some indication of the role he envisaged for Turkey and Greece in his strategic conception of the defense of Europe. Europe, Eisenhower told President Truman, was shaped like a long bottle, with Russia the wide part of the bottle, Western Europe the neck, and Spain the mouth of the bottle. The West controlled bodies of water (the North Sea and the Mediterranean) on either side of the bottle and had land on the far side of the water (England and North Africa) good for bases. The West had to rely on land forces in the center and apply great air and sea power on both flanks. As far as the Mediterranean was concerned, this meant giving arms to Turkey and Yugoslavia and supporting them with great air and sea power. If the Soviets tried to move ahead in the center, he would hit them very hard from both flanks, allowing the center to hold and forcing the Soviets to pull back.[39]

Turkey's potential role in the security of Europe was now perceived as increasingly significant. It also became increasingly feasible as the acquisition of sufficient Allied strength in Europe and the rate of the U.S. buildup made additional resources available to Turkey. By May 1951 President Truman had decided that the United States should press immediately for the inclusion of Turkey and Greece as full members of NATO.[40]

The rationale behind the NATO Council's unanimous decision in September 1951 to extend an invitation to Greece and Turkey to join NATO, and Greece and Turkey's formal admission to full membership in Feb-

---

[39] *FRUS*, 1951, V, 27–42, 108, 115; *FRUS*, 1951, III, 454, 479–85, 488–97, 523.

[40] See the conversation with Bayar, *FRUS*, 1951, III, 466–73; for the decision to support an increase of 40,000 men in the Turkish army, see *FRUS*, 1951, V, 1135–42; for the allocation of military aid ($1.4 billion over five years) to Greece, Turkey, and Iran (resulting from the guidelines of NSC 68 and made available under Title II of the Mutual Defense Assistance Act), see *FRUS*, 1950, I, 437–38, 466. For some of the key documents in the president's decision, see *FRUS*, 1951, V, 50–76, 102–104, 113–20, 1117–26, 1148–62; *FRUS*, 1951, III, 501–05, 511–15, 520–22, 575. See also Kilic, *Turkey and the World*, 158; Metin Tamkoç, *The Warrior Diplomats: Guardians of the National Security and Modernization of Turkey* (Salt Lake City: University of Utah Press, 1976), 232; *FRUS*, 1951, V, 1180; *FRUS*, 1951, III, 479 ff., 575–81, 691–92. With the appointment in December of Admiral Lord Mountbatten as commander in chief, Allied Forces, Mediterranean, the region's command arrangements were completed. Mountbatten was subordinate to SACEUR and commanded all naval forces in the Mediterranean except the U.S. Sixth Fleet, which was designed to support land forces and remained under Admiral Carney's Southern European Command. Mountbatten was responsible for the security of seaborne lines of communication. Peter C~lvocoressi, *Survey of International Affairs, 1952* (London: Oxford University Press, 1955), 50; Lewis, *Turkey*, 50.

ruary 1952, was interesting for what it revealed about how U.S. perceptions of the Middle East's Northern Tier had changed since the early days
of the Truman administration. At the time of the Truman Doctrine, Turkey was seen as the region's linchpin, the strongest anti-communist country on the periphery of the Soviet Union and the only country in the
eastern Mediterranean capable of substantial resistance to the Soviets.
With a capacity to put twenty-five divisions under arms in short order, it
constituted a deterrent to Soviet aggression and provided something of a
protective screen for the region. Loss of Turkey to the Soviet Union would
have given the Soviets a valuable strategic position in the region. If the
Soviets attacked Iran, which was virtually helpless, and Turkey remained
neutral, the Soviet right flank would have been protected. If Bulgaria
attacked Greece, Turkey would not have opposed Bulgaria unless intervention were dictated by the requirements of a larger security framework
that included the United States. Oil interests in the Gulf, meanwhile, would
have been vulnerable, and European economic viability threatened.

What was new in the 1950s was the conviction of a mutuality of benefits: Turkey and Greece on the one hand and Europe and the United
States on the other all stood to benefit. Many officials believed that the
United States was already committed to the security of Turkey. That was
the import of virtually every major decision of the administration in the
region since August 1946. But for the United States to ensure Turkey's
cobelligerency in the event of an attack on Europe, a U.S. security commitment was required. A security commitment was also necessary to secure access to Turkey's valuable bases and to close the Straits.[41]

Without a security commitment from the United States, U.S. officials
were concerned that Turkey would drift toward neutrality, as it had in
World War II, and as Iran appeared to be doing at the time under Prime
Minister Mossadeq.[42] If this happened, officials reasoned, the United States

[41] See Kenneth Condit, *The History of the Joint Chiefs of Staff: The Joint Chiefs of Staff
and National Policy, Vol. II, 1947–1949* (Wilmington, Del.: Martin Glazier, 1979), 288–
302; Gaddis, *Strategies of Containment*, 94; *FRUS, 1951*, I, 12; *FRUS, 1951*, III, 540,
569, 662; Hamilton Fish Armstrong, "Eisenhower's Right Flank," *Foreign Affairs*, July
1951, 651–63; and the article by C. L. Sulzberger, *New York Times*, 2 September 1951.

[42] Serious attention had continued to be given to Iran since 1945. For examples of such
concern in 1951, see *FRUS, 1951*, V, 103, 106, 264; *FRUS, 1951*, III, 526. See also the
testimony of George McGhee and Dean Acheson, *The Middle East, Africa, and Inter-
American Affairs* (Historical Series), vol. XVI, Selected Executive Session Hearings of the
Committee on Foreign Affairs, 1951–1956, U.S. House of Representatives, Washington,
D.C., 1980, 33, 50.

and Europe would lose the assistance of a powerful ally. Greece and Iran, if they were to be protected, required mutual defense arrangements with Turkey; this was possible only under a broader security arrangement of which the United States was a part. As members of NATO, Turkey and Greece would be important to SACEUR—both as a deterrent to a Soviet attack and as a threat to the Soviets' southern flank. If the region's military potential were integrated in a security framework, the Soviet Union would have to commit significant forces to protect its southern flank and its vital oil fields around Baku.[43] A security commitment to Turkey, therefore, constituted a far more effective deterrent than previous arrangements for resisting a Soviet attack, not only along the Middle East's entire Northern Tier, which provided a buffer for European and U.S. oil interests in the Persian Gulf, but in Europe as well.[44]

Finding a solution to the Palestine problem

If U.S. policy in the Near East was shaped by developments along the Northern Tier and by an increasingly clear conception of Turkey's unique geopolitical role in the balance of power, it was hopelessly muddled by developments in Palestine. Officials in the White House and the State Department, who saw eye-to-eye on the Northern Tier, were at variance over concerns that deserved presidential priority when it came to Palestine. These differences led to bewildering alterations in policy that at one point prompted the normally stolid Dean Rusk, then director of the Office of United Nations Affairs, to contemplate reserving a wing at a mental hospital in Washington, D.C. The consequence was aptly summarized in 1948 by Loy Henderson, who wrote Secretary of State George Marshall that Britain and the United States, "by following confused, contra-

---

[43] See the comments, later, by Prime Minister Menderes, *FRUS, 1951*, V, 220.

[44] The U.S. government, in examining the merits of the problem, looked at a host of concerns: provocation to the Soviet Union; organization and planning problems; the effect of widening obligations; the effect on regional countries such as Iran that were not included; the possible relaxation of Greek and Turkish efforts; increased demands for aid; and the lack of a common heritage. These concerns were dismissed. As in 1950, the United States also examined alternative arrangements; they, too, were dismissed. Admission to NATO was a quick and easy way of bringing Turkey and Greece into the overall defense picture; the Turks were already associated with NATO for planning purposes; they needed a credible deterrent and they wanted in; they wanted to be an integral part of the West, and their prestige was involved. These were the factors that led the United States to press immediately for the inclusion of Turkey and Greece as full members of NATO.

dictory, and opportunistic policies in the past, have added to the complications and injustices inherent in the situation."[45]

Part of an explanation for the abrupt shifts and inconsistencies in U.S.
policy begins with the past. Britain's professed "equality of obligation"
to Arabs and Jews, enshrined in the Balfour Declaration in 1917 and
incorporated in the British Mandate for Palestine, committed the British
to "view with favour the establishment in Palestine of a national home
for the Jewish people, . . . it being clearly understood that nothing shall
be done which may prejudice the civil and religious rights of the existing
non-Jewish [i.e., Arab] communities in Palestine." When the British government in 1947 decided to give up its mandate and depart from Palestine, Foreign Minister Bevin based his decision on two beliefs: that the
British could not reconcile these two obligations without American support and that the United States could not be relied on to support a settlement that failed to satisfy the proponents of Zionism.[46]

Britain's equality of obligation was shared to some extent by the United
States. Congress had approved the Balfour Declaration in a joint resolution in 1922. President Roosevelt, moreover, had undertaken two additional and equally irreconcilable commitments: He both endorsed the
idea of a Jewish state and promised King Abd Al-Aziz Ibn Saud that he
would neither help the Jews against the Arabs nor take any action in his
capacity as president that might prove hostile to the Arab people. When
President Truman inherited the contradictory commitments of his pre-
decessors, he might well have echoed Prime Minister Ramsay Mac-
Donald's observation to David Lloyd George in a debate over Palestine
in 1930, when the latter accused him of breaking the word of England:
"It was not a word we inherited. We inherited words, and they are not
always consistent."[47]

Compounding the problems posed by this legacy of equivocation were
several additional factors: President Truman's empathy for survivors of
the Holocaust, White House responsiveness to the interests and concerns
of the American Jewish community, and the State Department's sensitiv-

---

[45] Evan Wilson, *Decision on Palestine: How the U.S. Came to Recognize Israel* (Stanford,
Calif.: Hoover Institution, 1979), 11; *FRUS*, 1948, V, 1044, 1222, 1629–30.

[46] For background on British policy during the Mandate, see Christopher Sykes, *Crossroads
to Israel, 1917–1948* (Bloomington: Indiana University Press, 1965); and Michael Cohen,
Palestine and the Great Powers, 1945–1948 (Princeton: Princeton University Press, 1982).
See also Alan Bullock, *Ernest Bevin: Foreign Secretary, 1945–1951* (New York: W. W.
Norton, 1983), 44, 646, 841. For U.S. commitment, see *FRUS*, 1948, V, 690–91.

[47] Cordell Hull, *The Memoirs of Cordell Hull, Vol. II* (New York: Macmillan, 1948), 1536;
Wilson, *Decision on Palestine*, 45, 51, 180–81; Sykes, *Crossroads to Israel*, 118.

ity to the broad regional context within which U.S. policy toward Palestine would be implemented. Together these factors presented government officials with a fundamental problem: Humanitarian concerns, domestic political priorities, and wide-ranging interests in the emerging Third World, although not always compatible with each other, had to be reconciled in the context of the "national interest."

Regional specialists in the Department of State, whose professional training and responsibilities made them especially sensitive to the concerns of the Arabs, believed that the national interest required good relations with the Arab world. As a result, they worried that U.S. support for Zionist goals would alienate the Arabs, make them more receptive to the Soviets, and undermine the evolving U.S. efforts to contain Soviet influence in the Middle East. "There is no use in strengthening the arch [in Greece, Turkey, and Iran]," director of NEA's Division of Near Eastern Affairs Gordon Merriam wrote NEA director Loy Henderson in October 1946, "if we are going to kick out the pillars." Henderson agreed. A hostile attitude on the part of the Arabs, he wrote Under Secretary of State Robert A. Lovett in August 1947, "would threaten from the rear the position we are desperately trying to hold in Greece, Turkey, and Iran." A report by the Policy Planning Staff in January 1948, assessing the U.S. position on Palestine in light of the partition proposal by the United Nations Special Committee on Palestine (UNSCOP), elaborated on this consistent concern: The partition plan would afford the Soviets an opportunity to introduce forces into Palestine, outflank U.S. positions along the Northern Tier, threaten the stability of the entire eastern Mediterranean, and undermine the whole structure of security that had been set up in the Near East.[48]

Officials in NEA were sensitive to the plight of displaced persons, but they did not see Palestine as the exclusive solution to the problems confronted by European Jewry. In their view, the Jewish displaced person problem, if it were to be solved, required a comprehensive worldwide scheme as well as an acceptable solution to the Palestine problem as a whole. Because the Jewish displaced person problem was not within NEA's bureaucratic domain, officials in Henderson's office were only inciden-

---

[48] 15 October 1946 memo from Gordon Merriam to Loy Henderson, a xeroxed copy of which is in the author's possession; Wilson, *Decision on Palestine*, 99–100; *FRUS*, 1947, V, 800; and *FRUS*, 1948, V, 545–55; and Kenneth Ray Bain, *The March to Zion: United States Policy and the Founding of Israel* (College Station: Texas A&M University Press, 1979), 62. For the Turkish consul in Jerusalem's echo of this perception see *FRUS*, 1948, V, 1030.

tally concerned with aiding Holocaust survivors, whose goal of establishing a Jewish state they judged to be antithetical to U.S. interests. In contrast, finding an acceptable solution to the Palestine problem was one of their primary concerns, and like their British counterparts they believed it could be achieved only on the basis of consent by *both* Arabs and Jews. Political questions, in short, had to be settled first. This explains NEA's initial attachment to the notion of a binational state. Without the consent of both parties, Merriam and Henderson believed, the principle of self-determination deeply imbedded in U.S. foreign policy would be violated and the United Nations (U.N.) charter itself contravened.[49]

In November 1947 the United Nations General Assembly recommended adoption of the UNSCOP majority plan for the partition of Palestine. Arab rejection of this recommendation, however, led officials in NEA to conclude that partition could only be implemented by force. Because President Truman did not intend to deploy forces in Palestine, and many in the State Department and the Pentagon advised against it, these officials further concluded that partition was unworkable. It would result, they believed, in bloodshed, serious unrest, and instability that the Soviet Union could readily exploit. Partition not only would require a long-term U.S. commitment but also would damage overall U.S. security interests, which included Arab friendship, strategic lodgements in the Middle East, and access to Arabian oil.[50]

Loy Henderson, who like the British had come to believe that there was no solution to which both Jews and Arabs would acquiesce, had reluctantly gone along with partition. He continued to think, however, that a workable solution could evolve only after long and protracted discussion during which moderates could find common ground. This process, he believed, would be impeded if the United States took sides (i.e., supported partition) but it could be encouraged under trusteeship. When the situation in Palestine began to deteriorate in late 1947, Hen-

---

[49] 15 October 1946 memo from Merriam to Henderson; Wilson, *Decision on Palestine*, 37, 155; Bain, *The March to Zion*, 65, 200. In 1948 Arnold Toynbee told the Council on Foreign Relations that the partition of Palestine was "the *reductio ad absurdum* of territorial nationality." Peter Grose, *Israel in the Mind of America* (New York: Knopf, 1983), 263, 345. It is worth noting that only two Asian countries (India and Iran) were on the UNSCOP and that they opposed the majority plan.

[50] *FRUS*, 1948, V, 545–62, 573–81, 600–03, 619–25. On the question of force deployment, see *FRUS*, 1945, VIII, 724–25, 742–43; *FRUS*, 1946, VII, 644–45; *FRUS*, 1948, V, 797–800; Acheson, *Present at the Creation*, 179; Harry S. Truman, *Years of Trial and Hope* (Garden City, N.Y.: Doubleday, 1956), 149, 162; Cohen, *Palestine and the Great Powers*, 394; Robert J. Donovan, *Conflict and Crisis: The Presidency of Harry S. Truman, 1945–1948* (New York: W. W. Norton, 1977), 313.

derson's office looked once again at the possibility of a trusteeship. "Although there are many doubts about trusteeship," Merriam wrote Henderson in the spring of 1948, "no one has anything better to offer." A compromise solution, however, if it had ever had a chance, by this time had no hope. On the day after the United States proposed in the United Nations that partition be delayed, David Ben-Gurion, chairman of the Jewish Agency Executive (the governing body of the Zionist movement in Palestine), observed that the establishment of a Jewish state did not depend on the U.N. partition resolution but on the Jews' ability to emerge victorious: "It is we," he said, "who will decide the fate of Palestine." U.S. policy, in effect, had become irrelevant to events in Palestine.[51]

The Department of State's management of the Palestine question has been the subject of considerable criticism, some of which is merited. In the judgment of one historian, State and Pentagon officials exaggerated the *immediate* danger to U.S. oil interests and overestimated Soviet capacity to meddle in the region.[52] This may be true, but subsequent events have demonstrated that the *long-term* danger to Western oil interests was not exaggerated. Soviet options in the region, moreover, if overestimated at the time, significantly expanded under Stalin's successors—in part because of the legacy of U.S. policy toward the Palestine problem.

More cogent, perhaps, is the criticism that American diplomats, who were endlessly impressed by demonstrations and editorials in Arab capitals, derided similar expressions by Zionists in their own country as "playing politics." The result was a failure to develop an approach that accounted for popular sentiments in its recognition of realistic alternatives. Evan Wilson, who served on the Palestine desk in the 1940s, acknowledges that the thinking of officials in NEA did not sufficiently take into account the domestic political imperatives that were relevant to the Palestine question. "Nor did it take sufficiently into account," Wilson adds, "the driving force of nationalism among both Arabs and Jews." This failure—and in particular the failure either to comprehend the sig-

---

[51] *FRUS*, 1947, V, 1153–58, 1264–66, 1313–14; Aaron Miller, *Search for Security: Saudi Arabian Oil and American Foreign Policy, 1939–1949* (Chapel Hill: University of North Carolina Press, 1980), 194; Wilson, *Decision on Palestine*, 155–56; Grose, *Israel in the Mind of America*, 275; Cohen, *Palestine and the Great Powers*, 335.

[52] Ibn Saud, in a letter to Truman, had warned the United States in October 1947 that support for partition would result in a death blow to American interests in Arab countries, and the Arab League apparently considered the possibility of canceling British and American concessions in the Arab world. Despite these alarms, however, the king's immediate economic interests were bound up with the United States. Miller, *Search for Security*, xvii, 147, 169–70, 187–88, 190, 209–10, 282.

nificance of the Holocaust for world Jewry or to understand its implications for Zionism—led State Department officials to believe that a compromise solution in Palestine was feasible when it may have been impossible. In Wilson's retrospective judgment, a solution along the lines of a binational state was simply not an option after World War II. A failure to understand the imperatives of Zionism also led department officials to be overly optimistic about the ability of the United Nations to resolve disputes. In Wilson's view, a Jewish state was bound to come.[53]

Finally, the State Department was seriously misinformed about the military situation in Palestine. Secretary of State George Marshall, for example, saw grave risks and warned the Jewish Agency's Moshe Shertok against relying on the advice of his military. "Believe me, I am talking about things which I know," Marshall told him in May 1948. "You are sitting there in the coastal plains of Palestine while the Arabs hold the mountain ridges. . . . The Arabs have regular armies. They are well trained and they have heavy arms. How can you hope to hold out?" In a cabinet meeting in March 1951, Marshall (now Secretary of Defense) noted that twice in his career he had been seriously misinformed on the military potential of foreign powers. The first instance was the power of the French army in 1940; the second was the grave overestimate of Arab military strength in the recent conflict with Israel. The latter, he observed, constituted a gross failure of military intelligence.[54] In 1947–48, needless to say, poor information clearly complicated the judgment of NEA officials who were also seeking to avert what they felt was an impending bloodbath.

President Truman during these years was never convinced by the State Department's arguments on the Palestine question. His humanitarian instincts and attachment to the Bible inclined him, despite occasional irritability at Zionist pressures, to be sympathetic to the Jewish people's need to build a new life. Officials in the Department of State, he felt, were more concerned with the goodwill of the Arabs and the danger of

---

[53] Grose, *Israel in the Mind of America*, 215; Bain, *The March to Zion*, 91; Donovan, *Conflict and Crisis*, 378; Wilson, *Decision on Palestine*, 37, 151, 155–57. Bain, 199, 213, argues that the United Nations offered prospects for a collective solution to the Jewish refugee problem that could have minimized future conflict and made possible a just settlement. This judgment ignores, however, the strength of Jewish nationalism. Any compromise solution in Palestine, moreover, would have been difficult because it would have been opposed by both Arabs and Jews.

[54] Grose, *Israel in the Mind of America*, 287; memorandum for the president, 15 March 1951, President's Secretary's Files, Harry S. Truman Papers, HSTL; Wilson, *Decision on Palestine*, 157.

antagonizing them than with the suffering of the Jews. He believed that he could help the victims of the Holocaust find a home in Palestine, protect his political future in the United States, *and* safeguard the interests of the United States in the Middle East.[55]

The president's views deserve brief elaboration. To begin with, Truman did not fully understand either the history of the Palestine question or the dilemma inherent in the Balfour Declaration. As a result, he failed on occasion to comprehend the distinction between one diplomatic formula and another. Nor did he appreciate the perspective of the Arabs themselves. Unlike Roosevelt, he did not see the awkwardness of asking Arabs to accept Jewish immigrants in Palestine when the United States was reluctant to accept them. Nor was he sensitive to the fact that the admission of displaced Jews into Palestine or the creation of a Jewish state in Palestine represented actions that the Arabs had legitimate reason to regard as hostile.[56]

President Truman, because of his limited understanding of the Arab world, seems also to have been unwarrantedly optimistic about Palestine. Partition, for example, he initially regarded as opening the way for peaceful collaboration between Arabs and Jews along the lines of the Tennessee Valley Authority. In this, he was no different from many liberal Democrats such as Eleanor Roosevelt who, in opposition to Loy Henderson's warnings in 1947 about the U.N. majority plan, declared: "Come, come, Mr. Henderson. I think you're exaggerating the dangers. You are too pessimistic. A few years ago Ireland was considered to be a problem that could not be solved. Then the Irish Republic was established and the problem vanished. I'm confident that when a Jewish state is set up, the Arabs will see the light; they will quiet down; and Palestine will no longer be a problem."[57]

Although the president was intent on doing what was "right" when it came to Palestine, an objective view was difficult to achieve because the

[55]Truman, 135, 140, 145; Cohen, *Palestine and the Great Powers*, 53–54, 167; Zvi Ganin, *Truman, American Jewry, and Israel, 1945–1948* (New York: Holmes & Meier, 1979), pp. xv, 105; Grose, *Israel in the Mind of America*, 217; Miller, *Search for Security*, 199.

[56]Transcript of interview with Harry N. Howard, HSTL; Grose, *Israel in the Mind of America*, 146, 294–96; Truman, *Years of Trial and Hope*, 132–33, 156, 164. *FRUS*, 1946, VII, 714–17.

[57]Truman, *Years of Trial and Hope*, 156; and transcript of interview with Loy Henderson, HSTL; Wilson, *Decision on Palestine*, 116, 214; Bain, *The March to Zion*, 62, 202. Roosevelt, interestingly enough, considered himself something of an expert on the Middle East and believed he could straighten it out. For Roosevelt's views on Palestine, see Wilson, *Decision on Palestine*, chap. 4, and Grose, *Israel in the Mind of America*, chaps. 5 and 6.

environment in which President Truman operated, as Ernest Bevin recognized, was overwhelmingly supportive of the Zionist cause. The American Zionist Emergency Council (AZEC) and its 400 local committees,
their prominence among Jews of the world accentuated by the virtual
disappearance of European Jewry, worked hard in pressing the Zionist
case. The White House, in the latter half of 1947, for example, received
135,000 communications regarding Palestine, and in one three-month
period in 1948 received more than 300,000 postcards, nearly all of them
from Jewish interest groups and their supporters. As a result of AZEC's
efforts, 33 state legislatures passed resolutions favoring a Jewish state in
Palestine, while 40 governors, 54 senators, and 250 congressmen signed
petitions to the president.[58]

Zionists also set about "educating" Truman's former business partner
Eddie Jacobson to gain access to Truman. At the recommendation of the
president's administrative assistant David Niles, they focused their attention on Special Counsel Clark Clifford and found an avenue to Clifford
through his pro-tem aide Max Lowenthal. They briefed Niles and Clifford regularly, providing material that served as a basis for many memoranda to the president and even drafting some of Truman's statements.
Truman, at times, appears to have been unaware of the work of his aides,
whose actions in lobbying heavily for the partition of Palestine, for example, were at odds with instructions the president gave to the Department of State. The president's role in this episode, needless to say, is the
subject of considerable controversy.[59]

The president's responsiveness to Zionist influence was, aside from his
emotional predispositions, based on political reality. "I have to answer
to hundreds of thousands who are anxious for the success of Zionism,"
he told a number of State Department representatives on one occasion,
"I do not have hundreds of thousands of Arabs among my constituents."
Historians have pointed out numerous occasions in which Zionist pressures, both direct and indirect, influenced his decisions. These include
breaking away from the Morrison-Grady plan (which rejected partition
and spelled doom for a Jewish state), the president's Yom Kippur speech

[58] James McDonald's report on a conversation with the president, 27 July 1946, Clark
Clifford Papers, HSTL; John Snetsinger, *Truman, the Jewish Vote and the Creation of
Israel* (Stanford, Calif.: Hoover Institution, 1974), 5–6; Wilson, *Decision on Palestine*,
115; Grose, *Israel in the Mind of America*, 191; and *FRUS*, 1948, V, 691.

[59] Grose, *Israel in the Mind of America*, 230–31, 248–54, 270–71; Cohen, *Palestine and
the Great Powers*, 46, 162–63, 292–300, 354, note 13; Wilson, *Decision on Palestine*,
98, 125–27; Ganin, *Truman, American Jewry, and Israel*, 142–46; Donovan, *Conflict
and Crisis*, 329.

in 1946, support for the partition of Palestine in 1947, and the decision to recognize Israel in 1948.

Clark Clifford, one of his key advisers, has contested the assertion of one historian that Truman's policies were motivated by short-term political expediency rather than long-range national goals, arguing that political factors played only a minor role in Truman's broad national strategy for reelection in 1948. Clifford has cited as a case in point a memo he submitted to the president in November 1947 in which he argued that decisions on the Palestine problem should be based on intrinsic merit. He neglected to mention, however, his observations in that memo that the Jewish vote was important in New York, that no candidate since 1876 (except for Wilson in 1916) had lost New York and won the presidency, and that its forty-seven electoral votes were the first prize in any election. He also neglected to point out that although the president lost New York in 1948, the Jewish vote in Ohio, California, and Illinois was crucial to his reelection.[60]

Another factor that complicated the president's determination to do what was right was the predisposition of his advisers in the White House to share widely accepted stereotypes of Arabs. "You know that President Roosevelt said to some of us privately he could do anything that needed to be done with Ibn Saud with a few million dollars," the president's assistant David Niles wrote him in May 1946, failing to note that this judgment had changed considerably after Roosevelt's meeting with the king in February 1945. In that same memo Niles asserted that there would be very little opposition to the transfer of 100,000 displaced European Jews to Palestine; Niles also discounted the danger of unifying Muslims by such action on the grounds that "a good part of the Moslem world follows Gandhi and his philosophy of non-resistance." In another memo to the president, Clark Clifford noted that the United States appeared "in the ridiculous role of trembling before threats of a few nomadic desert tribes. ... Why should Russia or Yugoslavia, or any other nation treat us with anything but contempt," he wrote, "in light of our shilly-shallying appeasement of the Arabs?"

[60] Memo of 19 November 1947 from Clifford to Truman, Clark Clifford Papers, HSTL; Cohen, *Palestine and the Great Powers*, 46–47, 58, 64, 65n, 113, 128–32, 164–66; Grose, *Israel in the Mind of America*, 216, 288–93, 300–01; Ganin, *Truman, American Jewry, and Israel*, 101, 144–45; Donovan, *Conflict and Crisis*, 320; Bain, *The March to Zion*, 202; *FRUS*, 1946, VII, 682–83; Wilson, *Decision on Palestine*, 123, 142–43; Truman, 158; Snetsinger, *Truman, the Jewish Vote and the Creation of Israel*, 120–40; Clark Clifford, speech before the American Historical Association, 22 December 1976, Washington, D.C.

Briefs such as these—by advisers who had no sympathy for and knew little about the Arabs—may well have influenced the president, when he was confronted by domestic pressures and political constraints, to discount the importance of the Arabs and their rights in his overall scheme of what was just. The Morrison-Grady plan, he told more than one person, was the solution to the Palestine problem that he considered most fair; but he rejected this plan because it was politically unsupportable in the United States. Clearly, to do what was "right" was a difficult task.

One option other than a Jewish state that might have been available to displaced European Jews, as it had been to their persecuted brethren in earlier years, was immigration to the United States. Quotas, however, restricted Jewish immigration, and the president knew that the reaction in this country if he attempted to change those quotas would be divisive. One poll taken in January 1946 indicated that only 5 percent of respondents favored increased immigration from Europe. Another poll taken in 1946 found that only 43 percent favored allowing Poles, Jews, and other displaced persons to enter the United States. "I think there would be terrific resistance if we attempted at this time to bring even a small portion [of displaced European Jews] into our own country beyond the present quota limitations," David Niles wrote the president in May 1946. "I don't see how we can ask other countries [i.e., outside the Arab world] to do what we ourselves are unable to do." These observations imply that Arab views could be discounted; they also suggest that there was more than a grain of truth to Bevin's subsequent accusation that "The average citizen does not want them [i.e., Jewish immigrants] in the United States and salves his conscience by advocating their admission to Palestine."

President Truman, meanwhile, found it easier to discount Arab opposition to U.S. policy in the Middle East than to confront bigotry and anti-Semitism in the United States. This explains, perhaps, why his efforts in opening up immigration quotas were limited and why he did not push Congress to expand quotas for refugees. Only in 1947 did the White House begin a concerted campaign to produce extensive refugee settlement in the United States, and by June 1948 only 41,379 refugees (not all of whom were Jewish) had entered the United States under the president's executive order.

If the president was sensitive to domestic prejudice and more cognizant of the imperatives of Zionism than the Department of State, he remained insensitive to Arab concerns about the introduction of 100,000

Jews to Palestine and, because of domestic pressures, he refused to share British responsibility for the larger problem of finding a fair solution to the Palestine question. He ignored the principle of self-determination, which, presumably, he did not feel applied to the Arabs of Palestine, and he endorsed (but would not enforce) a partition plan that responded to Jewish needs but was manifestly unfair to the Arabs of Palestine.[61]

President Truman's support for partition, in contrast, gave international recognition to the Jewish claim of sovereignty in Palestine; his de facto recognition of Israel gave the state international legitimacy and began the special relationship between the United States and Israel. It was the Jews themselves, however, not Truman, who were responsible for bringing Israel into being. Partition probably would have come about even without his support. The result was also bound to reflect the relative strength of the parties involved. But the president does share responsibility for never attempting to initiate a long-term solution to the problem of Palestine. Subject to the dichotomous views of his bureaucracy and lacking the substantive knowledge to judge their validity, Truman pursued policies that only put off or mitigated problems he did not understand and could not solve.[62]

Oil, nationalism, and Britain's waning imperial power

The Palestine problem, one historian has observed, was a barometer that measured government sensitivities to a broad range of strategic concerns in the Middle East.[63] The strategic concern with the highest priority was

[61] John Morton Blum, ed., *The Price of Vision: The Diary of Henry A. Wallace, 1942–1946* (Boston: Houghton Mifflin, 1973), 407; unpublished manuscript, Henry Grady Papers, HSTL; Bain, *The March to Zion*, pp. xv, 53, 58–60, 88–91, 162, 197–98, 202; Wilson, *Decision on Palestine*, 137, 155; Cohen, *Palestine and the Great Powers*, 395; 27 May 1946 memo from David Niles to President Truman, reprinted in Abram L. Sachar, *Redemption of the Unwanted: From the Liberation of the Death Camps to the Founding of Israel* (New York: St. Martin's, 1983), 316–18; Edward Stettinius, Jr., *Roosevelt and the Russians* (Garden City, N.Y.: Doubleday), 289–90; and Wilson, *Decision on Palestine*, 50–56. For further discussion on immigration issues, see also: Grose, *Israel in the Mind of America*, 32–33, 120, 200–10, 338; Cohen, *Palestine and the Great Powers*, 14–15, 101–02, 118–19, 393; Sykes, *Crossroads to Israel*, 377–80; Donovan, *Conflict and Crisis*, 133–34. On the question of the fairness of partition see Wilson, *Decision on Palestine*, 112–13, 128, who notes that Jews were given 53 percent of the land area of Palestine although they owned only 7 percent of the land and constituted only one-third of the population.

[62] Ganin, *Truman, American Jewry, and Israel*, 146, 188–89; Donovan, *Conflict and Crisis*, 386; Wilson, *Decision on Palestine*, 148; Cohen, *Palestine and the Great Powers*, 44–45, 389, 393; Grose, *Israel in the Mind of America*, 192. See also note 55.

[63] Miller, *Search for Security*, 190, 209.

the containment of Soviet influence. Of lesser priority but nonetheless important were Western interests in and continued access to Persian Gulf oil. Because public U.S. support for Zionist objectives in Palestine threatened to undermine the containment policy and jeopardized access to Gulf oil, the State Department sought to improve relations with Arab oil states through private enterprise and looked increasingly to U.S. oil companies to promote U.S. interests in the region.

Historians have shown how U.S. oil policy served the special interests of competing interest groups both within and outside the government and established a pattern for future U.S. actions vis-à-vis Saudi Arabia and Middle East oil. The State Department, by subordinating the antitrust implications of unregulated business arrangements to the "national interest," made it possible for U.S. oil companies to secure increased markets and to acquire additional sources of supply. State officials supported the allocation of scarce steel resources for the Trans-Arabian pipeline linking Saudi oil to Western markets. Following the advent of the Korean War, they also encouraged a fifty-fifty profit-sharing arrangement between the Arabian American Oil Company (ARAMCO) and Saudi Arabia. As a result of these developments, the position of U.S. petroleum interests in Saudi Arabia was vastly improved. Ibn Saud received more revenue to aid in the modernization of Saudi Arabia, and progress was made toward the State Department goal of ensuring economic stability and containing the spread of communism in the area. The Defense Department, meanwhile, by obtaining increased Saudi production, conserved its strategic resources in the Western Hemisphere. Over time, the process of securing mutual interests gave birth to the special relationship between Saudi Arabia and the United States.[64]

Despite the developing U.S.-Saudi relationship, however, U.S. interests in the Middle East continued to be jeopardized not just by U.S. policy toward the Palestine problem but by U.S. relations with Britain. The United

[64] Ibid., xvi–xvii, 154–63, 188, 190–93, 201, 211–14, 273; Irvine Anderson, *ARAMCO, the United States, and Saudi Arabia: A Study of the Dynamics of Foreign Oil Policy, 1933–1950* (Princeton: Princeton University Press, 1981); and George McGhee, *Envoy to the Middle World: Adventures in Diplomacy* (New York: Harper & Row, 1983), 186. For speculation on the advantages of pursuing national advantage through arrangements other than private corporations, see Anderson, *ARAMCO*, 206–07, and Michael Stoff, *Oil, War, and American Security: The Search for a National Policy on Foreign Oil, 1941–1947* (New Haven, Conn.: Yale University Press, 1980), 215. For a critical view of U.S. oil policy, see David Sidney Painter, "The Politics of Oil: Multinational Oil Corporations and United States Foreign Policy, 1941–1954" (Ph.D. diss., University of North Carolina at Chapel Hill, 1982).

States and Britain, it may be remembered, had committed themselves to cooperate and to pursue parallel policies in the Near East. This was necessary if they were to maintain the balance of power and contain Soviet influence in the region. When George Marshall was secretary of state, the cornerstone of his policies in the Middle East was the maintenance of Britain's declining position to the greatest extent possible (Palestine, of course, was an important exception). Under his successor, Dean Acheson, this policy was unchanged.[65] In the later 1940s, however, nationalist forces in Iran and Egypt, with whom the United States sought better ties, had begun to resist the attempts by Britain to hold onto what was left of its empire and to contest treaties that had been negotiated under imperial pressures.

In Egypt, discontent over the establishment of Israel fueled passions over Britain's pervasive influence and focused on two legacies of the past: an Anglo-Egyptian treaty that gave Britain the right to maintain troops in Egypt until 1956 and a condominium agreement between Britain and the Sudan that was a facade for British rule. The Egyptians wanted the British out of Suez and "unity for the Nile Valley." The British, determined to maintain access to the Suez base, attempted to balance the inevitability of withdrawal with the requirements of defense. Their goal was a phased withdrawal in exchange for immediate access to military bases in the canal zone in the event of war. The United States, which shared British concerns about the consequences of withdrawal, sought a mutually satisfactory settlement that humiliated neither party while meeting both Western strategic concerns and Egyptian national demands. Through the concept of a Middle East Command (MEC), the United States and Britain sought to internationalize the issue in the context of a regional defense organization. They hoped to circumvent Anglo-Egyptian differences by substituting an Allied base for a British base and an Allied presence for a British presence in the canal zone. Egypt, however, was far removed from the Northern Tier and was preoccupied with Israel and Britain, not the Soviet Union. As a result, the MEC and a subsequent proposal, the Middle East Defense Organization, were stillborn. Encouraged by developments in Iran, the Egyptians in October 1951 abrogated the Anglo-Egyptian Treaty and the Sudan Condominium Agreement.[66]

[65] See note 18; McGhee, *Envoy to the Middle World,* 53, 55; transcript of interview with Loy Henderson, HSTL.
[66] Eden, *The Reckoning,* 258–59, 274; Peter Calvocoressi, *Survey of International Affairs,*

In many of the differences between Britain and Egypt, U.S. officials were aware of the liabilities of supporting Britain; because no other country was willing to assume Allied responsibilities in the region, however, they believed they had few options. Acheson, for one, believed that there was little he could have done to ameliorate the Anglo-Egyptian problem, and as long as the Anglo-American partnership was central to his policies he was probably right. Even so, there were limits. When skirmishes in January 1952 between Britain and Egypt resulted in bloodshed, the United States refused to grant Prime Minister Churchill's request to send "token" troops to the Suez. The British leader, whose Conservative government had come back into power partly as a result of British difficulties in Iran and Egypt, was still smarting over the British setback in Iran; he told Acheson that under his government "there might have been a splutter of musquetry," but the British would not have been kicked out of Iran. Three weeks later, after the British stormed a police headquarters at Ismailia, Acheson commented to the British ambassador that "the splutter of musketry apparently doesn't stop things as we have been told from time to time that it would." It didn't, and the Americans were extremely pessimistic about the situation in Egypt. In June 1952 the monarchy was overthrown, and although American officials hoped that a new regime signaled an opportunity to resolve Anglo-Egyptian differences, continued efforts to mediate those differences were not successful. Egyptian nationalism, the security of the Suez, Britain's position in the Middle East, and stability in the region together constituted an extremely difficult combination of concerns to blend together into a constructive policy.[67]

In Iran, a nationalist desire to exact a larger share of the profits from Britain's exploitation of Iran's oil resources clashed with Whitehall's insistence on retaining profitable control over them. Iran's opposition to the Anglo-Iranian Oil Company (AIOC) and attempt to exercise national control over the oil industry had been crystallized in the aftermath of World War II by a debate over revision of a 1933 agreement under which Iran received 16 percent of the royalties paid by AIOC. Although a proposed supplemental agreement in 1949 would have been the most favor-

1951 (London: Oxford University Press, 1954), 203–30; McGhee, *Envoy to the Middle World*, 365–87; Gaddis Smith, *Dean Acheson* (New York: Cooper Square, 1972), 347–48; Acheson, *Present at the Creation*, 563–64; Sachar, *Europe Leaves the Middle East*, 586; *FRUS*, 1951, V, 401; Bullock, *Ernest Bevin*, 156–57, 751–52, 831–32.

[67] *FRUS*, 1951, V, 402; 6 January and 27 January 1952 memos of conversations, Box 67, Acheson Papers, HSTL; Peter Calvocoressi, *Survey of International Affairs, 1952* (London: Oxford University Press, 1955), 220–21; Acheson, *Present at the Creation*, 566–67.

able of its kind when negotiated (Iran would have received 29.5 percent of the royalties), the Iranians rejected it. Debate over the agreement, meanwhile, catapulted the National Front and its leader Mohammed Mossadeq to the forefront of Iranian politics and led to nationalization of the oil industry. By October 1951 strikes had forced the British to close down and withdraw from the largest refinery in the world at Abadan, and a major crisis was at hand.[68]

Mossadeq, who became prime minister in 1951, had helped lead the opposition to Soviet oil concessions in the 1940s. In the 1950s, his longstanding, intense dislike of the British and their historical interference in Iranian politics was energized by the terms under which the British had exploited Iranian resources. The AIOC, which was Britain's largest overseas asset, was valued at somewhere between £81 million (the undepreciated book value) and £500 million (the replacement cost). In 1950 the AIOC produced 6 percent of the world's oil and provided Britain with something in the neighborhood of £100 million in foreign exchange earnings. Iranians were exercised by the fact that AIOC made larger payments to the British Treasury than to Iran, whose dividends in the late 1940s did not reflect increased production and higher profits. Other grievances included an inability to monitor AIOC activities and AIOC sales to the British Admiralty at reduced prices.[69]

Mossadeq's primary concern was with the political aspects of nationalization—with the sovereign right of Iran to control its own natural resources and rid itself of British dominance. This objective, he believed, was more important than the immediate economic benefits that could be gained by temporizing. Control of the oil industry was, in effect, a moral imperative that could not be compromised.[70]

The British were equally determined to thwart Mossadeq. Although eventually willing to accept the principle of nationalization, they claimed "just compensation," which they interpreted as including compensation for the concession itself and future profits from it. In short, the conditions under which they would accept nationalization would nullify the con-

[68] Smith, *Dean Acheson*, 330; Rouhollah Ramazani, *Iran's Foreign Policy, 1941–1973: A Study of Foreign Policy in Modernizing Nations* (Charlottesville: University Press of Virginia, 1975), 181–250.
[69] Ibid.; Calvocoressi, *Survey of International Affairs, 1951*, 292–337; Rouhollah Ramazani, *The United States and Iran: The Patterns of Influence* (New York: Praeger, 1982), 13; McGhee, *Envoy to the Middle World*, 355; Henry Grady M.S., Henry Grady Papers, HSTL; Painter, "The Politics of Oil," 476.
[70] Calvocoressi, *SIA, 1951*, 303; Ramazani, *The United States and Iran*, 16; Smith, *Dean Acheson*, 340.

cept. The British were concerned, ultimately, not over AIOC properties, the loss of which they could have absorbed, but over the precedent that the seizure of AIOC would set for British interests in the Gulf and throughout the world. They refused to accept a settlement in which Mossadeq benefited relative to rulers elsewhere who abided by their contracts. If the British had to choose between Iran's going communist or Britain's going bankrupt, which is how they defined the problem, they saw the former as less important than preserving the last remaining bulwark of British solvency: their overseas investments and properties.[71]

Britain's strategy for dealing with Mossadeq was predicated on the assumption that economic pressure would bring him to his knees; if the United States refused to assist him, Mossadeq would come around. A corollary of this line of thinking was a belief that Iran's economic standards were so low that the country's total collapse was not imminent. As a result, the British saw no urgency in the situation and viewed conciliatory actions as worse than doing nothing. Foreign Minister Anthony Eden, for example, rejected the argument of U.S. officials that the only alternative to Mossadeq was communist rule. He believed that satisfactory alternatives could be found and in the interim saw no agreement as better than one that did not support British objectives.[72]

U.S. policy toward the Anglo-Iranian dispute, in contrast, was governed by a sense of urgency. This had not always been the case. After the Azerbaijan crisis of 1946, State Department officials saw themselves struggling to maintain the status quo in Greece and Turkey and saw little basis for new commitments. Worldwide demands limited the funds and equipment available to Iran, whose absorptive capacity posed additional problems. U.S. officials, meanwhile, were unsympathetic with Iran's obsessive desires for parity with Turkey and irritated by Iran's ambiguous and overlapping requests for assistance, which outnumbered those of the rest of the seventeen countries under NEA's jurisdiction combined. U.S. attitudes began to shift, however, after the Korean War began and after the Soviet Union began to pursue a more moderate course of action toward Iran. By the fall of 1950 State Department officials began to pay more

[71] Acheson, *Present at the Creation*, 501; Smith, *Dean Acheson*, 340; Ramazani, *Iran's Foreign Policy*, 210, 229; 16 November 1951 memo for the president from James Webb, and attached telegram from Acheson to McGhee dated 10 November 1951, President's Secretary's File, Truman Papers, HSTL; and 4 December 1952 Memorandum of Meeting with Oil Company Representatives, Acheson Papers, HSTL.

[72] Telegram of 10 November 1951 and 4 December 1952 memo cited in note 71; Anthony Eden, *Full Circle: The Memoirs of Anthony Eden* (Boston: Houghton Mifflin, 1960), 219, 222, 236; McGhee, *Envoy to the Middle World*, 403.

attention to Iran's need for economic assistance and by the beginning of 1951 to worry over Iran's drift toward neutrality in the cold war.[73]

As the nationalization crisis unfolded, U.S. officials were increasingly irritated by Britain's attitude toward Iran, typical of which was the statement by AIOC's representative in New York that Britain had already made liberal concessions and would soon arrive at a point where the AIOC would have "nothing in the till." Acheson, who believed British policies to be persistently stupid, subsequently observed that ARAMCO had avoided such a situation in Saudi Arabia by "graciously granting that which it no longer had the power to withhold." AIOC representatives were less flexible, and U.S. officials, concerned with preventing the Soviets from gaining influence in and control of the Middle East, believed that the AIOC was subordinating broader political considerations to commercial interests. The main priority of the United States was preventing the loss of Iran to the free world. Desiring to prevent economic collapse and to preserve Iran's independence, the United States thwarted Britain's inclination to intervene militarily in Iran and attempted to persuade the AIOC to make real concessions. Nationalization, U.S. officials believed, had to be accepted. It was a sovereign right and should not be opposed if prompt and effective compensation were paid. This does not mean that U.S. officials were prepared to disrupt the system that distributed the world's oil. It means, rather, that they sought greater flexibility on the part of Britain and initially attempted to find formulas that would help to mediate differences.[74]

Following the election of a Conservative government in Britain in October 1951, however, the United States was reluctant to oppose Churchill's tough line toward Iran. Although U.S. officials were convinced that Mossadeq was sincere in seeking a solution that would allow him to avoid turning to the Soviet Union for assistance, they increasingly sided with Britain in a dispute where the issues appeared nonnegotiable. The United States made up for Britain's diminished refinery capacity and foreign exchange losses. By early 1952, U.S. policies were more closely aligned with Britain's, and American financial assistance to Iran was made con-

[73] *FRUS*, 1947, V, 924–27; *FRUS*, 1949, VI, 472–73; *FRUS*, 1950, V, 173–74, 447–51, 564–66, 586–87, 593–600, 604–07, 625–26; *FRUS*, 1951, I, 6–7, 68–69; see also James F. Goode, "United States-Iranian Relations, 1947–1951" (Ph.D. diss., Indiana University, August 1984).

[74] Acheson, *Present at the Creation*, 501, 506; McGhee, *Envoy to the Middle World*, 85, 269, 319, 330, 332, 393; *FRUS*, 1950, V, 14; *FRUS*, 1951, V, 309–15; 22 October 1951 memo for the president, President's Secretary's File, Truman Papers, HSTL. For differing British and American perceptions of Mossadeq, see Louis, 651–54, 680, 684.

tingent on Iran's reaching an agreement with Britain. Even so, at the end of 1952 the Truman administration was unwilling to consider a British proposal backed by Churchill and Eden to overthrow Mossadeq. Instead, it explored the possibility of finding a solution in collaboration with the major oil companies, while the JCS advocated a break with the British, arguing that animosity toward the British would be greater if the United States failed to act than if it did. Efforts to resolve the problem, however, failed. As Acheson observed in his memoirs, time ran out and the Eisenhower administration took over.[75]

Conclusion

President Truman's commitment to maintain the balance of power in the Near East was his administration's most important policy in the region. It constituted an assumption of responsibility that, to use Dean Acheson's words, was "decided rightly and vigorously followed through." The determination of men like Loy Henderson and Acheson to sustain that commitment throughout the early postwar period and, after the advent of the Korean War, the initiative of Assistant Secretary of State George McGhee in bringing Greece and Turkey into NATO, served to undergird the Truman administration's policies. Their primary objective was the

---

[75] Acheson, *Present at the Creation*, 508, 681, 685; Painter, "The Politics of Oil," 490–92, 508, 528–29; Eden, *The Reckoning*, 226; transcript of interview with Loy Henderson, Dwight D. Eisenhower Library, Abilene, Kansas; Kermit Roosevelt, *Countercoup: The Struggle for the Control of Iran* (New York: McGraw-Hill, 1979), 2, 3, 107–08, 110; 4 December 1952 memo cited in note 71; and 5 January 1952 Steering Group paper on Iran, President's Secretary's File, Truman Papers, HSTL. For British inspiration of the overthrow of Mossadeq, see C. M. Woodhouse, *Something Ventured* (London: Granada, 1982), 104–35, who contrasts the receptivity of the Truman and Eisenhower administrations to British proposals.

Technical and military aid continued but was not as critically needed as financial aid. Ramazani, *Iran's Foreign Policy*, 247. For the work of the Point Four Program in Iran, which by the end of the Truman administration had over sixty project agreements on technical assistance ranging from water piping and poultry production to veterinary services and locust control, see William Warne, *Mission for Peace: Point 4 in Iran* (New York: Bobbs-Merrill, 1956).

In his memoirs, McGhee observes: "In the years following World War II, Americans generally accepted without question the general propositions that democracy was every nation's ultimate goal, and that it could be achieved through economic development and mass education. Development aid, as much as military assistance, was recognized as a deterrent to the spread of Communism."

McGhee judges that aid to what he calls the "Middle World," which includes the Middle East, did not produce either democratic societies or development according to schedule, perhaps because the United States, frustrated by instability, inexperience, and corruption in recipient countries, lacked the patience to sustain a commitment to long-term programs.

containment of Soviet influence through support for the sovereignty and territorial integrity of the Northern Tier states. That objective was informed by an increasingly clear conception of Turkey's unique geopolitical position as a Near Eastern *and* a European country, with an important role to play in the defense of *both* regions.

If the United States had not stood firm in Iran and not confronted Soviet pressures in Turkey during the early postwar years, it is likely that Stalin would have been tempted to expand the Soviet sphere of influence in the Near East as he did in Eastern Europe and the Far East. "The fact that this did not happen when the British were driven to reduce their commitment drastically in 1947," Alan Bullock has observed, "does not prove the fears of 1945–46 to have been exaggerated or groundless." Firmness, in short, may well have put Stalin on notice that expansion to the south could be carried out only at the risk of confrontation.[76]

Soviet actions in Iran, following as they did Soviet expansion into Eastern Europe and the Far East, superseded the bounds of what a majority of the international community was prepared to accept. What would be done to oppose similar Soviet actions elsewhere along the Middle East's Northern Tier or Europe was not clear. That is why, despite its shortcomings, something like the Truman Doctrine may have been necessary when the British began to withdraw from the region. Whether Soviet pressures on Iran and Turkey can be justified by the Soviet Union's enormous losses during World War II or by its security needs depends on one's point of view. What is striking is the extent to which, in the eyes of those whose territorial integrity was in question, U.S. interpretations of events were seen as more accurate and U.S. concerns were seen as more legitimate than the interpretations and concerns of the Soviet Union. U.S. involvement in the affairs of Iran and Turkey, finally, was encouraged by those countries because their governments wanted the United States to serve as a counterweight to the Soviet Union, whose influence was resented and feared.

If the solid reputation that President Truman enjoys among most historians today can be attributed in part to his support for Iran and Turkey early in the cold war, it is also true, as one historian has noted, that his reputation "must stand on spheres other than Palestine."[77] The Palestine problem, it must be acknowledged, provided him with little room for maneuver. Although the plight of Europe's surviving Jews clearly neces-

---

[76] Bullock, *Ernest Bevin*, 156–57.
[77] Cohen, *Palestine and the Great Powers*, 389.

sitated heroic efforts on the part of the world community, the world's reluctance to accommodate them and the survivors' need for redemption from the traumas of the Holocaust ultimately pointed to a solution that could be effected only at the expense of the Arab majority in Palestine and against the wishes of the Arab world. Rectifying one injustice by helping to perpetrate another, U.S. policy supported the creation of a Jewish state while helping to sow the seeds of future conflict.

"The price for treating the Arab view-point as unimportant," Alan Bullock has observed of British policy during the Mandate, "has continued to be paid long after the British have left the Middle East."[78] The United States, needless to say, is one of those still paying that price, a good part of which was set by the 1948 war. The Palestine refugee problem, which was not anticipated and which U.S. officials assumed would be resolved in a year or two, proved unresponsive to economic approaches. In time, many observers would recognize the need of Palestinians for a homeland as parallel to the need of the Jews, and the sympathies of the United Nations, its ranks tripled by nations of the emerging Third World, would be profoundly altered. The problem itself, meanwhile, continues to defy solution. Its complexity also suggests why the Truman administration's efforts to ameliorate it resulted only in uneasy truces and in what Dean Acheson has characterized as "a long record of failure." According to Margaret Truman, the Palestine problem in some ways was the most difficult problem of her father's entire administration. "He did his best to solve it," she wrote in 1973, "and even today he admits that his best was probably not good enough." It wasn't, although, as she also noted, "perhaps the situation was impossible, from the start."[79]

If the Palestine problem was impossible, the larger region of which it was a part presented the Truman administration with a somewhat less hopeless but nonetheless formidable problem. Although increasingly involved in the affairs of Turkey and Saudi Arabia, the United States had few resources with which to undertake new commitments elsewhere in the Middle East. As a result, U.S. officials saw collaboration with Britain as central to the policy of containment. Such collaboration, however, impeded better U.S. relations with the region's emerging nationalist forces, whose differences with Britain threatened to undermine the very policy

---

[78] Bullock, *Ernest Bevin*, 169.
[79] Transcripts, Harry Howard, Fraser Wilkins, and George McGhee Oral History Interviews, HSTL; Acheson, *Present at the Creation*, 269; Margaret Truman, *Harry S. Truman* (New York: Pocket Books, 1974), 416.

that Anglo-American ties were designed to support. Although U.S. officials recognized that British relations with the Middle East had to be put on the basis of equality and attempted themselves to establish better relations with their Middle East counterparts, the priority that the Truman administration gave to Anglo-American relations dictated the course of action. To put it simply, the administration believed that the Soviet Union constituted a much greater threat to U.S. interests than did U.S. support for the vestiges of colonialism.[80]

In Egypt, there may have been few alternatives open to U.S. officials. In Iran, however, events could have taken a different course had the administration found a basis to support Iran before the nationalization crisis. This is a point made by former U.S. ambassador Henry Grady as well as by former Assistant Secretary of State George McGhee.[81] Once the situation in Iran reached crisis proportions, Anglo-American collaboration virtually compelled Mossadeq's increasing toleration of the Tudeh Party and sealed his fate.[82] A purported "alliance" between Mossadeq and the Soviet Union provided the pretext for his overthrow, but the evidence is not convincing and appears to have been exaggerated by the man who engineered his removal. McGhee, for one, does not believe that Mossadeq ever formed such an alliance. It is also possible that the Central Intelligence Agency misconstrued the implications of a traditional Iranian tactic of playing the great powers off against one another.[83] Mossadeq's own limitations, of course, contributed to his undoing. The deteriorating situation that led Britain and the United States to seek his overthrow unquestionably was exacerbated by his atavistic fear of British influence and his inability to compromise with the AIOC.[84] But U.S. support for British policies, it must be remembered, limited Mossadeq's options and forced him into a corner, precluding a viable liberal-democratic alternative to the shah. As a result, U.S. policies cannot escape major responsibility for the impasse in Iran when President Truman left office. The Eisenhower administration, in turn, bears the responsibility for tak-

---

[80] McGhee, *Envoy to the Middle World*, 181–204, 375, 383, 385.

[81] McGhee, *Envoy to the Middle World*, 71; Grady MS, Henry Grady Papers, HSTL.

[82] Barry Rubin, *Paved With Good Intentions: The American Experience and Iran* (London: Oxford, 1980), 57–59; and Richard Cottam, *Nationalism in Iran*, updated through 1978 (Pittsburgh: Pittsburgh University Press, 1964, 1979), 221–30.

[83] Roosevelt, *Countercoup*, 2; McGhee, *Envoy to the Middle World*, 391; and chapter II, Grady MS, Grady Papers, HSTL. Ramazani notes that as the United States drew closer to Iran, the appeal of playing off the Soviet Union against the United States and Britain proved irresistible. *Iran's Foreign Policy*, 199, 227, 245–48.

[84] Cottam, *Nationalism in Iran*, 272–73; 284.

ing a step that violated the principle of sovereignty that previous administrations had pledged to uphold, the consequences of which returned to
haunt the United States a quarter-century later.

A more assertive and fair-minded role in mediating the conflict between the AIOC and Mossadeq was fraught with problems, but it might
have made a major difference for the course of Iranian history and U.S.
policy in the Middle East.[85] Instead, the State Department was discouraged from continuously redefining the international situation. As the advent of conservative governments in Britain and the United States signaled a change in the public mood, unrealistic rhetoric, once used to
mobilize public opinion in support of sensible policies, came to determine
policy, and U.S. policy in Iran became symptomatic of the process.

[85] Woodhouse, *Something Ventured,* 131, notes that if the British could have foreseen the
consequences of the overthrow of Mossadeq, they would still have done the same thing
but would have forestalled the consequences. They did not foresee the shah's capricious
and tyrannical use of his strength; nor did they foresee that the British and the Americans
would fail to keep him on a reasonable course. Rather, what they foresaw in 1953 was
more like what happened in Afghanistan between 1973 and 1980: the overthrow of a
weak monarchy by nationalist forces, which were then overthrown by indigenous communists, who were then overwhelmed by the Red Army.

11

Toward a post-colonial order:
Truman administration policies toward
South and Southeast Asia

ROBERT J. McMAHON

When Harry S. Truman suddenly entered the White House in April 1945, he faced a staggering array of problems, many of which demanded immediate attention. Certainly the future of colonial rule in South Asia and Southeast Asia did not rank very high among them. Indeed, the administration of Franklin D. Roosevelt had already agreed not to challenge the reassertion of European colonial authority in Southeast Asia and not to pressure the British on the sensitive subject of Indian independence. The untested chief executive from Independence, Missouri, had no reason to question those decisions. Nor did he have cause to question the conventional wisdom that both areas were peripheral to core U.S. interests. To be sure, during World War II the United States evinced a growing interest in the colonial territories of southern Asia; not only did those regions possess a wealth of valuable natural resources—as the events leading up to Pearl Harbor amply attest—but American strategic planners called for an enhanced U.S. military presence in the postwar Pacific. Still, as the new president prepared for the daunting tasks ahead of him, most knowledgeable observers inside and outside the government anticipated that the U.S. stake in colonial Asia would remain circumscribed indefinitely.

They could not have been more mistaken. For Truman's presidency dramatically—and probably irrevocably—transformed America's approach to the world. When Truman left office in January 1953, it was difficult indeed to distinguish vital U.S. interests from secondary ones; given the administration's expansive definition of the Soviet threat, all interests appeared suddenly critical. By then the United States had embraced what one historian has called the doctrine of national security: a concept that "postulates the interrelatedness of so many different political, economic, and military factors that developments halfway around the globe are seen to have automatic and direct impact on America's core interests."[1] A study of the Truman administration's record in South and Southeast Asia provides an instructive microcosm of the "globalization" of U.S. foreign policy during the postwar era. Areas that had traditionally been of distinctly minor interest to Washington were transformed during the Truman years into critical cold-war battlegrounds, as the United States redefined its national security interests in the face of what it considered an unprecedented threat from the Soviet Union.

From anticolonialism to "noninvolvement"

During the war years, the Roosevelt administration came to view both South Asia and Southeast Asia as part of a broader problem: the future of the colonial empires. Although the administration never adopted a consistent policy toward this vexing problem, the president and other senior officials often publicly condemned imperialism while supporting the principle of self-government for all dependent territories. Roosevelt himself characteristically took the lead on this issue, alternately chiding British, French, and Dutch officials on past colonial practices while urging more enlightened postwar policies.

As with so many American foreign policy initiatives, Roosevelt's anticolonial approach represents a blend of idealism and self-interest. His attitude reflected a genuine revulsion toward what he viewed as the often inhumane treatment of subject peoples. He expressed moral outrage on numerous occasions concerning European colonial rule, often singling out French Indochina as a particularly grievous example. "France has had the country—thirty million inhabitants—for nearly one hundred years," he stormed at one point, "and the people are worse off than they

---

[1] Daniel Yergin, *Shattered Peace: The Origins of the Cold War and the National Security State* (Boston: Houghton-Mifflin, 1978), 195–96. On the Truman administration's failure to distinguish vital from peripheral interests, see John Lewis Gaddis, *Strategies of Containment: A Critical Appraisal of Postwar American National Security Policy* (New York: Oxford University Press, 1982). For an excellent discussion of the evolving American conception of national security, see Melvyn P. Leffler, "The American Conception of National Security and the Beginnings of the Cold War, 1945–48," *American Historical Review* 89 (April 1984): 346–81.

were at the beginning."[2] At the same time, the president's concern with the plight of dependent peoples was reinforced by a fear that the indefinite preservation of imperial rule would adversely affect U.S. interests in a stable and prosperous postwar world. Imperialism, FDR often remarked, simply sowed the seeds for future war. Furthermore, the continued existence of colonial trade blocs discriminated against U.S. commercial interests and directly challenged the U.S. vision of an open postwar world.[3]

Consequently, the Roosevelt administration initially sought to prevent a return to the pre-World War II status quo in the colonial areas of Asia. The president's repeated efforts to prod the British on the emotional issue of Indian independence, his gentler but equally determined entreaties to Queen Wilhelmina on the future of Dutch rule in the East Indies, his various trusteeship schemes for French Indochina and other areas, and his commitment to postwar independence for the Philippines all reflected this important policy objective.[4]

Well before his death, however, larger political, military, and strategic concerns prompted Roosevelt to modify substantially his approach to the colonial issue. The angry European response to any plan that would compromise territorial sovereignty in the colonial areas attenuated U.S. trusteeship planning. European intransigence deeply troubled the Roosevelt administration as it threatened not only to create severe strains within the wartime alliance but to open fissures that could undermine U.S. post-

---

[2] Cordell Hull, *Memoirs*, 2 vols. (New York: Macmillan, 1948), II, 1597. For FDR's Indochina policy, see Walter LaFeber, "Roosevelt, Churchill and Indochina, 1942–1945," *American Historical Review* 80 (December 1975): 1277–95; Gary R. Hess, "Franklin D. Roosevelt and Indochina," *Journal of American History* LIX (September 1972): 353–68; Christopher Thorne, "Indochina and Anglo-American Relations, 1942–1945," *Pacific Historical Review* XLV (February 1976): 73–96.

[3] These matters are discussed at length in a superb study by William Roger Louis, *Imperialism at Bay: The United States and the Decolonialization of the British Empire, 1941–1945* (New York: Oxford University Press, 1978). For a discussion of Roosevelt's anticolonialism, see also Willard Range, *Franklin D. Roosevelt's World Order* (Athens: University of Georgia Press, 1959), 102–19; Robert J. McMahon, *Colonialism and Cold War: The United States and the Struggle for Indonesian Independence, 1945–49* (Ithaca: Cornell University Press, 1981), 53–73; Gerlof D. Homan, "The United States and the Netherlands East Indies: The Evolution of American Anticolonialism," *Pacific Historical Review* 53 (November 1984): 436–44.

[4] For a discussion of FDR's policy toward India, see Gary R. Hess, *America Encounters India, 1941–1947* (Baltimore: Johns Hopkins University Press, 1971); Christopher Thorne, *Allies of a Kind: The United States, Britain, and the War Against Japan, 1941–1945* (New York: Oxford University Press, 1978); Kenton J. Clymer, "The Education of William Phillips: Self-Determination and American Policy Toward India, 1942–45," *Diplomatic History* 8 (Winter 1984): 13–35.

war plans as well, plans that depended to a great extent on harmonious relations with the imperial powers. "We could not alienate them in the Orient," Secretary of State Cordell Hull later recalled, "and expect to work with them in Europe."[5]

Strong opposition from within the U.S. government itself placed another brake on trusteeship planning. The Navy and War Departments insisted that U.S. national security required exclusive U.S. control over the Japanese-mandated islands in the Pacific and feared that insistence on the trusteeship formula would foolishly compromise that need. As a result of these critical considerations, the Roosevelt administration retreated from its aggressive anticolonial policy. Although it never completely abandoned its interest in effecting a liberalization of colonial rule, the United States jettisoned trusteeship planning and in early 1945 quietly informed the British, French, and Dutch that it would not contest their reassertion of sovereignty in southern Asia.[6]

Consistent with Roosevelt's blunting of American anticolonial pressures, at the Potsdam Conference of July and August 1945 President Harry Truman agreed to transfer responsibility for the liberation of the Dutch East Indies and the southern half of Indochina, along with Thailand, to the Southeast Asia Command of British Admiral Lord Louis Mountbatten. With this decision, Washington in effect surrendered the enormous political leverage that it could have used to reshape postwar Southeast Asia. The prime reason for the transfer in command responsibilities was undoubtedly the stated one: The Truman administration was marshaling all available resources for what it expected to be a protracted and bloody frontal assault on the Japanese home islands. In comparison with that overarching objective, involvement in the colonial territories of Southeast Asia proved a distinctly minor concern.

At the same time, political considerations probably reinforced those strategic ones. U.S. officials were aware that nationalist movements in Indochina and the East Indies had aspired to independence for decades. Some State Department specialists feared that if U.S. forces liberated those areas from the Japanese, they could find themselves forced to mediate between the conflicting demands of native nationalists and European colonialists. Because U.S. postwar plans required friendly relations with both the colonial powers and the developing nations, such an awkward entanglement could only be detrimental to Washington's interests.[7]

[5] Hull, *Memoirs*, II, 1559.
[6] Louis, *Imperialism at Bay*, 351–77.
[7] See, for example, Department of State memorandum, "Imperialism versus an Enlightened

It must be emphasized, however, that U.S. policy makers were almost completely unprepared for the depth and intensity of the nationalist rebellions that erupted in Southeast Asia in the wake of the Japanese surrender. Within days after the Pacific War reached its final denouement, nationalists in the East Indies boldly proclaimed an independent Republic of Indonesia. Two weeks later, Vietminh guerrilla fighters in Indochina followed suit, declaring independence for a Democratic Republic of Vietnam. Although some of the more astute Asian experts in the U.S. government had warned that the war would lead to intensified nationalist sentiment in these areas, none anticipated the rapid establishment of popular and broad-based local governments. Most top U.S. policy makers, preoccupied with more pressing matters, expected the reassertion of European authority to be relatively smooth and orderly. Poor intelligence on actual conditions in Southeast Asia reinforced that complacency. At least one official report even predicted that the Indonesians would greet their returning Dutch rulers as liberators.[8]

When it quickly became apparent during the fall of 1945 that the return to imperial rule in Southeast Asia would be neither smooth nor orderly, the Truman administration adjusted its policy to meet the new realities. Intent on maintaining warm relations with its European allies and yet unwilling to alienate colonial nationalists, the administration adopted a position of strict neutrality and noninvolvement. "Hands-off" would remain the keynote of U.S. policy toward the colonial upheavals in Southeast Asia until 1947. Thus, while conceding the legal right of France and Holland as "territorial sovereigns" to restore their prewar rule, the United States periodically indicated that it would favor any steps toward eventual self-government in both Indochina and the Indies.[9]

In fact, U.S. "neutrality" was never truly impartial. As Stanley Hornbeck, the Asian expert who served as U.S. ambassador to the Netherlands during the early postwar years, later recalled: The United States "in effect attempted to support neither side and yet favored one and hoped not

Colonial Policy in the Area of the South East Asia Command," 2 January 1945, Folder: "Southeast Asia, 1946–1948, U.S. Policy," in Records of the Office of Philippine and Southeast Asian Affairs, Record Group (RG) 59, Records of the Department of State, National Archives, Washington, D.C. (hereafter referred to as PSA Records, DSR); Charles Wolf, *The Indonesian Story: The Birth, Growth and Structure of the Indonesian Republic* (New York: John Day, 1948), 16.
[8] Office of Strategic Services (OSS), "Problems Arising from a Sudden Liberation of the N.E.I.," Research and Analysis Report no. 3229, 13 August 1945, DSR.
[9] See, for example, U.S. Department of State *Bulletin* 13 (23 December 1945), 1021–22.

unduly to offend the other."[10] When Sukarno, president of the infant Republic of Indonesia, asked President Truman to serve as a mediator, the United States summarily dismissed his appeal, explaining that such a request could come only from the "territorial sovereign." Similarly, when Vietnamese President Ho Chi Minh addressed a series of personal appeals for U.S. backing to Truman, the administration ignored them, reasoning that it would be improper to exchange communications with a government it did not recognize.

Perhaps no single issue better reflects the biased character of Washington's so-called hands-off policy than its stance on the controversial issue of Lend-Lease supplies. Beginning only weeks after Tokyo's capitulation, British and French troops in Vietnam and British and Dutch troops in the Indies freely used U.S. Lend-Lease equipment, including arms, to help restore colonial authority. When reports reached the United States that U.S. matériel was being used in clashes with nationalist forces, a storm of controversy was unleashed. The Truman administration responded belatedly by requesting the removal of all U.S. insignia from this equipment. Not surprisingly, this "Pontius Pilate" gesture, as one observer derisively characterized it, did little to stem growing nationalist misgivings with the direction of U.S. sympathies.[11]

To U.S. policy makers, studied noninvolvement appeared the only workable response to the nationalist revolts in Indochina and the East Indies. Those revolts, which constituted the first major challenge to the Truman administration's plans for postwar Asia, posed an insuperable dilemma for Washington. According to the administration's first policy paper on the subject, U.S. interests would best be served by "a Far East progressively developing into a group of self-governing states—independent or with Dominion status—which would cooperate with each other and with the Western powers on a basis of mutual self-respect and friendship." European efforts to restore the old colonial order would clearly undermine that long-term goal. Would the United States, then, press its allies to make commitments to eventual native self-rule even if they proved reluctant? Anticipating this problem, the paper acknowledged that "a

[10] Stanley K. Hornbeck, "The United States and the Netherlands East Indies," *Annals of the American Academy of Political and Social Science* 255 (January 1948): 132–33.
[11] James Byrnes to Walter Foote (U.S. consul general in the East Indies), 31 October 1945, 856E.00/10–2845, DSR; memorandum by John Carter Vincent (director of the State Department's Office of Far Eastern Affairs), 22 October 1945, *Foreign Relations of the United States, 1945*, VI, 1167–68 (hereafter cited as *FRUS*); Russell H. Fifield, *Americans in Southeast Asia: The Roots of Commitment* (New York: Crowell, 1973), 109–11; Junius B. Wood, "Twilight of Empire," *Nation's Business*, March 1946, 89.

problem for the United States is to harmonize, so far as possible and without prejudice to its traditional position, its policies in regard to two objectives: increased political freedom for the Far East and the maintenance of the unity of the leading United Nations."[12]

Left unexplored was the potentially contradictory nature of these policy objectives. Given the extreme sensitivity of the decolonization question in France and Holland—two countries, after all, that were just recovering from the shattering psychological and economic effects of prolonged German occupation—how could the United States realistically expect to pressure them in Southeast Asia and still maintain their staunch support in Europe? Yet if the colonial powers refused to make concessions to legitimate nationalist demands, the United States would soon have to choose between these conflicting policy objectives. The "hands-off" posture reflected U.S. reluctance to make that choice.

At that time, the manifest tilt toward the colonial nations reflected the sober calculation at the upper reaches of the Truman administration that European interests rated a distinctly higher priority than Asian ones. The steady deterioration of U.S.-Soviet relations during this period underscored the critical importance of cultivating reliable partners in Western Europe. Pressing European priorities—political, economic, and strategic—were inextricably linked to the emerging U.S. global foreign policy, formulated in response to perceived Soviet ambitions. In comparison, Southeast Asia seemed an annoying, and potentially divisive, sideshow. Besides, U.S. policy makers had reason to believe that enlightened self-interest would eventually compel the British, French, and Dutch to adopt colonial policies that would be consonant with U.S. interests.[13]

The Truman administration hoped that the U.S. record in the Philippines might serve as a model in that regard. Moving quickly to honor Roosevelt's wartime pledge, the United States, with great fanfare, granted independence to its Asian colony on 4 July 1946. The enormous influence

---

[12] Policy paper prepared in the Department of State, "An Estimate of Conditions in Asia and the Pacific at the Close of the War and the Objectives and Policies of the United States," 22 June 1945, *FRUS*, 1945, VI, 557–58.

[13] CIA Report ORE 25–48, "The Break-up of the Colonial Empires and Its Implications for US Security," 3 September 1948, President's Secretary's Files (PSF), Harry S. Truman Papers, Harry S. Truman Library (HSTL), Independence, Missouri. For the dominance of European concerns in American policy making, see George C. Herring, "The Truman Administration and the Restoration of French Sovereignty in Indochina," *Diplomatic History* 1 (Spring 1977): 97–117; George McT. Kahin, "The United States and the Anticolonial Revolutions in Southeast Asia, 1945–1950," in Yonosuke Nagai and Akira Iriye, eds., *The Origins of the Cold War in Asia* (New York: Columbia University Press, 1977), 347–49.

that the United States maintained in the Philippines after independence—
best symbolized by the massive U.S. military bases at Clark Field and
Subic Bay and the dependent economic relationship enshrined in the Bell
Trade Act—certainly suggests that the United States neither expected nor
desired a precipitous removal of European influence from the colonial
areas. Rather, U.S. policy makers sought the gradual transfer of political
authority to responsible, West-leaning native elites. In the view of U.S.
planners, such elites would best ensure long-term political stability while
protecting legitimate Western strategic and economic interests.[14]

That objective appeared near realization in the Indies when the Dutch
and Indonesians initialed the so-called Linggadjati agreement in November 1946. The United States quickly extended congratulations to both
parties for their statesmanship. By providing for the peaceful evolution
toward native self-rule, while maintaining intact Dutch political, military, and economic influence in the islands, the agreement appeared to
conform perfectly with U.S. policy objectives for colonial Asia. In contrast with the rapidly deteriorating situation in Indochina, where the brutal French bombing of Haiphong harbor that same month signaled the
beginning of outright warfare, Linggadjati indeed seemed to represent a
hopeful and rational precedent for other colonial powers to follow. It
was, in the words of former Under Secretary of State Sumner Welles, "the
most encouraging development of recent months."[15]

Equally encouraging to the United States was the evolution of a more
liberal British colonial policy under the leadership of Prime Minister
Clement Attlee. No colonial issue had proved more divisive during the
war than that of India's future; at times it threatened to embitter Anglo-
American relations. FDR persistently urged Winston Churchill during
the early years of the war to make an explicit commitment to postwar
independence, much to the prime minister's discomfiture. Despite Roosevelt's various efforts, including the dispatch of two presidential representatives on much publicized fact-finding missions, Churchill remained
intransigent on this highly emotional subject. Recognizing the depth of
his ally's feelings about the British empire and being unwilling to jeop-

---

[14] For an analysis of U.S.-Philippine relations during the Truman administration, see Stephen R. Shalom, *The United States and the Philippines: A Study of Neocolonialism* (Philadelphia: Institute for the Study of Human Issues, 1981).

[15] U.S. Department of State *Bulletin* XV (29 December 1946), 1188; memorandum to Under Secretary of State Dean Acheson, 27 November 1946, *FRUS*, 1946, VIII, 855–56.
Welles is quoted in Everett F. Drumright (first secretary of the U.S. embassy in London)
to Richard Allen of the British Foreign Office, 27 November 1947, FO 371 F17357/1/
61, Records of the British Foreign Office, Public Records Office, Kew, England.

ardize wartime harmony for an issue that was of distinctly secondary interest to Washington, Roosevelt relaxed his pressure by 1943. Ironically, by then, critics were accusing the president, with considerable justification, of turning his back on India and acquiescing in the ill-conceived British efforts to suppress the Indian independence movement.

The Truman administration accordingly welcomed the dramatic transformation in Britain's colonial policy that followed accession of Attlee in July 1945. Committing itself almost immediately to early independence for India and other Asian possessions, Attlee's Labour government moved toward that goal, albeit haltingly, throughout 1945 and 1946. Pleased with what it viewed as a progressive and realistic policy, the Truman administration only occasionally prodded London during this period, suggesting politely that it might move more speedily and boldly. Such friendly advice, however, was invariably offered in a low-key manner; U.S. officials carefully shied away from the confrontations of the war years.[16]

Much to the delight of U.S. officials, in December 1946 Britain announced its intention to grant independence to Burma and two months later publicly committed itself to full independence for India. Those decisions conformed perfectly with the U.S. vision of a peaceful and gradual evolution of southern Asia from colonialism to self-rule. Accordingly, Secretary of State George C. Marshall promptly congratulated the British for their statesmanship. In the hope that a gracious and orderly end to nearly two centuries of the British raj might have a catalytic effect on the French and the Dutch, Washington suggested several times that the British accelerate their timetable for Indian independence. Although the rapid ascent of Mohammed Ali Jinnah's Muslim League and the sheer complexity of the subcontinent's communal problems perplexed U.S. observers, the Truman administration supported Britain's controversial decision to create the independent Muslim state of Pakistan. American diplomats rejoiced at London's decision to grant independence to India and Pakistan on 14 August 1947. Finally, it appeared, a European power had recognized its own enlightened self-interest.[17]

---

[16] Hess, *America Encounters India*, 157–82. For the evolution of British policy, see R. J. Moore, *Escape from Empire: The Attlee Government and the Indian Problem* (Oxford: Clarendon Press, 1983).

[17] Memorandum of conversation between Marshall and the British ambassador, 20 February 1947, 845.00/2–2047, DSR; memorandum prepared for Marshall by the Office of Near Eastern, South Asian, and African Affairs, 24 February 1947, 711.45/2–2447, DSR; Department of State *Bulletin*, 9 March 1947, 50; Betty Miller Unterberger, "American

Developments in Southeast Asia at this juncture evoked considerably less optimism. In Indochina, full-scale guerrilla warfare raged throughout 1947. In Indonesia, the promising Linggadjati settlement, ratified by both parties in March 1947, collapsed shortly thereafter. Unwilling to acquiesce to nationalist demands for true independence, the Dutch, like the French, inexorably gravitated toward a military solution. Ignoring U.S. entreaties, on 20 July 1947 they suddenly launched a full-scale offensive against the Republic of Indonesia, quickly capturing substantial portions of the republic's territory and presenting the United States—and the world—with a fait accompli.

The United States viewed the colonial conflicts in Southeast Asia with alarm. To be sure, neither the French-Vietminh nor the Dutch-Indonesian struggle for power preoccupied the president or his senior advisers during the early cold-war years. With tension mounting between Washington and the Kremlin over such divisive areas as Eastern Europe, Germany, Iran, and Greece, top U.S. policy makers could hardly be expected to devote much attention to hostilities in far-off Southeast Asia. But Indochina and Indonesia were inseparably linked to other, more central, concerns. The political and economic stabilization of Western Europe (one of the leading postwar priorities for the United States) was intimately connected to the tumultuous developments in that region. A report prepared for President Truman in 1947 by the newly created Central Intelligence Agency emphasized this interrelationship. "Of important concern in relation to Western European recovery," it noted, "is the existing instability in colonial (or former colonial) areas upon the resources of which several European powers (the United Kingdom, France, and the Netherlands) have hitherto been customed to depend. . . . The continuance of unsettled conditions hinders economic recovery and causes a diversion of European strength into efforts to maintain or reimpose control by force."[18]

The United States and Indonesian independence

Given those interlocking concerns, it should not be surprising that, in the wake of the Dutch military action, the United States abandoned its hands-

Views of Mohammed Ali Jinnah and the Pakistan Liberation Movement," *Diplomatic History* 5 (Fall 1981): 313–36.

[18] CIA, "Review of the World Situation as it Relates to the Security of the United States," CIA 1, 26 September 1947, PSF, Truman Papers, HSTL; War Department memorandum, "The Situation in Southeast Asia as It Affects the Availability of Strategic Raw Materials," June 1947, folder: "Southeast Asia, 1946–1948, U.S. Policy," PSA Records, DSR.

off policy by offering its services as a mediator to the two parties. After failing to prevent the Dutch "police action" with its last-minute representations, the Truman administration reasoned that U.S. mediation might at least limit the damage of that ill-conceived assault and perhaps bring both sides back to the negotiating table. Still, the United States proffered its good offices only after the governments of India and Australia had called formally for action by the United Nations Security Council. Fearing that international debate on the Dutch offensive would prove contentious, and might compromise as well its cherished neutrality stance, the United States sought to preempt United Nations intervention by its unilateral mediation offer. But Indonesian leaders, wary of Washington's decidedly pro-Dutch orientation, opted instead for United Nations consideration, in effect rejecting the U.S. overture. Its initiative rebuffed, the Truman administration quickly shifted gears; if international involvement was unavoidable, then it would try both to limit and control the nature of that involvement. The subsequent action of the Security Council in forming a Good Offices Committee whose counsel would be strictly noncompulsory, with the United States in the strategic middle position on the three-nation grouping, well accommodated that new strategy.[19]

From the formation of the Good Offices Committee in October 1947 to the establishment of a sovereign nationalist government on 27 December 1949, the United States played a major, and ultimately decisive, role in the resolution of the Dutch-Indonesian conflict. The U.S.-sponsored Renville settlement of January 1948, signed on board a U.S. naval vessel after perceptible U.S. pressure on both sides, established a framework for a settlement. Much to the dismay of U.S. diplomats, the unilateral Dutch abrogation of that internationally sanctioned agreement in late 1948 culminated in their preemptive military offensive in December of that year. In response, the United States threatened to withhold its substantial economic and military assistance to the Netherlands unless the Dutch committed themselves clearly and irrevocably to Indonesian independence. Recognizing the necessity of U.S. support, the Dutch relented. In April 1949 they agreed to transfer sovereignty within months to an independent nationalist government. Before the close of the year they proved true to their word, although persistent U.S. pressure during the final negotiating stages was necessary to remove some lingering obstacles.[20]

[19] For an extended discussion of these points, see McMahon, *Colonialism and Cold War*, 168–205; Alastair M. Taylor, *Indonesian Independence and the United Nations* (Ithaca: Cornell University Press, 1960).
[20] See McMahon, *Colonialism and Cold War*, 206 ff.

That U.S. policy smoothed the path toward Indonesian independence is indisputable. Probably more than any other factor, the application of direct U.S. economic pressure early in 1949 compelled the Dutch to relinquish their prized colony.

It must be emphasized, however, that U.S. support for the Indonesian Republic came only very slowly and with the greatest reluctance. Before the second Dutch military offensive, the actions of the Truman administration consistently bolstered the position of the Netherlands. The statements of U.S. spokesmen at the United Nations as well as the actions of U.S. representatives on the Good Offices Committee reflected that bias. Marshall Plan aid to the Netherlands, which began to flow in the spring of 1948, hopelessly compromised any remaining pretense to neutrality. "The practical effect of ECA [Economic Cooperation Administration] aid on the political conflict," noted a State Department intelligence report in April 1948, "is to strengthen the economic, political, and military position of the Netherlands in Indonesia. . . . Reactions to ECA grants by the Dutch and by the Indonesians show that this effect is clearly understood by both sides."[21]

The reason for this marked U.S. tilt toward the Netherlands lies in the European orientation of Truman's foreign policy during this period. No initiatives during the early cold-war years were more important to the administration's overall foreign policy objectives than the Marshall Plan and the North Atlantic Treaty Organization. Those programs, designed to rehabilitate and strengthen Western Europe in the face of a perceived global Soviet threat, were indispensable to the administration's developing strategy of containment. As Dutch support was important, if not crucial, to the success of both programs, the Truman administration carefully avoided any rupture with its ally over the sensitive issue of colonial relations. The United States was not uncritical of Dutch policy, of course; it repeatedly urged the negotiation of an equitable settlement with the republic, pressured the Dutch to sign the Renville agreement, and warned against resorting to force before both police actions. Still, the administration operated within certain clearly defined parameters. As the State Department instructed its representatives in Indonesia prior to the signing of the Renville agreement: The "Netherlands is [a] strong proponent [of] US policy in Europe. Dept believes that [the] stability [of the] present Dutch government would be seriously undermined if Netherlands fails to

---

[21] U.S. Department of State, Office of Intelligence and Research, Division of Research for the Far East, "Political Implications of E.C.A. Aid to Indonesia," 29 October 1948, DSR.

retain very considerable stake in NEI and the political consequences of failure [of] present Dutch Govt would in all likelihood be prejudicial to US position in Western Europe."[22]

The sharp reversal in U.S. policy following the second Dutch police action occurred when it became clear to the administration that the new offensive jeopardized those European priorities. Appalled by the unilateral Dutch violation of an agreement backed by the United States, a vocal minority in Congress threatened to cut off funds to the European Recovery Program and block passage of the Atlantic pact in retaliation. The very cornerstone of the administration's foreign policy thus appeared likely to unravel as a result of what many U.S. policy makers considered a foolishly anachronistic resort to military muscle. Consequently, Secretary of State Dean Acheson bluntly informed his Dutch counterpart in a climactic meeting that an immediate change of policy would be essential for a continuance of U.S. economic support. "Money talked," as one U.S. diplomat later recalled wryly.[23]

Asian considerations joined with these European ones to hasten the abrupt change in U.S. policy. Most important in this regard was the abject failure of the Dutch to accomplish their military objectives. Months after the offensive began, guerrilla warfare in Java and Sumatra was intensifying, with Dutch forces actually on the retreat in some areas. A report by the National Security Council (NSC) predicted that the Dutch would prove unable to pacify the archipelago and in the process would likely strengthen the appeal of radical elements within the nationalist movement. Given the demonstrably moderate character of the Republic of Indonesia government, the NSC paper recommended that the administration support Indonesian independence as "the only channel lying between polarization and Stalinization." Recognizing that support for native self-rule would be "a difficult course," the NSC nonetheless judged it necessary in order to develop "an effective counterforce to communism in the Far East leading eventually to the emergence of [Southeast Asia] as an integral part of the free world."[24]

[22] Robert Lovett (acting secretary of state) to Frank P. Graham (U.S. representative on the Good Offices Committee), 31 December 1947, *FRUS*, 1947, VI, 1099–1101.
[23] Howard P. Jones, *Indonesia: The Possible Dream* (New York: Harcourt Brace Jovanovich), 111–12.
[24] NSC 51, "U.S. Policy Toward Southeast Asia," 29 March 1949, P&O 092 Asia, Planning and Operations Division Files, Modern Military Branch, National Archives.

The evolution of U.S. policy toward Indochina

Ironically, a similar blend of European and Asian concerns, shaped, as in Indonesia, by the administration's global strategy for containing the Soviet Union, prompted a sharply differentiated response to the Vietnamese struggle for independence. Until mid-1947 U.S. officials tended to view both of Southeast Asia's colonial conflicts in broadly comparable terms. With the advent of the first Dutch police action, however, U.S. policy toward the two struggles began to diverge markedly. The Truman administration inserted itself actively into the Indonesian imbroglio at that juncture while clinging to its hands-off posture in Indochina. Cautious optimism toward the prospects for a settlement in the Indies helps explain the adoption of an active U.S. policy toward that dispute; senior officials were far less sanguine about the possibility of a breakthrough in the French-Vietminh war. As Secretary of State Marshall conceded in a cable to the U.S. embassy in Paris early in 1947, the United States simply had "no solution of [the] problem to suggest."[25] In addition, United Nations consideration of the Indonesian question added a significant new dimension to that conflict. With the issue suddenly thrust before the world community, continuing American noninvolvement became increasingly untenable. By exercising its veto in the Security Council, France could, of course, easily circumvent any proposed international mediation of its colonial difficulties.[26]

The fact that Ho Chi Minh and many of his key advisers were avowed communists greatly exacerbated the U.S. policy dilemma in Indochina. Although U.S. diplomats privately acknowledged on numerous occasions that the French, like the Dutch, were guilty of "a dangerously outmoded colonial outlook and method," support for a communist-led nationalist movement was virtually unthinkable. To be sure, some Asian specialists in the State Department bravely advanced the thesis that Ho might emerge as an "Asian Tito." But such speculation, however prescient it might appear in retrospect, never was seriously considered by top administration planners. "It should be obvious," Marshall emphasized in a review of U.S. policy options, "that we are not interested in seeing colonial empire administrations supplanted by [a] philosophy and political organi-

[25] Marshall to the embassy in France, 3 February 1947, *FRUS*, 1947, VI, 67–68.
[26] For a comparison of U.S. policy toward Indochina and Indonesia during these years, see Evelyn Colbert, "The Road Not Taken: Decolonization and Independence in Indonesia and Indochina," *Foreign Affairs* 51 (April 1973): 608–28; McMahon, *Colonialism and Cold War*, 313–15.

zation directed from and controlled by [the] Kremlin." Implicitly, he and other leading officials assumed that all local communists were allied with, and served the interests of, the Soviet Union.[27]

With the intensification of the cold war in the late 1940s, the Truman administration desperately explored alternatives in Indochina. Its dilemma proved daunting. The "Asian Tito" option never attracted high-level support; at the same time, official approval of France's misguided efforts to return to the days of imperial glory appealed to only the mc st hopelessly uncritical Francophiles in the State Department. Yet most administration planners viewed some settlement as essential. The colonial war in Indochina was draining France's economy, thereby significantly curtailing its contribution to European recovery. U.S. officials often acknowledged with embarrassment, moreover, that Marshall Plan support was indirectly underwriting France's attempted suppression of Vietnamese nationalism.[28]

In the absence of any other clear alternatives, by early 1949 the Truman administration gradually acquiesced in France's so-called Bao Dai solution. That effort to create a non-communist nationalist alternative under the aegis of Bao Dai, emperor of Annam under the former French and Japanese colonial regimes, raised modest hopes in Washington. Those hopes were tempered, of course, by the realization that the much-maligned playboy emperor was a weak reed upon which to base a policy. Nonetheless, his emergence seemed to presage a softening in France's hard-line colonial policy, and by this time Washington was convinced that a French military victory was unattainable.

As a result, the Truman administration swallowed its misgivings and publicly backed the Elysée Agreement of June 1949, which called, albeit vaguely, for the transfer of authority to a nationalist government in Vietnam under Bao Dai's leadership. On 7 February 1950, the United States formally recognized the puppet Bao Dai government, along with the Kingdoms of Laos and Cambodia, as independent states within the French Union. The State Department, perhaps in an act of wishful thinking, called U.S. recognition "consistent with our fundamental policy of giving sup-

[27] Marshall to the embassy in France, 3 February 1947, *FRUS*, 1947, VI, 67–68. For a discussion of State Department consideration of the "Asian Tito" option, see Gary R. Hess, "The First American Commitment in Indochina: The Acceptance of the 'Bao Dai Solution,' 1950," *Diplomatic History* 2 (Fall 1978): 334–36, 342–43; Robert M. Blum, *Drawing the Line: The Origin of the American Containment Policy in East Asia* (New York: W. W. Norton, 1982), 118–23.

[28] Those dilemmas are clearly set forth in the Department of State's Policy Statement for Indochina, 27 September 1948, *FRUS*, 1948, VI, 43–49.

port to the peaceful and democratic evolution of dependent peoples toward self-government and independence."[29] On 8 May, the United States quietly announced the extension of military assistance to Bao Dai—and the French—beginning an ultimately tragic involvement in Indochina. The next month, after the outbreak of war in Korea, the Truman administration deepened that commitment.[30]

The evolution of the Truman administration's policy toward Indochina from strict noninvolvement to unconditional support for the French can be understood only within the context of a deepening cold war. As relations with the Soviet Union deteriorated steadily during the early postwar years, Truman and his advisers groped for an explanation of Soviet behavior. By late 1946, they became convinced that the ambitions of America's former partner in the Grand Alliance were limitless and that the threat posed to U.S. security by that inherently expansionistic state and its revolutionary ideology was unprecedented. In response, for the first time in its history the United States sought to formulate and execute an integrated global foreign policy. The intensification of the cold war in Europe during 1948 and 1949—with the Soviet coup in Czechoslovakia, the Berlin crisis, and the formation of NATO and the Warsaw Pact—heightened fears of outright military confrontation between the two superpowers. The successful detonation of a Soviet atomic bomb in mid-1949, followed quickly by the decisive victory of Mao Tse-tung's communists in China, underscored for Truman administration planners the gravity of the international situation.[31]

Viewed against that backdrop, the continuing hostilities in Indochina took on new significance. Leading U.S. policy makers increasingly saw the French effort there as part of the West's worldwide struggle to contain communist expansion. That Ho Chi Minh's forces had indigenous roots was incontestable but also largely irrelevant. What was important was the communist character of the nationalist movement—and the firm resolve of U.S. officials in the wake of Mao's shattering successes to pre-

[29] Memorandum from the Department of State to the French Foreign Office, 6 June 1949, *FRUS*, 1949, VII, Part 1, 39–45; *American Foreign Policy, 1950–1955: Basic Documents*, 2 vols. (Washington, D.C.: U.S. Government Printing Office, 1957), II, 2386; Fifield, *Americans in Southeast Asia*, 121–27; Hess, "The First American Commitment in Indochina," 336–48; George C. Herring, *America's Longest War: The United States and Vietnam, 1950–1975* (New York: Wiley, 1979), 12–15.

[30] For a detailed account of the complex legislative origins of the Truman administration's initial assistance program to the French, see Blum, *Drawing the Line*, 125 ff.

[31] These points are developed at length in many of the standard works on the origins of the cold war. See, for example, Yergin, *Shattered Peace*; Thomas G. Paterson, *On Every Front: The Making of a Cold War* (New York: W. W. Norton, 1979).

vent yet another triumph for the forces of international communism. "If Southeast Asia is also swept by communism," an NSC paper of December 1949 warned, "we shall have suffered a major political rout, the repercussions of which will be felt throughout the world. . . . It is now clear that Southeast Asia is the target for a coordinated offensive directed by the Kremlin."[32]

The tendency to view all local disorder through the prism of East-West conflict was reinforced by the outbreak of war on the Korean peninsula in June 1950. Although historians still debate the amazingly complex origins of that conflict, the Truman administration determined with remarkable alacrity that it represented a new stage in the aggressive designs of a Soviet-directed world communist movement. Consequently, only three days after the fighting broke out in Korea, Truman publicly announced four major decisions: U.S. forces would be sent to Korea; the U.S. Seventh Fleet would be dispatched to the Taiwan Strait; and increased aid would be provided to help the French combat the Vietminh and to help the Philippine government suppress the Huk insurgency. The implication of Truman's decisions is unmistakable. The enemy in Korea, Taiwan, Indochina, and the Philippines, in the administration's view, was the same: a unified, Kremlin-directed communist movement. Subtleties and shadings were lost in the rush to adopt a more active policy. The cold war in Asia had been joined.[33]

U.S. relations with South Asia

The inclination to view Asian affairs within an East-West context, a tendency greatly accentuated by the victory of the Chinese communists and the onset of the Korean War, also exerted a profound influence on U.S. relations with South Asia. Initially, the Truman administration accorded

---

[32] For the full text of this important statement of policy, NSC 48/2, dated 30 December 1949, see *FRUS, 1949*, VII, Part 2, 1215–20. Among the most incisive studies of the evolution of American strategy in the Far East during this period are John L. Gaddis, "Korea in American Politics, Strategy, and Diplomacy, 1945–50," in Nagai and Iriye, eds., *The Origins of the Cold War in Asia*, 277–98; Thomas H. Etzold, "The Far East in American Strategy, 1948–1951," in Etzold, ed., *Aspects of Sino-American Relations Since 1784* (New York: New Viewpoints, 1978), 102–26; William W. Stueck, Jr., *The Road to Confrontation: American Policy Toward China and Korea* (Chapel Hill: University of North Carolina Press, 1981); Michael S. Schaller, "Securing the Great Crescent: Occupied Japan and the Origins of Containment in Southeast Asia," *Journal of American History* 69 (September 1982): 392–414.

[33] For the latest scholarly assessments of the Korean War and its origins, see Bruce Cumings, ed., *Child of Conflict: The Korean-American Relationship, 1943–1953* (Seattle: University of Washington Press, 1983).

a low priority to the new nations of India and Pakistan. More pressing international flash points left Truman and his advisers little time to spend on those struggling young countries. The subcontinent, after all, had long been within the British sphere of influence, and, in the view of many U.S. experts, would probably remain there indefinitely. Even during the immediate postpartition period, however, American officials invariably measured the two new nations in terms of their potential contribution to larger cold-war priorities.[34]

Judged by that critical litmus test, India attracted far more attention than Pakistan. U.S. officials routinely speculated that India, with its vigorous leadership, rich natural resources, and vast size and population, was destined to play a major role on the world stage. They viewed Pakistan, in sharp contrast, as an anomalous creation whose ultimate survival was much in doubt. The U.S. chargé in Karachi reported in October 1947 that Pakistan's problems were so overwhelming they had already "assumed such proportions as to threaten the very existence of the new State."[35] Some American specialists considered Pakistan's eventual absorption into India to be a strong possibility.[36]

At the same time, other officials speculated that Pakistan might have considerable strategic value. That view, which found resonance especially in the military and intelligence communities, was based on two principal considerations: Pakistan's contiguous border with the Soviet Union, and hence the desirability of establishing air bases and intelligence-gathering facilities there, and Pakistan's proximity to the Persian Gulf, and hence its potential role in the defense of Middle East oil fields.[37]

The predominant view within the administration during the late 1940s, however, held that India was by far the larger and more valuable diplo-

[34] CIA Report SR-21, "India-Pakistan," 16 September 1948, CIA Reports File, Truman Papers, HSTL; Report by the State-Army-Navy-Air Force Coordinating Committee for the Near and Middle East, SANACC 360/14, "Appraisal of U.S. National Interests in South Asia," 1 April 1949, 890.00/8–2949, DSR; "The Position of the United States with Respect to South Asia," 24 January 1951, FRUS, 1951, VI, part 2, 1651–52; JCS 1992/48, 12 January 1951, G-3 092 Asia TS, Records of the Army Staff, RG 319, Modern Military Branch.

[35] Colonel N. R. Hoskot to the Department of the Army, 24 April 1948, 845F.00/4–2448, DSR.

[36] Hoskot to the Department of the Army, 14 February 1948, 845F.00/2–1448, DSR.

[37] Memorandum from the Joint Chiefs of Staff, 24 March 1949, Appendix C to SANACC 360/14, 890.00/8–2949, DSR; memorandum from Stephen Spingarn (of the White House staff) to Clark Clifford, 23 August 1949, Folder: "International Affairs—India," Stephen J. Spingarn Papers, HSTL; memorandum from Spingarn to Clifford, 25 October 1949, ibid.; "Notes on Pakistan," 26 October 1949, ibid.

matic prize in South Asia. The deepening cold war and the imminent success of the communist revolution in China tended to reinforce such thinking. "India," the CIA concluded in July 1949, was "a major Asiatic power" and was "alone in a position to compete with Chinese Communism for hegemony in Southeast Asia."[38] Leading administration planners indeed hoped that India would soon emerge not only as the principal ideological rival to China but as a bulwark against further communist expansion on the Asian mainland.

With the steady collapse of the Chinese Nationalists providing a dramatic backdrop, Indian Prime Minister Jawaharlal Nehru made his first official visit to the United States in October 1949. "There is no personality more important for the United States today than Pandit Nehru," wrote influential columnist Dorothy Thompson. "Every American word and gesture during Mr. Nehru's visit," she predicted, "will have repercussions from the Middle East to East and South Asia and Southern Africa. It is a diplomatic event of the most far reaching consequences."[39] Many U.S. policy makers agreed; the establishment of the People's Republic of China earlier that month, they reasoned, rendered India crucial to the containment of communism in Asia. "Mr. Nehru," emphasized Secretary of State Acheson in a memorandum for the president, "is today and will probably continue to be for some time the dominant political figure in Asia."[40] Philip Jessup, Acheson's close adviser, called Nehru "outstandingly the most vital and influential person for the accomplishment of U.S. objectives in Asia."[41] Although some policy makers sought to temper official expectations with the caveat that Nehru's trip was primarily intended as an educational one, the deceptively attractive notion that India now was the "cornerstone" or "fulcrum" of U.S. policy in Asia was difficult to suppress.[42]

Given such unrealistically lofty expectations, it is difficult to judge the Nehru visit as anything less than a serious setback for U.S. plans. Although Nehru's meetings with Truman, Acheson, and other leading

---

[38] CIA Intelligence Memorandum No. 197, "Implications for U.S. Security of Developments in Asia," 25 July 1949, CIA Reports File, Modern Military Branch.

[39] Quoted in State Department Briefing Memorandum, 3 October 1949, 845.002/10–549, DSR.

[40] Memorandum from Acheson to Truman, 18 August 1949, 845.002/8–1849, DSR.

[41] Memorandum by Jessup, 29 August 1949, 845.002/9–1449, DSR.

[42] Memorandum from George C. McGhee (assistant secretary of state for Near Eastern, South Asian, and African Affairs) to Dean Rusk (deputy under secretary of state), 26 September 1949, 845.002/9–2649, DSR; State Department Briefing Memorandum, 3 October 1949, 845.002/10–549, DSR.

American officials were unfailingly courteous, they yielded little of substance. Instead, they revealed quite starkly that on numerous critical international issues Nehru's views diverged fundamentally from those of the Americans. Nehru refused to budge from his policy of nonalignment, disagreed with his hosts on the nature of the Soviet threat, revealed his intention to recognize the new communist government in China at the earliest possible opportunity, and insisted that colonialism, not communism, was the gravest danger to world peace.[43]

On these and other issues U.S.-Indian relations foundered in the aftermath of Nehru's American tour. Reporting from New Delhi in April 1950, Ambassador Loy Henderson decried the "steadily increasing" Indian "feelings of unfriendliness" toward the United States. Not only were there major philosophical differences about foreign policy, but also he noted India's deep resentment about Washington's unwillingness to provide it with sufficient levels of economic assistance. India's friendly relations with China, its muted criticism of the Soviet Union, its lack of support for the United States during the United Nations debates on the Korean War, its uncooperative policies toward Indochina and Japan, and the tangled financial aid question all managed to heighten tensions between the two democracies. The same U.S. officials who had expressed so much hope for India on the eve of the Nehru visit could express little more than dismay in the months following the outbreak of war in Korea. The steady deterioration in relations between Washington and New Delhi so alarmed the British Foreign Office that in September 1950 a senior British diplomat remarked to his American counterparts that U.S.-Indian differences "constituted a running sore."[44]

Pakistan, in marked contrast, largely supported U.S. positions on world affairs during this period. Prime Minister Liaquat Ali Khan visited Washington in May 1950 (after the United States persuaded him to cancel a scheduled visit to Moscow) and proclaimed Pakistan's resolve "to throw all her weight to help the maintenance of stability in Asia." Although the

---

[43] Memorandum of conversation between Truman and Nehru, 13 October 1949, *FRUS*, 1949, VI, 1750–52; memorandum of conversation between Nehru and Acheson, 12 October 1949, 845.021/10–1249, DSR; memorandum of conversation among Nehru, Acheson, Jessup, and others, 19 October 1949, *FRUS*, 1949, VI, 1752–56; Howard Donovan (Chargé, New Delhi) to the State Department, 26 October 1949, 845.002/10–2659, DSR; Sarvepalli Gopal, *Jawaharlal Nehru: A Biography*, vol. II, *1947–1956* (Cambridge, Mass.: Harvard University Press, 1979), 59–64.

[44] Henderson to the State Department, 12 April 1950, *FRUS*, 1950, V, 1461–63; Acheson to the U.S. embassy in India, 21 April 1950, ibid., 1464–66; Record of Informal U.S.-U.K. Discussions, 18 September 1950, ibid., 202–03.

trip had been planned hastily in an effort to balance Nehru's visit, U.S. policy makers found themselves quite favorably impressed with the Pakistani leader's positions on major international issues and especially with his implied inclination to align his nation with the West. The contrast with Nehru's performance—as Liaquat well understood—could not have been much sharper. Unlike India, moreover, Pakistan supported the United States during the United Nations debates over Korea and during the subsequent negotiation of a Japanese peace treaty, thus serving to highlight even more starkly the differences between the two countries' international orientation.[45]

By 1951, a major test of the developing relationship between Washington and Karachi had emerged: Pakistan's interest in purchasing large quantities of U.S. military equipment. The Pakistanis were insistent on this point. In one emotional exchange with a State Department representative, a Pakistani diplomat exclaimed that the failure to acquire arms from the West would lead to grave problems for his government and might eventually force Pakistan to turn away from the West.[46]

The Truman administration found itself deeply divided on this question. The arguments against a favorable response to the Pakistanis were compelling: A major arms deal would inevitably alienate India which, despite its uncooperative policies, was still by far the larger, stronger, and more influential power; moreover, such a deal could easily jeopardize Washington's neutrality on the increasingly acrimonious Kashmir dispute. In addition, a large wheat loan to India in June 1951 and the appointment of the popular and energetic Chester Bowles as ambassador to India later that year seemed to signify a thaw in U.S.-Indian relations. At the same time, there were some equally important geopolitical factors to weigh. Pakistan had expressed its unequivocal desire to cooperate with the West—a tempting offer, given the anti-Western inclinations of so many

---

[45] Memorandum from McGhee to Acheson, 17 October 1949, 845.002/10–1749, DSR; memorandum from Acting Secretary of State James E. Webb to Truman, 31 October 1949, State Department Correspondence folder, Confidential File, Truman Papers, HSTL; memorandum from Acheson to Truman, 4 November 1949, Official File 48-T, ibid.; Department of State Policy Statement on Pakistan, 3 April 1950, *FRUS*, 1950, V, 1490–99; Avra Warren (U.S. Ambassador in Pakistan) to the State Department, 18 August 1950, ibid., 1501–02.

[46] Memorandum of conversation between Ambassador M.A.H. Ispahani and Donald D. Kennedy (director of the Office of South Asian Affairs), 18 October 1951, ibid., 2227–28; memorandum Frank C. Nash (assistant secretary of defense for international security affairs) to Secretary of Defense Robert Lovett, 23 October 1951, CD 092 (Pakistan), Records of the Office of the Secretary of Defense, Office of the Administrative Secretary, RG 330, Modern Military Branch.

Third World areas. Furthermore, as noted earlier, certain important elements within the U.S. government had long held that Pakistan potentially represented a major strategic asset. Air Force Chief of Staff Hoyt Vandenberg told Bowles in September 1951, before Bowles left for New Delhi, "We are going to give you some trouble out there in India because we have our eyes on bases in Pakistan." The administration's growing concentration on the defense of the Middle East at this time served to underscore Pakistan's strategic value.[47]

The latter factor was crucial. By early 1951, with a hot war raging in Korea and crises brewing in Iran and Egypt, the defense of the Middle East was rapidly emerging as a high-level priority for the Truman administration, and Pakistan's possible role in such a defense was assuming singular importance. On 2 April 1951, during a meeting in London with British Foreign Office representatives, Assistant Secretary of State for Near Eastern, South Asian, and African Affairs George C. McGhee noted that Pakistan's contribution "would probably be the decisive factor in ensuring defense of the area." The British agreed, indicating their belief that the defense of the Near East was "probably not possible without the effective support of Pakistan." Both American and British officials applauded Pakistan's well-trained army, martial tradition, strategic location, and eagerness to cooperate with the West. On 2 May, McGhee underscored these points during a meeting at the Pentagon. "With Pakistan, the Middle East could be defended," he stated flatly. "Without Pakistan, I don't see any way to defend the Middle East."[48]

Accordingly, throughout 1951 and 1952 the Truman administration wrestled with various plans for ensuring the defense of the Middle East, almost all of which included some form of Pakistani participation. After the proposed Middle East Command met determined resistance in late 1951 from Egypt and certain other Arab states, U.S.-sponsored regional defense efforts shifted to the so-called Middle East Defense Organization (MEDO). Well aware that the price of Pakistani cooperation would likely

[47] Letter from Bowles to McGhee, 8 November 1951, Folder 273, Box 98, Chester Bowles Papers, Yale University Library, New Haven, Conn.; memorandum from Bowles to Acheson, 6 December 1951, FRUS, 1951, VI, part 2, 2191–2202; Selig S. Harrison, "Case History of a Mistake," New Republic, 10 August 1959, 13.

[48] "Agreed Conclusions and Recommendations of the Conference of Middle Eastern Chiefs of Mission," Istanbul, 14–21 February 1951, FRUS, 1951, V, 59; Admiral Robert B. Carney (commander in chief, U.S. Naval Forces in the Eastern Atlantic and Mediterranean) and other commanders in chief in the Middle East to the British Chiefs of Staff and the U.S. Joint Chiefs of Staff, 13 March 1951, ibid., 94–95; memorandum of informal U.S.-U.K. discussions, 2–3 April 1951, ibid., 104–10; minutes of discussion at a State Department-Joint Chiefs of Staff meeting, 2 May 1951, ibid., 114–20.

be U.S. military assistance, in March 1952 the Defense Department entered into preliminary negotiations with Pakistani representatives regarding the feasibility of such an arms deal. The Truman administration came to an end, however, before plans for a MEDO were completed and before plans for a military assistance pact with Pakistan had advanced beyond the talking stage. Once again, fears of an adverse Indian reaction gave the administration pause in consummating the controversial arms deal.[49]

Frustrations in Southeast Asia

The Truman administration's failed efforts to enlist India in the containment umbrella and its flirtation with a Pakistani arms pact were mirrored in its search for reliable partners in Southeast Asia. In Indonesia, as in India, that search proved counterproductive. Following independence, relations between Washington and Djakarta appeared to be based on a firm foundation; certainly U.S. support for Indonesian independence, although belated, created an immense reservoir of goodwill. The rapid U.S. provision of much-needed economic, technical, and military assistance to the new government seemed to foreshadow an era of deepening ties between the United States and Southeast Asia's largest country. The Truman administration's interest in Indonesia was quite explicit, as Acheson informed Truman in January 1950: "The loss of Indonesia to the Communists would deprive the United States of an area of the highest political, economic and strategic importance."[50]

Those cold-war considerations were of course accentuated after the onset of the Korean War. Consequently, the United States sought on various occasions to enlist Indonesia within a contemplated U.S. alliance system in Asia. When the administration began discussing the prospects for a Pacific defense pact in 1950, Indonesia was regularly touted as a possible participant. Unfortunately for U.S. planners, Indonesia's determination to pursue a self-styled "active and independent" foreign policy clashed with any plans for aligning it with the West. Thus in October

---

[49] Harrison, "Case History of a Mistake," 14–15; G. W. Choudhury, *India, Pakistan, Bangladesh, and the Major Powers: Politics of a Divided Subcontinent* (New York: Free Press, 1975), 80–81; memorandum of conversation between Lovett and Mir Laik Ali, adviser to the Pakistani Minister of Defense, 23 July 1952, CD 092 (Pakistan), Records of the Office of the Secretary of Defense, Modern Military Branch; memoranda of conversations in New Delhi and elsewhere between Ambassador Bowles and Indian officials, 20 October 1951–20 March 1953, Folder 392, Box 104, Bowles Papers.

[50] Memorandum from Acheson to Truman, 9 January 1950, *FRUS*, 1950, VI, 964–66.

1950 Indonesian officials informed the United States that they were unwilling to accept military assistance under the Mutual Defense Assistance Program, because such aid would clearly imply taking sides in the cold war. In a particularly ill-conceived initiative, the United States tried nonetheless to conclude just such a pact with Indonesia in December 1951 only to have a preliminary agreement rejected as a violation of fundamental nationalist values. As a result of this incident, the West-leaning government of Prime Minister Sukiman, the most pro-American of Indonesia's early leaders, was toppled from power and nationalist resentment of U.S. machinations rose sharply. Coupled with the Truman administration's deference to the Netherlands on the supercharged issue of West New Guinea's ultimate disposition, the fall of the Sukiman cabinet increasingly strained the relations between Washington and Djakarta.[51]

The continuing quagmire in Indochina, meanwhile, proved even more disheartening to the Truman administration. It faced an unusually cruel predicament there. Without U.S. assistance the French position was likely to collapse; as a result, the communists would gain a foothold in Southeast Asia. Nearly all senior U.S. policy makers viewed this prospect as constituting a decisive cold-war defeat. Consequently, the administration inexorably deepened its commitment to the French. Following the initial aid decision of May 1950, Truman announced stepped-up deliveries, and he increased aid after the Korean War began. By late 1950 the United States had committed $133 million in aid to the French. Military reverses led the Truman administration in June 1952 to advance an additional $150 million in military assistance. Yet, despite this substantial U.S. commitment, the administration remained pessimistic about ultimate French prospects for concluding the war successfully. Only promises of increased autonomy for Vietnamese nationalists could reverse the unfavorable trend, U.S. officials believed, but the French proved absolutely intransigent on that point. Acheson conceded that the United States might ultimately "lose out" if it supported France's "old-fashioned colonial attitudes," but he was unwilling to exert pressure on a key European ally. Not only did the French often threaten to withdraw from Indochina entirely when subjected to what they viewed as unwarranted U.S. meddling, but their support was critical to the high-priority European Defense Community initiative, demonstrating once again how European interests

[51] *FRUS*, 1951, VI, part 1, 729 ff; Herbert Feith, *The Decline of Constitutional Democracy in Indonesia* (Ithaca: Cornell University Press, 1962), 198–207.

could override Asian interests. Thus Truman left office with the United States deeply embroiled in a colonial conflict, supporting approximately 40 percent of the French effort, with the military prospects poor, the political prospects worse, and the chances of a complete collapse growing daily.[52]

Conclusion

On the most basic level, Truman left to his successors a legacy of deepening American involvement in the affairs of South and Southeast Asia. The growing American stake in those regions was, by the time the Korean War had ended, inseparably linked to America's global effort to contain Soviet communist expansion. Given the veritable explosion in U.S. economic power and perceived strategic needs during World War II, some wider concern with developments in colonial Asia was probably inevitable. Political unrest and economic instability in those areas, moreover, had a direct and immediate bearing on the economic rehabilitation of Western Europe, a policy goal of commanding significance to the United States. It was the cold war, however, that lent force and urgency to U.S. diplomatic objectives in South and Southeast Asia. And it was the cold war that hopelessly distorted U.S. perceptions of the revolutionary forces that were rapidly transforming those regions.

Viewed on its own terms, the Truman administration's record in South and Southeast Asia is a mixed one. Despite its high hopes and vigorous efforts, the administration clearly proved unable to construct bastions of anticommunism in those regions. Nor with a widening conflict raging in Indochina can it be said that the administration achieved the order and stability that it so desperately sought. Yet Truman and his advisers could boast that none of the newly emerging nations of South and Southeast Asia—Vietnam excluded—had embraced communism, and none of those nations was gravitating toward the Soviet bloc. The neutralist inclinations of India and Indonesia deeply disturbed U.S. policy makers, to be sure; it can be argued, however, that both nations remained on friendlier terms with Washington than with Moscow and Peking. As Truman's

---

[52] U.S. Congress, Senate, *Review of the World Situation: 1949–1950, Hearings Held in Executive Session Before the Committee on Foreign Relations* (Washington: U.S. Government Printing Office, 1974), 266–68, 292–93; NSC 124/2, 25 June 1952, *The Pentagon Papers* (Senator Gravel Edition), 4 vols. (Boston: Beacon Press, 1971), I, 385–86; Herring, *America's Longest War*, 13–23.

tenure in office came to a close, the prestige and influence of the United States were substantially higher than those of the Soviet Union or China in nearly all the newly independent nations of southern Asia. Using the barometer of cold-war loyalties, then, the administration's record can perhaps be called moderately successful.

A broader perspective, however, is in order here. The eruption of nationalist movements in South and Southeast Asia following World War II was a historical development of truly epic proportions. The process of decolonization, in which the peoples of southern Asia took such a leading role, must rank among the most profound and far-reaching developments in modern world history. Certainly, Asian nationalist stirrings created numerous new problems and opportunities for U.S. policy makers. Consequently, one critical element in any overall assessment of the Truman administration's policies in southern Asia must be its response to the nationalist challenge.

Viewed from that perspective, those policies appear both ineffective and short-sighted. Certainly, one can argue that the administration deserves credit for helping to bring about the relatively peaceful transition from colonialism to independence. That so many nations could achieve independence within so short a period of time and with so little bloodshed is at least in part a tribute to the constructive role played by the United States. U.S. support for Indonesia's independence is perhaps its most striking accomplishment in this regard, although the Truman administration's quiet role in helping to speed independence for India, Pakistan, Burma, and Ceylon should not be overlooked.

The subordination of all other diplomatic goals by 1949–50 to a global geopolitical strategy for containing the Soviet Union, however, largely negated those positive accomplishments. Thus by the early 1950s, efforts to align India and Indonesia with the West led to strained relations with both new countries. The administration's consideration of a military assistance pact with Pakistan promised to cement relations with the world's largest Muslim nation but only at an enormous cost. And in Indochina the administration had committed itself to a cause that increasingly appeared doomed.

These policy failures stemmed from a common cause: a tendency to overlook the historical roots of local and regional developments in the rush to strengthen America's global defense posture vis-à-vis the Soviet Union. The revolutionary changes in southern Asia were thus seen through the invariably distorting lens of East-West conflict. Perhaps the supreme irony of the Truman administration's efforts to "contain" southern Asia is that they ultimately contributed to the region's instability, thus unwittingly undermining the very diplomatic goal that they were designed to achieve.

12

Occupied Japan and the cold war in Asia

JOHN W. DOWER

When Harry Truman succeeded Franklin Roosevelt as president in April 1945, the United States had just begun the systematic, low-level saturation bombing of Japanese cities. In the third month of his administration, the new president received word of the nuclear test at Alamogordo, thought immediately of biblical prophesies of the apocalypse, and immediately approved the use of the atomic bombs against Japan. As he phrased it in his belatedly discovered "Potsdam diary," written at the time he learned about the successful test, the Japanese were "savages, ruthless, merciless and fanatic." In a personal letter written a few days after Hiroshima and Nagasaki had been destroyed, the president explained that "when you have to deal with a beast you have to treat him as a beast." Following Japan's capitulation in mid-August 1945, the United States occupied the country as the overwhelmingly dominant force in a nominally "Allied" occupation and proceeded to initiate a rigorous policy of "demilitarization and democratization."[1]

Less than five years later, the Truman administration had identified Japan as the key to the balance of power in Asia—and Asia as capable of tipping the global balance in the direction of the Soviet Union. Before the

---

[1] On the Japanese as savages, see "Today Has Been a Historical One: Harry S. Truman's Diary of the Potsdam Conference" (introduced by Eduard Mark), *Diplomatic History* 4 (Summer 1980): 324; also Robert H. Ferrell, ed., *Off the Record: The Private Papers of Harry S. Truman* (New York: Harper & Row, 1980), 55–56. Truman's comment on having "to deal with a beast" was made in a letter dated 11 August 1945 and is quoted in Barton J. Bernstein, "The Atomic Bomb and American Foreign Policy: The Route to Hiroshima," in Barton J. Bernstein, ed., *The Atomic Bomb: The Critical Issues* (Boston: Little, Brown, 1976), 113. The policy of low-level incendiary bombing of Japanese urban areas began with the devastating air raid against Tokyo on 9–10 March 1945 and had been extended to more than sixty Japanese cities by the time the atomic bombs were dropped.

outbreak of the Korean War on 25 June 1950, Okinawa had been taken over as the key U.S. nuclear base in the Far East, the runways on airfields in Japan were being lengthened to accommodate the newest U.S. heavy bombers, policy toward occupied Japan had shifted from reform to economic reconstruction, plans were in the air to promote Japanese production of capital goods including military items for export, and the United States was urging Japan to rearm. In addition, policy makers in Washington were in general agreement on the urgent need to integrate Japan and Southeast Asia with one another economically and militarily, as part of a "great crescent" of anti-communist containment in Asia. As a number of contemporary observers noted, some wryly and some bitterly, the Americans seemed to be dusting off Japan's plans of the 1930s and early 1940s to integrate the southern areas in a great "co-prosperity sphere," which had brought World War II to Asia in the first place.

In September 1951, the United States and forty-seven other nations signed a nonrestrictive and relatively brief treaty of peace with Japan in San Francisco, thereby (pending ratification by home governments) formally ending the state of war between the Allied Powers and Japan. Simultaneously, as the essential quid pro quo for this "generous" peace treaty on the part of the United States, a bilateral United States-Japan Mutual Security Agreement was signed, permitting the maintenance of U.S. bases throughout sovereign Japan and anticipating future substantial Japanese rearmament. Because of this de facto military rider, the Soviet Union did not sign the peace treaty. Furthermore, because of disagreements among the Allies concerning policy toward China, neither the People's Republic of China nor the Chinese Nationalist regime ensconced in Taiwan were invited to the peace conference. In the months following the San Francisco conference, however, while Japan remained occupied, the conservative government of Shigeru Yoshida was effectively pressured into signing a bilateral peace treaty with the Chinese Nationalists and adhering to the U.S. policy of isolating and economically strangling communist China. In April 1952—ninety months after the end of World War II in Asia—the occupation of Japan formally ended and Japan reentered the global arena as the key U.S. ally in Asia.

At the time the occupation ended, it seemed to most observers, certainly on the Japanese side, to have been an unduly prolonged affair. Indeed, one of the major arguments in Washington for restoring sovereignty to Japan was that further delay would simply erode Japanese goodwill toward the United States and increase the possibility of Japan's sliding toward the Soviet Union. In retrospect, of course, we are inclined to weigh time differently and see this as a relatively short period in which momentous changes took place. In retrospect, too, it is also now apparent that Japan, less than seven years after sacrificing more than 2 million of its citizens and losing an empire, was about to embark on a period of accelerated economic growth that was actually facilitated by war: by breakthroughs in technology and labor skills that came about in mobilizing for "total war" beginning in the 1930s; by the destruction of old industrial plants in the U.S. air raids of 1944 and 1945, which paved the way for factory reconstruction at more modern and rational levels after 1945; by the stimulation that the Japanese economy received from war-related "special procurements" and "new special procurements" by the United States after the outbreak of the Korean War in 1950; and by the fact that the U.S. policy of incorporating Japan economically as well as militarily into a new Pax Americana in Asia also involved giving Japanese industrialists fairly generous access to U.S. licenses and patents.

This transformation from "savage" enemy to "freedom-loving" ally was breathtaking in many ways. It was not necessarily conceptually or psychologically disorienting to most Americans, however, because much of the basic rhetoric of the World War II years was simply reassigned. The communists were now portrayed as the savages who were conspiring to conquer the world (U.S. wartime propaganda had insisted not merely that Japan's goal was world conquest but that the Japanese had a "100-year plan" for accomplishing this). More peculiar to the Asian context, the Japanese now donned the "democratic, business-oriented" characteristics that had been assigned to America's wartime Chinese allies, while the Chinese, as communists, suddenly became inherently treacherous and fanatic, robotlike and antlike. The communist Chinese also absorbed much of the racist "Yellow Peril" animosity that had been directed against the Japanese enemy during World War II—now with the overlay, of course, of the "Red Peril" as well.

Even before the Truman administration ended, it was apparent that Japan was the only place in postwar Asia where U.S. policy could reasonably claim success. Judged on its own terms, the occupation had been unexpectedly amicable; and despite the so-called reverse course that marked the shift in U.S. policies from reform to rehabilitation of Japan as a cold-war ally, many of the initial democratic reforms remained intact. The government of Japan was conservative and staunchly anti-communist. And with the conspicuous exception of the left-wing parties and a good portion of the intelligentsia, who opposed the dilution of reformism and abandonment of the early ideals of demilitarization and neutrality, the Japanese people as a whole also appeared to look favorably on the United States. When Americans looked at the rest of Asia—at China, Korea, and Southeast Asia—Japan could not help but bring a sigh of relief. By comparison with the Soviet presence in Eastern Europe, moreover, Japan could be held up as a model of enlightened "free world" occupation policies.

Until perhaps the end of the 1960s, Western scholarship on U.S. policy toward Japan during the Truman administration tended to dwell on these positive accomplishments and was characterized by several lines of emphasis. The focus was on the occupation of Japan per se and, within this frame, on the positive American contribution to "democratization." The occupation was presented as a model of enlightened red-white-and-blue "social engineering," as suggested by the title of the most popular book on the subject, Kazuo Kawai's *Japan's American Interlude,* first published in 1960. The "reverse course" was not greatly emphasized (except as a necessary way of preserving the democratic reforms by stabilizing the economy), and the decision to remilitarize Japan was presented largely as a response to a Soviet threat to Japan and Asia. Because Japanese rearmament, the decision to maintain post-treaty U.S. bases in Japan, and the policy of trilateral linkage among Japan, Southeast Asia, and the United States all emerged as formal public policies after the outbreak of the Korean War, it was generally implied that they were responses to that conflict.

More recent scholarship on this period, in Japan as well as in the English-speaking countries, has by no means denied the "democratization" that occurred in postsurrender Japan, but in general it has taken a different tack in approaching occupied Japan as history. In good part, the revised approach derives from the opening of the U.S. archives on this period, along with a wealth of private papers, reminiscences, oral histories, and the like. To some extent, the new approaches also reflect the questions asked by a younger and more skeptical generation of scholars in the United States, who began to do archival work on early postwar U.S. policy in the wake of the Vietnam War. To risk some grand generalizations, it can be said that recent scholarship on U.S. policy toward Japan in the late 1940s and early 1950s (1) gives greater emphasis to the Japanese contribution to developments in occupied Japan, positive as well as negative, and at the popular as well as official levels; (2) is more attentive to the contribution of "middle-echelon leadership" on both the U.S.

and the Japanese sides, as well as to the influence of special-interest groups; (3) places U.S. policy toward occupied Japan firmly in the context of U.S. global policy; (4) traces almost all key strategic policies (such as Japanese remilitarization, U.S. bases in sovereign Japan, and integration of Japan and Southeast Asia) to before the Korean War; (5) emphasizes the economic as well as military considerations in U.S. planning for Asia (such as the "dollar gap" crisis of the late 1940s); (6) deemphasizes the fear of a direct Soviet attack on Japan on the part of U.S. planners while elevating the importance assigned to Japan in balance-of-power thinking; and (7) calls attention to some of the more hysterical U.S. proposals for Japan that emerged after the outbreak of the Korean War, such as the demand for a Japanese army of at least 300,000 men and the anticipation that Japan should and would soon emerge as an arsenal of select military items for non-communist Asia.

The implications of such interpretations are substantial. For example, the repressive aspects of the reverse course within the Japanese body politic have become more apparent to Western students and scholars. (They have always been emphasized in Japanese writings on the period.) Also, the fundamentally benign picture of Japan's being remilitarized in response to mounting tensions in Asia is called into question, because it is now apparent that the U.S. policy toward Japan also contributed to tension and confrontation in Asia in particular and in the cold war in general, especially from 1949 on (that is, before the Korean War and even before the Sino-Soviet pact of February 1950, which is often cited as evidence of the hostile intentions of the communist powers). Perhaps the single most concrete and consequential point that emerges from the recently opened archives is the extent to which, by the early 1950s, U.S. planners had come to see Japan and Southeast Asia as inseparable parts of the containment strategy. Southeast Asia needed the Japanese "workshop," it was argued, but even more significantly Japan needed secure access to the markets and raw materials of Southeast Asia, especially if it was not going to be allowed to reestablish intimate economic relations with China. When postwar U.S. policy toward Asia is examined from this perspective, Japan emerges as the greatest "domino" of all well before the Geneva Conference of 1954. It is now apparent that the initial U.S. commitment to counterrevolution in Southeast Asia, which eventually proved so tragic, cannot be fully understood without taking Japan into account.[2]

---

[2] An excellent annotated guide to the earlier literature is Robert E. Ward and Frank Joseph

Footnote continued from preceding page:
Shulman, eds., *The Allied Occupation of Japan, 1945–1952: An Annotated Bibliography of Western-Language Materials* (Chicago: American Library Association, 1974). Shulman also compiled a listing of "Doctoral Dissertations on the Allied Occupation of Japan, 1945–1952" for the 1978 MacArthur Memorial conference cited below. For a more succinct and recent list of basic published sources as of the early 1980s, see John W. Dower, *Japanese History and Culture from Ancient to Modern Times: Seven Basic Bibliographies* (New York: Markus Wiener Publishing, 1986), 199–222.

For general historiographic appraisals of Japanese as well as English scholarship on the occupation, see John W. Dower, "Occupied Japan as History and Occupation History as Politics," *Journal of Asian Studies* 34 (February 1975):485–504; and Carol Gluck, "Entangling Illusions: Japanese and American Views of the Occupation," in Warren I. Cohen, ed., *New Frontiers in American-East Asian Relations: Essays Presented to Dorothy Borg* (New York: Columbia University Press, 1983), 169–236. Short essays by Dower, Edwin O. Reischauer, Eiji Takamae, and Rinjirō Sodei in Harry Wray and Hilary Conroy, eds., *Japan Examined: Perspectives on Modern Japanese History* (Honolulu: University of Hawaii Press, 1983), 331–63, convey some of the interpretive diversity in the field today.

Among the most notable earlier influential accounts of the occupation are the various editions of Edwin O. Reischauer, *The United States and Japan* (Cambridge, Mass.: Harvard University Press, 1st ed., 1950); Kazuo Kawai, *Japan's American Interlude* (Chicago: University of Chicago Press, 1960); Frederick S. Dunn, *Peacemaking and the Settlement with Japan* (Princeton: Princeton University Press, 1960); and Robert E. Ward, "Reflections on the Allied Occupation and Planned Political Change in Japan," in Robert E. Ward, ed., *Political Development in Modern Japan* (Princeton: Princeton University Press, 1968).

I myself have dwelled in earlier writings, with more extensive notations, on some of the more revisionist themes mentioned here. See *Empire and Aftermath: Yoshida Shigeru and the Japanese Experience, 1878–1954* (Cambridge, Mass.: Council on East Asian Studies, Harvard University, 1979), 305–492; "The Eye of the Beholder: Background Notes on the U.S.-Japan Military Relationship," *Bulletin of Concerned Asian Scholars* 2 (October 1969): 15–31; "Occupied Japan and the American Lake, 1945–1950," in Edward Friedman and Mark Selden, eds., *America's Asia: Dissenting Essays on Asian-American Relations* (New York: Pantheon Books, 1974), 146–206; and "The Superdomino in Postwar Asia: Japan In and Out of *The Pentagon Papers,*" in Noam Chomsky and Howard Zinn, eds., *The Senator Gravel Edition of the Pentagon Papers,* vol. 5 (Boston: Beacon Press, 1972), 101–42. Howard Schonberger has made extensive use of government archives and private papers to illuminate U.S. decision making and the cold-war context of the occupation in a series of influential revisionist articles, among them the following: "Zaibatsu Dissolution and the American Restoration of Japan," *Bulletin of Concerned Asian Scholars* 5 (September 1973): 16–31; "The Japan Lobby in American Diplomacy, 1947–1952," *Pacific Historical Review* 46 (August 1977): 327–59; "American Labor's Cold War in Occupied Japan," *Diplomatic History* 5(Summer 1979): 249–72; "General William Draper, the 80th Congress, and the Origins of Japan's Reverse Course," paper presented to the International Conference on the Occupation of Japan, Amherst College, August 1980; "The General and the Presidency: Douglas MacArthur and the Election of 1948," *Wisconsin Magazine of History* 57 (Spring 1974): 201–19; "U.S. Policy in Post-war Japan: The Retreat from Liberalism," *Science and Society* 46 (Spring 1982): 39–59; and "John Foster Dulles and the China Question in the Making of the Japanese Peace Treaty," in Thomas W. Burkman, ed., *The Occupation of Japan: The International Context* (Norfolk, Va.: MacArthur Memorial, 1982), 229–54.

For detailed analysis of the emergence of a broad regional approach in U.S. economic planning toward Japan and postwar Asia, see William Borden, *Pacific Alliance: United States Foreign Economic Policy and Japanese Trade Recovery, 1947–1955* (Madison: University of Wisconsin Press, 1984); and Michael Schaller, *The American Occupation of Japan: The Origins of the Cold War in Asia* (New York: Oxford University Press, 1985). Schaller's book is an elaboration of his incisive article on pre-Korean War proposals to

As these observations suggest, a comprehensive study of the policies of the Truman administration toward Japan must move in several directions, encompassing both internal developments in occupied Japan and broader regional and global strategies. In the latter instance, a great deal more is involved than just the projected linkage of Japan and Southeast Asia, for this positive policy naturally developed against the background of reassessing U.S. policy toward China and Korea—developments that have been the subject of a number of recent monographs in English.[3] The regional dimension also involves international considerations of a slightly different order, namely, the response of U.S. allies such as Britain, Australia, and New Zealand to U.S. initiatives involving Japan and the rest of Asia. These countries, too, have opened their diplomatic archives in recent years, and it is more apparent than ever that their cooperation with the U.S. cold-war policy was frequently tempered by grave misgiv-

integrate the Japanese and Southeast Asian economies: "Securing the Great Crescent: Occupied Japan and the Origins of Containment in Southeast Asia," *Journal of American History* 69 (September 1982): 392–414.

The major forum in the United States for studies of occupied Japan has been the symposia sponsored by the MacArthur Memorial in Norfolk, Virginia. Symposia with published proceedings include *The Occupation of Japan and Its Legacy to the Postwar World* (1975); *The Occupation of Japan: Impact of Legal Reform* (1977); *The Occupation of Japan: Economic Policy and Reform* (1978); *The Occupation of Japan: Education and Social Reform* (1980); and *The Occupation of Japan: The International Context* (1982). For the proceedings of a 1977 conference on occupied Japan and occupied Germany, see Robert Wolfe, ed., *Americans as Proconsuls: United States Military Government in Germany and Japan, 1944–1952* (Carbondale: Southern Illinois University Press, 1984).

[3] Recent studies in English dealing with U.S. policy toward other parts of Asia in the first postwar decade and providing an important complement to the Japan-centered emphasis of this present essay include Akira Iriye, *The Cold War in Asia: A Historical Introduction* (Englewood Cliffs, N.J.: Prentice-Hall, 1974); Yonosuke Nagai and Akira Iriye, eds., *The Origins of the Cold War in Asia* (New York: Columbia University Press and University of Tokyo Press, 1977); Bruce Cumings, "Introduction: The Course of Korean-American Relations, 1943–1953," in Bruce Cumings, ed., *Child of Conflict: The Korean-American Relationship, 1943–1953* (Seattle: University of Washington Press, 1983), 3–55; Bruce Cumings, *The Origins of the Korean War: Liberation and the Emergence of Separate Regimes, 1945–1947* (Princeton: Princeton University Press, 1984); Bruce Cumings, "The Origins and Development of the Northeast Asian Political Economy: Industrial Sectors, Produce Cycles, and Political Consequences," *International Organization* 38 (Winter 1984): 1–40; William Whitney Stueck, Jr., *The Road to Confrontation: American Policy Toward China and Korea, 1947–1950* (New York: Columbia University Press, 1981); Dorothy Borg and Waldo Heinrichs, eds., *Uncertain Years: Chinese-American Relations, 1947–1950* (New York: Columbia University Press, 1980); Robert M. Blum, *Drawing the Line: The Origin of the American Containment Policy in East Asia* (New York: W. W. Norton, 1982); Nancy Bernkopf Tucker, *Patterns in the Dust: Chinese-American Relations and the Recognition Controversy, 1949–1950* (New York: Columbia University Press, 1983); Robert J. McMahon, *Colonialism and Cold War: The United States and the Struggle for Indonesian Independence, 1945–1949* (Ithaca: Cornell University Press, 1981). The maiden issue of *The Japanese Journal of American Studies*, published in 1981, was devoted to "United States Policy toward East Asia: 1945–1950."

ings. The rearmament of Japan caused shudders throughout non-communist Asia, to say nothing of the fear provoked in the communist countries. And the unilateral U.S. decision to promote Japanese economic reconstruction was not exactly received gleefully by Japan's former and future economic rivals in Asia. When it became clear that the United States had decided not merely to assist in the economic rehabilitation of Japan but to deflect such projected growth away from China and in the direction of Southeast Asia, the alarm was palpable, especially in London, where such a policy could be seen as yet another potentially devastating blow to the Sterling bloc. From this perspective, U.S. policy toward Japan also must be seen in the context of the decline of the British empire and the tensions that arose within the Anglo-American camp as the Pax Britannica gave way to a Pax Americana.[4]

Although the transformation of Japan from bitter enemy to cold-war ally may seem natural in retrospect, this reversal of policy did not occur all of a piece; nor was it arrived at without controversy within U.S. decision-making circles; nor was it a policy without ambiguities—including resentment on the part of many Japanese conservatives who felt they were being denied true sovereignty, and lingering doubts on the U.S. side about how far Japan could be trusted. Even as U.S. planners came to assign Japan a crucial role in the global balance of power, in both a negative and positive sense (denying Japan to the Soviet Union's sphere

---

[4]The most concise introduction to disagreement (as well as agreement) on occupation policy among the allies of the United States is an early official publication: U.S. Department of State, *The Far Eastern Commission: A Study in International Cooperation, 1945–1952* (Washington, D.C.: D.O.S. Publication 5138, 1953). In 1982, the government of New Zealand published a mammoth (almost 1,800 pages) collection of pertinent documents as volume 2 of *Documents on New Zealand External Relations,* edited by Robin Kay and subtitled *The Surrender and Occupation of Japan.* British attitudes toward occupied Japan are closely examined in Roger W. Buckley, *Occupation Diplomacy: Britain, the United States, and Japan, 1945–1952* (Cambridge: Cambridge University Press, 1982). Australia's position was the subject of an earlier monograph by Richard N. Rosecrance, *Australian Diplomacy and Japan, 1945–1951* (Cambridge: Cambridge University Press, 1962). The published proceedings of the fifth of the MacArthur Memorial conferences, cited in note 2, contain many papers on the international aspects of the occupation.

Although the Japanese Ministry of Foreign Affairs has adopted a policy of selective declassification of archives pertaining to the occupation, scholars are still greatly hampered in gaining access to basic primary materials scattered throughout the Japanese bureaucracy. Petitions calling for more open and convenient access have been presented to the government by Japanese and non-Japanese specialists on the occupation—notably in 1980 and 1983—but thus far the response has been essentially tokenistic; numerous materials have been made available on microfilm, but most of this is of little or no interest to scholars. The Soviet archives on the period are, of course, completely closed; and (with certain minor exceptions such as the Wellington Koo papers at Columbia) the internal Chinese record is also inaccessible to researchers.

of influence and using Japan against the Soviet "bloc"), they remained nervous about Japan's "ideological" inclinations. Extremists of either the Left or the Right, it was feared, might still assume power in the future. Thus, while the bilateral United States-Japan security treaty signed at San Francisco in 1951 was first and foremost an anti-communist pact, it simultaneously functioned as a vehicle for controlling Japan by perpetuating its military subordination to the United States in every conceivable direction: strategic planning, matériel procurement, technological development, and the continued presence of U.S. forces in and around Japan. Similarly, the security treaties that the United States negotiated with the Philippines and Australia-New Zealand in 1951 also served the double function of assuring these allies of U.S. assistance in the event of either communist or Japanese aggression. At the time they were negotiated, in fact, these parallel security pacts were requested by the Asian nations involved primarily out of alarm at the specter of a remilitarized and revanchist Japan.

From the perspective of Washington, the U.S. relationship with Japan also was plagued by the legacy of one of the early ideals of the occupation: the pacifist sentiment embodied in the famous "no war" clause (Article Nine) of the new constitution that General Douglas MacArthur and his staff had pressed upon the Japanese in 1946. Although U.S. officials quickly came to lament this dramatic exercise in "demilitarization," the Japanese people as a whole continued to embrace Article Nine, in spirit if not to the letter, and resisted its abrogation or amendment. Their recollection of the hardships and horrors of the war in Asia and the Pacific remained keen, as did their skepticism of overly zealous appeals to remilitarize in the name of "defense." The symbolic significance of Article Nine in postwar Japanese politics cannot be overemphasized, and Japan's conservative government lost no opportunity to use this in resisting the heavy pressure for rapid remilitarization that the United States exerted after June 1950.

In the pages that follow, the fascinating developments that took place within occupied Japan will be mentioned only in passing; primary attention will be given to Japan's place in the strategic thinking of the Truman administration. Recent country-oriented studies of postwar U.S. policy toward China, Korea, and Southeast Asia as a rule point to the year or so before the Korean War as marking a watershed in U.S. planning. Certainly the documents of the time reveal officials as temperamentally diverse as George Kennan, Dean Rusk, and Louis Johnson all lamenting the "country by country" approach toward Asia that existed in 1949 and into 1950, and it is from this time on that the contours of a more integrated, regional approach to Asia become conspicuous.[5] Strategic policy toward Japan not only fits this pattern but can be analyzed more precisely as having evolved through four stages between the end of the war in 1945 and the end of the occupation in April 1952: (1) concentration on the "demilitarization and democratization" of Japan and projection of a disarmed and "neutral" Japan in the future (August 1945 to mid-1947); (2) a "soft" cold-war policy, in which the primary emphasis was placed on denying Japan to the Soviet sphere (mid-1947 to 1949); (3) a "hard" cold-war policy, in which Japan was assigned a positive, active role in the U.S. anti-communist strategy (mid-1949 to September 1951); and (4) an integrated cold-war policy, in which the concrete mechanisms of regional military and economic integration were actually created—including the peace treaty and various security treaties of 1951–52, the coordination of U.S. military and economic policies, and the firm commitment to containment of China through the creation of a trilateral nexus linking the United States, Japan, and Southeast Asia (beginning in the latter part of 1951). Obviously, the roots of each "stage" can be found in earlier periods.

Demilitarization and democratization, 1945–1947

Well before World War II ended, it was widely assumed that the United States would maintain strategic control of the Pacific Ocean—an assumption that was blithely captured at the popular level in a wartime American song entitled "To Be Specific, It's Our Pacific." U.S. military planners gave close attention to the key islands in the Pacific over which they desired to maintain unilateral control indefinitely, but such planning did not extend to Japan per se. Until the final stages of the war, plans for postsurrender Japan anticipated an "Allied" occupation in which the United States would play the leading role, but China, Britain, and possibly the

---

[5] For Kennan and Rusk, see Committee on International Relations, House of Representatives, *Selected Executive Session Hearings of the Committee, 1943–50*, vol. 8 (United States Policy in the Far East, part 2), 160, 512; cf. ibid., 242, for Dean Acheson on the same problem. Louis Johnson's famous blast at the lack of a coordinated policy was delivered on 10 June 1949, when the Defense Department adopted a hard stance on Asian policy in the form of the famous "NSC 48." Cf. Kenneth W. Condit, *The Joint Chiefs of Staff and National Policy, 1947–1949*, vol. 2 of the official *The History of the Joint Chiefs of Staff* (Wilmington, Del.: Michael Glazier, 1979), 516; also U.S. Department of Defense, *United States-Vietnam Relations, 1945–1967*, 8: 217–18.

Soviet Union (if it entered the war before Japan surrendered) would all have a serious place.[6]

When Japan's capitulation became a reality, however, the Truman administration took a strong stand against a multinational occupation in any meaningful sense. The United States refused to consider dividing Japan into zones of occupation as had been done in Germany, demanded that all of occupied Japan be placed under a U.S. supreme commander, and balked at the creation of a genuinely influential international control commission. There was some grousing at this on the part of other Allied powers, and the creation of an essentially tokenistic superstructure of international supervision was not completed until early 1946, by which time the bureaucratic apparatus of de facto unilateral U.S. control was firmly in place.[7]

Looking ahead to the rise of cold-war tensions between the United States and Soviet Union, it is noteworthy that Stalin did not make a great issue out of the U.S. assumption of a dominant position in Japan and the Pacific. Although the Soviet Union requested a joint U.S.-Soviet supreme command in Japan, and asked that the northern island of Hokkaido be made a Soviet zone of occupation, Stalin accepted Truman's flat rejection of these requests with little more than a shrug. And although legally entitled to send a Soviet military contingent to Japan as part of the nominally Allied occupation force, the Soviet dictator declined to do so on the grounds that this would inconvenience General Douglas MacArthur, who had been designated supreme commander. In the exchanges that took place over the control apparatus for occupied Japan between August 1945

---

[6] For presurrender planning, see U.S. Department of State, *Foreign Relations of the United States* [hereafter *FRUS*], 1944, V, 1186–1289, and 1945, VI, 497 ff. Hugh Borton, a central figure in the State Department group that drafted most of the presurrender plans for Japan, has written two informative essays on this subject: "Preparation for the Occupation of Japan," *Journal of Asian Studies* 25 (February 1966): 203–12; and *American Presurrender Planning for Postwar Japan* (New York: Occasional Papers of the East Asian Institute, Columbia University, 1967).

Some of the public discussion concerning postwar U.S. bases is summarized in Dower, "Occupied Japan and the American Lake"; the archival record on this is introduced in Melvyn P. Leffler, "The American Conception of National Security and the Beginnings of the Cold War, 1945–48," *American Historical Review* 89 (April 1984), especially 349–56. The song title is recorded in Colin Shindler, *Hollywood Goes to War: Films and American Society, 1939–1952* (Boston: Routledge and Kegan Paul, 1979), 35.

[7] The formal policy of unilateral U.S. control of the nominally "Allied" occupation was set forth in State-War-Navy Coordinating Committee (SWNCC) 150/2 ("United States Initial Post-Defeat Policy Relating to Japan") of 12 August 1945; *FRUS*, 1945, VI, 609–12. International participation eventually took the form of a multination Far Eastern Commission that met in Washington and a four-delegate (United States, China, U.S.S.R., and Commonwealth) Allied Council in Tokyo. Neither was a control commission.

and early 1946, the Soviets gave numerous signals that they hoped the United States would accept their acknowledgment of a legitimate U.S. sphere of interest in Japan and the Pacific as a quid pro quo for American acknowledgment of the Soviet Union's reasonable security concerns in Eastern Europe. This conciliatory stance was consistent with the restraint the Russians displayed in Korea in August 1945, when Stalin held his forces at the thirty-eighth parallel although they could have occupied the entire Korean peninsula easily before the U.S. forces arrived. Stalin's willingness to recognize the Nationalist regime of Chiang Kai-shek as the sole legitimate government of China in August 1945 and to promise eventual withdrawal of Soviet troops from Manchuria also impressed some observers at the time as being unexpectedly conciliatory. As it turned out, the Truman administration was not inclined to acknowledge that there was any comparability in the assumed spheres of influence of the two nations.[8]

Journalistic accounts from the early months of the occupation often refer to gossip and scuttlebutt concerning Japan as the "staging area for the next war," and it is indeed possible to find U.S. officials who raised the question of Japan's future importance as an anti-Soviet military base at an early date. Navy Secretary James Forrestal turned this matter over in his mind in the early summer of 1945, for example; in the State Department, John Davies introduced the prospect of Japan as a future *place d'armes* in August 1946.[9] The mainstream of U.S. strategic planning for Asia from 1945 to 1947, however, remained grounded in the passions and assumptions of the recent war: notably, hatred and fear of Japan and lingering hope that China would emerge as a strong ally of the United States and capable "policeman" in Asia. Until well into 1946, and in

---

[8] Much of the *FRUS* volume for 1945 is devoted to these issues. The Soviet attempt to equate its own position in Eastern Europe with the American sphere in Japan and the Pacific emerges most strongly in the cables of the U.S. ambassador to Moscow, Averell Harriman. President Truman acknowledged the essentially moderate Soviet position in his *Memoirs: Year of Decisions* (New York: Signet, 1955), especially 490.

[9] On the "staging area," see Harold Issacs, *No Peace for Asia* (Cambridge, Mass.: MIT Press, 1947, reprinted 1967), 39, 119. Cf. Mark Gayn, *Japan Diary* (New York: William Sloane Associates, 1948), 42 (diary entry for 20 December 1945), 119 (21 February 1946), 212 (10 May 1946), 237–40 (27 May 1946); James Forrestal, *The Forrestal Diaries*, edited by Walter Millis (New York: Viking, 1951), 56 (May 1945); *FRUS*, 1946, VI, 285–86, 301–04, 337–39 (for the *place d'armes* memo and related discussion). Michael Schaller offers numerous other early U.S. statements concerning using Japan as an anti-Soviet base or ally in chapter 3 of *The American Occupation of Japan*, the most striking of which are the report of a meeting between General MacArthur and presidential envoy Edwin A. Locke in October 1945 and a February 1946 report from Tokyo by U.S. Treasury Department envoy D. R. Jenkins.

some circles much later, the *place d'armes* men were drowned out by a potent phrase that carried over from the war years, namely, the "permanent and complete" disarmament of Japan. The genealogy of this idealistic rhetoric is beyond the scope of this essay, but it is well to recall how immensely popular it was during the war. President Roosevelt, with characteristic grandiloquence, had declared this to be the Allied goal for both Germany and Japan; Senator Arthur Vandenberg called for "permanently and conclusively and effectively disarming Germany and Japan" in the famous speech of January 1945 in which he announced his support for a bipartisan foreign policy in the postwar era; the Potsdam Declaration of July projected the "complete disarmament" of Japan; and citizens' lobbies and the media readily embraced the prospect of a permanently defanged Axis foe.[10]

The agenda for Japan was in fact much broader than mere disarmament per se. Until the very eve of Japan's surrender, U.S. military planners still expected that the war in Asia might continue for another year or year and a half. Consequently, they were caught somewhat by surprise by Japan's surrender. Due in good part to the impressive activities of a small State Department group led by Hugh Borton and George Blakeslee of the Far Eastern Division, however, planning for postsurrender Japan at the lower levels of the bureaucracy was in fact well advanced when the war ended. Scores of position papers dealing with specific aspects of the Japanese state and society already had been reviewed by the critical intergovernmental committee in these matters—the State-War-Navy Coordinating Committee (SWNCC)—and these became the basis for a wide range of proposed reforms in occupied Japan. As the Borton-Blakeslee group and SWNCC saw it, disarmament was but one aspect of the task of ensuring a peaceful Japan in the future, for true demilitarization re-

---

[10] Roosevelt and Churchill spoke vaguely of the future disarmament of the Axis in the Atlantic Charter of August 1941, and on 7 January 1943 Roosevelt told Congress that Germany, Italy, and Japan "must be disarmed and kept disarmed," a declaration cited by many publicists; cf. William C. Johnstone, *The Future of Japan* (New York: Oxford University Press, 1945), 31. For Senator Vandenberg's speech, see the *New York Times* for 11 January 1945. There was indeed some ambiguity as to whether U.S. policy called for "permanent" disarmament of Japan, but the Potsdam Declaration of 26 July 1945 stated that the Japanese military would be "completely disarmed," and SWNCC 150/2 of August 12 stated that U.S. policy was "to accomplish the permanent and complete disarmament and demilitarization of Japan." The revised instructions sent to MacArthur on 29 August and made public on 22 September similarly said that "Japan will be completely disarmed and demilitarized." See *FRUS*, 1945, VI, 552, 610; Also Government Section, Supreme Commander for the Allied Powers, *Political Reorientation of Japan, September 1945 to September 1948* (Washington, D.C.: U.S. Government Printing Office, 1949), 2: 423–24, 431.

quired "democratization" as well. The fundamental assumption here was that the repressive structure of the prewar Japanese state had created a "will to war" (as Assistant Secretary of State Dean Acheson phrased it shortly after Japan surrendered), whereas democracies—by which was meant bourgeois democracies with a thriving middle class—did not practice oppression.[11]

The initial U.S. occupation policy of demilitarization and democratization rested on such sweeping assumptions. In the many instances where the policy directives emanating from Washington were couched in broad and somewhat ambiguous terms, moreover, MacArthur and his staff in Tokyo tended to interpret them as a mandate for genuinely drastic reform, on occasion of a more radical nature than Washington seems to have had in mind. MacArthur's prestige and messianic style, coupled with the Eurocentrism of the Truman administration, gave the occupation staff in Japan unusual leeway for approximately two years, until the latter part of 1947. And although the general may have fumed about liberal programs in his homeland under President "Rosenfeld," as he reportedly was wont to call his former commander in chief, as a reformer in the Japanese milieu MacArthur proved to be exceptionally receptive to the recommendations of a small coterie of American liberals and New Dealers. Some of the most dramatic and consequential reforms carried out under the early democratization program, such as the sweeping land reform of 1946–47 and the new constitution promulgated in 1946, actually were given their radical edge in MacArthur's headquarters in Tokyo.

By almost every appraisal at the time, the early democratization program as a whole was fundamentally progressive. War criminals were brought to trial. Some 200,000 alleged militarists and ultranationalists were purged from public life. On the economic front, in addition to the land reform, laws were enacted in support of labor unionization and the right to strike; the oligopolistic zaibatsu holding companies were dissolved; and policies were announced calling for economic deconcentration, industrial demilitarization, and severe reparations to Japan's war victims. Politically, even the Communist Party was made legal, and "grass-

---

[11] On SWNCC and the Borton-Blakeslee group, see citations in note 6 above and the analysis in Akira Iriye, *Power and Culture: The Japanese-American War, 1941–1945* (Cambridge, Mass.: Harvard University Press, 1982). The basic SWNCC (later SANACC) documents are available on microfilm in thirty-two reels under the title *SWNCC (State-War-Navy Coordinating Committee)/SANACC (State-Army-Navy-Air Force Coordinating Committee) Case Files, 1944–1949* (Wilmington, Del.: Scholarly Resources, Inc., 1977).

roots" democracy was to be promoted through police decentralization, educational reform, and the strengthening of local autonomy. Under the new constitution, which went into effect in early 1947, the emperor became a "symbol" of the state, the country renounced the resort to war as a means of solving disputes, and the people of Japan were granted a broad array of rights that in some instances (such as explicit acknowledgment of the equality of women) went beyond U.S. constitutional guarantees. In the realm of demilitarization more prosaically defined, occupation authorities moved quickly to repatriate and demobilize the Imperial army and navy, destroy military stocks, and abolish the entire military establishment. Their zealousness was such that, in one of the more notorious excesses of the demilitarization program, apparently on instructions from the War Department, they smashed the great cyclotron in the "Riken" laboratory in Tokyo and dropped the pieces in the ocean.[12]

---

[12] MacArthur's "President Rosenfeld" habit is recounted in an irreverent reminiscence by the general's former military secretary, Faubion Bowers, in "The Late General MacArthur, Warts and All," *Esquire,* January 1967, 90ff. The initial demilitarization and democratization policies are covered at length in a variety of official sources. The best known of these is the invaluable two-volume narrative summary and documentary collection prepared by MacArthur's headquarters and published in 1949 as *Political Reorientation of Japan, September 1945 to September 1948.* Two volumes authored by State Department officials were published under nongovernment imprints while the occupation was still under way: Edwin M. Martin, *The Allied Occupation of Japan* (New York: American Institute of Pacific Relations, 1948), and Robert A. Fearey, *The Occupation of Japan, Second Phase: 1948–50* (New York: Macmillan, for the International Secretariat, Institute of Pacific Relations, 1950). Between 1950 and the end of the occupation in early 1952, MacArthur's staff also prepared a useful and often overlooked official history that eventually included fifty-five monographs about specific aspects of the occupation; the series is available on microfilm from the National Archives under the collective title *History of the Non-Military Activities of the Occupation of Japan.* A neglected source on the military aspects of repatriation and demilitarization is *MacArthur in Japan: The Occupation: Military Phase,* "Volume 1—Supplement" of *Reports of General MacArthur* (Washington, D.C.: U.S. Government Printing Office, 1966).

The following nonofficial studies are also useful for specific aspects of occupation policy: Richard Minear, *Victor's Justice: The Tokyo War Crimes Trial* (Princeton: Princeton University Press, 1971); Phillip R. Piccigallo, *The Japanese on Trial: Allied War Crimes Operations in the East, 1945–1951* (Austin: University of Texas Press, 1972); Hans H. Baerwald, *The Purge of Japanese Leaders under the Occupation* (Berkeley: University of California Publications in Political Science, 8, 1959); Meirion and Susie Harries, *Sheathing the Sword: The Demilitarization of Postwar Japan* (New York: Macmillan, 1987); Ronald Dore, *Land Reform in Japan* (New York: Oxford University Press, 1959); Eleanor Hadley, *Antitrust in Japan* (Princeton: Princeton University Press, 1970); Eleanor Hadley, "Zaibatsu" and "Zaibatsu Dissolution," *Encyclopedia of Japan* (Tokyo: Kodansha, 1983) 8: 361–66; T. A. Bisson, *Zaibatsu Dissolution in Japan* (Berkeley: University of California Press, 1954); Chitoshi Yanaga, *Big Business in Japanese Politics* (New Haven, Conn.: Yale University Press, 1968); Chalmers Johnson, *MITI and the Japanese Miracle: The Growth of Industrial Policy, 1925–1975* (Palo Alto: Stanford University Press, 1982);

There were, to be sure, exceptions to the sweeping demobilization program that seem noteworthy in retrospect. Reliance on the Japanese for minesweeping in the waters around Japan, for example, preserved the nucleus around which a future navy could be reconstructed. The military "demobilization boards" themselves kept remnants of the Imperial army and navy employed and provided a body of records that proved useful later when the decision was made to create a new Japanese military beginning in 1950. Certain Japanese staff officers found a new home in the U.S. occupation bureaucracy itself, especially the Counter-Intelligence Section (G-2), where they were employed in such tasks as preparing historical accounts of the recent war. Many Japanese officers were "debriefed" as a matter of course, and in one appalling instance—involving officers and scientific researchers in the murderous "Unit 731," which had conducted lethal medical and biological-warfare experiments on prisoners of war in Manchuria (killing an estimated 3,000 in the process)—blatant war criminals were granted immunity from prosecution in return for disclosure of their special knowledge. Outside Japan, in parts of both China and Southeast Asia (especially the French- and British-controlled areas), the repatriation of scores of thousands of Japanese sol-

Martin Bronfenbrenner, "Occupation-Period Economy (1945–1952)," *Encyclopedia of Japan* 2: 154–58; Miriam Farley, *Aspects of Japan's Labor Problems* (New York: Institute of Pacific Relations, 1950); Joe B. Moore, *Japanese Workers and the Struggle for Power, 1945–1947* (Madison: University of Wisconsin Press, 1983); Solomon Levine, *Industrial Relations in Postwar Japan* (Champaign: University of Illinois Press, 1953); Solomon Levine, "Labor," *Encyclopedia of Japan*, 4: 343–49; John M. Maki, transl. and ed., *Japan's Commission on the Constitution: The Final Report* (Seattle: University of Washington Press, 1980); Theodore Cohen, *Remaking Japan: The American Occupation as New Deal*, ed. Herbert Passin (New York: Free Press, 1987); Justin Williams, Sr., *Japan's Political Revolution under MacArthur: A Participant's Account* (Athens: University of Georgia Press, 1979); Alfred C. Oppler, *Legal Reform in Occupied Japan: A Participant Looks Back* (Princeton: Princeton University Press, 1976); "Legal Reforms in Japan during the Allied Occupation," special reprint volume of *Washington Law Review* (1977); Kenzō Takayanagi, Ichirō Ohtomo, and Hideo Tanaka, eds., *Nihonkoku Kempō Seitei No Katei* (Yuhikaku: 1972; volume 1 of this two-volume work on "The Making of the Constitution of Japan" contains basic English-language documents pertaining to constitutional revision from the papers of Milo E. Rowell, covering the period from December 1945 to the end of February 1946); Kurt Steiner, *Local Government in Japan* (Palo Alto: Stanford University Press, 1965); Robert Ward and Yoshikazu Sakamoto, eds., *Democratizing Japan: The Allied Occupation* (Honolulu: University of Hawaii Press, 1987).

For case studies of prewar-postwar continuities in the political economy of Japan, see Dower, *Empire and Aftermath;* Johnson, *MITI and the Japanese Miracle;* Andrew Gordon, *The Evolution of Labor Relations in Japan: Heavy Industry, 1853–1955* (Cambridge, Mass.: Council on East Asian Studies, Harvard University, 1985); Sheldon M. Garon, "The Imperial Bureaucracy and Labor Policy in Postwar Japan," *Journal of Asian Studies* 43 (May 1984): 441–57.

diers was delayed for months and sometimes even years, as many of these unfortunate pawns found themselves enlisted to fight against indigenous communist or national liberation movements.[13]

In the light of Japan's later remilitarization, these exceptions to the demobilization and demilitarization program are suggestive and perhaps symbolic. At the time, however, they did not reflect the main thrust of U.S. strategic policy. In fact, for reasons that still remain somewhat obscure, this first stage of U.S. policy toward occupied Japan witnessed a rare occurrence: the literal putting into practice of rhetorical promises, namely, the promise of imposing "complete and permanent disarmament" upon Japan. This took the form of Article Nine of the new Japanese constitution, which, in its final form (after passing through MacArthur's headquarters, the Japanese cabinet's experts, the Japanese parliament, and a parliamentary committee), read as follows:

ARTICLE 9. Aspiring sincerely to an international peace based on justice and order, the Japanese people forever renounce war as a sovereign right of the nation and the threat or use of force as means of settling international disputes.

---

[13]Continuities in military staffing are best summarized in Ikuhiko Hata's Japanese-language monograph *Shiroku—Nihon Saigunbi* (1976: Bungei Shunjū). In English, the Navy carryovers are documented in James E. Auer, *The Postwar Rearmament of Japanese Maritime Forces, 1945–71* (New York: Praeger, 1973). On the "Hattori clique" in the occupation's G-2 Section, see Dower, *Empire and Aftermath*, 387.

For "Unit 731," which has received considerable publicity in Japan in recent years, the basic analysis in English is available in two articles by John W. Powell: "Japan's Germ Warfare: The U.S. Cover-up of a War Crime," *Bulletin of Concerned Asian Scholars* 12 (October–December, 1980): 2–17, and "Japan's Biological Weapons: 1930–1945," *Bulletin of the Atomic Scientists* 37 (October 1981): 43–53. Powell shows conclusively that occupation authorities agreed not to prosecute Japanese scientists and officers who had engaged in lethal experiments with POWs in exchange for technical information about the results of the experiments. Some of the lesser figures associated with Unit 731 were captured by the Russians when they invaded Manchuria in August 1945 and placed on trial in the so-called Khabarovsk war-crimes trials, the results of which were publicized in 1949 and published in a lengthy English-language summary in 1950 (*Materials of the Trial of Former Servicemen of the Japanese Army Charged with Manufacturing and Employing Bacteriological Weapons*, Foreign Languages Publishing House, Moscow). During the Korean War, when the communists accused the United States of experimenting with bacteriological warfare, it was also suggested that Shirō Ishii, the former head of Unit 731, was actively collaborating with the Americans.

The retention, abuse, and indoctrination of hundreds of thousands of Japanese POWs by the Soviet Union was widely publicized from around 1947 to 1949 and is generally well known. Less attention has been given to the retention—and frequently anti-communist military deployment—of Japanese in China and Southeast Asia. For a recent corrective to this lacuna, see Donald G. Gillin with Charles Etter, "Staying On: Japanese Soldiers and Civilians in China, 1945–1949," *Journal of Asian Studies* 42 (May 1983): 497–518. On Japanese POWs under British control in Southeast Asia as late as 1947, cf. *FRUS*, 1947, VI, 192–93, 255–56.

In order to accomplish the aim of the preceding paragraph, land, sea, and air forces, as well as other war potential, will never be maintained. The right of belligerency of the state will not be recognized.

The precise genesis of Article Nine is one of the tantalizing puzzles of the occupation. At the same time, the whole process of constitutional revision in occupied Japan is an excellent example of the ambiguity of U.S. policy for Asia in the immediate postwar years and of the way this ambiguity often enabled MacArthur and his staff in Tokyo to promote their own ideals. In one of the earliest basic documents sent to Tokyo to guide MacArthur (SWNCC 150/2 of August 1945), the objective of "complete and permanent" disarmament of Japan was reiterated. In a later policy document that suffered some untidy revision at the hands of the multinational Far Eastern Commission sitting in Washington (SWNCC 228 of January 1946), however, the concept of total and permanent demilitarization was muddied by reference to future prerogatives of the civilian branch of the Japanese government. MacArthur's command thus received mixed instructions on this critical issue. Indeed, on the issue of constitutional change in general it received no blueprint but only a general mandate for revision. The first draft of the new Japanese constitution was composed in English in the Government Section of MacArthur's headquarters, in a hectic and heady two-week period at the beginning of February 1946. Specialists on occupied Japan disagree on whether the idea of the "no war" clause originated with MacArthur himself or with one of the key officers in the Government Section (Charles Kades or Courtney Whitney), or possibly even with the then Japanese prime minister, Kijūrō Shidehara. No matter who may have been responsible for the original idea, however, it is clear that Article Nine originated in Tokyo and would never have become part of the national charter of Japan without MacArthur's blessing.

The "no war" clause of the draft constitution caught Washington by surprise and provoked the aforementioned discussion of Japan as a future *place d'armes* in 1946. By and large, however, Article Nine did not cause consternation in Washington, for it not only crystallized wartime promises concerning the complete and permanent disarmament of Japan but also was consistent with plans that were then being drafted in the State Department for the long-term (meaning twenty-five to forty years) international supervision of a disarmed Japan. No major planner in Washington prior to 1947 envisaged the serious rearmament of Japan in the near future, and those few who speculated that this might be desirable later simply assumed that it would be relatively easy to amend Article Nine.[14]

The survival of the "spirit of Article Nine" as a decisive feature of the subsequent relationship between Japan and the United States is the greatest and most ironic legacy from this first stage of postwar relations between the two countries. At the same time, another major feature of the eventual military arrangement also had emerged at a very early date, namely, the decision that the Bonin and Ryukyu islands (including Okinawa) would be treated differently from the rest of Japan. Top-level U.S. planning in 1945–46 did not project the long-term maintenance of U.S. military bases in the four main islands of Japan, but from the very end of the war the Bonins and Ryukyus were singled out as being of critical strategic importance to the United States, although it apparently was not until 1948 that Okinawa became formally designated as one of the three major bases "from which to launch a strategic air offensive employing atomic weapons."[15]

The soft cold-war policy, 1947–1949

On the first anniversary of Japan's surrender, General MacArthur announced that the Japanese people already had undergone a "spiritual revolution" that "tore asunder a theory and practice of life built upon two thousand years of history and tradition and legend." If the nation continued to pursue the great middle road of democracy, it would soon emerge as a "powerful bulwark for peace." Six months later, in March

[14] The origin of Article Nine has been most attentively addressed by Theodore McNelly. See "The Renunciation of War in the Japanese Constitution," *Political Science Quarterly* 77 (September 1962): 350–78; his more recent speculations (in both Japanese and English) in *Hōritsu Jihō* 51 (May 1979), 178–81, 256–60; and his comments in the *Daily Yomiuri* of 3 May 1980. On the draft disarmament treaty, cf. *FRUS, 1946,* VIII, 150–55, 227–28 (G.B.), 236 (China), 253–54, 326–32, 348–49, 356, 376. The basic "Draft Treaty on the Disarmament and Demobilization of Japan" was made public on 21 June and submitted to the Far Eastern Commission on June 24. The United States continued to reaffirm its support of a long-term disarmament treaty into 1947 (*FRUS, 1947,* VI, 237, 450–53, 478–79), but this had become a dead issue by midsummer, when George Kennan et al. brought about a reconsideration of occupation policy, as discussed in the following section on the soft cold-war policy.

[15] On Okinawa and the Ryukyus, cf. James F. Schnabel, *The Joint Chiefs of Staff and National Policy, 1945–1947,* vol. 1 of *The History of the Joint Chiefs of Staff* (Wilmington, Del.: Michael Glazier Inc., 1979), 335; Condit, *The Joint Chiefs of Staff and National Policy,* 495 (on JCS 1619/24 of September 1947) and chapter 9 (on the "Broiler," "Halfmoon," and "Fleetwood" plans); and *FRUS, 1947,* VI, 495–96, 537–43 (PPS 10 October 1947).

1947, MacArthur informed a press conference that the time had come to end the occupation and permit Japan to fulfill this grand destiny. As was often the case, the supreme commander's grand pronouncement had a highly personal and subjective underside, for at this juncture MacArthur had his eye on the impending presidential primary elections in the United States, in which he hoped to emerge as the Republican candidate. The March call for an early peace with Japan coincided closely with the enunciation of the Truman Doctrine for Europe and served as impetus to a flurry of activities that can be most charitably described as the peace-treaty charades of mid-1947. In the course of public and private debate over the prospects of an early peace with Japan, U.S. officials really began for the first time seriously and systematically to consider Japan's future role in the cold war.

Four aspects of the peace-treaty flurries of mid-1947 seem especially noteworthy. First, it became apparent that State Department planning for a future peace settlement with Japan remained in the mold of World War II thinking. The basic draft peace treaties for Japan that were being worked on within the department at this time (under the direction of Hugh Borton) were extremely long, and bristled with provisions for post-treaty international supervision and controls over "sovereign" Japan. They amounted, in a word, to a "punitive" peace.

Second, despite the cumbersome and still tentative nature of these internal drafts, the State Department responded to public pressure in July 1947 by calling for an international conference on Japan that (1) was scheduled for a time when Britain and the Commonwealth nations already had prior commitments, and (2) was procedurally unacceptable to the Soviet Union, because in the Soviet view it ignored prior understandings that these matters would first be considered by the wartime "Big Four" (the United States, Soviet Union, Britain, and China) before being submitted to a larger multinational forum. These procedural issues became a cause for charges of bad faith on all sides, and in this setting for the first time U.S. officials and politicians considered the notion that it might be appropriate to anticipate a "separate peace" with Japan—that is, a peace settlement on terms that would be unacceptable to the Soviet Union.[16]

---

[16] For MacArthur's statements, see *Political Reorientation of Japan,* 2: 756, 765–66. The peace-treaty debate is extensively documented in *FRUS,* 1947, VI. On the "separate peace" concept, cf. ibid., 476–77, 479–85, 489–502; also *Department of State Bulletin,* 24 August 1947, 395.

In a third related development, the Japanese—including not only government officials but also the presumedly "symbolic" and nonpolitical emperor himself—took the initiative to convey to the Americans their willingness to accept some sort of separate peace arrangement if necessary. These secret Japanese proposals, which in many respects anticipated by roughly four years the broad contours of the San Francisco settlement of 1951, hinted at a bilateral military agreement with the United States and the development of Okinawa as a major U.S. military bastion. To scholars of the occupation, these activities are of interest for a number of reasons. They call attention to the positive Japanese contribution to the policy-making process; offer an unusually vivid case study of politicking by the emperor through his personal advisers; and reveal that both the Japanese government and Imperial Household were willing from an early date to trade away true sovereignty for Okinawa in exchange for an early end to the occupation in the rest of Japan. As many Japanese critics see it, the special treatment accorded Okinawa beginning right after the war—its intense militarization and Americanization—makes it proper to see post-World War II Japan as a "semi-divided" country. Moreover, the Japanese ruling groups, as the record now clearly indicates, did little or nothing to prevent this from happening. On the contrary, they were all too willing to use Okinawa and its people, who have always been regarded as second-class citizens, as bargaining chips.[17]

Finally, the peace-treaty issue of 1947 focused attention on Japan and drew a new group of U.S. planners into the picture, many of whom hitherto had been preoccupied with policy making for Europe. Even as the United States publicly was blaming the Soviet Union for impeding progress on a peace settlement with Japan, these new national-security advisers were arguing behind the scenes not only that the Borton group's draft treaty was totally outdated but also that an early peace with Japan was out of the question. The United States itself was unprepared to talk concretely about a peace settlement with Japan in mid-1947, and it is for this reason that its public gestures to the contrary can only be described as a charade.

[17] The 1947 Japanese initiatives are described in various Japanese sources, including the valuable "insider" account by Kumao Nishimura, *San Furanshisuko Heiwa Jōyaku* (1971: vol. 27 of the Kajima Kenkyūjo Shuppankai series *Nihon Gaikō Shi*). In English, see Martin Weinstein, *Japan's Postwar Defense Policy, 1947–1968* (New York: Columbia University Press, 1971), chapter 2. The emperor's role was first made public by Eiichi Shindō in the April 1979 issue of the Japanese monthly *Sekai*. Eiji Takamae, the "dean" of Japanese specialists on the occupation, among others, has called attention to Okinawa and the "semi-divided" nature of post-1945 Japan.

Over the course of the next several years, the vision of a disarmed and neutral Japan remained a potent one in the public arena, partly because of General MacArthur's continued reaffirmation of this ideal. Although the supreme commander's presidential aspirations had been dashed by a stunning defeat in the Republican primary election in Wisconsin in April 1948, he remained very much in the public eye and as zealous a proselytizer as ever concerning the dream of turning Japan into a unique symbol of peace in the modern world. In his scenario, Japan's "disarmed neutrality" would be protected by the positioning of United Nations forces in key Pacific islands, including Okinawa. MacArthur's famous description of Japan as the "Switzerland of the Pacific" actually was made as late as March 1949, but by then time had passed him by. Still, whether out of pacifist ideals or, more commonly, lingering fear and mistrust of Japan, few American officials were ready to rush pell-mell into the wholesale rehabilitation of Japan as a cold-war ally.[18]

In Washington, the most articulate spokesmen for the new vision of Japan included the State Department's George Kennan and high civilian bureaucrats in the Department of the Army led by Secretary Kenneth Royall and Under Secretary William Draper. The "Kennan touch" was first applied to Japan policy in a decisive way in October 1947 in a paper on the peace-treaty issue for the State Department's Policy Planning Staff (PPS 10). The position set forth there became the basis for the National Security Council documents that governed Japan policy in 1948 and into 1949 (the NSC 13 series), and covered a wide range of sensitive policy issues. Kennan and his aides opposed an early end to the occupation, partly on the grounds that Japan's present economic instability made it ripe for communist penetration, and they foresaw the possibility of having to impose peace terms "unilaterally" later. While recognizing the necessity of long-term U.S. military control of certain islands peripheral to Japan, as well as of at least the northern part of Okinawa, PPS 10 indicated that the long-term presence of U.S. forces in the main four islands

---

[18] MacArthur's comments on security matters appear at great length in the *FRUS* volumes and the files of the Joint Chiefs of Staff in the Modern Military Records branch, National Archives. Many of the basic JCS documents are available in fourteen microfilm reels as *Records of the Joint Chiefs of Staff, part 2, 1946–1953, The Far East* (Frederick, Md.: University Publications of America, 1980). For the "Switzerland of the Pacific" statement, see the *New York Times*, 2 March 1949; this quotation appeared, it should be noted, in an interview in which MacArthur proposed an offshore island chain of defense in Asia very similar to that which Secretary of State Acheson described on 12 January 1950—including the Philippines, the Ryukyus, Japan, and the Aleutians, and neglecting Taiwan and Korea.

of Japan might not be necessary. The paper also proposed that any future peace treaty with Japan should avoid post-treaty supervision but at the same time reaffirm the principle of complete Japanese disarmament. The Kennan group also recommended that the reparations program should be terminated quickly to end uncertainty and to stimulate capital investment and economic recovery.[19]

By June 1948, this policy had evolved into NSC 13 ("Recommendations with Respect to U.S. Policy toward Japan"). This called for a brief, general, and nonpunitive peace treaty in the indefinite future; reaffirmed the necessity of maintaining long-term military control over not only Okinawa but also the great naval facilities at Yokosuka (south of Tokyo) as well, but deferred decision on post-treaty bases throughout the four main islands; advocated strengthening the Japanese "police"; and announced a shift in occupation priorities from reform to economic recovery.[20]

While this broad policy directive was worming its way to the surface in the National Security Council, numerous economic studies and proposals that addressed the economic reconstruction of Japan in more concrete terms were piling up on the desks of the national-security managers. As early as March 1947, an important internal State Department report known as the Martin Plan called attention to the changing nature of the world economy and the impending "dollar gap" crisis in Asia. With this in view, the report argued, it was desirable to promote Japan's future economic stability by actively developing its capacity to export capital goods to the nondollar markets of Asia.[21]

The Martin Plan was important as an early intimation of many economic considerations that would emerge as dominant over the course of time: the recognition of Japan's heavy dependence on U.S. aid, the fear that the dollar-poor countries of Asia would collapse unless more sophisticated patterns of interregional integration were developed, and the perception that in the future Japan would have to rely more on the export of machine goods and the like than on the export of textiles and light-industrial products as in the prewar period. In return for such exports,

---

[19] PPS 10 is printed in *FRUS*, 1947, VI, 537–43. See also PPS 28 of 25 March 1948, the key transitional policy paper between PPS 10 and NSC 13; *FRUS*, 1948, VI, 691–719.

[20] NSC 13 is reproduced in *FRUS*, 1948, VI, 775–81. The key documents in the series are NSC 13 (2 June 1948), NSC 13/1 (24 September 1948), NSC 13/2 (7 October 1948; approved by President Truman two days later), and NSC 13/3 (6 May 1949).

[21] For the "Martin Plan," see *FRUS*, 1947, VI, 184–86. This evolved into the State Department's SWNCC 381 of 22 July 1947, which the Army criticized as too soft in SWNCC 384 of 9 October; ibid., 265–66, 302–04.

Japan would import raw materials and cheap manufactures from the less developed countries of Asia.

Similar arguments came from other directions. Almost simultaneously with the Martin Plan, for example, the Army received an economic report from MacArthur's Economic and Scientific Section in Tokyo that also recommended curbing inflation and attaining a "balanced Japanese economy" by revising the reparations program and promoting Japanese production of capital goods earmarked for export. These prospects were thrown into the arena of public debate in a famous speech by Dean Acheson on May 8, in which the then assistant secretary of state, with his gift for the sharp aphorism, linked Europe with Asia while separating the cold war from the old war—all in a single stroke. There was no getting around the fact, Acheson declared, that Japan and Germany had to be developed as the "workshops" of Asia and Europe, respectively. How this was to be done, and how extensively and how rapidly, was debated within both the civilian and military bureaucracies in the months that followed, resulting in a small flood of reports and position papers that became the basis for swinging Congress behind the policy of promoting Japanese economic reconstruction in 1948. In June 1948, under the new Economic Recovery in Occupied Areas program, Congress appropriated $108 million that, for the first time, could be used specifically for economic recovery in occupied Japan. That same month Congress also approved a Natural Fibers Revolving Fund (P.L. 820) totaling $150 million that eventually was used to support massive exports of American raw cotton to Japan—a pump-priming program with obvious sectional appeal in Congress, although it did not reflect the emerging emphasis on promoting growth in Japan's nontextile sectors.[22]

As NSC 13 revealed, by 1948 the question of the future military disposition of Japan was being addressed on three levels: Okinawa, post-

---

[22] The SCAP study entitled *A Possible Program for a Balanced Japanese Economy* was sent to Army authorities on 27 March 1947; SCAP Records (in the National Archives in Suitland, Maryland), RG 331, Box 6670. In the convoluted genealogy of these internal studies and recommendations, this evolved into the so-called "Green Book" of October 1947 (*Possibility of a Balanced Japanese Economy*), and eventually the influential "Blue Book" of November 1948 (*Program for a Self-Supporting Japanese Economy*); cf. SCAP Records, RG 331, Boxes 7689, 7692, 8361. The text of Acheson's famous "workshop" speech appears as an appendix in Joseph M. Jones, *The Fifteen Weeks* (New York: Harcourt Brace and World, 1955).

For closely documented studies of the early recovery program, see Borden, *Pacific Alliance*, chapter 2; Schaller, "Securing the Great Crescent" and *The American Occupation of Japan;* Schonberger, "General William Draper, the 80th Congress, and the Origins of Japan's Reverse Course"; and the *Foreign Trade* volume (Monograph 50) in SCAP's *History of the Non-Military Activities of the Occupation of Japan.*

treaty U.S. bases in the rest of Japan, and Japanese rearmament. Okinawa was by this time explicitly identified as the primary forward base in U.S. nuclear strategy in the Far East. While the importance of continued U.S. access to the airfields in the rest of Japan was publicly discussed by top officials such as Draper, no formal decision had been made on this. And the issue of Japanese rearmament had been raised but shelved, emerging only obliquely in NSC 13 in the context of strengthening Japanese police forces against potential internal subversion.

Many formerly classified documents confirm that by 1948 the defense establishment was pushing fairly firmly in the direction of long-term U.S. bases in Japan and Japanese rearmament. As early as the spring of 1947, the JCS (Joint Chiefs of Staff) had identified Japan as the one country in Asia capable of holding the "ideological opponents" of the United States at bay while a major offensive was waged in the West. For that reason, the military planners observed, "of all the countries in the Pacific area Japan deserves primary consideration for current United States assistance designed to restore her economy and her military potential." Secretary of Defense Forrestal requested a study of limited military rearmament for both Japan and Germany in February 1948, and by May had received a lengthy and extremely frank response under the name of Secretary of the Army Royall, in which the Army planners not only supported post-treaty bases and constitutional revision that would permit future Japanese rearmament but also went on to emphasize the importance of developing new markets and sources of raw materials for Japan abroad. Nonetheless, when this document came before the JCS in October (accompanied by a copy of MacArthur's views opposing rearmament), the rearmament of Japan was rejected as impractical under present circumstances. The rearmament policy was not approved until early 1950 and not actually urged upon the Japanese government until June 22 of that year—three days before the outbreak of the Korean War.

Certain military officers did openly proclaim their desire to enlist the Japanese as an active military ally from an early date. For example, in 1948 General Robert Eichelberger, commander of the Eighth Army in Japan (who had described the Japanese enemy as "monkeys" in his wartime letters), publicly called for a Japanese army of 150,000 men. Such men, he said, would be the sort of military force every commander dreams of leading—an appalling and terrifying remark to the rest of Asia. In the internal documents of this period, however, even those who were advocating "limited military rearmament" for Japan took care to emphasize the necessity of controlling and restraining whatever remilitarization might be allowed. Distrust of Japan remained a conspicuous feature of this second stage of U.S. planning.[23]

In what ways, then, was the cold-war policy of this second stage "soft" in comparison with the eventual San Francisco settlement? In the case of both long-term bases in Japan and Japanese rearmament, the answer is obvious: Neither policy had yet been adopted by the U.S. government, and both still had strong and persuasive critics (including Kennan and most of his State Department colleagues, as well as MacArthur and many of his key aides). In addition, despite the fact that Japan was now identified as the future "workshop" of Asia—and despite vague references to a Marshall Plan for Asia—the soft policy did not offer a coherent vision of regional anti-communist economic integration in Asia. On the contrary, it was assumed until 1950, and in some U.S. and Japanese circles even later, that Japan would and should establish substantial economic ties with China, no matter what regime controlled the mainland. No positive steps were taken to integrate Japan and Southeast Asia until much later; and no concrete, systematic attempt to stabilize the Japanese economy and gear industry for export production was actually undertaken until January 1949, when the Detroit banker Joseph M. Dodge arrived in Tokyo to initiate the famous (or, to some, notorious) "disinflation" policy known as the Dodge Line. Although reparations policy began to be watered down beginning in 1947, the formal "postponement" of this program, which was so inhibiting to prospective Japanese investors and entrepreneurs, did not occur until May 1949. Indeed, NSC 13 itself was not approved by President Truman until October 1948 (as NSC 13/2), and well into the spring of 1949 policy makers in Washington were still lamenting that there had been virtually no progress in its actual implementation.[24]

---

[23] Okinawa's key position was spelled out in the secret strategy code-named "Halfmoon." Draper discussed the airfields in a 17 May 1948 speech entitled "Japan's Key Position in the Far East" (MacArthur Memorial Collection). The "ideological opponents" reference appears in JCS 1769/1 on 29 April 1947; *FRUS*, 1947, I, 745. Cf. Schaller, *The American Occupation of Japan*, 90, 104. Royall's important long memorandum of 18 May 1948, entitled "Limited Military Rearmament for Japan," appears under JCS 1380/48 of 25 October 1948 in the JCS archives, RG 218 (Geographic File 1946–47), Box 127. Further opposition to Japanese rearmament by MacArthur's staff, tendered on 23 December 1948, appears as JCS 1380/54 of 6 January 1949. Eichelberger's notorious 1948 comment is cited by Kazuo Kawai in *Pacific Affairs*, June 1950, 119; for the "monkey" reference, see Jay Luvaas, ed., *Dear Miss Em: General Eichelberger's War in the Pacific, 1942–1945* (Westport, Conn.: Greenwood Press, 1972), 8–9.
[24] The Joseph Dodge Papers in the Detroit Public Library are a major resource for analyzing

Perhaps most striking, the soft cold-war policy minimized the overt threat of Soviet aggression against Japan and instead emphasized the possibility of Japan's "going Communist" because of its own internal instability. As Kennan and others were quick to emphasize, Japan appeared extremely precarious economically and thereby politically precarious as well. Inflation was out of hand; lingering uncertainty over occupation policy in the areas of reparations and economic deconcentration stifled capital investment; foreign trade, stymied by occupation controls, hardly existed; and labor, caught in the inflationary spiral, appeared to be moving in an increasingly radical direction. In one of the more ideologically entertaining vignettes from this period, the "liberal" Kennan visited Japan in early 1948 and concluded that the "conservative" MacArthur was promoting policies conducive to communism. It was this vision of Japan as economically unstable and thereby ripe for communization *from within* that motivated the abandonment of some of the initial democratic and reformist policies of the occupation and the adoption instead of policies conducive to capitalist stabilization and reconstruction.[25]

This nervous and occasionally even apocalyptic vision of Japan as economically vulnerable, politically unstable, and ideologically unreliable was especially unsettling because it coincided with the enunciation in U.S. circles of an absolutely fundamental thesis: that Japan was the key to the balance of power in Asia. Beginning around 1948, this balance-of-power argument was developed roughly as follows: (1) Japan, with its skilled manpower and great industrial and war-making potential, was the critical power in Asia. (2) In grand global terms, however, Asia ranked neither first nor even second in strategic importance to the United States. On the contrary, the European theater took priority, followed by the Near and Middle East. In military terms, this called for a "strategic offense in the West and strategic defense in the East." (3) In this global scheme, Japan was more important to the Soviet Union than to the United States. (4) Consequently, the primary U.S. objective where Japan was

economic policy toward Japan from the beginning of 1949. Critical earlier "reverse course" economic missions, discussed in the standard literature, were led by Clifford Strike (producing the "Strike Report" of February 1947 and "Overseas Consultants Report" of February 1948, both calling for reduced reparations); Percy Johnston (resulting in the "Johnston Report" of April 1948); and Ralph Young (leading to recommendations for stabilization and a fixed exchange rate in June 1948). For the less-than-dynamic implementation of NSC 13, cf. *FRUS*, 1949, VII, 724–27, 754, 808–12, 815; also JCS 1380/59 of 10 February 1949 in RG 218 (1946–47), Box 122.

[25] Kennan's own *Memoirs 1925–1950* (Boston: Little, Brown, 1967) are very clear on this; cf. chapter 16.

concerned was not to make Japan a part of the U.S. offensive capability but rather, more simply, to keep Japan out of the Soviet sphere.

This concept of the *negative* importance of Japan (the need to "deny" it to the enemy) meant—and still means—that even apart from any positive contribution to U.S. objectives, the United States could never conceive of "writing off" Japan, for this would mean incalculable gain for the Soviet Union. John Foster Dulles later became fond of citing a phrase attributed to Stalin in 1925 to buttress this line of thinking ("The way to victory over the West is through the East"), and the concept was repeated again and again in the U.S. policy papers prior to 1950. As late as December 1949, for example, one of the basic papers pertaining to Asia (NSC 48/1) observed that "if Japan, the principal component of a Far Eastern war-making complex, were added to the Stalinist bloc, the Soviet Asian base could become a source of strength capable of shifting the balance of world power to the disadvantage of the United States." Even more succinctly: "The Asian power potential is more valuable to Russia than to the United States." An analysis by the Central Intelligence Agency (CIA) dated May 1949 spelled the same thesis out in fuller detail:

Control of Japan's industrial machine would be more valuable to the USSR than to the US, not only because the USSR has more immediate need of the products of Japan's industry but also because the USSR will be in effective control of the area (chiefly northern China, Manchuria and Korea) whose natural resources Japanese industry can utilize most efficiently. For this reason, long-range US security interests dictate the denial of Japan's capacity, both economic and military, to USSR exploitation. . . . The difficulties and cost to the United States of making Japan the center of a Far Eastern war-making complex, and the fact that Japan's industry—measured in terms of realizable steel production—is only 5 percent of US, probably would make denial of the Japan complex to the USSR, rather than full exploitation of Japanese industry as an auxiliary to US war production, the dominant US strategic consideration. Japan's industrial plant would be of much greater positive value to the USSR than to the US; it would, in fact, be for the Soviet Union the richest economic prize in the Fast East.[26]

To call such a policy soft is not meant to minimize either its dynamics or its impact on the attentive public. The British and Chinese (of all political persuasions), as well as the Soviets, voiced concern about the specter of Japanese remilitarization beginning in early 1948, and before the

[26] Central Intelligence Agency, "The Strategic Importance of the Far East to the US and the USSR" (4 May 1949), Modern Military Records, National Archives; "The Position of the U.S. with Respect to Asia" (NSC 48/1), reprinted in Thomas H. Etzold and John Lewis Gaddis, eds., *Containment: Documents on American Policy and Strategy, 1945–1950* (New York: Columbia University Press, 1978), 252–69.

end of that year the Soviets were citing Western press accounts in denouncing what they termed the U.S. military policy of surrounding China with a "defensive ring" stretching through Japan, Taiwan, the Philippines, Siam, Burma, and India. In the United States, a small, well-organized, and highly effective "Japan lobby" had emerged by 1948 under the name of the American Council on Japan, with excellent access to government, Congress, business and financial circles, and the media. And in Japan itself, the shift from reform to reconstruction was signaled by antilabor actions beginning in 1947 and, in 1948, the near-abandonment of one of the central announced policies of the demilitarization and democratization agenda: enforcement of a vigorous program of economic deconcentration.

Because of a variety of technical and political complications, the policy of democratizing the Japanese economy by eliminating excessive concentrations of economic power was almost stillborn. The basic enabling legislation for deconcentration was not even enacted until December 1947, by which time it was already wreathed in controversy. Although 325 companies were designated for investigation and possible reorganization in February 1948, by mid-April the policy had been almost completely reversed and occupation authorities were instructed that banks were to be totally excluded from the purview of the law and, in the words of a confidential internal memorandum, "no more than twenty companies were to be subject to reorganization under the law and these were to be chosen on the basis that they were interfering with Japanese economic recovery." By July, 225 of the 325 designated firms had been removed from designation, and eventually only 11 of the original 325 companies were ordered to split and another 8 to make minor organizational changes. One of the members of a Deconcentration Review Board composed of U.S. businessmen sent to Japan in May 1948 to terminate the program expressed the prevailing sentiment in a memorandum that described the antitrust legislation as "bordering on (if not actually) the methods used by so-called communist States today." In the words of one of the original supporters of the program, written as these events unfolded, "Facts of the last war faded . . . and conjectures on the next war took their place."[27]

Although the archival record concerning the decision to abandon the

---

[27] Cf. *Soviet Press Translations* 4 (1949), 615–16, for the Soviet response. The major article on the American Council on Japan is Schonberger's "The Japan Lobby in American Diplomacy, 1947–1952" (note 2 above). For economic deconcentration, see Hadley (note 12 above), especially *Antitrust in Japan*, 166, 172, 174, 180.

economic democratization program contains the usual good portion of blunt and colorful confidential quotations, it is more important to keep in mind that this reversal of policy was plain for all to see. It flew in the face of Acheson's old "will to war" hypothesis concerning the structural roots of Japanese aggression, while giving concrete meaning to his more recent vision of the Japanese "workshop." And, every bit as much as the specter of a remilitarized Japan, it caused alarm and protest through most of the rest of Asia.

The hard cold-war policy, 1949–1951

The reconsideration of policy toward Japan obviously occurred at a time when U.S. officials were becoming profoundly pessimistic about trends elsewhere in Asia. In essence, they were envisaging the old Greater East Asia Co-Prosperity Sphere (including Japan itself) turning Red and being harnessed to the Soviet Union: references to a "Communist Co-Prosperity Sphere" or to communist-influenced "Pan-Asiatic tendencies" actually appear in U.S. documents from this period.[28] At the same time, U.S. officials now were also beginning to think explicitly of Japan's role in a future global conflict between the United States and the Soviet Union—and from this it was only a short step to the logical next stage in strategic planning: the notion that it was not only necessary to deny Japan to the enemy but also essential to incorporate Japan in a positive manner in the U.S. cold-war strategy. When this step was taken, it marked the end of the soft cold-war policy.

The "hard" or "positive" cold-war policy line involving Japan can be dated from June 1949, when, shortly after Secretary of Defense Louis Johnson had called for a coordinated policy "to contain communism" in Asia, the Joint Chiefs of Staff submitted a strong and controversial statement of U.S. security needs in Japan to the National Security Council. In this document, NSC 49, the Joint Chiefs declared that America must maintain strategic control of an "offshore island chain" in Asia, with all of Japan playing a pivotal role in this chain as a forward staging area from which U.S. military power could be launched against the Soviet Union. NSC 49 also endorsed the creation of a Japanese military and indicated that eventually this military could be expected to play a significant role in the event of a global war between the United States and

---

[28] For the fascinating revival of "co-prosperity sphere" rhetoric, cf. Schaller, *The American Occupation of Japan*, 145, 179–80, 201, 205.

Soviet Union. In such a conflict, Japan would tie down the Soviets on their eastern front and thus prevent them from concentrating their forces against the United States and Europe in the west (unlike World War II, when the Soviet-Japanese neutrality pact had freed Russia in the east). This argument that Japan must play an *active* role in U.S. military policy—in contrast to the soft cold-war policy, with its relatively passive emphasis on denying Japan to the communist enemy—was concisely expressed in a basic JCS document of November 1949 that declared Japan "will be not only oriented toward the United States but also be actively allied with us in event of global war" (JCS 1380/75). Such thinking had indeed surfaced earlier, but now the Pentagon was placing it at center stage.[29]

After the outbreak of the Korean War one year later, the concept of the "offshore island chain" became a hotly debated issue in connection with a famous speech given by Secretary of State Acheson on 12 January 1950. On that occasion, Acheson had spoken of a defense perimeter in Asia that extended from the Aleutians through Japan and the Ryukyus to the Philippines. Because he left out South Korea, the secretary was later criticized for having invited the communist attack. It is understandable that this point of omission has attracted retrospective attention, but this has tended to obscure the positive thrust of the speech: the fact that the secretary's strategic line explicitly included Japan and Okinawa. At the time Acheson spoke (a matter of months after the Soviet Union had become a nuclear power and the People's Republic of China had been established), the United States was concretely building up its military capability on Okinawa and the four main islands of Japan.[30]

This does not mean that there was unanimity in U.S. decision-making circles at this time. Following the presentation of NSC 49, the Pentagon and the State Department fell into a quarrel over policy toward Japan that was not resolved until September 1950, although both sides were in general agreement before then on the necessity of Japanese rearmament and long-term U.S. military bases in Japan. The more subtle aspect of the disagreement concerned how to appraise and respond to the psychological and political inclinations of the Japanese. Could Japan be incorporated most effectively in the anti-communist camp by prolonging the oc-

[29] NSC 49 (15 June 1949) and 49/1 (30 September 1949) are reprinted in Etzold and Gaddis, *Containment*, 231–36. For JCS 1380/75 (30 November 1949), see RG 218 (1946–47), Box 127.

[30] Dean Acheson, *Present at the Creation: My Years in the State Department* (New York: W. W. Norton, 1969), 355–58.

cupation indefinitely, it was asked, or would a contrary policy of granting a peace treaty in the near future be more effective? In the view of the JCS, U.S. strategy in Asia now required exclusive and extensive control of airfields throughout the Japanese archipelago, plus the cautious development of Japanese forces for self-defense. At the same time, however, the military frankly acknowledged that they were not confident that Japan would remain democratic or was sincerely committed to the anti-communist cause. Because they needed Japan but could not trust the Japanese, talk of a peace treaty was premature.

State Department officials did not challenge their military colleagues' skeptical view of the Japanese, as a circular cable to diplomatic posts abroad from the secretary of state himself in May rather crudely revealed. "Japs will either move toward sound friendly relations with non-Commie countries," Acheson suggested, "or into association Commie system in Asia." As the diplomatic wing of the bureaucracy saw it, however, indefinitely prolonging the occupation might simply provoke the Japanese to the point where they would indeed become more favorably disposed to aligning with the "Commie system."

In its first formal response to NSC 49 (NSC 49/1 of 30 September 1949), the State Department reiterated its misgivings about the reliability of Japan's pro-Western orientation, concurred that the Japanese would have to develop their own self-defense capacity, rejected the argument that it was premature to start planning for a Japanese peace treaty, and expressed grave misgivings about the vast network of bases that the Pentagon wished to maintain indefinitely in Japan. General MacArthur, while backing off from his earlier idealistic stance, argued that adoption of the Pentagon's positive policy would threaten the communist countries and imperil Japan. "In any war," the general commented in January 1950 in response to the general thesis advanced in NSC 49, "regardless of what happened their [the Japanese] islands would be destroyed."

Thousands of pages of "Secret" and "Top Secret" arguments were devoted to these issues, but it should be noted (1) that the general principles (if not numbers) of long-term U.S. bases in Japan and Japanese rearmament had been agreed on by the first part of 1950 and (2) that the whole world was aware of the direction of the debate. By February 1950, several multimillion-dollar construction projects funded by congressional appropriations were under way to enlarge airfields and lengthen runways in Okinawa and Japan proper (and, as an attractive by-product, simultaneously stimulate Japanese economic recovery through construction contracts). At the same time, a series of well-publicized official U.S. missions visited Okinawa and Japan, including, from 31 January to 10 February, the Joint Chiefs of Staff. The JCS Chairman, Omar Bradley, was quoted in the *New York Times* as observing that "the former enemy appeared to be not only the strongest bastion but just about the only tangible thing left of the fruits of victory in the Pacific." Privately, the quotations were even pithier. In January 1950, when making the case for economic aid to Japan before the National Advisory Council, Joseph Dodge described Japan as a "springboard and source of supply." An investigative report to the Committee on Appropriations of the House of Representatives that same month identified Japan as the "west coast" of the United States.[31]

In Japan, prominent intellectuals organized against these trends as early as January 1950 by forming a Peace Problems Symposium (*Heiwa Mondai Danwakai*), which became the vanguard of the postwar Japanese peace movement. The Japanese government, conversely, sought to reassure the Americans of the wisdom of an early peace treaty by taking two bold initiatives, one secret and the other public. On 2 May the Japanese secretly offered to support post-treaty U.S. military bases in Japan, having concluded that the Americans would never end the occupation without such a guarantee. The Japanese informed the Americans that they had consulted leading legal authorities and been assured that post-treaty U.S. bases would not violate the Japanese constitution. Then, on 1 June, the Foreign Ministry issued a white paper that expressed Japan's willingness, if necessary, to accept a peace treaty not signed by all belligerents—in other words, to accept a separate peace without the participation of the Soviet Union.

The Japanese government was not at that point willing to undertake rearmament, however, as the conservative prime minister, Shigeru Yo-

[31] The position of the military is set forth in NSC 49, JCS 1380/75, JCS 1380/77 (10 December 1949), and NSC 60 (7 December 1949). For Acheson's cable, see *FRUS, 1949*, VII, 736–37; cf. ibid., 724–29, for a useful summary of the State Department's support of a bilateral treaty, U.S. bases in Japan, and eventual Japanese rearmament. MacArthur's January 1950 response to NSC 49 appears in *FRUS, 1950*, VI, 1110. The statement by Omar Bradley appeared in the *New York Times* on 7 February 1950. For Dodge's statement to the National Advisory Council, see the "Appropriations" file, Box 1, Joseph Dodge Papers for 1950. The House Appropriations Committee report (16 January 1950) is among the Dodge papers in the Japanese Ministry of Finance collection. For the resolution of the long bureaucratic impasse, see *FRUS, 1950*, VI, 1278–82 (JCS 1380/89 of 18 August 1950); 1282–88 (the State Department response); and 1293–96 (the joint Defense-State memo to the president of 7 September). NSC 60/1 of 8 September 1950, by which President Truman authorized the government to proceed with negotiations for a peace treaty with Japan, marked the formal end of the stalemate.

shida, made emphatically clear to John Foster Dulles on 22 June. Dulles had been brought into the Truman administration in May as a special adviser to help resolve the deadlock between the Pentagon and the State Department and to prevent the peace treaty issue from becoming embroiled in partisan politics. He chose to urge the Japanese to rearm as virtually the first item of business on his first visit to Tokyo. Yoshida enlisted MacArthur's support in turning the request aside, and MacArthur, in turn, urged Dulles to consider rehabilitating Japan's idle war-related factories instead. Thus, when the North Koreans launched their blitz across the thirty-eighth parallel, post-treaty bases, Japanese rearmament, and now even Japan's industrial remilitarization were all already on the table.[32]

Actually, there was even more on the table. In the final days of 1949 the National Security Council had distributed a lengthy summary paper on "The Position of the United States with Respect to Asia" (NSC 48/1). This, plus a wealth of prior and subsequent documents, carried projections concerning Japan's future economic role in the containment of communism in Asia to a new level of thinking. NSC 48/1 offered a succinct three-part summation of the strategic importance of Asia to the United States: Control there would enhance the war-making potential of the Soviets; development of indigenous anti-communist forces would reduce Soviet influence, save the United States money, and provide forces in the event of war; and certain raw materials available in Asia (especially tin and rubber) were of value to the United States. The catch phrase of basic military policy remained "a strategic offense in the 'West' and a strategic defense in the 'East.' "

NSC 48/1 was the master statement both of the balance-of-power thesis pivoting on Japan and of U.S. anxiety concerning Japan's political and ideological propensities. Traditional social patterns "antithetical to democracy" remained strong in Japan, it was stated, and the country might easily veer to the political right or political left. The United States could only hope to hold it to a middle-of-the-road course. The paper acknowledged that the Soviet Union did not pose a direct military threat to Japan or to the rest of Asia for the foreseeable future, and it also recognized potential sources of friction between the Soviet Union and China. As

---

[32] For activities on the Japanese side, see Dower, *Empire and Aftermath*; Nishimura, *San Furanshisuko Heiwa Jōyaku*; Michael M. Yoshitsu, *Japan and the San Francisco Peace Settlement* (New York: Columbia University Press, 1982); and Takeshi Igarashi, "Peace-Making and Party Politics: The Formation of the Domestic Foreign Policy System in Postwar Japan," *Journal of Japanese Studies* 11 (Summer 1985): 323–56.

prior position papers had argued, Japan was expected to have to engage in substantial trade with China in the future. Indeed, such Sino-Japanese trade, subject to restrictions on strategic materials, could serve U.S. purposes by making important Chinese commodities (such as tungsten, antimony, tung oil, and bristles) available to the United States, while drawing China closer to the capitalist economies. Although not mentioned in NSC 48/1, it is apparent from other archival sources that as of this date planners such as Kennan also looked forward to "the re-entry of Japanese influence and activity into Korea and Manchuria" as being "in fact, the only realistic prospect for countering and moderating Soviet influence in that area."[33]

Beginning in the latter part of 1949, however, and with mounting intensity thereafter, planners in Washington began to look to Southeast Asia rather than China as the critical area for Japan's future economic expansion. NSC 48/1 concluded with a general reference to the desirability of accelerating the integration of the Japanese economy with that of South and Southeast Asia; an earlier draft had noted even more precisely "the mutually beneficial character of trade of a triangular character" linking the United States, Japan, and Southeast Asia. The triangular metaphor became a key one in the months and years ahead, although this "triangle" actually had four corners: Southeast Asia, as other documents made clear, in good part meant the European colonies. Indeed, when the emerging blueprint of trilateral U.S.-Japanese-Southeast Asian integration was spoken of as an Asian version of the Marshall Plan or European Recovery Program, as also was frequently done, this, too, was somewhat misleading. In the first place, the United States did not regard the countries of Southeast Asia as in any way equivalent to the shattered but industrially advanced nations of Western Europe; only Japan had this advanced capitalist potential. More subtly, given the colonial structure of Southeast Asia and its perceived economic importance to Europe, U.S. promotion of the security and economic development of the area could more accurately be seen as a supplement—but also possibly a detriment—to the European Recovery Program, rather than simply a "little Marshall Plan" for Asia. As a report on the subject prepared in mid-1948 pointed out, the dollar earnings of Malaya, Indochina, and Indonesia played an important role in alleviating the dollar gap in trans-Atlantic

---

[33] NSC 48/1 (23 December 1949) and NSC 48/2 (30 December 1949) are reprinted in Etzold and Gaddis, 252–76. Kennan's observation, made in October 1949, is quoted in Cumings, *Child of Conflict*, 23; cf. 26, 35–37.

trade that plagued the British, French, and Dutch. The question that arose repeatedly in interagency discussions of promoting Japanese economic integration with Southeast Asia was whether this, too, would help the European nations by strengthening the Southeast Asian economies, or harm them by giving Japan a decided competitive edge in the southern reaches of its old "co-prosperity sphere."

Like the issues of Japanese rearmament and post-treaty bases, recommendations to promote the integration of the Japanese and Southeast Asian economies can be traced back to early 1947 but were not lifted to the level of "hard" policy until mid-1949. The State Department introduced the concept of a "great crescent" of containment extending from Japan through Southeast Asia to Australia and India in March 1949 (PPS 51); the National Security Council distributed (but did not formally adopt) this concept the following July as NSC 51. Background commentaries on the concept made it clear that Southeast Asia would function primarily as a market and source of raw materials for both Japan and Western Europe. Even as Kennan was contemplating checking Soviet influence in Northeast Asia by promoting Japan's economic reintegration with Korea and Manchuria, he was simultaneously giving attention to "the terrific problem of how the Japanese are going to get along unless they again reopen some sort of empire to the south." At precisely the same time (October 1949), the CIA was talking about subsidizing the return of Japanese investors and trading companies to Southeast Asia, where their pre-1945 experience would serve them in good stead. On a parallel line, at least in the symbolic sense of resuscitating the architects and technocrats of the Japanese empire, even as the Joint Chiefs of Staff and State Department were arguing that the United States could not afford to intervene militarily to save the Chinese Nationalists on Taiwan (a policy stated in NSC 48/1 and reiterated in basic NSC policy papers for China in March 1950), former Japanese military officers who had fought in the China War were secretly being sent to Taiwan to advise Chiang Kai-shek on how to retake the mainland.[34]

Tracy Voorhees, Draper's successor as under secretary of the army,

[34]The earlier draft of NSC 48/1 is quoted in Cumings, 36. Both Schaller and Borden document the emergence of the trilateral policy in great detail; for a concise summary, see Schaller's "Securing the Great Crescent," especially 398 ff., for references to the European dimension of the linkage and the global problem of the "dollar gap." Kennan's comments on reopening a Japanese "empire to the south" are quoted in Cumings, "The Origins and Development of the Northeast Asian Economy," 18. The use of former Japanese military men by the Chinese Nationalists in Taiwan is discussed in Hata, *Shiroku— Nihon Saigunbi*, 162–65.

quickly identified the Japanese-Southeast Asia nexus as crucial to future anti-communist regional integration of Asia and devoted much of his time from the beginning of 1950 to designing an integrated military and economic aid package that would promote such interdependence. His proposals, too, made clear, again prior to June 1950, that the Japanese workshop was now being viewed as a potential arsenal for non-communist Asia, with military items being among the capital goods that Japan could export to its neighbors in the south. The first of many overlapping U.S. missions to study the feasibility of such anti-communist regional integration was dispatched to Southeast Asia and Japan in January 1950; and the first U.S. commitment of military aid to Indochina, Indonesia, Thailand, and Burma, made in early 1950 under the Military Assistance Program, was undertaken in the context of these broader considerations. Shortly before the Korean War began, the State Department tentatively approved the creation of a huge "special yen fund" that was to be integrated with U.S. aid programs in a manner that would make the raw materials and markets of Southeast Asia more readily accessible to Japan.[35]

As in other critical areas of postwar U.S. planning (such as NSC 68 of April 1950, which called for tripling the U.S. military budget), the great significance of the Korean War insofar as Japan was concerned was that it facilitated and accelerated the implementation of policies that had already been introduced and largely agreed upon at the highest levels. Japanese rearmament was initiated in July. The State-Defense deadlock over a peace treaty was solved by September, with the Pentagon agreeing that Japan's allegiance could be best secured by an early peace treaty. The Japanese economy, which had been "disinflated" under the Dodge Line but appeared to be heading for a recession or even a bona fide depression, was pulled out of the doldrums by a dramatic "Korean War boom" (which coincided with the introduction of quality-control techniques by the American statistician J. Edwards Deming); and extremely ambitious plans were made, although not always carried out, for the long-term industrial remilitarization of Japan.

Domestically, the hard cold-war policy was reflected in numerous areas of occupation policy, most notably actions designed to weaken the labor

---

[35] For Voorhees and the intensified activities of early 1950, see Schaller, *The American Occupation of Japan*, 213–33; also Borden, *Pacific Alliance*, 124–42. For the "special yen fund," see *FRUS*, 1950, VI, 1223–27.

movement and more radical Left. This accelerated internal "reverse course" also was clearly in train well before the Korean War began. Legislation enacted earlier in the occupation to protect organized labor was watered down beginning in the latter part of 1948. Starting at the end of 1949, the occupation authorities and Japanese government collaborated in a "Red Purge" of public employees that resulted in dismissal of some 11,000 workers by June 1950; the great majority of these victims of occupation-style "McCarthyism" were union activists. In the wake of the Korean War, the Red Purge was extended to the private sector and resulted in the firing of almost exactly the same number of activist workers. While the Red Purges were being directed against the political Left, the "de-purge" of persons who had hitherto been prohibited from holding public or corporate office on the grounds of alleged militaristic or ultranation-alistic activities was initiated. In a fitting symbol of the swiftly changing political climate, the Japanese bureaucratic apparatus that had been cre-ated at the start of the occupation to handle the investigation and purge of persons deemed culpable of having contributed to repression and aggression before Japan's surrender was redirected to focus on persons associated with the political Left from 1949.[36]

In April 1951, the CIA summarized Japan's place in American stra-tegic planning as follows:

Because of the strategic location of Japan, its industrial capacity, and its large pool of trained civilian and military manpower, Japan's ultimate political align-ment will be a decisive factor in the balance of power in the Far East. If the Communists controlled Japan, they could:

a. Safeguard the Communist controlled territory in Northeast Asia;

b. Breach the US defense line in the western Pacific;

c. Strengthen the industrial and military power of the Soviet bloc, particularly in respect to shipping and sea power with the Far East;

d. Facilitate Communist aggression in South and Southeast Asia; and

e. Free Communist forces for deployment elsewhere.

If, on the other hand, Japan were to be rearmed and aligned with the West:

---

[36] Deming, later honored as the "father" of statistical quality-control practices in Japan, was invited by the Union of Japanese Scientists and Engineers in 1949 to teach industrial statistics in Japan; he convened his first eight-day seminar on the subject in Tokyo in July 1950 (attended by 220 engineers). The outbreak of the war two weeks earlier fortuitously provided a setting of military-related mass production and rapid industrial reconstruction that permitted the "Deming method" to be adopted, as it were, at the ground floor. For aspects of the "reverse course" in domestic occupation policy, cf. Dower, *Empire and Aftermath*, 332–33 (the purge and depurge), 338–41 (labor policy), 365–66 (the "Red Purge").

a. The West would benefit from the fact that the industrial and military resources of the nation were retained in friendly hands;

b. Japan would provide a potential base for Western military power in Northeast Asia;

c. The US would be able to protect its defense outposts in the Western Pacific; and

d. Other non-Communist countries would be encouraged in their fight against the spread of Communism.[37]

The CIA study went on to speak of the theoretical capability of Japan to raise an army of up to a half-million within six months or a year after the country had agreed to rearm. Furthermore, the agency concluded that there were "enough trained workers in Japan to operate an industrial plant as large and productive as that maintained during World War II. ... We estimate that within 12 to 18 months, a considerable portion of Japan's former capacity to produce weapons and ammunition for the use of ground and naval forces could be restored." The report also observed that South and Southeast Asia could "contribute significantly toward meeting Japanese requirements for food and such raw materials as iron ore, rubber, bauxite, tin, and cotton, and, to a lesser degree, petroleum," provided the area did not come under communist control.

Other internal reports not only accepted such projections but also urged something close to their full realization within the near future. Thus, the JCS reports in the months prior to the San Francisco conference made it clear that the military deemed it essential "to use Japan as a base for military operations in the Far East, including, if necessary, operations against the mainland of China (including Manchuria), the USSR, and on the high seas, regardless of whether such use is under United Nations aegis." At the same time, the U.S. government looked forward to the establishment of a Japanese army of 300,000 to 325,000 men in ten fully equipped combat divisions by 1953. General Matthew Ridgway, who succeeded MacArthur in the spring of 1951, declared emotionally, "Upon such an Army, in the final analysis, the entire Far East will be dependent for stability and protection." The creation of such a force, Ridgway went on, "with fighting spirit and ability equivalent to that displayed by Japanese Forces in World War II," was "paramount" over any other long-range project in the Far East. As a matter of course, it was assumed in all

---

[37] Central Intelligence Agency, "Feasibility of Japanese Rearmament in Association with the United States" (20 April 1951), *FRUS, 1951*, VI, part 1, 993–1001.

confidential U.S. documents from this period that Japanese remilitarization should and soon would be preceded by revision of Article Nine.[38]

The integrated cold-war policy, 1951–1952

Almost two years elapsed between the outbreak of the Korean War in June 1950 and end of the occupation of Japan in April 1952, and it was not until fairly well into 1951 that U.S. policy toward Japan and Asia actually transcended the "nation by nation" approach that so many policy makers had lamented and assumed more or less integrated form. The centerpiece of this coordinated regional policy was the peace treaty signed with Japan at San Francisco in September 1951, along with the three security treaties that accompanied this and linked the United States militarily with Japan, with the Philippines, and with Australia and New Zealand. Later the United States would also make security arrangements with South Korea (1953), the Nationalist regime on Taiwan (1954), and key countries of Southeast Asia (1954). Overall, these military pacts formed a patchwork pattern; there was no counterpart in Asia to the integrated structure of NATO.

The peace treaty that Japan signed with forty-eight nations in San Francisco followed the prescriptions set down by Kennan and his Policy Planning Staff in 1947; it was concise and nonpunitive, free of any provisions for post-treaty controls, and designed to give Japan every opportunity to emerge as a stable and prosperous member of the family of noncommunist nations. No one at the time, of course, anticipated how greatly Japan would prosper under its regained sovereignty. On the contrary, in the early 1950s both U.S. and Japanese officials remained generally pessimistic about the future prospects of Japan's "shallow economy." At the same time, no one really foresaw exactly how the bilateral military relationship between the United States and Japan would unfold. It was not until the early months of 1952 that the actual details of the post-occupation U.S. presence in Japan were worked out, and the extensiveness of the military installations demanded by the Americans far exceeded Japanese expectations. For understandable reasons, neither the U.S. nor the Japanese government publicized the fact that Japan's status

---

[38] *FRUS*, 1951, VI, part 1, 1258–59 (Chairman of the JCS to Secretary of Defense, 17 July 1951); cf. ibid., 1432–36 (JCS to Secretary of Defense, 12 December 1951). For Ridgway, see ibid., 1451–53 (20 December 1951).

under the bilateral security treaty and its enabling "administrative agreement" was less equitable than the status of any other nation that entered into a postwar security agreement with the United States—a condition that persisted until the security treaty was revised in 1960.

The United States-Japan security relationship also did not develop precisely as expected on another, more consequential front: Japanese rearmament. Although the United States initially assumed that its goal of a 300,000-man Japanese ground force would be met by 1953, the conservative Japanese government resisted pressure for such rapid remilitarization and continued to do so over the ensuing decades. This resistance is well known, but the full range of reasons that Japanese leaders offered from the start is generally less well appreciated. In addition to arguing that the Japanese public would not tolerate such rapid remilitarization and that the economy could not support it, Prime Minister Yoshida also confided that he feared the United States would expect Japan to send troops to Korea if a large army suddenly materialized. (Japanese minesweepers did in fact participate secretly in the war.) Moreover, much like the queasy State Department and Pentagon advisers who worried about Japan's ideological propensities, the prime minister also worried that too-rapid expansion would enable the new military to become infiltrated by "Reds." Furthermore (in marked contrast to his American allies), Yoshida was acutely sensitive to the terror and hostility a suddenly revived Japanese army would provoke throughout the rest of Asia, especially among those erstwhile anti-communist allies who still bore the physical and psychological scars caused by the debauchery of the imperial forces and their civilian camp followers. Finally, then and thereafter, Japan's leaders also argued that such blatant and extensive militarization as the Americans demanded would require constitutional revision. Article Nine could be reinterpreted as permitting the maintenance of "national police" or "self-defense" forces, they argued, but not the immediate creation of an army one third of a million men strong; and it would be political suicide for the ruling conservatives to attempt to force constitutional revision on a public that was already leery about how far the "reverse course" might go. As they had ever since the prospect of Japanese rearmament was first seriously broached in 1947–48, U.S. officials agreed that Japanese remilitarization on the scale desired required that the constitution be revised. They were not convinced, however, that this was actually as far beyond their capabilities as the conservatives claimed.[39]

[39] Cf. Dower, *Empire and Aftermath*, especially 369–400.

Militarily, the occupation thus did give way to a "fortress Japan" much as many Pentagon planners had hoped from mid-1949—but a fortress in which the Japanese garrison never became the substantial force Washington desired. As U.S. policy makers had predicted ever since the "separate peace" concept was first mentioned in 1947, the linking of the "generous" peace treaty to the bilateral United States-Japan security treaty was unacceptable to the Soviet Union, which attended the San Francisco conference but did not sign the peace treaty. The relationship between the San Francisco settlement and Japan's relations with China was less predictable and more convoluted, but ended in Japan's isolation from China—against the wishes of most Japanese, including the conservative leadership. If the Japanese government's successful resistance to pressure for more massive remilitarization showed the limits of U.S. power, Japan's inability to pursue an independent China policy, despite its desire to do so, revealed the coercive and seductive power of the new Pax Americana in Asia.

The containment of communist China represented the critical negative face of the integrated cold-war strategy in Asia. The evolution of this policy, culminating in 1951–52, can only be briefly summarized here. Until early 1950, both military and civilian U.S. planners generally assumed that Japanese trade with mainland China was inevitable, was essential to helping Japan escape the dollar gap and attain economic stability, and might even be valuable in the cold-war context (by reintroducing Japan into Manchuria and North China as a "buffer" against the Soviet Union and by helping to "wean" the Chinese communists away from the Soviets and toward the capitalist camp). Much of this line of thinking was embodied in NSC 41 of March 1949 and reiterated in NSC 48/1 and 48/2 the following December. In the months prior to the Korean War, as the U.S. position toward China hardened, the Japanese were required to follow a stricter list of embargoed goods in their trade with China; nonetheless, Sino-Japanese trade showed a conspicuous upturn in 1950, even after the Korean War began.

Although occupied Japan was naturally forced to adhere to the full embargo on trade with China following China's entry into the war in November 1950, it was still assumed in many quarters that Sino-Japanese relations would and should be resumed once the Korean War ended. Given the political volatility of the China issue within the United States and disagreements on the subject between the United States and its leading allies of the time, neither the communist nor the Nationalist

Chinese were invited to the San Francisco peace conference. The Japanese attended the conference, however, with the understanding that they would later be able to decide on their own what policy they wished to pursue toward China. This was also the British understanding of the situation. By December 1951, however, it had been brought home to the Japanese that if they did not commit themselves to relations with the regime in Taiwan, they faced probable rejection of the peace treaty in the U.S. Congress—and thus an indefinitely prolonged occupation.

During the final months of the occupation, the Japanese therefore negotiated an independent peace treaty with the Chiang Kai-shek regime, along the lines of the San Francisco treaty. While this was taking place in Taipei, U.S. officials were secretly preparing the ground for locking Japan firmly into the economic containment of China. This policy culminated in September 1952 in the creation of CHINCOM (the "China Committee"), an adjunct to the secret CG ("Coordinating Group") and COCOM ("Coordinating Committee") mechanism whereby the United States and its allies planned trade controls against the Soviet bloc. Under the CHINCOM arrangement, Japan did not simply agree to adhere to the lists of embargoed items that the other nations agreed upon; it was actually forced to agree to much more extensive restrictions on trade with China than any of America's other allies.[40]

With the China market thus abruptly cut off, first by China's entry into the war in Korea and then by fiat from Washington, the long-contemplated plan of integrating the Japanese and Southeast Asian economies suddenly became a matter of urgent concern in both Washington and Tokyo. Viewed from this perspective, the integrated policy can be said to have been introduced to the world in the early months of 1951, when it was publicly christened with the somewhat misleading formal name of "U.S.-Japan economic cooperation." This concept became the keynote of much top-level Japanese economic planning over the next several years, and it was understood by all concerned that U.S.-Japanese collaboration in the promotion of economic development in Southeast Asia was a critical part of the cooperative policy.

The first Japanese economic mission to the nations to the south was dispatched by occupation authorities in mid-1951, and the prospects of

[40] Concerning Japan and the containment of China, see ibid., 400–14; Schonberger, "John Foster Dulles and the China Question in the Making of the Japanese Peace Treaty"; and Yoko Yasuhara, "Myth of Free Trade: COCOM and CHINCOM, 1945–1952" (Ph.D. diss., University of Wisconsin-Madison, 1984). The issue is voluminously documented in FRUS, 1951, VI, part 1, and FRUS, 1952–1954, XIV.

a revived co-prosperity sphere (but now one that replaced rather than included China) taxed the imagination and energies of innumerable Japanese officials. In one of the revealing small touches of the San Francisco peace settlement, John Foster Dulles reintroduced the issue of the suspended reparations program, but with a twist. Japan, it was agreed, would pay reparations to its recent victims, but out of current production and with the primary objective of using these payments as an entering wedge for penetrating the Southeast Asia economies.[41]

As it turned out, Southeast Asia did not materialize as an immediate replacement for the closed-off China market, partly because of the weakness of these nations' economies and partly because the Southeast Asians nursed bitter memories and the reparations negotiations were protracted. What did materialize was an unexpected and immensely dynamic form of cold-war economic integration sparked by the conflict in Korea: the sudden burst of U.S. "special procurements" in Japan after June 1950 and, what was even more significant, the routinization of such military-related purchases under the rubric "new special procurements" beginning in mid-1951. In the ten years from 1951 through 1960, military procurements and expenditures pumped some $5.5 billion into the Japanese economy. This contributed greatly to military, economic, and technological integration among Japan, the United States, and the rest of the non-communist world; and although the planners worked it into shape, the initial impetus was unplanned. As the Japanese conservatives were fond of saying, the war in Korea was—for them—an unexpected "gift of the gods."[42]

[41] On the "U.S.-Japan economic cooperation" policy, see Borden, *Pacific Alliance,* 143–65, and Dower, *Empire and Aftermath,* 415–36. For reparations as a potential boon to the Japanese economy, cf. *FRUS,* 1951, VI, part 1, 1315–16.

[42] For procurement figures, see Borden, 230.

13

The Truman administration and the Korean War

BARTON J. BERNSTEIN

In his January 1953 farewell address, President Harry S. Truman cited his many momentous decisions, including dropping the atomic bomb on Japan; applying containment through the Truman Doctrine, Marshall Plan, and NATO to "save" Europe; integrating Japan and West Germany into a United States-led international system; and expanding military budgets and foreign military aid. "Most important of all," he declared, "we acted in Korea." The administration's commitment of U.S. troops to that war "established to the Kremlin," he contended, "the determination of free peoples to defend themselves."[1]

The Korean War erupted openly on 25 June 1950, when the North Korean forces attacked South Korea on the recently divided peninsula. That invasion, following a few years of insurrections in South Korea and border incursions by both North and South Korea,[2] propelled the Truman administration during the next five days to intervene in what was basically an ongoing revolution and civil war.

Despite some Republican criticism, Truman refused to seek a declaration of war and soon labeled this military intervention a "police action." But he did want international legitimation, and thus his government gained United Nations (UN) Security Council resolutions (with the Soviet Union absent) declaring the North Korean attack a "breach of the peace," calling on nations "to help repel the armed attack," and creating a U.S.-directed UN command. In fact, the UN exercised no authority

[1] Truman, Farewell Address, 15 January 1953, in *Public Papers of the Presidents: 1952–53* (Washington: U.S. Government Printing Office, 1966), 1197–1200.
[2] John Merrill, "Internal Warfare in Korea, 1948–1950: The Local Setting of the Korean War," in Bruce Cumings, ed., *Child of Conflict* (Seattle: University of Washington Press, 1983), 133–62. For a dispute about which side actually attacked first, see Jon Halliday, "Commentary," in ibid., pp. 163–68.

over the actual conduct of the war, and nations other than the United States and South Korea never contributed more than about 6 percent (fewer than 40,000 troops) of total Allied forces.[3]

The war spurred the administration to redefine other commitments abroad. It increased aid to the French in Indochina and to the Philippines to put down left-wing revolutions, reversed its recently announced policy of disengagement from Nationalist China (Taiwan) and decided to support Chiang Kai-shek, expanded military aid to Europe, and pushed for substantial European rearmament. The war meant the globalization of military containment—in effect, the massive U.S. rearmament policies called for in spring 1950 in the then secret (now declassified) National Security Council (NSC) Paper 68.[4]

In the summer and early autumn of 1950, as U.S. troops and their South Korean allies began winning battles, both the administration and General Douglas MacArthur, the U.S. commander in the Pacific, decided to move beyond the original war aim of liberating South Korea and chose to cross the thirty-eighth parallel, the dividing line between the two Koreas, to unify the peninsula. After Chinese communist "volunteers" unexpectedly entered the war in late October, U.S. leaders became distressed, but they regained their optimism when the Chinese forces broke off the engagement in early November. That optimism did not collapse until late November when "volunteers" massively entered the war and routed the United Nations forces.

Soon after this bloody turn of the tide, the war became unpopular in the United States. Angry and frustrated citizens frequently demanded escalation or withdrawal. The dialogue was both rancorous and narrow. Virtually none questioned the legitimacy of U.S. participation, only the wisdom of committing troops and pursuing limited war. After the virtual elimination of the domestic political Left in the few years before the war, the American political culture provided no ground for basic challenges or even probing questions: Wasn't this a revolution and civil war, and not aggression? Were the Soviets the instigators?

After the tide of war improved for the United States in late winter, an unhappy Truman, long chafing from dealing with the arrogant Mac-

---

[3] Walter Hermes, *Truce Tent and Fighting Front* (Washington: U.S. Government Printing Office, 1966), 513.

[4] Also see Robert Jervis, "The Impact of the Korean War," *Journal of Conflict Resolution* 24 (December 1980): 563–92. NSC 68, 14 April 1950, is printed in United States, Department of State, *Foreign Relations of the United States* (henceforth *FRUS*), 1950, I, 234–92.

Arthur, fired him for insubordination because he had tried to block a settlement in Korea and because Western allies feared his reckless ways. Nevertheless, the administration periodically (but secretly) flirted with MacArthur's strategies for a wider war and ultimately appointed another general, Mark Clark, who also hankered to take the war across the Yalu River.

During Truman's last twenty-one months in office, his administration struggled to achieve an armistice while restraining Syngman Rhee, South Korea's president, from sabotaging the effort. Truman could not obtain the armistice on the terms he demanded, and his requirement of voluntary repatriation of prisoners of war probably blocked a May 1952 settlement and prolonged the war into mid-1953. The war also unleashed ugly disputes in the United States, cost the United States billions of dollars and thousands of lives, and further narrowed the U.S. political consensus. But to Truman and his defenders then, and to many now, it was a necessary war to stop Soviet aggression and to protect the interests of the United States and its developing alliance system.

Now, four-and-a-half decades after Truman became president and almost four decades after he committed U.S. forces to the war, it is appropriate to analyze his major decisions in intervening, expanding, and conducting the war. Why, for example, did his administration withdraw troops from Korea in June 1949 and then return them in June 1950 to fight? Why did the administration rebuff efforts at a settlement in summer 1950 and, instead, soon expand the war into the North and toward the Yalu River? Was MacArthur chiefly responsible, as Truman and Dean Acheson later charged, for the November 1950 debacle? How committed was the administration, as it publicly contended, to keeping the war limited? Why did Truman introduce, and stick to, the demand for voluntary repatriation of prisoners of war? Running through the analysis of these problems are larger issues about the roles of domestic politics, concerns about the alliance, and the power of ideology in shaping the administration's behavior. And, finally, in this volume focusing on Truman and his presidency, it seems necessary to address, at least briefly, value-laden questions about the wisdom of his decisions in the Korean War and whether he overlooked better alternatives for the United States.

The evolution of the policy of containment toward Korea

Only very attentive rank-and-file Americans, who knew about the U.S.-Soviet disputes leading to the creation of the two Koreas and the administration's efforts to wring large Korean aid bills from Congress, recognized that Korea had become important to the Truman administration well before June 1950. Even most of these people did not know that the U.S. military occupation had overthrown left-leaning local governing committees in South Korea, blocked and reversed a social revolution there, relied heavily on former Japanese collaborators, and ultimately helped put into power Syngman Rhee, a shrewd and authoritarian leader.[5]

The policy of containment, formally enunciated in the March 1947 Truman Doctrine speech, was actually being considered for Korea in 1946. Indeed, from early 1947 until 25 June 1950 the issue within the administration was how, not whether, to apply containment there. In this argument, military officials frequently urged the withdrawal of U.S. troops but usually supported military and economic aid, while State Department officials campaigned for the continued stationing of those troops in Korea and the granting of military and economic aid.

As early as September 1946, presidential aide Clark Clifford recommended the strategy of containment for Europe and Asia, including Korea. "The United States," he wrote, "should support and assist all democratic countries which are in any way menaced or endangered by the U.S.S.R." Arguing that "military support in case of attack is a last resort," he turned first in his analysis to "some trouble-spots" in Asia. The United States should continue to strive for "a reconstructed and democratic Japan and a unified and independent Korea." The United States would have to make "a diligent and considered effort . . . if Soviet penetration and eventual domination [are] to be prevented."[6]

While declaring the Truman Doctrine, the president actually limited his aid program to Greece and Turkey. But in the secret congressional hearings, Dean Acheson, then under secretary of state, did include Korea loosely within the doctrine. The administration was already considering a large military aid program to shore up South Korea. "The line has been clearly drawn [in Korea] between the Russians and ourselves," Acheson argued and thus implied that U.S. power and prestige were already engaged.[7]

---

[5] The best analysis of the events in 1945–46 is Bruce Cumings, *The Origins of the Korean War* (Princeton: Princeton University Press, 1981); cf., Charles Dobbs, *The Unwanted Symbol* (Kent, Ohio: Kent State University Press, 1981), 30–46.

[6] Clark Clifford, "American Relations with the Soviet Union," report to the president, September 1946, printed in Arthur Krock, *Memoirs* (New York: Funk and Wagnalls, 1968), 479. The paper was drafted by George Elsey and generally endorsed by George Kennan. (Kennan, "Comments on the Draft Entitled 'American Relations with the Soviet Union,' " 16 September 1946, George Elsey Files, Harry S. Truman Library [hereafter HSTL].)

[7] Acheson in U.S. Senate, Committee on Foreign Relations, Historical Series, *Legislative*

Sharing this analysis, the Joint Chiefs of Staff (JCS) concluded that Korea was a country where "we alone have for almost two years carried on ideological warfare in direct contact with our opponents, so that to lose this battle would be gravely detrimental to U.S. prestige, and therefore security, throughout the world." For the JCS, the importance of Korea was not primarily its substance (its resources, population, or economic value to Japan) but its symbolism—what a loss there would betoken for our West European Allies, "which are of primary and vital importance to our national security." To the JCS, the concept of security was not simply military but also political and psychological. Doubts about U.S. power and will could erode informal alliances elsewhere and undermine trust. But because Korea would not be a good place for the United States to fight, according to the JCS, Korea should receive economic assistance *only* if America had the resources left after assisting countries of "primary" importance, including West European nations and Japan. In JCS calculations, Korea ranked fifteenth when judged by this expanded definition of "national security."[8]

The concept of containment meant different things to different groups within the administration, depending on the perceived value (economic, military, political) of an area and the cost and type of assistance in applying containment there. As a result, in April 1947, Secretary of War Robert Patterson, while operating within the containment framework, could urge withdrawal of U.S. troops from Korea at "an early date" because the United States, and especially the War Department budget, could not afford the costs. He acknowledged the political value of Korea but minimized its military value: It would not be a good place to fight in a general war, and because the planners believed that any future war with the Soviets was likely to be a general war, U.S. troops should be removed. In contrast, the State Department, stressing Korea's political value, used delaying tactics and emphasized the importance to U.S. prestige of retaining South Korea. What was at issue, basically, was a dispute over the components of "national security," with each part of the bureaucracy emphasizing the concerns primarily in its domain.[9]

Origins of the Truman Doctrine, 80th Cong., 1st sess., 22. For earlier thinking about aid, see "Memorandum by the Special Inter-Departmental Committee on Korea," 25 February 1947, in *FRUS*, 1947, VI, 608–18.

[8] Joint Strategic Survey Committee, JCS, "United States Assistance to Other Countries from the Standpoint of National Security," 29 April 1947, in *FRUS*, 1947, I, 744–45.

[9] Secretary of War (Patterson) to Acting Secretary of State, 4 April 1947, File 740.00119 Control (Korea), Department of State Records (hereafter DS Records), Record Group

In early 1948, the military analysts triumphed by gaining Truman's approval of NSC 8, which called for withdrawal of U.S. forces by 31 December, continued economic assistance to Korea, and the effort to gain UN support for unification there. This NSC paper did not abandon containment in Korea, but it did abandon the *military* component of the policy while expressing the vague hope that Korea could be kept out of communist clutches. The United States, the paper warned, should not get so involved in Korea as to become embroiled in a war there even though a communist triumph on the peninsula "would enhance the political and strategic position of the USSR with respect to both China and Japan and adversely affect the position of the U.S. in this area and throughout the Far East, and might well lead to a fundamental alignment of forces in favor of the Soviet Union throughout that part of the world." Put bluntly, the need to maintain U.S. prestige and to check Soviet power had to yield to exigency.[10]

By autumn, continuing political and economic deterioration in South Korea, as well as a major rebellion in one area, pushed State Department officials to plead successfully for a delay in the U.S. troop withdrawal. Only the U.S. presence, they argued, might stave off collapse and buy the newly created South Korean government time, with U.S. economic assistance, to stabilize South Korea.[11]

This State Department argument was strengthened by related Asian developments—the imminent fall of Chiang Kai-shek's Nationalist government on the mainland and the "reverse course" for Japan—that made Korea more important. If South Korea fell, warned Max Bishop, chief of the Division of Northeast Asian Affairs in the State Department, Japan would be bordered on three sides by communist territories, which would mean that the communists would use trade, political persuasiveness, and racial similarity to suck Japan into the Red orbit. Bishop's analysis was an economic and political, not a military, domino theory.[12]

Japan would need markets—Southeast Asia, Korea, and even Taiwan.

(hereafter RG) 59, National Archives (hereafter NA). Also see Report by the Ad Hoc Committee on Korea, "United States Policy in Korea," 4 August 1947, in *FRUS*, 1947, VI, 738–42.

[10] NSC 8, 2 April 1948, in *FRUS*, 1948, VI, 1164–69.

[11] John Muccio to Secretary of State Marshall, 28 October and 12 November 1948; and Charles Saltzman to General Wedemeyer, 9 November 1948, in *FRUS*, 1948, VIII, 1317–18, 1325–27, and 1324.

[12] Max Bishop, chief of Division of Northeast Asian Affairs, to W. W. Butterworth, director of the Office of Far Eastern Affairs, 17 December 1948, with draft memorandum, in *FRUS*, 1948, VIII, 1338–41.

As one U.S. official explained in late 1948, "Our first concern must be the liberation of Manchuria and North Korea from communist domination," because this area could be so valuable economically in the reconstruction of Japan and its integration, as an industrial junior partner, in the U.S.-led international capitalist system. In this formulation, the aim was not simply containment in Korea but also "liberation."[13]

Despite growing interest in protecting Korea for its value in the economic reconstruction of Japan, U.S. military officials continued to plead for an early withdrawal of troops from South Korea because it had "little strategic interest." The Truman-approved compromise, hammered out in NSC 8/2 in March 1949, seemed a victory for the military—withdrawal of troops by late June. The new guidance emphasized that the troop withdrawal should be *presented* as "in no way . . . lessening . . . US support of the Government of the Republic of Korea."[14]

That spring, Truman and Acheson resisted Rhee's pleas and threats for a security pact and the continued stationing of U.S. troops in South Korea. U.S. leaders resented Rhee's threats and mistrusted him, but they did not believe they were abandoning South Korea.[15] Rather, they believed that U.S. aid would shore up South Korea and possibly make it (in Truman's words) "a beacon to the people of northern Asia in resisting the control of the communist forces which have over-run them."[16]

What would happen if North Korea attacked South Korea after U.S. withdrawal? Truman and most others in the administration had skirted this problem by assuming that an attack was unlikely. Directly addressing this question in June 1949, the Department of the Army proposed that the United States should take the issue of aggression to the United Nations but that U.S. military intervention (termed "police action" in the paper) was "militarily unsound" and *"should be considered* [only if] all other methods have failed."[17]

---

[13] Economic Cooperation Administration (signed Joe) memorandum, 3 November 1948, Dean Acheson Papers, Box 27, HSTL, called to my attention by Bruce Cumings.

[14] NSC 8/2, 22 March 1949, in *FRUS, 1949*, VII, part 2, 969–78.

[15] Acheson to Muccio, 9 May 1949, *FRUS, 1949*, VII, part 2, 1014; and Acheson to Muccio, 13 May 1949, in File 501B (Korea), DS Records.

[16] Truman, "Special Message to the Congress Regarding Continuation of Economic Assistance to Korea," 7 June 1949, *Public Papers: Truman*, 1949, 276–78. Also see Undersecretary of State James Webb to Truman, 18 June 1949, President's Secretary's Files (PSF), HSTL.

[17] Department of the Army to Department of State, 27 June 1949, File 740.00119 Control (Korea), DS Records (emphasis added). For background, see Chief of Staff, Army, to JCS, 10 June 1949, JCS 1776/2, P&O 091 Korea File, RG 319.

This suggestion of a police action is important. Until then, the military had assumed that war in Korea would be part of a world war and thus that Korea was the wrong place to fight. Now, for the first time, the concept of a limited war on the peninsula appeared in U.S. military planning. Intervention, for the military, was still "militarily unsound," but it might be considered if necessary.

To U.S. leaders, such an attack, as the army's paper noted, would be regarded as aggression. To the Korean Left, however, it could be the continuation of a revolution carried on by new means. As U.S. leaders knew, Rhee's forces were especially busy in late 1949 suppressing revolutionary activity within South Korea. They largely succeeded in eliminating the Left in South Korea and thus ending the threat of revolution there.[18]

On 12 January 1950, in presenting a major address on the U.S. Far Eastern policy, Secretary of State Dean Acheson reaffirmed the U.S. economic commitment to South Korea. He placed it outside the defense perimeter of areas where the United States would automatically fight, but he ambiguously noted that the people of the attacked area would be expected to resist first and then to rely "upon the commitments of the entire civilized world under the Charter of the United Nations." His carefully phrased statement, emerging from a handful of drafts of the speech cast over about a week, had been calculated to stress South Korea's own resources and to leave the question of U.S. military intervention murky. He did not expect an attack from the North. He did not trust Rhee to refrain from starting a war, and perhaps he did not yet know what the administration should do if the North did attack.[19]

Officials in the State Department had already begun to think along the lines of limited war. "Limited rather than total war" should be our concern, George Kennan, head of the State Department's Policy Planning Staff, had concluded. The double blows of Chiang's ouster from mainland China and the Soviet development of its atomic bomb in August 1949 underscored such concerns. Well before work began in early 1950 on NSC 68, U.S. officials were thinking about limited war, worrying about the Soviets or their proxies nibbling away parts of the "free world," and

---

[18] John Merrill, "Internal Warfare in Korea," in Cumings, ed., *Child of Conflict*, 152–55, 159. Merrill also notes the powerful use of amnesty to siphon off support for the Left.
[19] See drafts by Acheson and others, Dean Acheson Papers, Yale University, New Haven, Conn.; and Department of State Press Release 34, 12 January 1950; cf. Acheson, *Present at the Creation: My Years in the State Department* (New York: W. W. Norton, 1969), 354.

stressing that the United States must develop both the military forces and the political will to resist such aggression.[20]

Most often, as in NSC 68 (completed in April 1950), when policy makers considered the likely threats in Asia, they focused on Southeast Asia, not Korea. At the time, Southeast Asia, beset by a revolution against the French and valuable economically to Japan, seemed the most likely test. The logic of this analysis and the power of self-exhortation could lead U.S. policy makers to intervene in Korea if the crisis erupted there instead. They were not eager for a crisis, but they (especially Acheson) were becoming prepared, psychologically and ideologically, for a crisis, and they had long assumed that South Korea represented a significant U.S. interest in the cold war. By mid-1950, there was a willingness to go into a shooting war—to link military containment to economic containment.[21]

The decisions to go to war

When war broke out in Korea on Sunday, 25 June, U.S. Ambassador John Muccio cabled Washington to report that this was not just another border incident but a major attack.[22] In Washington that Saturday evening (fourteen hours behind Korean time), when Secretary of State Acheson learned the news, he telephoned President Truman, then vacationing in Missouri, gained his approval to seek a UN resolution charging North Korea with a "break of the peace," but also told Truman that there was no need for him to return to Washington.[23]

In Tokyo, General Douglas MacArthur, U.S. commander in the Pacific, had little initial interest in the events in Korea. He treated them as a minor matter, not requiring his attention and certainly not betokening a substantial American war.[24] Unlike MacArthur, John Foster Dulles, a

---

[20] NSC 48/1, 26 October 1949, in NSC Papers box, and printed in Department of Defense, *United States-Vietnam Relations, 1945–1967* (Washington: U.S. Government Printing Office, 1971), Book 8, 225–64; and NSC 48/2, 30 December 1949, in *FRUS*, 1949, VII, 1215–20.

[21] Cf. James Matray, *The Reluctant Crusade* (Honolulu: University of Hawaii Press, 1985), 151–226.

[22] Ambassador in Korea (Muccio) to Secretary of State, 25 June 1950, File 795.00, DS Records.

[23] Harry S. Truman, *Memoirs*, vol. 2, *Years of Trial and Hope* (Garden City: Doubleday, 1956), 332; and Acheson, *Present at the Creation*, 403–05.

[24] John Allison, *Ambassador from the Prairie or Allison in Wonderland* (Boston: Houghton Mifflin, 1973), 129–30, 136. Also see MacArthur's slightly later response, MacArthur to Irwin, 25 June 1950, Box 71, George Elsey Papers, HSTL.

prominent Republican then in Tokyo negotiating the Japanese peace treaty, immediately called for committing U.S. troops if South Korea could not repel the attack, even though "this risks Russian counter moves." In a cable also signed by John Allison, director of the State Department's Division of Northeast Asian Affairs, Dulles told Washington, "To sit by while Korea is overrun by unprovoked armed attack would start disastrous chain of events leading most probably to world war."[25]

Not until Sunday morning, when the situation in Korea seemed worse, did Acheson urge Truman to return to Washington, and they agreed to call a meeting of top advisers for that evening. Looking back on his memorable Sunday flight to Washington, Truman later recalled that he had spent his airborne hours thinking of other acts of aggression—Japan's invasion of Manchuria in 1931, Mussolini's invasion of Ethiopia, and Hitler's march into the Saar and his overthrow of Czechoslovakia and Poland. The lessons of history, drawn partly from the 1930s, seemed clear to Truman. "It occurred to me" on that flight, Truman later said, that if the "Russian totalitarian state was intending to follow in the path of the dictatorships of Hitler and Mussolini, they should be met head on in Korea."[26]

Despite Truman's conviction that the Soviets had planned or instigated the invasion, there was no evidence, then or even now, that the Soviets had done so. Indeed, the most supportable interpretation is that the Soviets, though providing necessary military equipment, largely acceded to Kim's plans. Nikita Khrushchev later reported in his memoirs that Kim Il Sung, the North Korean leader, had planned the invasion, predicting that it would "touch off a revolution in the South." When Kim asked Stalin for support, the Soviet ruler had delayed, asked Kim to think it over, discussed it with Mao, and then finally granted approval. "The war wasn't Stalin's idea, but Kim Il Sung's," Khrushchev has emphasized.[27] To Kim, the attack (much like John F. Kennedy's later hopes for the Bay of Pigs) was not to conquer but to liberate South Korea—to touch off what he believed was a festering revolution. To the Soviets, this Korean venture should have seemed low-risk and attractive—unlikely to provoke U.S. intervention and likely to reunite the peninsula under com-

[25] Dulles-Allison cable quoted in Allison, *Ambassador from the Prairie*, 137.
[26] Truman, transcript for memoirs: re Korea, 21 August 1953, Post-Presidential Papers, HSTL.
[27] Nikita Khrushchev, *Khrushchev Remembers* (Boston: Little, Brown, 1970), 367–69; cf. John Merrill, review of *Khrushchev Remembers*, in *Journal of Korean Studies* (1981), 183–84.

munist leadership, thus creating a counterweight to Mao's China and possibly inspiring leftists in Japan to block the U.S.-planned treaty.

U.S. leaders never even considered that Kim might have been acting in semi-independence and had perhaps "jumped the gun" and attacked before the Soviets expected—that he was actually conducting a civil war, the continuation of a Korean revolution of the Left. The Korean War was primarily a local war conceived and initiated for Korean reasons. To U.S. leaders, such ideas—if they had been entertained, and they were not—would have seemed bizarre. Ideology served as the prism through which experience was viewed, and that ideology for U.S. leaders stressed a near-monolithic communism under Soviet direction. From the Soviet Union, for example, U.S. Ambassador Alan Kirk speedily cabled his analysis: The attack was a "clear-cut Soviet challenge which . . . US should answer firmly and swiftly as it constitutes direct threat [to] our leadership of free world against Soviet Communist imperialism."[28]

Within hours of learning of the attack, State Department analysts agreed that the North Korean government "is absolutely under Kremlin control and [thus this] move against South Korea must be considered a Soviet move." Like Kirk, these advisers stressed the threat to U.S. credibility and will, especially (in this order) in Japan, Southeast Asia, and Europe. "Soviet military domination of all Korea," they warned, "would give Moscow an important weapon for intimidation of the Japanese in connection with Japan's future alignment with the US."[29]

At Truman's Sunday night (25 June) meeting with his major advisers—Acheson, Secretary of Defense Louis Johnson, the service secretaries, the Joint Chiefs, and some State Department Asian specialists—all agreed that the Soviets had directed the attack and they focused on Soviet motives. A test of American will? A probe preparatory to an attack elsewhere?[30]

[28] Ambassador to the Soviet Union (Kirk) to Secretary of State, 25 June 1950, File 795.00, DS Records; cf. Foreign Office to Oliver Franks, 27 June 1950, FO 371/84080, Public Record Office, Kew, London (hereafter PRO).

[29] Department of State, Intelligence Estimate 7 ("Korea"), 25 June 1950, FRUS, 1950, VII, 146–51. For prewar analyses, see E. Drumwright, "Estimate of Soviet Intentions toward South Korea," 4 May 1950, File 795B, DS Records.

[30] Philip Jessup, Memorandum of Conversation, 25 June 1950, FRUS, 1950, VII, 157–61, which paraphrases participants' statements. This is the source for subsequent paragraphs on this meeting. Twenty-five years later, former under secretary of state James Webb argued that Acheson had restrained Truman's desire that night for more warlike action (Webb to John Snyder, 25 April 1975, General Correspondence file—S Folder, Webb Papers, HSTL).

That night, as throughout the week of crisis, Acheson shaped the agenda and the dialogue. Outlining the issues, he gained Truman's support for sending more military equipment to Korea (which MacArthur was already doing) and having the navy evacuate Americans while the air force protected the evacuation. The president deferred decisions on two other Acheson proposals—expanding aid to Indochina and moving the Seventh Fleet to the Taiwan Straits. They agreed that the air force should make contingency plans "to wipe out the Soviet air force in the Far East" and that State and Defense should make a survey to determine where the Soviets might next act.

At this session, most U.S. planners seemed delighted at the prospect of the challenge. "We must draw the line somewhere," asserted General Omar Bradley, JCS chairman, who received the approval of the president for his words. Bradley concluded "that Russia is not yet ready for war. The Korean situation offered as good an occasion for action in drawing a line as anywhere else." But some military men warned against getting involved in a land war. Bradley himself "questioned the advisability of putting in ground troops particularly if large number were involved." Secretary of the Army Frank Pace and Secretary of Defense Johnson joined Bradley, with Johnson warning bluntly that he "opposed . . . committing ground troops in Korea." None probed this military counsel, for Truman and Acheson were not interested in such warnings.

Admiral Forrest Sherman, chief of naval operations, stressed that Korea was "a strategic threat" to Japan and recommended using the navy in the war. He thought that the "Russians do not want war now but if they do they will have it." General Hoyt Vandenberg, air force chief of staff, acknowledged that the Soviets might enter the war, agreed "that we [must] stop the North Koreans," acknowledged that atomic bombs would be required to knock out Soviet bases in the Far East, and seemed to be itching for the air force to be sent to the war.

Although the pressures for U.S. intervention in the war were building among U.S. officials, some advisers were also warning the administration not to challenge Soviet prestige directly. They wanted to give the Soviets room to maneuver, feared locking them into an intractable position, and recommended against charging the Soviets with responsibility for the war. This strategy, advisers hoped, might allow the Soviets to stay out of the war or possibly even to call it off.[31]

[31] Ambassador to the Soviet Union (Kirk) to the Secretary of State, 26 June 1950; and

Truman was moving slowly and steadily—perhaps in ways he did not foresee—to a greater commitment in Korea. "Korea," he told an aide on Monday, 26 June, "is the Greece of the Far East. If we are tough enough now, if we stand up to them like we did in Greece three years ago, they won't take any next steps. But if we just stand by, they'll move into Iran and they'll take over the whole Middle East. There's no telling what they'll do, if we don't put up a fight right now."[32]

With the situation in Korea worsening, the president met again with his advisers. At their Monday night session, he committed the air force and navy to the war in the South, agreed to place the Seventh Fleet in the Taiwan Straits, thus ending the policy of disengagement from Chiang, and increased aid to Indochina and the Philippines. The administration believed that the United States could not afford communist triumphs in these areas, for U.S. prestige and power would seem impaired. And in the case of Taiwan, with its powerful lobby in America, how could Truman explain a military commitment to aid Korea, from which he had recently withdrawn forces, if he did not also protect Chiang? The new informal alliance between Taiwan and the United States was conceived in political necessity for the Truman administration, not in affection and trust.[33]

At the Monday night session, General J. Lawton Collins, army chief of staff, stressed that "the military situation was bad" and warned that the air force might not be able to reverse the tide of war. Acheson said "that it was important for us to do something even if the effort was unsuccessful." Secretary Johnson agreed, saying that "even if we lose Korea this action would save the situation." Johnson, cautious, believed that the military commitment should by sharply limited, that troops should not be deployed, and that even a limited commitment would reestablish the credibility of U.S. power and will.

Truman pushed beyond such cautious counsel. He said he had "done everything he could for five years to prevent this kind of situation. Now the situation is here and we must do what we can to meet it." He was

Ambassador to France (Bruce) to Secretary of State, 26 June 1950, *FRUS*, 1950, VII, 169–70, 174–75. Also see Commonwealth Relations Office telegram, 27 June 1950, FO 371/84081, PRO.

[32] George Elsey, "President's Conversation with George M. Elsey," 26 June 1950, Elsey Paper, HSTL.

[33] Philip Jessup, Memorandum of Conversation, 26 June 1950, *FRUS*, 1950, VII, 178–83, which paraphrases participants' statements. This is the source for subsequent paragraphs on the 26 June meeting.

willing to meet the test, to stand up to the Soviets by opposing what he deemed their proxy force. He had not formally made the next major decision, the commitment of ground troops, but he seemed ready to do so, if necessary. For him, his successes in defeating what he defined as earlier Soviet challenges—the Truman Doctrine for Greece and Turkey, the airlift to overcome the Berlin blockade—emboldened him to meet this test.

When Truman met with congressional leaders on Tuesday, 27 June, he made it clear that "the United States was now committed to defend South Korea." Explaining this escalating commitment, Acheson said that many West European governments were in "a state of near-panic as they watched to see whether the United States would act or not." "If we let Korea down," Truman argued, "the Soviets will keep right on going and swallow up one piece of Asia after another. We had to make a stand some time, or else let all of Asia go by the board. If we were to let Asia go, the Near East would collapse and no telling what would happen in Europe." Although his military advisers were unsure whether the United States had adequate forces to meet the threat, Truman cavalierly assured the congressmen that it did.[34]

Late Tuesday evening, the Security Council (with the Soviets absent), at the behest of the United States, provided legitimation for Truman's military intervention in Korea by calling upon UN nations "to help repel aggression." Led by the United States, the Security Council rejected Yugoslavia's resolution for UN mediation of the dispute, including an invitation to North Korea to participate in the UN mediation process.[35]

Slowly, Truman was edging closer to the commitment of ground troops in the war. At a special NSC meeting on Wednesday, 28 June, according to Philip Jessup, Truman said that "if the difficulties in Korea increased instead of our meeting with quick success, he didn't intend to back out unless there should develop a military situation which we had to meet elsewhere."[36]

Nearly every day during this critical week, as the reports of deterioration in Korea reached the White House, Truman expanded the U.S. commitment. On 29 June, he acceded to Secretary of the Air Force Thomas Finletter's request to let the air force cross the thirty-eighth parallel and

---

[34] Elsey, notes on 27 June 1950 meeting, Elsey Papers, HSTL. On foreign responses, also see Department of State, "Summary of Telegrams," 27 June 1950, PSF, HSTL.

[35] Resolutions in *FRUS*, 1950, VII, 211.

[36] Jessup, "Meeting of the NSC in the Cabinet Room at the White House," 28 June 1950, Acheson Papers, HSTL.

to the JCS request to deploy troops to establish a beachhead at Pusan.[37] Acheson had supported both requests. The only remaining question was whether a great number of U.S. ground troops would be needed, and that judgment rested on the progress of the war—the success of the North Koreans and the failure of the South.

In large measure, what liberated Truman to expand his commitment was Thursday's Soviet message, which State Department specialists interpreted to mean that the Soviet Union would not intervene in the war. The Soviet communication seemed mild, stating that the "Soviet Government adheres to the principle of the impermissibility of interference by foreign powers in the internal affairs of Korea."[38] According to State Department specialists, the United States would be free to "save" South Korea and reaffirm containment without stumbling into a world war. Strangely, Chou En-Lai's statement, interpreted in Washington as "perhaps indicating that Chinese troops would be thrown into the fighting," did not give Truman, Acheson, and their aides pause. Then, as later, their concern was primarily the Soviet Union, not China.[39]

At lower levels in Washington, there was bellicosity, indeed almost recklessness. On 29 June, at a session of the NSC consultants, for example, advisers talked about bombing Manchuria if China entered the war, possibly using the atomic bomb. They even said that it might not be a bad time for war with Russia. "If we caught Chinese Communists in South Korea," according to George Kennan, who had recently stepped down as director of the Policy Planning Staff, "we could . . . even bomb in Manchuria." Major General Richard Lindsay, deputy director for strategic plans, warned that "if we bombed in Manchuria with conventional bombs we would lose some of our capability of using atomic weapons if they later became necessary." He implied that the best targets would be destroyed and thus the atomic bomb would not dramatically demonstrate its impact. Kennan, while forecasting that the Soviets would probably "exploit Asiatic satellites against us . . . because there was no risk involved for the USSR," also remarked that if the Soviets "got into a war now they would have stumbled in, and in the long run this might be the best decision for us." Apparently he meant that the Soviet Union

[37] Jessup, "Meeting of the NSC in the Cabinet Room at the White House," 29 June 1950, File 795.00, DS Records.
[38] Soviet message cited in Ambassador Kirk to Secretary of State, 29 June 1950, *FRUS, 1950*, VII, 229–30.
[39] Jessup, "Meeting of the NSC in the Cabinet Room at the White House," 29 June 1950, File 795.00, DS Records.

was weaker in 1950 than it would be later, and therefore it would be easier to defeat with less damage to the United States.[40]

Truman and his close advisers were not so daring or reckless in June, but the president and Acheson were ready to commit ground troops. The triggering event was the Friday request, on 30 June, from General MacArthur, who, having just surveyed the spreading wreckage of South Korean forces, asked Washington to authorize the dispatch to Korea of a U.S. regimental combat team and two divisions. Awakened in the middle of the night, Truman, without consulting aides, promptly approved the request for the combat team. After an early morning meeting with Acheson, Johnson, the Joint Chiefs, and a few others, the president also authorized the two divisions.

Meeting with congressional leaders a few hours later, Truman strangely chose to conceal this momentous decision. He informed them that MacArthur "has been authorized to use certain supporting ground units." He explained disingenuously, "Our present plan is just to keep communications and supply lines open" in Korea. At this meeting, Senator Kenneth Wherry, a McCarthyite Republican from Nebraska, demanded that Truman consult Congress before he committed a substantial number of troops, and Truman promised to do so. While concealing his morning decision, Truman said there had been a weekend crisis a few days before and he had had to act without consultation. "I just had to act as Commander-in-Chief, and I did."[41]

Before Truman's decision of 30 June, Senator Robert A. Taft, a prominent GOP conservative called "Mr. Republican," announced that he feared that the administration might move to war without a declaration of war. Believing that modern Democratic presidents had usurped the Constitution, Taft pleaded unsuccessfully for such a declaration before a commitment of force.[42] Truman and Acheson, later explaining that they had feared that the declaration might be delayed by time-consuming debate, argued that they had to act promptly in the national interest. Congress could be too slow; the executive had to seize the initiative.[43]

On 1 July, the day after Truman's decision, John Foster Dulles pri-

---

[40] "Memorandum of National Security Council Consultants' Meeting," 29 June 1950, Policy Planning Staff Files, DS Records, and printed in *FRUS, 1950*, I, 327–30. This memo actually paraphrases the participants' statements.

[41] Elsey, notes on 30 June 1950 meeting, Elsey Papers, HSTL, partly summarizing Truman's words.

[42] Taft in *Congressional Record* (28 June 1950), 81st Cong., 2d sess., 9319–23.

[43] Acheson, *Present at the Creation*, 415.

vately questioned it. The commitment of troops might mean the overextension of U.S. military power, he warned some administration advisers. Reversing his advice of 25 June, Dulles was echoing MacArthur's counsel, given to Dulles just a few days earlier in Tokyo, that the United States could not be a land power in Asia and should not get involved in a land war there. Wouldn't Korea be another Dunkirk? Dulles asked military leaders. How many troops would be needed? How long might the war last? Evading these pointed questions, the military leaders explained that they had reversed their 1949 endorsement of withdrawal of forces from Korea because political leaders—Truman and Acheson—wanted to commit troops to the war.[44]

Truman and Acheson were the guiding spirits in making this decision. Military leaders acceded. They had strategic doubts but shared the consensus on the need to stop communism. By Sunday or Monday, 25 or 26 June, they understood that Truman did not want to hear their wary counsel, so they stopped raising questions and expressing doubts.

Under Truman and Acheson, the administration plunged the nation into war to establish credibility to block likely Soviet moves elsewhere; and to make clear that the United States would not accede to Soviet attacks or aggression by proxy in the Middle East, Asia (especially Japan), and Europe. In short, action in Korea was an important symbol; when they thought about its substance, their primary concern was about Korea's strategic location in regard to Japan—a communist Korea, pointed like a dagger, could threaten Japan psychologically and militarily. Beyond that, they recognized that Korea had an important role in the Asian economy and that the loss of Korea could disrupt the Pacific basin and especially injure Japan's economy. For them, in summary, Korea was the first of the dominoes.

In June 1950, U.S. domestic politics supported the administration's commitment and even reinforced the administration's inclinations during the week. Fears of McCarthyite attacks, following charges about the "loss" of China, may have subtly helped to push Acheson and Truman in the direction that for other reasons they wished to go. Their toughness in Korea might defuse possible attacks and reestablish the fierce anticommunist credentials of the administration. But domestic politics did not compel the administration to send troops into the war.[45]

---

[44] John Foster Dulles, Memorandum of Conversation, 1 July 1950, Dulles Papers, Seeley Mudd Library, Princeton University.

[45] Cf. Stephen Pelz, "America Goes to War, Korea, June 24–30, 1950: The Politics and Process of Decision" (Woodrow Wilson Center Paper 1979), 31–42; and see Sen. Joseph

Had Truman and Acheson wished to avoid this commitment, they could have devised strategies for protecting themselves politically at home. They could have easily parried charges that the administration had left South Korea militarily unprepared. Because many congressmen, especially Republicans linked to the China lobby, had resisted the Korean aid bill earlier that year, the administration would have found it easy to blame the GOP for failing to protect South Korea. And the administration might have skillfully co-opted some Republicans by privately warning them of the perils of intervention—that, as Dulles feared, another Dunkirk was possible.

Significantly, in late June 1950, few major newspapers, politicians, or columnists were out in front of the administration in proposing U.S. military intervention in the war. Many called vaguely, but always vaguely, for support for South Korea. Support could mean equipment, money, and words. They did not urge deployment of the navy and air force before 26 June, when the administration took such action, or of ground troops before 30 June, when Truman committed them. On 27 June, for example, after surveying the media and the mainline politicians, the State Department reported that few of those surveyed recommended committing troops and many contended that the United States "should stop short of involving American troops. . . . A meeting of Republican members of Congress agreed that 'the incident' should not be used as a provocation for war."[46]

Between 26 and 30 June the domestic political situation was sufficiently fluid that the administration, after sending equipment to South Korea, might have chosen either military intervention with ground forces or nonintervention. Whichever route the administration chose, it could have shaped the dialogue within the anti-communist culture at home. Intervention fanned the flames of expectations and built fires of hope that would ultimately injure the Truman administration.

Containment, liberation, and the route to debacle

Containment was a doctrine of resistance to communism with the hope of creating "the seeds of destruction" within the communist system. This doctrine could easily spill over into liberation—the speedy rollback of

O'Mahoney to Truman, 27 June 1950, and reply, 28 June 1950, PSF, HSTL. Pelz's interpretation of this O'Mahoney-Truman exchange seems strained and unconvincing.

[46] Division of Public Affairs, Office of Public Affairs, "Public Comment on the Korean War," 27 June 1950, File 611.95, DS Records. This analysis has been supplemented by my own analysis of major newspapers for 24 June–1 July 1950.

communist influence. In Korea, a policy instituted in late June 1950 to restore the status quo ante quickly turned into a quest for unification and liberation.

In July, with UN forces struggling at the southern end of Korea, Truman and Acheson rejected the British and Indian proposals for a settlement in the war, because the terms included admission of China to the United Nations. Acheson explained that such a concession would "whet Communist appetites and bring on other aggressions elsewhere." The British, fearful that the United States would become too involved in Korea and thus unable to meet more important challenges in Europe, argued that Acheson and Truman were unwisely missing an opportunity to weaken the Soviet-Chinese alliance by making an overture to China.[47]

Even if Truman and Acheson had wanted to let China join the United Nations, endorsing such a move would have provoked great antagonism in the United States and charges of appeasement. Domestic politics reinforced the Truman-Acheson inclinations, and the continuing war kept open the options for rearming the United States and Western Europe. It was not that Truman and Acheson cynically rejected a settlement that summer in order to achieve these other goals, but rejection strengthened their arguments for rearmament.

Even before U.S. troops ended the rout in mid-summer and began moving back toward the thirty-eighth parallel, many U.S. leaders looked forward to crossing the parallel and uniting the peninsula. MacArthur's bold mid-September victory at Inchon nourished these hopes. Occasional warnings from Kennan and Paul Nitze, among others, could not dampen the enthusiasm of John Allison; Dean Rusk, assistant secretary of state for Far Eastern affairs; and, most important, Acheson and Truman.[48]

Liberation of Korea was part—but not an essential part—of Acheson's assertive foreign policy, which also included larger military budgets for the United States and its European allies, the rearmament of Germany, a peace treaty with Japan plus bases there, and assistance to France to put down the revolution in Indochina. Unification of Korea would be a valuable triumph. It would weaken communist morale, protect and expand markets for Japan, and remove the threat of a partly communist Korea aimed at Japan. In Asia and Europe, according to Acheson's strategy, communism would be halted, perhaps even rolled back.

[47] Acheson, *Present at the Creation*, 418–19. See also British cabinet minutes, 18 July 1950 in C.M. 49 (50), CAB 128/18, PRO.
[48] George Kennan, *Memoirs, 1950–1963* (Boston: Little, Brown, 1972), 47–53; John Allison to Paul Nitze, 24 July 1950, File 795.00, DS Records.

Would China or the Soviet Union block this strategy in Korea? Acheson judged that the Soviets would probably not intervene, and he was sure that China would not. His analysis of China's actions was a curious amalgam of hopeful assumptions producing unwarranted conclusions. He assumed that the Soviet Union alone sponsored the North Korean attack and therefore that China had no stake in defending North Korea or in stopping the United States from uniting Korea. As he repeatedly and publicly lectured the Chinese, Acheson believed that the great threat to China was Soviet imperialism, not the United States.[49] Even Truman, who privately believed that the Chinese government was "nothing but a tool of Moscow," also publicly tried to reassure the Chinese leaders: "We hope ... that China ... will not be misled or forced into fighting against the American people, who ... are their friends."[50]

In September, the administration began to make plans to cross the thirty-eighth parallel and unite the recently divided nation. At first, the plans reflected anxieties (which mostly concerned possible Soviet entry), but these were assuaged as the month wore on and UN forces met successes.[51] The decision in Washington corresponded with the hopes and expectations of MacArthur who, after his dramatic victory at Inchon, did not wish to be denied the opportunity of vanquishing the North Koreans, establishing U.S. superiority, and thus, in his formulation, teaching the Soviets a lesson and blocking communist aggression elsewhere. MacArthur, a general with a staunch domestic constituency, would have been difficult to restrain from moving toward unification, but there was no conflict between him and Washington, because everyone sought the same goal and believed that it could be achieved.

They all minimized or ignored China's warnings that it would intervene if U.S. forces crossed the parallel.[52] Truman, Acheson, and George Marshall, now secretary of defense, did worry about General MacArthur's attempts to redirect U.S. policy elsewhere in Asia and to plead

[49] Acheson, interview of 10 September 1950, in Department of State *Bulletin* 23 (18 September 1950): 460–61.

[50] Truman to Sen. Arthur Vandenberg, 6 July 1950, PSF, HSTL; and Truman, speech of 1 September 1950, in *Public Papers: Truman*, 1950, 613.

[51] NSC 81, 1 September 1950, and NSC 81/1, 8 September 1950, in NSC Papers box, Military Records Branch, NA; JCS to MacArthur, 27 September 1950 (two messages), JCS 92762 and 92801, CCS 383.21 Korea (3-19-45), Records of the Joint Chiefs of Staff, RG 218, NA. For British support, see Bevin to Attlee, 22 September 1950, FO 800/511; and Bevin to Nehru, 27 September 1950, FO 371/84098, PRO.

[52] For traditional views, see William Stueck, "The March to the Yalu: The Perspective From Washington," in Cumings, ed., *Child of Conflict*, 207–37; and Richard Neustadt, *Presidential Power* (New York: Wiley, 1964). Also see Acheson to Neustadt, 9 May 1960, reply, 29 July 1960, and Acheson's response, 13 September 1960, Acheson Papers, Yale.

his case and injure the administration at home. To restrain MacArthur from such disruptive ventures and to bask in the reflected glory of the general's recent victories, President Truman, with his party facing the November 1950 elections, flew halfway around the world in mid-October to meet with MacArthur. In their conversations, the president and the general did not dwell on China's entry into the war, which everyone deemed unlikely, but on how soon they could end the war, how many American troops could then be sent to Europe, and how a united Korea should be economically reconstructed.[53]

In late October, the unexpected occurred: Chinese communist "volunteers" did attack the UN forces in Korea. But U.S. policy did not change. There was a flurry of fear, a burst of reassessment, but no call for retreat. Soon after Chinese forces broke off the battle on 7 November, U.S. policy makers returned to their earlier optimism. On 9 November, for example, they canvassed various possibilities (even negotiations with China) but decided that there was no crisis, certainly no imminent disaster. MacArthur did not intimidate and thus bar the JCS and Acheson from revising the general's orders and halting his march toward the Yalu. Rather, these Washington leaders persuaded themselves that no massive Chinese entry could occur, and that victory was still within grasp; their estimates and MacArthur's nicely dovetailed.[54]

This optimism is revealed in the minutes of Acheson's discussion with his associates on 21 November. That day, just a week before the massive Chinese intervention, Acheson and Marshall agreed that MacArthur should continue marching toward the Yalu, and they discussed whether to create a buffer zone along the Yalu *before* or *after* victory.[55] MacArthur was authorized to move toward the Yalu, but the Joint Chiefs did suggest that he might pull back after reaching the Yalu, if there was no effective resistance, and thus he could create a de facto buffer zone. When MacArthur, desiring a complete victory, counseled his superiors that

[53] "Substance of Statements Made at Wake Island Conference on 15 October 1950," printed in *FRUS, 1950*, VII, 948–60. Also see Acheson, "Meeting with the President," 9 October 1950, Acheson Papers, HSTL; and "Note on the Wake Island Conference," 13 September 1950, PSF 244, HSTL.

[54] Joint Chiefs of Staff to Secretary of Defense Marshall, 9 November 1950, File 795.00, DS Records; cf. CIA, "Chinese Communist Intervention in Korea," 8 November 1950, *FRUS, 1950*, VII, 1101–06. On British estimates, see Bouchier to Chiefs of Staff, 10 November 1950, FR 1015/G 296, FO 371/84070, PRO.

[55] Jessup, "Memorandum of Conversation," 21 November 1950, *FRUS, 1950*, VII, 1204–08. Also see Peter Farrar, "Britain's Proposal for a Buffer Zone South of the Yalu in November 1950: Was It a Neglected Opportunity to End the Fighting in Korea?" *Journal of Contemporary History* 18 (1983): 327–51.

they were being unduly cautious, they backed down from their suggestion.[56]

Like Acheson and Marshall, MacArthur wanted to assert U.S. strength;
their major *expressed* differences were on how to settle the war after
defeating the enemy in Korea. But unlike Acheson, Marshall, and the
JCS, all of whom wanted to stop near the Yalu, MacArthur seemed to be
seeking to extend the war to China—precisely as China feared and as the
administration promised would not happen.

U.S. promises (statements by Truman and Acheson) that China's borders would be inviolate were unconvincing to China, as its public declarations in mid-November made clear. How could China trust America,
the Chinese publicly asked, when Truman was supporting Syngman Rhee,
who had pledged that UN armies would cross the Yalu?[57]

On 28 November, China made it dramatically clear that U.S. promises
had not met its needs. That day, frustrating MacArthur's promises and
Acheson's aims of easy unification of the peninsula, about 250,000 Chinese
troops attacked the UN forces. "We face an entirely new war," a desperate and unhappy MacArthur cabled Washington. The United States had
moved into a debacle.[58]

In later years, Acheson and other administration stalwarts, as well as
many independent analysts, would blame the disaster on MacArthur.[59]
It was his fault, but not his alone. Washington and he shared the same
aims, the same information, and the same estimates of likely Chinese
behavior. It might have been politically difficult for the administration to
restrict MacArthur's advance in mid-November, but what is most important, Acheson and others did not want to do so. They did not want to
restrain him because they were sure that he would be successful and thus
they saw no reason for great caution.

Truman and Acheson had refused to interpret the initial Chinese intervention of late October and early November as a warning. Even after
the late November debacle, they insisted that the Chinese action was
"unprovoked aggression," not a response to U.S. provocation. When Asians
and Europeans in 1950 argued that China had intervened to protect interests that seemed threatened by U.S. action, Acheson, in words similar

[56] J. Lawton Collins to MacArthur, 24 November 1950; and MacArthur to JCS, 25 November 1950, *FRUS, 1950*, VII, 1222–24, 1231–35.
[57] *Survey of the Mainland China Press* (Hong Kong: American Consulate General).
[58] MacArthur to JCS, 28 November 1950, *FRUS*, VII, 1237.
[59] See, e.g., Stueck, "March to the Yalu," 225–37; Neustadt, *Presidential Power*, 120–41;
Acheson, *Present at the Creation*, 464–68.

to MacArthur's, bitingly dismissed such explanations as an unwillingness to face "hard facts."[60]

Struggle over a wider war

The massive Chinese entry of late November 1950 enraged and alarmed Americans, provoked more thoughts about using nuclear weapons, unleashed pleas by MacArthur and others for a wider war, and frightened European allies who feared a global conflict.

In Washington, amid the sense of panic in late autumn, advisers talked about abandoning Korea and Taiwan. Acheson, himself, was eager for a cease-fire but feared that the United States would lose prestige by requesting it. Puncturing the gloom, Admiral Forrest Sherman emphasized that "we had lost the campaign, but not a war." He proposed that the United States "tell the Chinese Communists to get out of Korea or face war" against its heartland.[61]

Acheson, stressing U.S. global interests, feared extending the war to China and risking the intervention of the Soviet Union. "Then we would fight without allies on our side," he warned. He chafed that "we are fighting the second team [China], whereas the real enemy is the Soviet Union." He even suggested that the Soviet Union might want America to get into a deeper war with China and thus squander resources that otherwise would help build up Europe.

The fear of a domino effect—psychological and geographical—dominated thinking in Washington. JCS Chairman Bradley warned that a defeat in Korea could mean losing Taiwan and Indochina. "The Germans are already saying that we are weak," he complained. "Appeasement is gaining in Europe." For most advisers, the great fear was that a defeat in Asia would injure U.S. interests in Europe, still the primary long-run concern of U.S. global policy.

General J. Lawton Collins, army chief of staff, had already warned his associates that the United States might use atomic weapons, and he had called secretly for the selection of targets.[62] In what may have been a

[60] Acheson, *Present at the Creation*, 464–68.
[61] Jessup, Memorandum of Conversation, 3 December 1950, *FRUS*, 1950, VII, 1323–34, which paraphrases participants' statements. This is also the source for the next two paragraphs.
[62] Army Chief of Staff to Joint Chiefs, "Possible Employment of Atomic Bombs in Korea," 20 November 1950, CCS 383.21 Korea (3-19-45), Records of the JCS, NA. Also see General Reuben Jenkins, "Department of the Army Policy Concerning the Employment

calculated threat, Truman implied at his press conference on 30 November that he might drop nuclear weapons in Korea.[63] His statement provoked some hostile mail but also considerable enthusiasm in the United States.[64] But in Europe it produced horror. British Prime Minister Clement Attlee rushed to Washington to urge caution. The resulting Anglo-American communiqué, patching over differences, expressed Truman's hope that nuclear weapons would not be necessary.[65]

Perhaps wisely, Truman never stipulated under what conditions he might use such weapons. If thousands of U.S. troops had been confronted with annihilation or surrender, as had almost happened to a marine division in December, he would have felt sorely tempted to use the weapons. For him, as for many U.S. leaders, the major constraints were the likelihood of Soviet nuclear retaliation and the defection of NATO allies.

Truman also had to deal with his Pacific commander, whose desires to widen the war frightened NATO allies and threatened the alliance itself. Truman never trusted MacArthur, feeling that he "is a supreme egotist, who regards himself as something of a god."[66] Truman's strategy was to try to avoid clashing with MacArthur while restraining the general's more dangerous impulses. An open confrontation, the president feared, could injure the administration at home, where MacArthur had substantial support, and impair U.S. prestige abroad.

MacArthur's bureaucratic strategy was to stretch and twist Washington's orders, to feign innocence and surprise when he was lectured or scolded, and to continue guilefully to push for the policies he desired. Unlike Truman and Acheson, MacArthur, after a flurry of wild talk about withdrawing from Korea, wanted to win the war as the tide of battle changed in favor of the UN forces during the late winter. While the administration prepared to accept a divided Korea, MacArthur became more eager to press on to victory. He still sought "liberation." Whereas his Washington superiors understood that a quest for victory in Korea would

of Atomic Weapons in the Korean Operation," 20 November 1950, G-3, 335.2 TS, Records of the Army Staff, RG 319, NA.

[63] Truman, press conference, 30 November 1950, in *Public Papers: Truman, 1950,* 727, 738–40. I am indebted to Roger Dingman and Bruce Cumings for pushing me to reconsider my earlier analysis that Truman simply slipped at this conference and to consider that he was probably intending to threaten.

[64] Ruckh to George Elsey, 4 and 12 December 1950, Elsey Papers, HSTL. Gallup polls of 12–17 November 1950, in George Gallup, ed., *The Gallup Poll* (New York: Random House, 1972), II, 950.

[65] Attlee-Truman communiqué in *Public Papers: Truman, 1950,* 740; cf. Elsey notes on cabinet meeting, 1 December 1950, Elsey Papers, HSTL.

[66] Eben Ayers diary, 1 July 1950, Ayers Papers, HSTL.

weaken the U.S.-led alliance in Europe, MacArthur believed that victory in Asia would make Europe more secure by establishing faith in U.S. power and will.

On 23 March 1951, MacArthur sabotaged the administration's plan for seeking a truce in Korea when he demanded that the communists surrender and threatened otherwise to defeat them on the battlefield. The same week, he sent to Speaker Joe Martin, a Republican, a letter (not made public until 5 April) rejecting the administration's policy of limited war in Korea. He recommended using Nationalist Chinese troops and attacking China. "[If we lose this war to communism in Asia] the fall of Europe is inevitable," he warned. "Win it—and Europe most probably would avoid war and yet preserve freedom . . . we must win. There is no substitute for victory."[67]

MacArthur's proposal was actually quite similar to the secret counsel given to Truman by the JCS and W. Stuart Symington, chairman of the National Security Resources Board, in mid-January, when the UN forces had seemed near defeat. The JCS had wanted to blockade China, aid Chiang Kai-shek's forces in attacking China and, if necessary to save U.S. troops, expand the war to China. Symington had reached beyond these notions to prepare a bold global plan that included attacks on China and a nuclear ultimatum to the Soviet Union. If the United Nations or the Allies opposed this strategy, Symington urged unilateral U.S. action. "Any further aggression," the United States should inform the Soviet Union in an ultimatum, "would result in the atomic bombardment of Soviet Russia itself." Such a warning, Symington promised, would deter Soviet aggression, reassert U.S. leadership in the "free world," and establish "moral justification for the use of . . . atomic bombs."[68]

MacArthur had probably learned from his Washington contacts of the proposals by the JCS and Symington. Even though the gloom of January had lifted by March as UN troops pushed back the enemy, MacArthur had reason to believe that his bellicose strategy would find support within parts of the government and in sections of the Republican party. He may have believed that he could coerce Truman into changing his policy and fighting to victory.

[67] MacArthur to Joseph Martin, 20 March 1951, in Joint Senate Committee on Armed Services and Foreign Relations, *Military Situation in the Far East*, 82d Cong., 1st sess., 3182.

[68] NSC 101 (JCS memorandum), 12 January 1951; and NSC 100, 11 January 1951, PSF and Department of State Files (under FOIA). For later similar views by Symington, see Symington to Joe Alsop, 29 January 1952, Box 9, Alsop Papers, Library of Congress.

No other American general could have escaped being dismissed for such behavior. But the Joint Chiefs, as well as Truman, recognized the dangers of removing MacArthur—possible injury to the Japanese peace negotiations, outrage in America, attacks on the president, and more domestic battles about the purposes of war. So MacArthur's 23 March announcement provoked only a mild rebuke from Washington. He was reminded that he had to clear all policy pronouncements with Washington and informed that any communist request for armistice negotiations should be reported to Washington for a decision.[69]

But on 5 April, when Speaker Martin released MacArthur's letter, the administration was again challenged and embarrassed. "MacArthur shoots another political bomb," Truman complained in his diary. "This looks like the last straw. Rank insubordination." He wanted to fire MacArthur immediately, but apparently he concealed his desire even from close advisers.[70] Both Secretary Acheson and W. Averell Harriman, a trusted presidential adviser, urged immediate dismissal of the arrogant general. Secretary of Defense Marshall and General Bradley, presumably more wary of the backlash at home and injury to the war effort abroad, counseled caution and delay. They proposed that Marshall should write MacArthur "a confidential letter . . . pointing out the difficult position in which he was placing the government."[71]

The strategy of caution soon dissolved. The Joint Chiefs, although not eager for confrontation with the general, agreed "from a *military view only* . . . that General MacArthur should be relieved." They knew that they could not trust MacArthur, and thus they had even withheld from him a contingency order for a retaliatory bombing of Chinese air bases if the communists made a large air attack on U.S. forces in Korea. The Chiefs had feared that MacArthur would "jump the gun," and later explain that he had thought he was acting under orders. According to Bradley, the Chiefs believed that if MacArthur were not relieved, civilian control of the military would be jeopardized.[72] Truman himself seems to have waited for JCS approval before acting. To cashier the popular general, he knew, would produce a powerful political backlash in America.

[69] See untitled memoranda, 24, 26, 27 March 1951, Acheson Papers, HSTL.
[70] Truman, "Diary, 1951," 6 April 1951, Post-Presidential Papers (Memoirs), HSTL.
[71] "Memorandum for the Record," with excerpts from Bradley's diary, 7 April 1951 (hereafter "Bradley's diary"), JCS Papers, Pentagon; cf. Truman, "Diary," 6, 7, 8 April 1951.
[72] "Bradley's diary," 8 April 1951; and "Memorandum for the Record," n.d. ("Forrest Sherman's diary," 8 April 1951), Box 1 Forrest Sherman Papers, Naval Archives, Washington, D.C.

And the support of the Joint Chiefs, precisely because they were techni-
cally limiting their counsel to the "military view," would help justify his
act and protect him from some political assaults.

Truman's firing of MacArthur unleashed vicious charges against the
White House. The president was hanged in effigy in countless cities. The
returning general, treated like a conquering hero, was honored by ticker-
tape parades and even invited to address a joint session of Congress. He
pleaded his case in interminable congressional hearings.

In a burst of malicious whimsy, one administration adviser poured out
his frustration in a sardonic memorandum:

(Schedule for Welcoming of General MacArthur): 12:30, Wades ashore from
Snorkel submarine; 12:31, Navy Band Plays "Sparrow in the Treetop" and "I'll
be Glad You're Dead, You Rascal You"; 12:40, Parade to the Capitol with General MacArthur riding an elephant; 12:47, Be-heading of General Vaughan at the
rotunda; 1:00, General MacArthur addresses Members of Congress; 1:30–1:49,
Applause for General MacArthur; 1:50, Burning of the Constitution; 1:55,
Lynching of Secretary Acheson; 2:00, 21-atomic bomb salute; 2:30, 300 nude
D.A.R.'s leap from Washington Monument; 3:00, Basket lunch, Monument
grounds.[73]

At the time, the Truman-MacArthur controversy was widely misinter-
preted as a *constitutional* conflict over civilian versus military authority.[74] It was not. MacArthur never challenged the constitutional order of
civilian authority; he challenged Truman's judgment. As a hero, Mac-
Arthur had the political power to do so. Nor was MacArthur unique
among that generation of World War II heroes in possessing political
power. General Dwight D. Eisenhower, too, had great power, and Bradley had some. MacArthur was unique, however, in openly using his personal prestige, while in uniform, to oppose and undercut the president's
policies.

Ultimately the administration, aided by Marshall and Bradley, was
able to defeat MacArthur politically by bringing the political weight of
the JCS to bear against him. The JCS, as anyone conversant with Washington knows, is not just a military body. It is a military body that, because of its expertise and prestige, can act in profoundly political ways—

[73] Elsey, "Schedule for Welcoming General MacArthur," n.d. (April 1951), Elsey Papers,
HSTL.
[74] Cf. John Spanier, *The Truman-MacArthur Controversy and the Korean War* (New York:
W. W. Norton, 1965), 257–81; and Gabriel Kolko, *The Roots of American Foreign
Policy* (Boston: Beacon, 1969), 34–35.

to gain budgets, define international events, block programs, and shape foreign policy.

The issues raised by MacArthur—of taking the war to China—would not disappear in America. Had critics of the administration strategy understood that prominent advisers (most notably the Joint Chiefs and Symington) flirted with a similar strategy, Truman and Acheson might have been in even deeper political trouble at home. By concealing the earlier disputes and keeping the records secret, the administration managed to draw an overly sharp contrast between the bellicose MacArthur and the cautious administration.

The uneasy quest to end the war

"How is America to be victorious in Korea?" Congressman Albert Gore, a loyal Democrat, asked the president in mid-April 1951. "Korea has become a meat grinder of American manhood," lamented Gore. His solution was to call for what he labeled "something cataclysmic"—a radiation belt dividing the Korean peninsula and the possible use of atomic weapons.[75] Despite his seemingly outlandish proposal, he was pleading, along with many others, for a settlement of the conflict in Korea.

Having long since surrendered their 1950 hopes for victory in Korea, Truman and Acheson aimed to gain an armistice on decent terms: a divided Korea near the thirty-eighth parallel, exchange of prisoners of war, inspections to ban the introduction of more foreign troops, and the ultimate withdrawal of foreign forces. By spring 1951 they concluded that there was no purpose in continuing the costly war, because the ground forces were roughly stalemated and any UN escalation on the ground was likely to provoke the introduction of more Chinese "volunteers" and a higher level of violence. The war was unpopular both with Americans and with the nation's allies. It was killing U.S. and Allied soldiers, squandering resources, souring U.S. politics, spurring domestic inflation, threatening the U.S. belief in collective security, and straining relations within NATO.

Armistice negotiations opened in early July 1951 and, to the surprise of many people, dragged on for nearly two years. At first, the United States (acting for the United Nations) quarreled with China and North Korea over formulating an agenda and then over drawing the armistice

[75] Albert Gore to President, 14 April 1951, Official File 692A, HSTL. For administration thinking about using nuclear weapons, see Roger Anders, *Forging the Atomic Shield* (Chapel Hill: University of North Carolina Press, 1987), 127–41, 156–61.

line—at the thirty-eighth parallel, as the United States had earlier suggested, or farther north, as the United States demanded in July as compensation for its air supremacy. Unable to agree on placing the line, they agreed simply that it would be along the final line of battle, and thus each side found good reason to continue trying to gain small chunks of territory.

Washington's chosen negotiators were military officers—inflexible, intolerant, and self-righteous. Spurred on first by General Matthew Ridgway and then by General Mark Clark, his successor, the negotiators did not want to negotiate but to stipulate, not to bargain but to offer intractable positions. "More steel and less silk," Ridgway counseled the JCS. He explained that the United States must insist "on the unchallenged logic of our position [which] will yield the objectives for which we honorably contend." To his dismay, Washington was more willing to bargain.[76]

By January 1952, with only a few issues still in dispute, Acheson believed that an armistice was imminent. If it was not soon achieved or if China later violated it, Acheson contemplated bombing and blockading China. In discussions with Prime Minister Winston Churchill, Acheson sought British approval for this strategy. But Churchill, fearing the loss of Hong Kong and the prospects of a wider war, resisted U.S. entreaties.[77] Churchill also worried about the use of nuclear weapons. He probably found little comfort in General Bradley's reply, according to the minutes, that "it was not our intention to use these bombs, *since up to the present* no suitable targets were presented. . . . If the situation changed in any way," Bradley admitted, "a new situation would arise." In the United States, as Churchill undoubtedly knew, a majority favored using atomic bombs in the war. Such action would have destroyed NATO.[78]

As the armistice negotiations dragged on, Truman poured his frustration into his diary. Compelled in his actual policy to show restraint, he sketched in the privacy of his diary a Walter Mitty-like fantasy of delivering an ultimatum to the Soviets: all-out war unless there was a speedy settlement. "Moscow, St. Petersburg [Leningrad], Vladivostock, Pekin[g],

[76] CINCFE to DEPTAR, is November 1951, C57216, and JCS to CINCFE, 13 November 1951, JCS 86804, CCS 383.21 Korea (3-19-45), Records of the JCS, NA.
[77] Acheson, "Memorandum of Conversation at British Embassy, Sunday, 6 January 1952," 7 January 1952, Herbert Feis Papers, Library of Congress.
[78] Ibid.

Shanghai, Port Arthur, Dairen, Odessa, Stalingrad, and every manufacturing plant in China and the Soviet Union will be eliminated."[79]

By spring 1952 the issues had narrowed, basically, to one dispute—whether prisoners of war would be free to choose to return to their presumed homeland (voluntary repatriation) or whether they would be automatically returned. That issue stymied negotiations and prolonged the war for about fifteen months.

Truman and Acheson sincerely believed in the principles of voluntary repatriation. It would be unconscionable, they concluded, to return unwilling prisoners of war, who might be mistreated or killed. Freedom of choice, an American value, could be imposed. They expected that the defection of communist troops would embarrass China and North Korea and possibly establish a precedent so that communist nations might never again go to war lest their armies melt away. For the president and secretary of state, this new position on repatriation—a radical departure from established procedures—would also constitute a powerful symbolic victory for the West.[80]

U.S. military leaders, as well as U.S. negotiators at Panmunjom, had warned Truman and Acheson that this new position could bar a settlement and delay the return of American prisoners of war. For the U.S. military, repatriation of their own soldiers was the "paramount" concern. Truman and Acheson did not foresee that their stand on voluntary repatriation would prolong the war for more than a year and thus help destroy the administration politically. They believed, wrongly, that the communists would accede after possibly a few months of wrangling.[81]

The position on voluntary repatriation was not politically forced on the president. That position did nicely coalesce, however, with the emerging demand of some Republican congressmen, who independently desired the same policy.[82] But if Truman had wanted to avoid this commitment, he could have maneuvered to do so. He could have warned these Republicans that they were risking an extended war and delaying the return of American prisoners of war in order to save enemy soldiers who

---

[79] Truman Diary, 27 January 1952, PSF, HSTL. Also see ibid., 18 May 1952.

[80] Barton J. Bernstein, "The Struggle over the Korean Armistice: Prisoners of Repatriation?" in Cumings, ed., *Child of Conflict*, 274–305.

[81] Ibid., 279–84.

[82] About sixty senators had signed a petition by Senator William Jenner (R.-Ind.) opposing forcible repatriation, but their position never gained public attention. "Draft Memorandum Covering Meeting of Secretary Acheson, Secretary Lovett . . . ," n.d. (about mid-November 1952), Acheson Papers, HSTL.

had tried to kill Americans. Why sacrifice American soldiers? he might have asked.

Truman and Acheson, as well as their military advisers, had not foreseen that so few enemy prisoners of war (only about 70,000 of 132,000) would agree to repatriation. Earlier, advisers had predicted about 116,000, and U.S. negotiators at Panmunjom had even mentioned that number. Had the United States been able to provide about 100,000, including about 16,000 unwilling Chinese, a settlement could probably have been achieved in the summer.[83]

Blocked in negotiations, the administration sought to force a settlement on U.S. terms by bombing North Korean cities and villages as well as key hydroelectric plants on the Yalu. Although the war on the ground was generally stalemated, with neither side launching a major offensive, the United States believed that military coercion could be the handmaiden of tough negotiations. Pyongyang, the North Korean capital, was a favorite target of the heavy bombings.[84]

"If we can stay firm [on the prisoner-of-war issue] we can tear them up by air," Robert Lovett, the new secretary of defense, explained to the cabinet. "We are hurting them badly. . . . If we keep on tearing the place apart, we can make it a most unpopular affair for the North Koreans. We ought to go right ahead."[85]

Frustrated in its effort to achieve the desired armistice, the administration also confronted the deft opposition of Syngman Rhee. A fervent patriot reluctant to give up his vision of a united Korea under his own rule, Rhee periodically threatened to withdraw his troops from the U.S. command, thus leaving Allied forces to fight on alone, or to disrupt the armistice after it was achieved. At the behest of Washington, Mark Clark, the new commanding general in the Pacific, prepared a plan to overthrow Rhee. The Korean leader, deftly skirting the precipice of danger, managed to avoid triggering the plan. He was aided by the facts that the United States did not have a substitute South Korean Leader to impose and that a high-handed coup, so contrary to the American rhetoric of democracy and self-determination, would have embarrassed Truman at home.[86]

---

[83] Bernstein, "Struggle over Korean Armistice," 283–88, 293–95.

[84] Ibid., 291–94; cf. Henry Kissinger, *Nuclear Weapons and Foreign Policy* (Garden City, N.Y.: Doubleday, 1958), 33–45; and Bernard Brodie, *War and Politics* (New York: Macmillan, 1973), 90–104.

[85] Matthew Connelly, "Notes on Cabinet Meeting," 12 September 1952, Connelly Papers, HSTL.

[86] Barton J. Bernstein, "Syngman Rhee: The Pawn as Rook; The Struggle to End the Korean War," *Bulletin of Concerned Asian Scholars*, January–February 1978, 38–41.

Clark himself, supporter of MacArthur's earlier recommendations for expanding the war across the Yalu, wanted to widen the war by attacking Manchuria and North China with both nuclear and conventional bombs. "I consider it necessary," he informed the Pentagon in October 1952, "that plans be made for the use of atomic weapons. . . . I do believe that serious consideration should be given to removal of the restriction on the employment of atomic weapons."[87] Fearful of a wider war, the administration rejected his bellicose counsel.

Although Truman was not a candidate in the 1952 presidential election, the war was a major campaign issue, and a settlement might have greatly helped the Democrats. Yet neither Republican nor Democratic congressional and presidential candidates, either publicly or privately, criticized the administration for its insistence on voluntary repatriation. There was a comfortable consensus that the United States, as Truman had explained publicly, could not surrender this principle and send prisoners of war to their death.

The Truman administration failed to achieve an armistice on the desired terms, and the war dragged on for six months after the politically repudiated president had departed from the White House. Ultimately, President Dwight Eisenhower, probably aided by Stalin's death, U.S. tactics of bombing key irrigation dikes, and the use of nuclear threats,[88] gained the settlement that Truman and Acheson had been denied—an armistice with voluntary repatriation. About 50,000 prisoners (including 14,700 Chinese) did not return home.[89] Eisenhower, succumbing to Rhee's blackmail, also gave the wily autocrat the mutual security pact he had

---

[87] Clark to Chief of Staff, Army, "Operation Plan CINCUNC No. 8–52," 16 October 1952, attached to JCS 1776/330, 30 October 1952, CCS 383.21 Korea (3-19-45), Records of the JCS, NA.

[88] For continuing controversy on whether there were nuclear threats and whether they succeeded, see Barry Blechman and Robert Powell, "What in the Name of God Is Strategic Superiority?" *Political Science Quarterly* 97 (Winter 1982–83): 590–97; Edward Friedman, "Nuclear Blackmail and the End of the Korean War," *Modern China* 1 (1975): 75–91; James Shepley, "How Dulles Averted War," *Life* 40 (16 January 1956), 71–72; Barton J. Bernstein, "New Light on the Korean War," *International History* 3 (April 1981): 272–77; Edward Keefer, "President Dwight D. Eisenhower and the End of the Korean War," *Diplomatic History* 10 (Summer 1986): 267–89; and John Lewis and Xue Litai, *China Builds the Bomb* (Stanford, Calif.: Stanford University Press, 1988), chapters 1–2.

[89] The official U.S. army history cites 22,604 (14,704 Chinese and 7,900 North Koreans) as rejecting repatriation. But the meaningful numbers are much larger, because Rhee had released 25,000 North Koreans in June and the United States also released about 38,000 civilian internees, including *some* prisoners of war. It is impossible to determine how many of the released internees were really POWs. See Acheson in Princeton Seminars transcript, 14 March 1954. Hermes, *Truce Tent and Fighting Front*, pp. 514–15, indicates that 82,493 (6,670 Chinese and 75,823 North Koreans) chose to return home.

long desired and thus committed the United States to the long-term pledge to containment in Korea.

Conclusions and speculations

President Truman and Secretary Acheson, as well as their advisers and most other Americans, desired to stop communism and to roll it back *when such action seemed safe*. Containment could easily turn into liberation when opportunity seemed to beckon. Many of the domestic political disputes over the conduct of the war focused on the safety or danger of seeking liberation in Korea.

Americans shared a common faith that their welfare—indeed, their economic and political systems—depended on an "open door" world. Such a view was quite supple and allowed different emphases; some were heavily political, and others economic-political. Whereas many Americans stressed the antidemocratic character of communism and viewed it (or at least its Soviet embodiment) as imminently expansionist, policy makers were likely to perceive events in a more complex framework of international political economy and to dwell on threats to the international system—the disruption of markets, the closing off of trade, the pressures on allies, and ultimately the injury to the U.S. economic system.[90] That framework led them to resist the Soviet Union, to oppose indigenous left-wing movements in the Third World, and to see the events in Korea primarily through the prism of the cold war and thus to misunderstand the Korean War.

Yet this ideology did not dictate the administration's critical decisions on the war. Truman's own ideology could have accommodated different responses. If Truman and Acheson had had less faith in U.S. power and in its capacity to triumph, these leaders, like some of their military advisers, might have been more cautious.

Truman the Democrat did not greatly differ from Eisenhower the Republican with respect to the international world he wished to create, but

[90] Cf. William Appleman Williams, *The Tragedy of American Diplomacy* 2nd rev. ed. (New York: Dell, 1972), especially 8–16; Gabriel Kolko, *Roots of American Foreign Policy*, 48–87; Robert Tucker, *The Radical Left and American Foreign Policy* (Baltimore: John Hopkins University Press, 1971). So far, despite great controversy over the applicability of an "open door" framework, with portions of the Left arguing instead for structural-economic imperatives and mainstream analysts integrating pieces of the framework on an ad hoc basis, there has been no systematic effort, in research or in theory, to distinguish *elite* "open door" beliefs from *rank-and-file* "open door" understanding and to discuss the strength of anticommunism within these two related kinds of thinking.

Truman had more confidence in the use of U.S. military power and less fear of war. Temperament and experience may have been critical factors in explaining why Truman went to war in Korea in 1950 and why Eisenhower, chastened by the Korean War, avoided war in Indochina in 1954.

The Korean War helped embitter U.S. politics, pushed European rearmament, raised military budgets, and killed more than 50,000 Americans and many more Koreans and Chinese. By framing the flames of anticommunism in America, the war narrowed the domestic political dialogue and helped establish a dangerous precedent for presidents to conduct substantial undeclared wars, in this case, a "police action."

Looking back over these years, it is tempting to ask whether key U.S. decisions could and should have been different. In considering this question, there is merit in focusing on three sets of critical decisions—entry into the war in late June 1950, the commitments during the summer and autumn of 1950 to expand the war across the thirty-eighth parallel and to the Yalu, and the choice in 1952 to insist on voluntary repatriation of prisoners of war before accepting an armistice.[91]

In June 1950, President Truman could have avoided committing the United States to the war without producing a backlash at home or disrupting the alliance system. Indeed, at that time, perhaps the administration should have followed the advice it had formulated in 1948 in NSC 8: "The US should not become so irrevocably involved in the Korean situation that any action taken by any faction in Korea could be considered a casus belli for the US." Unfortunately, between early 1948 and June 1950, Acheson and Truman had subtly caused that cautious position to erode by expanding in their own minds the terms of containment.

In the summer and early autumn of 1950, especially after MacArthur's dramatic triumph at Inchon, the administration might have had greater domestic political difficulty in halting at the thirty-eighth parallel and accepting a divided Korea. Many Americans, including administration advisers, wanted a strategy of liberation. But had Truman and Acheson taken seriously China's warnings and informed congressional leaders of both parties of the lurking dangers, perhaps a bipartisan consensus could have been established to stop at the parallel. Desiring to transform containment into liberation, however, the administration instead savored the prospect of imminent success and cavalierly dismissed China's warnings.

Had Truman and Acheson in 1952 not insisted on the voluntary re-

---

[91] For another view, see Eliot Cohen, "The Hot Cold War," *New Republic*, 2 May 1988, 34–38; cf. Rosemary Foot, *The Wrong War* (Ithaca, N.Y.: Cornell University Press, 1985).

patriation of prisoners of war, a position that domestic politics did not initially require, the war would probably have ended in spring or summer 1952. Many lives would have been saved, and the administration would have suffered less opprobrium.

Operating in this risky realm of counterfactual history, it is worth speculating whether, if Truman had not entered the Korean War, domestic politics in the 1950s would have been less rancorous, and whether if the UN forces had halted at the thirty-eighth parallel, the rapprochement with China might have occurred by the late 1950s, under a Republican administration. Missed opportunities—paths not taken—are worth contemplating, at least briefly, in a volume dedicated to analyzing, understanding, and assessing the Truman administration, because the implementation of containment and liberation in Korea had unforeseen costs for Truman and for the United States.

To many Americans and others, however, the benefits may seem substantial enough to have justified intervention in 1950, for otherwise South Korea would not have been "protected" from communism and probably would not have achieved the rapid economic growth (a miracle, some say) of recent years. Truman himself expected that his vigorous efforts on behalf of anticommunism would shape assessments of his presidency, and he viewed his action in Korea as "most important of all."

About the authors

BARTON J. BERNSTEIN is Professor of History and Mellon Professor of Interdisciplinary Studies, Stanford University, and editor of *The Politics and Policies of the Truman Administration* (1971) and *The Atomic Bomb* (1976).

PAUL BOYER is Merle Curti Professor of History and Senior Member of the Institute for Research in the Humanities, University of Wisconsin–Madison, and author of *By the Bomb's Early Light: American Thought and Culture at the Dawn of the Atomic Age* (1985) and *Urban Masses and Moral Order in America, 1820–1920* (1978).

WILLIAM H. CHAFE is Professor of History, Duke University, and author of *The Unfinished Journey* (1987) and *A History of Our Time* (1984).

JOHN W. DOWER is Joseph Naiman Professor of History and Japanese Studies, University of California, San Diego, and author of *War Without Mercy: Race and Power in the Pacific War* (1986) and *Empire and Aftermath: Yoshida Shigeru and the Japanese Experience, 1878–1954* (1979).

JOHN LEWIS GADDIS is Professor of History, Ohio University, and author of *The Long Peace* (1987).

CRAUFURD D. GOODWIN is James B. Duke Professor of Economics, Duke University, and author, with Michael Nach, of *Absence of Decision* (1983).

ROBERT GRIFFITH is Professor of History, University of Massachusetts–Amherst, and author of *The Politics of Fear: Joseph R. McCarthy and the Senate* (2d ed., 1987) and *Ike's Letters to a Friend: 1941–1958* (1984).

ALONZO L. HAMBY is Professor of History, Ohio University, and author of *Beyond the New Deal: Harry S. Truman and American Liberalism, 1945–1953* (1973) and *Liberalism and Its Challengers: F.D.R. to Reagan* (1985).

Bruce R. Kuniholm is Professor of History and Public Policy, Duke University, and author of *The Origins of the Cold War in the Near East* (1980) and *The Near East Connection: Greece and Turkey in the Reconstruction and Security of Europe* (1984).

Michael J. Lacey is Secretary of the Program on American Society and Politics at the Woodrow Wilson International Center for Scholars.

Nelson Lichtenstein is Associate Professor of History, Catholic University of America, and author of *Labor's War at Home: The CIO in World War II* (1982) and *On the Line: Essays in the History of Auto Work* (1988).

Robert J. McMahon is Associate Professor of History, University of Florida, and author of *Colonialism and Cold War: The United States and the Struggle for Indonesian Independence, 1945–49* (1981).

Charles S. Maier is Professor of History, Harvard University, and author of *Recasting Bourgeois Europe: Stabilization in France, Germany, and Italy in the Decade after World War I* (1975), *In Search of Stability: Explorations in Historical Political Economy* (1987), and *The Unmasterable Past: History, Holocaust, and German National Identity* (1988).

Robert A. Pollard is an Economic Officer in the U.S. Foreign Service. He is serving in the Trade Office of the U.S. Department of State, specializing in issues related to the economic integration of the European Community planned for 1992. Pollard is the author of *Economic Security and the Origins of the Cold War, 1945–1950* (1985).

Index

447